W9-DIZ-413

Human Rights: Moral or Political?

Human Rights: Moral or Political?

EDITED BY
Adam Etinson

OXFORD
UNIVERSITY PRESS

OXFORD

UNIVERSITY PRESS

Great Clarendon Street, Oxford, OX2 6DP,
United Kingdom

Oxford University Press is a department of the University of Oxford.
It furthers the University's objective of excellence in research, scholarship,
and education by publishing worldwide. Oxford is a registered trade mark of
Oxford University Press in the UK and in certain other countries

© the several contributors 2018

The moral rights of the authors have been asserted

First Edition published in 2018
Impression: 1

All rights reserved. No part of this publication may be reproduced, stored in
a retrieval system, or transmitted, in any form or by any means, without the
prior permission in writing of Oxford University Press, or as expressly permitted
by law, by licence or under terms agreed with the appropriate reprographics
rights organization. Enquiries concerning reproduction outside the scope of the
above should be sent to the Rights Department, Oxford University Press, at the
address above

You must not circulate this work in any other form
and you must impose this same condition on any acquirer

Published in the United States of America by Oxford University Press
198 Madison Avenue, New York, NY 10016, United States of America

British Library Cataloguing in Publication Data
Data available

Library of Congress Control Number: 2017954187

ISBN 978–0–19–871325–8

Printed and bound by
CPI Group (UK) Ltd, Croydon, CR0 4YY

Links to third party websites are provided by Oxford in good faith and
for information only. Oxford disclaims any responsibility for the materials
contained in any third party website referenced in this work.

Contents

Contributors   ix

Introduction   1
Adam Etinson

Part I. The Relevance of History

1. Rights, History, Critique   41
    Martti Koskenniemi

    1.1 Doing Without an Original: A Commentary
        on Martti Koskenniemi   61
        Annabel Brett

2. Human Rights in Heaven   69
    Samuel Moyn

    2.1 Philosophizing the Real World of Human Rights:
        A Reply to Samuel Moyn   88
        John Tasioulas

    2.2 Genealogies of Human Rights: What's at Stake?   103
        Jeffrey Flynn

Part II. The Orthodox–Political Debate

3. Human Rights: A Critique of the Raz/Rawls Approach   117
    Jeremy Waldron

    3.1 On Waldron's Critique of Raz on Human Rights   139
        Joseph Raz

4. Assigning Functions to Human Rights: Methodological Issues
    in Human Rights Theory   145
    James W. Nickel

    4.1 On Being Faithful to the "Practice": A Response to Nickel   160
        Adam Etinson

5. Beyond the Political–Orthodox Divide: The Broad View   174
    Andrea Sangiovanni

    5.1 Human Rights in Context: A Comment on Sangiovanni   200
        Rainer Forst

Part III. Morality and Law

6. Taking International Legality Seriously: A Methodology
    for Human Rights 211
    Allen Buchanan & Gopal Sreenivasan

    6.1 Instrumentalism and Human Rights: A Response to Buchanan
        and Sreenivasan 230
        Erasmus Mayr

7. The Turn to Justification: On the Structure and Domain of
    Human Rights Practice 238
    Mattias Kumm

    7.1 Human Rights and Justification: A Reply to Mattias Kumm 262
        Samantha Besson

8. Appreciating the Margin of Appreciation 269
    Andreas Follesdal

    8.1 The Margin of Appreciation Revisited: A Response to Follesdal 295
        George Letsas

Part IV. Ideals and their Limits

9. Dwelling in Possibility: Ideals, Aspirations, and Human Rights 313
    Kimberley Brownlee

    9.1 In What Sense Should Respect for Human Rights Be Attainable?
        A Response to Brownlee 327
        Rowan Cruft

10. The Nature of Violations of the Human Right to Subsistence 337
    Elizabeth Ashford

    10.1 Remarks on Elizabeth Ashford's "The Nature of Violations of
         the Human Right to Subsistence" 363
         Daniel Weinstock

Part V. The Challenges of Politics

11. Reflections on Human Rights and Power 375
    Pablo Gilabert

    11.1 Reflections on Human Rights and Power: A Commentary 400
         Elizabeth Frazer

12. The Hazards of Rescue   409
     C. A. J. Coady

     12.1 The Politics of Humanitarian Morality: Reflections on
           "The Hazards of Rescue"   429
           Vasuki Nesiah

Part VI. Individuals, Borders, and Groups

13. Human Rights and Collective Self-Determination   441
     Peter Jones

     13.1 Linking Self-Determination and Human Rights: Comment
           on Peter Jones   460
           Will Kymlicka

14. Human Rights, Membership, and Moral Responsibility in
     an Unjust World: The Case of Immigration Restrictions   469
     Alex Levitov & Stephen Macedo

     14.1 The Slippery Slope of Statist Cosmopolitanism: A Response
           to Levitov and Macedo   489
           Seyla Benhabib

Index   501

Contributors

ELIZABETH ASHFORD, University of St Andrews
SEYLA BENHABIB, Yale University
SAMANTHA BESSON, University of Fribourg
ANNABEL BRETT, University of Cambridge
KIMBERLEY BROWNLEE, University of Warwick
ALLEN BUCHANAN, Duke University
C. A. J. COADY, University of Melbourne
ROWAN CRUFT, University of Stirling
ADAM ETINSON, University of St Andrews
JEFFREY FLYNN, Fordham University
ANDREAS FOLLESDAL, University of Oslo
RAINER FORST, Goethe University Frankfurt
ELIZABETH FRAZER, University of Oxford
PABLO GILABERT, Concordia University
PETER JONES, Newcastle University
MARTTI KOSKENNIEMI, University of Helsinki
MATTIAS KUMM, New York University
WILL KYMLICKA, Queen's University
GEORGE LETSAS, University College London
ALEX LEVITOV, Independent Scholar
STEPHEN MACEDO, Princeton University
ERASMUS MAYR, Fiedrich-Alexander University Erlangen-Nüremburg
SAMUEL MOYN, Yale University
VASUKI NESIAH, New York University
JAMES W. NICKEL, University of Miami
JOSEPH RAZ, Columbia University/King's College London
ANDREA SANGIOVANNI, King's College London
GOPAL SREENIVASAN, Duke University
JOHN TASIOULAS, King's College London
JEREMY WALDRON, New York University
DANIEL WEINSTOCK, McGill University

Introduction

Adam Etinson

Moral *or* political? Can't human rights be both moral *and* political—and can't they be so in a variety of senses? It is plausible to think so. But one could be forgiven for assuming that philosophers have come to think otherwise.[1]

Over the past decade or so, philosophers have grown divided over the question of how to properly conceive of human rights. On the one hand, there are "orthodox"[2] theorists (sometimes referred to as "naturalistic,"[3] "humanist,"[4] "traditional,"[5] "old-fashioned,"[6] or "philosophical"[7]). These theorists think of human rights as natural rights: moral rights that we have simply in virtue of being human. On the other hand, there are "political"[8] theorists (sometimes referred to as "practical,"[9] "institutionalist,"[10] or "functional"[11]) who think of human rights as rights that play a distinctive role, or set of roles, in modern international politics: setting standards of political legitimacy,[12] serving as norms of international concern,[13] and/or imposing limits on the exercise of national sovereignty.[14]

Some may wonder why it is worth reading what philosophers have to say about these matters. After all, wouldn't it be better if we spent our time promoting human rights, or doing human rights "work," rather than engaging in intellectual debates about what such rights *really* are (if it even makes sense to ask such a question)?

This is a legitimate concern. But the Orthodox–Political debate, as I shall refer to it here, is not blind to it. In some ways, the debate shows that philosophers too are puzzled about their role when it comes to human rights. And this is at least partly due to the multifaceted nature of human rights themselves—their involvement in various domains of human life and thought.

In one guise, human rights present themselves to us as a bundle of supposedly natural or objective moral facts—facts that determine what we owe to each other as

---

[1] A special thanks to James W. Nickel and Rowan Cruft for helpful comments on an earlier version of this introduction.

[2] Tasioulas 2010.   [3] Beitz 2009; Liao & Etinson 2012.   [4] Gilabert 2011.   [5] Raz 2010.
[6] Buchanan & Sreenivasan in this volume.   [7] Jones 1996.   [8] Raz 2010; Valentini 2011a.
[9] Beitz 2009; Wenar 2005.   [10] Sangiovanni 2007.   [11] Griffin 2008, p. 27; Tasioulas 2012.
[12] Dworkin 2011, pp. 332–9; Williams 2005, pp. 62–4.   [13] Beitz 2009, p. 109.
[14] Rawls 1999, pp. 78–82; Raz 2010, p. 328.

human beings. The human right to freedom from slavery, for instance, looks a lot like this.[15] It prohibits the enslavement of anyone by anyone, and it does so (by all appearances) objectively: the normative force of the prohibition, or the "wrongness" of slavery, does not depend on its recognition by any group or person, let alone any popular moral code, institutional system, or positive body of law. Slavery was not any less of a human rights violation when (not all that long ago) most of the planet thought that it was morally and legally permissible to hold slaves.

Seen in this light, human rights look like a topic in moral philosophy, one that can be approached with the traditional tools of the armchair philosopher: principled reasoning, moral intuition, and (when necessary) empirical information to help *apply* abstract norms to specific circumstances. This vision fits nicely with the Orthodox conception of human rights, which emphasizes their status as moral rights. And philosophers, on this view, have a reasonably clear intellectual and practical role to play when it comes to human rights: like natural rights theorists of the past, philosophers can be expected to tell us what human rights there are, why (and how) they exist, and what they concretely require of us.

But human rights present themselves to us in other guises as well. In addition to seeming morally real, or part of what the British legal philosopher H. L. A Hart called "critical" morality, human rights are also standards that many people around the world happen to *believe* in, which makes them part of various "positive" or popular moralities too.[16] Moreover, human rights are deeply embedded in contemporary politics and law—both domestically, regionally, and internationally.[17]

The fact that human rights are today explicitly recognized norms of popular morality, political practice, and legal institutions throughout the world—the fact that it is now perfectly meaningful to speak of things like human rights "culture," human rights "practice," the human rights "movement," and human rights "law"—is of enormous practical and theoretical significance.

It is of practical significance because it is hard to imagine how the promise of human rights will ever be fulfilled *without* things like real-world belief in their importance, as well as recognition in politics and enforcement through law. These are the chief mechanisms through which human rights are realized, or *not* realized.

It is of theoretical significance for a number of reasons. First, contrary to Platonic stereotypes, philosophers, like other theorists, do take an interest in the world around them. The recent surge in scholarship on human rights—not just in philosophy but also in history, law, political science, and international relations—has a great deal to do with the recent success of human rights as a *public* idea. If it were not for the increased profile of human rights in political rhetoric, the popular imagination, the media, and law, contemporary scholars of human rights would probably have devoted their

---

[15] Article 4, *The Universal Declaration of Human Rights* [UDHR] (1948); Article 8, *The International Covenant on Civil and Political Rights* [ICCPR] (1966/1976).

[16] Hart 1994, p. 301.

[17] For a comprehensive overview, *see*: Alston & Goodman 2012; Nickel 2007, ch. 1.

energies elsewhere—certainly, a large edited volume like this is unlikely to have found its way into existence. And this is no doubt as it should be, which raises a second point.

Sometimes we want philosophy to help us interpret or make sense of our ideals and practices as they *are*. At other times we quite reasonably want philosophy (as well as literature and the arts, etc.) to operate in a *normative* mode—that is, to help us reimagine our ideals and practices as they *ought to* be. Once we home in on the public life of human rights as a key object of theoretical interest, however, we might wonder how best to *normatively* appraise it. We can always try to imagine human rights practice, human rights law, or the human rights movement as they might (ideally) be. But this should be more than a haphazard effort. What are the standards against which these phenomena should be judged?

One answer, perhaps the most obvious one, is that we should judge the public reality of human rights by how well it lines up with the *moral* reality thereof. After all, if there is a moral human right to freedom from slavery, then presumably popular morality, politics, and law should reflect this. And this seems to be true of countless other moral human rights as well.

But this suggestion overlooks the fact that the positivization of human rights has a logic of its own. Like other kinds of law, human rights law is something more than just a vehicle for the expression of moral standards. The law is a public instrument that, among other things, is designed to facilitate stable and predictable social relations. Unlike moral norms, which might be enforced in any number of ways, legal norms are typically enforced by means of coercive power.[18] And given the public role of law, there may be good reason for it to avoid ruling on issues that are marked by strong dissensus. Morality, by contrast, does not seem to operate under this same constraint; it can be as controversial as it turns out (or as we take it) to be.

With this in mind, perhaps not all (moral) human rights are well suited for legal protection. For instance, as John Tasioulas, a key champion of the Orthodox conception of human rights, has argued, the human right to a fair say in important family decisions (e.g., about the division of spousal labour) is morally plausible but nonetheless ill-suited for legal recognition.[19] Despite their far-reaching effects and enormous potential for unfairness, such decisions are extremely difficult to regulate and (in any case) strike us as importantly "private."

In other instances, there may be good reason to codify a legal human right that has no direct moral counterpart. For example, as Gopal Sreenivasan and Allen Buchanan suggest in this volume, a legal human right to health has various potential benefits *beyond* the promotion and/or protection of health itself: these may include improvements in

---

[18] It is true that international human rights law is not coercively enforced in the way that domestic law typically is. That said, the norms of international human rights law are designed to be incorporated into domestic law, where they (standardly) *would* be coercively enforced (*see:* Article 2, ICCPR; Article 2, ICESCR). Thus, in a very important sense, these legal norms are developed with the aim of coercive enforcement in mind.

[19] Tasioulas 2012, p. 2. Sen (2004, pp. 326–8) makes a similar point.

happiness, social solidarity, economic productivity, and the more general realization of a just and humane society, etc. Perhaps these aggregate benefits, if real, are enough to justify the enactment of a legal human right to health *even if* it turns out that there is no equivalent moral right, as some contend.[20]

At the very least, these considerations complicate the task of evaluating human rights law. They suggest that responsibly measuring its success (or ideal content) is *more* than just a matter of seeing how well it conforms to, expresses, or enforces human rights morality—that we cannot know what legal human rights there should be simply by knowing what moral human rights there are, and vice versa. And perhaps something like this is true of popular morality and politics as well. After all, not all good moral causes make for good political platforms, institutional projects, or social movements.

For instance, one prominent complaint about the human rights movement is that, for all its noble intentions, its focus on basic liberties and social services distracts us from more pressing "structural" injustices, including historically unprecedented levels of global and domestic economic inequality.[21] Perhaps there really are ways in which the belief in (or practical pursuit of) human rights—via popular morality, social mobilization, and/or political institutionalization—can have adverse effects overall. And perhaps these adverse effects give us reason to rethink how (or even whether) morally justified human rights should be institutionalized and socially disseminated.

All of this leaves the role of the philosopher somewhat unclear when it comes to evaluating the public life of human rights. Even if we suppose (no doubt contentiously)[22] that philosophers are capable of moral expertise—and, in particular, expert knowledge of the moral requirements of human rights—this would still not guarantee them insight into what human rights *politics* and *law*, or what the human rights *movement*, ought to be like. The independent life and logic of these real-world phenomena makes their evaluation a special task of its own, perhaps one that philosophers (or at least moral theorists) are in no privileged position to pursue.

This is the kind of observation that motivates the Political approach to human rights. According to one of its most prominent defenders, Joseph Raz, the Political approach acknowledges that contemporary human rights "practice" (largely a *legal* phenomenon, in his view)[23] cannot be evaluated on the basis of moral insight alone. Just as it would be strange to evaluate the content of the law without some understanding of the functions of law in general, Raz suggests that contemporary human rights practice ought to be evaluated under the light of a faithful understanding of what it is that the practice aims to *do*.

Following John Rawls, the original proponent of this approach,[24] Raz argues that the main function of human rights practice is political: to make states answerable to the international community when it comes to their treatment of individual persons.

---

[20] Buchanan & Sreenivasan in this volume. *Also see:* Buchanan 2013, p. 53.
[21] For a broad discussion, *see:* Gilabert in this volume, Sec. 2.2.4. *Also see:* Moyn 2015 & 2018.
[22] *See e.g.* McGrath 2008; Nussbaum 2002; Singer 1972.
[23] Raz in this volume. *Also see:* Etinson in this volume, for a broader discussion.   [24] Rawls 1999.

With this function in view, Raz outlines the standards against which the practice should be judged. *Genuine* human rights—those which ought to be recognized by the practice if they are not already—consist in the set of individual moral rights that can be justifiably held against states in this way, i.e. as potential defeaters of state sovereignty. Evaluating contemporary human rights practice is ultimately a matter of figuring out which moral rights these are, and then seeing whether or how well they are represented in the practice itself.[25]

Understood in this way, Raz's theory appeals to relatively ordinary moral and political considerations. It requires us to think, on the one hand, about which individual moral rights (if any) should be a matter of state responsibility, and on the other, about when (if ever) the failure to meet such responsibilities should render a state liable to external interference or review.[26] No doubt, these are complex calculations, but they draw on ordinary normative considerations (about the grounds of individual moral rights, and of state sovereignty, etc.) that apply in various contexts, not just contemporary human rights practice.

Some proponents of the Political approach think that this is a mistake. According to Charles Beitz, for example, taking the normative independence of contemporary human rights practice seriously requires evaluating it entirely on its own terms—that is, in light of concepts and considerations that are unique (or "*sui generis*") to the practice itself.[27] For Beitz, even the concept of *rights* operative in the practice is unique and unbeholden to standard theoretical understandings thereof.[28] This might make the practice look deficient from various well-established theoretical points of view, but, as Beitz argues, so much the worse for the establishment: "Why should we insist that international human rights conform to a received philosophical conception rather than interpret them, as they present themselves, as a distinct normative system constructed to play a certain special role in global political life?"[29]

The Orthodox–Political debate, then, is as much about the nature and limits of philosophy as it is about human rights. It is as much a debate about how to theorize human rights—and to what end—as it is about human rights themselves. In part, the debate reflects recent trends in moral and political philosophy: trends that have opened up questions about how normative or "utopian" philosophical theory should be,[30] about the role of moral theory (and "truth") in politics,[31] and about the relevance of political institutions to political theory.[32] But most of all the debate reflects the innate complexity of its subject matter—the *many lives* of human rights, as it were.

The title of this volume, then, is not meant to assert any kind of fundamental opposition or contradiction. Rather, it is meant to highlight this innate complexity,

---

[25] Raz 2010, p. 327.   [26] Raz 2010, pp. 335–6.   [27] Beitz 2009, p. 12, 197.
[28] Beitz 2009, p. 119.   [29] Beitz 2009, p. 61.
[30] *See e.g.* Estlund 2014; Rawls 1999, esp. pp. 11–23; Valentini 2012.
[31] *See e.g.* Rawls 2005; Raz 1998; Quong 2010.
[32] *See e.g.* Cohen 2010; James 2005; Sangiovanni 2007; Valentini 2011b; Waldron 2013.

the philosophical debate that has grown out of it, and the many questions it continues to raise.

*   *   *

This volume has two central aims. First, it aims to make new headway in the Orthodox–Political debate, moving it beyond its current state of progress. The bulk of that work can be found in Part II, which is where the most direct contributions to the debate have been gathered. The second aim of the volume is to provide a state-of-the-art discussion of a number of important topics that are closely connected to the Orthodox–Political debate, but not normally a focal point thereof. That work can be found in Parts I, III, IV, V, and VI.

So far, the Orthodox–Political debate has focused on questions about the nature of human rights (What *are* human rights?), their grounds (What *justifies* their normative existence or authority?), their content (What human rights are there?), and about the aims and methods of a philosophical theory of human rights in general. But as a debate that is, at its core, instigated by the complex status of human rights as both critical standards of morality, on the one hand, and positive standards of law, politics, and popular morality, on the other, it in fact raises a much broader set of questions.

This volume explores a handful of key topics within that broader set. These include questions about: the relevance of the real-world history of human rights to their philosophical comprehension (Part I); how to properly understand the relationship between human rights morality and law (III); how to balance the aspirational or "utopian" character of human rights—their description of an *ideal* world—with the requirement that they be feasible in the here and now (IV); the role of human rights in a world shaped by politics and power (V); and how to make sense of the ascription of human rights to both individuals, on the one hand, and political communities, on the other (VI).

In exploring these adjacent topics, the volume aims not just to deepen our understanding of some important questions about human rights, but also to exploit the opportunity this provides for interdisciplinary engagement. Several of the author-commentator pairings in the volume place scholars from different disciplines (including history, philosophy, international law, political science, and legal theory) into direct dialogue with one another on a shared topic. Human rights have become an extraordinarily active area of research in a wide variety of disciplines, but the coordination and communication of research *across* disciplinary boundaries is rare and frequently prone to misunderstanding. Working across these boundaries, or at least trying (as several authors in this volume do) to figure out how research on human rights in any one discipline bears on research in others, is an important task in its own right. It is also crucial to determining just where philosophical theory fits into the impressive range of work currently being done on human rights, both intellectually and practically, which is a key preoccupation of the Orthodox–Political debate itself.

*   *   *

The remainder of this introduction aims to give the reader some sense of the content of the volume, of how it builds on current scholarship, and highlights key starting points for critical reflection.[33]

I. The Relevance of History

The volume begins with a series of contributions that tackle the question of how the history of human rights bears (or should bear) on the philosophy thereof. What relevance, if any, do *historical claims* about human rights (e.g. about the series of events that lead to the UN General Assembly's adoption of the Universal Declaration of Human Rights on December 10th, 1948) have to the *conceptual claims* (e.g. about the nature of human rights) that philosophers tend to be interested in?

It is easy to picture philosophers (concerned, as one might imagine, strictly with timeless and universal truths) adopting a hard-line stance here: one that denies that philosophy, properly understood, ought to take *any* account of historical facts about human rights. But interestingly, philosophers have by and large gone a different route. Historical claims about human rights have in fact played a prominent role in the Orthodox–Political debate. For example, in Raz's view, one of the main problems with Orthodox theories of human rights is their anachronism. By understanding human rights to be (in essence) natural rights, Raz argues that such theories fail to capture the special functions that human rights have come to play in international legal and political practice *today*. In other words, if Orthodox theories ever did provide a valid benchmark against which to evaluate human rights practice, in Raz's view they no longer do; the practice has changed in ways that render such theories irrelevant or obsolete.

Raz tries to provide us with what he thinks are the right criteria for evaluating human rights practice in a given *historical period*: one that starts roughly at the end of the Second World War—or, at the very latest, after the collapse of the Soviet Union[34]—and continues into the present day. During this period, Raz suggests that for the first time in history it has become internationally conventional to treat the violation of certain individual rights (called "human rights") as grounds for intervention in a state's sovereign affairs.

As already mentioned, Raz takes this to be the "distinctive" function of human rights practice.[35] And even though other proponents of the Political approach, such as Charles Beitz and John Rawls, offer subtly different accounts of this function,[36] their historical focus is much the same.[37] All three of these thinkers see themselves as capturing, in theoretical terms, an important historical *shift* in the international order that

---

[33] For a state-of-the-art and comprehensive overview of contemporary philosophical debates about human rights, *see:* Cruft, Liao, & Renzo 2015.

[34] Raz 2015, p. 217.   [35] Raz in this volume.

[36] *See:* footnotes 12, 13, and 14 in this introduction.   [37] *See:* Beitz 2009, p. 13; Rawls 1999, p. 79.

began sometime after the end of the Second World War, and which saw human rights take on a new regulatory role in global politics and law.

Orthodox theorists do not necessarily deny the reality of this shift, nor are they disinterested in the history of human rights. On the contrary, Orthodox theorists, just like their Political counterparts, are keen to capture (in theory) the distinctive functions attributed to human rights (in legal and political practice) since the end of the Second World War.[38] Where Orthodox and Political theorists differ is in their reading of *which* of these functions are worth incorporating into the *concept* of human rights and which are not.

Orthodox theorists accept that human rights have been ascribed new and important institutional roles over the last half-century or so. What they deny is that these changes are of *conceptual* significance, or that they should (in some fundamental way) govern our evaluation of the practice.

Rather than emphasize the theoretical significance of historical *shifts*, Orthodox theorists tend to emphasize the significance of certain *continuities* across the historical trajectory of human rights. For example, James Griffin, a key proponent of the Orthodox approach, argues that the modern (post-1948) idea of human rights is identical to its Enlightenment era predecessor:

> The notion of human rights that emerged by the end of the Enlightenment—what can reasonably be called the Enlightenment notion—is the notion we have today. There has been no theoretical development of the idea itself since then. It is not, of course, that there have been no developments of any sort. The League of Nations developed, through treaties, basic mechanisms for the international protection of human rights. The United Nations, through the Universal Declaration and subsequent instruments, created a largely agreed list of human rights, which has had wide ramifications in political life. International law now embodies human rights and has developed complex institutions of adjudication. And so on. But despite the many changes, none has been to the idea itself. The idea is still that of a right we have simply in virtue of being human, with no further explanation of what "human" means here.[39]

Tasioulas, for his part, makes broadly similar claims about the continuity between the contemporary idea of human rights (which he identifies, at its core, with a "distinctive moral sensibility") and the natural rights tradition.[40]

So part of what underlies the Orthodox–Political debate, then, is not so much a historical disagreement as a disagreement about the *theoretical significance* of (some events in) the postwar history of human rights. As such, the debate raises profound (and not at all obvious) questions about how and why history matters, as it were, and in particular how and why it matters for a philosophical theory of human rights. The two main chapters and three commentaries in this first Part of the book set out to answer these very questions.

*   *   *

---

[38] Griffin 2008, p. 29; Tasioulas in this volume, Sec. I.
[39] Griffin 2008, p. 13.   [40] Tasioulas 2012, p. 26.

Orthodox and Political theorists take an interest in the history of human rights because they believe that *evaluating* public practice requires historical perspective. Theorists on both sides agree that a philosophical conception of "human rights" that bears no resemblance to the historically contingent notion that has taken root in global politics, law, and society would fail to exert any *meaningful* critical leverage on the latter.[41]

This failure can be understood in different ways.[42] On the one hand, it may be a *semantic* failure: a wildly unfamiliar theory of human rights (one that, say, portrayed them as the rights of only a small subset of all living persons) is unlikely to come across as a theory of *human rights* at all; contemporary audiences will intuitively dismiss it as "changing the subject"—as confusing apples with oranges.

On the other hand, it may be a failure of *focus*: a theory interested in determining what rights should be recognized by, say, international human rights law (IHRL), ought to take account of the real-world (and historically contingent) consequences of recognizing rights in *that* environment. For instance, if we learn that the norms of IHRL are meant to be incorporated into domestic and regional law,[43] this gives us a reason to think that IHRL should recognize rights (like the right to social security) that can typically be protected by domestic institutions. In general, a theory that aims to evaluate the public practice of human rights needs to keep these and other historically contingent features of the practice in focus; otherwise, its recommendations will be "so remote from the practice of human rights as to be irrelevant to it."[44]

In the first chapter of the volume, Martti Koskenniemi suggests that studying the history of human rights is crucial to *more* than just meaningful philosophical engagement with public practice—history is, in fact, a valuable *replacement* for abstract philosophical theory. In Koskenniemi's view, there is not much to be gained from using philosophical reasoning to approach questions about what human rights are, why they exist, what they require of us, and how best to enact them in public life. When we try to do this, he suggests, even a cursory survey of the philosophical literature will show that we run into intellectual dead ends and interminable debates. Against this (gloomy) background, Koskenniemi argues that we can look to history as a way out—a way of answering some of the questions philosophy puts before us but without becoming bogged down in impossible abstractions.

Koskenniemi uses three episodes in the history of human rights (spanning from the 16th to the 18th centuries) to illustrate what he thinks we can learn, generally speaking, from historical analysis. What these episodes show, in his view, is that rights claims, even when advanced under the most rigorous philosophical auspices, are ultimately tools of politics and a product of historical forces. Rights claims come in on all sides of political conflicts—both as a way of challenging entrenched interests and advancing them—and so the illuminating thing to understand about rights, Koskenniemi asserts,

---

[41] Beitz 2009, p. 61; Griffin 2008, p. 29; Raz 2010, p. 324; Tasioulas in this volume, Sec. I.
[42] *See:* Etinson in this volume, Sec. V.   [43] *See:* fn. 18.   [44] Raz 2010, p. 323.

is not how they *should* be used but rather how they *are* used, and how they help political actors achieve certain ends in concrete historical circumstances.

In her helpful commentary, Annabel Brett suggests that Koskenniemi's dismissal of philosophy is less absolute than he makes it out to be. Brett suggests that Koskenniemi is opposed to "legislative" philosophical theories of human rights (theories that tell us "what human rights *are*," once and for all) but would accept a more speculative type of philosophy that offers "an imaginative construction of how human rights might be thought of, if we want to make a better world for living in." If this is a call for epistemically modest and historically informed philosophical work, then it should be welcomed. But it is hard to see how a philosophical theory of human rights can be purged of any "legislative" aspect—that is, any judgment as to how such rights ideally *ought* to be practised and/or understood.

Nor is it clear that Koskenniemi has offered us good reasons for thinking that it should. Philosophy may be difficult, and its conclusions subject to seemingly interminable debate, but the same is true of other disciplines, including history. And Koskenniemi's insightful historical observations about the realpolitik functions of human rights discourse might plausibly be used as an *aid* to (rather than as a *replacement* for) normative inquiry into how current legal-political practice might be improved, and in particular how it might learn from past mistakes—a claim powerfully defended by Pablo Gilabert and C. A. J. Coady in Part V of this volume.

Like Koskenniemi, Samuel Moyn thinks that history provides us with valuable insight into the nature and functions of human rights. But unlike Koskenniemi, Moyn clearly believes that philosophy has an important role to play here too—at least so long as it avoids the dangers of excessive abstraction. Moyn's request is that philosophers approach human rights with the aim of being both faithful and *helpful* to public practice. He asks, of theorists, that they both accurately interpret the publicly shared understanding of human rights (in law, politics, and society, etc.), as well as offer suggestions about how it might be improved, particularly in ways that will enhance the *realization* of human rights—their transformation of the "world itself."

In order for philosophical theory to do this, Moyn argues, it needs to be highly alert to its historical moment. Philosophers need to think carefully about the historical forces that allowed human rights to break out as a popular (or "salient") idea in the past, the factors that have limited their realization or fulfilment thus far, and the circumstances (and conceptual modifications) that might well allow them to break out as a more popular and realizable ideal in the future.

In a sense, then, Moyn wholly agrees with the main participants in the Orthodox–Political debate: historical awareness is crucial for meaningful critical engagement with public practice. But he also highlights a special virtue of such awareness: its capacity to help theorists solve the very important practical problem of realizing human rights in a recalcitrant world.

Moyn is right to think that philosophy can make an important contribution to this task. Philosophical attempts to understand, critique, and reimagine human rights can help practitioners set basic goals as well as evaluate different strategies of implementation. But it is not obvious that philosophers should be so interested in developing theories of human rights that are palatable to the public at large, or that fit with (what we might call) the current historical "zeitgeist," in the way that Moyn suggests. Doing so may (possibly) make philosophical theories of human rights easier to realize, but it may also diminish their critical power or normative plausibility.

Furthermore, as John Tasioulas notes in his reply to Moyn, realizing human rights is a *multi*-disciplinary effort. It requires skill, effort, data, favourable circumstance, leadership, institutions, and human ingenuity that vastly outstrip anything philosophical insight alone can provide. With that in mind, Moyn's argument for a philosophy of human rights that (with the aid of history) is in charge of transforming both the world of ideas *and* the world itself may seem to trade on an overinflated understanding of the discipline.

That said, Moyn's argument serves as an important provocation for philosophers, one that forces them to address productive questions about the role of philosophy in the study and advancement of human rights, and about the role of history in philosophy. In his overview of this first Part of the volume, Jeffrey Flynn highlights some of the ways in which the disciplinary objectives of history and philosophy can both intersect and diverge in the context of human rights.

II. The Orthodox–Political Debate

Part II of the volume takes a direct look at the Orthodox–Political debate itself. The debate operates at four different levels, each of which addresses a different set of questions. These include questions about (i) the *nature* of human rights, (ii) their *grounds*, (iii) their *content*, and (iv) the *aims* and *methods* of a philosophical theory of human rights in general.

These questions are not entirely insulated from one another. If, for example, one adopts an Orthodox understanding of (i) the *nature* of human rights, understanding them to be moral rights that we have simply in virtue of being human, this exerts logical pressure on one's understanding of (ii) and (iii): presumably, the existence of such rights will depend on certain facts about human nature (a claim about *grounds*), and only those moral rights that are grounded in such facts will qualify as genuine human rights (a claim about *content*).

So there is a natural order of operations here; it makes good theoretical sense to start out by identifying (i) the nature of human rights, and to proceed onwards from there, allowing the dominoes to fall accordingly. But philosophical claims about the "nature" or "concept" of human rights can be opaque until we say something about their scope and purpose, as well as about the kind of evidence that can be marshalled in their favour—that is, until we say something about (iv).

For instance, when Orthodox theorists tell us that human rights are moral rights that we have simply in virtue of being human, it helps a great deal to know that this is not just a brute philosophical stipulation, but rather an attempt to home in on an understanding of human rights that embodies various *virtues*: (a) historical resonance,[45] (b) fidelity to contemporary legal and political practice,[46] (c) theoretical determinacy,[47] (d) broad acceptability,[48] and (e) ethical or normative plausibility.[49] Similarly, when Political theorists say that human rights are individual moral rights that limit the exercise of national sovereignty, it helps just as much to know that this is an attempt to identify the role of "human rights" within the specific context of (b) contemporary international politics and law.[50]

In a sense, these details of scope and purpose form part of the *meaning* of claims about the nature of human rights; they help us understand what such theoretical claims ultimately amount to. Furthermore, these meta-theoretical details tell us something about how to *evaluate* claims about the nature or concept of human rights—that is, about the kind of evidence that can be marshalled in their favour, or to their discredit. All of this is crucial to making rational engagement possible.

For this very reason, most theorists in fact start by identifying (iv)—the scope, purpose, and evidentiary grounds of their theory of human rights—and then move on from *there*. Beitz, Griffin, Raz, and Tasioulas all preface their theoretical claims with (meta-theoretical) declarations of aim and approach.

Indeed, Raz and Beitz think that what ultimately distinguishes a Political conception of human rights from its Orthodox counterpart is its stance on questions of just this type (iv). In their view, Political theories of human rights are distinguished not by what they say about the basic nature of such rights, but rather by their underlying commitment to saying something that, again, captures the functions attributed to "human rights" in contemporary international legal and political practice, whatever these ultimately turn out to be.[51]

This might seem puzzling given that, as already noted, Orthodox theorists like Griffin and Tasioulas *also* appear to share an interest in modelling these functions. And puzzling it is. The fact that Beitz and Raz take themselves to be offering not just a different philosophical theory, but a fundamentally different *kind* of philosophical theory from their Orthodox counterparts, highlights an important weakness of the debate so far. Despite their prefatory focus on questions of aim and approach, participants in the Orthodox–Political debate have rarely specified just how their answers to such questions *compare* to those of their interlocutors. This has left the debate vulnerable to basic misunderstanding and cross-talk. And several commentators have seized on this in recent years, arguing that Orthodox and Political theories of human rights are compatible in ways not recognized by their main proponents.[52]

The contributions in this second Part of the volume directly address these two crucial *levels* of the Orthodox–Political debate. First, they address the core question of how best to conceive of (i) the nature of human rights. And second, they shed valuable

---

[45]   *See:* Griffin 2008, ch. 1.   [46]   *See:* fn. 38.
[47]   Griffin 2008, pp. 2, 14–20.   [48]   Tasioulas in this volume, Sec. I.
[49]   Griffin 2008, p. 2, 4; Tasioulas in this volume, Sec. I.
[50]   Raz 2010, p. 327; Beitz 2009, pp. 42–4, 102–6.
[51]   Idem.   [52]   Liao & Etinson 2012; Gilabert 2011.

light on the meta-theoretical issue of (iv) what theorists are really doing (and what they *should* be doing) when they construct a philosophical theory of human rights that answers questions of this first sort, and others. Several contributions also address the claim that Orthodox and Political theories are at cross-purposes, or ultimately compatible with one another.

*   *   *

Jeremy Waldron's chapter wrestles directly with the *first* level of debate. There, the key issue, as he puts it, is to figure out what sense to make of the term "human" in human rights. Waldron presents us with two broad alternatives, which roughly correspond to the options presented by Orthodox and Political theories but also frame them in a new light.

One option is the "human bearer" approach (aka the Orthodox view), which understands human rights as rights *born* by all persons in virtue of their humanity. The other option is the "human concern" approach, which takes human rights to be the proper *concern* of all human agents—a concern that (as the Political view suggests) cannot be successfully rebuffed by appeals to national sovereignty.

These alternatives do not exhaust the contemporary theoretical landscape. For one, there is a common type of view that is plausibly categorized as "Political"—because it defines human rights as rights that serve the overtly political function of setting necessary standards of legitimate governance[53]—but that does not seem to fit within Waldron's binary schema. Nonetheless, the schema does effectively embrace the leading theoretical alternatives currently on offer, including those Waldron wants to criticize: Raz and Rawls's *concern*-based theories of human rights.

Waldron interestingly points out that debates about the nature of human rights cannot ultimately be resolved by appeal to the ordinary or everyday meaning of the term. He agrees with Raz that, analytically speaking, "the whole field is a bit of a mess."[54] As Waldron sees it, "The question is not: What does the "human" in "human rights" *really mean*? The question is: what is the more convenient and illuminating use to make of the term in this context?"

If we take this point seriously, perhaps we should think of Orthodox and Political accounts of human rights as presenting us with something *less* than a full analytic definition thereof—that is, something less than the necessary and sufficient conditions under which any right qualifies as a *human* right. We might instead think of these accounts as describing "characteristic" or even contingent features of such rights in particular circumstances.[55]

Even on this score, however, Waldron thinks we should be wary of following Raz and Rawls in linking human rights to a specific kind of actionable *concern* on the part

---

[53] *See:* fn. 12.

[54] "There is not enough discipline underpinning the use of the term 'human rights' to make it a useful analytical tool." (Raz 2010, pp. 336–7.)

[55] *See:* Nickel's chapter in this volume for one possible way of making sense of this suggestion.

of others, particularly in the international arena. Waldron's chapter meticulously high-lights various costs or "inconveniences" of doing so: costs that include losing sight of the *individualism* of human rights—that is, the normal thought that these are rights that every human being, considered as a discrete individual person, can be said to have—and the implication of a (false) discontinuity between human rights and consti-tutional rights. Together, these concerns present a powerful challenge to the Political account of human rights, or at least to one version of it.

In his reply, Joseph Raz suggests that Waldron has misunderstood the basic point of developing a Political account. Raz denies having any interest in the question of what sense should be made of the "human" in human rights, or what the characteristic or core features of such rights might be. Instead, he insists that he is strictly interested in the legal and political *practice* of human rights, and in identifying the normative stand-ards against which that practice should be judged—standards that, he thinks, are not (fully) captured by the *moral* human rights affirmed by Orthodox theorists.

But Raz's provocative response to Waldron may overstate things. After all, Raz *is* interested in identifying characteristic or core features of human rights; it is just that he confines his focus to those "human rights" explicitly recognized in contemporary international politics and law. And most importantly, it is not clear that Waldron's focus is any different, particularly given his more general interest in the analysis of *legal* (rather than purely moral) concepts.[56]

James W. Nickel's chapter takes a less partisan stance on the Orthodox–Political debate. Nickel's interest is wholly in questions of type (iv). That is, his chapter sheds light on the differences in aim and approach that *underlie* type (i) conceptual disagree-ments about the nature of human rights—differences of just the kind Raz brings up in his reply.

Nickel points out that Orthodox and Political accounts of human rights can plaus-ibly be seen as having different *aims* or areas of "focus." For instance, Griffin's Orthodox theory identifies features or functions (mainly, the protection of normative agency) attributable to human rights, understood as a set of authoritative moral norms, in *any* time period. His focus is atemporal.[57] It also identifies features that such rights would have across a range of contexts of application—or "spheres" of life, as Nickel calls them. These include not just international but also domestic and interpersonal affairs.[58] Political theorists like Rawls, Raz, and Beitz, by contrast, are more constrained in their focus. Their theories aim to capture features (such as the limitation of national sovereignty) attributable to human rights as they operate in modern times (post-1948), and particularly in *international* politics and law.

Understood in this way, Nickel argues, Orthodox and Political theories might be seen as offering compatible and even mutually correct accounts of human rights. But unlike some other recent work on the compatibility of Orthodox and Political

---

[56] *See e.g.* Waldron 2012, pp. 13–15, to pick one example.   [57] Griffin 2008, pp. 50–1.
[58] Ibid., p. 170.

perspectives on human rights,[59] Nickel is careful not to suggest that his observations necessarily *resolve* the debate. Instead, he simply exhorts theorists to be more transparent about issues of focus, and to be more sharply aware of how their choice of focus compares to that of others—an issue that is all too important if the integrity of current philosophical debates is to be maintained going forward.

Adam Etinson's response casts some doubt on the conciliatory power of Nickel's analysis. Nickel's chapter implicitly draws on an accommodating master-view of human rights on which various orientations of focus are possible. But this master-view might be rejected by Political theorists, such as Charles Beitz and John Rawls, who think of human rights as (essentially) norms that govern the behaviour of states under modern circumstances—that is, as norms that operate in the contemporary international domain *exclusively*. In this respect, Nickel's analysis may be more of a *participant* in the Orthodox–Political debate than it pretends to be.

This does not stop Nickel's analysis from providing significant insight. And Etinson's commentary deliberately uses it to shed light on the meaning, justification, and importance of a poorly understood feature of the Orthodox–Political debate: the (ubiquitous) notion that philosophical theories of human rights should be "faithful to the practice" thereof. Etinson identifies and critically examines two independent arguments for this notion—one based on semantic, and the other on focus-related considerations of just the kind explored by Nickel.

Andrea Sangiovanni's chapter ambitiously covers questions of type (i) *and* (iv). Its most striking contribution is the addition of an *alternative* to the Orthodox and Political accounts of human rights: what Sangiovanni calls the "Broad View." The Broad View of human rights is distinguished by its *accommodating* power (hence the label). Its core conceptual claim (i) is that human rights are "those moral rights that ought to be of universal moral, legal, and political *concern*." So Sangiovanni seems to offer us a version of what Waldron calls the "human concern" approach to human rights.

But the type of "concern" at issue here is far more open-ended than it is on Waldron's view. Since many types of moral rights should plausibly concern us all, some human rights, according to the Broad View, will be moral rights that we have simply in virtue of being human (Orthodox), and others will be moral rights that limit the exercise of national sovereignty (Political). Human rights include rights of *both* these types, and more. In this way, the Broad View *subsumes* its Orthodox and Political counterparts.

Sangiovanni offers an array of interesting reasons for adopting this exceedingly broad understanding of human rights. But one of its key motivations is the diversity and breadth of human rights practice itself. Like Orthodox and Political theorists, Sangiovanni believes that a theory of human rights ought to be adequately faithful to the practice thereof. Unlike those theorists, however, he believes that the practice is *too* broad and diverse to be captured by any concept of human rights as *specific* as those of Orthodox and Political views.[60]

---

[59] *See* fn. 52.   [60] See Tadros 2015 (p. 445), for a similar point.

Some practitioners have little interest in whether or not the rights they affirm are grounded in considerations of humanity. Others will have little interest in whether they override considerations of sovereignty. And there is nothing wrong with this; in Sangiovanni's view, there simply is no deep moral unity underlying the various activities and interests of human rights practitioners.

This is a provocative claim. It questions an assumption that seems to be widely shared in the Orthodox–Political debate: that there *is* a single (reasonably specific) concept of human rights governing the "practice." At the very least, Sangiovanni is right to flag this assumption as one worthy of serious examination.

But the Broad View faces challenges of its own. One is, ironically, a problem of fidelity. The theory is so deliberately vague and open-ended that it seems to stretch well beyond any normal sense of the boundaries of human rights talk itself. For instance, since the welfare of animals is plausibly of universal moral concern, Sangiovanni's theory will include *non*-human animals among the bearers of *human* rights—a highly counterintuitive result. Other worries about the extraordinary breadth of the view are highlighted by Rainer Forst in his incisive commentary.

III. Morality and Law

The major instruments of human rights law (whether domestic, regional, or international) are often thought of as vehicles for the implementation of pre-existent moral rights. There are various reasons why this is so.

First, it is undergirded by the apparent "suprapositivity"[61] of human rights—their possession of a normative authority (i.e. a moral existence or validity) that *transcends* their embodiment in law. As mentioned in Section I of this Introduction, the human right not to be enslaved seems to have just this type of authority. We have a duty to respect it even if the law fails to acknowledge as much. And it is natural to say the same about many other human rights as well. This opens up the possibility that human rights can *motivate* or *justify* their own legal embodiment; their suprapositivity makes them capable, at least in principle, of calling for the creation of law, rather than just being creatures of it.

A second key observation is that human rights law portrays *itself* as a medium for the enactment of suprapositive rights. The two core instruments of international human rights law (the ICCPR and ICESCR), for instance, both present themselves as engaged in the "recognition"—rather than the creation or stipulation—of human rights: "the equal and inalienable rights of all members of the human family."[62] And these rights are said to "derive from the inherent dignity of the human person."[63] This claim seems to imply that international human rights law is grounded in a moral status

---

[61] Neuman 2003, p. 1868. *See also:* Cruft, Liao, & Renzo 2015, p. 5; Griffin 2008, p. 54.
[62] ICCPR, Preamble; ICESCR, Preamble.   [63] ICCPR, Preamble; ICESCR, Preamble.

or value that exists beyond it (hence its "inherence"), and that gains expression and protection through it.[64]

In addition to all of this, thinking of human rights law as a vehicle for the implementation of human rights morality is a very natural way of understanding its function as a *distinct* area of law. Generally speaking, areas of law are developed in response to, and defined by their service of, certain identifiable needs. International Aviation Law, for instance, addresses the need for universal standards governing air travel, air traffic safety, and associated activities.

In the case of human rights law, broadly speaking, the relevant need seems to be that of articulating, enforcing, regulating, and monitoring compliance with *human rights*, understood as (among other things) a set of pressing moral rights that require universal recognition. This is not the only way of understanding the distinctive role of human rights law, nor are these the only reasons for doing so, but it is a natural view that many philosophers, lawyers, and legal theorists have found attractive.[65]

However natural this thought may be, the relationship between human rights morality and law has come under intense scrutiny in recent years. Two questions in particular have received special attention. First, there has been controversy over whether (a) *all* moral human rights require legal recognition. And second, there has been some discussion about whether (b) *only* moral human rights can justify the enactment of legal human rights—that is, about whether human rights law serves justifiable purposes *beyond* that of implementing human rights morality.

The first claim (a) has received considerable and longstanding support.[66] According to many, moral human rights—and indeed, moral rights in general[67]—are something like "laws in waiting."[68] They are the kind of moral norms that *ought* to be incorporated into law and coercively enforced, if they are not already.

As already mentioned in this introduction, however, not all moral human rights seem worthy of legal recognition. Consider, again, the right (among spouses) to an equal or fair say in important family decisions.[69] This certainly seems like a human right—one that all human beings are entitled to—but it nonetheless appears unworthy of *legal* recognition. Not only would it be extremely difficult for courts of law to adjudicate a right of this sort, such adjudication would interfere with the privacy of family life in ways that seem more broadly damaging or inappropriate. Similar concerns come up in the case of other plausible human rights, such as the right of mature children to

---

[64] There is plenty of room for disagreement here. (*See e.g.* Waldron 2012 and Waldron 2015, who thinks of human dignity as a principally *legal* doctrine.) I am simply articulating what I take to be a natural reading of this claim.

[65] *See e.g.* Cranston 1983 pp. 16–17; Griffin 2010, p. 353; Lauterpacht 1950, p. 74; Neuman 2003, pp. 1868–9; Nickel 2007, p. 10; Wellman 2011, ch. 4.

[66] *See e.g.* Cranston 1983, p. 16; Hart 1955, pp. 177–8; Habermas 2010, p. 470; Martin 1989, p. 83.

[67] Hart 1955.　　[68] The phrase is from Sen 2004, p. 326.

[69] The example is borrowed from Tasioulas 2012, p. 2.

(parental) respect for their autonomy,[70] or the right of all human beings to respect in general.[71]

There is a way in which these examples can be accommodated by (a). Much depends on how we interpret the normative strength of the claim. If (a) is read *strongly*, as asserting that there is always a *conclusive* case in favour of positivizing any moral human right, then the prospect of accommodation is closed, and we have to decide whether to reject the examples or to reject (a).

On the other hand, if the claim is read more *weakly*, as suggesting only that there is always a *pro tanto* or *prima facie* case in favour of positivizing any moral human right, then the possibility of accommodation remains open. Indeed, arguably, the examples cited above are simply ones in which pro tanto reasons in favour of legal positivization are defeated by weighty concerns about justiciability, appropriate forms of punishment, and/or the value of privacy, etc. Perhaps there always *is* a pro tanto case in favour of legally recognizing moral human rights—or any moral right, for that matter—just not always a conclusive one.

While this conciliatory strategy might work, at least in principle, it is not clear that it provides us with insight into the thinking of any actual proponent of (a). This is because authors that defend (a) have rarely specified its *strength*—that is, whether they endorse the weak or strong version thereof. Jürgen Habermas, for instance, says variously that human rights are "oriented" towards, "designed" for, and uniquely amenable to institutionalization and coercive enforcement.[72] But none of this really clarifies the normative strength of their alleged legalistic orientation.

There is no absolute need for reconciliation here of course. One plausible reaction to the examples is simply to reject (a) in both its weak and strong forms. And, indeed, if the examples are convincing, this may well be the more plausible way to go. After all, it is not obvious that there is even a *pro tanto* case to be made in favour of legally implementing the right to an equal or fair say in important family decisions, and considerably less obvious that this right is somehow a "law in waiting," uniquely oriented towards or designed for coercive legal enforcement.

Instead, we might take the examples to illustrate the plausibility of adopting a less legalistic understanding of moral human rights, and of moral rights in general. On one such understanding, a moral right simply identifies what some duty-bearer(s) owe, or are morally required to provide, to some right-holder(s). The question of whether (and how) that duty should be enforced by third parties is left entirely open to additional argument and circumstances. On another such understanding, moral rights do necessarily call for *some* form of third-party (i.e. social or institutional) enforcement, but not necessarily legal enforcement in particular. Perhaps in many or most instances legal measures will be appropriate, but in others we may find that enforcement via less formal social customs and attitudes is more advantageous.

---

[70] Griffin 2010, pp. 354–5.   [71] Buchanan & Sreenivasan in this volume, Sec. 4.
[72] Habermas 2010, p. 470.

This last understanding of moral rights has a strong following and dates at least as far back as John Stuart Mill.[73] When applied to moral human rights in particular, it makes ample room for the diversity of ways in which human rights find recognition and protection in the real world: through monitoring and information-sharing, public criticism and condemnation (or so-called "jawboning"),[74] popular mobilization, and other informal mechanisms. As Tasioulas mentions in this volume, the widely endorsed 2011 "Guiding Principles on Business and Human Rights," developed by Professor John Ruggie, are a good example of this.[75] These principles assign ambitious responsibilities for respecting human rights to business corporations, but they do not establish legal obligations of any sort. Rather, they aim to be effective by setting clear behavioural expectations that can serve as a focal point for social and political action.

The Millian understanding of moral rights is still compatible with their having *some* special orientation towards law. For instance, we might think of moral human rights as *generally* deserving (as a statistical and contingent matter) of legal recognition, or we might single out some *subset* of moral human rights as deserving of legal recognition, even if we accept that not all human rights are.[76]

The contributions in this third Part of the volume do not challenge the idea that moral human rights may call for diverse (potentially non-legal) forms of recognition, protection, and implementation. Their focus is instead on the moral functions of *legal* human rights—those human rights that *are* recognized in law. They approach this topic in two main ways. First, they examine whether (b) these functions are *restricted* to that of expressing correspondent moral human rights, or whether they include more than this. And second, they offer an account of the specific values realized by various *systematic features* of human rights law. Both of these projects offer a macroscopic supplement to well-known work on the value (and *dis*value) of *particular* legal human rights, including the right to health,[77] the right to democracy,[78] and the right to periodic holidays with pay,[79] among many others.

*   *   *

Allen Buchanan and Gopal Sreenivasan's discussion starts from the assumption that international human rights law (IHRL) is an *instrument* or *tool*, one that serves a variety of moral purposes. Against the grain of the suggestion made earlier in this Section of the Introduction, however, they argue that the implementation of pre-existent moral human rights is *not* an essential part of what IHRL does.

---

[73] Mill 1989, p. 14; Sen 2004, pp. 320–8; Tasioulas 2012, p. 2.   [74] Nickel 2006, pp. 271–4.

[75] Tasioulas in this volume, Sec. III.

[76] One view on which any such affirmation is impossible is that of Samantha Besson, according to whom moral human rights only exist *once* they have been given legal recognition. On this view, in other words, moral human rights are "children" rather than "parents" of their legal counterparts. *See*: Besson 2011.

[77] Brownlee 2015; Hassoun 2015; Wolff 2012.

[78] Benhabib 2011; Christiano 2011; Cohen 2010; Gilabert 2012.

[79] Cranston 1983, pp. 7, 12–13; Griffin 2008, p. 209; Risse 2009; Waldron 1993, pp. 12–13.

In their view, IHRL consists in a set of legal entitlements that: (i) individuals hold primarily against their state; (ii) become binding on states through a process of ratification; and (iii) can limit the exercise of sovereignty even within a state's own borders. Given that there might plausibly be a wide range of moral reasons to enact any given legal entitlement of this sort—as discussed in the case of the right to health—Buchanan and Sreenivasan argue that there is no reason why these entitlements should be limited to ones that correspond to pre-existent moral human rights, or even to moral rights in general. Thus, they deny (b), or what they call "the mirroring view": the idea that the only justifiable moral reason for enacting an international legal human right is that it corresponds to a pre-existent moral human right of similar content and character.[80]

In denying (b), Buchanan and Sreenivasan take themselves to be overturning a kind of orthodoxy within the philosophy of human rights, one that cuts across the Orthodox–Political divide. And indeed, to the extent that rejecting (b) involves rejecting the intuitive idea that legal human rights are a vehicle for the expression and protection of pre-existent moral human rights, Buchanan and Sreenivasan do reject a commonly held view.

But there is in fact little reason to think that this commonly held view stands or falls on the truth of (b). IHRL *can* be a vehicle for the expression, recognition, and enforcement of pre-existent moral human rights—indeed, this can even be its characteristic purpose, or *most* of what it does—even if it is sometimes justifiable to enact a legal human right that has no obvious moral counterpart. We may even find, as Erasmus Mayr suggests in his comments, that justifiable international legal human rights always *do* express corresponding moral human rights, despite this not being a strict or straightforward necessity. There is no logical contradiction here. Nor is it clear that any actual author holds the restrictive "mirroring view" (b).[81] But even if Buchanan and Sreenivasan overestimate the revisionary nature of their position, their discussion helpfully identifies some of the central complexities involved in morally evaluating the content and structure of IHRL.

Mattias Kumm's chapter takes on just this evaluative task. His interest is in diagnosing the "moral point" of three structural or pervasive features of human rights law, with a special focus on the European system in particular. These features include: (i) the broad *scope* of legal human rights—their guarantee of much more than just minimally decent forms of existence; (ii) the fact that some legal human rights are regarded as subject to justifiable *infringement*, provided certain proportionality requirements are met; and (iii) the extensive *variation* both in terms of the formulation and judicial interpretation of human rights across jurisdictions and strata of human rights law.

Kumm's central suggestion is that we should interpret these practices as mandated by a conception of justice centered on the idea of a universal "right to justification"—a

---

[80] *Also see:* Buchanan 2013, pp. 14–23.
[81] Griffin, who Buchanan and Sreenivasan suggest can "naturally" be read as holding this view, explicitly denies it in at least one instance: Griffin 2010, p. 351. So too does Raz in this volume.

constructivist principle of Kantian inspiration that has recently been championed by Rainer Forst.[82] According to this basic right or principle of justice, political and legal institutions ought to be constructed in accordance with norms that free and equal persons can reasonably be expected to accept. For Kumm, legal human rights are a crucial vehicle through which the content of such norms is decided and expressed. And this makes them not only a central part of politics and law but also a key object of reasonable disagreement themselves. It is this (moral) centrality and (epistemic) contestability, Kumm suggests, that explains both the origin and value of features (i), (ii), and (iii) above: the broad invocation of human rights; their curtailment in cases of conflicting objectives; and extensive disagreement about their content.

Kumm presents this account as the "best justification" of the practice we have, not just as one possible moral justification thereof. In order to successfully demonstrate this, however, Kumm not only has to address possible gaps between his constructivist principle and the practices he seeks to vindicate—gaps that Samantha Besson, in her commentary, insists are real; he also needs to address *other* possible ways of justifying (i), (ii), and (iii). And this includes offering some argument to those who are not already convinced that Kantian constructivism (or some version thereof) provides the best framework for thinking about justice in general.

Kumm's analysis is further complicated by a simultaneous interest in both moral justification (the *value* of x) and historical explanation (the *origins* of x). Though it may only do so implicitly, Kumm's chapter attempts to uncover a logic that both justifies and *explains* key features of contemporary human rights practice. These are two very different tasks, however, and Kumm rarely engages in the kind of historical evidence-gathering (e.g. about the intentions of key drafters, politicians, judges, and practitioners, etc.) necessary to accomplish the latter. In fairness, Kumm admits that his account offers only the beginnings of a complete argument. And in the meantime, it outlines an impressively comprehensive framework for evaluating human rights law.

Andreas Follesdal's chapter, like Kumm's, has a strong European focus. But Follesdal's interest is in gauging the value of a more singular and specific legal phenomenon: the so-called "Margin of Appreciation" (MA) doctrine famously practised by the European Court of Human Rights (ECtHR). The MA requires the ECtHR to show a degree of deference, under certain conditions, to the judgement of a domestic authority when determining whether it is in compliance with its treaty obligations under the European Convention on Human Rights (ECHR). In so doing, the doctrine effectively allows for member states to interpret and implement the ECHR in different ways. And for this reason it has been an object of both strong praise and condemnation.[83] Follesdal nimbly explores a broad array of arguments on either side, but his leading hypothesis is that the leeway it provides can be justified by a general principle of respect for democracy, and particularly for democratic decision-making at the domestic level.

---

[82] *See:* Forst 2012.   [83] *See e.g.* Benvenisti 1999; Letsas 2006; Shany 2006; Wilkins 2002.

This justification has its limits, however. As Follesdal explains, when there is no good evidence to suggest that a state's action, law, or policy is backed by genuinely democratic support, or if basic democratic rights are themselves at stake, the ECtHR should refuse to grant the state a MA on that issue. In such "undemocratic" situations, the principle of respect for democracy no longer speaks in favour of the MA, and may indeed prohibit it.

Follesdal's account has the advantage of being valuably specific about what it is that makes the MA an attractive doctrine; he avoids the natural temptation of simply grounding this on the broad value of national "sovereignty"—indeed, as George Letsas suggests in his extensive commentary, a case built on respect for sovereignty may fail outright. But Follesdal's account also faces some hurdles. It is not easy, after all, to measure the democratic character of a judicial decision, piece of legislation, let alone of an entire state. Judges, for one, are often appointed rather than elected, making their democratic credentials especially hard to assess. And even if we want regional courts like the ECtHR to be making these kinds of measurements, there is a serious risk that very few actual states will qualify as sufficiently democratic to be granted an MA— that is, unless the bar is set quite low. The risk here is that justifiable applications of the MA would be so rare as to render the doctrine almost practically irrelevant.

IV. Ideals and their Limits

Human rights are *ideals*. They set standards of conduct (and also of belief, attitude, and emotion)[84] to which various agents are expected to conform. But how demanding are human rights? How far must we travel, as it were, to fulfil them? Is this even possible? For a volume that is about the relationship between the normative reality of human rights, on the one hand, and their imbrication in the concrete worlds of law, politics, and popular morality, on the other, these are central questions.

Most theorists agree that human rights are subject to a "practicability" or "feasibility" test. And a key reason for this is the plausibility of the common assumption that "ought implies can"—that a person or institution cannot be obligated to do the impossible.[85] For example, one can hardly be obligated to rescue a child that is drowning on the other side of the planet. The sheer physical impossibility of such an act makes it an implausible object of duty. But human rights are standardly understood to correlate with duties; without duties, there can be no rights. And so human rights are naturally subject to such concerns about feasibility. As Maurice Cranston, one of the earliest authors to write on this topic, explains: "If it is impossible for a thing to be done, it is absurd to claim it as a right."[86]

---

[84] Not only is the UDHR framed (at least partly) as an educational document to be used for teaching or promoting belief in human rights, it also aims to promote certain moral *attitudes*: Article 1, for instance, demands that all human beings "act towards one another in a *spirit* of brotherhood" (my emphasis). For a defence of the idea that love is a requirement of human rights, *see* Liao 2015.

[85] For a classic critique, *see*: Sinnott-Armstrong 1984.   [86] Cranston 1973, p. 66.

But even if we accept the idea that human rights must be feasible, we can still reasonably ask *how* feasible they must be. Cranston himself believes that a genuine human right must be achievable (a) for *all* persons (b) *today*. For example, since (in his view) the widely proclaimed human right to periodic holidays with pay satisfies neither of these conditions, it is not a genuine human right.[87]

But this is an implausibly strong test. Even the universally recognized human right to bodily security seems likely to fail it, given that part of what this right requires is adequate institutional *protection* against attack (via effective law enforcement, legislative action, a competent criminal justice system, etc.), and providing this for every last person on the planet is probably not possible today, though it may one day be so.

The alternative is to adopt some weaker version of the feasibility test. And there is good reason to think that it should be quite a bit more flexible than Cranston's. One reason to think so is that there are often concrete steps that can be taken to make presently *in*feasible rights feasible in the near or distant future. For example, even if we cannot currently grant the human right to periodic holidays with pay to all persons, there are still steps (through advocacy, institution building, campaigning, etc.) that we can take today to make this a more universally realizable right in the future. When such steps are possible, when a right has this partial degree of feasibility, it seems feasible *enough* to perform the basic functions of (and thus count as a legitimate instance of) a right: it can assign meaningful and actionable duties to agents, even if these duties have an essentially forward-looking character.

Indeed, several authors have taken these observations to be grounds for thinking that human rights generate two distinct categories of duties: (i) "direct" duties to respect or fulfil human rights, and (ii) "indirect" duties to make respecting or fulfilling them a more feasible task in the future.[88]

The contributions in this fourth Part of the volume tackle two outstanding questions in this area of debate. First, they examine the common line of thought defended just above—that is, the idea that human rights must be feasible in at least *some* sense. And second, they ask how human rights can have the sort of dualistic normative character described just a moment ago. How can human rights *both* require (i) full and immediate respect or satisfaction (as in the case of, say, the right not to be tortured) while also setting (ii) long-term goals towards which we are expected to work in an incremental fashion (as in the case of, say, the right to periodic holidays with pay)? Is there any fundamental incoherence here?

*   *   *

---

[87] Cranston 1973, p. 66. The right is recognized in the UDHR, Article 24, and the ICESCR, Article 7(d).
[88] *See:* Beitz 2009, p. 121; Gilabert 2009, pp. 676–8. The distinction maps on fairly well to the juridical distinction between "minimum core" and "progressive realization" rights. *See:* Committee on Economic, Social and Cultural Rights, "General Comment No. 3" (1990).

Kimberley Brownlee's chapter takes on the first of these questions. Against the grain of a good deal of contemporary theory,[89] Brownlee argues that human rights need not pass *any* feasibility test, weak or strong. This is because, as she argues, contrary to what most assume, human rights do not need to be feasible in order to meaningfully and legitimately guide action; there is, in other words, nothing particularly "absurd" about claiming a right to the impossible. Indeed, as she explains, there are in fact many ideals that are unattainable and yet fully capable of guiding action.

One example, in her view, is the ideal of being a good parent, which she takes to be a so-called "sustainability ideal" in that it requires *sustained* fulfilment. It is of course impossible to *always* be a good parent. Even the very best parent will suffer intermittent lapses. And yet, it seems obvious that the ideal of being a good parent, suitably fleshed out, can serve as a meaningful and worthy guide to action nonetheless. Brownlee's claim is that human rights are like this too. Like sustainability ideals, they require *continuous* respect or satisfaction—which, as she explains, is impossible. Even if a government can succeed for a time at fully securing its citizens' human rights to, say, political participation and due process, "there will inevitably be circumstances in which some people are either denied due process or illegitimately disenfranchised due to errors or prejudices." But these inevitable lapses, and the consequent unattainability of human rights ideals, do not undermine their action-guiding character. Thus, not only are human rights infeasible, their being so is little cause for concern.

Brownlee's argument moves from the observation that (a) *flawless* compliance with human rights is impossible to the assumption that (b) compliance with human rights is infeasible *simpliciter*. But this move may be too quick. As Rowan Cruft points out in his response to Brownlee, even if full or perfect compliance with human rights is impossible, this would not rule out their being feasible in other "lesser" ways. Indeed, if it were not at least possible to *approximate* human rights ideals—like those of sustainably securing citizens' rights to political participation and due process—then, as Cranston points out, it would hardly seem rational to pursue them.

So there is reason to think that even Brownlee's understanding of human rights requires that they be feasible in *some* respect, which undermines her attempt to transcend contemporary debates about the stringency of the feasibility test altogether. Even if this is correct, however, it still leaves intact her provocative suggestion that *full* respect for human rights is an ideal out of reach for human individuals and institutions.

The main goal of Elizabeth Ashford's chapter is to defend subsistence rights (to basic food, housing, healthcare, etc.) against those who would dismiss them as "secondary" or even counterfeit ("manifesto") human rights.[90] Attacks of this sort have been advanced on various grounds, but Ashford's interest is in those grounded in the (apparent) non-*urgency* of subsistence rights, particularly when compared with traditional liberty rights.

---

[89] *See:* Gilabert 2009 for an excellent overview.
[90] *See e.g.* Cranston 1973, ch. 8; Feinberg 1970, pp. 254–6; O'Neill 2005.

As she points out, liberty rights (like the right not to be tortured) have an obvious air of urgency about them: they are rights of the utmost moral priority and must be immediately complied with. However, subsistence rights (like the right to adequate healthcare) appear to have a more aspirational character: they are rights towards which we are meant to *work*, in a progressive, step-by-step manner. The concern, then, is that subsistence rights generate goal-like duties of type (ii) rather than genuine rights-based duties of type (i) and that, because of this, including them in standard lists of human rights risks "diluting" the moral force thereof. With subsistence rights in the mix, human rights appear to lack consistent moral urgency, and may (all too conveniently) be glossed over as rights that can be "deferred" as long-term projects in the works.

Ashford addresses these concerns in two main ways. First, she argues that subsistence or welfare rights are not *alone* in having an aspirational component. As mentioned, protecting liberty rights (such as the right to bodily security) is just as much of a long-term, progressively realizable project as is securing the means of subsistence for all. The development of an effective criminal justice system is a complex, incremental, and resource-intensive task. So, even if the aspirational aspect of human rights is something to lament, subsistence or welfare rights are not *solely* responsible for it.

Second, Ashford argues that, like other human rights, subsistence rights *combine* both aspirational and peremptory components. As she explains, developing Shue's tripartite analysis of rights,[91] (a) the institutionalized *protection* of individuals against life-threatening deprivation may be a long-term project, but (b) the duty not to *deprive*, and (c) certain instances of the duty to *aid* the deprived, are "primary" duties of the utmost moral urgency, on par (in Ashford's view) with the duty not to torture.

Thus, the best way to avoid casting all human rights under the glow of their aspirational component is to be more clear-eyed and discerning about the *variety* of duties they are capable of generating. Ashford makes a good case for this variety, and also for the urgency of coordinated action and institution-building that addresses global subsistence needs today. But she leaves untouched the complicated question of *what* individuals are concretely required to do (e.g. advocate, vote, mobilize, aid, donate, etc.), and *how much* is required of them, in light of these obligations—a crucial next step in her analysis. Among its other valuable contributions, Daniel Weinstock's commentary helpfully illustrates some of the practical uncertainties we are likely to face here.

V. The Challenges of Politics

Part IV addressed the question of whether, and to what extent, human rights are constrained by facts about what is feasible or possible for (would be) duty-bearers. If, as many believe, human rights are so constrained, then it is likely that *political* facts will be included in this set.[92] It would be strange if human rights required the politically

---

[91] Shue 1996a.   [92] *See*: Gilabert 2009, pp. 664–7.

impossible or even unworkable: for instance, government by perfect consensus in large-scale societies.

But political facts do more than just limit the scope of what human rights can sensibly require. Human rights, on any familiar understanding, require political recognition and institutional enactment. And, for better or worse, they are pursued by actors that must navigate a world shaped by the forces of politics, warts and all. As such, human rights face a number of political challenges: not only is (a) their content constrained by the limits of political or institutional possibility; even once their content is decided, (b) their realization depends, to a substantial degree, on their political fortunes; and, more broadly, (c) the formulation and pursuit of human rights inevitably have political consequences, and may be subject to dangerous political pitfalls, that merit serious consideration.

One of the more widely discussed political challenges facing human rights is (b): the fact that their satisfaction depends (at least in part) on the will and capacity of political agents, particularly nation-states. The challenge is a grave one, especially if it is true that, as many believe, even when states do have the ability to comply with human rights, the political *will* is rarely there.

One popular argument for this cynical conclusion is furnished by so-called "realist" presuppositions about the behaviour of states in the international domain. According to realist theories of international relations, states act entirely in accordance with their perceived self-interest. And since there is currently no global human rights enforcer capable of making compliance with (costly) human rights standards a reliably rational choice for self-interested state actors, realists conclude (what is already supported, in their view, by considerable independent evidence) that states lack the will to comply therewith.[93] The overall implication is that, however morally appealing they may be, human rights will be politically neglected for the forseeable future.

In recent years, several prominent scholars of international law have challenged this realist picture. For instance, Beth Simmons has argued that state compliance with international human rights standards can be incentivized even in the absence of global enforcement mechanisms, such as foreign intervention, international sanctions, monitoring, and public condemnation, etc. As she explains, *domestic* mobilization— public protest, grassroots activism, litigation, lobbying, etc.—can act as a powerful enforcement mechanism of its own.[94]

In other work, Ryan Goodman and Derek Jinks have argued that the ("soft") power of *acculturation*—essentially a form of peer pressure that operates within the international community—has been and can be a crucial factor promoting compliance with international human rights law.[95] If these scholars are right, then we can more or less accept the realist's Machiavellian assessment of the motivating sources of state

---

[93] *See:* Beitz 1979, pp. 11–67, and Coady 2008, ch. 1, for excellent discussions. For a recent example of a realist perspective on human rights, *see:* Posner 2014.

[94] Simmons 2009.   [95] Goodman & Jinks 2013.

behaviour, as well as acknowledge the lack of (coercive or "hard") power backing compliance with human rights at the international level, *without* concluding that human rights standards are doomed to be shirked by state actors; the reality would be more complicated and hopeful than that.

Realism has been used to highlight other political challenges for human rights as well. Most prominently, realists have suggested that human rights standards are not only flouted but also *manipulated* by states in ways that further their self-interest. For instance, it is often said that human rights—or, rather, claims about the violation thereof—are (and have been) used by powerful states to justify aggressive international actions that, at bottom, are motivated by the prospect of material and/or political self-gain.[96] Here the concern is not, as it was just above, that human rights are politically impotent. On the contrary, the concern is that human rights are, in a sense, all too effective in politics, or rather effective in the wrong way. If we think of the manipulation of human rights by state actors as a (potentially ever-present) *risk*, this looks like a political challenge of type (c): that is, a dangerous political pitfall that afflicts their international formulation and pursuit.

These are two key political challenges for human rights. There are of course many others—including Rawlsian concerns about the need for a *stable* international consensus on human rights.[97] The contributions in this fifth Part of the volume catalogue, in illuminatingly fine-grained detail, the immense variety of political challenges in this area. But just as important as this, and against the (highly polemical) grain of scholarship on this topic, they also devote constructive attention to the question of what *implications* we should draw from these challenges: that is, the question of what these challenges ultimately mean for the theory and practice of human rights, and what, if anything, can and should be done about them.

Is the manipulation and disregard for human rights by political agents a defect of the rights themselves or (perhaps more plausibly) of human beings and political institutions? Does the regularity of such events imply, as Raymond Geuss has suggested, that human rights are merely a "kind of puffery or white magic"?[98] Do states that have a (e.g. colonial) history of manipulating human rights standards to their own political advantage lose the moral standing to promote human rights internationally today?[99] Are the political challenges facing human rights surmountable, manageable, or intractable? And if they are not intractable, how should they be met?

* * *

Pablo Gilabert's chapter develops a constructive analysis of the normative and theoretical implications of what he calls "power-related" worries about human rights. Having observed that human rights are both shirked and manipulated by powerful political

---

[96] *See e.g.* Douzinas 2007; Mutua 2002, esp. ch. 1; Zolo 2010, esp. pp. 563–5.

[97] Rawls 1999, esp. pp. 121–3; Cohen 2004.   [98] Geuss 2001, p. 144.

[99] My thanks to Rowan Cruft for raising this question.

agents with alarming regularity, Gilabert notes that we can respond to this fact in three general ways.

First, we can think of it, as Geuss does, as an indication that human rights do not *exist* (normatively speaking)—that is, that they do not qualify as norms that we genuinely *ought* to respect. Second, we can think of it as an indication that human rights "practice"—broadly, the modern project of explicitly recognizing and promoting human rights in international law and politics—should be *abandoned*. And third, we can think of it as an indication that human rights practice ought to be *(re)shaped* in ways that address concerns about its political neglect, subversion, and abuse.

Gilabert favours the third response. The first, he thinks, is indefensible. Not only does it (very implausibly) assume that states can rid themselves of the moral obligation to respect human rights by regularly shirking it, it also fits poorly with the general tone of scholarship on this topic. In nearly all cases, authors that document the abuse, neglect, and manipulation of human rights by the powerful treat this as a *lamentable* fact. And presumably this is because, at bottom, they believe that human rights (or something very much like them) *exist*—that is, that states really ought to do the sort of things that human rights typically require of them, such as grant fair trials, refrain from torture, tolerate dissent, and offer basic services, etc.

Gilabert also finds the second response uncalled for. As he suggests, there is, as of yet, simply not enough evidence available to know whether human rights practice merits abandonment: whether overall it has done more harm than good, or whether (even if it has) it will clearly continue to do so.

In order to develop and give substance to the third response, Gilabert looks at a variety of power-related concerns about human rights, and tries to see how the practice might be reshaped in ways that address them. The chapter identifies a number of helpful desiderata of this sort. But perhaps its key observation is that power should not simply be seen, as it often is, as an *obstacle* to be constrained and eventually overcome, but also as something that the practice ought to *harness* and distribute in ways that help fulfil the promise of human rights.

Gilabert thinks empowerment should be "built into" the human rights project. Not only should individuals and groups be empowered (i.e. provided with the means) to acquire the objects of their human rights; they should also be able to play an active role in their elaboration and identification. Thus, *political* rights to equal representation and participation—to have one's voice "heard" in the public domain—should be seen as a central part of the human rights project, in Gilabert's view.

In her comments, Elizabeth Frazer argues that political rights will have to be supplemented by political *knowledge*—particularly knowledge of complex "power structures" that perpetuate various forms of domination in society—if Gilabert's democratic vision is ever to be achieved. That seems right, but Gilabert's proposal requires other forms of supplementation as well. While individual democratic rights (and political knowledge) are a sensible way of addressing concerns about various imbalances of power within the *domestic* context of the nation-state, it is not obvious how they are meant to work at the *international* level, where the prospect of genuinely democratic institutions is hugely remote, and which is the focus of so many of the worries Gilabert sets out to address in the first place.

C. A. J. Coady's chapter explores some of the political and moral risks ("hazards") involved in efforts to implement human rights through acts of rescue, whether in the form of aid or military intervention. Coady identifies a number of such risks, which he labels "moralisms." Moralisms are, in essence, moral beliefs and practices that fail to take account of relevant prudential considerations. In the context of rescue, Coady argues, with the help of powerful historical examples, that we ought to be particularly careful to avoid pitfalls like the moralism of "deluded power" (which involves the false belief that moral conviction on its own has the power to do substantial good in the world), of "unbalanced focus" (which involves an undue fixation on some moral considerations at the expense of others), of "abstraction" (which involves insufficient attention to the concrete circumstances in which one aims to act), and of "imposition" (whereby an outsider's vision of the needs and/or desires of a community is unduly imposed upon it).

Coady is moderate and sensible in his treatment of these concerns. The solution, in his view, is not to *abandon* rescue efforts altogether[100]—although in her comments Vasuki Nesiah suggests that Coady should be more profoundly concerned about the growing prominence of "rescue" as a human rights imperative. Instead, like Gilabert, Coady recommends that we use these critical observations *constructively*, to formulate lessons that can help improve decision-making and rescue efforts in the future.

If we accept, as Coady does, that rescue is sometimes necessary even though it may well lead to disaster, whether as a result of moralism or any other failure, then his constructive approach is indispensable. Clearly, we ought to think about how to do necessary work well. The looming challenge is to figure out how best to institutionalize and develop the enlightened sense of prudence or caution that Coady argues for, but (and this is no small feat) without letting it transform, when practised, into a paralytic aversion to rescue that he sees no reason to embrace.

VI. Individuals, Borders, and Groups

Most agree that human rights are typically held by *individual* human beings, principally against the state. That is, after all, true of most of the rights one finds in key international human rights documents like the UDHR, ICCPR, and ICESCR.[101] And critics have taken note. The ostensible individualistic orientation of human rights brought them firmly into the crosshairs of the so-called "communitarian" critique of rights that flourished during the 1990s. Drawing partly on Marx,[102] communitarians

---

[100] *See e.g.* Zolo 2010.
[101] *See:* Nickel 2007, ch. 1; Nickel 2014, sec. 1, for a longer list of prominent features of such rights.
[102] *See:* Gilabert in this volume, for a brief discussion.

insisted that the affirmation of individual rights distracts us from the importance of "community," social responsibility, socio-economic equality, and the basic inter-dependence of human beings.[103]

These criticisms have been vigorously contested.[104] And the communitarian critique is at least partly undermined by the fact that affirming rights simply *is* a way of affirm-ing certain social responsibilities. Rights, or rather "claim rights," of which human rights are mostly composed, logically correlate with duties—duties owed to the rights-bearer by some agent or set thereof.[105] And so issues of social responsibility and human interdependence are, in a very basic sense, never far from view when rights claims are at stake, regardless of whether these are individual claims or not.

Another fact that undermines the communitarian critique is that human rights instruments are designed to protect and promote community life in various ways. The UDHR recognizes rights to nondiscrimination (Article 1), equality before the law (Article 7), freedom of association (Article 17), and freedom of thought and expression (Article 18), all of which are crucial to the flourishing of minority groups.[106] The ICCPR—leaning on the Convention on the Prevention and Punishment of the Crime of Genocide (1948)—recognizes "genocide" (the targeting of a specific group for destruc-tion) as a grave and punishable crime under international law (Article 6). And the ICCPR explicitly recognizes the rights of "ethnic, religious or linguistic minorities ... to enjoy their own culture, to profess and practice their own religion, or to use their own language" (Article 27).

Perhaps most notable of all, both the ICCPR and ICESCR recognize (in Article 1, no less) the rights of "peoples" to political self-determination: "to freely determine their political status and freely pursue their economic, social, and cultural development." One of the remarkable features of this right, as well as some of those listed above, is that it is clearly assigned to *groups* rather than individual persons. The right grants an entitlement of self-rule to a "people"—a political collective—not to any one person as such. This represents a strong break from the general focus on individual rights in inter-national human rights law, and provides it with a striking communitarian component.

But the inclusion of group rights within standard lists of human rights also opens up difficult questions of its own. For one, (i) it raises questions about who, or rather *what*, can hold human rights. The ICCPR and ICESCR might assign human rights to groups, but how does this fit with other features often attributed to such rights: for instance, that they are held (a) *universally* by all persons, including by those who (for any number of reasons) *lack* membership in a political group; or that they are held (b) *naturally*, simply in virtue of one's humanity, and therefore not as a result of contin-gent facts about group affiliation? Upon reflection, the inclusion of group rights in

---

[103] *See e.g.* Glendon 1991, ch. 4; Etzioni 1993, pp. 1–23; Yew 1992.

[104] *See e.g.* Alston & Goodman 2012, pp. 509–30; Donnelly 2013, chs. 7, 12; Gould 2004, ch. 5; Shue 1996b, pp. 218–19; Taylor 1999.

[105] *See:* Hohfeld 1923, pp. 36–8; Feinberg 1970.

[106] *See:* Nickel 2007, ch. 10 and Donnelly 2013, ch. 3, for good discussions on this.

standard lists of *human* rights may seem like a category mistake, and in some cases also a moral mistake.[107]

Second, (ii) the recognition of group rights generates special normative tensions within human rights doctrine. The right of peoples to self-determination is naturally understood to include a right to *border* control—to set rules that determine the conditions of entry, visitation, passage, immigration, and exit. It's hard to imagine how a group could be genuinely self-determining *without* the ability to exercise some degree of control over such matters. But this right (to exclude) comes into conflict with other human rights that guarantee freedom of movement *across* borders: for instance, the right to *leave* any country,[108] as well as the right to seek and enjoy asylum from persecution.[109]

In a sense, then, the demands of international human rights sit on either side of political borders; they are a source of duties to let outsiders in and of permissions to keep them out. It is not unusual for human rights to generate conflicting practical demands—as they famously do, for instance, in the case of the human rights to security[110] and to privacy.[111] But any such tension calls for an effort to "balance" competing claims, which requires careful evaluation of the considerations at hand.

These questions about how (and indeed *whether*) human rights serve the interests of political groups engage a core focus of this volume: the *political* dimensions of human rights. To date, (i) the status of group rights within the human rights corpus remains a controversial question,[112] and (ii) the normative or practical tensions generated by the affirmation of such rights have been a source of energetic and unresolved debate.[113] The contributions in this sixth and final Part of the volume aim to make progress on both of these key issues.

*   *   *

Peter Jones's chapter examines whether the right of peoples to self-determination can properly be thought of as a *human* right: question (i). Jones is interested in whether a case can be made for the *moral* existence of such a human right, but assumes that a favourable answer to this question would justify its legal recognition as well—an assumption that, as noted in Section III of this introduction, can reasonably be disputed.

Jones argues that group rights like the right to self-determination can indeed be understood as human rights, but only under certain conditions. One such condition, in his view, is that the right be "collective" in a special sense: not in virtue of being borne by a single corporate entity, but rather as a result of being a right that individuals

---

[107] Consider, for instance, the ECtHR's 2011 decision that a corporation, the Yukos Oil Company, holds human rights [in *Yukos Universal Limited (Isle of Man) v The Russian Federation*]. My thanks to Rowan Cruft for bringing this example to my attention.

[108] UDHR, Article 13; ICCPR, Article 12.   [109] UDHR, Article 14.

[110] UDHR, Article 3; ICCPR, Article 6, 9.   [111] UDHR, Article 12; ICCPR, Article 17.

[112] *See e.g.* Buchanan 2013, p. 77; Donnelly 2013, ch. 3; Griffin 2008, ch. 15; Newman 2011; Nickel 2007, ch. 10.

[113] *See e.g.* Abizadeh 2008; Benhabib 2004; Carens 2013; Miller 2005; Risse 2008.

hold jointly, and *only* jointly. This condition is important, Jones argues, because it means that the human right of peoples to political self-determination is ultimately born by *individual* human beings, which he thinks is an essential feature of human rights in general.

Another condition is that the right concern itself only with what Jones calls the "determination principle." This principle requires that there be a one-to-one match between the people whose collective lives are determined in a certain territory and those who do the determining. In effect, it grants a right to self-determination to all extant political groups, regardless of their composition, history, and current geographical extension. However, the principle takes no position on what Jones calls the "issue of selfhood"—that is, the question of which specific units of population qualify as "peoples" deserving of political constitution in the first place. Jones argues that the determination principle can be brought within the compass of human rights thinking, but that the issue of selfhood cannot.

The reason for this, he explains, is that we are unlikely to discover any general rules that allow us to determine which groups deserve to be politically constituted as a "people" and which do not. The territory of the world is not fairly or justly divided. Many populations have been wrongly stripped of territories and political control that they deserve—that much is clear. Nonetheless, it is often difficult to know exactly *where* just borders should lie, or exactly *which* populations (and *sub*-populations) deserve to keep or newly gain political independence as a result of their special history, identity, or status as a "people." If any answers are to be found here, they are likely to be highly contextual, historically contingent, and will often be morally hazy. This makes the issue of selfhood an unsuitable topic for *human rights* doctrine, in Jones's view— which he thinks of as oriented towards more universalistic and less morally ambiguous concerns—though he admits that the issue can and should be approached with other normative tools.

As Will Kymlicka points out in his commentary, this is a severe restriction. If the purpose of the human right to collective self-determination is to protect peoples against unjust interferences with their sovereignty, then the issue of selfhood cannot really be avoided. After all, as Kymlicka points out, some of the most insidious violations of sovereignty—such as annexation and forced settlement—target the *composition* of the demos; they strip political power from a people without quite violating the determination principle itself, since in theory they may allow the (altered) demos to self-govern. Surely, Kymlicka argues, the human right to collective self-determination should protect peoples against such forms of international aggression, and so take the issue of selfhood on board.

Kymlicka's criticism is grounded in his provocative claim that the chief purpose of international human rights norms is to remedy or address fundamental injustices created by the international legal-political order itself, and that a significant portion of these injustices include violations of selfhood of the kind described just above. But we can question Jones's position on its own grounds.

Jones argues that violations of selfhood should not be covered by the human right to collective self-determination because this would force human rights practitioners to tackle highly contextual and morally ambiguous problems. But this seems like an odd reason to limit the right. Many core human rights, such as the right to an adequate standard of living,[114] merely point the way towards what will inevitably be a highly contextual determination of what individual human beings need to adequately flourish in specific circumstances. And international human rights documents contain limitation clauses precisely because the pursuit of such rights is readily understood to mire agents in morally ambiguous predicaments that require costly sacrifices and sometimes even the infringement of human rights themselves.[115] If the realization of human rights is already a highly contextual and morally hazardous affair, then there is little reason to think that the human right to collective self-determination should be spared from this.

Alex Levitov and Stephen Macedo's chapter delves into some of the concrete normative ambiguities we are likely to encounter as a result of recognizing the human right to collective self-determination. Levitov and Macedo are specifically interested in the apparent conflict between this right, which seems to grant peoples a permission to *exclude* outsiders, and other human rights (or normative considerations) that guarantee universal freedom of movement *across* borders: question (ii).

Levitov and Macedo believe that this normative conflict is real. But they develop a framework (which they call "cosmopolitan statism") within which it is meant to be managed, if not entirely resolved. The distinguishing feature of their position is that it invests the state, and our obligations to compatriots, with paramount normative significance (hence its "statism"), while *also* acknowledging ambitious duties towards outsiders (hence its "cosmopolitanism"). This latter set of duties include (a) natural duties of rescue, (b) natural duties to assist outsiders in domestic institution-building, and (c) duties of reciprocity, which include duties to engage outsiders fairly, to address past wrongs, and to improve international institutions so that reciprocally fair inter-state relations are easier to establish.

Because Levitov and Macedo acknowledge such strong obligations *both* to compatriots and to outsiders, the conflict that they aim to arbitrate turns out to be a "hard case." So much so that they are keen to stress the "reasonableness" of multiple approaches to it—that is, multiple immigration schemes that balance these duties in different ways, from more closed to more open.

Given this reasonable plurality, they argue, states deserve a wide degree of discretion, or freedom from external interference, in deciding just what type of immigration scheme to adopt. Indeed, following language familiar from Rawls,[116] Levitov and Macedo suggest that states should even be free to adopt *unreasonably* or *unfairly* restrictive immigration policies, providing these don't fall into the domain of the "fully

---

[114] UDHR, Article 25; ICESCR, Article 11.
[115] UDHR, Article 29; ICESCR, Article 4; ICCPR, Article 18.   [116] Rawls 1999, pp. 74–5.

unreasonable." *Fully* unreasonable immigration policies, Levitov and Macedo explain, violate the human rights of outsiders, which is intolerable.

Thus, for instance, a state may refuse to grant entry to low-skilled migrant workers whose basic needs are already met at home, but it cannot refuse entry to individuals fleeing persecution, which would amount to a clear violation of their human rights. And to make sure that states stay well within the boundaries of the reasonable when it comes to immigration, Levitov and Macedo suggest that immigration policies should be regularly vetted by multilateral international organizations specifically charged with this task, and capable of imposing reputational and material penalties when states fall short.

In her wide-ranging commentary, Seyla Benhabib points out that immigration policies determine more than just how many outsiders will be allowed into a state, and under what conditions; they also determine how outsiders are treated once they gain entry, whether legally or illegally. Benhabib turns our attention from non-citizens outside our borders to those who are already here among us, and she persuasively argues that states should have no discretion when it comes to respecting the human rights of domestic non-citizens, including their socio-economic human rights: "by penalizing unsanitary and exploitative work conditions, and by expediting the integration of undocumented migrants into the social network of the country in question through state or city-issued identity cards, the issuance of social security numbers, etc."

Interestingly, Benhabib also points out that states that fully respect the human rights of domestic non-citizens may paradoxically see a reduction in immigration, since this is likely to reduce the availability of cheap, exploitative labour. These observations provide an important complement to Levitov and Macedo's analysis of border policy.

There is an ambiguity that courses through Levitov and Macedo's discussion of the human right to collective self-determination. On one understanding of the right, it grants peoples a permission to exclude non-citizens (whether at home or abroad) from entry or full membership. But Levitov and Macedo adopt a more ambitious interpretation of the right, as one that grants peoples a permission to *unfairly* exclude outsiders from entry or full-membership—essentially, a permission to do wrong.

This is not an implausible interpretation of the right. But it is far from inevitable. And moreover, Levitov and Macedo's focus on the extent of peoples' freedom to be unfair or unreasonable distracts their analysis from the question of just what a fair and reasonable immigration policy should look like in the first place. Readers looking for an answer to the latter question rather than the former will want to hear more.

References

Abizadeh, Arash (2008) "Democratic Theory and Border Coercion," *Political Theory*, Vol. 36, No. 1, pp. 37–65.

Alston, Philip & Goodman, Ryan (2012) *International Human Rights* (Oxford: Oxford University Press).

Beitz, Charles R. (1979) *Political Theory and International Relations* (Princeton: Princeton University Press).

Beitz, Charles R. (2009) *The Idea of Human Rights* (Oxford: Oxford University Press).

Benhabib, Seyla (2004) *The Rights of Others: Aliens, Residents and Citizens* (Cambridge: Cambridge University Press).

Benhabib, Seyla (2011) "Is There a Human Right to Democracy? Beyond Interventionism and Indifference" in Claudio Corradetti (ed.), *Philosophical Dimensions of Human Rights: Some Contemporary Views* (Cambridge: Cambridge University Press), pp. 191–213.

Benvenisti, Eyal (1999) "Margin of Appreciation, Consensus, and Universal Standards," *New York University Journal of International Law and Politics*, Vol. 31, No. 1, pp. 843–54.

Besson, Samantha (2011) "Human Rights: Ethical, Political...or Legal?" in D. Childress (ed.), *The Role of Ethics in International Law* (Cambridge: Cambridge University Press), pp. 211–45.

Brownlee, Kimberley (2015) "Do We Have a Right to the Political Determinants of Health?" in Rowan Cruft, S. Matthew Liao, & Massimo Renzo (eds), *Philosophical Foundations of Human Rights* (Oxford: Oxford University Press), pp. 502–15.

Buchanan, Allen (2013) *The Heart of Human Rights* (Oxford: Oxford University Press).

Carens, Joseph (2013) *The Ethics of Immigration* (Oxford: Oxford University Press).

Christiano, Tom (2011) "An Instrumental Argument for the Human Right to Democracy," *Philosophy and Public Affairs*, Vol. 39, No. 2, pp. 142–76.

Coady, C. A. J. (2008) *Messy Morality: The Challenges of Politics* (Oxford: Oxford University Press).

Cohen, Joshua (2004) "Minimalism About Human Rights: The Most We Can Hope For?" *The Journal of Political Philosophy*, Vol. 12, No. 2, pp. 190–213.

Cohen, Joshua (2010) "Is There a Human Right to Democracy?" in *The Arc of the Moral Universe and Other Essays* (Cambridge, Mass.: Harvard University Press), pp. 349–73.

Cranston, Maurice (1973) *What are Human Rights?* (London: The Bodley Head).

Cranston, Maurice (1983) "Are There Any Human Rights?" *Daedalus*, Vol. 112, No. 4, pp. 1–17.

Cruft, Rowan, Liao, Matthew, & Renzo, Massimo (2015) "Introduction" in Rowan Cruft, S. Matthew Liao, & Massimo Renzo (eds), *Philosophical Foundations of Human Rights* (Oxford: Oxford University Press), pp. 1–45.

Donnelly, Jack (2013) *Universal Human Rights in Theory and Practice* (Ithaca, NY: Cornell University Press), Third Edition.

Douzinas, Costas (2007) *Human Rights and Empire: The Political Philosophy of Cosmpolitanism* (Milton Park: Routledge-Cavendish).

Dworkin, Ronald (2011) *Justice for Hedgehogs* (Cambridge, Mass.: Harvard University Press).

Estlund, David (2014) "Utopophobia," *Philosophy and Public Affairs*, Vol. 42, No. 2, pp. 114–34.

Etzioni, Amitai (1993) *The Spirit of Community* (New York: Crown Publishers).

Feinberg, Joel (1970) "The Nature and Value of Rights," *Journal of Value Inquiry*, Vol. 4, No. 4, pp. 243–60.

Forst, Rainer (2012) *The Right to Justification: Elements of a Constructivist Theory of Justice*, tr. Jeffrey Flynn (New York: Columbia University Press).

Geuss, Raymond (2001) *History and Illusion in Politics* (Cambridge: Cambridge University Press).

Gilabert, Pablo (2009) "The Feasibility of Basic Socioeconomic Rights: A Conceptual Exploration," *Philosophical Quarterly*, Vol. 59, No. 273, pp. 659–81.

Gilabert, Pablo (2011) "Humanist and Political Perspectives on Human Rights," *Political Theory*, Vol. 39, No. 4, pp. 439–67.

Gilabert, Pablo (2012) "Is There a Human Right to Democracy? A Response to Joshua Cohen," *Latin American Journal of Political Philosophy*, Vol. 1, No. 2, pp. 1–37.

Glendon, Mary Ann (1991) *Rights Talk: The Impoverishment of Political Discourse* (New York).

Goodman, Ryan & Jinks, Derek (2013) *Socializing States: Promoting Human Rights Through International Law* (Oxford: Oxford University Press).

Gould, Carol C. (2004) *Globalizing Democracy and Human Rights* (Cambridge: Cambridge University Press).

Griffin, James (2008) *On Human Rights* (Oxford: Oxford University Press).

Griffin, James (2010) "Human Rights and the Autonomy of International Law" in Samantha Besson & John Tasioulas (eds), *The Philosophy of International Law* (Oxford: Oxford University Press)pp. 339–57.

Habermas, Jürgen (2010) "The Concept of Human Dignity and The Realistic Utopia of Human Rights," *Metaphilosophy*, Vol. 41, No. 4, pp. 464–80.

Hart, H. L. A. (1955) "Are There Any Natural Rights?" *Philosophical Review*, Vol. 64, No. 2, pp. 175–91.

Hart, H. L. A. (1994) *The Concept of Law: Second Edition*, with a Postscript edited by Penelope A. Bulloch and Joseph Raz (Oxford: Oxford University Press).

Hassoun, Nicole (2015) "The Human Right to Health," *Philosophy Compass*, Vol. 10, No. 4, pp. 275–83.

Hohfeld, Wesley (1923) *Fundamental Legal Conceptions* (New Haven: Yale University Press).

James, Aaron (2005) "Constructing Justice for Existing Practice: Rawls and the Status Quo," *Philosophy and Public Affairs*, Vol. 33, No. 3, pp. 281–316.

Jones, Peter (1996) "International Human Rights: Philosophical or Political?" in Simon Caney, David George, and Peter Jones (eds), *National Rights, International Obligations* (Boulder, Colo.: Westview Press), pp. 183–204.

Lauterpacht, Hersch (1950) *International Law and Human Rights* (London: Stevens & Sons). Reprinted in: Alston, Philip & Goodman, Ryan (2013) *International Human Rights* (Oxford: Oxford University Press), pp. 150–7.

Letsas, George (2006) "Two Concepts of the Margin of Appreciation," *Oxford Journal of Legal Studies*, Vol. 26, No. 4, pp. 705–32.

Liao, S. Matthew (2015) *The Right to be Loved* (Oxford: Oxford University Press).

Liao, S. Matthew & Etinson, Adam (2012) "Political and Naturalistic Conceptions of Human Rights: A False Polemic?" *The Journal of Moral Philosophy*, Vol. 9, No. 3, pp. 327–52.

Martin, Rex (1989) "Human Rights and Civil Rights" in Morton E. Winston (ed.), *The Philosophy of Human Rights* (Belmont: Wadsworth), pp. 75–85.

McGrath, Sarah (2008) "Moral Disagreement and Moral Expertise" in *Oxford Studies in Metaethics, Volume 3* (Oxford: Oxford University Press), pp. 87–108.

Mill, John Stuart (1989) *On Liberty and Other Writings*, ed. Stefan Collini (Cambridge: Cambridge University Press).

Miller, David (2005) "Immigration: The Case for Limits" in Andrew I. Cohen and Christopher Heath Wellman (eds), *Contemporary Debates in Applied Ethics* (Malden, Mass.: Blackwell).

Moyn, Samuel (2015) "Human Rights and the Age of Inequality" in Doutje Lettinga & Lars van Troost (eds), *Can Human Rights Bring Social Justice? Twelve Essays* (Amsterdam: Amnesty International Netherlands), pp. 13–19.

Moyn, Samuel (2018) *Not Enough: Human Rights in an Unequal World* (Cambridge, Mass.: Harvard University Press).

Mutua, Makau (2002) *Human Rights: A Political & Cultural Critique* (Philadelphia: University of Pennsylvania Press).

Neuman, Gerald (2003) "Human Rights and Constitutional Rights: Harmony and Dissonance," *Stanford Law Review*, Vol. 55, No. 5, pp. 1863–900.

Newman, Dwight (2011) *Community and Collective Rights: A Theoretical Framework for Rights Held by Groups* (Oxford: Hart Publishing).

Nickel, James W. (2006) "Are Human Rights Mainly Implemented by Intervention?" in Rex Martin & David Reidy (eds), *Rawls' Law of Peoples: A Realistic Utopia?* (Oxford: Blackwell Publishing), pp. 263–78.

Nickel, James W. (2007) *Making Sense of Human Rights: Second Edition* (Oxford: Blackwell Publishing).

Nickel, James W. (2014) "Human Rights" in Edward Zalta (ed.), *The Stanford Encyclopedia of Philosophy*. Available online.

Nussbaum, Martha C. (2002) "Moral Expertise? Constitutional Narratives and Philosophical Argument," *Metaphilosophy*, Vol. 33, No. 5, pp. 502–20.

O'Neill, Onora (2005) "The Dark Side of Human Rights," *International Affairs*, Vol. 81, No. 2, pp. 427–39.

Posner, Eric A. (2014) *The Twilight of Human Rights Law* (Oxford: Oxford University Press).

Quong, Jonathan (2010) *Liberalism Without Perfection* (Oxford: Oxford University Press).

Rawls, John (1999) *The Law of Peoples: With "The Idea of Public Reason Revisited"* (Cambridge, Mass.: Harvard University Press).

Rawls, John (2005) *Political Liberalism: Expanded Edition* (New York: Columbia University Press).

Raz, Joseph (1998) "Disagreement in Politics," *American Journal of Jurisprudence*, Vol. 43, No. 1, pp. 25–52.

Raz, Joseph (2010) "Human Rights without Foundations" in John Tasioulas & Samantha Besson (eds), *The Philosophy of International Law* (Oxford: Oxford University Press), pp. 321–39.

Raz, Joseph (2015) "Human Rights in the Emerging World Order" in Rowan Cruft, S. Matthew Liao, & Massimo Renzo (eds), *Philosophical Foundations of Human Rights* (Oxford: Oxford University Press), pp. 217–32.

Risse, Mathias (2008) "On the Morality of Immigration," *Ethics and International Affairs*, Vol. 22, No. 1, pp. 25–33.

Risse, Mattias (2009) "A Right to Work? A Right to Leisure? Labour Rights as Human Rights," *Law & Ethics of Human Rights*, Vol. 3, No. 1, pp. 1–39.

Sangiovanni, Andrea (2007) "Justice and the Priority of Politics to Morality," *The Journal of Political Philosophy*, Vol. 16, No. 2, pp. 2–28.

Sen, Amartya (2004) "Elements of a Theory of Human Rights," *Philosophy and Public Affairs*, Vol. 32, No. 4, pp. 315–56.

Shany, Yuval (2006) "Towards a General Margin of Appreciation Doctrine in International Law?" *European Journal of International Law*, Vol. 16, No. 5, pp. 907–40.

Shue, Henry (1996a) *Basic Rights: Subsistence, Affluence, and U.S. Foreign Policy* (Princeton: Princeton University Press) Second Edition.

Shue, Henry (1996b) "Thickening Convergence" in D. K. Chatterjee (ed.), *The Ethics of Assistance: Morality and the Distant Needy* (Cambridge: Cambridge University Press), pp. 226–7.

Simmons, Beth (2009) *Mobilizing for Human Rights: International Law in Domestic Politics* (Cambridge, Mass.: Harvard University Press).

Singer, Peter (1972) "Moral Experts," *Analysis*, Vol. 32, No. 4, pp. 115–17.

Sinnott-Armstrong, Walter (1984) "'Ought' Conversationally Implies 'Can'," *The Philosophical Review*, Vol. 93, No. 2, pp. 249–61.

Tadros, Victor (2015) "Rights and Security for Human Rights Sceptics" in Rowan Cruft, S. Matthew Liao, & Massimo Renzo (eds), *Philosophical Foundations of Human Rights* (Oxford: Oxford University Press), pp. 442–58.

Tasioulas, John (2010) "Taking Rights out of Human Rights," *Ethics*, Vol. 120, No. 4, pp. 647–78.

Tasioulas, John (2012) "Towards a Philosophy of Human Rights," *Current Legal Problems*, Vol. 65, No. 1, pp. 1–30.

Taylor, Charles (1999) "Conditions of an Unforced Consensus on Human Rights" in J. R. Bauer & D. A. Bell (eds), *The East Asian Challenge to Human Rights* (Cambridge: Cambridge University Press), pp. 124–47.

Valentini, Laura (2011a) "In What Sense Are Human Rights Political? A Preliminary Exploration," *Political Studies*, Vol. 60, No. 1, pp. 180–94.

Valentini, Laura (2011b) "Global Justice and Practice-dependence: Conventionalism, Institutionalism, Functionalism," *Journal of Political Philosophy*, Vol. 19, No. 4, pp. 399–418.

Valentini, Laura (2012) "Ideal vs. Non-ideal Theory: A Conceptual Map," *Philosophy Compass*, Vol. 7, No. 9, pp. 654–64.

Waldron, Jeremy (1993) *Liberal Rights: Collected Papers* 1981–1991 (Cambridge: Cambridge University Press).

Waldron, Jeremy (2012) *Dignity, Rank and Rights* (Oxford: Oxford University Press), ed. Meir Dan-Cohen.

Waldron, Jeremy (2013) "*Political* Political Theory: An Inaugural Lecture," *The Journal of Political Philosophy*, Vol. 21, No. 1, pp. 1–23.

Waldron, Jeremy (2015) "Is Dignity the Foundation of Human Rights?" in Rowan Cruft, S. Matthew Liao, & Massimo Renzo (eds), *Philosophical Foundations of Human Rights* (Oxford: Oxford University Press), pp. 117–38.

Wellman, Carl (2011) *The Moral Dimensions of Human Rights* (Oxford: Oxford University Press).

Wenar, Leif (2005) "The Nature of Human Rights" in Andreas Follesdal & Thomas Pogge (eds), *Real World Justice: Grounds, Principles, Human Rights, and Social Institutions* (Dordrecht: Springer), pp. 285–95.

Wilkins, Burleigh (2002) "International Human Rights and National Discretion," *Journal of Ethics*, Vol. 6, No. 1, pp. 373–82.

Williams, Bernard (2005) *In The Beginning Was the Deed: Realism and Moralism in Political Argument* (Princeton: Princeton University Press).

Wolff, Jonathan (2012) *The Human Right to Health* (New York: W.W. Norton & Co.).

Yew, Lee Kwan (1992) "Democracy, Human Rights, and the Realities." Speech delivered at the creation of the Asahi Forum, Tokyo, 20 November 1992.

Zolo, Daniel (2010) "Humanitarian Militarism?" in Samantha Besson & John Tasioulas (eds), *The Philosophy of International Law* (Oxford: Oxford University Press), pp. 549–69.

PART I

The Relevance of History

1

Rights, History, Critique

Martti Koskenniemi

What are human rights? Where do they come from? How can we know them, or know if we "have" them? (And what does "having a right" mean?) Any discussion of the nature or role of rights tends very rapidly to lead to questions that seem soluble only by taking a stand on some pretty tough issues that have been debated for at least 2,000 years of Western political thought. Although some do suggest, or at least imply, that we are now finally in a position to give good responses to questions such as these, most would think it ridiculous to expect that we may have legitimate recourse to right-talk only once this has actually taken place. Surely it is possible to talk meaningfully of rights even in the absence of any firm philosophical founding. Here as elsewhere, *Gelassenheit*—just "letting it be"—has much to say for itself. There is much in the world that we do although we cannot quite explain why we do so. Perhaps all we can say about rights, at least for now, is that something like them needs to be supposed for the other things we do in or think about the world to make sense. This would make them articles of a pragmatic faith, referring back to nothing grander than the effortless intimacy we have with our practices. But why would this be wrong? Is not asking those grander questions just to have missed the postmodern boat?[1]

But even if a kind of unthinking, pragmatic faith might sometimes be useful, it is not always available. Famously, faith is not born out of a wish to have it. Once such hard questions have been posed, it is difficult to forget them. The genie is out of the bottle and we find ourselves struggling with it. This may not happen as long as we talk with those with whom we agree. But often we use rights in contexts of disagreement, to defend entitlements that have been denied or to attack claims that seem unfounded. Rights-language has distributive consequences. In an otherwise utilitarian policy-environment, rights indicate preferences that, we believe, should not be overridden by whatever net benefits a policy might offer. This is why everyone has a great interest in translating their preferences into rights. Without an authoritative list of such preferences,

---

[1] Marie-France Dembour has usefully identified four approaches to human rights—thinking of them as "natural" or as aspects of "protest", part of a "deliberative" politics or simply a "discourse". Only the first two "believe in" rights while the latter two use rights as policy-instruments. Dembour 2006, pp. 232–71.

however, there is no limit to the translation process. In the end, all social conflict will appear as rights-conflict. At that point, it begins to seem imperative to find an answer to questions such as: "What really is a 'right' (in contrast to a mere 'preference')? How do we know them? Do they exist in some hierarchy? What values determine their position?" The pragmatic attitude "if it works do not fix it" no longer suffices. Instead we seem to need an urgent response to questions such as "Works for whom? With what cost?"

A return to philosophy will hardly prove helpful. The twentieth century has not been kind to the idea that the resolution of social conflicts should take place by abstract reasoning. Indeed, philosophy today may have altogether given up such ambition and the best political and legal theory works with contextual vocabularies that are as messy as the world they propose to organize. Speaking in a universal language has come to appear as an effort to exercise hegemony.[2] Hence, I think, the increasing recourse to anthropology and sociology in rights-analysis.[3] Hence also the impressive recent surge of histories of rights.[4] It is this last move that I shall adopt and whose significance I shall discuss briefly in this chapter. Perhaps, if rights cannot be grounded on faith or philosophy, we might at least think of them historically, as part of the normative organization of a period. Much new historical work has looked for the origin of our present obsession with individual (human) rights. That origin has been found in different periods. Were "human rights" part of Roman (civil) law?[5] Or did they only emerge in the process or recovery of that law in the twelfth and thirteenth centuries? Did they belong to Canon law or emerge only with the nominalist attack upon Thomistic rationalism?[6] Should the first significant articulation of the idea of human rights be credited to the Spanish scholastics?[7] Or would it be more appropriate to focus on Protestant ideas about resistance to authority in the sixteenth century?[8] Should Hobbes or Grotius be heralded—for good or ill—as the intellectual fathers of the idea of individual (natural) rights?[9] Or did the idea of such rights emerge only with eighteenth-century Enlightenment, the American Bill of Rights (1776), or

[2] I have elaborated this more in Koskenniemi 2005, pp. 113–24.

[3] See e.g. Merry & Goodale 2007; Kennedy 2008; Halme-Tuomisaari 2010.

[4] For a useful overviews, see Slotte & Halme-Tuomisaari 2015; Moyn 2012, pp. 123–40.

[5] See e.g. Giltaj 2011.

[6] The view that rights emerged in the context of the Franciscan poverty dispute within the Catholic debates on natural law has been powerfully made in Tierney 1997. See also Reid Jr 1991–2, pp. 37–92. Against the (now old) view that subjective rights emerged with Ockham and the "moderns", Peter Garnsey has concluded that "Romans did possess the concept of property rights and individual rights in general", Garnsey 2007, p. 194. This is not the place to examine these arguments. Instead, there is reason to emphasize, from a legal point of view, the ease with which positions about objective law can be rewritten in terms of the subjective rights of those who are to benefit from the enforcement of (objective) law. This is why there is (contra Tierney 1997, pp. 208–16) in fact no "paradox" in the way conciliar "collectivism" could produce a theory of individual rights.

[7] See Brett 1997.   [8] See e.g. Witte 2008, pp. 545–70.

[9] This is the view of that most insistent critic of rights-individualism, Michel Villey. See e.g. Villey 1983.

the French *Déclaration des droits de l'homme et du citoyen* (1789)?[10] What about the connection between the emergence of human rights and the abolition of slavery, or the rise of the various humanitarian movements in the nineteenth century?[11]

Others have argued that there is no such long trajectory of "rights" passing through history at all. They have suggested that rights should be seen as part of twentieth-century institutional politics—perhaps that it "began" in the debates on minority protection within the League of Nations, or the passing of the 1948 Universal Declaration on Human Rights (UDHR), and as a reaction to Hitlerite racial aggression.[12] Others have claimed that our present rights talk should be seen in even more recent light—as part of an effort to marry free market liberalism and religious conservatism in the postwar era, an offshoot of 1970s cold war strategies or the ideological foundation for 1990s institutional developments in international human rights law.[13]

The turn to history in order to understand rights today is surely useful, though not as an effort to search for the origin of our present rights-practices. That would presuppose the self-evidence of our present rights—the very starting-point that was questioned— and reduce the past into its immature "predecessor". History is useful not because it "originates" or "foreshadows" present practices but because it provides illustrations of the ways in which a political vocabulary (such as rights-language) can be used for the accomplishment of different tasks. There are serious interpretative questions about the meaning and relations of "natural rights", "individual rights", "subjective rights", and "human rights" in different periods. They resemble each other, but are also different. While political philosophy seeks to clarify the differences and resemblances in its pursuit of a good rights-vocabulary, history, or at least conceptual history, seeks to locate rights in the contexts of contestation where they have been used to defend or attack distributive schemes and claims of jurisdiction. History does not resolve today's problems. But it may relieve us from the anxiety that a loss of faith in rights as providing a ready-made set of answers to social conflict may engender. It brings them down from a conceptual heaven and shows them as parts of a human world where they give shape and meaning to our agendas and pursuits. What we should think of them, or how they might be implemented in a world of scarce resources will still remain a matter of political judgement.

To answer the question "what are human rights?" without becoming entangled in endless philosophical conundrums it is possible to focus on the use of the rights-idiom in the practical contexts where political or professional actors have had recourse to it. They may have done this to make a claim, to support a preference or to attack an adversary; they may have wished to defend or challenge some use of power. In this chapter I will describe some such uses. But I recognize also the limits of this type of contextual history. What is the relevant "context"? Is it that of scholars and jurists or

---

[10] See Hunt 2007. See also the discussion of the Jellinek–Boutmy debate regarding the proper origin of rights in either the American or French revolutions, in Kelly 2004, pp. 493–529.

[11] See Martinez 2012. But see also Moyn 2012.   [12] Mutua 2002, pp. 15–17.

[13] For an instant classic, see Moyn 2010. See also Duranti 2017.

that of political, military, or economic power? Should we look at agents or structures? How should the object be delimited, and from what perspective ought we to examine it? In making such choices, contextual history approaches its rivals by beginning to think about history *normatively*—singling out more or less relevant aspects of the past by reference to contemporary concerns.[14] I do not think there is any closure: norms and histories feed into each other endlessly. But I think that emphasis on history is specifically needed in the human rights field to rid it from its persistent ideological commitment to thinking by reference to some timeless human essences enshrined in "universal" and "inalienable" norms, a commitment sometimes genuine but often contrived and cynical.

I. How To Do Things with Rights—Three Examples

A. *Rights in a Counter-Reformation mode: Spanish sixteenth century*

Three challenges faced unified Spain at the turn of the sixteenth century. Expansion in the Americas was not only hugely costly but posed serious ideological and religious questions about the expanse of the world and the striking differences in the beliefs and ways of life of its populations. Problems with regard to the management of a transcontinental empire were accompanied by concerns of conscience relating to the expansion of trade and commercial culture that were impossible to alleviate within prevailing religious doctrines. The rapid spread of Protestantism in the Habsburg realm suggested that neither set of problems was efficiently resolved by the Church or by traditional ideals of Christian rulership. But Spain was also home to Europe's intellectual powerhouse, the University of Salamanca, where scholars such as Francisco de Vitoria (1485/92?–1545) and Domingo de Soto (1494–1560) applied the most up-to-date humanist teachings to respond to the challenges faced by their monarch who was in 1519 crowned Emperor and *Dominus mundi*.

The Salamanca scholars were regularly consulted by the Emperor, members of the imperial elite and leading merchants about the concerns raised by the novel practices.[15] To strengthen the Church's intellectual and moral leadership it was important that their responses would fit with inherited religious views but also not outlaw territorial and commercial expansion or complicate the struggle against Protestantism. At the heart of their solutions to problems about the government of the "Indies", about just war and about the ethics of commerce (trade, banking, insurance, and so on) was a notion of subjective right, *dominium* in its two related forms, sovereignty and property (*dominium jurisdictionis* and *dominium proprietatis*). Humans had been created free, Vitoria and Soto argued, which meant they possessed *dominium in actionum*

---

[14] For a useful critique of contextualism in legal history, see especially Orford 2013a and Orford 2013b. See further e.g. Jay 2011, pp. 557–71; Tomlins 2012, pp. 31–68.

[15] See e.g. Martinez Peñas 2007. For this chapter, see also Koskenniemi 2011a, pp. 1–36.

suarum—dominion over themselves and their actions.[16] This enabled them to set up social institutions that would enable them to lead good and virtuous lives. God had originally foreseen that humans would live in peace, sharing all things in common. With the Fall, however, this became impossible. There was constant conflict and humans had to work in order to make their living. To protect themselves and to organize the attainment of their welfare, they had to divide things. First they created sovereign communities whose ruler had *dominium* over his subjects. This right was not absolute, however. Nor did it emerge from God—as Protestant heretics argued—but from the community itself.[17] Political rights also extended to the Indians of the new world so that Spaniards had no right to intervene in the government of those communities without special justification.[18] Alongside political communities, humans also used their freedom to create private property rights. These provided Vitoria and Soto the basis on which to discuss the law and the ethics of the novel commercial practices, questions such as just price, the morality of buying cheap and selling dear, of taking profit for exchanging currency, and so on.[19] What emerged from the work of the Salamanca theologians was a powerful theory of universal subjective rights that became the foundation both of political and private power and could be defended—as Vitoria made clear—by just war.[20]

As a summary of the works of the Spanish theologians, the Jesuit Francisco Suárez (1548–1617) made express the point of the priority of subjective rights (of *dominium*) over other normative directives. The original situation of no political *dominium* and common property had been based on ("objective") natural law. This, however, had only a "negative" character which meant that it did not prohibit *divisio rerum* (or as Vitoria put it, it had only the character of recommendation—"concessio"),[21] which is why it left "the matter to the management of men, such management to be in accordance with reason".[22] This, however, posed an additional problem. If sovereignty and property were based on purely human acts, had natural law then nothing to say about revolution or theft? Well, that did not follow. Early on in his work Suárez introduced a distinction between *ius* as law and *ius* as subjective right of *dominium*. When natural law provides

---

[16] See Vitoria 1934/1952, Tomo III, Q 62 A 10–11 (69–71) and Soto 1964, § 10 (100). For extended commentary, see Brett 1997.

[17] Although the prince's jurisdiction (*dominium*) over his subjects did originate from God, the transfer of that power to any particular prince took place through the community. See e.g. Vitoria 1992 11. As Soto points out, civil power is created "mediante lege naturae per civilem republicam", in de Soto 1967, Bk IV Q IV A 2 (302b).

[18] See especially Vitoria 1992, pp. 250–1.

[19] Vitoria's views on private property and commercial expansion are discussed at length in his lectures. See Vitoria 1934/1952, Tomo III (especially Q61 and 77–8). Parts of the commentaries are now published also as Vitoria 2006. For a discussion of the role of Vitoria and Soto as founders of a private rights-based economy, see further Miguel 1998, pp. 124–44.

[20] Vitoria 1992, pp. 281–2, 'On the Law of War', Vitoria 1992, pp. 295–308.

[21] Suárez 1944, Bk II Ch. XIV, § 14 (276–7). Skinner 1977, pp. 153–4. Vitoria 1934/1952, Comentarios III Q 62 A 1 § 20 (77).

[22] Suárez 1944, Bk II Ch. XIV, § 6 (270).

for the latter, it also provides for protection to whatever has been produced by it. After the intervention of *divisio rerum* natural law's non-derogable power now attaches to it, too, so that resistance to authority or stealing will become an evil, subject to punishment.[23] The "advantage" gained by fallen humanity from sovereignty and property is thus ratified by the binding force that natural law attaches to subjective rights.[24]

The subjective rights of the Spanish theologians helped to deal with the concerns of conscience among contemporaries triggered by violent expansion in the Indies and the widening network of global trade based on private profit-seeking. Even if freedom, equality, and common ownership still remained ideals of natural law, this did not mean, as the theologians carefully explained, that they would have actually prohibited the establishment of political commonwealths with secular sovereigns, or the division of properties so as to enable the creation of worldwide contractual dependency networks. Sovereignty and property may not have their origin in nature but they were justified creatures of liberty and individual rights. As such they could be situated in the teleological frame of supernatural happiness that brought varied forms of political and economic power under the ideological supervision of the Catholic Church.

B. Rights, Protestantism, and trade: Dutch seventeenth century

But the Habsburg realm of which Spain had become part in 1519 remained unable to maintain itself as a viable empire. With the Peace of Augsburg (1555), Protestantism found a permanent foothold in Germany and the revolt of the Protestant part of the Netherlands was consolidated by 1587–8 as Spanish attention was turned to England and France instead. By that time, the United Provinces had been able to establish themselves as a formidable military and economic power that was challenging Iberian dominance in the East Indies.[25] A key role in the rise of the United Provinces was played by the civil ethos of Dutch Protestantism. It united the interests of the state with those of the mercantile class, supporting the creation of an overseas trade network that would account for the future prosperity of the rebel provinces. The ideological background was provided by theories of resistance to tyranny that were also endorsed in the elaborate system of rights that lay at the heart of the writings of Hugo Grotius (1583–1645). Grotius came from a wealthy, well-connected family and had been trained in humanist and Stoic ideals. As a young man, he had been taken as apprentice and assistant to the Dutch Stadtholder Johan van Oldenbarneveldt, in which role he had above all to mediate between the Protestant factions struggling for leadership in the young state.[26] From 1604 he had also been engaged as legal adviser to the East India Company (VOC), developing an elaborate legal defence for the Company's violent operations against Portuguese and Spanish shipping that he had

---

[23] Suárez 1944, Bk II Ch. XIV § 13 (275–6).   [24] Suárez 1944, Bk II Ch. XIV § 13 (276).
[25] See e.g. Israel 1985, pp. 38–79.
[26] Grotius' life is written in many places. A good condensed summary is Eysinga 1952.

based on the right of self-preservation (including the preservation of property) as the most important rule of natural law.[27]

In his main work *De jure belli ac pacis* (1625) Grotius followed Suárez by outlining three meanings of the expression "*ius*". First is *ius* as the object of justice—*quod iustum est*—"that which is just".[28] Like Suárez, Grotius then made reference to a notion of *ius* that was synonymous with that of "law"—*idem valet quod Lex*. This described any legal norm that was valid in the community concerned.[29] But most interesting was the third (second in the order of presentation) notion of *ius*, one that exists as a *"[q]ualitas moralis personae competens quad aliquid iuste habeandum vel agendum"*, a moral quality that human beings may "have" and carry with themselves wherever they go. This may exist in two modes, a "perfect" one that Grotius called *facultas* and an "imperfect" one that he labelled *aptitudo*.[30] The former included the power that humans have on themselves (personal liberty) as well as over one's property. Every human being possessed such *facultas* by virtue of merely being human. The network of relations between *facultates* was covered by what Grotius calls "expletive" justice: the horizontal system of inter-individual relations characterized by the exercise of such subjective rights on the one hand, and everyone's duty to respect their use, on the other.[31]

Such *facultates* contrasted with mere "*aptitudo*" that Grotius received from the Aristotelian notion of distributive justice (relabelled "allocative" justice) that governed the vertical relations between public power and the subject. Or in Grotius' own words:

> *Attributive Justice,* styled by *Aristotle* [...] *Distributive,* respects Aptitude or *imperfect Right,* the attendant of those Virtues that are beneficial to others, as Liberality, Mercy, and prudent Administration of Government.[32]

An "*aptitudo*" respected the merits or the needs of a person but it could not be enforced by public authorities. It did not therefore ground a properly speaking "legal" relation at all.[33] In other words, natural subjective rights belonged to the realm of inter-individual justice and were both universal and binding as strict law, while entitlements based on attribution by the community, resulting from considerations of justice or charity, remained matters of value and choice. They may have moral or ethical force but do not ground any strong claim against the State. Nor can they be enforced against *facultates*, especially against rights of *dominium*.[34]

---

[27] Grotius 2006, Prolegomena (22–3).

[28] Grotius 2005, Bk I Ch. I § III.I (136). Interestingly, the "just" is defined in a negative way—"that which may be done without injustice to an enemy", injustice being defined as what is "repugnant to a Society of reasonable Creatures", ibid.

[29] Haggenmacher 1997, p. 75.   [30] Grotius 2005, Bk I Ch. I § IV (138).

[31] Grotius 2005, Bk I Ch. I § V (138–9) and Preliminary Discourse, VIII (86).

[32] Grotius 2005, Bk I Ch. I § VIII (143).   [33] See Haggenmacher 1997, p. 74.

[34] To illustrate this distinction Grotius added in the 1631 edition of *De jure belli ac pacis* the story of Cyrus who had to adjudicate between two boys fighting over two coats. Cyrus decided to give the bigger coat to the bigger boy and the smaller coat to the smaller boy. In this he was corrected by his tutor. The task was not to attribute the coats in accordance with what Cyrus might have thought each had an entitlement according to allocative—that is to say, distributive—justice. The task was to give each boy the coat that

In Grotius, then, we can find a well-developed system of individual (human) rights that not only justified Dutch commercial expansion but was specifically intended to create a universal system of rights, operated by contract, which it was the task of public power to facilitate and enforce. This Grotius expressly contrasted to any distributive scheme that public power might develop. As is well known, Grotius also supported a "contractual theory of absolute sovereignty".[35] Nature, he wrote, led humans to contract on the establishment of a political community. But although the *foundation* of civil community was in natural right, once the rights have been contracted, the life of the community was determined by sovereign power.

For those who had incorporated themselves into any Society, or subjected themselves to any one Man, or Number of Men, had either expressly, or from the Nature of the Thing must be understood to have tacitly promised, that they would submit to whatever either the greater part of the Society, or those on whom the Sovereign Power had been conferred, had ordained.[36]

In Grotius, a naturalist theory of individual rights was made to accomplish two things. One was the establishment and justification of a worldwide system of private commercial relations. The smooth operation of this system, as Grotius frequently remarked, was part of God's providential design to bring people together and to provide them with goods and happiness.

God has not bestowed his Gifts on every Part of the earth but had distributed them among different Nations, that Men wanting the Assistance of one another, might maintain and cultivate Society. And to this End has Providence introduced Commerce.[37]

Alongside this universal system that entitled the Dutch to penetrate maritime areas formerly held under Iberian monopoly, private rights likewise justified the Dutch rebellion against their former master, the Habsburgs. But once the rebellion was over—as it largely was by the time Grotius wrote—what was needed was doctrine of a strong centralized government that could keep in check the various religious factions that still continued to tear the young (and in some way quite artificial) state apart. A universal empire of private commercial relations, and a firm notion of state sovereignty—both were received by Grotius from a sophisticated argument from individual (human) rights. Because those rights were no longer based on an overall teleology of supernatural happiness in the afterlife, as they had been with the Spanish writers (whom Grotius closely followed), this deprived the Church from its position as the final authority on their use.

---

belonged to him, over which he had the subjective right of *dominium*. The task of the State was not to distribute property according to some allocative principle but to give effect to the relations of *dominium* as they existed in the network of relations of commutative justice that governed the relationships of subjective right holders to each other. The King, in other words, was not entitled to intervene by an act of redistribution. Allocative justice could not be exercised over expletive justice. To do this was to violate the strict right the smaller boy had to the bigger coat. A relationship of rights is prior to any relationship of attribution. The King may tax his subjects for the good of the community but not in order to distribute wealth among his subjects. Grotius 2005, Bk I Ch. I § VIII.2 (146–7).

[35] Loughlin 2010, p. 75.   [36] Grotius 2005, Preliminary Discourse XVI (93).
[37] Grotius 2005, Bk II Ch. II § XIII (444).

C. Rights, Empire, and revolution: eighteenth century

The vocabulary of rights provided a convenient instrument to address both European state-building and expansion that could only with difficulty be brought under larger theological or imperial frames. The idea of ownership of one's freedom, understood as a faculty, would easily extend to the right to contract over the establishment of a commonwealth at home as well as to acquire and dispose of property everywhere.[38] In both Catholic and Protestant realms ideas about objective justice—justice as the object of what we do—were in the course of sixteenth and early seventeenth centuries translated into subjective (*dominium*) rights that would be natural to all humans and applicable across the world through the operation of what was often called the *jus gentium*.[39] In the Spanish scholastics and their Jesuit followers as well as in Grotius, Melanchton, and Calvin's disciples subjective natural rights would provide building-blocks for the justification of civil power at home as well as a conception of what Suárez called "*respublica humana*" within which individual right-holders could freely travel and transact on their properties everywhere. In Spain, the theologians' principal concern had been to develop a meticulously up-to-date casuistry for the moral assessment of new types of activities in which Christians had been participating as a result of conquest and commercial expansion. In the United Provinces, Grotius removed this casuistry from its original theological context and used it as part of a system of (subjective) natural rights in which providence would see to the ultimate compatibility of the pursuit of self-preservation with an all-encompassing sociability. As the latter's Saxon follower Samuel Pufendorf (1632–94) would explain, with human beings who are both weak and self-loving, the rational conclusion was to become sociable—that is to say, to set up social institutions whose official justification would always look back to the original liberties of their founders.[40] Whether natural liberty encompassed also the right of selling oneself to slavery (as the apologists of Portuguese slave trade explained) was a disputed question. But most natural right went into justifying firm political rule over confessionally split societies with the objective of *salus publica*.

In England, the coincidence of John Locke's (1632–1704) influential writings on individual rights with his interest and advocacy of English colonization in the Americas has long been known. There probably is no reason to attribute to Locke the kinds of imperialist designs that would emanate from ideas of racial supremacy or civilizing progress.[41] The main target of his *Two Treatises* was the theory of divine kingship against which Locke set up all individuals' universally valid natural rights. Unlike in the continental traditions, these rights would continue to play a role also in the government of political commonwealth.[42] Nevertheless, the criteria through which he derived rights to property on land and sovereign authority over a community, somehow always eluded the Indians. Native Americans may indeed have shared humanity and

---

[38] See further, Pagden 2003, pp. 171–99.   [39] See especially Brett 2011, pp. 76–89.
[40] Pufendorf 1672/1994, Bk II Ch. 3 § 14–24, pp. 151–7.   [41] Armitage 2012, pp. 84–111.
[42] Locke 1924, e.g. 2.169–74 (204–6).

natural rights with Englishmen. But this did not mean that their agricultural or hunting activities would have provided them exclusive entitlement to lands desired by Englishmen or that their communities would have qualified as political common-wealths with sovereign rights against foreign intruders.[43]

Locke instituted the eighteenth-century practice of using the contrast of "slavery" and "rights" as a combat call against absolutism and in favour of a commercial society whose backbone would be a vibrant merchant elite. Therefore, by far the most important (universal, human) right in his system was the right to private property—even if it always remained subject to some limitation by its having been instituted by God for the preservation of individuals and humankind at large.[44] Human beings enter society, Locke famously wrote, for "the enjoyment of their properties in peace and safety".[45] From this he received a conclusion quite opposite to that of Grotius and many later naturalists, namely that the right was not exhausted by the social contract but remained valid as a right *against* the legislature, prohibiting rule "by extemporary arbitrary decrees" as well as the taking of property, including through taxation, without consent.[46] To lose one's natural rights in a political community would count as enslavement—and it would be absurd to think that originally free individuals would ever have accepted the institution of political sovereignty for such purpose.

In post-Westphalian Germany natural law would legitimate the post-confessional state. Following Pufendorf, Christian Thomasius and other jurists at such early Enlightenment universities as Halle or Göttingen postulated a state of nature in which free individuals contracted among themselves over the establishment of political com-munities and setting up (usually absolutist) rulers to govern them ("*Gesellschaftsvertrag*" and "*Untewerfungsvertrag*"). Until the 1770s and 1780s natural rights were understood above all in terms of the original liberty that was channelled to State institutions for the realization of the functional objectives of *salus publica* and state purpose (*Staatszweck*). They remained, however, usually without legally binding force against the ruler. Towards the end of the century constitutionalists began to argue for the normative force of rights even within the state, through the spread of the rhetoric of freedom ("*Freiheit*") in legal and political discourse, inspired by the revolutionary experiences in America and France.[47] This did not necessarily inject them with revolutionary character. In March 1791 the Imperial Chancellery in Vienna, for example, published a statement to the effect that it was evident that all individuals enjoyed human rights but that they became no better by being shouted by mobs: "the rights of human beings and of citizens are nowhere better secured than in the heart of [the Emperor] Leopold".[48]

---

[43] For the classic discussion, see Tully 1993, pp. 137–76.

[44] Locke 1924, 2.31 (131–2). See further Tully 1980, pp. 121–4.   [45] Locke 1924, 2.134 (183).

[46] Locke 1924, 2. 136, 138, 140 (183, 185, 189).

[47] For a full discussion of the contrast between "old" (1648–1770) and "new" (1770–1815) uses of natural law and natural rights in Germany, see Klippel 1976.

[48] "die Rechte der menschen und Bürger sind nirgends sicherer bewahrt als im Herzen Leopolds (II)", Brauneder 2006, p. 162.

The natural rights idiom had become familiar in France especially after the translations of Grotius and Locke, as well as the writings of Jean-Jacques Burlamaqui (1694–1748), became available to the reading public. By the 1720s and 1730s, French jurists had learned to pepper their arguments with points about the rights of their clients.[49] However, unlike in Germany, natural law never became a university discipline in France.[50] This was in part because of its association with Huguenot policy, in part owing to what the society of the salon viewed as its pedantic scholasticism. Voltaire and Rousseau understood it as conservative, if not strictly reactionary. On the other hand, literary invocations of a golden age were nevertheless often expressed in the languages of "humanity" and "natural liberty" so as to attack the ills of the old regime.[51] Diderot, Montesquieu, and Rousseau all had a complex debt to the natural law tradition. It was only later in the century that individual natural *rights* arose as a significant *topos*. One context in which it did so was that of the economic theories of the Physiocrats who, as part of their criticisms of mercantilism and advocacy of free trade, highlighted the rights of contract and property as the only acceptable foundation for a modern economy. Nothing puts more clearly the universalist pathos of the new doctrine of natural rights than the brief essay by a leading "Économiste", Pierre Samuel Dupont de Nemours (1739–1817), later Inspector General of Commerce, and a tireless propagator of free trade in France and later in the United States.[52] He began with the anti-Hobbesian dictum that a natural society existed between humans that was formed out of their needs and interests and was prior to any convention between them.

Dans cet état primitif les hommes ont des droits et devoirs réciproques d'une justice absolue parce qu'ils sont d'une nécessité physique & par conséquent absolue pour leur existence.[53]

The natural society of humans was expressed in their reciprocal rights and duties that good government would put in a harmonious relationship. In the natural society all humans had the liberty to pursue their subsistence; they also had the right of property over things they had achieved through their labour. The rights were anterior to any convention and could not be taken away by convention, either. In Dupont's dramatic formulation, the human sovereign was incapable of legislating anything new—"car les lois sont toutes faites par la main de celui qui créa les droits & les devoirs".[54] Positive laws were powerless to contradict the laws of freedom and property; all they could (and should) do was to declare their content and to enforce them.[55]

---

[49] On the spread of natural rights in French legal advocacy (with statistical data on legal process in Dijon), see Schmale 2006, pp. 94–6.

[50] See e.g. Heilbron 1995, pp. 42–6, 67–8.

[51] See Edelstein 2011, pp. 58–9; Heilbron 1995, pp. 96–100. And further Edelstein 2009.

[52] For a useful discussion, see Giraudeau 2008, pp. 225–42.   [53] Dupont 1768, pp. 17–18.

[54] Ibid., p. 30.

[55] Hence there was no reason to separate between legislation and enforcement; valid legislation was always also enforcement of the prior system of natural rights and obligations. Dupont 1768, pp. 31–2. For the absolute natural rights doctrine of the leading jurist among the Physiocrates, Pierre-Paul Lemercier de La Rivière, see Koskenniemi 2012, pp. 61–3.

But if individual rights operated well as a claim by the "moderns" to support the move to a commercial society, they were equally available as a republican instrument to support political renewal on the left. Abbé Gabriel Bonnot de Mably (1709–85), one-time friend of Rousseau's, and the author of an early commentary on *Droit public de l'Europe*, turned into a fierce critic of the old regime in a dialogue with the fictitious Englishman "Lord Stanhope", putting forward a radical project of political renewal in pursuit of individual political rights after the English model. To the Frenchman who agreed on the basic rights but voiced doubts about the ability of Frenchmen to make constructive use of them, "Stanhope" responded that there was a duty on every patriot to employ the rights they possessed and not to rely on authority; rights crystallized in active citizenship and a novel constitution had to give room for activism as the core of a system of republican rights.[56] The French revolutionaries had read their Mably, their Rousseau and their sentimental literatures in which the rhetoric of rights flourished— deciding to preface the constitution they had decided to adopt with a declaration of rights, a task they thought to perfect first in a few heated days in August 1789 but to which the conduct of the revolution itself forced them to return in 1793 and in 1795.

The drafting of the *Declaration on the Rights of Man and Citizen* by the French National Assembly and Convention, as Marcel Gauchet has shown, was intended to accomplish a number of paradoxical objectives. It was to provide an ideological basis to a novel power, the Nation that would represent "all"—while simultaneously laying the limits of that power vis-à-vis the citizens. As a result, the debates on the relations of "rights" to "duties", and of freedom-rights to the rights of "assistance" from the Nation that were repeated almost verbatim in 1789, 1793, and 1795, came to define the pattern of parliamentary politics everywhere in Europe. Fluctuating between more and less radical and conservative tendencies, between the "Left" and the "Right", the deputies often found refuge in ambivalent formulations that linked rights with corresponding obligations or stressed that "free individuality" was possible only in a society that provided equal resources to everyone. A founding on individual freedoms, for Jacobin patriots, could only mean complete subservience of everyone to the Nation—while the express inclusion of individuals' "duties" would, for Thermidorean revisionists, provide a definite sphere for the roles of each. The deputies grappled with formulations that derived the rights—and thus the constitution they would preface—from nature and from society alternatively, thus suggesting that political problems were ultimately philosophical in nature. And yet, proposed philosophical formulations gave no concrete indication regarding the policies to be adopted. The deputies' anxiety about the governmental tasks they were trying to accomplish was reflected in the proposal, still debated on the last day of the Thermidorean drafting process in 1795, that at issue was not the adoption of a "law" at all, but a "basis of the social contract" or the declaration of a "theory".[57]

---

[56]   De Mably 1789. For the context, see Baker 1990, pp. 88–91.   [57]   Gauchet 1989, p. 315.

The wisdom and the paradox of this last suggestion arose again with the passing of the Universal Declaration of Human Rights in 1948, where one of the principal post-war proponents of the idea of a declaration, Hersch Lauterpacht, lamented that the rights were included in an instrument that was a mere General Assembly resolution and as such not binding as law, that in fact the passing of the declaration by the Assembly offered the only conceivable context in which UN member states could stand up to declare, with all due solemnity, that they loved these rights, but were not bound by them.[58] Yet had the rights been the object of a treaty, new problems would have arisen. At that point, they would have become subject to all the problems concerning national ratification and reservations as well as the interpretative principles of the 1969 Vienna Convention on the Law of Treaties; their amendment and indeed their validity would have been anchored in the fluctuations of UN diplomacy. Surely to exist as the *foundation* of politics, they should not be understood as an effect of political interests and bargains...

II. The Power and Weakness of Rights: Some Conclusions

The discussion in Section I highlights the almost infinite variability of the contexts in which rights-vocabulary may be available to support some causes or preferences against others. In the United Nations, for example, the direction of rights-activity has fluctuated from a Western stress on civil and political rights, to a more inclusive stress on their "indivisibility" from economic, social and cultural rights, to a 1970s–1980s post-colonial "revisionism" that read rights as instruments for economic justice and "development", and finally into an alignment in the 1990s with the preferences of UN human rights treaty bodies.[59] Rights have both supported and challenged the power of religious institutions. They have been a key ideological instrument to support private property against extractions by the king or public power, as well as a basis to challenge the inequality of property and the power of money. In early modern Germany, rights were invoked to defend individual liberty but also to retrench a firm central power assigned to look after the security and happiness of the citizens. During the European Enlightenment rights supported revolution but also state-building and then, as now, the two things have often gone together. As much as rights have defended individuals against their communities, they have also underwritten the community's power to demand that individuals respect its traditions: liberalism, republicanism, and even socialism have thrived on rights.

Because rights are everywhere, it is impossible to use them to show a single line of progress. It is a fantastic but significant fact that although "slavery" had been a continuously reiterated trope of the French Enlightenment, standing for everything the

---

[58] Lauterpacht 1950.   [59] For aspects of this history, see Whelan 2010.

enlighteners were against, that discourse coexisted quite peacefully with the enslavement of Africans in the French West Indies throughout the eighteenthth century, up into and beyond the revolution of 1789. In fact, the number of slaves imported to the Caribbean was never higher than in the last quarter of the eighteenth century when it rose to 419,500.[60] The call to break the "chains of serfdom" meant emancipation at home, not putting an end to colonial slavery. Rousseau, for example, had nothing to say in the whole of his career about the system of enslavement in the Caribbean that was the source of the sugar he enjoyed.[61]

The coexistence of rights with enslavement and other kinds of massive suffering is of course not a thing of the past but a palpable aspect of the present. As Susan Marks has pointed out, between the 1990s and now the tone of rights-speech has moved from romance to tragedy, not only because there has not been "enough" rights-speech but owing to problems (such as those surveyed in this chapter) *within* rights-speech itself.[62] To explain this, it may be useful to start with acknowledgement that the common discourse about rights being "universal, inalienable and indivisible" is an intellectual stopgap and a political dead end. It looks towards a world of harmony where the right of all humans—that is to say the preferences of all—would organize themselves harmoniously and in a coterminous way. Neither conceptual logic nor historical experience supports such a view. Since Kant, and perhaps earlier, the view that rights exist in harmony has been an aspect of rationalist imagination whose political force may have been formidable, but which has lent itself to assist whatever cause and agenda. Because it denies the reality of conflicts, explaining them as misunderstandings about everyone's real preferences, it has complicated, instead of facilitated, their resolution.

No doubt, rights theorists have long since recognized that the way to utopia is not opened by assuming a pre-existing harmony where none exists. The process of redescribing some interests or preferences as "rights" has been and continues to be about struggle and compromise in which some claimants win, others lose. It may be easy to understand why, sometime in the 1960s or 1970s, a powerful rights-rhetoric arose to trump the deformalized administrative processes through which the government of welfare societies was to be arranged. What Max Weber analysed at the beginning of the twentieth century as the increasing complexity and fragmentation of modern society and the related deformalization of modern law, the turn from generally applicable "rules" to contextually sensitive anti-formal principles of proportionality, good faith, and optimal result, empowered law-appliers in a way that created the call for new absolutes. "You may not override my interest even if that were in the interests of the community. This is so because my interest embodies a right." The massive translation of "interests" into "rights" in the late twentieth century was occasioned precisely by

---

[60] The number is from Nimako & Willemsen 2011, p. 22. See further Blackburn 2011 p. 161 and generally Benot 2005.

[61] Buck-Morss 2009, pp. 29–34.   [62] Marks 2011.

the hope that in this way they could be made untouchable, lifted outside politics altogether. But there is no limit to this translation, which is why the world of politics became saturated by rights-claims. For every claim of right, the burden that is to fall upon somebody for honouring it may be seen as a violation of the rights of the latter. Every increase of the right to freedom of somebody is felt as an encroachment on the right to security of someone else. And so on. There is no social conflict in which both sides could not, with some plausibility, invoke their interest as a "right". The result has been the rise of the bureaucratic management of rights through ubiquitous practices of "balancing" whose criteria are received from an institutional bias that cannot be articulated by the rights whose limit and content it sets.[63]

And yet it is also obvious that behind every (subjective) human right lurks an "objective" right that invokes some idea of the good society in which the preference captured by the right is supposed to flourish. Freedom of speech is meaningful only in a society with a well-functioning and accessible system of communication—but what it means to have such is an issue of policy. To make a reality of civil and political rights involves more than periodic elections and often—as the "Arab Spring" suggests—wholesale transformation of societies where some will win, others lose. And of course economic and social rights refer back to contested views about just distribution, techniques of economic management and even the objectives to be attained. Only by reference to such larger—one is tempted to say "structural"—objectives and values is it possible to finally prefer some rights (and their attendant institutional projects) to others.

Marxian critics used to argue that it was a big problem with rights that they tended to prefer individuals over groups, positing the egoistic and alienated individual as the ideal to which everyone should aspire but which then perpetuated the exploitative relations of capitalist society.[64] Although the power of that critique has not been exhausted, it is nevertheless the case that the spread of rights to cover goods of a collective type, including economic and social rights (however lacking in implementation), has mitigated that concern and expanded the range of preferences rights-talk can be used to defend. More important, perhaps, is the way that rights-talk's focus on things we "have" or (to follow Grotius) "faculties" we "possess", seems obsessively concerned with identities rather than the structural determination of those identities. Rights-talk may support our capacity to exercise a religion we profess, to express an opinion or to support a party we prefer, or to use a property we have—that is to say, to be "true" to ourselves and our life projects. But it is blind to the conditions within which we come think of ourselves as "religious" in a particular way, members of a party, property-owners or persons with specific opinions. This, I think, is an important aspect of the intellectual dead end that rights bring with them. They claim to protect our (person, group) identities and preferences *without ever questioning how we came to*

---

[63] I have discussed these matters in more detail in Koskenniemi 2010 & 2011b. The best discussion of the turn to "balancing" in rights-technologies is Kennedy 1997.

[64] See Marx 1994, p. 41.

have them. They are so close, so intimate with our assumed selfhood that they make it impossible for us to situate ourselves in any larger context—especially the context of an ubiquitous identity-producing power.

It is here, I think, that historical studies of the uses of rights-vocabularies become helpful. Raymond Geuss recently pleaded against abstract political theory that focuses on ideal states and moral commitments and in favour of historically informed studies of the uses of political concepts—such as "human rights"—in actual controversies. For, as he put it,

[t]he reasons for why we have most of the political and moral concepts we have (in the form in which we have them) are contingent, historical reasons, and only a historical account will give us the beginnings of an understanding of them and allow us to reflect critically on them rather than simply taking them for granted.[65]

Historical studies of rights, I would like to claim, have two kinds of properties that break the intellectual dead-ends involved in abstract philosophical exercises around the topic. They open up those larger contexts in which we can see rights perform (or failing to perform) social functions by advancing some causes against other causes, supporting interests, projects, and programmes that have real importance to the actors in historical dramas. They show that rights not only overlap and conflict but that this is often their very point. The most important human rights violations do not just "happen" to some people but are logical and accepted consequences of particular policies. They are not the product of impersonal forces but "planned misery", outcomes of choices that account for the wealth and power of others.[66] Shifting focus in this way from victims to perpetrators is easiest in historical studies that locate rights as aspects of imperial or commercial expansion, religious war, colonial exploitation, revolution or retrenchment, state-building, and so on. Chronology helps to attain distance and genealogy makes that which happened seem not necessary at all, but the contingent result of struggle and choice.

But historical studies also illustrate the processes whereby people attain certain identities and preferences—how they come to think of themselves as "Catholics" or "Protestants", "Indians" or "Turks", men and women. Early scholastic thought under-stood *dominium* fundamentally as the individual's ownership of their identity and used the attendant notion of "liberty" to justify the new social roles that sixteenth-century Spaniards were adopting in a commercially and militarily expanding Europe. Similarly, the eighteenth-century conception of natural rights opened for Europeans a way to think of themselves as virtuous republicans or cosmopolitan operators in a commercial "system," choices and subject-positions within which increasingly minute differentiations counted for the European modernity that soon became "modernity" *tout court.* The new histories of human rights, I think, are valuable in marking out how the structure of that modernity came about but also how it became invisible by the

---

[65] Geuss 2008, p. 69.   [66] Marks 2008, pp. 281–307; Marks 2011, pp. 57–78.

fact of attention being directed to individuals, their preferences and projects, their identities and "rights". In these ways history performs a classical critical service. It situates rights-vocabularies in the contexts of their uses, drawing out the winners and the losers, and points to the structures that situate people in these groups.

References

Armitage, David, "John Locke: Theorist of Empire?", in Sankar Muthu (ed.), *Empire and Modern Political Thought* (Oxford: Oxford University Press, 2012).

Baker, Keith Michael, "A Script for the French Revolution: The Political Consciousness of Mably", in *Inventing the French Revolution: Essays on French Political Culture in the Eighteenth Century* (Cambridge: Cambridge University Press, 1990).

Benot, Yves, *Les Lumières, l'esclavage, la colonisation* (Paris: Découverte, 2005).

Blackburn, Robin, *The Overthrow of Colonial Slavery, 1776–1848* (London: Verso, 2011).

Brauneder, Wilhelm, "Vom Nutzen des Naturrechts für die Habsburgsmonarchie", in Diethelm Kilippel (ed.), *Naturrecht und Staat: Politische Funktionen des europäischen Naturrechts* (Munich: Oldenbourg, 2006).

Brett, Annabel, *Liberty, Rights and Nature: Individual Rights in Later Scholastic Thought* (Cambridge: Cambridge University Press, 1997).

Brett, Annabel, *Changes of State: Nature and the Limits of the City in Early Modern Natural Law* (Princeton: Princeton University Press, 2011).

Buck-Morss, Susan, *Hegel, Haiti and Universal History* (Pittsburgh: University of Pittsburgh Press, 2009).

Carr, Craig L. & Michael J. Seidler, *The Political Writings of Samuel Pufendorf* (Oxford: Oxford University Press, 1994).

Dembour, Marie-France, *Who Believes in Human Rights? Reflections on the European Convention* (Cambridge: Cambridge University Press, 2006).

Dupont de Nemours, Pierre Samuel, *De l'origine et des progrès d'une science nouvelle*, (London: Desaint, 1768).

Duranti, Marco, *The Conservative Human Rights Revolution: European Identity, Transnational Politics, and the Origins of the European Convention* (Oxford: Oxford University Press, 2017).

Edelstein, Dan, *The Terror of Natural Right: Republicanism, the Cult of Nature & the French Revolution* (Chicago: Chicago University Press, 2009).

Edelstein, Dan, *The Enlightenment: A Genealogy* (Chicago: University of Chicago Press, 2011).

Eysinga, W. J. M., *Hugo Grotius: Eine biographische Skizze* (Basel: Schwabe, 1952).

Garnsey, Peter, *Thinking about Property: From Antiquity to the Age of Revolution* (Cambridge: Cambridge University Press, 2007).

Gauchet, Marcel, *La Révolution des droits de l'homme* (Paris: Gallimard, 1989).

Geuss, Raymond, *Philosophy and Real Politics* (Princeton: Princeton University Press, 2008).

Giltaj, Jakob, *Menschenrechten in het romersche recht?* (Nijmegen: Wolf, 2011).

Giraudeau, Martin, "Performing Physiocracy: Pierre Samuel Dupont de Nemoius and the Limits of Political Engineering", 3 *Journal of Cultural Economy* (2008), 225–42.

Grotius, Hugo, *The Rights of War and Peace* (Indianapolis: Liberty Fund 2005 [1625]).

Grotius, Hugo, *Commentary on the Right of Prize and Booty*, ed. & introd. M. J. V. Ittersum (Indianapolis: Liberty Fund, 2006 [1604–6]).

Haggenmacher, Peter, "Droits subjectifs et système juridique chez Grotius", in Luc Foisneau, *Politique, droit et théologie chez Bodin, Grotius et Hobbes* (Paris: Kimé, 1997).

Halme-Tuomisaari, Miia, *Human Rights in Action: Learning Expert Knowledge* (Leiden: Brill, 2010).

Heilbron, John, *The Rise of Social Theory* (Cambridge: Polity, 1995).

Hunt, Lynn, *Inventing Human Rights: A History* (New York: Norton, 2007).

Israel, Joachim, *Dutch Primacy in World Trade* 1585–1740 (Oxford: Clarendon Press, 1985).

Jay, Martin, "Historical Explanation and the Event: Reflections on the Limits of Contextualization", 42 *New Literary History* (2011), 557–71.

Kelly, Duncan, "Revisiting the Rights of Man: Georg Jellinek on Rights and the State", 22 *Law & Hist. Rev.* (2004), 493–529.

Kennedy, David, *The Rights of Spring* (Princeton: Princeton University Press, 2008).

Kennedy, Duncan, *Critique of Adjudication (fin-de-siècle)* (Cambridge, Mass.: Harvard University Press, 1997), 316–33.

Klippel, Diethelm, *Politische Freiheit und Freiheitsrechte im deutschen Naturrecht des* 18. *Jahrhunderts* (Paderborn: Schönigh, 1976).

Koskenniemi, Martti, "International Law in Europe: Between Tradition and Renewal", 16 *European Journal of International Law* (2005), 113–24.

Koskenniemi, Martti, "Human Rights Mainstreaming as a Strategy for Institutional Power", 1 *Humanity. An International Journal of Human Rights, Humanitarianism and Development* (2010), 47–58.

Koskenniemi, Martti, "Empire and International Law: The Real Spanish Contribution", 61 *University of Toronto Law Journal* (2011a), 1–36.

Koskenniemi, Martti, "The Effect of Rights on Political Culture", in *The Politics of International Law* (Oxford: Hart, 2011b), 133–52.

Koskenniemi, Martti, "The Public Law of Europe", in H. Lindemann et al. (eds), *Erzählungen vom Konstitutionalismus* (Baden-Baden: Nomos, 2012).

Lauterpacht, Hersch, *International Law and Human Rights* (London: Praeger, 1950).

Locke, John, *Two Treatises of Government* (London: Everyman's, 1924).

Loughlin, Martin, *Foundations of Public Law* (Oxford: Oxford University Press, 2010).

Mably, Abbé de, *Des droits et des devoirs du citoyen* (Paris: Lacombe, 1789).

Marks, Susan, "Exploitation as an International Legal Concept", in Marks (ed.), *International Law on the Left: Re-Examining Marxist Legacies* (Cambridge: Cambridge University Press, 2008).

Marks, Susan, "Human Rights and Root Causes", 74 *Modern Law Review* (2011), 57–78.

Marks, Susan, "Human Rights in Disastrous Times", in James Crawford & Martti Koskenniemi, *The Cambridge Companion on International Law* (Cambridge: Cambridge University Press, 2011).

Martinez, Jenny S., *The Slave Trade and the Origin of International Human Rights Law* (Oxford: Oxford University Press, 2012).

Martínez Peñas, Leandro, *El confesor del rey en el antiguo régimen* (Madrid: Editorial Complutense, 2007).

Marx, Karl, "On the Jewish Question", in Marx, *Early Political Writings*, ed. J. O'Malley (Cambridge: Cambridge University Press, 1994).

Merry, Sally Engle & Mark Goodale (eds), *The Practice of Human Rights: Tracking Law Between the Global and the Local* (Cambridge: Cambridge University Press, 2007).

Miguel, Cirilo Flórez, "La escuela de Salamanca y los orígenes de la económia", in Francisco Gómez Camacho & Ricardo Robledo (eds), *El pensamiento económico en la escuela de Salamanca* (Salamanca: Ediciones Universidad Salamanca, 1998).

Moyn, Samuel, *The Last Utopia: Human Rights in History* (Cambridge, Mass.: Harvard University Press, 2010).

Moyn, Samuel, "Of Deserts and Promised Lands: The Dream of Global Justice", *The Nation* (March 19, 2012).

Moyn, Samuel, "Substance, Scale, and Salience: The Recent Historiography of Human Rights", 8 *Annual Review of Law and Social Science* (2012).

Mutua, Makau W., *Human Rights: A Political and a Cultural Critique* (Philadelphia: University of Pennsylvania Press, 2002).

Nimako, Kwame & Glenn Willemsen, *The Dutch Atlantic: Slavery, Abolition and Emancipation* (London: Pluto Press, 2011).

Orford, Anne, "The Past as Law or History? The Relevance of Imperialism for Modern International Law", in Emmanuelle Jouannet & Hélène Ruiz-Fabri (eds), *Tiers-Monde: Bilan et perspectifs* (Paris: Société de Législation Companée, 2013a).

Orford, Anne, "On International Legal Method", 1 *London Review of International Law* (2013b), 167–97.

Pagden, Anthony, "Human Rights, Natural Rights and Europe's Imperial Legacy", 31 *Political Theory* (2003), 171–99.

Pufendorf, Samuel, "On the Law of Nature and of Nations" (1672), in Carr & Seidler 1994.

Reid, Charles J., Jr., "The Canonistic Contribution to the Western Rights Tradition: An Historical Inquiry", 33 *Boston College Law Review* (1991–2), 37–92.

Schmale, Wolfgang, "Naturrecht und Staat in Frankreich", in Diethelm Klippel (ed.), *Naturrecht und Staat: Politische Funktionen des europäischen Naturrechts* (Munich: Oldenbourg, 2006).

Skinner, Quentin, *The Foundations of Modern Political Thought*, vol. II (Cambridge: Cambridge University Press, 1977).

Slotte, Pamela & Miia Halme-Tuomisaari (eds), *Revisiting the Origins of Human Rights* (Cambridge: Cambridge University Press, 2015).

Soto, Domingo de, *Relección 'De dominio': Edición crítica y Traducción, con Introducción, Apéndices e Indices, por Jaime Prufau Prats* (Granada: Universidad de Granada, 1964).

Soto, Domingo de, *De iustitia et iure* Libri decem/*De la justicia y el derecho en diez Libros*, introd. P. V. Diego Carro, Spanish trans. P. M. Gonzalez Ordonez (Madrid: Reus, 1967 [1556]).

Suárez, Francisco, "On Laws and God the Lawgiver", in *Selections from Three Works*, vol. II, trans. G. L. Williams et al. (Oxford: Clarendon, 1944).

Tierney, Brian, *The Idea of Natural Rights: Studies in Natural Rights, Natural Law and Church Law* 1150–1625 (Grand Rapids, Mich.: Eerdmans, 1997).

Tomlins, Christopher, "After Critical Legal History: Scope, Scale, Structure", 8 *Annu. Rev. Law. Soc.* (2012), 31–68.

Tully, James, *A Discourse on Property: John Locke and his Adversaries* (Cambridge: Cambridge University Press, 1980).

Tully, James, *An Approach to Political Philosophy: Locke in Contexts* (Cambridge: Cambridge University Press, 1993).

Villey, Michel, *Le Droit et les droits de l'homme* (Paris: PUF, 1983).

Vitoria, Franciso de, *Comentarios a la Secunda secundae de Santo Tomás*, Edición preparada por Vicente Beltrán de Heredia (Salamanca: n.pub., 1934/1952).

Vitoria, Francisco de, *Political Writings*, ed. A. Pagden and J. Lawrance (Cambridge: Cambridge University Press, 1992).

Vitoria, Francisco de, *Contratos y usura* (Pamplona: EUNSA, 2006).

Whelan, Daniel J., *Indivisible Human Rights: A History* (Philadelphia: University of Pennsylvania Press, 2010).

Witte, John, "Rights, Resistance, and Revolution in the Western Tradition: Early Protestant Foundations", 26 *Law & Hist. Rev.* (2008), 545–70.

1.1

Doing Without an Original
A Commentary on Martti Koskenniemi

Annabel Brett

How can history help us with human rights? What *are* human rights, anyway? This is the bind that Martti Koskenniemi outlines at the beginning of his contribution. History—or at least, history conceived in a certain way—seems to demand an identifiable subject of which to *be* the history. But the present-day 'human rights phenomenon' is so amorphous as to defy that demand. Human rights are different things to different people, and to insist that they are one thing and not the other is immediately to take either a political or a philosophical position (or both). Not that there is anything wrong with that, per se: as Koskenniemi stresses, politics will always, ultimately, be involved, somewhere; and, although his chapter throughout adopts a critical tone towards philosophy, his words imply that it is a certain *kind* of philosophy to which he objects, and which indeed has lost credibility more generally. This is the kind of 'legislative' philosophy that asserts what human rights *are*, rather than offering an imaginative construction of how human rights might be thought of, if we want to make a better world for living in. The trouble is that it is this kind of philosophy that tends to be implicated in histories of a certain kind, histories that search for 'origins'. In its naive form, this kind of history thinks of its subject much as if it were an adult human being. Here is person X, now; to tell the story of X, we need to go back to when he or she was born, find the birth certificate, identify the parents, then trace his or her progress through childhood, adolescence and early adulthood until the present day. What we get is not so much a history as a *biography* of human rights. Such a story is happy to refer to 'context', but only in the sense of the circumstances for a life lived, a life that has an essential unity that transcends all circumstances.

Not all 'origins' stories are naive in this way, of course; neither in history more generally, nor in intellectual history more particularly. Thus, for example, Richard Tuck's 1979 classic, *Natural Rights Theories: Their Origins and Development*,[1] uses the organic metaphor but evades the organic analogy by taking as its subject not 'natural

---

[1] Tuck 1979.

rights' but 'natural rights theories': how people have construed natural rights from the first time that we can identify such an idiom in use. It is no longer the history of an 'idea', but the history of people doing something, and doing something with words. As such it is a product of the deep change wrought in the practice of intellectual history by the movement known as the 'Cambridge School', and especially perhaps by Quentin Skinner, owing to his deliberately iconoclastic attack on the older 'history of ideas'.[2] The word that tends to be associated with this movement is 'context', the demand to read texts in context: to understand them as speech acts designed to do something at a particular time and in a particular place. But equally important is 'text' itself: the concentration on language rather than on thought as the subject of intellectual history. As such, the Cambridge School is not unique but one moment in a broader twentieth-century movement that we know as the 'linguistic turn'. Its specific debts are to the 'speech act' theory of John Austin and John Searle, but also to the later Wittgenstein and his notion of a 'language game', a shared system of signs *and* 'the actions into which it is woven',[3] in which meaning is inevitably public rather than private. It is within such a game that an individual speaker makes his or her move, the 'speech act' that has a particular context. But the game itself has a context too. In both ways, context becomes part of the meaning, rather than existing as a kind of environment for an 'idea'. It is a history, not just of language, but of language-in-use.

As Koskenniemi notes, this history—like any history—is not free of normative commitments. For all but the most simple speech acts, there are plural and overlapping contexts, just as there are plural and overlapping language games in which they might participate. Our decision to understand the intentionality of a text in one or the other of these, and our prior decision to focus on the particular texts that we do, are choices that involve, at a very basic level, our understanding of what is important and what is not, and can be much more overtly political.[4] I would add that doing history this way has a philosophical dimension as well. To explore the language of one or a series of texts, or an entire language game in itself, is to interpret and to reimagine a way of seeing the world, to engage our own language with that of the past to create something that opens shafts not only into the past but within the present as well. It is the antithesis of 'legislative' philosophy, but it is philosophical nonetheless. 'Our language can be seen as an ancient city: a maze of little streets and squares, of old and new houses, and of houses with additions from various periods; and this surrounded by a multitude of new boroughs with straight regular streets and uniform houses.'[5] To explore a past idiom is like exploring an old street; but it is a street in our city, nonetheless, and we re-inhabit our own language as we do so.

In this perspective, then, 'human rights' is not an idea, but an element of present language, one so pervasive as to form an entire 'way of talking', or language game, in itself. What kind of history does that way of talking have? In previous centuries there

---

[2] Skinner 1969.   [3] Wittgenstein 1968, § 7.   [4] Consider, for example, Skinner 1998.
[5] Wittgenstein 1968, § 18.

has been talk of natural rights, the rights of man (though one might more properly perhaps refer to 'the Rights of Man', to catch the eighteenth-century flavour of the idiom), and other kinds of rights; but we do not seem to have *human* rights before the mid-twentieth century. The language is not wholly without precedent in the nineteenth century, but that precedent cannot be made to do any clear explanatory work; there seems to be no relation between any previous deployment of the term 'human rights' and its efflorescence in the late 1930s and 1940s, culminating in the Universal Declaration of 1948.[6] The context for the Declaration is the politics of the Second World War, already looking forward to the cold war era. In this context they could appear either as a new universal language, created by a multiplicity of voices, designed to capture the progressive ideals of all nations; or as some kind of dystopian Orwellian newspeak, forged (in both senses) to legitimate a new hegemony. Indeed, recent research on the Declaration points dispiritingly in this direction. But here we come upon another aspect of language: its ability to float free of its original context and wash up on alien shores, there to be appropriated by different people and put to very different uses, to legitimate things quite other than those originally intended. (Though it has an inveterate habit of floating off yet again.[7]) The history of appropriation subsequent to 1948 is, precisely, the history of human rights: a short one. Why does it need to be any longer?

Well, there is a little bit more to be said about the Universal Declaration. As a 'Declaration', it harks back to two previous, and celebrated declarations, both from the late eighteenth century and both of which invoke rights belonging to all 'men' (or 'Men'): the American 'Declaration of Independence', and the French 'Déclaration des Droits de l'Homme et du Citoyen'.[8] Many of the phrases in the body of the text also echo eighteenth-century formulations: 'equal and inalienable rights', 'the right to life, liberty' (if not 'the security of the person'), 'no one shall be subjected to cruel, inhuman or degrading treatment or punishment'. These might therefore seem to be the same 'rights of man' that the eighteenth century recognized, even if the title of the Universal Declaration calls them by the un-eighteenth-century term 'human rights'. Indeed, René Cassin, one of its drafters, never failed to think of them as *les droits de l'homme* and to deplore the marginalization of that term in favour of 'human rights'.[9] From this perspective, the French translation might look more like the original. But in fact the

---

[6] See Moyn 2010 for this thesis, with which I broadly agree, although Moyn holds that the efflorescence of human rights really only dates to as recently as the 1970s, when they were taken up as the eponymous 'last utopia' by Western reformers, despairing of any other. This argument threatens, however, to suggest that these latter-day Western human rights, with their function of protecting the vulnerable against the excesses of state power, just *are* human rights, bypassing any other post-1948 appropriations of the idiom. The same position with regard to their protective function is also what serves to disqualify natural rights and the rights of man from being human rights: Moyn argues that these seventeenth- and eighteenth-century rights function towards the power of the state rather than against it. But this for/against the state is too simple a criterion; natural rights *can* function against the state, but they do not do so by 'protecting the vulnerable.' Rather, they signal the limits of the moral obligation of a subject. See Brett 2015.

[7] See Derrida 1982 for a classic exploration of the ability of language *always* to exceed context.

[8] For the idea of a 'declaration', see Armitage 2007 and references there.   [9] Sluga 2011.

key point about the Declaration is that it defies our search for an original as a source of meaning. The eighteenth-century rights it appears to suggest are linked with social and economic rights that the eighteenth century never even dreamed of. The text is not at home in any historical political language ('idiom' or 'rhetoric'), just as it is not at home in any 'natural' language (a misnomer, because such languages too have a history, and a political history at that). It is this that accounts for the peculiar blankness of the text, and the peculiar meaninglessness of human rights more generally. People make of them what they will, and use them how they will: the situation of anomie with which Koskenniemi begins.

As we have seen, a history of language rather than ideas cannot help us out here with a longer story of 'origins'. It might, however, have value in other ways. One approach might be to explore the contours of different historical rights idioms—say, natural rights, or the rights of man—including, as an essential part of this enterprise, the contexts in which they were deployed. It might then offer some kind of critical fix on the meaning of (that is: the way we use) human rights today. For example, there is a widespread assumption that 'natural rights' and 'human rights' are the same thing, since the former belong to all human beings by nature and the latter to all human beings as such. But not only is it not clear, conceptually speaking, that the two locutions amount to the same thing;[10] historically speaking, the claim that a right is 'natural' or 'by nature' implicates it in a complex causal story and a series of conceptual contrasts—nature/grace, nature/city—that are centrally involved in the legitimizing power of the discourse. It is the very opposite of isolating the 'human being as such'. Moreover, the appeal to nature can sometimes pull against the distinction between the human and the animal, which is so powerfully drawn in other ways. An exploration of the sense of the 'natural'—and by implication the 'human'—in these terms could serve as to give us a critical perspective on the way that we ourselves invoke the category of the human in the phrase 'human rights'. As Koskenniemi notes more generally, it will still be up to our political judgement whether we want to continue to invoke it or not; but if we do, at least we may do so with more awareness of what we are doing, of what building we are occupying, to continue Wittgenstein's analogy—and can history ever hope to offer more?

Koskenniemi does not choose this approach, however. He does indeed imply that to take a historical perspective we need to look at other kinds of rights—'natural rights', 'individual rights', 'subjective rights'—which have similarities and differences with human rights. But the similarities and differences are not spelled out or directly explored. Koskenniemi implies that this is the task of philosophy, whereas the task of history is to locate those idioms in their historical contexts (a sharper break between history and philosophy than the above approach would posit). We need, that is, to see what they are *doing*. One might initially feel that this side-stepping move on the question of the 'human' in 'human rights' evades the whole issue, but I shall suggest that

---

[10] See Geuss 2001, pp. 139–40.

there is a rationale for it, one that becomes clear only at the end. We have, precisely, to go through history first, and to do so without a precise referent for our enquiry—which, we come to see, *is just what it is* to go through history.

Bracketing the issue of the 'human', then, the rights idioms that Koskenniemi examines in context all have the basic feature of attributing rights to individuals outside (or at least, not deriving from) their membership in a specific political entity. It is this that allows them to play their key ideological role in the construction (and regulation) of political entities. But history shows up the hollowness of this rhetoric. What is 'outside' political entities is itself political, and so these kinds of rights are not, as they claim to be, either supra-political or pre-political. When we see them in use—*and we cannot see them anywhere else*—we show them on the contrary as implicated in political action and political history. As Koskenniemi makes clear in his concluding section, this is also to see them as weapons of war. We tend to think of rights as belonging to the victims of violence, but history shows that they belong to the perpetrators just as much.

The three examples offered of 'doing things with rights' illustrate this. The first two, the theologians of the Spanish 'School of Salamanca', and the Dutch humanist Hugo Grotius, are related, since the context, on Koskenniemi's understanding, is broadly the same—the justification of commercial empire—and, in consequence, so are the twin leitmotifs of property and sovereignty.[11] The natural rights idioms of both, despite their different modulations, depict human beings as natural commercial subjects, furnished with rights over things in the form of *dominium* or property. One of the key features of such rights, which differentiates them from human rights, is their alienability: they are there to be swapped and traded; they justify commercial empire by being themselves part of the commerce. It is the original possession of rights, and the on-going capacity to have them, rather than actually *having* the rights now, which is key to the concept of the 'human' involved. The only truly inalienable right is self-defence, and this, both in some of the scholastics and in Grotius, treads the boundary between the human and the animal, rather that clearly delineating it.[12]

This type of natural right operates in what to us is an astonishingly fluid conception of the zone beyond the boundaries of a political community, boundaries that are not themselves marked in the way we would expect. The line between inside and outside, and between public and private, is very thin, facilitating the kind of entrepreneurial 'venture' that marks early-modern colonial activity. Indeed, the political community, the commonwealth, is also, in part, a kind of 'venture', understood as created by the coming-together of individuals for the sake of a better life, and involving a transfer of *dominium* or liberty (itself a form of *dominium*). Only in part, however: the fluidity of both sovereignty and commerce are, as Koskenniemi notes, stabilized by a teleology of supernatural felicity or providence. Neither sovereignty nor commerce is an end in

[11] Commercial empire has long been recognized as a (although not the only) context for Grotius's natural rights theories; Koskenniemi's innovative view of the scholastics suggests the same for them. See Koskenniemi 2011.

[12] See Brett 2015; Doyle 2010.

itself; they have their ultimate legitimacy through their place within a broader narrative running from creation to salvation, a narrative in which human nature itself is situated, together with its concomitant capacities and original rights. For all these reasons, these natural capacities and rights might belong to all human beings, at least to begin with; but the imagination behind them is very different from that of human rights.

In Koskenniemi's handling, the eighteenth century marks the diffusion of these rights idioms and their incorporation into other vocabularies, centrally among them that of liberty as a political value. This process begins with Locke, who combined the natural rights idiom with the slavery-tyranny antithesis central to republican thought. Natural rights—especially that of property—could then operate *within* the common-wealth, the proper space of republican politics. By the early eighteenth century, however, the sixteenth- and seventeenth-century sense of the fragility of the political adventure had given way to a greater sense of political stability.[13] 'Natural liberty' was still there as a political concept, but no longer carried the revolutionary overtones that it did for Hobbes or Locke. Rather Koskenniemi shows how, in Germany, it could be deployed as an academic reference in the service of the existing order. In France, outside a university context, the appeal of the locution seems to lie instead in the continuing resonance of 'nature' within a broader narrative of humanity, a narrative that could be put to work in the justification, yet again, of commerce. Finally, the French revolution made plain that natural rights had not lost their political teeth, the political place that Locke had created for them in a republican antithesis between slavery and tyranny. And yet the linking of this language to 'Nation' or 'Patrie' meant that the revolutionary force of natural rights was worlds away from Locke's entrepreneurial picture of a 'Company' of individuals in the state of nature voluntarily forming into a 'Political Society'.[14]

Koskenniemi offers four main thoughts as a conclusion to his historical survey. The first two flow directly from the mode of analysis he has adopted: that rights are used for all sorts of things, in all sorts of different contexts, so that they cannot be squeezed into any single line of progress; and that rights are a part of conflicts, not outside them, let alone a solution to them. The third conclusion represents a historically inflected resolution to the issue of whether rights are ends in themselves. Koskenniemi argues that no right represents an ultimate value; that behind every subjective right there lies 'some idea of a good society', a 'structural' objective or value, which is what finally grounds what we choose to call a right. The historical inflection of the argument lies in two aspects: the first, that it does not take any rights as given, and then ask whether they are ultimate values; the second, that it does not pursue any philosophical condi-tions on what might count as an ultimate value. Rather (and I think this is the sense of 'structural'), no rights are given, but are implicated in ways of thinking normatively that are also ways of thinking politically. Both of these are a product of history; they can be resisted—we have a choice—but only if we *know* our history.

---

[13]   See the first two chapters of Baumgold 2010; cf. the evocative title of Simmons 1993.
[14]   Locke 1988, p. 333.

This brings us to Koskenniemi's final, and most far-reaching, conclusion, which is that the problem with rights as something we 'have' is that they privilege identity over structural determinations of identity. History helps us here because it addresses precisely these processes of structural determination. Thus, whereas the previous point concerned the way we think about a good society, this one concerns the way we think about ourselves; and the point is that rights have a corrosive effect on this dimension of our reflection. Rights as something we 'have' is a locution that distorts our understanding of the connection between rights and our identity. It is implicit in Koskenniemi's final analysis, though he does not spell it out, that the connection goes both ways: from who we are to the rights we have; but also from the rights we have to who we are. In other words, selves have rights, but rights also create selves. The trouble with the rights-locution—rights as something we have—is that it entices us, appealingly, to focus on (and to celebrate) the first connection, but not the second: we do not see ourselves for their creatures. We prefer to think that we are human beings, and have human rights, than that we have human rights and that this casts, historically, the very human beings that we are. The historicity of the *subject* of rights is Koskenniemi's ultimate Foucauldian counter to the 'timeless essence' of humanity that human rights claim, and the reason for that side-stepping move we noted earlier on. It is only by stepping out of '*human* rights' that we can properly see what is involved in claiming them. Both our rights, and we ourselves, are the product of history, a history of language that is at the same time a history of politics and conflict. This is what we miss in the idea of rights as something we have. Rights in this way of talking are always in the present tense. But we ourselves are not exclusively in the present tense: we have been, and we will be, and this shapes the 'now' of who we are and what rights we have. If we do not want them, or if we want others, Koskenniemi implies, the fight is on that far more difficult and shifting ground.

References

Armitage, D. *The Declaration of Independence: A global history* (Cambridge, Mass.: Harvard University Press, 2007).

Baumgold, D. *Contract theory in historical context* (Leiden: Brill, 2010).

Brett, A. 'Human rights and the Thomist tradition', in P. Slotte and M. Halme-Tuomisaari eds, *Human rights and other stories* (Cambridge: Cambridge University Press, 2015).

Derrida, J. 'Signature event context', in Derrida, *Margins of philosophy*, tr. A. Bass (Chicago-Brighton UK: University of Chicago Press/Harvester Press, 1982).

Doyle, J. P. 'Suárez on human rights', in Doyle, *Collected studies on Francisco Suárez* 1548–1617 (Leuven: Leuven University Press, 2010).

Geuss, R. *History and illusion in politics* (Cambridge: Cambridge University Press, 2001).

Koskenniemi, M. 'Empire and international law: The real Spanish contribution', *Toronto Journal of International Law* 61 (2011), 1–36.

Locke, J. *Two treatises of government*, ed. P. Laslett (Cambridge: Cambridge University Press, 1988).

Moyn, S. *The last utopia: Human rights in history* (Cambridge, Mass.: Harvard University Press, 2010).

Simmons, A. J. *On the edge of anarchy: Locke, consent and the limits of society* (Princeton: Princeton University Press, 1993).

Skinner, Q. 'Meaning and understanding in the history of ideas', *History and Theory* 8 (1969), 3–53.

Skinner, Q. *Liberty before liberalism* (Cambridge: Cambridge University Press 1998).

Sluga, G. 'René Cassin. *Les droits de l'homme* and the universality of human rights, 1945–1966', in S.-L. Hoffmann ed., *Human rights in the twentieth century* (Cambridge: Cambridge University Press, 2011).

Tuck, R. *Natural rights theories: Their origin and development* (Cambridge: Cambridge University Press, 1979).

Wittgenstein, L. *Philosophical investigations*, tr. G. E. M. Anscombe (Oxford: Basil Blackwell, 1968).

2

Human Rights in Heaven

Samuel Moyn

But perhaps, I said, there is a model of it in heaven, for anyone who wants to look at it and to make himself its citizen on the strength of what he sees. It makes no difference whether it is or ever will be somewhere, for he would take part in the practical affairs of that city alone.

—Plato, *Republic* (1992: 263)

The theologian may indulge the pleasing task of describing Religion as she descended from Heaven, arrayed in her native purity. A more melancholy duty is imposed on the historian. He must discover the inevitable mixture of error and corruption which she contracted in long residence upon earth, among a weak and degenerate race of beings.

—Edward Gibbon (1994: 1: 416)

As premises of an incipient international architecture and a notable political movement, human rights today clearly have old roots, indeed ones dating back centuries. It is well known that at the most abstract level—including the foundational claim that individuals have moral entitlements that in turn implicate duties of protection to be borne by others—philosophers historically gave most attention to "human rights" in natural law traditions of early modern or even medieval vintage. It was long ago, indeed, that philosophers had the best case to guide, rather than follow, practical developments, offering a theory of rights as principles of moral justification before that theory was of any serious political relevance. For it is also true that rights became a politically operative justification of the nature of citizenship only in the late eighteenth century, and did not take on the character of ground rules for the global community conceived either as a collection of states or a larger transnational order until some point after 1945. Rhetorical though human rights most frequently remain, one of the most significant phenomena of the era straddling the end of the Cold War has been the prospect of an international regime, monitored and improved by a transnational movement, in which rights not only attach abstractly to individuals in virtue of their humanity, but are actually enjoyed by them in some meaningful respects if and when states fail. It was part of the campaign to imagine and create such a regime—the pursuit of protection beyond borders—that human rights became famous. And it is largely in light of this campaign that philosophers have returned, after a long absence of interest, to the field of rights theory (see Moyn 2010, esp. pp. 214–16 on Anglo-American philosophy).

What this sketch omits, of course, is how contested human rights—defined either as some of our moral norms or as the slogan of some of our political enterprises—have long been, and not simply because of the failure to enforce them. The history of philosophy provides an excellent (in fact perhaps the best) vantage point on this truth. For since the early modern period when rights were indeed theorized in earnest as constituents of natural law, their fortunes have been decidedly mixed, if not entirely disastrous, among canonical thinkers. To the extent that they were not wholly absent, rights generally figured in these traditions as outmoded metaphysics and pious fictions. Between the 1790s and the 1970s, for example, it is hard to find premier thinkers, even in the stereotypically hospitable precincts of Anglo-American liberalism, who volunteered to salvage the theoretical credentials of rights. Our time is the exception, not the rule, in the enthusiasm of its philosophers to do so—and to argue with one another about the most plausible approach to "a philosophy of human rights." It is in view of this novel priority that two developments in current philosophy and political theory with which I am concerned in this chapter take on their true significance.

The first is an exciting current attempt to renew the premises of the recent efflorescence of philosophical attention to human rights—to hit the reset button, as it were, before the field goes too far in the wrong direction. In our own day, philosophers now see the need to correct the logic of *their own discovery* of human rights over the past few decades alone with a proper logic of justification. In the bulk of this chapter, I will survey this current campaign—with most attention to John Tasioulas's call (2012) to save human rights from their profoundly flawed proximate articulations in his own philosophical community. I argue that, while a plausible self-correction within the precincts of their philosophical guild, it ironically converts the philosophy of human rights into a project of normative justification alone, and away from the project of conceptualizing them as the political enterprise they also clearly are—and which originally prompted philosophical interest in human rights in the first place.

In the end of the chapter, I turn from contemporary philosophy to current political theory, in order to examine calls for a new "realism" to supplement or displace contemporary philosophical emphasis on normative justification—an emphasis of precisely the sort that Tasioulas, James Griffin, and others recommend when it comes to human rights. I argue that, historically, the struggle for human rights of recent decades has always been a compromise—as all interesting and relevant political movements are—between utopianism and realism. The most pressing matter, I contend in conclusion, is what sort of compromise between them will propel human rights further than they have gone so far. Both the contemporary return to abstract normativity and the "realist" correction to it distract from this all-important imperative of compromise.

The fortunes of human rights politics have not normally depended on the normative account philosophy currently seeks. And those politics, both in their successes and their failures, have shown the falsehood of the choice between utopianism and realism.

Outsiders, like myself, comment on the discussions of professional philosophers at their own peril, and at the risk of disqualifying incompetence. But I have courted that risk in what follows in search of what is valuable for all those interested in human rights, and not simply for philosophers, in a prominent current impulse within the guild. At a minimum, my goal is to insist that philosophers have an honest answer to what broader purposes they are serving when they bring their unique skills to a fraught global debate—and what risks of their own they incur given the temptation of falling back on their talents for affirming normativity and clarifying norms rather than explaining what the rest of us do with them in a complex world of passion and force. Slightly more boldly, the point is to call for an alternative version of philosophy— including an alternative philosophy of human rights—that embraces the situation that outsiders acknowledge as an unavoidable condition: caught in the rough and tumble or outright strife of politics, in a historically constituted world, that even philosophy cannot escape.

Human Rights as Normative Principles and Interests

A good many philosophers today have shouldered the mission of saving human rights from John Rawls. In itself this development is ironic. He did so much to introduce rights-based normativity to the philosophical agenda in *A Theory of Justice* (1971) that it may seem surprising that he is attacked today for not doing enough. But the crucial fact is that his theory of rights was based on a domestic "joint venture" which accepted the modern world of nation-states as the set framework of global order. In his famous original position, all sorts of things are absolved for the sake of legitimate choice, but nation-states remain. In *A Theory of Justice* proper he neither mentioned "human rights" (in fact I doubt he knew at the stage he wrote the book about the Universal Declaration of Human Rights of 1948) nor envisioned many rules for the world beyond those of traditional international law such as *pacta sunt servanda*.[1] Years later, he made more room for "humanitarian intervention" than before—as a device of an order in which human rights (which he now referenced) define a minimum code of conduct that all states must satisfy in order to avoid being subject to justified foreign intervention. But early and late, Rawls's thought was based on a fundamental distinction between rights in a polity and so-called human rights: "Human rights are distinct," Rawls wrote, "from the rights of liberal democratic citizenship" (1999, p. 79). Or, as the leading Rawlsian Charles Beitz put the same point, human rights are best conceived of

---

[1] Rawls 1971. He took over his account of global order from a canonical rendition of international law, one that barely mentioned human rights when updated in the 1960s for the edition Rawls used. See Brierly 1965.

as "revisionist appurtenances of a global political order composed of independent states" (Beitz 2009, p. 179). They are add-ons after the historical fact and analytical project of conceptualizing rights at home.

Though Rawls was certainly responsible for the revival of rights in Anglo-American philosophy, in other words, it was in a way that starkly distinguished them from the "international human rights" that became prestigious after he wrote his masterpiece. And it is for this reason that, in the current philosophy of human rights, a leading item on the agenda is to return to rectify Rawls's original "mistake." Human rights, according to a significant philosophical impulse, are the same whether at home or abroad. To consider this impulse, let us turn to a defining landmark of the current agenda, John Tasioulas's rich and compelling inaugural lecture as Quain Professor of Jurisprudence at University College London, significantly entitled "Towards a Philosophy of Human Rights."

Tasioulas hopes, like Jeremy Waldron in his closely kindred chapter in this volume, to rescue human rights from Rawls (Waldron in this volume).[2] Tasioulas denounces what he calls the "functional" approach to human rights, which reduces them (at least as a matter of definition) to their significance for the international system now con-stituted as a world of states—as if they were not first of all moral entitlements of individuals considered separately from their institutionalization in political affairs. Indeed, Tasioulas insists that it is a deep error to reduce human rights to their political functions generally—at home as well as abroad. "Human rights are relevant to assessing the status and performance of governments," he acknowledges, "including their legitimacy, and in making judgments about the assistance we owe to people in other countries and, in more extreme cases, about the justifiability of intervening in, or even declaring war against, foreign states. But it is not written into the concept of a human right that they perform these other functions. One can adequately grasp what a human right is without reference to its political uses. Whether and to what extent a particular human right should play any such political role is a matter of substantive argument; it is not something constitutive of its nature as a human right" (2012, p. 18; cf. 29 for a similar statement).

Analogously, Waldron criticizes a "human concern" as opposed to a "human bearer" model of what makes rights human rights, on the grounds that the former reduces them to their role in triggering the interest of the international system or external act-ors or (assuming that concern already exists) rebutting the criticism that outsiders have no business in meddling in a state's sovereign affairs. Like Tasioulas, Waldron worries that mortgaging "human rights" to their internationalist uses, as Rawls did, inserts an unacceptable hiatus between them and rights simpliciter, "unhelpfully sidelin[ing] a number of conditions that are quite properly thought crucial to the modern human rights idea—such as the individualism of rights and the continuity

---

[2] In mentioning the points of commonality between Tasioulas and Waldron, I do not mean to associate the latter with all of the former's views I discuss in this chapter.

between human rights and the rights recognized and remedies provided under the auspices of national law" (Waldron in this volume).

Both Tasioulas and Waldron lay the blame for the reduction of human rights to their political functions (and especially their international political functions) at Rawls's feet.[3] It is important to be clear that neither author offers this criticism as part of the now familiar "cosmopolitan" response to Rawls, in which rights politically accrue to human beings for the sake of global distributive justice or even a global political order in which national sovereignty is marginalized or treated as a normatively insignificant intermediary. Rather their point is much more definitional: human rights are a matter of moral entitlement, and it is the entirely prior and most abstract level of inquiry at which philosophers should begin their work, rather than accept the concrete and specific historical realities in which human rights got defined as international rights supplementing those announced and enacted through state citizenship. Even were it to turn out that Rawls was separately correct that the sole function of human rights is sometimes to rebut a presumptive norm of non-interference in an order of sovereign states, it could not possibly follow that human rights should be philosophically defined in the first instance in terms of that function.

It is thus also important to be clear that neither Tasioulas nor Waldron thinks (or at any rate should) that the problem with the "functionalist" or "concern" model of human rights is that its partisans make no room for other sorts of rights.[4] Obviously, Rawls like others who take this broad approach believe that the (typically more gener-ous) sorts of rights enjoyed by citizens politically or even the normative entitlements humans are owed in view of their status as humans simply need to be distinguished from what are colloquially called human rights—principles of the international system that, among other things, explain why sometimes foreign moral and legal orders are justifiably subject to external opprobrium or even force of arms. Rawls and the others are seeking, not to deny a large universe of rights, but to *reserve* the concept and term of "human rights" for what they have typically and specifically meant in recent polit-ical debates. A more inclusionary definition, Rawls might have replied to Waldron, could "unhelpfully sideline" what is distinctive about today's human rights that makes philosophically clarifying them a newer and different project than a more abstract rights theory. In turn, Tasioulas and Waldron worry that this reservation misses precisely the philosopher's proper goal of proffering a theory of normative principles at first separate from its implications for the international order (or even its political implications generally).

---

[3] Both are also intensely concerned with a short essay by Joseph Raz outlining a theory of human rights as norms whose violation legitimates international intervention in general (not merely military intervention in particular), while both acknowledge that Charles Beitz is the figure who has, in *The Idea of Human Rights*, most carefully developed Rawls's "minimalism" (Raz 2010b; see also Beitz 2009 and Raz 2010a).

[4] For example, Tasioulas acknowledges that Raz "seemingly presupposes the existence of universal moral rights" (2012, p. 22).

If this brief reconstruction is correct, neither side has a knockdown argument against the other but rather (and merely) a preferred emphasis. In particular, the debate is not really about whether the rights of citizenship share *some* features with human rights—clearly Rawls thought they did. The very fact that both sets of entitlements are called rights means they share some characteristics. But this does not exclude the possibility that they differ in more important ways. The argument, in short, is really about the importance for specific theoretical purposes of eroding the border between the two groups of rights in view of the fact, contingent but all-important, that international human rights politics in our time have been constituted in an interstate order featuring national political communities in a global space. There is no doubt that Tasioulas and Waldron are correct that there is good reason to see analogy and homology, especially the more abstract one gets, between rights and human rights. They are even persuasive that philosophers may properly care most about the analogy or homology (or even identity) one wins through abstraction. But they may not adequately consider what losses one risks, for the quite distinct communities of philosophers and others, when one detaches philosophy from the very international human rights politics that—among its minor consequences—stoked philosophical interest in the topic to begin with.

Philosophia Perennis versus Politics and History

At stake is whether the current campaign to "defunctionalize" human rights—at least as a matter of definition—undermines or at least postpones inquiry into how human rights fit in our historical and political situation, for the sake of assurance or reassurance that they can be known and affirmed apart from that situation. Philosophy, that is, gives itself the task of verifying the existence of norms, not interpreting the specific world in which they have gained purchase (including to the point of prompting our leading philosophers suddenly to fold them into their traditional concern with normative theory).

Tasioulas is beautifully clear on how the current reconceptualization affects our sense of the historical origins of human rights (see also Besson and Zysset 2012). Once functionalism is given up, he reports, there are "strong continuities between human rights and natural rights. Both are, fundamentally, moral rights possessed by all human beings simply in virtue of their humanity."[5] Humorously criticizing my own emphasis on the explosion of human rights as internationally salient and mobilizing principles since the 1970s, Tasioulas writes: "Here I feel somewhat as Bernard Williams did in responding to a sociologist's claim that quarks rose from the activities of particle physicists—'the 1970's is rather late for the beginning of the universe'" (2012, p. 26).

---

[5] "I reject the increasingly popular view that the Universal Declaration ushered in a new concept..." (Tasioulas 2012, p. 26).

For Tasioulas, Plato deserves credit for insisting that moral principles are eternal no matter when we discover them; and while it may have taken some centuries, the Aristotelian Middle Ages are owed deepest respect, in spite of their apparently extraneous Christianity, for hitting on the natural rights of individuals. In fact, on inspection, there is so long a tradition of belief in the morally objective entitlements of individuals that one might wonder what the point of the Universal Declaration of Human Rights was—besides mastery of the obvious. Indeed, Tasioulas boldly declares, it has caused distraction when it attracts celebrations as an alleged breakthrough that needs to be explained—as if humanity before had no inkling that there were moral realities and that the basic values called human rights were them (2012, p. 26). As for my point that almost nobody, not least among philosophers, cared about the Universal Declaration for decades, I have simply redoubled the distraction.

On this account, apparently, history is mere trivia about how we came to develop our knowledge about (and institutionalize our practices around) human rights, parallel in triviality to the details like how people came to know about quarks and assign them importance. Recent enforcement against violations beyond borders in a second moment, or even struggle for rights within national borders before then, provide the plot of a modest tale that, from this perspective, is of some moral grandeur but hardly the stuff of the exclusive philosophical interest that Rawls and his followers have shown in them. Certainly they justify no distinction *in principle* between rights at home and abroad. The logic of discovery of moral reality, let alone diverting but hardly foundational stories about how people in history got the world to conform better to that moral reality, just isn't relevant to the logic of its existence or justification, and philosophers should defend the autonomy and priority of the latter as their topic.

These arguments seem irrefutable on their own terms. In fact I think the current attempt to defend the normative validity (and comparatively old dating) of human rights makes considerable sense for philosophers—whose task it often is to deliberate about the existence and means of defense of norms, whether or not they ever achieve any "functional" importance. But there are two points worth making, one concerning that philosophical task when it comes to human rights considered on its own, and the other concerning its worldly setting and broader importance outside the frequently picayune debates of philosophers.

First off, it is not totally obvious—though it suddenly seems nearly incontrovertible to philosophers after long disinterest and contempt—that human rights are the correct norms for them to justify. It is not even obvious that philosophers are supposed to be defending moral truth in any version (some have doubted it). To the extent that moral objectivity might be false or its current defenders might be wrong that human rights are the obvious content of the moral truths that they must defend, historical trivia surely matters a lot. For morality suddenly becomes local, timebound, and contingent. For his part, it is hardly convincing for Williams to simply dismiss out of hand the revolution after Thomas Kuhn that led to famous works like Andrew Pickering's *Constructing Quarks* (1984) (as if the whole enterprise of the post-positivist philosophy and history of science were absurd and worthless). And even if Williams was right in this scepticism, it does not seem straightforward that the same sarcasm is due those who deny or bracket the assertion of incontestable moral realities.

More important, the vast majority of moral realists in human history have defended radically different contents in their doctrines than individual human rights in general, let alone our contemporary list in particular. The Platonic-Christian West was mainly oppressive from the perspective of rights, especially contemporary rights. To that extent, trivia about the recent construction of our values (through the functionalization of morality among other processes) looks more and more like an important account of how our current moral realists came to adopt the local and temporary beliefs they have.[6] Tasioulas would understandably like to commune with moral reality, and sees philosophers from Plato through Thomas Aquinas as inadvertently laying the foundation for the conceptualization and justification of our current value system (however much they themselves would have rejected it as abhorrent). But historians would prefer to bet that, like all the other moral realists who preceded him, Tasioulas will soon seem a quaint product of his time. Philosophers themselves, realists or otherwise, indeed might be relied upon to *resist* the popularity of human rights in our day—which, whatever else is involved, seem a trend that requires as much critical interrogation as normative clarification. Western philosophy began with Socrates's ironic doubts about popular morality, not Plato's realist metaphysics; and for that matter the history of modern thought, so often critical of rights, suggests that a "philosophy of human rights" needs to constantly entertain the possibility that our short-term enthusiasm for them is misplaced.

That said, many historians are interested in human rights because they know how politically different the forms are that our desire to institutionalize abstract morality—notably the freedom and equality of human beings in modern times—has taken. Tasioulas and Waldron seem correct that, from an abstract enough point of view, human rights share much with rights traditions that preceded them. Who ever doubted it? But Tasioulas's desire for the unity of rights traditions couldn't

---

[6] I leave for another occasion Tasioulas's important contention that historians like me are nihilists in bracketing the truth of human rights in trying to explain their rise. For 2,000 years the right answer to the question of why we are living in a Christian world was simply that Christianity is true. When he founded modern historiography, Edward Gibbon, whom Tasioulas himself invokes, responded that by postponing that answer we could gain space to understand the range of verifiable factors at work (which surely include the subjective understanding of actors, quite apart from the truth of that under-standing). Tasioulas's response to this invocation of Gibbon is that the bracketing might have made sense for Christianity, but it would not for human rights: the one was false where the other is true. But Gibbon's point was that we could not wait for the authority of belief to pass to bracket it; and it remains best for history to proceed by considering the fullest range of causes for phenomena—not least since subjective belief in the moral truth of one's cause is a prevalent constituent of action no matter what the cause. Even were Tasioulas correct that it is crucial to evaluate the truth of subjective belief as a condition of explanation, it could not possibly pre-empt the search for *other* factors—and could not excuse philosophers from interest in those factors when it comes to why they suddenly believe in human rights today.

possibly absolve historians from charting the changing functions and rise in salience of human rights—or philosophers from pondering them. To dismiss attention to the novel "functionalization" of rights in the name of their medieval philosophical discovery is simply to isolate one topic for philosophical inquiry while ruling out others, starting with functionalization itself and the diverse and sometimes opposed forms it has taken. (The functionalization of human rights in the Atlantic revolutions that canonized them abetted a politics of sovereignty, whereas human rights have become famous in our day, as Rawls understood, as part of a search for ways to limit sovereignty, just as the current "responsibility to protect" redefines or contains it, and some even hope human rights indicate the possibility of a politics beyond its terms) (Moyn 2010, chap. 1 and *passim*).

To believe that an act of definitional legerdemain saves us the trouble of meditating on the recency and currency of our interest in human rights, and these human rights in their most contemporary political forms, is to change the topic rather than solve a problem. It is much like claiming that once the Internet has been placed in the broader framework and longer history of human sociability and communication in all their manifold forms, then its origins are not only older but different than seemed to be the case when it was considered on its own as the very significant departure it obviously is. The proper response to such a claim is that, however old human communication and sociability are, what is new about the Internet is still brand new and potentially controversial and worth explanation (and, if necessary, worry). The same applies to human rights. Until yesterday, the norms that Tasioulas plausibly insists on returning to their medieval or even ancient origins in a sempiternal account of the human good hardly existed in the functional forms they have taken on now.

At times Tasioulas gestures towards a more nuanced understanding of human rights as a "sensibility" but it is remarkable that his default attitude is not to work out the extremely complex relations between normativity, culture, and practice but to fall back on his apparent commitment to the objectivity of morals as if there were no problem in explaining moral change, even before and apart from any "functionalization" has occurred. While he refers to human rights as a moral sensibility, one that potentially need not implicate any commitment to moral objectivity, Tasioulas does not separate the two clearly and if anything implies that they are deeply connected. Perhaps the most remarkable moment in his essay, indeed, is his praise for Thomist Alasdair MacIntyre for providing something like the proper framework for conceptualizing human rights today. Apparently MacIntyre erred only in his conclusion that the values of modernity, Enlightenment, and human rights were excluded by his commitments, since (as it now turns out) human rights are the near the core of a defensible moral realism (2012, p. 12). Unless Tasioulas believes the history of philosophy from Plato to Thomas Aquinas actually saves us the trouble of understanding the relationship between *the very idea* of an individual human right and the conceptual evolution of the contents of such an entitlement and the way the world has changed in order to honour it, then the assertion of moral objectivity turns out to solve fewer intellectual problems than one might like.[7] Similarly, one might contend that defining human rights as moral principles and interests in the abstract, and thus connecting them with the natural rights and citizenship rights that were their first functions, does not rule out philosophical interest in their plural and most recent functionalizations—including their international ones. And to be fair, Tasioulas does conclude with a call for investigation of the plural functions normative entitlements have had, do have, and presumably might have. All the same, the emphasis on his "defunctionalizing" campaign is so intense that it easily leaves the impression that the affirmation of moral norms for its own sake is at the heart of what a "philosophy of human rights" is going to be about.

Tasioulas's de-functionalizing recommendation distracts from political challenges if it ends up mainly exchanging investigation of historical and contemporary meaning as if philosophical reassurance about the existence of the norms—human rights in heaven, so to speak—were not merely the first but also the main task. Just as Tasioulas's antediluvian account of human rights succeeds only on condition of his substitution of a non-functionalist definition of human rights—as Tasioulas himself acknowledges—so definitional work hardly changes the fact that there is and ought to be intense political debate about what our specifically institutionalized human rights imply and should imply.[8] That abstract individual entitlements that humans enjoy by nature are both the moral and historical source of "human rights" in their diverse forms over time is, for anyone concerned by this debate, simply a non sequitur. Of course it is the case that treating human rights as a class of abstract moral entitlements changes when they were propounded. Focusing on their transformation into the basis of political authority shifts attention to the eighteenth century, just as emphasizing their internationalization moves the clock further still into the twentieth century—and even the 1970s. To the extent, then, that a philosophy of human rights dislocates them from the place and time-bound specificity that has made them a suddenly powerful phenomenon, the less purchase philosophy has on how to defend or extend (or criticize or revise) this phenomenon. In his insistent moral realism and call for old roots, Tasioulas does not acknowledge, let alone guard against, this risk.

The Context and Politics of Abstraction

In any case, philosophers too live in the thick of history and politics. The current campaign to save human rights from Rawls seems to me actually to help justify the chronology of human rights to which recent historical study has given rise—or actually

---

[7] In certain respects the earlier Tasioulas was much clearer than in his newer lecture about the importance of modernity and the political transformations it involved in drastically changing expectations so much as to alter humanity's sense of its most basic entitlements (2007, p. 76, where he speaks of the "temporally constrained universality" of human rights).

[8] "Partly, these historians are led astray by functionalism..." (2012, p. 26). But if the intention is to understand the history of the political functions of human rights, then functionalism properly defines the enterprise rather than poses an obstacle to it.

to push the clock forward since the story of the search for "a philosophy of human rights" dates from the 1990s and is achieving special intensity only at the moment. "On a rhetorical level at least, the idea of human rights has emerged as a ruling idea of our age," Tasioulas notes, effectively acknowledging *the entire premise* of the new historiography focusing on recent developments. And "[p]hilosophers are relative latecomers to the contemporary human rights scene" (2012, pp. 2–3).

The belatedness of philosophers also turns out to mean that the unfolding of their debate itself reflects a revealing path-dependence—a phenomenon to which philosophers are as subject as anyone else. That the corrective burden to overcome Rawls's "mistake" has to be shouldered at all, one might suggest, is the best proof available that contemporary philosophy is strongly conditioned by an influential definition of human rights as ones in the international system urged by an international movement— indeed sometimes reduced, as Rawls risked doing, to the 1990s interest in humanitarian intervention—and now by a felt need to correct that premise *post hoc*. The fact that Tasioulas had to ask whether human rights are "essentially triggers for intervention," as Rawls largely saw them, reveals that his own philosophical work is deeply connected to the historical and political events that first determined how and why human rights became a current topic at all.[9] From this angle, there are two possible and troubling implications of the current attempt to develop a philosophy of human rights that absconds from the very specific historical context in which philosophers have suddenly become interested in the topic.

One is that philosophers—illustrating their own embedding in politics and history in spite of themselves—are responding to a new but equally specific historical context. Another is that they succeed in achieving a philosophy of rights as normative entitlements far more distant from the political movement that first inspired them— which makes the project of normative justification something of a retreat from the political aspirations of the human rights revolution out of which the philosophy of human rights itself was born. Both of these possibilities are live and reveal different potential defects of the current enterprise. These implications further elaborate the contrast above between the *déformation professionelle* of philosophers in seeking the security of normative affirmation and the imperative of the historically-minded social disciplines that focus instead on the fate of normative beliefs in practice notwithstanding whatever commitment to moral objectivity they might (or might not) presuppose.

What is the political and historical context, one might ask, in which the attempt to de-functionalize or de-internationalize human rights is occurring? If the very fact of the rescue mission proves the relevance of the historical moment in which Rawls worked, then one might naturally ask what historical changes—what features of the current moment—have prompted the rescue mission itself. It is happening primarily,

---

[9] I allude to the title of one of Tasioulas's preparatory essays (2009)—a question that also serves as a leitmotif of Waldron's worry about defining human rights primarily in terms of crossborder concern.

I think, because of a widespread fear of the ill-repute into which the history of post-Cold War international affairs have sunk human rights, after an equally widespread age of hasty enthusiasm. In spite of the moral consciousness raising that human rights have involved, and possibly some moral victories, people are more aware every day that they have been as much entangled in great power politics as they offer a way beyond that depressing world. The age of liberal interventionism is a mixed bag, as more and more mainstream observers are willing to say. Convincing though it is on its own terms, the definition of human rights independent of their functions, one might suggest, resembles not a little the old Marxist claim that it is important to focus on the immaculate truth of its ethical idea now that its enacted programme seems something other than what it appeared at first. Human rights cannot be essentially triggers for intervention because intervention has rarely worked very well.

Now let us turn from the political context of abstraction to its political (ir)relevance. In fairness, it is crucial to note that officially Tasioulas is committed to an account of human rights respectful of their current political meaning, even though the contemporary enterprise of human rights history provokes Tasioulas to rise to a defence of moral objectivity (and therefore the sempiternity of moral norms discovered long ago). Implicitly, Rawls adopted his separation between citizens' rights and human rights accepting what he understood to be their distinctive political implications in the debate of his era, and offering what he took to be philosophically informed justification for certain political beliefs of that 1990s moment.[10] As Beitz, his follower, has best emphasized, the virtue of this approach to the philosophy of human rights is that it followed "practice"—how the world establishes the setting for philosophy (2009, chaps. 2, 5, and *passim*). Similarly, Joseph Raz has indicted the philosophical attempt to "ground" human rights apart from their characteristic practical meaning in contemporary global affairs in part because that attempt eventuates in abstraction "so remote from the practice of human rights as to be irrelevant to it" (Raz 2010b, p. 323). Tasioulas, however, also wants to be faithful to practice. He simply thinks Rawls and Raz are mistaken about what it is.

And to a large extent he is right. Even in the 1990s, when Rawls wrote, his reduction of human rights to norms that justify foreign intervention and a few other purposes reflected scandalous ignorance. Officially, Tasioulas's essay is intended to "make sense" of "contemporary human rights culture," not simply abscond from it for the sake of normative truth divorced from the world as it is. Perhaps surprisingly given his rejection later in the essay of much of any interest in the recent and specific circumstances in which human rights have become politically relevant (as opposed to morally conceivable), Tasioulas begins his essay with a strong plea for relevance: "Because much philosophical work on human rights exhibits this fixation on abstract theoretical structures, it often results in a disappointing non-engagement: a failure to bring into

---

[10] For an exceptionally cutting presentation of the geopolitical circumstance that Rawls's thinking reflected, see Anderson (2005, esp. pp. 22–3).

focus human rights as that notion is understood in the wider culture in which it has its home" (2012, p. 3). But it turns out on inspection that Tasioulas's absolutely proper call for a "philosophy of human rights" faithful to what human rights mean in practice remains at several removes from it.

Amazingly, the primary role of the appeal to "practice" in Tasioulas's argumentation is to *rebut functionalization*—in the name of a definition of human rights as fundamental moral norms. In particular, in response to Raz, Tasioulas insists that the role of human rights in determining which entitlements transcend those of state citizenship was never intended to be the sole function of the norms—indeed that function was never even dominant.[11] Of course, this is no argument for de-functionalizing human rights at all, only to be more sensitive to all the different ways that human rights function. Rawls's own mistaken restriction of the functions of human rights to cross-border concern or military intervention is no commentary on a functional emphasis—on the contrary. And Tasioulas hardly redeems his own call to be truer to the dense realities of human rights culture in making this the sole appeal to practice in his essay.[12] Ironically, then, the interest in practice is not only allied to but also ironically transposed into a project of normative abstraction. What at first seems a fundamental departure from the initial premises of the field, saving it from Rawls's already belated focus on foreign intervention to achieve a truer appreciation of the huge range of human rights practice, looks on second glance like another version of cloistered abstraction. To put it differently, practice serves Tasioulas, at least in this essay, to justify abstraction and a return to traditional normative theory, not to motivate empiricism and the search for a politically relevant theory.

In the end it is clear what has gone wrong: a Platonic imperative to defunctionalize human rights, asserting moral realities whether or not useful to anyone, has prevailed over the philosophical imperative to be faithful and helpful to practice—and above all to the *functional intricacy* of human rights today. Tasioulas reasonably complains that the normative moment in human rights risks occlusion by a functional orientation, but this concern hardly rules out a corresponding worry that the normative orientation philosophers have been willing to show so far is insufficient and uninformed. From that perspective there is not too much functionalism in the current philosophy

---

[11] Tasioulas is not altogether convincing in these arguments. He selectively cites two drafters of the Universal Declaration purporting to show that they were neutral about the political architecture in which human rights were to have bearing, ignoring the general context of their work as state diplomats. Tasioulas also appeals to Beth Simmons's (2009) view of human rights practice but ignores that *the entire point* of her research is to show how the *international architecture* established by *human rights treaties* supposedly affords domestic actors tools they could not have had working under their own power. For a reconstruction of human rights in the 1940s stressing their statism, see Moyn 2010, chap. 2; for my criticism of Simmons, see Moyn 2012.

[12] Similarly, James Nickel sees the multiplicity of functions of human rights not as a reason to abandon functionalism but rather as a reason to abandon mono-functionalism: i.e., defining human rights in light of their performance of one single function, rather than a host of (potentially constantly evolving) functions. See Nickel in this volume.

of human rights; there is far too little.[13] And the question that naturally follows is what it would mean to elaborate a philosophy of human rights genuinely faithful to the realities of global human rights culture.

Utopianism and Realism

The negligence of the landscape of human rights practice is, I believe, an unintended commentary on an ambivalence about the basic goals of the philosophical venture—or perhaps more accurately a tension between disciplinary goals and public relations. One impulse, usually dominant in actual philosophical work, is to win the intraphilosophical struggle for the best theoretical account of our norms, which ultimately drives Tasioulas into a kind of *philosophia perennis*. But the other impulse is to reflect on the historically constituted and politically debatable realities of a specific time and place—including today's human rights architecture and movement—in order to help them evolve in the best manner. The trouble is that these two impulses often point in alternative directions.

While disciplines are always entitled to their own intramural debates, what seems important to philosophers may not matter to anyone else. Tasioulas says about his own approach that the price of not endorsing it is "forfeit[ing] the opportunity to exert any meaningful critical leverage" on human rights culture as it stands (2012, p. 3). But how does the vindication of the status of human rights as age-old moral entitlements embrace this opportunity, when it comes to any burning debate today? After all, merely saving human rights from their reduction to the function of (armed) interventionism, or their broader role in authorizing external concern, is a threshold correction. It is no proxy for the discovery of the hugely complex and finely differentiated terrain of human rights in our time.

Most of all, then, a move towards an alternative philosophy of human rights would require a careful empiricism, one far more attentive to the huge amount of information and interpretations a now massive number of scholars have offered about how "human rights culture" works from place to place. When one reflects on how little of this information—differentiated in its geographical setting and multidisciplinary in its academic articulation—makes it into contemporary mainstream attempts to offer philosophical clarity and rigour, the result is potentially embarrassing. It is fully as embarrassing as the lack of clarity and rigour in other fields: as one might put it, a philosophy of human rights without adequate information is empty, just as the fields which dutifully gather that information are blind without philosophy. In his own inaugural lecture on assuming the Chichele Professorship in Social and Political Theory at the University of Oxford, Waldron (2013)—cutting across his argument for basing the philosophy of human rights on chiefly normative premises—has called

---

[13] The chief exception to this remark is, again, Beitz 2009, but it has tended to get short shrift in comparison to Rawls and Raz, as Tasioulas's and Waldron's essays exemplify.

for the sort of attention to institutions that legal and political theory are better at providing than traditional moral inquiry into virtue, principles, and interests. In my view he might have added mobilization *outside* institutions, a focus on which is irreplaceable in the human rights context. Both the institutional and mobilizational dimensions of contemporary human rights practice are indispensable in reckoning with it.

In this land that the parties to current debates still tend to see from afar, a philosophy of human rights might well discover—at least if my own historical argument about origins is correct—a modestly utopian movement in need of understanding and guidance. Though not without precedents, that movement emerged recently; and it faces quandaries about how to advance further in the world. It is here that a philosophy of human rights, precisely on the basis of its normative justification of human rights precepts, could take a further step of offering a political theory of human rights—theorizing the political functions human rights should have after learning enough about the political functions they do have.

And yet in the world of political theory in our day, a commitment to something called "realism" is resurgent. It reacts to the normative abstractions of contemporary philosophy with a call for supplementing and sometimes entirely displacing ethics with insights into strategy, power, and violence.[14] The main observation I want to make in parting is that the human rights movement has always known how controversial it is in its normative commitments as well as how canny it needs to be to advance them; and the primary philosophical question that movement needs help in solving it is not whether it is based on (old or new) normative values but whether it needs various sorts of correction both on the normative and practical side.

Characterizing human rights as a contemporary "utopia" is obviously to use that term in a specific way. For one thing, it does not regard that label as a charge—a narrow and controversial understanding of what utopianism is, and one not particularly faithful to the utopian tradition.[15] To define utopia in terms of its irrelevance to reality—as Plato implausibly did by placing norms in heaven as if their presence there sufficed—has often led to the defensive reply that human rights are indeed germane to the real world.[16] At the same time, the broader tradition of utopianism has refused the notion that proximity to the actual world as it stands is a condition of significance. Clearly, as Tasioulas says, human rights today are mostly rhetorical. But it is precisely the promise of justice they provide that makes them both utopian and relevant.

The slowly developing human rights architecture was devised and erected by and for states; and it was, for a long time, sterile in its outcomes and impotent in its

---

[14] The main landmarks are Geuss 2008 and Williams 2005. For assessments, see Galston 2010 and B. Honig and M. Stears 2011.

[15] See, for example, Claeys 2011.

[16] One of the pioneering philosophically-minded commentators on the human rights movement addressed the problem in this way (Nickel 1982). For a defence of the Platonic form of utopianism that insists on the value of ideal theory even (or especially) if it is irrelevant, see Estlund 2014.

capacity to inspire. For this reason, the potential of that architecture—a potential set up, as Tasioulas would have it, in medieval times by the abstract notion of individual moral entitlements—was, until something changed, essentially inert. Then a new sort of movement with transnational aspirations arose, subverting both states and the designs of the international architecture states had created, and made human rights transnationally relevant. This movement did so not because it was the first political movement in history—hardly. (It was certainly not the first try at functionalizing a controversial moral realism either!) Rather, the culture of human rights took its place alongside competing mobilizational ventures, but enjoyed massive rhetorical success, especially insofar as it claimed global exclusivity in the realm of norms and commanded attention as totalitarianism entered crisis and atrocity abroad finally became intolerable for a broad public. It was, as I have described elsewhere, "the last utopia."

But it also enjoyed success because of its strategic bent—its "realist" commitment to advance its programme in a world of contending normative visions which have traditionally resorted to persuasion, manipulation, and sometimes force to succeed. To mention only one example, it was of overwhelming importance that the organized human rights movement *abjured* violence—unlike so many movements in history, including prior rights movements—and more generally that it officially insisted that it remain neutral about the nature of the good life in order to define a set of basic constraints on any actual or imaginable regime or society. The movement certainly ascended on the basis of normative conviction. But if those who invented the contemporary human rights culture were utopians, they were Machiavellians too, devising a strategy that would allow their brand of transformation to differ from the world as it was but also from alternative political agendas—often by strategically denying that their aims were strategic at all. In propitious circumstances, human rights exploded, pluralizing in their constituencies and forms, in part out of the crisis of competing agendas and in part as a result of their own escalating success. Tasioulas is right that human rights became through this process "a ruling idea of our age" but it was through a mobilizational effort in specific circumstances: in the service of a specific normative vision as well as on the basis of a complex realist gambit.

If this (admittedly controversial) view about the conditions of their currency today is correct, the main quandary about human rights now, one that philosophers as much as anyone else are eligible to solve, is whether and how to correct them normatively and practically. For the most significant fact about human rights today is that the original synthesis of moral norms and realist strategies allowed by its architecture and adopted by its pluralizing movements has had far more success on the rhetorical level than otherwise. Human rights have done far more to transform the terrain of idealism than they have the world itself (Moyn 2010, p. 9, and chap. 4 for the details). The disappearance of some outrageously oppressive regimes may be a significant victory that the idea of human rights can claim (or, given historical controversies around why evil states from the communist Soviet Union to Moammar Gaddafi's Libya fell, may not). But the obstacles human rights have faced in doing more have so far proved daunting. For this reason, awareness of the dense reality of human rights culture should force its partisans to face the possibility that its original normative framing was in some way flawed or incomplete and that it was allied to a realist strategy that was in some way limited or even self-defeating.

No matter how far the contemporary scholarly discipline I have considered in these reflections has moved "towards a philosophy of human rights" in recent years, it has not reached this problem—not by a long shot. On my account, however, it is the most momentous one there is. It not only exceeds in relevance but it also rivals in difficulty the undoubtedly important and interesting problem as to how one might normatively justify human rights. For most observers, anyway, the quandary of normative justification about human rights is deep in the background of—and its resolution is irrelevant to—the raging debate about their functional purposes today (or, more accurately, their failure to achieve more of these purposes).

It is not my aim, at least here, to endorse any particular stance in that debate. I have argued elsewhere that what made international human rights so powerful in robbing some regimes of legitimacy has made them less useful at improving others—including our own. On the normative plane, the individualism of human rights, on which Waldron insists, historically did more work to buttress the right of private property—precisely the right that most obstructs the redistributive aims dear to progressives even in the age the latter champion "economic and social rights." And on the strategic plane, the denial of human rights to be a political agenda, so as to be above the fray, entailed certain limits on their ability to mobilize followers to transcend the indictment of the worst regimes (Moyn 2010: epilogue). But instead of pursuing these arguments, my goal here is to point out the significance of the debate itself, and how different contemporary philosophy would look if the guild were to take it seriously, rather than follow the path-dependent arguments that ironically appear to be leading the field back into the defence of normativity for its own sake—as if the gravitational pull of philosophy's Platonic sources were so powerful that the field could never range too far from home. Such an alternative philosophy of human rights would begin from the premise that a normative heaven is not the place to keep our utopias, especially since the human rights movement demonstrated the applicability of idealism to politics and history before philosophers finally and recently decided to theorize in its wake.

Important as normative inquiry is for philosophers and scholars generally, it does not appear that human rights practice needs it much. And in the face of realist critics of normativity, similarly, the human rights movement has always known there was no choice to make between morality and enactment: it has always offered both together. What is increasingly controversial—indeed normatively and practically pressing—is the specific alliance between them that the movement offered, which appears to face stark limits in allowing it to redeem its promises.

Conclusion

Most often, philosophers are latecome followers. Never has that been more true, perhaps, than in the sudden rise of philosophical interest in human rights, after long neglect. In deference to this fact, philosophers could make their inquiry more open to the recurrent insight that they, too, live in the midst of an unfolding history, in the thick of a built institutional scheme, and in the heat of a contestatory political space, not apart from them.

Conceiving of philosophy as another aspect of the struggle of human beings to set the terms of their lives together cannot mean the irrelevance of normativity, to be sure, as the most brazen realists tend to assume. I regard international human rights as a joint normative and political enterprise and perhaps the signature such project of our time. Far from wishing to leave the world untransformed, or sticking close to an extant reality, international human rights are the slogan of a modestly utopian enterprise. Even if it arose on the ruins of more robust utopianisms, both within and among states, to trivialize its transformative ambition is to misunderstand it. To regard human rights this way does not simply force one to see how recent a political enterprise it is. It also encourages a debate about what sort of utopianism to endorse. But if the sort realism that denies the purchase of normativity altogether misses the need for this debate, this cannot mean that the philosophical demand for normative justification is sufficient unto itself. An essential contention here, therefore, is that there is no way to choose between utopianism and realism. They depend on one another.

That human rights have been closely identified with an international movement and the international sphere since the 1970s and, with special force, the end of the Cold War is thus not the result of John Rawls's philosophical mistake. Rather, it is because human rights were never simply moral principles; they were also a suddenly appealing and transnationally emergent political enterprise to change the world. In spite of the deep taproots of human rights as normative principles and interests, the international enterprise based on them is a new growth. Indeed, the internationalization of rights understood as a political enterprise was the primary factor in shifting philosophers themselves away from their inattention to or disdain for rights generally across modern history. And this enterprise has always proceeded as a compromise between utopianism and realism, not a choice of one over the other. Once philosophers learn this, and engage human rights culture in its full intricacy, they could cross the threshold to try to help everyone else.

References

Anderson, P. (2005). "Arms and Rights: Rawls, Habermas, and Bobbio in an Age of War," *New Left Review* n.s., 31: 5–40.

Beitz, C. R. (2009). *The Idea of Human Rights* (Oxford University Press).

Besson, S. and Zysset, A. (2012). "Human Rights Theory and Human Rights History: A Tale of Two Odd Bedfellows," *Ancilla Iuris*, special issue, 204–19.

Brierly, J. C. (with Waldock, H.). (1965). *The Law of Nations: An Introduction to International Law*, 6th edn (Oxford University Press).

Claeys, G. (2011). *In Search of Utopia: The History of an Idea* (Thames and Hudson).

Estlund, D. (2014). "Utopophobia," *Philosophy and Public Affairs* 42/2: 113–34.

Galston, W. (2010). "Realism in Political Theory," *European Journal of Political Theory* 9/4: 385–411.

Geuss, R. (2008). *Philosophy and Real Politics* (Princeton University Press).

Gibbon, E. (1994). *The History of the Decline and Fall of the Roman Empire*, ed. David Womersley, 3 vols. (Penguin).

Honig, B. and Stears, M. (2011). "The New Realism," in J. Floyd and M. Stears (eds), *Political Philosophy versus History? Contextualism and Real Politics in Contemporary Political Thought* (Cambridge University Press).

Moyn, S. (2010). *The Last Utopia: Human Rights in History* (Harvard University Press).

Moyn, S. (2012). "Do Human Rights Treaties Make Enough of a Difference?" in C. Douzinas and C. Gearty (eds), *Cambridge Companion to Human Rights Law* (Cambridge University Press).

Nickel, J. W. (1982). "Are Human Rights Utopian?," *Philosophy and Public Affairs* 11/3: 246–64.

Pickering, A. (1984). *Constructing Quarks: A Sociological History of Particle Physics* (University of Chicago Press).

Plato. (1992). *Republic*, trans. G. M. A. Grube and C. D. C. Reeve (Hackett).

Rawls, J. (1971). *A Theory of Justice* (Harvard University Press).

Rawls, J. (1999). *The Law of Peoples* (Harvard University Press).

Raz, J. (2010a). "Human Rights in the Emerging World Order," *Transnational Legal Theory* 1/1: 31–47.

Raz, J. (2010b). "Human Rights without Foundations," in S. Besson and J. Tasioulas (eds), *The Philosophy of International Law* (Oxford University Press).

Simmons, B. (2009). *Mobilizing for Human Rights: International Law in Domestic Politics* (Cambridge University Press).

Tasioulas, J. (2007). "The Moral Reality of Human Rights," in T. Pogge (ed.), *Freedom from Poverty as a Human Right: Who Owes What to the Very Poor?* (Oxford University Press).

Tasioulas, J. (2009). "Are Human Rights Essentially Triggers for Humanitarian Intervention?," *Philosophy Compass* 4/6: 938–50.

Tasioulas, J. (2012). "Towards a Philosophy of Human Rights," *Current Legal Problems* 65: 1–30.

Waldron, J. (2013). "*Political* Political Theory: An Inaugural Lecture," *Journal of Political Philosophy* 21/1: 1–23.

Williams, B. (2005). *In the Beginning Was the Deed: Realism and Moralism in Political Argument* (Princeton University Press).

2.1

Philosophizing the Real World of Human Rights
A Reply to Samuel Moyn

John Tasioulas

The post-World War II human rights phenomenon has in recent years become the focus of an outpouring of academic interest that spills across a number of disciplines—not only law and philosophy, but also history, theology, political science, anthropology, and international relations, among others. This is without doubt a positive development, since the major questions to which that phenomenon gives rise are by no means the exclusive preserve of any one academic specialization. However, as Samuel Moyn's chapter in this volume, written with his customary learning and flair, vividly illustrates, productive cross-disciplinary dialogue on this apparently common subject-matter is not easily achieved. In this reply I will indicate some of the ways in which Moyn mistreats arguments that I advanced in 'Towards a Philosophy of Human Rights', the text that is his primary target.[1] My comments are offered with the aim of furthering a broad agenda that I believe we both share, which is that the academic study of human rights should critically engage with the discourse and practice of human rights in the real world.

I

Although philosophers address certain familiar questions about human rights, those questions are not helpfully seen as exhaustive of human rights' theoretical and practical interest. Presumably, philosophers focus on these questions not because they take them to be the most important in some unqualified sense, but rather because they are those with which, as philosophers, they are best equipped to make headway. To that extent, no aspersions are cast on the validity of questions they tend to ignore, such as the historical

---

[1] Tasioulas 2012b, pp. 1–30.

origins of human rights discourse or the legitimacy of the existing international human rights legal regime. In 'Towards a Philosophy of Human Rights', I focused on two broad questions about human rights that have occupied centre-stage in philosophical debates over the last decade. The first is a question about the *nature* of human rights: what is the core concept or idea of a human right? What distinguishes such rights within the general class of normative standards? The second is a question about the *grounds* of human rights. Once we have a clearer grasp of the nature of human rights, under what conditions, if any, are we justified in asserting the existence of norms of this kind? Charles Beitz's *The Idea of Human Rights* is primarily an exemplary philosophical study of the first question, just as James Griffin's *On Human Rights* is of the second.

In 'Towards a Philosophy of Human Rights', and other work, I have ventured answers to both of those questions that swim against strong currents in the contemporary philosophy of human rights. As to the nature of human rights, I defend the orthodox view that they are moral rights possessed by all human beings simply in virtue of their humanity. This contrasts with newly emergent functionalist views, inspired largely by John Rawls and most fully developed by Beitz, that cast human rights in terms of some fairly specific political function(s), such as benchmarks of political legitimacy or triggers for international concern or intervention. In response to the question of the grounds of human rights, I oppose the foundationalist view, according to which such rights have importantly distinctive grounds as compared with other moral norms. Contrary to foundationalists such as Griffin, I argue that the grounds of human rights are pluralistic, embracing both a moral element (basic human dignity) and a diversity of prudential elements (universal human interests).

In his chapter, Moyn does not explicitly disentangle my treatment of the questions of nature and grounds. In any case, he seems to be mainly concerned with the first question, which he occasionally unhappily refers to as a 'definitional' enterprise. But what is at issue is not a search for necessary and sufficient conditions for applying the phrase 'human rights'. Rather, it is a question of conceptual elucidation: a matter of identifying what it is to have an adequate grasp of the concept of a human right, something which one may possess without having the words 'human rights' or any other phrase readily translatable by those English words. Something more needs to be said, however, about this conceptual project, since it is highly likely that the discourse of human rights involves a multiplicity of different concepts, each of which might with some plausibility be presented as 'the' concept of human rights.

The conceptual investigation I am engaged in, contrary to the impression conveyed by Moyn, does not begin by considering human rights from the heavenly perspective of eternity. Instead, it starts from Moyn's own preferred starting-place: the rich and complex discourse of human rights that has come to prominence since the Universal Declaration of Human Rights. This discourse is neither exclusively one of law nor of high politics; instead, it also embraces the activities of ordinary people in day-to-day encounters, the campaigns of human rights activists, and so on. And the project asks whether this discourse can be interpreted as involving some core or focal concept of a 'human right'. This is a concept that can be mobilized to make ethical sense of, and potentially justify, that discourse, and in relation to which other conceptualizations of 'human rights' are importantly derivative. The project is not a cheerleading exercise; instead, it leaves open the sceptical possibility that ultimately no such concept or justification is available. Moreover, it is just one kind of intellectual project regarding human rights; there may be many other viable projects, and more important projects, besides this one.

The desiderata bearing on the project of uncovering such a concept are complex and potentially in tension. They include, on the one hand, a desideratum of charity or normative plausibility: a concept whose applications can be well grounded is, other things being equal, to be preferred to one that cannot. Even if ultimately we feel compelled to reject the human rights project root and branch, our rejection will itself be convincing only if we have first sought to discover the most attractive interpretation that project can be made to bear. To this extent, it is no embarrassment that the identification of the core concept is responsive to evaluative concerns, rather than some value-free exercise in conceptual divination (cf. Moyn p. 76). On the other hand, there is a constraint of ecumenism: other things being equal, it should be possible to interpret people with otherwise highly divergent views about the grounds, content and practical implications of human rights as sharing this same concept, which operates as a common plateau that makes their disagreements genuine. And, of course, there is an overarching desideratum of fidelity: the proposed focal concept must 'fit' enough of the post-UDHR thought and practice of human rights to be eligible as an account of the core idea.

Now, as already mentioned, I have defended an orthodox account of the nature of human rights, one according to which they are moral rights possessed by all human beings simply in virtue of their humanity. The positive dimension of the defence elaborates on this deceptively simple formula so as to render it maximally plausible; the negative part highlights problems faced by rival conceptualizations, including the political view of human rights. To the latter end, I have offered both wholesale and retail arguments. Wholesale arguments identify problems afflicting the general class of political views—for example, that they make the discourse of human rights parasitic on the idea of certain institutional structures (such as the state or a system of states), whereas perfectly intelligible deployments of that discourse, by anarchists or cosmopolitans, urge the abolition of those very same structures. Retail arguments identify problems for specific versions of the political view, such as the ultra-minimal list of human rights that issues from Rawls's account of human rights as norms of intervention and legitimacy, or the idiosyncratically broad construal of the principle of sovereignty presupposed by Joseph Raz's contention that human rights permit interventions that are ordinarily prohibited by that principle.[2]

---

[2] See the discussions of Rawls and Raz in my articles 'On the Nature of Human Rights' (Tasioulas 2012a) and 'Towards a Philosophy of Human Rights' (Tasioulas 2012b).

Moyn, for his part, obviously adheres to some yet-to-be fully specified version of the political view of contemporary human rights discourse. At one point, he remarks that Rawls's account straightforwardly identifies what human rights 'have typically and specifically meant in recent political debates' (p. 73). But this claim runs up against the notorious implication of that account, explicitly drawn by Rawls himself, that most of the rights listed in the UDHR are merely 'liberal aspirations' and not 'human rights proper'.[3] Awareness of the difficulties confronting received versions of the political view breaks out near the end of the chapter when Moyn endorses the idea, which he ascribes to James Nickel, that objections to it can be met by appealing to a multiplicity of political functions, not just a single one (p. 81, fn12). This suggestion is puzzling, however, since Rawls appeals to the *dual* functions of triggering intervention and setting a benchmark for legitimacy. Still, Moyn can be read as calling for a multiplication of *disjunctively* specified functions beyond Rawls's dualist scheme. But this proposal seems, if anything, to reinforce the wholesale objection to the political view noted above. Now, if the multiple political functions of human rights are indeed specified disjunctively, this may indeed go some way towards deflecting the retail objections, for example, familiar human rights that are not aptly construed as triggers of (military) intervention might nonetheless be bases for some kind of international 'concern'. But the risk is that this advantage comes at the cost of undermining the integrity of the concept of human rights by incorporating within it a hotch-potch of functions drawn from the vagaries of existing practice. Will any function to which the language of human rights is put in contemporary practice count as part of the very concept of such a right? If so, the difference between the functions that are integral to the concept and those that are not will be lost.

This foray into the nitty-gritty of the debate about orthodox and political views of human rights just recounted is, however, an atypical moment in Moyn's chapter. For, in general, he is silent both about the positive case I mounted for orthodoxy and the arguments I brought against the political view in its various guises. At one level, this may simply reflect sheer incredulity on his part that anyone who takes the post-war discourse of human rights at all seriously could fail to embrace a version of the political view. But, of course, I am hardly alone in adhering to orthodoxy or the associated idea that the concept of a human right is importantly continuous with that of a natural right. Both views are also endorsed by a number of philosophers of otherwise highly divergent orientations, such as John Finnis, James Griffin, Onora O'Neill, Amartya Sen, A. John Simmons, Jeremy Waldron, and Nicholas Wolterstorff, as well as by leading historians of human rights, including Tony Honore and Brian Tierney. Moreover, the political view has been trenchantly criticized by some of these philosophers, just as historians and lawyers have expressed scepticism about Moyn's companion thesis that the idea of human rights was born in the late 1970s—a product of the Carter adminitration's foreign policy aimed at sparking the American nation's moral regeneration

---

[3] Rawls 1999, pp. 65.

after the calamity of the Vietnam War—and are conceptually *sui generis* with respect to the natural rights tradition.[4]

In my judgement, unsurprisingly, the orthodox view merits the tribute of critical scrutiny of the arguments advanced in its favour. One possible reason why Moyn largely refrained from paying it is that he contrasts orthodoxy with views that I have called 'functionalist', and he takes it as obvious that the discourse of human rights is characteristically invoked to perform certain functions. But the project of limning the concept of human rights is not one of cataloguing the various uses—legitimate or not—to which speakers put that concept. Instead, it is concerned only with those functions that are necessary elements of the concept, such that failure to grasp them would betray a defective grasp of the concept itself. On the orthodox view, human rights do have a function: they are a class of duties owed to all human beings in virtue of some fact about the latter (for example, their moral status or their interests). The function of identifying duties owed in this way to all human beings is integral to the concept of a human right. Additionally, the orthodox view can embrace the idea that the concept embodies the claim that society ought in some sense to recognize and uphold these duties. Now, it is perfectly compatible with all this that human rights are commonly and even justifiably invoked as standards that perform various other functions, such as triggering intervention, even though these additional functions are not integral to the concept of a human right. Moreover, these non-integral functions may nonetheless be very important in understanding and evaluating the contemporary human rights culture, and so eminently deserving of attention.[5] But they are no more part of the concept of a human right than a potential role in a system of mutually assured destruction is part of the concept of a nuclear weapon.[6] Of course, it is a delicate question which of the uses of the concept of a human right reflect features integral to its nature, but that is precisely the question addressed by the substantive arguments whose presence in my work Moyn barely acknowledges.

II

Even assuming that Moyn misinterpreted or failed to engage sympathetically with my philosophical project in the ways indicated in Section I, this by no means wholly defuses the general dissatisfaction with that project expressed in his chapter. The latter crystallizes in the sense that this project fails to address and illuminate contemporary realities. A related concern is that it supposedly provides very little in the way of

[4] See e.g. Blackburn 2011, pp. 126–38; Alston 2013, p. 2043; McCrudden 2015.

[5] There seems to be a pervasive assumption in Moyn's chapter that I must judge to be unimportant any feature of human rights discourse that is not captured by the concept of a human right. But that some aspect of human rights discourse does not have *conceptual* significance does not preclude it from having tremendous significance of other kinds, such as political significance.

[6] It is notable that one of the most sophisticated versions of a 'political' view of human rights, that developed by Jean Cohen, applies only to a proper sub-set of human rights, where the broader category of human rights is picked out in terms friendly to orthodoxy (Cohen 2013, ch. 3).

guidance in addressing some of the deepest practical challenges that we confront in making human rights discourse a useful instrument in hastening the emergence of a better, more just world. So, towards the end of his chapter, Moyn identifies the 'most momentous' problem afflicting the real-world human rights phenomenon, one that recent philosophical work—of which my article receives the ambiguous compliment of being emblematic—has 'not reached... not by a long shot' (p. 85):

[T]he main quandary about human rights now, one that philosophers as much as anyone else are eligible to solve, is whether and how to correct them normatively and practically. For the most significant fact about human rights today is that the original synthesis of moral norms and realist strategies allowed by its architecture and adopted by its pluralizing movements has had far more success on the rhetorical level than otherwise. Human rights have done far more to transform the terrain of idealism than they have the world itself... [T]he obstacles human rights have faced in doing more have so far proved daunting. For this reason, awareness of the dense reality of human rights culture should force its partisans to face the possibility that its original normative framing was in some way flawed or incomplete and that it was allied to a realist strategy that was in some way limited or self-defeating.   (pp. 84–5)

Whether or not one agrees with the implicit pessimistic assessment of the human rights culture in this passage, it is arguable that Moyn purchases it too cheaply—by setting the bar of success unrealistically high. This assessment, including the worry about self-defeatingness, presumably reflects the ironical upshot of his book, *The Last Utopia: Human Rights in History*. According to Moyn's provocative narrative in that work, the emergence of human rights in the 1970s was trammelled up with their character as an 'apolitical', moral response to the failures of earlier political visions, principally communism. However, in time they came to inherit all of the challenges of those earlier visions, with the result that they now proliferate uncontrollably as would-be solutions to all of our political problems. Whatever one makes of the historical accuracy of this supposed 'transition from antipolitics to program' (Moyn 2010, p. 224), it is clear that Moyn conceives of human rights as a totalizing ideology, a 'worldview that [seeks] to provide an answer to any area of global concern' (p. 221). It is doubtful, however, that a charitable construal of human rights morality would conceptually lumber it with such grandiose aspirations. Instead, human rights would be one kind of globally relevant norm among others, some of them not primarily rights-based (for example, humanitarian or public good concerns) and others not primarily anthropocentric in character (for example, environmental concerns).

Notice also the personalizing locution in the quoted passage, according to which 'human rights' are held responsible for doing, or failing to do, this or that. One might with no less cogency say that justice, equality, fairness, mercy and love have not 'done enough' to transform the world as it is. By my lights, however, this way of speaking conflates human rights, understood as genuine normative demands, and the fallible practical measures through which we seek, successfully or not, to fulfil them. From this perspective, the question is not what human rights can do for us, but what we can do to realize our human rights. These reservations aside, the question of how we might better realize the demands of human rights in the world as it is is, without doubt, an important one—perhaps it is *the* most important question about human rights. But the relationship of philosophical inquiry to that ultimate practical question is not simple, but rather heavily mediated in at least two ways.

First, in addressing that question, we must give or presuppose answers to a large number of other questions, not all of them immediately practical. Some are staples of philosophical inquiry. I have so far only discussed those about the nature and grounds of human rights. In addition, there are questions about such matters as: the specification of associated duties and the principles guiding their allocation to particular duty-bearers; the role of human rights in practical deliberation, including potential conflicts among human rights or between human rights and other considerations; the way in which the universal morality of human rights can properly accommodate cultural differences without unduly blunting its critical edge; the principles that properly guide the legal or other institutional embodiment of human rights, whether in domestic legal systems, national constitutions, or international law; and the design of mechanisms for ensuring compliance with institutionally embedded human rights, including through measures such as intervention or punishment in the event of their violation, among others. Moreover, in addressing these questions, as well as others besides, philosophy is but one of the disciplinary perspectives on which we need to draw; others include political science, economics, psychology, law, and so on. For example, it is one thing to establish a general normative framework for assessing the legitimacy of international human rights law; it is quite another thing to apply it in relation to any existing international human rights legal regime. The latter enterprise will need to draw extensively on empirical evidence about the efficacy of the regime in question, something beyond the philosopher's domain of expertise.[7] Now, Moyn recognizes that exponents of other disciplines are also eligible to address his 'momentous' question; but my point here is that no discipline can credibly address it single-handedly, that it implicates a diversity of further questions, different aspects of which are more profitably addressed by exponents of some disciplines rather than others, which leaves us with the difficult and ongoing task of weaving together the various strands of a multi-disciplinary dialogue.

Second, the relationship between philosophical theory (or academic inquiry more generally) and the realities of political and other practices cannot consist in the one-way dictation of practical instructions by theorists to agents. A philosophical treatise on human rights cannot plausibly aspire to be a practical blueprint for achieving a human rights utopia. Beneath Moyn's castigations of contemporary philosophy of human rights for its supposed disengagement from political realities, I suspect there lurks the countervailing ideal of philosophers as Platonic guardians legislating for

---

[7] An impressive recent example of the kind of study I have in mind is Simmons 2009, which I discuss briefly in my article 'Human Rights, Legitimacy, and International Law' (Tasioulas 2013).

the world. Here, Moyn sets up the philosopher for a fall that is as inevitable as it is humiliating. But philosophy's ambitions cannot be anything like so grandiose; instead, it should offer conceptual and normative arguments that provide a basis for a clear-sighted and justified commitment to human rights, as well as a general framework within which important practical questions for the pursuit of human rights can be formulated and addressed. But none of this, however well executed, can substitute for a variety of personal and institutional virtues that go far beyond the mere 'application' of philosophically generated principles. These virtues include the need for statesmanship on the part of political leaders, with its ineffable capacity for sound judgment in identifying and seizing opportunities for advancing human rights in specific historical circumstances;[8] the need for courageous and determined struggle on the part of activists grappling with concrete humans rights abuses such as extreme poverty, sexism and racism; and, no less important, there is the crucial role of an engaged and enlightened democratic community in sustaining a deeply grounded human rights ethos. Beyond the need for practical wisdom and virtue, there is also just the plain fact that sound normative principles systematically under-determine practical outcomes, with the consequent need to devise various fair and effective institutional means of reaching a decision when their guidance peters out. For these reasons and more besides, philosophy and intellectual inquiry more generally—however engaged with the problems of the world—is no substitute for practical politics aimed at transforming our social and personal lives.

In short, an adequate assessment of what philosophy can contribute to Moyn's 'most momentous question' must reckon more that he does with two realities: first, that philosophy is one of many academic disciplines addressing a great multiplicity of questions concerning human rights in a many-sided enterprise that involves a significant division of labour; and, second, that the sound deliverances of these disciplines, even taken as a whole, heavily underdetermine the concrete practical steps needed adequately to realize human rights in the world as it is.

III

The remarks in Section II were pitched at an abstract level, corresponding to Moyn's very general formulation of his dissatisfaction with the contemporary philosophical human rights scene. Still, many will share his impatience with the emphasis I and other philosophers have placed on the questions of the nature and grounds of human rights and, even more so, with the orthodox account of their nature. So, the criticism might now take a more specific form: a philosophical approach that privileges these

---

[8] 'It is the task of the student of philosophy to articulate and express the permanent conditions and the real interests of a well-ordered society. It is the task of the statesman, however, to discern these conditions and interests in practice. The statesman sees deeper and further than most others and grasps what needs to be done' (Rawls 1999, p. 97).

concerns and, in particular, one that sets out from an orthodox view of human rights, is ill-equipped to make a significant contribution to answering the 'momentous question' identified by Moyn. I put to one side the obvious response that—of course—no philosophy of human rights should be confined to addressing just the questions of nature and grounds. What more might be said?

I turn briefly to the grounds of human rights before moving on to their nature, and the orthodox account of it, which is Moyn's chief bugbear. Moyn begins with the moderate observation that his 'most momentous' question 'exceeds in relevance... but also rivals in difficulty the undoubtedly important and interesting problem of how one might normatively justify human rights' (p. 85). Within a few paragraphs, however, this is ramped up to a general dismissal of the wider significance of the justificatory enterprise: 'Important as normative inquiry is for philosophers and scholars generally, it does not appear that human rights practice needs it much' (p. 85). Given his characterization of the 'most momentous' question, it is all the more puzzling why Moyn belittles the contribution that reflection on the grounds of human rights can make to engaging with that question, a contribution whose potential significance is not restricted to 'philosophers and scholars'. Precisely because of the deep and diverse challenges confronting the discourse of human rights, we need to address the question of their grounds. How else to vindicate our commitment to human rights? How else to patrol the boundary between universal human interests and human rights, given the self-undermining tendency of human rights claims to proliferate endlessly? How else to evaluate the institutional and other political mechanisms that have been adopted to embody and implement human rights standards? How else to respond to the widespread resistance to human rights on the basis that they represent the ideological advance-party of Western imperialism?[9] Hence, for example, the welcome critical scrutiny that philosophers and others have in the last few years directed at the widely echoed claim that human dignity is the foundation of human rights.[10] Among other things, such scrutiny may help us to understand the extent to which human rights are subject to trade-offs against other concerns within moral and political deliberation, a theme whose 'real-life' urgency Moyn rightly stresses. Yet Moyn's line of argument may wrongly tempt us into underestimating the value of such contributions, and how they might eventually seep into the wider human rights consciousness to good effect, on the misplaced ground that they do not directly 'solve' his 'most momentous' question.

---

[9] Indeed, I would go further, and agree with Christopher McCrudden, that an adequate historical narrative of human rights must draw on some account of their normative basis, since this crucially bears on the kind of explanation—sceptical or vindicatory—that we give of why people came to believe in human rights. The failure to mobilize such an account, according to McCrudden, is the deepest problem with Moyn's *The Last Utopia*, and the point at which his thesis of the discontinuity of human rights from natural rights is most vulnerable (McCrudden 2015). Unfortunately, constraints of space prevent me from taking up this theme in the present commentary. However, it is vitally important to stress that commitment to an objective grounding for human rights in no way entails the optimistic historicist thesis that their eventual triumph is likely, let alone inevitable. For a discussion of this last point, see Tasioulas 2012, pp. 30–3, edited by Sellers.

[10] See e.g. McCrudden 2013.

Turn now to Moyn's main irritant, the orthodox view that human rights are universal moral rights, i.e. moral rights possessed by all human beings simply in virtue of their humanity, and discoverable by ordinary (or natural) moral reasoning. On this view, the concept of a human right is importantly continuous with that of a natural right, which is itself the focus of a tradition that stretches back at least to the medieval period, if not earlier. Moyn's complaint is well encapsulated by the question: 'how does the vindication of the status of human rights as age-old moral entitlements embrace this opportunity [to use philosophical theory in order to exert critical leverage on the existing human rights culture], when it comes to any burning debate today?' (p. 82). Surely, the complaint goes, the focus on these 'age-old' entitlements, in abstracting from the conditions distinctive of the world in which the contemporary human rights idiom operates, will yield severely impoverished returns for the major questions of the here-and-now. On this telling, an orthodox theorist seems like an aged aristocrat obsessed with investigating obscure corners of his genealogy, oblivious to the fact that his dilapidated ancestral pile is falling apart around him.

However, this objection can be met if we distinguish, as Moyn fails to do, between the antiquity of the concept of a human right and the temporal scope of judgements deploying it. It is indeed an implication of the orthodox view that the concept of a human right turns out to be an old one, in the sense that we can find something very like this concept at work in the natural rights tradition. We are familiar with this kind of continuity from the case of other moral-political concepts: for example, intellectual historians, including Moyn, find it informative to trace a recognizably democratic form of government all the way back to fifth-century BC Athens. The broad concept of democracy—something like, say, Amartya Sen's idea of 'government by discussion'[11]— remains intact across time, even if people's sense of what that concept properly requires in their historical circumstances (political participation by women and the propertyless, periodic elections, one-person-one-vote, etc.) undergoes seismic shifts. Moreover, in developing my version of the orthodox view, I have stressed that it is perfectly acceptable to impose temporal constraints on the class of human beings whose rights one is seeking to identify.[12] Hence, contemporary human rights discourse, I claim, is usually best understood as addressing the rights possessed by all human beings within the context of modernity. This is why the orthodox view does not succumb to the objection that it can only appeal to the meagre set of human rights meaningfully possessed by all human beings throughout human history, even Stone Age cavemen or denizens of medieval hamlets.[13] This objection would have great force if human

[11] See Sen 2009, ch. 15, which distinguishes the broader notion of democracy as 'government by discussion' from narrower 'organizational' conceptions that focus on procedures such as balloting and elections.

[12] See e.g. my articles, 'The Moral Reality of Human Rights' (Tasioulas 2007), and 'On the Nature of Human Rights' (Tasioulas 2012a). Moyn seems to think (fn. 19) that my defence of orthodoxy is a departure from the temporally constrained view, whereas in fact it is part of the former's fuller elaboration. Similar themes are present in the work of James Griffin (Griffin 2008, pp. 37–9, 44) and David Miller (Miller 2008, ch. 7).

[13] See e.g. Beitz 2003, pp. 36–46.

rights were being equated with natural rights, in the restricted sense of rights that are possessed even in a pre-political state of nature. But that is only one specific variant of the natural rights tradition, and no such equivalence is asserted by my version of the orthodox view.

If we mobilize an orthodox concept of human rights with associated temporal constraints, we are in a position to take the full measure of a sensible point repeatedly emphasized by Moyn, i.e. that human rights thought has to be attuned to 'realist' considerations in elaborating its utopian ideal. This is a point that recent orthodox theorists have openly embraced, contrary to the unworldly image of them presented by Moyn. So, for example, I have elaborated on the 'threshold' that enables us to pass from universal human interests to duties generated by those interests that are owed to all human beings.[14] This threshold involves feasibility constraints as to what is possible to secure through the imposition of duties, as well as what would be excessively burdensome so to secure. In both cases, judgements of possibility and burden can be made more tractable and practically relevant by being indexed to broadly contemporary conditions regarding such matters as available resources, institutional capacities, and level of technological development. This explains why a human right to an adequate standard of living may be plausibly ascribed to human beings today, but not to Stone Age cavemen or medieval serfs, and perhaps also not to a future humanity suffering from the irreversible depredations of climate change. It is also why literal understandings of the human right to health, as demanding the 'highest attainable' level of mental and physical health, grossly over-reach. More generally, the threshold is the key bulwark in stemming the 'proliferation' of human rights claims that threatens to strip the discourse of its force and significance. And naturally, in arriving at reliable estimations of possibility and burden, it will be necessary to factor in information yielded by a range of academic disciplines, including notably economics, law, history, and political science.

Even if this is enough to address Moyn's more sweeping objections to the orthodox view, can we point to specific ways in which it helps address any 'burning debate' on human rights today? Well, in a way, a major contention of my work has been that it is immensely clarifying for contemporary human rights discourse not to conceptually tether them to intervention or legitimacy. Their relation to assessments of the latter issues is substantive, not conceptual. For reasons that are unclear to me, Moyn says this is merely 'a threshold correction' (p. 82). On the contrary, I see this as an important step in combating what often looks like the liberal interventionist and neo-conservative hijacking of the idea of human rights. In any case, let me offer another, more concrete, illustration: the 'Guiding Principles on Business and Human Rights', which were

---

[14] See my articles 'Towards a Philosophy of Human Rights' (Tasioulas 2012b) and 'On the Foundations of Human Rights' (Tasioulas forthcoming).

devised by Professor John Ruggie in response to a mandate from UN Secretary-General Kofi Annan and published to widespread endorsement in 2011.[15]

One of the most difficult and pressing questions in the era of globalization is the applicability of human rights norms to increasingly powerful non-state actors, prominent among them multinational corporations. Human rights advocates have often presupposed a statist and legalist paradigm. On this view, long-entrenched in the international law of human rights, and endorsed at a conceptual level by many adherents of the political view of such rights, states are the primary, if not necessarily the exclusive, bearers of the duties associated with human rights, and these duties centrally require them to enact legislation that binds other agents in furtherance of human rights objectives.[16] So conceived, human rights do not directly bind corporations; instead, they are obligated to comply with laws enacted by the relevant state in fulfilment of the latter's duty to promote human rights compliance.[17]

By at least the 1990s, however, this statist-legalist paradigm started coming under immense strain, especially as allegations of serious corporate human rights violations began to mount. There was not simply the problem of weak or ill-governed states that did not ratify human rights treaties, or that failed to enact or enforce laws reflecting their demands. The situation was complicated by two collective action problems. First, states have an economic incentive not to impose human rights constraints through legislation if this would cause valuable economic activity within their borders to migrate to less scrupulous jurisdictions. Second, corporations themselves have an economic

[15] 'Guiding Principles on Business and Human Rights: Implementing the United Nations' "Protect, Respect, and Remedy" Framework, 2011'. The next few paragraphs are indebted to the rich, partly autobiographical, discussion of these matters in Ruggie 2013.

[16] The statist assumption is common ground to leading advocates of the political view, such as Beitz, Rawls, and Raz (although Rawls speaks of 'peoples' rather than 'states'). Meanwhile, the legalist assumption is explicitly endorsed by Habermas and Raz, among others: '[H]uman rights have an inherently juridical nature and are conceptually oriented toward positive enactment by legislative bodies' (Habermas 2001, p. 122); '[O]f all our moral rights only rights that should be respected and enforced by law are identified as human rights' (Raz 2010, pp. 31–47, 43). For a critique of statism/legalism, see my Tasioulas 2012a and 2012b. In *The Last Utopia: Human Rights in History*, Moyn also appears to deploy a concept of human rights locked into the statist-legalist paradigm. This might be overlooked, because he sharply distinguishes human rights from natural rights, and construes the latter as 'statist' insofar as they provide moral foundations for the sovereignty of the nation-state. Human rights, by contrast, are interpreted as providing a basis for the external abrogation of state sovereignty: 'the central event in human rights history is the recasting of rights as entitlements that might contradict the sovereign nation-state from above and outside rather than serve as its foundation' (Moyn 2010, p. 13). But even as they subordinate the state system to a structure of global governance, human rights must presumably for Moyn conceptually presuppose that system, as they do in the sophisticated political view of human rights developed by Charles Beitz, according to which the practice of human rights is a 'revisionist appurtenance of a world order of independent, territorial states' (Beitz 2009, p. 128). In addition, Moyn's understanding of human rights is legalist, insofar as he makes clear that the idea of human rights, when it comes into its own in the late 1970s, involves the idea of a 'utopia of supranational governance through law' (Moyn 2010, p. 81).

[17] Although the statist and legalist view is a feature of international human rights *law*, it is worth mentioning that such law arguably recognizes direct obligations on the part of corporations when the human rights violations in question reach the level of international crimes, e.g. war crimes, genocide, torture, extra-judicial killings, etc.

incentive not to comply with human rights demands voluntarily unless they can be assured their competitors will also do so. Now, one classic way of resolving collective action problems is through enforceable law, and indeed many human rights activists have called for a multilateral treaty regime on business and human rights. However, there are seemingly insuperable obstacles to negotiating such a treaty, at least in the foreseeable future, given ideological disagreements and the absence of suitable incentives. In the meantime, something urgently needs to be done to address the problem of corporate human rights abuses.

Ruggie's innovative principles offer a solution to this problem by breaking the stranglehold of the statist-legalist paradigm of human rights. On the one hand, the principles impose an *independent* corporate responsibility to respect human rights, one that applies independently of the fulfilment of the duties imposed on states. In brief, it requires business enterprises to act with due diligence in order to avoid human rights violations and to address any adverse impacts on human rights with which they are involved, including those caused by businesses to which they are linked. On the other hand, the principles abandon the legalist assumption: they are not legally binding but rather aspire to be politically authoritative, providing a focal point for securing convergent expectations and behaviour regarding corporate human rights responsibilities. Ruggie does not preclude binding legal norms in this area, such as multilateral treaties, but he anticipates they will likely operate as 'precision instruments' within a regulatory framework that is not exclusively or predominantly legal in character. Moreover, the principles do not require that there always be legally enforceable remedies for corporate human rights violations. Judicial redress is one among a variety of contemplated remedial mechanisms, alongside civil and corporate mechanisms, in a system of 'polycentric governance'.

Now, not only does Ruggie depart from the statist and legalist assumptions taken for granted by many proponents of the political view of human rights, he also explicitly appeals to the orthodox view of human rights developed by Amartya Sen as a justification for doing so:

[Sen] does not believe that the very idea of human rights is or should be confined to their role as either laws' antecedents or effects. To do so would unduly constrict—Sen actually uses the term 'incarcerate'—the social logics and processes other than law that derive enduring public recognition of rights. I share Sen's view.   (Ruggie 2013, p. 8)

Of course, Ruggie's principles are no panacea;[18] among various concerns, I would highlight the problematic idea that the principles are grounded merely in 'social expectations', as opposed to the objective values that justify any such expectations. But they are nonetheless an innovative and promising new step in human rights governance, a constructive attempt to overcome the limitations of the statist-legalist paradigm. Moreover, they are not merely attractive on their intrinsic merits, they have also

---

[18] For a helpful discussion of the issues, see McCorquodale 2013, pp. 287–315.

secured a remarkable degree of support among relevant 'stakeholders', a crucial fact in light of their projected function as an authoritative global 'focal point'. In 2011 the principles were unanimously endorsed by the UN Human Rights Council, and have also been approved by influential bodies such as the OECD, the European Commission, and the American Chamber of Commerce. The principles highlight the advantages of an orthodox understanding in shaping human rights governance in a globalizing world in which the capabilities of states and the efficacy of traditional legal remedies are variously diminished or strained. From this perspective, ironically, it is the statism and legalism characteristic of many political views that is revealed as passé in tethering human rights to outmoded assumptions about institutional capacities and enforcement mechanisms. Nor are the Ruggie principles an isolated example of the value of an orthodox approach. The same repudiation of the statist-legalist paradigm can be found, for example, in feminist deployments of human rights critiques within the private sphere or in concerns about torture and other egregious human rights violations being committed by agents in the context of failed states. What these various examples underline is that the fulfilment of human rights requires the creation of a sustaining culture far beyond anything contemplated by that paradigm.

Samuel Moyn's charge that the orthodox view is inconsequential for the great contemporary questions of human rights ultimately misses its mark. On the contrary, it is precisely by formulating a concept of human rights abstracted from certain institutional particularities that we best equip human rights thought to respond creatively and flexibly to the challenges confronting their fulfilment in the world today. The alternative approach, one that assimilates the very idea of human rights to existing institutional structures and policies, risks discarding the vital kernel of truth in human rights morality along with the chaff of yet one more ill-fated blueprint for constructing utopia.

References

Alston, Philip. 'Does the Past Matter? On the Origins of Human Rights'. *Harvard Law Review* 126, no. 7 (2013).

Beitz, Charles. 'What Human Rights Mean'. *Daedalus* 132, no.1 (2003).

Beitz, Charles. *The Idea of Human Rights* (Oxford: Oxford University Press, 2009).

Blackburn, Robin. 'Reclaiming Human Rights'. *New Left Review* 69 (2011).

Cohen, Jean. *Globalization and Sovereignty: Rethinking Legality, Legitimacy, and Constitutionalism* (Cambridge: Cambridge University Press, 2013), ch. 3.

Griffin, James. *On Human Rights* (Oxford: Oxford University Press, 2008).

'Guiding Principles on Business and Human Rights: Implementing the United Nations' "Protect, Respect, and Remedy" Framework, 2011', accessed 28 November 2014, <http://www.ohchr.org/Documents/Publications/GuidingPrinciplesBusinessHR_EN.pdf>.

Habermas, Jürgen. *The Postnational Constellation* (Cambridge, Mass.: MIT Press, 2001).

McCorquodale, Robert. 'Pluralism, Global Law and Human Rights: Strengthening Corporate Accountability for Human Rights Violations'. *Global Constitutionalism* 2, no. 2 (2013).

McCrudden, Christopher (ed.). *Understanding Human Dignity* (Oxford: Oxford University Press, 2013).

McCrudden, Christopher. 'Human Rights Histories: Integrating Law, Politics, and Morals'. *Oxford Journal of Legal Studies* (2015).

Miller, David. *National Responsibility and Global Justice* (Oxford: Oxford University Press, 2008), ch. 7.

Moyn, Samuel. *The Last Utopia: Human Rights in History* (Cambridge, Mass.: Harvard University Press, 2010).

Rawls, John. *The Law of Peoples* (Cambridge, Mass.: Harvard University Press, 1999).

Raz, Joseph. 'Human Rights in the Emerging World Order'. *Transnational Legal Theory* 1, no. 1 (2010).

Ruggie, John G. *Just Business: Multinational Corporations and Human Rights* (London: WW Norton & Co., 2013).

Sen, Amartya. *The Idea of Justice* (New York: Allen Lane, 2009), ch. 15.

Simmons, Beth. *Mobilizing for Human Rights: International Law in Domestic Politics* (Cambridge: Cambridge University Press, 2009).

Tasioulas, John. 'The Moral Reality of Human Rights'. In Thomas Pogge (ed.), *Freedom from Poverty as a Human Right* (Oxford: Oxford University Press, 2007).

Tasioulas, John. 'On the Nature of Human Rights'. In G. Ernst and J.-C. Heilinger (eds), *The Philosophy of Human Rights: Contemporary Controversies* (Berlin: de Gruyter, 2012a).

Tasioulas, John. 'Towards a Philosophy of Human Rights'. *Current Legal Problems* 65, no. 1 (2012b).

Tasioulas, John. 'Human Rights, Legitimacy, and International Law'. *American Journal of Jurisprudence* 58, no. 1 (2013).

Tasioulas, John. 'On the Foundations of Human Rights'. In Rowan Cruft et al. (eds), *The Philosophical Foundations of Human Rights* (Oxford University Press, forthcoming).

2.2

Genealogies of Human Rights
What's at Stake?

Jeffrey Flynn

"In order to understand properly what we are about, we have to understand how we got where we are."

Charles Taylor, "Philosophy and Its History"

"There is a struggle for the soul of the human rights movement, and it is being waged in large part through the proxy of genealogy."

Philip Alston, "Does the Past Matter? On the Origins of Human Rights"

How is the history of human rights relevant to doing philosophy of human rights? In her commentary on Martti Koskenniemi, Annabel Brett notes how a certain type of "legislative philosophy," which tries to tell us precisely what human rights *really are* (a kind of conceptual transcendence), often goes hand in hand with a certain type of history, which begins with the origins of human rights in the distant past and traces their progressive development up to their culmination in the present (a kind of historical transcendence). Even when such stories refer to "context," the core of the narrative is often about "an essential unity that transcends all circumstances."[1] In contrast to this focus on continuity, attention to discontinuity—to the distinct ways in which rights have been invoked within different historical contexts—tends to breed scepticism about any philosophical approach that would define human rights in terms of something that transcends those contexts. This is precisely what we find in Koskenniemi's provocative contribution, in which he combines that scepticism with an analysis of the different ways rights were used in three definitive episodes in the Western history of rights.

---

[1] Brett in this volume, p. 61. I began this chapter while a Member of the School of Social Science at the Institute for Advanced Study (Princeton, NJ). I am grateful for support from the Institute as well as Fordham University for a Faculty Fellowship during 2013–14. I am extremely grateful to Adam Etinson for extensive comments on earlier versions and for inviting me to write this commentary. I also want to thank Sam Moyn and John Tasioulas for their comments on an earlier draft.

But this way of viewing things obscures the possibility of philosophical approaches that attempt to identify something that transcends particular contexts while also remaining sensitive to historical discontinuities. This is one of John Tasioulas's aims in his recent work. Samuel Moyn, I take it, remains unconvinced. It is a privilege for me to comment on four such distinguished contributors to not only their respective fields, but to the flourishing interdisciplinary conversation on human rights. As that exciting conversation grows, however, it is all too often hindered by mutual miscomprehension. So one of my aims here is to identify points at which the interlocutors may be talking past each other, in particular Tasioulas and Moyn when it comes to discussing the function of human rights. More generally, I want to try to get a better grasp on how various ways of doing the history of human rights are relevant to various ways of doing the philosophy of human rights.

Substance, Scale, and Function

At the core of recent debates over the relevance of history to thinking about human rights are various claims about continuities or discontinuities between contemporary human rights discourse and earlier appeals to rights. Because the stakes differ by discipline, assessing such claims in a general way is not easy. There is little reason to think a single answer would apply across disciplinary boundaries. Consider the attempt to identify something *significant* about human rights that transcends the ways in which the language of human rights or natural rights has been deployed in various historical contexts. The criteria for assessing what counts as significant will vary not only by discipline but also with the distinctive aims of different projects within the same discipline. In political philosophy, for example, Rawlsians and their critics disagree about the significance of post-1948 developments in the history of human rights. In history, some intellectual historians ponder over philosophical abstractions while other historians concentrate on more concrete matters. Hence, making general claims about significant degrees of continuity across history faces a dual challenge: the first challenge, of identifying something meaningful about human rights that transcends historical contexts in the first place, is exacerbated by a further challenge, of trying to say something meaningful to interlocutors in other disciplines with different ideas about what would count as significant. Something similar is surely true for generating meaningful interdisciplinary discussion about the significance of certain types of historical discontinuity.

Clearly there are both continuities and discontinuities between today's invocations of human rights and various iterations of rights in the past, but the relevance of any particular continuity or discontinuity depends on what one is trying to do. Take, for instance, two common aims of historians that would be thwarted if their investigations of the past were guided by the idea that our current conceptions of human rights are entirely continuous with earlier conceptions of rights. First, to adequately *understand* the various ways rights-talk has been used in the past, as Koskenniemi attempts to do in his chapter, one has to be careful about letting current conceptions seep into interpretations of the past.[2] A second common aim of historians is to *explain* some historical change. For instance, in trying to explain the recent surge in human rights rhetoric in the 1970s—one of Moyn's primary aims in *The Last Utopia* (2010)—long-standing continuities will likely have less explanatory power than discontinuities.[3]

How should we proceed, then, in trying to have an interdisciplinary conversation about human rights and their history? I want to start with a distinction Moyn has recently developed as a way of clarifying his own position and suggest some ways it might be helpful for addressing specific issues raised in the debate with Tasioulas as well as more generally for thinking about the relation between the history and the philosophy of human rights. Moyn distinguishes three modes of doing the history of human rights depending on whether one focuses on substance, scale, or salience.[4] The first and until recently dominant form has been substantive history, which focuses on identifying and tracing developments with regard to the concept and content of rights. This kind of history might focus on the historical development of the general idea of individual rights, or of particular rights like freedom of religion, or packages of rights like civil and political rights. Scalar history, on the other hand, tracks changes in our understanding of the scope of rights (their scale or geographical range of application), while salience history focuses on the degree to which rights-talk has been taken up as a language of ideology and struggle. In stressing the importance of the latter two approaches, to which his own book contributes, Moyn maintains that

only a history of human rights oriented to scale and salience can capture not only how the idea was propounded or the practice started, but also how it came to fit the imagination and reorient the actions of large swaths of people, informing their everyday thought and lives, and legitimating one sort of moral world over another both at home and abroad.[5]

Scale and salience are both ways of capturing not just the concept or content of human rights but the degree to which they inspire social movements (salience) to pursue particular political projects (on a national versus a global scale).

Moyn credits the historian Lynn Hunt with making a decisive move toward supplementing substance with salience history. In her book, *Inventing Human Rights* (2007), she extends the subject matter for historians of human rights beyond cataloguing when particular rights claims were first made toward understanding and explaining deeper social transformations.[6] Her main argument is that the emotional responses of eighteenth-century readers of novels were transformative in ways that paved the way for their commitments to the Rights of Man. Notably, this move places the rise of the Rights of Man within a broader transformation of humanitarian sentiment

---

[2] For Koskenniemi's further reflections on methodological challenges to writing the history of international law, see Koskenniemi 2013.

[3] Moyn 2010.   [4] Ibid.   [5] Ibid., p. 6.   [6] Hunt 2007.

in the eighteenth century, a topic of interest to historians that predates interest in "human rights."[7]

In supplementing substance with salience, however, Moyn argues that Hunt failed to account for the issue of scale that is so important to understanding contemporary invocations of human rights. There simply was no international human rights movement in the eighteenth century. Moyn maintains that recent historical scholarship on the 1940s reverses the imbalance in Hunt insofar as it stresses the scalar move made by the Universal Declaration and subsequent developments to make human rights part of the international legal and political order, even though it failed to confront the issue of salience. International human rights were declared in the 1940s (the scalar move), but there was no international human rights *movement* until the 1970s (increasing salience). This is why Moyn distinguishes in his book between "human rights," whose scale is the globe, and "revolutionary rights" or the Rights of Man, whose scale was the nation-state, and then attempts to explain why human rights took on such salience in the 1970s.

So how does Moyn's distinction relate to the philosophy of human rights? Most philosophers of human rights take as their central task the aim of clarifying the concept and justifying the content of human rights. Substance history can be relevant to this endeavour by providing raw materials for philosophical debates about how human rights should be conceived or which rights should count as such. Philosophers can point to historical sources simply as a way of identifying when certain ideas were first put forward or draw on texts and historical episodes for insights and arguments that may still be relevant today. When Tasioulas claims that the "orthodox" definition of a human right—as a moral right possessed by all human beings simply in virtue of their humanity—is "importantly continuous with that of a natural right," we can read this as an appeal to substance history.[8] In terms of substance (using the term here to capture either the concept or the content of human rights), there are indeed continuities between human rights today and earlier rights traditions. Moyn acknowledges this point when he says that Tasioulas is "correct that, from an abstract enough point of view, human rights share much with rights traditions that preceded them," adding, for emphasis, "Who ever doubted it?"[9] Here he is reiterating the extent to which scale and salience are his primary concern, not the claims of substance history.

Rawlsian functionalists, by focusing on developments in international law and politics since 1948, clearly take the scalar move to the international level as a decisive enough shift to make it central to the meaning of human rights today. In the most sophisticated functionalist approach, Charles Beitz's *The Idea of Human Rights* (2009), Beitz argues that a philosophy of human rights that is guided by older concepts, such as natural rights or the Rights of Man, runs the risk of missing what is novel about

---

[7] For more on Moyn and Hunt in relation to human rights and humanitarianism, see Flynn 2012.
[8] Tasioulas in this volume, p. 91.   [9] Moyn in his volume, p. 76; see also p. 69.

contemporary human rights practice.[10] He maintains that investigating past conceptions is not pointless by any means, only that we should not assume that analysing those conceptions "would be an investigation of human rights in the sense in which they occur in contemporary public discourse."[11] Using Moyn's terminology, we might say that a central disagreement between Tasioulas and Beitz is over whether this scalar change—or any other scalar change, for that matter—is of essential significance to the concept of human rights or not.

On this front, Tasioulas makes an interesting distinction between integral and non-integral functions:

> The project of limning the concept of human rights is not one of cataloguing the various uses—legitimate or not—to which speakers put that concept. Instead, it is concerned only with those functions that are necessary elements of the concept, such that failure to grasp them would entail a defective grasp of the concept itself.[12]

Defining which functions are necessary elements of the concept of human rights is a core dispute between orthodox and functionalist approaches. That is, Beitz would presumably argue that failure to grasp the ways in which human rights function in our political discourse today—as a language for expressing international concern and potentially triggering intervention—is indeed to have a defective grasp of the concept.[13] My primary aim here, however, is not to adjudicate this philosophical debate, but to consider how historians and philosophers can even engage in a common conversation on this terrain—and more specifically, to identify points at which Tasioulas and Moyn are talking past each other. One such point is when the function of human rights is discussed.

Tasioulas reads Moyn as committed to a philosophical position on the essential meaning of human rights that aligns him with philosophical functionalism, maintaining in the current volume that Moyn "obviously adheres to some yet-to-be fully specified version of the political view of contemporary human rights discourse."[14] And in an earlier essay Tasioulas claimed that historians like Moyn "are led astray by functionalism, especially the version which interprets human rights as essentially limitations on state sovereignty or triggers for some kind of international action."[15] Tasioulas is certainly not wrong to say Moyn is interested in the contemporary political functions of human rights. But why should we think Moyn has been "led astray" by a particular philosophical position on the meaning of human rights? Regardless of whether functions are essential or not to the concept of human rights, focusing on such functions is the name of the game for many historians and precisely what we should hope

---

[10] Beitz 2009, pp. 44–5.   [11] Ibid., p. 11.   [12] Tasioulas in this volume, p. 92.

[13] Beitz does not simply catalogue the various ways in which speakers use the concept today, but sets out to capture "what an ordinarily competent participant in the discourse of human rights would understand herself to be committed to if she were to acknowledge that a human right to such-and-such exists" (2009, p. 11). On Beitz's methodology of relying on the contemporary discourse and practice of human rights to identify the "discursive role" of human rights, see 2009, pp. 9–11, 102–17.

[14] Tasioulas in this volume, p. 91.   [15] Tasioulas 2012, p. 27.

they would do, as Koskenniemi does in his chapter. As Moyn puts it in his chapter, "Tasioulas's desire for the unity of rights traditions couldn't possibly absolve historians from charting the changing functions and rise in salience of human rights — or philosophers from pondering them."[16] I will return to the question of whether philosophers can be absolved from pondering such things as salience. The point I want to stress here is that Moyn need not take any position at all on the essential nature or meaning of human rights in order to do history, nor is it clear that he has. Charting the changing functions of "human rights" over time is simply not the same thing as defending functionalism in philosophical debates between orthodox and functionalist approaches. In fact, from the perspective of doing history, it is not clear that Moyn could even begin to explain what he aims to explain in *The Last Utopia* if he were not attuned to such changes.

Failure to see this as his focus is of a piece with a common misreading of Moyn's project, one that makes it an excessively easy target by reading him as claiming that there is absolutely no continuity between today's human rights and earlier concepts of rights—a position he clearly disavows in his contribution to this volume. Some of Moyn's rhetoric in *The Last Utopia* makes the common misreading understandable, but one would have to ignore key passages to read the book this way. He states early on that the book is about the "practical outcomes" of proclaiming human rights and the kinds of politics and programmes they inspire.[17] More specifically, he characterizes his aim in terms of showing that "human rights *as a powerful transnational ideal and movement* have distinctive origins of a much more recent date."[18] Although he did not deploy the substance-scale-salience distinction in the book, this passage surely makes it clear that the focus was to be scale and salience. Unfortunately, it seems as if Tasioulas still fails to see this in his contribution to the current volume, citing "historians and lawyers" who have "expressed scepticism about Moyn's companion thesis that the idea of human rights was born in the late 1970s…and is conceptually *sui generis* with respect to the natural rights tradition."[19] This reading of Moyn on the concept of human rights would have him doing bad substance history rather than acknowledging his focus on scale and salience.[20]

If Tasioulas misconstrues Moyn's rationale for focusing on functions, Moyn surely goes too far in his critique of Tasioulas's attempt to de-functionalize the definition of human rights. Tasioulas rightly replies that Moyn has misunderstood his original aims in deploying a concept of human rights that is sufficiently abstract that it can accommodate multiple functions and plural foundations. Even if Moyn is right to claim that the move to abstraction is a move away from being directly relevant to contemporary issues,

---

[16]   Moyn in this volume, p. 76–7.

[17]   Moyn 2010, p. 1. In this, Koskenniemi was a direct influence on the book's framework. See Moyn 2010, p. 293 n. 3.

[18]   Moyn 2010, p. 7, italics added.   [19]   Tasioulas in this volume, pp. 91–2.

[20]   This misreading may also underlie Philip Alston's critique of what he calls Moyn's "big bang" theory, the "basic assumption" of which is that human rights emerged "almost out of nowhere in 1977" (Alston 2013, p. 2074).

Moyn is wrong to place so much emphasis on this. The move to abstraction, *taken by itself*, is not the move that is meant to make the theory relevant to contemporary practice. It is the subsequent flexibility made possible by that abstraction, to engage with an emerging and dynamic practice, and the fruits of that engagement, that is the true test of relevance. As Tasioulas concludes his commentary, it is "precisely by formulating a concept of human rights abstracted from institutional particularities that we best equip human rights thought to respond creatively and flexibly to the challenges confronting their fulfilment in the world today."[21] That Tasioulas should claim this in the end is not surprising, for when he argues that his more abstract concept of human rights is actually more flexible than functionalist approaches that bind the concept of human rights to contemporary functions or institutional arrangements, he has already taken the core of the functionalist challenge to heart. That is, he clearly acknowledges the importance of the contemporary functions of human rights by trying to make his account more flexible on this front than functionalist approaches are themselves. This is one of the central virtues of Tasioulas's approach: he shows how concern for contemporary roles and institutional arrangements—and so sensitivity to certain historical discontinuities—can also be accommodated by more orthodox philosophical approaches to human rights. When it comes to discussing the function of human rights, then, Tasioulas and Moyn are often talking past each other.

Salience History as Genealogy

Thus far, I have focused mainly on the relevance of substance and scale histories. But is salience history relevant to doing philosophy of human rights? One could simply argue that salience history has nothing to do with defining the concept of human rights, whether one takes an orthodox or functionalist approach to the philosophy of human rights. Although substance history can provide points of reference for orthodox and functionalist approaches, and scalar history provides an essential point of reference for functionalists, salience history would seem to have little to offer either endeavour. This may be correct. Nonetheless, I want to conclude with a few reflections on what to make of salience history in relation to philosophy. This will also allow me to highlight some further affinities between Moyn and Koskenniemi.

In his chapter here and in other work, Koskenniemi shares with Moyn the aim of doing critical history. But Koskenniemi also refers more specifically, in his conclusion, to the power of "genealogy." One could simply use this term to refer to the general idea of exploring something's origins, but Koskenniemi specifically notes how "genealogy makes that which happened seem not necessary at all, but the contingent results of struggle and choice," in addition to illustrating "the processes whereby people attain

---

[21] Tasioulas in this volume, p. 101. I maintain a similar point in my own work on human rights. Although I defend Habermas's general approach to human rights, I argue against his juridical model in favour of a more flexible approach that does not bind the concept of human rights to particular legal institutions. See Flynn 2014, ch. 5.

certain identities and preferences."[22] In making this point, he invokes two of the classic moves of genealogy as a critical mode of doing philosophy.

First, there is the historicizing move, the force of which depends on whether revealing the contingent conditions of emergence affects the meaning or value of some concept, value, or practice thought to be universal. Second, there is the challenge to the identity of the readers—the ones for whom the value is valuable—that is generated by putting their self-understanding in historical perspective.[23] So Nietzsche famously raised the question of the "origin of morality" as a way of posing the question of the "*value* of morality," challenging his readers by historicizing their self-conceptions as modern moral agents.[24]

One way in which Koskenniemi and Moyn attempt to achieve their critical aims is through the power of genealogy in this sense. Both draw attention to how particular conceptions of rights enabled people to commit themselves to certain political projects or, more fundamentally, how contingent historical processes simultaneously produced such people and such commitments. Koskenniemi highlights, for instance, the ways in which the scholastic concept of *dominium*, conceived in terms of individual ownership of one's identity, was used to "justify the new social roles that sixteenth-century Spaniards were adopting in a commercially and militarily expanding Empire."[25] More generally, Brett rightly characterizes the challenge Koskenniemi poses in terms of his linking the history of rights to the history of the selves who see themselves as "having" rights. This is a genealogical mode of critique insofar as it aims to historicize, as a product of conflict, contingency, and politics, an identity that many simply take for granted.[26]

Something similar is going on with Moyn's salience history, which is not a history of ideas in the traditional sense of telling us the story of where our ideas came from. It is more like genealogy in the sense of telling us the story of where people like us, committed to certain ideas in specific ways, came from. The opening page of *The Last Utopia* contains this line: "Over the course of the 1970s, the moral world of Westerners shifted, opening a space for the sort of utopianism that coalesced in an international human rights movement that had never existed before."[27] The story of that shift is not primarily a story about the definition of a concept or even the origins of a concept, but about how the terrain of idealism and activism shifted in ways that led many to express their aspirations for a better world in the language of human rights. It is telling that Moyn begins the Epilogue of his most recent collection of essays with this claim: "to know

---

[22] Koskenniemi in this volume, p. 56.   [23] See Saar 2008, p. 302.

[24] Nietzsche 1998, Preface, §5, p. 4.   [25] Koskenniemi in this volume, p. 56.

[26] I would argue that the genealogical challenge Koskenniemi raises is not intended to be entirely subversive in a Nietzschean way, but more of a problematizing genealogy. Here I have in mind a distinction between three modes of genealogy—subversive, vindicatory, or problematizing—as developed in Koopman 2013. Koskenniemi himself continues to stress the need for a utopian, context-transcending aspect to critical legal theory in Koskenniemi 2013, p. 216. Likewise, I do not think Moyn should be read as trying to entirely subvert commitment to human rights, though some have read him this way. See Benhabib 2013 and Moyn 2013. For an attempt at a vindicatory genealogy of human rights, see Joas 2013.

[27] Moyn 2010, p. 1.

what to make of human rights in the future, the first step is to understand what they have made us."[28] This posits genealogy as a key step in the process of critically reflecting on the significance of human rights today.

Of course, philosophers of human rights who focus primarily on defining the concept and content of human rights may not see any use at all for salience history carried out in a genealogical mode. But I think we should view normative justification and genealogy as two types of critical tool, each of which provides a different way of understanding and evaluating our commitments. We can directly evaluate our commitments by considering whether the reasons underlying them can withstand critical scrutiny. But we can also consider how particular kinds of commitment were made possible or encouraged by specific historical and political circumstances and what that says about us or how that might inform our understanding about where we want to go from here. More pointedly, Moyn and Koskenniemi challenge philosophers to consider what *kinds of theorizing* have been made possible or encouraged by changing historical and political contexts, and how important taking that historical perspective is for fostering critical distance on our own theoretical activity.

In conclusion, I want to propose two topics raised by salience history that might profit from more interaction between philosophers and historians. First, one strength of salience history is that it brings out the affective dimension of commitment to human rights. Hunt's main argument is that changing habits of feeling in the eighteenth century enabled the kind of empathy across difference that provided the affective basis for the commitment to equal rights. Moyn, along with others' work on the "breakthrough" moment of human rights in the 1970s, can be read alongside recent work on the explosion of humanitarian sentiment during this period in trying to better understand the development of various ways of expressing concern for the suffering of distant strangers in the latter half of the twentieth century.[29] It would surely be fruitful to integrate work by historians on the ways in which moral sentiments like compassion and indignation have been effectively mobilized, revealing both their promise and their peril, with that of philosophers on the nature and value of moral and political emotions.[30]

Second, another strength of salience history is that it homes in on real movements and struggles for rights. But this approach needs to be extended. As important as it is to situate the rise of the Western human rights movement within a better historical understanding of the emergence of various forms of global concern, this is not the only context for thinking about their salience. For one thing, it tends to view human rights primarily from the perspective of mobilizing for the rights *of others*. What about the perspective of those struggling for their own rights? In his contribution to this volume, Jeremy Waldron contrasts the "human bearer approach," according to which human

---

[28] Moyn 2014, p. 136.

[29] See, for instance, Heerten 2015. Historically informed social science is important here too. See Fassin and Rechtman 2009 and Fassin 2012.

[30] On the latter, see, for instance, Nussbaum's focus on compassion in Nussbaum 2013.

rights are those rights held by all humans in virtue of their humanity, with the "human concern approach," according to which human rights are those rights whose violation is properly the concern of all human beings.[31] Moyn and others have contributed to the history of the shift corresponding to the rise of the concern approach. But a certain kind of salience history might also help us better understand the human bearer approach, in terms of the history of struggles to achieve the standing associated with being a rights-bearer and debates over what such standing entails, both in domestic and international legal orders. Waldron rightly maintains that the concern and bearer approaches need not be incompatible. Perhaps enhancing our historical understanding of both, including continuities and discontinuities between them, could enhance our philosophical deliberations about both. And with shared understandings of distinctions like bearer versus concern, or substance, scale, and salience, perhaps philosophers and historians could engage in a fruitful conversation that might even be relevant to realizing human rights in the real world.

References

Alston, Philip (2013), "Does the Past Matter? On the Origins of Human Rights," *Harvard Law Review*, Vol. 126, No. 7, pp. 2043–81.

Beitz, Charles (2009), *The Idea of Human Rights* (Oxford University Press).

Benhabib, Seyla (2013), "Moving beyond False Binarisms," *Qui Parle: Critical Humanities and Social Science* Vol. 22, No. 1, pp. 81–93.

Fassin, Didier (2012), *Humanitarian Reason: A Moral History of the Present* (University of California Press).

Fassin, Didier, and Richard Rechtman (2009), *The Empire of Trauma: An Inquiry into the Condition of Victimhood* (Princeton University Press).

Flynn, Jeffrey (2012), "Human Rights in History and Contemporary Practice: Source Materials for Philosophy," in *Philosophical Dimensions of Human Rights* (Springer), ed. Claudio Corradetti.

Flynn, Jeffrey (2014), *Reframing the Intercultural Dialogue on Human Rights: A Philosophical Approach* (Routledge).

Heerten, Lasse (2015), "'A' as in Auschwitz, 'B' as in Biafra," in *Humanitarian Photography: A History* (Cambridge University Press), ed. Heide Fehrenbach & Davide Rodogno.

Hunt, Lynn (2007), *Inventing Human Rights: A History* (W. W. Norton).

Joas, Hans (2013), *The Sacredness of the Person: A New Genealogy of Human Rights* (Georgetown University Press).

Koopman, Colin (2013), *Genealogy as Critique* (Indiana University Press).

Koskenniemi, Martti (2013), "Histories of International Law: Significance and Problems for a Critical View," *Temple International & Comparative Law Journal* Vol. 27, pp. 215–40.

Moyn, Samuel (2010), *The Last Utopia: Human Rights in History* (Harvard University Press).

Moyn, Samuel (2012), "Substance, Scale, and Salience: The Recent Historiography of Human Rights," *Annual Review of Law and Social Science* Vol. 8, pp. 123–40.

---

[31] Waldron in this volume.

Moyn, Samuel (2013), "The Continuing Perplexities of Human Rights," *Qui Parle: Critical Humanities and Social Science* Vol. 22, No. 1, pp. 95–115.

Moyn, Samuel (2014), *Human Rights and the Uses of History* (Verso).

Nietzsche, Friedrich (1998), *On the Genealogy of Morality*, ed. and trans. M. Clark and A. Swenson (Hackett).

Nussbaum, Martha (2013), *Political Emotions: Why Love Matters for Justice* (Harvard University Press).

Saar, Martin (2008), "Understanding Genealogy: History, Power, and the Self," *Journal of the Philosophy of History* 2, pp. 295–314.

Tasioulas, John (2012), "Towards a Philosophy of Human Rights," *Current Legal Problems* Vol. 65, No. 1, pp. 1–30.

PART II

The Orthodox–Political Debate

3

Human Rights
A Critique of the Raz/Rawls Approach

Jeremy Waldron

I

What does the term "human" mean in human rights? The most familiar answer is that human rights are rights all humans have by virtue of their humanity (their being human). They are rights that humans have whatever society they live in, however they are governed, and whatever stage of economic development their society happens to be at. Unlike legal rights and constitutional rights, they are not supposed to differ from country to country, depending contingently on positive laws and constitutions. They are rights that belong to human beings as such.

I say this is the most familiar understanding, but it is certainly not free of difficulty. Indeed, it is often thought that the category of human rights, so defined, may be empty. For consider three points.

(i) Humans evolved as a species hundreds of thousands of years ago. For most of that time, it hardly makes sense to think of human beings as right-holders; certainly they didn't think of themselves in those terms and they didn't have governments they could hold rights against. The conditions and circumstances of their lives have varied enormously over that period. Even 10,000 years ago, if humans might be said to have had any rights, they would be quite different in character from the rights humans are now thought to have. Of course rights-claims are normative, not descriptive. We are not talking about how Cro-Magnon man was actually treated by his peers and rulers (if he had any). We are not even talking about Cro-Magnon man's thoughts about his rights; human rights are rights that humans have, not that humans think they have. Still, many will say that the attribution to Cro-Magnon man of the rights that we take to be human rights today makes no sense. The circumstances of *his* human being and of *his* human life are so different from the circumstances of ours, that the very idea of trying to establish a normative list of rights we share with him is misconceived.

(ii) Something similar confronts us even today when we try to concoct such a normative list in the face of the variety of ways there are of being human. Humans live now in so many ways and they are so disparately situated in such different social, cultural, economic, political, and legal environments; they lead such different kinds of life; and even the idea of leading a life (in our sense of personal autonomy) has such different patterns of application across the human family—that the task of specifying a common set of rights on the basis that "one size fits all" seems insuperable.

(iii) Even if we confine our attention to one class of modern human societies— say, advanced Western democracies—we still run into difficulties with the idea of a single set of rights that it makes sense to attribute to all the human inhabitants of such societies. For the human inhabitants of these societies include not just able-bodied adults exercising what we think of as distinctively human powers, but tiny babies, humans who suffer from profound disabilities, the very old and the demented who have lost any capacity for reasoned thought or the ability to understand the living of their lives. It may seem that if we are looking for rights that can be attributed literally to all human beings (in a given class of modern societies), the rights in question won't be much more expansive than rights that may plausibly be attributed to all animals. Either that, or we have to venture into metaphysical or religious conceptions that relate rights to the momentous importance of human beings as such—their importance to God, for example—irrespective of their particular capacities. But there is something unsatisfactory about hitching the idea of human rights to any particular theology when it is supposed to be a theory for the whole world.

These difficulties have prompted some political philosophers to wonder whether the term "human" in human rights might not be doing some quite different work. One possibility is that "human" refers not to the right-bearers (and their humanity) but to the class of people for whom violations of these rights are properly a matter of concern. Certain rights, it may be thought, are or ought to be matters of general concern among humans: As Kant put it, "a violation of right on one part of the earth is felt in all."[1] The idea is that there is a class of rights such that no human should be indifferent to the violation of any right in that class. These rights are called "human rights" because humans are called on to support them.

So we have two quite different approaches to the term "human" in "human rights." On the first type, which I shall call "the human bearer approach," rights are designated as human rights because they are rights held by all humans in virtue of their humanity. On the second type, which I shall call "the human concern approach," rights are designated as human rights because they are rights whose violation is the proper concern of

---

[1] Kant 1996, p. 330 (8: 360).

all humans. Of course there is no reason why these two approaches cannot be combined. I will indicate something along these lines at the end of the chapter. But there are versions of the human concern view that define a starker alternative.

For some adherents of the human concern approach, the relevant human concern about rights is not just a matter of disapproving of their violation. It is *practical polit-ical* concern: these theorists say that human rights are rights whose violation appro-priately elicits *action* on the part of the rest of humanity against the violators. More specifically, views of this kind focus on the response of governments and international agencies. The idea is that we can define a class of rights such that no government, nor any other human agency or organization, is ever required or permitted to say that the violation of one of these rights is none of their business, no matter where it occurs. Action by a government or an agency in support of such rights is never precluded by the fact that the government or agency is an outsider to the relation between the right-bearer whose rights are being violated and the government that is responsible for violating them. So we define a right, R, as a human right when we think that, not only that any human person, but also any outside government or agency has authority to respond to and maybe interfere with another government's violation of R. If we don't think of R in this way, then—on the view we are considering—we are saying in effect that R is not a human right.

In this chapter, I am going to consider several variants of this approach. Though it offers an interesting basis for defining rights as human rights, I shall show that it too faces certain difficulties. These difficulties may cast doubt on the wisdom of abandoning the human bearer approach. Certainly the difficulties I will identify with the human concern approach are worth examining. If the human concern approach is to be made viable, these difficulties have to be confronted and I think better answers have to be supplied than the proponents of this approach have so far been able to come up with. The best-known proponents of the human concern approach are John Rawls, in *The Law of Peoples*,[2] and Joseph Raz in an article entitled "Human Rights without Foundations."[3] Others have followed their lead to a certain extent: I shall also talk a little about the work of Charles Beitz in his book *The Idea of Human Rights*.[4]

None of them uses the label "human concern." Rawls, I think, would be happy with the term "political" to describe his approach to human rights, to differentiate it from the more philosophical approaches that focus on the character of humanity as such. Raz labels what I have called the human bearer view "the traditional doctrine" and he follows Rawls in developing what he thinks of as a "political conception" in contrast to that, though he distances himself from John Rawls's own account in a number of respects. Beitz talks of a "practical," as opposed to a "naturalistic" (human nature) conception of human rights. The terminology doesn't matter: my "human

---

[2] Rawls 1999a, p. 80.   [3] Raz 2010a, at pp. 336–7.   [4] Beitz 2009, pp. 96ff.

concern approach" is no doubt the most abstract label; it is supposed to highlight the fundamental character of the contrast.[5]

Labels aside, I will try not to neglect the differences between these theorists. But I want to begin with a quite crude version of the human concern approach. It is not a version that any scholar will own up to holding. (As we shall see, Rawls's formulation comes close.) But it is a version that is in circulation informally, and it is often used in conversation among theorists to display what is distinctive about the human concern approach. For me, the advantage of the view I am about to outline is that it highlights in rough and visible form some of the difficulties that, I think, almost all versions of the human concern approach are likely to face.[6] In Section II, I shall sketch out the view I want to consider. In Section III, I identify various difficulties that it gives rise to. Then, in Section IV, I shall consider a more cautious version of the human concern approach to see if it can avoid the difficulties I have identified.

II

According to the version of the human concern approach that I have in mind, a right is properly described as a human right if the appropriate response to its violation by an otherwise sovereign state is *armed interference* by an outside state or an international organization aimed at remedying or punishing or preventing the continuance of the sovereign state's violation. I shall call this "the armed intervention version of the human concern approach" (the Armed Intervention View, for short).

I am not attributing the Armed Intervention View to anyone in particular. John Rawls comes close to it in *The Law of Peoples*. He says that one role of human rights is to specify limits to state sovereignty and to the principle of non-intervention associated with state sovereignty. "Their fulfilment is a necessary condition of a regime's legitimacy," and it is "also sufficient to exclude justified and forceful intervention by other peoples, say by economic sanctions or, in grave cases, by military force."[7] On Rawls's account, when certain rights are violated by the government of a state, that government loses any standing to complain about interventions by other governments aiming to vindicate the rights in question against the first government. That's Rawls's theory of the "human" in human rights, and (as I say) it is quite close to the Armed Intervention View, distinguished only by his willingness to contemplate measures, like economic sanctions, that fall just short of military intervention.

---

[5] One reason for the broader "human concern" label is to pick up an aspect of Joseph Raz's recent writing on the subject where he says—in Raz 2010b, at p. 41—that "[o]ne of the most important transformations brought about by the pursuit of human rights has been the empowerment of ordinary people, and the emergence of a powerful network of nongovernmental as well as treaty-based institutions pressurising states and corporations…in the name of individual rights."

[6] It is a bit like the strategy suggested by Socrates in *The Republic* (368d–e)—looking first at some large letters scrawled out on a rough surface to illuminate the detail of some fine print elsewhere.

[7] Rawls 1999a, p. 80.

Notice that the Armed Intervention View (and views like it) understands rights as human rights solely on the basis of the remedy appropriate for their violation. That in itself is not a problem. We do something like this as a matter of course when we distinguish legal rights from rights that are merely moral, and also in some countries when we distinguish constitutional rights from ordinary legal rights. The term "legal rights" directs us to remedies provided by courts; "constitutional rights" directs us to remedies that may include judicial review of legislation; and "human rights," on the approach we are considering, directs us to remedies provided by members of the international community. The remedy associated with a given right is always an important feature of the right: *ubi ius, ibi remedium.*[8]

Some may see it as a problem that the Armed Intervention View makes into a matter of definition what many think should be an open question. Surely, whether outside intervention is an appropriate response to a given set of violations is something for us to argue about. In some circumstances such a drastic remedy may be appropriate; in other circumstances it may be more sensible to look for remedies internal to the polity in question. Perhaps we should argue this through as a practical matter rather than distracting ourselves with the claim that something conceptual turns on the outcome of our deliberation about remedies. But I am reluctant to press this point, because the contrast here between analytic propositions and propositions that are open to substantive argument is not hard and fast. Joseph Raz has stipulated that it may not be plausible to regard either the human concern view or its traditional rival as an analytic proposition: he says "[t]here is not enough discipline underpinning the use of the term 'human rights' to make it a useful analytical tool."[9] On either side, we are arguing about how to approach the issue of the relation between human rights, distinctively human interests, and the actions of the international community. I don't think either side should be interested in making this or contesting it as a matter of definition.[10]

One advantage of the Armed Intervention View is that it connects up quite naturally to the idea that human rights are *important* rights. Joseph Raz has remarked that there is no guarantee that human rights are important if they are understood along the lines of the human bearer approach: "Neither being universal, that is rights that everyone has, nor being grounded in our humanity, guarantees that they are important."[11] He criticizes some recent attempts to define the importance that human rights are supposed to have on the basis of interests held by all humans; he thinks we should give up

---

[8] Cf. Dicey 1982, p. 118.   [9] Raz 2010a, at pp. 336–7.

[10] In any case, it is sometimes unclear whether a statement about the practical or political significance of the violation of human rights is intended as definitional of "human rights." Ronald Dworkin, in his unpublished paper "Human Rights and International Law" (<http://habermas-rawls.blogspot.com/2010/10/dworkin-on-human-rights-international.html>) countenanced the idea that respect for human rights was a necessary condition for the legitimacy of a regime. But he was reluctant to say that this was true as a matter of definition and, generally speaking, he was quite averse to settling matters such as these on a definitional basis.

[11] Raz 2010a, p. 323.

on that enterprise.[12] The alternative view, it seems, offers a better account of importance, or rather a better way of setting the threshold of importance that a right must have to be a human right. A right has to be important for its violation to be connected to the possible overriding of national sovereignty, since overriding sovereignty is a high-stakes matter (as far as the sovereign state in question is concerned, as far as the intervening state is concerned, and as far as the world community is concerned). Nothing could justify it unless it possessed a degree of importance capable of standing against the importance of sovereignty itself and the considerations that ordinarily inhibit (and ought to inhibit) humanitarian intervention. Indeed, as John Rawls emphasizes, this particular criterion of importance—or anything like it—will tend to isolate as "human rights" only a subset of the rights that are traditionally given that designation. He suggests that, of the Universal Declaration of Human Rights, only the right to life and the right not to be tortured are clear instances of human rights; Articles 4 (anti-slavery), 7 (non-discrimination), 9 (protection from arbitrary arrest), and 10–11 (due process) may or may not be in this category "pending issues of interpretation," while the remaining provisions, including the socioeconomic provisions count as "liberal aspirations" rather than human rights.[13] A page or so earlier, he offers an even more restricted list: "a special class of urgent rights, such as freedom from slavery and serfdom, liberty (but not equal liberty) of conscience, and security of ethnic groups from mass murder and genocide."[14] James Nickel has called this an ultraminimalist conception of human rights.[15] To those who defend an approach like this, it is supposed to be one of its virtues that it picks and chooses among the traditional menu of human rights with great discrimination.[16]

Of course even rights in the subset that Rawls identifies are often not supported by humanitarian intervention. It is notorious that humanitarian intervention does not always take place when it should: the Western powers' failure to act in Rwanda in 1994 is a good example. Intervention by one sovereign state in response to rights violations is still a relatively rare occurrence. Also, we cannot rule out the possibility that some nation or nations will intervene militarily in the sovereign affairs of another (in part citing human rights justifications) when such interference is inappropriate: the US-led invasion of Iraq in 2003 is an example of this. But the Intervention View defines rights as human rights on the basis of what the international community *ought* to do about them not on the basis of what the international community does do or is likely to do. It is a normative rather than a predictive approach to an understanding of human rights.

On the other hand, proponents of views of this kind often say they don't want their understanding of the "human" in human rights to be divorced too much from actual practice in international affairs. Raz says, for example, it is "observation of human rights practice" that shows that human rights are taken to be "rights which ... set limits

---

[12] Raz 2010a, pp. 323–7.   [13] Rawls 1999a, p. 80 n.
[14] Ibid., p. 79.   [15] Nickel 2007, p. 98.
[16] In this chapter I do not consider the various theories about the basis of the importance of certain rights that are produced by defenders of the approach I am considering. But of course any defender of the human concern approach must have such a theory.

to the sovereignty of states."[17] This does not necessarily make the view a predictive one; Raz's point seems to be that the appropriate normative proposition is one that we should infer from some of the normative talk that takes place in human rights practice. Something similar can be said about Charles Beitz's assertion that "[w]e inspect the practice of human rights because we are interested in the way participants in this practice understand the practical inferences to be drawn from assertions about human rights."[18] Again, this does not mean that we treat present practice as beyond criticism; however, it does seem to require that any criticism be immanent rather than advanced from a normative perspective that is not acknowledged within the practice.

There is the further question of what sort of normativity we are speaking of here. Is R a human right when intervention is morally *required* in response to a violation of R? Or is R a human right when intervention is *permitted* in response to a violation of R. I guess I can define the artificial position I'm setting up any way I like. But it is worth considering the sort of normativity that views of this sort have in mind. The normativity of Rawls's view seems to involve permission rather than obligation: what a violation of a human right does is to disable the principle of non-intervention; it removes a reason which would ordinarily make such intervention impermissible.[19] Raz, however, couches his view more affirmatively. He says he takes "human rights to be rights which set limits to the sovereignty of states, in that their actual or anticipated violation is a (defeasible) reason for taking action against the violator in the international arena."[20] And Beitz talks of "a pro tanto reason" to interfere.[21] This seems to imply that, in the absence of reasons to the contrary, non-intervention in response to a violation of one of these rights would be wrong. And maybe this accords with human rights practice, which talks these days of a "*responsibility* to protect" not just a right or permission to do so.[22] (I emphasize again that neither Beitz nor Raz nor even Rawls holds the Armed Intervention View in an unqualified form. My questions are partly about the shape of the views (of this kind) that they do hold in order to highlight choices that would have to be made about the formulation of the Armed Intervention View or anything like it.)

III

I turn now to some criticism and difficulties. Though I am going to discuss these as they affect the Armed Intervention View, grasping them is important I think for any variant of the human concern view that anticipates *some* form of official international action in response to human rights violations. In this section, I will consider both criticisms that relate specifically to the Armed Intervention View and criticisms that, having been evoked by that view, may seem to apply to any sort of interventionist

---

[17] Raz 2010a, p. 332.   [18] Beitz 2009, p. 105.   [19] Rawls 1999a, p. 37.
[20] Raz 2010a, p. 328.   [21] Beitz 2009, p. 109.
[22] 2005 *World Summit Outcome*, United Nations General Assembly, 60th session, §§ 138–9. See Evans 2006. See also *The Responsibility to Protect: Report of the International Commission on Intervention and State Sovereignty* (International Development and Research Center, 2001).

approach. Only in Section IV will I consider whether retreating to a more modest version enables the human concern view to avoid criticism along these lines.

(1) Intervention for reasons other than rights

Humanitarian intervention is a very special kind of remedy and it would not be surprising if it seemed appropriate for some otherwise important rights and not for others. I noted earlier Raz's observation that a view like his helps explain why being a human right is likely to mean being an important right.[23] But importance is not a one-dimensional idea. I think that Raz had in mind moral importance. But rights (and rights violations) may be important in other ways too: for instance, they may be important because of their geopolitical significance. Some rights violations such as ethnic cleansing have the potential to destabilize large regions of the world beyond the borders of the state that is guilty of the violations. Others, like the violation of the right not to be tortured, are morally awful, but do not necessarily have a regionally disruptive character. I am convinced that, on account of its distinctively disruptive character, ethnic cleansing is more likely to generate humanitarian intervention than torture is, because decisions about humanitarian intervention are seldom motivated just by attention to the moral importance of the rights that are being violated. They are motivated also (and often overwhelmingly) by potential ill-effects of violations on the interests of intervening states. No doubt this is as it should be: humanitarian intervention is rare anyway and it is never going to be motivated just by abstract altruism. I think a case can be made, not only that intervention won't happen in the absence of destabilizing effects, but that it probably shouldn't happen except when such effects threaten to accrue. But it seems odd to hold the "human" in "human rights" hostage to geopolitical factors in this way.

We should also bear in mind that there may be grounds for the appropriateness of humanitarian or other outside intervention which are hardly rights-based at all. Generalized and potentially contagious instability in a country may be a reason for intervention; so may failures of good governance such as rabid kleptocracy or a collapse of state institutions. We should not be seduced by the popularity of rights-discourse into thinking that the theory of rights exhausts the normative theory of good governance, including those aspects of good governance in a country that are properly of great interest to its neighbours. Of course, one might undertake to jam any ground for intervention into a rights-formula, and perhaps that can always be done; but it may not be an illuminating characterization.

Defenders of the Armed Intervention View may be unconcerned that there are also non-right-based grounds for humanitarian intervention. But it makes the theory look rather ad hoc, if it turns out not only that many of the rights we thought were human rights are not human rights on this account, but also that right-based grounds for humanitarian intervention are usually entangled with other grounds. If it turns out

---

[23] See text accompanying note 11.

that—whatever the rhetoric—the most likely predictor of humanitarian intervention is the destabilizing character of conditions in the target country (whether rights violations are involved or not), then we may seem to be concocting a conception of human rights that really doesn't map on to significant features of political reality. And that may sacrifice important advantages—such as fidelity to practice—that the human concern approach claims for itself.

One final point in this regard. As I have noted, it is important to some of the defenders of the human concern approach that they maintain a realistic connection to the realities of human rights practice. But it is equally important, given the shape of the view, that they maintain a realistic connection to the realities of humanitarian intervention. And the fact is that the most fervent defenders of the "Responsibility to Protect," do not envisage human rights violations as such (under any definition of "human") as the appropriate trigger for intervention. The famous article 139 of the 2005 World Summit Outcome document refers to intervention "to protect populations from genocide, war crimes, ethnic cleansing, and crimes against humanity."[24] These phenomena certainly comprise human rights violations; but the violations trigger intervention only when they take place en masse, and the reason for deeming intervention appropriate *only* when they take place en masse seems to have more to do with the destabilizing impact of massive population-wide abuses rather than the fact that rights as such are at stake.

(2) Contingency and circumstances

Even when rights are in play, judgements about the appropriateness of humanitarian intervention will involve an awful lot of other factors as well. We know that such interventions are in fact very rare in spite of the huge number of what most of us regard as human rights violations in the world. They are rare because their costs are very high, they are often politically unpopular, their chances of success are low, they tend to get out of hand and require the intervening power to take much more responsibility for governance in the target country than it may have intended to, and they often do more harm than good—indeed they sometimes end up just empowering another echelon of rights violators. Any country contemplating humanitarian intervention has to consider all this. It has to make a global calculation ranging over an enormous number of factors. These factors may vary dramatically in their bearing on particular cases. My question is: Are all these factors to be taken into account in using the appropriateness of intervention as the criterion for designating a given right, R, as a human right? If so, should we expect the designation of R as a human right to vary in the same sort of way?

There are two possibilities. (A) Maybe the designation of a right as a human right reflects an all-things-considered judgement about the appropriateness of humanitarian intervention in a particular case. Or (B) maybe it reflects only a *pro tanto* view about the appropriateness of intervention based on the character of the right itself.

---

[24] See note 22.

Now, version (A) of the Armed Intervention View is going to be a little counter-intuitive. As things stand, we identify rights as human rights using general descriptions—like the right to free speech or the right not to be tortured. We don't usually refer to them as the right to free-speech-in-Kosovo or the right not-to-be-tortured-in-Iraq. But if the designation of a right as human depends on the all-things-considered appropriateness of humanitarian intervention to vindicate that right, then a given right will turn out to be a human right in some settings but not in others, depending on how the array of considerations relevant to the justification of humanitarian intervention plays out in each setting. The right not to be tortured might prove to be a human right in Iraq in 2003, but what we usually identify as the same right might prove not to be a human right in Syria in 2013 because (at the date of writing: May 2013) the practicalities argue against humanitarian intervention against the atrocities of the Assad regime.

As I say, it seems counter-intuitive to have the predicate "human" apply to rights in this contingent and situational fashion. And this is not just because we are accustomed to thinking of rights as human (or not) on a more settled basis, but because of the kinds of factors that are likely to enter into the relevant judgement. For example, I have heard it said that the technological possibility of drone warfare makes humanitarian intervention easier, which means it may be appropriate, all things considered, for a wider range of cases. Do we really want to draw from this the inference that certain rights become human rights which were not so in the days before drones? Or, I have heard it said that humanitarian intervention is less appropriate when it is likely to encounter substantial and prolonged opposition than when the offending government whose territory is to be invaded is weak. (This is not just a predictive matter; the justification for military intervention always depends in part on the prospects of success and the likelihood of there being a protracted war as a result.) Do we really want to have to infer from this that rights are more likely to count as human rights when they are asserted against a weak government than when they are asserted against a government capable of offering protracted military resistance to humanitarian intervention?[25]

Is there a way for proponents of the Armed Intervention View to avoid committing themselves to apply the term "human" to certain rights on the basis of all-things-considered situational judgements about humanitarian intervention?

(B) Well, maybe the Armed Intervention View can be focused on the right itself as one factor among others that enters into the political calculation about the appropriateness of humanitarian intervention. The idea might be that we designate R as a human right by virtue of the fact that it is appropriate for the prevention or punishment of violations of R to enter positively into calculations about humanitarian intervention. Even if other factors such as cost or danger or the potential loss of blood and treasure outweigh the advantages of stopping or punishing violations of R, still it may make sense to say that

---

[25] Some defenders of the human concern view seem comfortable with results along these lines. Joseph Raz, for example, acknowledges that "one immediate consequence of the [human concern] conception is that human rights need not be universal or foundational," although I am not sure he envisages their being quite as contingent as this. See Raz 2010a, p. 332.

R (understood now in a general way) is a constant and serious factor in connection with possible humanitarian intervention and that this is why it is put into this special class of rights (viz., human rights). This would mean that rights do not go into and out of the "human rights" classification on the basis of contingent considerations about political cost, available technology, etc. Raz seems to have this in mind when he says we should understand human rights as "rights which set limits to the sovereignty of states, in that their actual or anticipated violation is a (*defeasible*) reason for taking action against the violator in the international arena."[26]

On this variant, it will be a further question whether a right has to have a certain minimum weight in relation to the other kinds of factors that are relevant to decisions about humanitarian interventions before it can be counted as a human right. If the answer were "no," then almost every right would be a human right, since there might theoretically be a case for intervention on its behalf whenever the countervailing costs were zero. Perhaps we should set a threshold that reflects at least the nominal significance of infringing another country's sovereignty, so that R would count as a human right only if its importance were sufficient to override at least the normal considerations that weigh in favour of sovereignty. It would have to have enough importance to outweigh what we might think of as the standard costs of infringing the sovereignty of a violator-state. I worry, however, that if we go down this road, it may be very hard to disentangle these standing costs from the pragmatic considerations that argue against humanitarian intervention in particular cases. The two are not independent; the relation between them would seem to be at least inductive. This is because the importance of sovereignty is not a wholly abstract matter; it is itself partly pragmatic and itself partly responsive to world conditions, the state of the system of states, the likely costs of interventionist warfare in current circumstances, and so on.

(3) Selling short the individualism of rights

One of the most disturbing features of the Armed Intervention View is the way it sells short the individualism of human rights. I don't mean individualism as opposed to collectivism; I mean the individualism that insists on the trumping importance of each single individual's right, irrespective of what is happening to other individuals.

Consider a particular right which almost everyone accepts should be regarded as a human right—the right not to be tortured (R_t). Almost all of us accept that when some individual is tortured a human right is violated. But I don't think anybody believes that when *just one person* is tortured, humanitarian intervention by outside forces is justified to stop that torture or punish it. There is never any question of humanitarian intervention to vindicate just one person's right. Does this mean that the general impression that R_t is a human right is a mistake, according to the Armed Intervention View?

---

[26] Raz 2010a, p. 328 (my emphasis). Again I hasten to add that Raz's own view is much more subtle than the Armed Intervention View we are considering; nevertheless his view does seem to be (B)-shaped rather than (A)-shaped.

No doubt if hundreds or thousands of people were being tortured, there might be some prospect of humanitarian intervention. So, a predicate that applies to rights in virtue of the appropriateness of humanitarian intervention makes most sense as applied to large clusters of individual rights: we might say a cluster of rights violations (comprising hundreds or thousands of instances) counts as a cluster of *human* rights violations if it tends to justify humanitarian intervention. But the logic will be awkward: we will not be able to infer from the fact that R is a member of a cluster of human rights that are being violated that R itself is a human right, considered as something held by just one individual. Or if we do infer that, we will run the risk of implying something quite misleading, namely that the violation of R in and of itself tends to justify humanitarian intervention, which is seldom if ever the case.

I think this is a very serious difficulty. The great advantage of rights-talk has always been the way it forces us to focus on individual wrongs, wrongs done to individual persons, rather than evaluating societies on the basis of the way they treat their members in aggregate terms. True, the Armed Intervention View does not adopt the worst sort of aggregation—trading off the wrongness of rights violations against the possible advantages that may accrue to a society therefrom. It is aggregative only in the sense that it sums up a large number of rights violations as a precondition for designating them as violations of *human* rights. But the "human" now follows the particular remedy, which is a response to the aggregate, rather than the right which was always understood to be individual.

Those who adopt something like the view I am considering show some awareness that there is a problem here. We don't find Rawls, for example, saying that rights count as human rights when individual violations of them generate a certain level of international concern. Instead he says of human rights that "[a]ny *systematic* violation of these rights is a serious matter and troubling to the society of peoples as a whole," and that the normal principle of non-intervention does not apply to states where "serious violations of human rights are *endemic*."[27] Similarly Charles Beitz states what he calls his "practical conception" in these terms: "Whatever else is true of human rights, they are supposed to be matters of international concern in the sense that a society's failure to respect its people's rights *on a sufficiently large scale* may provide a reason for outside agents to do something."[28] And theorists of humanitarian intervention say something similar: J. L. Holzgrefe defines humanitarian intervention as "the threat or use of force across borders by a state . . . aimed at preventing or ending *widespread* and grave violations of the fundamental human rights of individuals."[29] Individuals are mentioned here, but only widespread violation of their rights triggers the case for intervention.

One can imagine a number of possible responses from proponents of the Armed Intervention View.

---

[27] Rawls 1999b, p. 32 (my emphasis) and Rawls 1999a, p. 38 (my emphasis).
[28] Beitz 2009, pp. 105–6 (my emphasis).   [29] Holzgrefe 2003, p. 18 (my emphasis).

(i) Verbally, the position can be stated and the problem finessed with a formula that attributes human-ness to individual rights in virtue of something that is true of the violation of many such rights. It is easy enough to say of any individual right that it has the property φ where φ= {*if enough rights of this kind are violated, then outside interference will be justified*}. Then one can say one says that R is a human right just in case R has the property φ. Thus one person's right not to be tortured counts as a human right just because outside interference is justified when many such rights are violated. It works formally, but the manoeuvre feels tricky and it smells disreputable. Property φ is concocted just to make this theory work.

(ii) Alternatively, the Armed Intervention View may embrace the individualism of human rights, and talk about the violation of one individual right tending *pro tanto* to justify intervention—even though the *pro tanto* case won't ever add up to an actual case for intervention until it is accompanied by hundreds or thousands of other instances. At least that restores the normativity of individual rights. But it is a minimal normativity, and we have lost sight of any sense that individual rights as such have momentous trumping importance. We saw earlier that Raz prided himself on offering an account that illuminated the importance of rights.[30] But now that seems to be an illusion, at least as far as the Armed Intervention View is concerned: it illuminates only the importance of large clusters of rights violations.

(iii) A third possible response is to cram all the individualism into the concept of a right as such. Certainly various normative conclusions do follow from the fact that it is *a right* that is being violated.[31] The idea of a right is that someone has a duty just in virtue of some individual's (the right-bearer's) individual interest, and the right-bearer should have an (individual) remedy whenever there has been a failure of this duty (as owed to him or her).[32] The idea is that all this is securely in place when we start our analysis of the "human" in "human rights." So, it might be said, whether a right is human or not does not affect the point that each individual right has normative consequences considered in and of itself. All the idea of a human right adds is that there is, *in addition*, the prospect of an intervention-remedy for large clusters of violations. I think this response is fine as far as it goes. It envisages human rights having individual-level remedies qua rights (qua legal rights, for example, or qua constitutional rights). But it does leave the strange impression of a gap between the way rights work within a state (individual importance, individual remedies) and the way they work from the outside in human rights practice. And that leads to my final criticism.

---

[30] See text accompanying note 11.

[31] In a recent article, Raz makes it quite clear that his account of the "human" in human rights presupposes his more general account of rights as such (Raz 2010b).

[32] See Raz 1986, pp. 165ff.

(4) The implied discontinuity between human rights and constitutional rights

John Rawls observed in *The Law of Peoples* that a view like his distinguishes sharply between human rights, on the one hand, and "constitutional rights or the rights of liberal democratic citizenship, or... other kinds of rights that belong to certain kinds of political institutions," on the other.[33] Rights in the second category operate within a society to provide assurances for ordinary individuals, by legally constraining the actions of government and by providing a facility for making legal claims in a country's courts when those rights are infringed. These functions are quite different from those that are indicated by the use of "human" to designate certain rights (on the human concern approach). In the case of the Armed Intervention View, the difference is stark: it is the difference between an ordinary law suit for (say) judicial review of executive action—which many of us regard as business as usual inside a legal system—and the intrusion of military force into a country from the outside, which always has to be regarded as extraordinary.

I said before that Raz regards it as an important feature of views of this kind that they pay attention to the practice of human rights. He says "[t]he task of a theory of human rights is... to establish the essential features which contemporary human rights practice attributes to the rights it acknowledges to be human rights."[34] But human rights practice does not acknowledge a gap of this kind between human rights and constitutional rights. Often there is a continuity between the rights designated as human rights and the rights designated as constitutional rights: in the United Kingdom, for example, rights that are used internally as the basis of judicial review of governmental action are set out in something called "the *Human* Rights Act."[35] And as Gerald Neuman has argued, human rights documents and national rights documents (whether the latter are labelled "human rights" or not) are often seen as complementary positivizations of basically the same idea. Fundamental rights are positivized as constitutional rights so that ordinary individuals are given certain assurances within their society about fundamental aspects of their freedom and well-being, by virtue of the fact that governments are legally and *internally* required to act in a constrained manner; they are positivized to provide a legal basis for individual claims to respond to violations of these assurances.[36] And the point of positivizing basically the same rights in international human rights charters, such as the ICCPR, is to guide and direct the provision of these internal assurances and internal remedies in each country's constitutional law. It is remarkable that, for all his professed interest in human rights practice, Raz fails to acknowledge that the primary instruction contained in the ICCPR so far as sovereign states are concerned is to direct them "to take the necessary steps, in accordance with [their] constitutional processes... to adopt such laws or other measures as

---

[33] Rawls 1999a, p. 79.   [34] Raz 2010a, p. 326.
[35] See also the argument of Griffin 2010, at p. 344.   [36] Neuman 2003, p. 1863.

may be necessary to give effect to the rights recognized in the present Covenant" and "[t]o ensure that any person whose rights or freedoms as herein recognized are violated shall have an effective remedy."[37]

On the Armed Intervention View this continuity and this orientation is lost completely. The positivization of fundamental rights in human rights law is supposed to convey quite a different message—that the outside world will respond in various non-legalistic ways to violations of rights. It is supposed to draw attention to the limits of state sovereignty and warn sovereigns of the prospect of outside intervention. Never mind that there is nothing in the great international charters that can remotely be interpreted in that way. The Armed Intervention View insists on this discontinuity despite the fact that nothing like it exists in practice.[38]

IV

No one, I said, will own to holding the Armed Intervention View. Even Rawls, who came very close to it in *The Law of Peoples*, pulled back from regarding the appropriateness of armed intervention as the sole criterion for designating a right as a human right. He spoke of military force "in grave cases," but he also envisaged a continuum of "justified and forceful" pressure including diplomatic activity and economic sanctions.[39]

Other versions of the human concern view are more moderate. Joseph Raz says that he is following Rawls when he takes "human rights to be rights which set limits to the sovereignty of states, in that their actual or anticipated violation is a (defeasible) reason for *taking action* against the violator in the international arena."[40] But "taking action" can include many things short of military intervention. He says that "human rights set some limits to sovereignty, but do not necessarily constitute reasons for all measures, however severe, against violators." For instance, Razian intervention might include forceful criticism or public denunciation of one government by another. However, the logic of the position is the same as the Armed Intervention View. The criticism or denunciation must be such that it would ordinarily be ruled out by respect for the target state's sovereignty:

[W]hen states act within their sovereignty they can, even when acting wrongly, rebuff interference, invoking their sovereignty. Crudely speaking, they can say to outsiders: whether or not I (the state) am guilty of wrongful action is none of your business. Sovereignty... protects states from external interference. Violation of human rights disables this response, which is available to states regarding other misdeeds.[41]

---

[37] ICCPR, Art. 2.

[38] Maybe Rawls's misconception of the relation between human rights and constitutional rights (in *The Law of Peoples*, p. 38) is understandable, given the common (though mistaken) view in the United States that the two are really quite separate enterprises. See also Waldron 2012, pp. 120–3. There is less excuse for this misconception among British and European scholars.

[39] Rawls 1999a, p. 80.   [40] Raz 2010a, p. 328.   [41] Raz 2010a, p. 328.

How do these more nuanced versions of the human concern approach fare in addressing the various difficulties that we saw afflicting the Armed Intervention View?

(1) Intervention for reasons other than rights

The first difficulty I mentioned—that external military action is often as much a response to regional instability as to the violation of any particular class of rights— really applies only to the Armed Intervention View. But there may be versions of it that attach to any expressions of official action by the international community. If we pull back to a less extreme version of the human concern approach, involving for example just external criticism, we may not find it easy either to associate the human concern approach with any particular delimited class of basic rights or to identify a form of outside response that reacts distinctively to rights violations as opposed to other kinds of concern.

Obviously the weaker the form of reaction we are considering, the larger the range of rights that may be the basis of the reactive concern. One can imagine a scrupulous outsider responding critically to everything it hears about the violation of rights— any rights—in a given country. The position we are considering assumes that the sovereignty of the target country insulates it from some such criticisms and entitles it to say to the outside world, "Even if this is a rights violation, it is none of your business." But though this may once have been a credible thing for a rights violator to say—and although some countries, notably China, act as though it is still a credible thing for them to say when rights violations in that country come to outside attention (I am going to call this the Chinese position)—many people no longer accept this, even in principle, as an incident of sovereignty. This is certainly true of many people in the human rights community, some of whom are prepared to throw overboard the whole idea of sovereignty and not just this particular aspect of it.[42] Raz, Rawls, and others may criticize them for doing this; but the more they do that, the less benefit they can claim from their respect for the actual practice of the human rights community. The trouble is that the versions of the human concern view that we are now exploring seem to need the Chinese position to be available, otherwise they will not be able to associate the criterion of legitimate outside criticism with the specification of a proper subset of rights. But that need arises only out of the exigencies of the theoretical position they have adopted, not out of any sensitive attention to how sovereignty-claims are actually treated in practice.

On the other hand, even if we accept something like the Chinese position about sovereignty and criticism, it may legitimately be displaced by considerations other than the violation of rights. States may regard it as permissible to officially criticize other states for egregious failures of good government or to draw attention to institutional collapse in the target state, even when rights are not at stake or even when the primary basis of such criticism has nothing to do with individual rights. The human

---

[42] See e.g. Henkin 1999, p. 1.

concern view is always in danger of conceiving international reaction or expressions of international concern with its own preoccupation with the subject of human rights. But if it is going to live up to its claim of a realistic engagement with practice, it is going to have to come to terms with the fact that rights are not always (and should not always be) uppermost in the mind of governments when they respond to the failings of other governments.

(2) Contingency and circumstances

The second difficulty was about the situational contingency of judgements about humanitarian intervention, and the relationship between rights violations, as one factor in the judgement about whether to intervene, and all the other factors that go into that judgement. On the more moderate view we are considering, judging the appropriateness of outside criticism may not involve as many other factors or other factors as serious as those involved in judgements about military action. But there will still be other factors involved besides rights, and they will vary from situation to situation. Two countries, X and Y, violate right R and a third country has to consider whether to express official concern. If the third country is a trading partner of country X (but not of country Y) or if it is engaged in delicate negotiations on some other issue with country X, it may be both unlikely (and inappropriate, when the economic or diplomatic stakes are high enough) for it to express the same level of public concern about the same violation in X and Y. Are we to infer that the violated right is a human right in country Y but not in country X? Few will be willing to embrace this conclusion, given the delicacy and contingency of the judgements that are likely to be involved.

So presumably defenders of the human concern will want to adopt (B), the second of the options I set out when I considered this as an objection to the Armed Intervention View:[43] we say that a right is a human right if its being violated is a reason for an outside government or agency to publicly criticize the government that violates it, even though the appropriateness of such criticism may appropriately be offset by factors other than the sovereignty of the target government. Once again, though, it will be very difficult to specify the threshold that puts a right into this class and very difficult to distinguish the factors that inform the setting of this threshold from other pragmatic, political, economic, and diplomatic considerations that enter into the particular calculation. I said earlier that doctrines of sovereignty are partly based on pragmatic considerations. That may be especially true when we are talking about sovereignty as a barrier to public criticism, as opposed to sovereignty as a barrier to military intervention: to the extent that it is acknowledged at all, sovereignty as a barrier to public criticism is partly a matter of inter-state civility and *politesse* and that will be difficult to separate from judgements about the particular state of relations between the two countries in question. The problem is exacerbated too by the fact that official criticism of one state by another can cover a range of actions from the withdrawal of ambassadors

---

[43] See text accompanying note 26.

through various kinds of official démarche all the way down to the raising of some issue in private consultations between the ministers of the respective countries.

(3) Selling short the individualism of rights

The third objection I set out—the objection that humanitarian intervention is usually a response to a large aggregate of rights violations and not to rights violations one by one—may seem to pose slightly less of a difficulty for the more moderate view. Although governments mostly criticize other governments for clusters of rights violations, sometimes the criticism focuses on some individual violation considered on its own. True, these are usually celebrity cases involving people like Aung San Suu Kyi, where the predicament of one well-known figure, often a dissident leader, has caught the attention of the world. The importance of such cases should not be denied. Equally, however, we should not lose sight of the ordinary egalitarianism of rights. Rights are supposed to be attributed to individual men, women, and children, even when they are among the lowest ranks of their society, the humblest, the most ordinary, the least glamorous and well known of their countrymen. Of course outside governments can only respond with official criticism to cases that they know about, and the cases they respond to will always be a skewed sample of the violations that actually take place. The worry is that this seems central to and characteristic of the approach we are considering, whereas a good theory of human rights should surely make it seem marginal and problematic.

(4) The implied discontinuity between human rights and constitutional rights

We saw that, on the Armed Intervention View, there was a considerable gap between the idea of human rights and the idea of constitutional rights. The account we are now considering offers the prospect of closing that gap. It is easier to envisage a dovetailing of external and internal remedies when the external remedy is official criticism than when it is military intervention. Formal denunciation from the outside often seems appropriate when internal remedies are exhausted. It works in something approaching an appellate mode. This is true of regional decision-making such as decisions of the European Court of Human Rights and global determinations by, for example, the UN Human Rights Committee. And it may even be true, in some fashion, of diplomatic démarches and denunciations. There are formal mechanisms in the ICCPR which enable state parties to complain of each other's rights violations;[44] and with regard to some regional instruments, like the ECHR, states have competence to commence law suits in respect of another state's violations of human rights.[45] Also, it is not just criticism and denunciation. As Beitz has emphasized, outside states and international institutions also offer affirmative assistance to countries that are finding it difficult to

---

[44] ICCPR Articles 41–4; but not widely used. See also Waldron 2012, pp. 129–30.
[45] E.g. *Republic of Ireland v. United Kingdom*, ECtHR, Series A, No. 25, 18 January 1978.

satisfy human rights standards or that lack the capacity to satisfy them, as things stand.[46] Outside assistance can be oriented both to the internal establishment of the appropriate standards and to the mechanisms that will enable them to be more effectively upheld.

But then there is a question about whether the closing of the gap between internal and external responses puts paid to the idea that external responsiveness defines human rights in a distinctive way. For it is not at all clear that this version of the human concern approach will enable us to pare down the traditional list of human rights to anything like a Rawlsian minimum.[47] Particularly when we emphasize Beitz's point about outside concern taking the form of affirmative assistance as well as criticism or denunciation, we find that virtually all the rights on the traditional list of human rights satisfy this criterion, including the socioeconomic rights that the Rawlsian version disdained. Indeed, the process may be too accommodating. On some accounts, outside criticism of the informal sort may be an appropriate response to the violation of *any* right within a community, even ordinary legal rights like rights of property. Outside criticism of countries for failing to adhere to the Rule of Law is commonplace. We may criticize a government for failing to observe the rule of law which may include failures to uphold the rights defined by its own constitution or statutes. Does this make those rights human rights? Surely not.

That point aside, a more general problem with the present approach is that it may not after all offer a genuine alternative to the traditional way of defining human rights. Often when governments are criticized for violating rights, the criticisms come because the rights in question are understood to be human rights; they are not human rights because the criticism is thought appropriate. Agencies like the UN Human Rights Committee bring to their consideration of the behaviour of sovereign states a list of rights already regarded as human, with which they then examine the record of each government. And the same seems to be true of individual countries' criticisms of one another. On the website of the US Department of State, for example, we are told that

annual Country Reports on Human Rights Practices—the Human Rights Reports—cover internationally recognized individual, civil, political, and worker rights, as set forth in the Universal Declaration of Human Rights and other international agreements. The U.S. Department of State submits reports on all countries receiving assistance and all United Nations member states to the U.S. Congress in accordance with the Foreign Assistance Act of 1961 and the Trade Act of 1974.[48]

So an account of the sort we are considering is in some difficulty, at least if it is supposed to be a reflection of practice. It does not follow that the traditional human bearer account is correct (as an account of the way "human" is used in human rights practice).

---

[46] Beitz 2009, p. 109.

[47] Rawls 1999a, p. 80 n. See text accompanying notes 13–16 in the current chapter.

[48] <http://www.state.gov/j/drl/rls/hrrpt/> (last visited May 17, 2013).

But it would not be surprising if it were. For the international agencies, and the State Department and its equivalents in other countries, do use a common set of criteria to judge and comment from the outside on individual governments' records with regard to individual rights. They talk and act as if one size fits all—as if the rights-based evaluation of human arrangements, anywhere and in any contemporary circumstances, were a matter of applying a list of rights that any human is understood to have.

V

I believe that the points developed in Sections III and IV should lead us to reject the proposal to define a right as a *human* right simply in virtue of the type of external response that is appropriate when it is violated. Proposals of this kind face too many difficulties: they associate the "human" in human rights with conditions—like local destabilization and diplomatic and military effectiveness—that don't really relate to the delineation of an important *subset of rights*; and they unhelpfully sideline a number of conditions that are quite properly thought crucial to the modern human rights idea—such as the individualism of rights and the continuity between human rights and the rights recognized and remedies provided under the auspices of national law.

The criticisms I have made are not knock-down refutations of the position I have been considering. As already noted, there is no question of one side being right and the other wrong in virtue of the logic of the phrase "human rights." Joseph Raz is right: analytically, the whole field is a bit of a mess.[49] The question is not: What does the "human" in "human rights" *really mean*? The question is: what is the more convenient and illuminating use to make of the term in this context? Some of the ideas picked out by the human concern view are surely important, and it may well be that we should seek eclectically some sort of combination of approaches, with a set of rights being identified as human rights both (a) in terms of their being rooted in distinctively human interests, on the one hand, and (b) in terms of their violation being an appropriate subject of global human concern.[50] The best features of the human concern view can be incorporated helpfully into such an eclectic account, without the distraction, the omissions, or the selling short of various accepted features of human rights discourse that a criterion based exclusively on the appropriateness of intervention would seem to involve.

---

[49] Raz 2010a, pp. 336–7: "There is not enough discipline underpinning the use of the term 'human rights' to make it a useful analytical tool."

[50] As far as I can tell, Raz's essay "Human Rights in the Emerging World Order" offers an account of this type; I think it represents a sort of retreat from his position in "Human Rights without Foundations," not least in his suggestion that "[t]he importance of human rights...is in affirming the worth of all human beings" (Raz 2010b, p. 41) and in his willingness to look for a sense of universality—e.g., in his claim that human rights may be "synchronically universal" (ibid.)—that responds to some of the questions raised concerning the human bearer view.

Finally, none of these arguments I have put forward against interventionist versions of the human concern view make the difficulties with the human bearer view that we began with go away. (i) We still have to grapple with the problematic universality of a human bearer view (even if it is used, as I have just suggested, in an eclectic position). We still have to address the issue about attributing rights to Cro-Magnon man. (ii) We still have to consider the problem of universality in relation to different ways of being human and of leading a human life even in the modern world. (iii) And we still have to figure what to say about the issues of profound disability that seem to make some members of the human family unlikely bearers of the rights we usually regard as human rights. These problems continue to affect the human bearer approach, whatever we say about intervention and human concern.

My view is that these three issues just need to be grappled with. There is not going to be any easy disposal of them; but it is incumbent on those of us who remain committed to the human bearer approach to do the hard work that grappling with them will involve and to dispel the impression that is sometimes conveyed by our opponents that it is well known upfront that all such work is hopeless. Some progress is being made already; much remains to be done. What I don't find helpful, however, is the implicit suggestion in the versions of the human concern approach that I have been considering, that grappling with these problems is neither necessary nor worthwhile in thinking about why we call certain rights *human* rights.

References

Beitz, Charles, *The Idea of Human Rights* (Oxford: Oxford University Press, 2009).

Dicey, Albert Venn, *Introduction to the Study of the Law of the Constitution* (Indianapolis: Liberty Fund, 1982).

Evans, Gareth, "From Humanitarian Intervention to the Responsibility to Protect," *Wisconsin International Law Journal*, Vol. 24, No. 3 (2006), pp. 101–20.

Griffin, James, "Human Rights and the Autonomy of International Law," in Besson and Tasioulas (eds), *The Philosophy of International Law* (Oxford: Oxford University Press, 2010), pp. 339–57.

Henkin, Louis, "That 'S' Word: Sovereignty, and Globalization, and Human Rights, Et Cetera," *Fordham Law Review*, Vol. 68, No. 1 (1999), pp. 1–14.

Holzgrefe, J. L., "The Humanitarian Intervention Debate," in J. L. Holzgrefe and Robert Keohane (eds), *Humanitarian Intervention: Ethical, Legal and Political Dilemmas* (Cambridge: Cambridge University Press, 2003).

Kant, Immanuel, "Toward Perpetual Peace," in Immanuel Kant, *Practical Philosophy*, ed. Mary Gregor (Cambridge: Cambridge University Press, 1996).

Neuman, Gerald, "Human Rights and Constitutional Rights: Harmony and Dissonance," *Stanford Law Review*, Vol. 55, No. 5 (2003), pp. 1863–900.

Nickel, James, *Making Sense of Human Rights*, 2nd edn (Oxford: Blackwell Publishing, 2007).

Rawls, John, *The Law of Peoples* (Cambridge, Mass.: Harvard University Press, 1999a).

Rawls, John, "The Law of Peoples," in The Belgrade Circle (ed.), *The Politics of Human Rights* (London, Verso, 1999b).

Raz, Joseph, *The Morality of Freedom* (Oxford: Oxford University Press, 1986).

Raz, Joseph, "Human Rights without Foundations," in Samantha Besson and John Tasioulas (eds), *The Philosophy of International Law* (Oxford: Oxford University Press, 2010a), 321–39.

Raz, Joseph, "Human Rights in the Emerging World Order," *Transnational Legal Theory*, Vol. 1, No. 3 (2010b), pp. 371–92.

Waldron, Jeremy, *Partly Laws Common to all Mankind: Foreign Law in American Courts* (New Haven: Yale University Press, 2012).

3.1

On Waldron's Critique of Raz on Human Rights

Joseph Raz

Had Prof. Waldron's chapter not been entitled '...a critique of the Raz...approach' I would not have known that it is. Much of what he says seems sensible, and some of it supports, mostly indirectly, my views. To give just two examples: Prof. Waldron correctly observes that (a) the importance of a right (and I should add: of a right violation—the two should not be confused) is typically determined by a variety of considerations, stemming from different sources of moral concern (he declines to consider any view about the importance of rights—fn. 16), and that (b) the case for taking action to protect a right or to remedy its violation is affected by matters other than the importance of the right or its violation. I am making these observations in my own way, and they differ in detail, but are consonant in the main with Waldron's remarks in Section III (1). He also observes (in the same section) that acts that are sometimes undertaken, or should be undertaken, to protect a right or to remedy its violation, can also be taken for other reasons (e.g. I may owe you money to make good wrongful damage to your property, or because it is the price of a property that I am buying from you). What is puzzling is why Waldron should think that any of this constitutes a difficulty for any view about human rights, or indeed for any view about rights, including the crazy 'armed intervention view', which by his own account no one holds, and to which he dedicates the larger part of his chapter.

Another helpful observation is offered by Waldron when considering the implications of the view (held by me) that human rights are individual rights that set limits to sovereignty, and that means that their violation can be a reason for action that would otherwise be blocked by sovereignty. He wonders how it can be that any right is not a human right: would not the violation of any right count in favour of overriding sovereignty at least in some circumstances? He writes: 'Perhaps we should set a threshold that reflects at least the nominal significance of infringing another country's sovereignty, so that R would count as a human right only if its importance were sufficient to override at least the normal considerations that weigh in favour of sovereignty. It would have to have enough importance to outweigh what we might think of as the standard costs of infringing the sovereignty of a violator-state. I worry, however, that if we go down this road, it may be very hard to disentangle these standing costs from the pragmatic considerations that argue against humanitarian intervention in particular cases' (III (2)). And he proceeds to outline one difficulty. But the easy life is not a recognized aspiration of political theory, and the fact that theoretical distinctions are sometimes difficult to apply has always been recognized. Note that Waldron's worries do not show that the distinction will be difficult to apply to all rights.

There are other sensible observations in the chapter that would be of interest to students of human rights. I mentioned the two above because they help with my puzzle: why does Prof. Waldron think that his chapter raises serious objections to my views about human rights?[1] Part of the explanation is: because he thinks that the two observations present serious objections to a type of human rights theory that he takes my view to belong with. If they are, as I suggested, observations about some elementary features of any remotely plausible account of rights then obviously they are no objection to any theory of human rights, unless it is inconsistent with human rights being rights. I do not think that mine is so inconsistent, and there is no sign that Waldron thinks so either.

The more fundamental explanation of the puzzle is that Prof. Waldron gives me a compliment that I do not deserve. His comments on my views are generally expressed in a moderate and thoughtful way throughout. But the undeserved compliment is that he takes me to be engaged in the same enterprise that he himself undertakes, and which he thinks is the right enterprise to pursue. He writes: 'The question is not: What does the "human" in "human rights" really mean? The question is: what is the more convenient and illuminating use to make of the term in this context?' (Section V). That is not what I was doing when writing on human rights, nor is it a question that I would recommend to others. I will briefly explain what I was trying to do, and how Waldron's misunderstanding of my aim undermines the relevance of his comments on my work.

Here is the task: there is what I call 'a human rights practice', comprising ratifying conventions, enacting legislation, and adopting other measures in the name of human rights; litigating, implementing, applying, and so on, those so-called human rights measures; advocating observance and incorporation into law of other so-called human rights, and more. The practice has gathered ever-increasing pace since the end of the Second World War, so that the role and significance of the rights identified in common discourse as 'human rights' in the political life of many countries and in international

---

[1] For the reader less interested than I am in my own views the chapter poses a more serious puzzle: Why does Prof. Waldron think that his article supports his conclusion that the best theory of human rights would understand them as rights that belong to all human beings in virtue of their humanity alone? He starts with listing some of the many arguments that have been levelled against that view, and concludes that since the view is right we had better work hard to answer the criticism. That conclusion is based on the fact that he identified, as he thinks, some serious difficulties with a few alternative views, difficulties that he correctly observed are not conclusive objections to these alternatives. There seems to be something missing in this argument.

relations have been transformed. As a result, those engaged with the practice have mostly failed to notice the way it can no longer be normatively justified in terms of the ideas that dominated thought about human rights before the War, and that (the need for different justifications), it seems to me, turns out to be not a bad thing. The absence of a coherent body of doctrine underpinning the practice makes little difference to those involved in it. In the hands of pressure groups, NGOs, litigators, advocacy groups, and others, its evolution has the characteristics of the evolution of the common law. One thing leads to another, governed by analogical reasoning, and some vague sense of moral orientation. The theoretical-normative task is to establish what normative considerations govern the practice, namely what considerations determine which of the measures included in it should be there, and which should not, how it should be developed, how it should be applied, and the like.

You may say that the correct doctrine of human rights, i.e. of the rights that all people have in virtue of their humanity, sets out the considerations that normatively govern the practice. That is the view of several, perhaps most, of the theorists who are engaged with it. I think that their theories are mistaken. In my 'Human Rights without Foundations' that Waldron discusses I criticized two contemporary accounts, and some of my arguments apply to other accounts as well. More generally the disagreement has to do with a broader understanding of the place of rights in the normative domain. I am with those who think that for the most part rights play a local, derivative role, that their existence depends on values and their applications to particular historic circumstances. That rights are historically conditioned, is consistent with the possibility that there are rights held by all human beings in virtue of their humanity, but the historical dependence of rights implies that most of the rights that are taken to be human rights are not of that kind. More importantly, the truth or falsity of philosophical human rights theories (including all those that I criticize) is irrelevant to the general doctrine about the right way to assess the human rights practice. Even true human rights theories should not be the standards by which to judge human rights practice.

Imagine that various legal provisions giving legal effect to certain rights because they are thought, by the authorities adopting those legal provisions, to be human rights are not in fact human rights. Various theorists conclude that because those rights are not human rights, their legal implementation should be repealed. I argued that this is a non sequitur. Suppose, for example, that there is no human right to adequate housing.[2] It does not follow that the legal right to adequate housing should be repealed. It may be a very good right based on considerations that have nothing to do with human rights. Approving of that right in that way means approving of it for reasons different from those that led to its adoption, reasons different from those of many of its defenders.

---

[2] It is legally recognized as a human right in article 11 (1) of the Covenant for Economic, Social and Cultural Rights. See for its meaning Committee on Economic, Social and Cultural Rights, General Comment 4, The right to adequate housing (Sixth session, 1991), UN Doc. E/1992/23, annex III at 114 (1991).

Of course, if it is in fact a right held by all people in virtue of their humanity alone, if cave dwellers in the Stone Age had a right to decent housing that is fine, and the legal implementation of the right can be defended on those grounds as well. My point is merely that if it is not a human right it may still be a right that it is justified to implement or protect by legal means. Similarly, it does not follow from the fact that a right is a human right that it should be protected by legal means. There are numerous legal norms defended today on grounds different from those that led to their adoption. For example, possibly the law against murder was adopted because it was believed that human life was made sacred by God. That should not lead atheists to call for the repeal of the law. It is justified even though its originators, and many of its current defenders, are mistaken (according to the atheists) about the reasons that justify it.

For the task that I explained, the important point is not to expose the mistakes about traditionally conceived human rights, even though they should be exposed. The important point is to understand that the task is to strive to find a comprehensive normative perspective from which to evaluate human rights practice as it is and as it should become. The task is mishandled when it is assumed that it consists in developing the correct account of human rights (meaning the rights held by all people in virtue of their humanity) and judging the practice by it.

I then suggested that the distinctive element of human rights practice is its role in international relations. Why so? Not because the rights with which human rights practice concerned itself do not apply between individuals or between individuals and corporations, or individuals and the state. They do. It was partly because it seemed that international relations were more radically changed by the practice than the moral understanding of relations among individuals or between them and corporations or the states they are found in. But there is another more theoretical reason for focusing on international relations: In international relations those rights were orphans in a way that they were not in domestic relations. Our understanding of the standards we apply to interpersonal conduct has evolved, and hopefully deepened, but it has not been indebted to ideas about human rights. Similarly constitutional rights emerged through improved understanding of the role and function and limits of government, again largely independently of ideas about human rights. If you believe in some traditional human rights ideas you may think that they support all those standards and rights. But loss of confidence in human rights ideas is unlikely to shake your confidence in those standards and rights, nor should it. There are other familiar ways of arguing for them. Not so with the rights emerging in international law and applying to the relations between individuals and states and other international bodies.

Many people would say that the same rights apply for the same reasons in international relations. The problem is that in international law they were unenforceable because they used to be blocked by the doctrine of state sovereignty, as it emerged with the European settlement in the wake of the religious wars, usually dated to the Peace of Westphalia. There are various highly important features to the development of human rights practice beyond the gradual growing respect for important moral standards.

One of them is that human rights practice is one, though not the only, development exerting pressure towards giving individuals independent standing in international law. But in both practice and theory the more radical development the practice of human rights heralded was the erosion of the previously accepted ideas about the scope of sovereignty. Again, this development is not alone. The growth of functional organizations (like the WTO) and of regional ones (like the EU) with powers to develop new law binding states independently of their consent also erodes sovereignty. But that does not diminish the importance of the role of human rights practice in the process, given that it is a feature of international human rights that their violation within a state is a reason for actors, states and others, outside that state to intervene, including in ways that would have been previously considered an inappropriate interference in the internal affairs of the offending state.

As Waldron remarked, the limits of sovereignty are disputed, and in fact have always been. My suggestion about the normative principles that govern human rights practice was that their understanding goes hand in hand with a better understanding of the normative grounds of state sovereignty, and its scope. I have myself contributed little, perhaps nothing, to that task. My contribution was to point to the interrelations between the two and to the need for a theory that will deal with both issues together.

I will not detain you with other matters dealt with in my writing about the human rights practice. Waldron rightly identifies my claims about the relations between human rights (or rather the human rights practice) and sovereignty as central to my account, and that is what I was trying to clarify here. It follows that, contrary to his understanding of my article, I do not take fidelity to the practice to be a desirable feature of an account of human rights, let alone as relevant to deciding what sense it is desirable to attribute to 'human' in that context. Rather, human rights practice is what the theoretical account is about.[3] To repeat what I suggested as the task for a normative theory of the practice: it is to establish the criteria by which the practice should be judged. They may lead to the conclusion that it should be abandoned, not a conclusion that can be justified by fidelity to the practice. Of course, the task assumes that possibly different practices are governed by different normative criteria, and that presupposes that we can distinguish between them, that they have characteristics that possibly subject them to different normative criteria. And my reflections on the practice of international human rights were partly aimed at identifying features of the practice that affect the considerations by which it should be judged.

---

[3] For example, he misunderstands my point in the following observation: 'proponents of views of this kind often say they don't want their understanding of the "human" in human rights to be divorced too much from actual practice in international affairs. Raz says, for example, it is "observation of human rights practice" that shows that human rights are taken to be "rights which ... set limits to the sovereignty of states." ' As a result he thinks that the logic of my view requires fidelity to some other aspects of practice. But it requires no fidelity to any aspect of international practice. It just has to be about that practice, and in my view that means that it should be about a practice which takes certain rights to set limits to sovereignty.

Prof. Waldron both regards my views as a version of what he calls the human concern approach and claims that I made some observations about the human concern approach (e.g. fn. 22, but it is not the only place). The second is simply mistaken. I never said anything about it, if only for the simple reason that I did not know of such an approach. My own approach is not an instance of that approach, for reasons that should by now be clear. In a way, it is not about human rights at all. It is about the practice of human rights. In my mind this is partly because theories of human rights are faulty, and in any case largely irrelevant to a normative assessment of the very important practice of human rights. Of course, we would expect the normative theory of human rights practice to determine which normative considerations are relevant to the evaluation of the practice and its desirable development, and if there are rights that all humans have in virtue of their humanity alone they will feature in the theory, along with other normative considerations. But they are not in themselves such a theory.

Therefore, the task I undertook assumed from the beginning the possibility, and according to my understanding of morality, the inevitability, that the normative standards that govern human rights practice are not the ones that many human rights theorists share, and indeed my understanding diverges from the official rhetoric that pervades human rights practice, and the views of a number of its activists. As a result it is, on the one hand, no criticism of my view that it does not conform to aspects of the common ideology and rhetoric surrounding the practice, parts of which are suffused with the thought that the practice deals with the rights of all humans held in virtue of being human. But, on the other hand, some may think that that speaks against my understanding of my task. And if I thought that there is some hope for theories of rights of that kind, in a way that would qualify them to govern the practice of human rights, I would have agreed.

4

Assigning Functions to Human Rights

Methodological Issues in Human Rights Theory

James W. Nickel

To explain what human rights are, theorists often identify distinctive functions or uses that human rights serve. Disagreements about such uses have been prominent in recent debates between "political" and "orthodox" conceptions of human rights.[1] Political conceptions of human rights assign one or more constitutive *political* functions to human rights, frequently at the international level. Orthodox conceptions are more closely associated with the natural rights tradition, hold that the justification of at least some political and legal rights is based on analogous moral rights, reject limiting the roles of human rights to the political realm, and are not adverse to philosophical theories of human rights that rely on controversial values such as autonomy or equality. Still, orthodox views also sometimes assign essential or central functions to human rights such as protecting human dignity or autonomy.

My goal in this chapter is to not to resolve or transcend the debate between orthodox and political conceptions of human rights. It is rather to call attention to some of its deficiencies, particularly in the assignment of roles to rights, and to suggest some ways in which the debate could be improved. Section I develops a framework for understanding functional claims and using them in philosophical explanations of norms. Sections II and III discuss the roles that James Griffin, John Rawls, and Charles Beitz ascribe to human rights and their grounds for doing so. A fuller discussion of authors in this area would cover Joseph Raz, John Tasioulas, and others as well but I do not undertake that here.[2] The concluding Section IV suggests several ways to improve the debate.

---

[1] Orthodox views are also sometimes labelled "naturalistic" and "humanist." For participants in the debate and discussions of it, see the references at the end of this chapter.

[2] Raz 2010, Tasioulas 2013.

I. Framework

A. *Assigning functions and roles*

Explanations of a concept, practice, or artefact often identify uses or functions. For example, someone who wants to know what a saw is might be told that it is a hard thin movable blade with teeth whose function is cutting hard materials. Functional (or partially functional) explanations are indispensable for some concepts, including "saw." Often, however, it is an open question whether a functional explanation or definition is necessary. And what seems to be a functional *definition* may just be a useful illustration of a concept's typical uses.

A function (role, use, job) is a type of doing, work, or production. An ascription of a role or function will typically start by naming or describing a kind of thing such as a bell, a saw, a number, a comma, or a right. Let's call this the *subject*. Such an ascription continues by naming or describing some type of action or doing that the subject does or is used to perform. A minimal functional statement would consist of a noun, a verb, and an object as in "Saws cut hard materials." The subject of a statement about the functions of saws may be saws in a completely generic and unqualified sense—all saws anywhere and anytime from any point of view. Or the focus may be narrower. Functional claims often presuppose or impose temporal restrictions, limit spheres of use, and adopt distinctive points of view. .

Statements about functions often explain the process or mechanism whereby the subject produces an output or product. Lots of things other than saws are used for cutting hard materials (e.g. axes, shears, torches, laser beams) so we need to add some description of *how* saws work such as "by moving a hard blade that has teeth." Let's say that this is the *mechanism or process* whereby saws cut. Complex systems have many subordinate mechanisms and processes that work together to produce the end product(s). In describing the mechanisms that serve some function it will often be necessary to explain their composition by referring to metals, chemicals, or electrical currents—things that are not functionally defined. Because of this, many functional definitions will be only partially functional.

Things with functions typically have users: persons or agencies who monitor and control their operation and perform needed maintenance and updating. Most human concepts, artefacts, and norms are not fully automated systems that start, stop, run, and repair themselves on their own. If a lot of people use a thing over an extended period their uses are likely to be various. Think of all the uses other than providing transportation that automobiles have. These include portable office; place to eat, drink, and sleep; waiting room; storage closet; and murder weapon. And even if some uses are the standard or typical uses, users frequently invent new ones. Botox (botulinum toxin) was first used as a poison, then as a way of treating crossed eyes, and still later as a way of easing wrinkles and treating migraines. Polyfunctionalism is normal, unless we are describing functions in extremely abstract terms.

Things having multiple functions and uses are common. The human hand is polyfunctional; it has a multitude of functions in many spheres of life. If we listed verbs that involve doing things with one's hand(s), the list would be extremely long. There is not much prospect, consequently, of assigning a single *distinctive* function to human hands—even at an abstract level. Grasping-and-ungrasping is an important function, but there are uses of hands such as poking, rubbing, and pointing that do not involve grabbing and letting go. Sometimes polyfunctional things can be assigned very abstract functions, as when we say that the function of the hand is manipulating the physical environment. But such abstract functions are often unilluminating and too inclusive—as this example illustrates. Thousands of things manipulate the physical environment.

Monofunctionalism gets its attraction from the goal of explanatory simplicity. Elegant explanations do not look like laundry lists. Abstract monofunctionalism might allow one to achieve both. It could be very inclusive while preserving the appearance of monofunctionalism. But if you make the account too broad and abstract it will be unilluminating (like "computing" as an account of what computers do or "manipulating" as what hands do).

If one concept falls entirely under a broader concept (if its extension is a proper subset of the broader concept's extension) then whatever functions the broader concept has will be inherited by the narrower concept. For example, the generic function of saws will be inherited by bandsaws and chainsaws. This kind of inheritance may be important for human rights since they seem to fall under broader concepts such as norm, directive, and right.

There are several criteria a theorist can appeal to in defending a claim about something's function or role. The most obvious one is facts about a thing's use. An empirical study of what saws are used for would reveal, I expect, that the most frequent use is cutting hard materials. Their uses by magicians and musicians are much less common. A second criterion, available for things with designers and authors, is the designer's or author's intention. For legal norms, this is the criterion of legislative intent. A third criterion is importance or centrality. Even if surgeries for cosmetic purposes came to outnumber those for repairing injuries and treating diseases, we might still think of the latter as the main role of surgery because of its greater importance in medical practice. Finally, a particular function might be prescribed for a practice because it gives greater coherence and clearer boundaries to that practice. These four criteria for assigning functions can yield different and competing results.

B. *Ascribing functions to human rights*

Two theorists, both writing about human rights, can nevertheless attend to different aspects or areas of operation. Let's call this a difference in *focus*. The result may be that apparently conflicting claims fail to contradict each other. Choice of focus covers the temporal frame, the *spheres* in which human rights operate, the level of abstraction at which a theorist proceeds, and special points of view. Different choices can result in differing accounts of what human rights are, their main users, and their end products. As we will see, human rights theorists vary in the temporal frame they assign to human rights.

Further, theorists can choose among spheres such as interpersonal relations, national politics and law, and international politics and law. Choice of these may be influenced by disciplinary affiliations. One way in which accounts of the functions of human rights can differ is that some theorists may be attempting to explain the generic function(s) of human rights in all the spheres in which they operate while other theorists may have the more limited goal of describing the functions of human rights within a particular sphere such as international relations. Finally, a theorist can take some special point of view such as effective enforcement and sketch the nature of human rights from that perspective.

We have seen that if a feature or function falls under a broader category then it inherits the features and functions of that category. Human rights are *norms*. This suggests that a function of human rights is *directing* the behaviour of persons and institutions. Further, at least most human rights are rights, with whatever features and functions that implies.[3] Rights direct behaviour in distinctive ways. They focus on the benefit to the rightholder(s) and often give rightholders control over whether they wish to accept the benefit.

For a system of human rights to work in directing behaviour there need to be mechanisms and processes that promulgate rights, teach people about them, monitor compliance with them, and sanction violators. The forms these activities take will vary by spheres such as law and morality, just as the forms sawing takes vary from carpentry to metalworking to surgery. This shaping of behaviour by human rights is likely to produce adventitious results such as providing work (paid or not) for lawyers and human rights activists.

Human rights have features that make them unlikely to have a single function unless it is very abstract. The most important of these features is that human rights on all accounts are plural, they come in *lists* of specific rights. Each specific right has its own distinctive content and function(s). The subjects covered by standard lists of constitutional and human rights include security, fairness in criminal law, fundamental freedoms, political participation, equality before the law and nondiscrimination, education, meeting basic needs in areas such as nutrition, health, and economic opportunities, and protecting minorities against extermination, enslavement, subordination, and discrimination. Distilling down to one the roles of these diverse norms is very difficult—and even if achieved may come at the cost of such great abstraction as to make proposed generic functions unilluminating or far too inclusive.

One attraction of identifying generic functions for human rights is that if we know the general function(s) of human rights then we'll know how to evaluate and justify

---

[3] On these see Wenar 2013.

them. For example, if the functioning of international human rights generally involves sanctions or intervention then the justification of those rights will have to justify those measures.

II. Griffin: Assigning Roles within Orthodoxy

One might think that political theories of human rights ascribe functions to them and that orthodox theories decline to do this. James Griffin, in his valuable recent book, *On Human Rights*, is a clear counterexample to this way of drawing the distinction since he holds an orthodox view but assigns a generic function to human rights.[4] Griffin's theory is teleological in that it justifies human rights in terms of their service to a very important value—operative human autonomy or "normative agency." For such a justification to succeed human rights must succeed in serving this function. Griffin explicitly says that the role of human rights "is to protect normative agency, both our capacity for it and our exercise of it."[5] We will see, however, that this is more a prescription than a description.

Griffin ascribes five characteristics to human rights. First, he thinks of human rights as *moral* rights, not as purely political or legal notions. They are successors to the Enlightenment notion of a natural right (but without its theological content) and involve "ethical judgments as applied to the assessments of our societies."[6] Griffin recognizes that universal human rights are often used in criticizing or holding accountable other countries for their treatment of their residents, but he does not take this international political role as definitional. Second, Griffin thinks of human rights as *claim rights*—as rights having correlative duties held by persons and institutions.[7] Third, a human right is a right that "we have simply in virtue of being human"— although this is qualified to apply only to humans who have normative agency or autonomy.[8] Human rights cannot be special rights resulting from promises or personal connections and must be (nearly) universal rights—ones possessed by every human who enjoys at least a threshold level of normative agency or personhood.[9] Fourth, human rights have a minimalist character that keeps them from being too demanding and that distinguishes them from mere ideals.[10] Griffin is critical of long lists of putative human rights and of what he calls the "ballooning of the content" of specific rights.[11] Finally, human rights are resistant to trade-offs, but not entirely. They are not absolute but they are very strong.[12]

The functions of human rights vary in accordance with their level of abstraction, but according to Griffin the distinctive, generic function of human rights is (or, if it isn't already, should be) protecting—directly or indirectly—the development, maintenance, and exercise of normative agency or autonomy. Having normative agency is having a

---

[4] Griffin 2008.   [5] Ibid., p. 183.   [6] Ibid., pp. 1–2.
[7] Ibid., pp. 48, 51.   [8] Ibid., pp. 2, 277.   [9] Ibid., pp. 48, 50.
[10] Ibid., p. 53.   [11] Ibid., p. 220.   [12] Ibid., pp. 76, 36.

functioning capacity to choose, evaluate, deliberate, plan, revise, pursue, and follow one's own course in life.[13] Griffin uses several names to describe this capacity—normative agency, autonomy, autonomous agency, status as a self-determiner, and personhood.

Griffin thinks that tying all human rights to this capacity will give them clearer limits and greater unity and coherence. When a particular generic function is used to demarcate human rights it will follow that every valid human rights claim will be a claim to have that role performed, directly or indirectly, in each particular case. Other functions may be performed as well, but they are adventitious. For example, if the protections of autonomy, freedom, and welfare that human rights provide also serve to promote equality, that may be welcomed, but it is not in Griffin's view part of what human rights are *for*.

Griffin says that normative agency is one ground of human rights but that "practicalities" are another.[14] Accordingly, we can describe the generic function that he assigns to human rights as protecting normative agency while taking account of practicalities.

Griffin's view is orthodox because he holds that (1) today's human rights practice is a development of the natural rights tradition going back many centuries; (2) the role of human rights is not exclusively political (limited to legal and political rights at the international level); and (3) philosophical accounts of human rights need not avoid perfectionism or reliance on comprehensive philosophical views that are controversial.

Griffin is primarily a moral philosopher rather than a political or legal philosopher and this shows in what he takes human rights theory to be, namely an area of philosophical ethics that has applications in national and international politics and law. He says that he is "looking for the notion of human rights that fits into the best ethics that we can establish."[15] Griffin's focus has a time frame that is very long, going back to the late Middle Ages.[16] The result of this is a different conception of human rights practice from the one, oriented towards twentieth-century developments at the international level, used by theorists such as Rawls and Beitz who defend political conceptions of human rights. Further, Griffin's view of the spheres in which human rights operate is broad. It is not limited to law and politics or to international relations.[17] He believes that human rights do and should have useful roles within countries and within institutions such as hospitals and families. For example, he believes that a parent could violate a child's human rights by refusing to allow him or her to go to school.[18] The focus of Griffin's theory is sufficiently different from the ones used by Rawls and Beitz to make it easy for them to talk past each other.

A major and unresolved issue in contemporary human rights theory is historical. It concerns the uniqueness of the developments in human rights discourse that began with the Universal Declaration in 1948, continued with regional human rights treaties such as the European Convention of Human Rights (1950), the American Convention (1969), and the African Charter (1981), developed further with the International

---

[13] Ibid., p. 32.   [14] Ibid., pp. 33–8.   [15] Ibid., p. 2.
[16] Ibid., pp. 9, 19, 26, 30.   [17] Ibid., p. 24.   [18] Ibid., p. 165.

Covenants of 1966, the UN treaties on the rights of women and minorities, and the development of important human rights bodies and courts within international organizations. Are these developments best seen, as Griffin probably sees them, as just the scaling up of ideas and practices that were present much earlier? Or are they better seen as very new and distinctive and thus as requiring separate treatment that emphasizes their legal and political dimensions. Political conceptions of human rights tend to take the latter view. They need not deny the importance of antecedents in the history of ideas, historic bills of rights, and political movements such as the anti-slavery movement, the labour movement, and the women's movement, but they see these antecedents as lacking crucial political and legal dimensions, particularly at the international level, that did not flower until the second half of the twentieth century.

Griffin describes the products of realizing human rights at three levels of abstraction. At the level of specific rights, each human right has a distinctive function. For instance, the right to freedom of expression protects speech and expression and the right to education ensures the availability of educational opportunities. At this level there are as many specific functions as there are specific rights. At a middle level of abstraction Griffin sets out three "highest-level human rights," namely the right to autonomy, the right to liberty, and the right to "minimum material provision."[19] The role of these abstract rights is to protect three broad areas of or conditions for functioning normative agency. One of them protects the capacity for autonomy; another protects the freedom needed to exercise one's autonomy; and the third ensures the minimum material conditions needed for the development, operation, and maintenance of one's autonomy. And finally, as we have seen, there is the most abstract level where the generic function or functions of human rights are found. The end product, when human rights are realized, is the protection of autonomy or normative agency as qualified by practicalities.

This is a pleasingly clear structure, and there is little doubt that protecting people's normative agency or autonomy is one important role of human rights. Nevertheless, showing that it is or should be the *defining* role or justifying purpose of human rights is difficult. If the test is giving an empirically accurate description of the jobs that human rights norms currently perform, Griffin's monofunctionalism will be less plausible than its polyfunctionalist alternatives. I believe that providing protections for basic welfare, dignity, and fairness or basic equality would also make the list. Different social and political groups with their various commitments and preoccupations have contributed to the formulations and protections of human rights with the result that human rights have messy boundaries, a tendency towards expansion, and seem to promote a variety of values including welfare, fairness, equality, and good government.

If the claim is that normative agency *should* be the single justifying purpose of all human rights, this seems exceptionally hard to argue. Griffin suggests that it would be good if normative agency played this role (1) because it can; (2) because this role's level

[19] Ibid., pp. 149–52, 180.

of importance is uniquely high; and (3) because it would give human rights a distinctive job that would set them apart from other moral norms. I won't argue these claims here, but I think that (1) is excessively narrow, particularly its denial that promoting fairness is a role of human rights.[20] I accept that normative agency is an important basis for human rights but reject the idea in (2) that it has unique importance; and deny the presumption in (3) that human rights need some single distinctive function that separates the work they do from that done by all other norms. Griffin does not address the question of how much cross-sphere commonality there is between moral and political/legal human rights; he just assumes that there is a lot.[21]

III. Rawls and Beitz on the Roles of Human Rights

This section discusses the roles and functions assigned to human rights in the theories of John Rawls and Charles Beitz. I treat them together because Beitz's theory of the nature of human rights is a much more extended, sophisticated, and methodologically self-conscious development of the Rawlsian approach.

A. Rawls

In *The Law of Peoples* John Rawls says that Human rights are "a special class of urgent rights."[22] Rawls's focus is *international* human rights—ones that have developed and are at work in the global arena. *The Law of Peoples* is a normative reconstruction of international law and politics within today's global system, and hence it is no surprise that almost all of the roles Rawls ascribes to human rights occur in the international sphere. Further, Rawls's focus is *contemporary* human rights.

In *The Law of Peoples*, Rawls was attempting to develop a conception of international human rights that is not guilty of liberal parochialism and that countries around the globe could find attractive. To this end, Rawls gives an abbreviated list of specific human rights that leaves out important protections for liberty and equality. Further to this end he offers an account of the justification of international human rights that avoids controversial normative and metaphysical assumptions. He suggests, in effect, that people and governments should not worry about exactly what human rights are or about the philosophy behind them but just look at what they *do*. Once the world's diverse peoples and their representatives in international negotiations focus on the good that human rights can do at the international and national levels they will, he hopes, be more favourably inclined to accept them.

As a political philosopher writing about international norms, Rawls has nothing to say about the roles of human rights in the sphere of interpersonal relations. Rawls may have been stipulating a limited focus when he says "Human rights *in the Law of*

---

[20] Nickel 2012, 2015.
[21] On the relations between moral rights and human rights, see Buchanan 2013.
[22] Rawls 1999, p. 79.

Peoples... express a special class of urgent rights." (my italics). In all his writings Rawls advocated and used a methodology that involves working up principles for limited spheres as a way of making large problems more manageable. For example, his account of justice in *A Theory of Justice* is limited to what he calls the "basic structure" of society.[23] It does not attempt to explain the concept of justice in its full range of uses. As I read him, Rawls was not attempting to describe or prescribe a generic function to human rights of every type. His exclusive focus was the functions of human rights in international law and politics.

There is nothing wrong with this focus. Indeed, it may be wise to work towards a generic function for human rights in all spheres by seeing first how they work in particular spheres. But it would have been better if Rawls had made clearer his exact focus and whether or not he was suggesting that the international rights he theorized are the only human rights. Rawls could argue, of course, that there is not enough similarity between human rights in international law and politics and human rights in other spheres for a generic function of all human rights to be plausible. This, however, is a controversial proposition that needs to be argued, and Rawls never defends it.

In Rawls's account the users of human rights are all actors on the global stage. They include states and their representatives such as presidents, foreign ministers, and diplomats, and international bodies such as the various organs of the United Nations, and international lawyers and scholars. Secondary users include legislators, judges, political critics, and NGOs at the national level.[24]

Broadly, Rawls tells us that the constitutive roles of human rights at the international level are to (1) help define in various ways the normative structure of the global system by providing content to normative concepts such as legitimacy, sovereignty, permissible intervention, and membership in good standing in the society of peoples; and (2) help to provide criteria for how countries may be sanctioned for serious human rights violations.

One way to explain the roles a norm plays in some area of practice is to explain what it does when it is complied with in good faith and what happens when it is violated. To do this we can use a large set of conditional statements. The if-clause of each one of these conditionals would identify some circumstances, some agents, and some acts the agents perform. The then-clause identifies practical consequences that do or should follow. Rawls proceeds in this way, but focuses on negative consequences for violators rather than on the beneficial consequences for countries that mostly comply or for the rightholders. If a country (C) engaged in systematic and serious violations of one or more human rights then other countries and international bodies such as the United

---

[23] Rawls 1971, pp. 6–10.

[24] Rawls does not say much about the roles human rights play *within* countries, although his view presupposes that they have many such roles. Griffin identifies some of them when he says that human rights "quite obviously have a point intra-nationally: to justify rebellion, to establish a case for peaceful reform, to curb an autocratic ruler, to criticize a majority's treatment of racial or ethnic minorities" (Griffin 2008, p. 24).

Nations Security Council would have permission and perhaps some positive probability of their acting to:

(1) deny C full membership in good standing in the international community
(2) deny the legitimacy of C's government
(3) intervene in C's domestic affairs through diplomatic and economic sanctions, and in extreme cases through military intervention, without violating C's sovereignty—since human rights set limits to national sovereignty.[25]
(4) not tolerate C's internal rights-violating practices—since human rights set limits to the tolerance other countries are required to practice.[26]

Rawls ascribes a cluster of related roles to human rights, and hence it is best to think of his view as polyfunctional. When we assign functions to human rights using conditional statements we have to decide which antecedent circumstances to pick. Rawls mostly focuses on what happens when human rights are violated and identifies some broad consequences within international relations that would appropriately follow such violations. A theorist could equally well start, however, with an if-clause pertaining to a country that very regularly supports and upholds human rights and trace how that would be beneficial in international relations for such a country. These consequences might be that its domestic law and practices are taken as models of good practice, its leadership in international human rights bodies and activities is eagerly sought, it gets high marks when it reports to treaty bodies, and it generally wins when it litigates issues before international human rights courts.

Rawls focuses excessively on what in this chapter I have called subordinate mechanisms and processes. What human rights achieve within international politics in response to violations is not their most important product. What matters ultimately is what human rights do for people in terms of ensuring things such as freedom from discrimination, freedom of thought and belief, and access to education. If rational individuals in Rawls's "original position" were asked to choose a list of human rights rather than principles of justice, these are the sorts of outcomes they would be considering.

B. Beitz

In *The Idea of Human Rights*, Charles Beitz develops a theory of the nature of human rights that shares many similarities with Rawls's view.[27] Like Rawls, Beitz does not treat human rights in the interpersonal sphere and he deals with human rights practice only in terms of political and legal developments after 1948.

Beitz says that his view borrows Rawls's basic insight that we can develop a view of human rights by attending "to the practical inferences that would be drawn by competent participants in the practice from what they regard as valid claims of human rights."

---

[25] Rawls 1999, p. 80.
[26] Ibid., p. 79. Another role—of a somewhat different character—is providing a cut-off for duties of assistance to "burdened societies" (Ibid., pp. 115–19). I am indebted to Adam Etinson for this point.
[27] Beitz 2009.

These inferences for action or practice inform the account of the meaning of the concept of human rights.[28] By practical inferences Beitz means inferences about what one should say and do, the reasons for action that human rights provide. The focus is not on what human rights are at some deep philosophical level; it is rather on how they *work* by guiding actions within a recently emerged and still evolving discursive practice.[29]

Human rights are mostly rights, so let's consider what Beitz takes a right to be. I say "mostly" because Beitz thinks that human rights tend to be more indeterminate than other rights and because he thinks that some human rights are only manifesto rights.[30] Beitz focuses on *claim* rights, ones that have associated duties or responsibilities. Beitz's most general description of claim rights is in a passage in which he says that ordinarily a valid claim of right conveys "information about the nature and importance of the benefit that would be provided or the harm avoided by compliance with the right's requirements, the identify of the agents whose conduct is regulated by the right, the conduct required of them, and the kinds and range of circumstances in which it could be permissible not to comply."[31] This passage makes clear that Beitz views claim rights as having rightholders or beneficiaries and as focusing on the benefit that the rightholder should receive. This makes them beneficiary-oriented. Further, claim rights have addressees or bearers of duties or responsibilities. Finally, claim rights have normative content; they identify the conduct required of the addressees, are sources of reasons for action, and sometimes have the ability to exclude competing reasons as irrelevant.[32] Beitz calls this the supply side of rights.

Let's now turn our attention to *human* rights. Beitz takes these rights to be less "information rich" than ordinary legal rights, leaving more to be worked out at the application stage. Second, human rights generally have high priority. Because they are based in important or urgent interests, their protection may reasonably be considered to be a political priority.[33] Third, human rights are universal in the sense of being "assertable by more-or-less anyone in the world."[34] Fourth, the primary dutybearers for human rights are countries. "There is no serious indeterminacy about the location of the first-level responsibilities: they rest with the governments of states."[35] For nonstate actors human rights can generate reasons for action but not duties to act. Finally, for Beitz human rights are not a fundamental moral category or part of one. "Human rights operate at a middle level of practical reasoning, serving to organize these further considerations and bring them to bear on a certain range of choices."[36]

Beitz identifies his focus as the contemporary discursive practice of human rights, and goes beyond a list of rights to include norms and practices, some of them

---

[28] Beitz 2009, p. 103.   [29] Ibid., p. 124.
[30] Ibid., p. 117–2; on manifesto rights see Feinberg 1973, p. 67 and pp. 94–5.
[31] Beitz 2009, p. 119.   [32] Ibid., pp. 109, 115, 118, 127.   [33] Ibid., p. 137.
[34] Ibid., p. 71.   [35] Ibid., p. 118.   [36] Ibid., pp. 127–8.

informal, governing how various parties should act in order to promote and uphold human rights. These norms and practices govern, for example, areas of human rights practice such as the propagation of human rights, their interpretation, their application and adjudication, responding to criticisms of human rights, and—perhaps most importantly—responding to serious violations of human rights. Beitz says that "human rights are potential triggers of transnational protective and remedial action and should be suitable to function as justifications of it."[37]

A distinctive feature of Rawls's view was a somewhat abbreviated list of specific human rights.[38] Beitz does not follow Rawls in this respect. He agrees with Rawls that the requirements of human rights are weaker than the requirements of social justice. But Beitz denies that human rights are minimalist in other respects.

Beitz rejects orthodox theories that interpret international human rights as the "public, doctrinal expression of a distinctive underlying order of moral values conceived as rights."[39] He believes that orthodox theories treat human rights as theoretically deeper than they actually are. I believe that Griffin is largely immune to this criticism since while holding that human rights have a deep philosophical root in the value of normative agency he fully accepts that most specific human rights appearing in standard lists of human rights are derivative, middle-level principles that are substantially influenced by practicalities.

Beitz suggests that human rights are public international norms open to a variety of justifications and do not presuppose any philosophical view about their basis.[40] Beitz accepts Rawls's idea that a philosophical account of human rights should avoid as far as possible controversial assumptions about the grounds of human rights. The emphasis of philosophical explication should be on what human rights do, not on their grounds or what they ultimately are. In this way human rights remain more open to acceptance by people from around the world with their diverse religious and philosophical traditions.

I agree that it is good for human rights *declarations and treaties* to be philosophically shallow in this way, but I do not see why this applies to philosophical theories of human rights. Such theories do not have the practical importance that declarations and treaties do (even if some philosophers wish they would). Few people read human rights theory so its practical impact is very limited. And smart practical people are readily able to accept attractive norms while dismissing philosophical views of the grounds of those norms that they find controversial or unappealing. I submit that philosophy, including political philosophy, should be allowed to follow its own traditions as a highly theoretical subject dealing in deep and fundamental questions. Philosophical controversy should be celebrated and enjoyed by those who appreciate it. Liberal philosophers, like philosophers of other stripes, are entitled to choose the level of

---

[37] Ibid., p. 65.
[38] On this see the discussion of the "list question" in Nickel 2007, pp. 92–105.
[39] Ibid., p. 103.   [40] Ibid., pp. 21, 105.

depth and abstraction at which they wish to work and to try to find deep grounds for their views about human rights.

Beitz improves on Rawls by giving adequate attention to the end-product or justifying purpose of the practice of human rights, which he takes to be protecting people's urgent interests.[41] Human rights are "requirements whose object is to protect urgent individual interests against certain predictable dangers ('standard threats') to which they are vulnerable under typical circumstances of life in a modern world order composed of states."[42] This broad idea of urgent interests has a good fit with the idea—which I just criticized—of keeping human rights theory as uncontroversial as possible so that it can provide a widely acceptable international basis for human rights. Success in protecting these urgent interests gives normative force to valid claims that one's human rights be respected and protected.

When we turn to mechanisms and processes, Beitz has lots of plausible things to say. He describes human rights as matters of international concern, serving as standards to which the international community may hold states' institutions accountable and generating reasons for action to protect them and to criticize and sanction violations. "This transnational action-justifying role is definitive of the function of human rights in the normative discourse of global politics."[43] Human rights can justify (or generate *pro tanto* reasons for) interference in the domestic affairs of countries that violate human rights. Thus human rights have an "interference-justifying" feature.[44]

Beitz and Griffin seem to be using different criteria for justifying functional claims. Beitz attempts to make human rights practice intelligible by sticking closely to the facts about how human rights norms are currently used internationally. Griffin is looking to what would make human rights practice coherent and give it a distinctive, well-demarcated role. If Griffin overdoes prescription, Beitz relies too heavily on description.

IV. Conclusion

There is little reason to expect that the debate between political and orthodox conceptions of human rights will be soon be ended with victory by one side or the other. Indeed, I would not wish for this debate to cease because there are still many issues to be explored. Further, the research programmes the two sides propose are both valuable and illuminating—and are compatible in many if not all respects.[45] Evidence of this is found in the excellence of both Griffin's book and Beitz's. There is much to learn from both.

I would, however, like to see the debate turn to addressing some of the underlying disagreements. These deeper conflicts include issues such as whether human rights theory should assume that there are justified and knowable universal moral rights or be agnostic about this; how closely universal moral rights, if there are any, relate to

---

[41] Ibid., pp. 119, 134.   [42] Ibid., p. 109.   [43] Ibid., pp. 43–4.
[44] Ibid., p. 109.   [45] Gilabert 2011; Liao and Etinson 2012.

political and legal human rights and their justification; the best justificatory framework for human rights (e.g. consequentialism, teleology, contractualism, deontology); which disciplines are best positioned to theorize human rights (e.g. international relations, law, philosophy of law, political philosophy, normative ethics, metaethics, intellectual history); and what avoiding parochialism and ethnocentrism requires of philosophical theories of human rights.

Better awareness of and explicit debate about focus—as I have called it—would also help. Griffin, Rawls, and Beitz all attempt to base their accounts at least partially on the nature of human rights practice. But, as we have seen in this chapter, Rawls and Beitz focus on human rights as they developed politically and legally during the twentieth century, while Griffin's focus is much broader and includes interpersonal rights. Given that difference, it is not surprising that they give different accounts of what human rights are and do. Progress here requires arguing about the distinctiveness of twentieth-century developments and whether they require treatment that is *sui generis*.

Further, self-consciousness and explicit debate about disciplinary orientations and methods would be helpful. Rawls and Beitz are political philosophers with strong interests in international politics and law. Their accounts attempt to describe key features of contemporary human rights practice at the international level. Griffin works from the perspective of normative ethics and constructs an account of human rights within ethics . This makes it unsurprising that Griffin's view of human rights includes the interpersonal sphere and is highly prescriptive or reconstructive.

Finally, assigning functions or roles to rights could be done with much more sophistication and caution and supported with more and better arguments. A starting assumption should be that assigning functions to human rights is at most one part of giving an adequate account of what human rights are. Another starting assumption should be that human rights are polyfunctional. Attempts to assign a single unifying function are likely to be too abstract to provide much illumination. We saw that there are multiple criteria available for selecting functions and that particular theorists seem to give greater weight to some of them than to others. These criteria include how frequently a particular kind of use of human rights occurs, designers' and users' intentions, the importance of the function to the overall practice, and giving greater unity and coherence to the practice. Debates about the roles or functions of human rights would better and deeper if the criteria a theory relies on for selecting roles were identified, elaborated, and defended.

References

Beitz, C. 2009. *The Idea of Human Rights*. Oxford: Oxford University Press.

Buchanan, A. 2013. *The Heart of Human Rights*. Oxford: Oxford University Press.

Feinberg, J. 1973. *Social Philosophy*. Englewood Cliffs, NJ: Prentice Hall: 67–95.

Gilabert, P. 2011. "Humanist and Political Perspectives on Human Rights," *Political Theory* 39: 439–67.

Griffin, J. 2008. *On Human Rights*. Oxford: Oxford University Press.

Liao, M. and Etinson, A. 2012. "Political and Naturalistic Conceptions of Human Rights: A False Polemic?," *Journal of Moral Philosophy* 9: 327–52.

Nickel, J. 2007. *Making Sense of Human Rights*, second edition. Malden, Mass.: Blackwell Publishing.

Nickel, J. 2012. Review of Griffin, *On Human Rights, Philosophical Review* 121: 461–3.

Nickel, J. 2015. "Personal Deserts and Human Rights," in R. Cruft, S. M. Liao, and M. Renzo, eds, *Philosophical Foundations of Human Rights*. Oxford: Oxford University Press.

Rawls, J. 1971. *A Theory of Justice*. Cambridge, Mass.: Harvard University Press.

Rawls, J. 1999. *The Law of Peoples*. Cambridge, Mass.: Harvard University Press.

Raz, J. 2010. "Human Rights without Foundations," in S. Besson and J. Tasioulas, eds, *The Philosophy of International Law*, Oxford: Oxford University Press, pp. 321–38.

Tasioulas, J. 2013. "Human Rights, Legitimacy, and International Law," *American Journal of Jurisprudence* 58 (1): 1–25.

Wenar, L. 2013. "The Nature of Claim Rights," *Ethics* 123: 202–29.

4.1

On Being Faithful to the "Practice"
A Response to Nickel

Adam Etinson

I

With characteristic lucidity and good sense, James Nickel's chapter sheds much needed light on some murky issues in the philosophy of human rights. Philosophical debates about human rights have focused on roughly four sets of issues. First, and most prominently, there have been disagreements about the *nature* of human rights: that is, about what human rights are, and what makes them different from other norms. Second, there have been disagreements about the *grounds* of human rights: that is, about what considerations, if any, speak in favour of their normative existence or authority. Third, there have been disagreements about *content*: for instance, about whether social and economic rights are in fact human rights, or even "rights" at all.[1] And fourth, there have been disagreements about the *aims* and *methods* of a philosophical theory of human rights in general.

Disagreements of this fourth kind proceed at a higher level of abstraction. That is, they are not about the nature, grounds, or content of human rights per se, but about how enquiry into such matters should proceed and be understood. They also remain obscure and less well developed than debates of the first three kinds. Nickel's chapter directly addresses this important deficit in the literature.

Nickel argues that reticence about questions of aim and approach can lead (and has led) to avoidable misunderstanding and cross-talk among philosophers of human rights. I think he's right about this.[2] When basic claims about human rights are advanced with different criteria in mind—e.g., when one theorist aims for ethical plausibility, another for historical accuracy, and a third for consistency with contemporary international law—this ought to be explicitly acknowledged. Otherwise, theorists risk talking past one another.

Nickel's chapter illustrates this point nicely. Consider, for example, his discussion of John Rawls and James Griffin. Rawls claims that human rights are distinguished by their ability to justify external interference in a state's internal affairs.[3] Griffin, on the other

---

[1] O'Neill 2005.   [2] Liao & Etinson 2012.   [3] Rawls 1999b, §10.

hand, claims that their distinguishing feature is that they protect the universal value of personhood or normative agency.[4] On the face of it, these claims are contradictory, or at least hard to reconcile—Griffin certainly thinks so.[5]

But on Nickel's analysis this contradiction becomes less obvious. This is because, in Nickel's view, Rawls and Griffin are not really theorizing the *same thing*. Rather, they are focused on different aspects or applications of human rights. Rawls's focus is on human rights as they operate in contemporary international politics. Griffin's focus, however, is on human rights as norms that operate more broadly in ethical life, including in the interpersonal domain. Once these differences in focus are taken into account, Rawls's and Griffin's respective theories of human rights no longer seem so incompatible. Indeed, they seem more like complementary (and quite possibly mutually accurate) explorations of a multi-purpose idea.

Nickel's hope, one that I share, is that his analysis will motivate theorists of human rights to pre-empt any danger of cross-talk by making theoretical focus a more explicit and established topic of discussion.

II

Nickel's chapter aims to help us along in this task by providing us with some orienting concepts and observations. Perhaps the most significant of these is its overarching assertion, already implicit above, that the roles of human rights are likely to *vary* depending on one's focus, i.e. depending on the relevant temporal frame of reference, sphere of operation, level of abstraction, and point of view. In Nickel's view, human rights are best understood as "polyfunctional" norms. What one sees in them, and what they *do*, will in large part depend on context.

As plausible as this may seem, it is not a claim that will sit well with everyone. In particular, it cuts against an increasingly common tendency to understand human rights in ways that *limit* their possible extension across time and (what Nickel calls) spheres of life. For instance, in his recent work, Charles Beitz urges us to think of human rights as norms that govern the behaviour of states under modern circumstances.[6] For Beitz, Griffin's affirmation of the validity of (at least some) human rights across history (including very distant history),[7] and his application of such rights to the interpersonal sphere (where they would prohibit, among other things, common crimes like murder),[8] are something akin to a category mistake. Human rights are, on Beitz's picture, just *not* the sort of norms that operate in those contexts.[9]

Nickel's understanding of human rights, by contrast, is far more capacious. But this comes at a dialectical cost. Nickel's chapter asks us, in effect, not just to be more explicit about theoretical focus, but also to accept an accommodating master-view of human

---

[4] Griffin 2008, ch. 2.   [5] Ibid., pp. 22–7.   [6] Beitz 2009, p. 109.
[7] Griffin claims that human rights are rights we would possess even in a hypothetical "state of nature" (2008, pp. 50–1).
[8] Griffin 2008, p. 170.   [9] For a similar view, *see:* Sangiovanni 2007, p. 17.

rights on which various orientations of focus can be made intelligible. Even if it only does so implicitly, this broad view of the scope of human rights—or of their *range* of application—makes Nickel a *participant* in, rather than just an observer of, the debate between Political and Orthodox theorists of human rights. This is because any account of the essential nature of human rights (i.e. of *what* human rights are) that is going to pass muster on such a view will have to limit itself to features or roles that human rights possess in *all* of the spheres in which they operate; presumably, a conceptually basic feature of *x* does not come and go depending on the context.

As one might expect, these enduring features or roles are highly abstract. Nickel mentions two such features in the present chapter: (i) that human rights are *norms* and, in particular, *rights*, and (ii) that they are *plural* in that they come in lists. Elsewhere, he notes two other generic features of human rights: that they are (iii) *universal* and (iv) *high-priority* rights.[10]

As far as defining characteristics of human rights go, these four features are plausible. They also come very close to characterizing human rights in the way that Orthodox theorists (like Griffin and Tasioulas) typically do, i.e. as rights possessed by all human beings simply in virtue of their humanity.[11] But they stop well short of defining human rights in the way that Political theorists suggest we should, and this is to be expected.

Political theorists (like Rawls, Raz, and Beitz) define human rights in light of their role or function in contemporary international politics, whether this is to serve as a benchmark of political legitimacy,[12] a focus of international concern,[13] or a trigger for intervention.[14] The role of human rights in contemporary international affairs may be very important, but it is clearly too limited to serve as a *basic* or *defining* feature of such rights if we think of them as norms that operate across vastly different spheres of life and periods of history, including periods in which modern nation states do not even exist.[15]

In this way, the broad and polyfunctional picture of human rights invoked in Nickel's chapter *intervenes* in the Orthodox–Political debate. Perhaps the greatest dialectical weakness of his chapter is that it banks on the sheer self-evidence of this contested but appealing picture, without actively defending it.

III

Nickel observes that human rights can be assigned definitive roles in two basic senses: *descriptive* and *normative*. In the former case, one identifies features and/or functions that *are* attributed to human rights in some real-world domain (e.g. international law, popular morality, etc.). In the latter case, one identifies features and/or functions that *ought to be* attributed to human rights therein. This is an important distinction, as

---

[10] Nickel 2014a, Sec. 1.   [11] Griffin 2008; Tasioulas 2012.   [12] Rawls 1999b, p. 80.
[13] Beitz 2009, p. 109.   [14] Rawls 1999b, p. 80; Raz 2010, p. 328.   [15] Nickel 2014a, Sec. 1.

these are very different claims and, at least on the face of it, require different kinds of evidence.

One of the remarkable features of recent philosophical work on human rights is that it has become increasingly hard to tell which of these two kinds of claims theorists are trying to advance. A central source of confusion in this area is that, with very few exceptions, theorists who assign roles to human rights in a *normative* sense still rely on *descriptions* of the real-world roles of human rights as evidence for such assignments. That is, even theorists who present us with an idea of what human rights we *ought to* recognize (and of what those rights *ought to* do) still tend to base that vision on an empirical look at what human rights *are* recognized in the world around us (and what *they* do). In this way, virtually all human rights theorists pride themselves on faithfully rendering in theory what human rights are (or do) in "practice": so much so that "fidelity to the practice" has come to be seen as a primary virtue of any theoretical account of human rights.

It is natural for a descriptive account of the roles of human rights to be grounded in empirical data about their real-world use. But it is not as obvious that a normative account of human rights should be so grounded, or at least not primarily so. One reason is that such an account would be "normative" only in a limited sense. It would be unable, for instance, to ground any *wholesale* critique of contemporary human rights practice. It may still be able to generate something like an *immanent* critique thereof; after all, the real-world practice of human rights itself recognizes normative standards to which it may be upheld, and of which it may fall short. Still, we might reasonably wonder whether the possibility of immanent critique is adequate here. What if some of the characteristic real-world uses of human rights (e.g. their role as triggers for intervention, or as standards of development) are ultimately ones that we would rather they *not* perform? A theory of human rights that is faithfully modelled on the practice thereof may be incapable of accommodating such critical observations.

And yet fidelity to the practice of human rights is, again, a methodological dogma of sorts. It is hard to find a theorist *not* committed to it. Several Political theorists understand this kind of fidelity to be the defining feature of their view. For instance, as Joseph Raz, a prominent defender of the Political view, writes:

The task of a theory of human rights is (a) to establish the essential features which contemporary human rights practice attributes to the rights it acknowledges to be human rights; and (b) to identify the moral standards which qualify anything to be so acknowledged. I will say that accounts which understand their task in that way manifest a political conception of human rights.[16]

But this kind of methodological commitment is not exclusive to the Political view. John Tasioulas, who defends the Orthodox approach, claims that any "credible account must exhibit an appropriate level of *fidelity* to the human rights culture that

---

[16] Raz 2010, p. 327.

has flourished post-1945..."[17] And Griffin, also in the Orthodox camp, opts for what he calls a "bottom-up" approach to the theory of human rights: "one starts with human rights as used in our actual social life by politicians, lawyers, social campaigners, as well as theorists of various sorts" and constructs a theory from there.[18]

So there is widespread agreement among philosophers that a theory of human rights (whether descriptive *or* normative) should emulate or be faithful to the practice thereof. But what motivates this agreement? *Why* is "fidelity to the practice" such an important theoretical goal, and *how* important is it really?

In what remains of this commentary, I want to use Nickel's chapter as a springboard for addressing these two questions about the ideal of fidelity. My sense, very much in line with that of Nickel, is that human rights theorists have not dealt with these meta-theoretical questions explicitly enough, and that current and future debates would be improved if that were to change.

IV

The first thing to (at least try to) clarify is what theorists mean by human rights "practice." There is no single answer to this question. The term is handled in slightly different ways in each case. The best way to see this is to start by considering what would be covered by the term on its broadest definition. Consider Nickel's own highly comprehensive definition in a recent article.[19] Nickel suggests that human rights practice can be seen as having five main components: (i) ethical beliefs and attitudes; (ii) action and activism; (iii) law; (iv) political practice; and (v) journalistic and scholarly work. When theorists refer to human rights "practice," it is plausible to think of them as referring to either some or all of this.

That said, there is a noticeable centre of semantic gravity here. The "practice" of human rights is most often understood in political and, in particular, *legal* terms. It is normally taken to refer to (something like) "the contemporary political project of creating an international law of human rights that promotes decent treatment of people by their government."[20] This focus—which most clearly embraces elements (ii), (iii), and (iv)—is in some ways already connoted by the term itself. After all, there are other popular ways of referring to human rights "practice." We might well refer, as many do, to human rights "culture," the human rights "movement," or human rights "discourse." But these terms seem to connote something broader than the "practice" as such.

The idea of a human rights "movement," for instance, evokes images of popular mobilization and political activism (the African-American Civil Rights Movement being a point of comparison)—stressing elements (i) and (ii). And the notions of human rights "culture" and "discourse" naturally connote something even broader than that: certainly (i) ethical beliefs and attitudes, but also a systematic way of interpreting

---

[17] Tasioulas 2009, p. 939 (original emphasis).   [18] Griffin 2008, p. 29.
[19] Nickel 2014b.   [20] Nickel 2007, p. 1.

or "seeing" the world, a marker of identity, and something that has a presence in the broader domains of (v) civil society, the media, and academia.

Nickel is probably right to think that the notion of human rights practice can in principle be stretched to include all of this, but nonetheless the term is most naturally used, it seems to me, to refer to the international legal and political practices (e.g. declarations, treaties, formal institutions, non-governmental organizations, and activist efforts, etc.) that have developed around the idea of human rights since the end of the Second World War.

This narrower political-legal interpretation of the term is dominant in the literature. Beitz understands the practice of human rights to be an international "public political project" designed to regulate the behaviour of states. The project consists in a set of legal-political norms and a (growing) "discursive community" that recognizes and advocates for them.[21] It is doubtful that (v) journalistic and scholarly work plays much of a role here.

Raz, for his part, adopts a highly legalistic interpretation of human rights practice that seems to exclude even (i) ethical beliefs and attitudes, or what he calls the "common ideology and rhetoric surrounding the practice." On Raz's view, the practice consists in: "ratifying conventions, enacting legislation and adopting other measures in the name of human rights; litigating, implementing, applying and so on, those so-called human rights measures; advocating observance and incorporation into law of other so-called human rights, and more."[22] Allen Buchanan's account is similarly legalistic, placing international human rights law at the very "heart" of human rights practice.[23]

Orthodox theorists like Griffin and Tasioulas seem to pay indirect homage to this narrow reading by avoiding the term "practice" altogether. Griffin, for instance, speaks of being faithful to human rights "discourse" rather than human rights "practice." And this, I think, is probably because he is interested in being faithful not only to contemporary politics and law, but also to the idea of human rights that emerged in the (i) ethical doctrines and (v) scholarly work of the Enlightenment tradition.[24] Something similar may be true of Tasioulas, who, as noted above, has spoken of being faithful to post-1945 human rights "culture" rather than the "practice" per se.[25] Given his identification of human rights with a "distinctive ethical sensibility," it is clear that his interests also lie beyond the domains of politics and law (although they certainly include them).[26]

These observations are meant to help bring the idea of human rights "practice" into sharper relief. They are also meant to illustrate how the boundaries of the practice are

---

[21] Beitz 2009, pp. 8–13, 42–4. "Since the end of World War II, this practice has developed on several fronts: in international law, in global and regional institutions, in the foreign policies of (mostly liberal democratic) states, and in the activities of a diverse and growing array of nongovernmental organizations (NGOs) and networks" (Beitz 2009, p. 1).

[22] Raz in this volume.   [23] Buchanan 2013, pp. 5–9.   [24] Griffin 2008, ch. 1.

[25] Tasioulas 2009, p. 939.   [26] Tasioulas 2012, pp. 4–5.

drawn in subtly different ways in different cases. In the end I don't think we should make too much of these differences. Tasioulas and Griffin may use the alternative terms of "culture" and "discourse" to highlight the real-world phenomena that their theories aim to be faithful to, but, as Nickel's comprehensive definition shows, these are plausibly just ways of referring to human rights practice on some broader understanding thereof. And more importantly, I doubt that any of these theorists would deny that the *most* crucial thing, when it comes to fidelity, is that a theory manages to capture the core features attributed to human rights by contemporary international human rights law, and by the political practices surrounding it. So the basic thrust of the idea remains the same in all cases.

V

Why, then, should a theory of human rights be faithful to human rights practice? As mentioned in Section III, the answer may be obvious in some cases. Some theories of human rights may have strictly *descriptive* or *interpretative* aims—such as explaining the influence of European human rights law on domestic law and policy in the United Kingdom. And it is not difficult to see why this would often be so. Human rights have a rich life in the political, legal, and social world around us, and it is entirely normal for theorists to take an interest in that life and to try to give an account of it. This can only be done by empirically "looking" at human rights practice (or some aspect of it), trying to discern its governing purposes and ideas, and examining its results. For such theories, fidelity to the practice is straightforwardly mandated by their basic aim and subject matter.

But Orthodox and Political theorists cannot avail themselves of this simple response. No theorist standardly placed under either heading is interested *solely* in describing or interpreting contemporary human rights practice. As the quote in Section III indicates, Raz's theory aims to identify criteria (or "moral standards") that can be used to determine what rights *should* (or should *not*) be recognized as human rights by contemporary human rights practice, regardless of whether they already are so. His theory is meant to offer *guidance* to, and to provide a possible framework for *criticism* of, the practice. And the same is true of Griffin's and Tasioulas's Orthodox theories, as well as Rawls's and Beitz's versions of the Political approach.[27] Griffin, for example, wants to *remedy* the indeterminacy of our contemporary understanding of human rights, and presents his theory as a way of bringing order to an unruly status quo.[28]

If these theorists are trying to identify a *normative* benchmark against which contemporary human rights practice can be judged, why are they so keen to make sure that this benchmark is faithful to the practice *as it is*? As far as I can tell, there are two

---

[27]   *See:* Griffin 2008, ch. 11; Tasioulas in this volume; Beitz 2009, ch. 6; Rawls 1999b, §1 (on the idea of a "realistic utopia").

[28]   *See:* Griffin 2008, pp. 1–6.

main arguments for this implicit in the literature. One is (a) *semantic* and the other is based on considerations of what Nickel calls (b) *focus*.[29]

(a) The Semantic Argument

The semantic argument starts by noting that we already share at least *some* idea of what a "human right" is, and of what human rights there are. Evidence for this can be seen in the simple fact that not all rights intuitively strike us as "human": for instance, the right to veto legislation passed by the United States Congress is clearly *not* a human right—it is not *universal* enough to plausibly count as one. Once we recognize that there is at least some conceptual discipline underlying the use of the term "human rights" in contemporary language and thought, however, we also ought to acknowledge the constraints that this imposes on human rights theorizing. What it implies, generally speaking, is that a theory of human rights will only *register* as such if it achieves some degree of fit with the ordinary concept of human rights. Otherwise, it will come across (at least to its audience, if not to its author) as a theory of "something else."

The reason that this generates an argument for theoretical fidelity to the *practice* is that the ordinary concept of human rights (to the extent that there is one) seems largely conditioned by the practice itself—that is, by the specific *lists* of individual rights that are proclaimed as human rights in various areas of law, by the likely (or publicly stated) *consequences* of respecting or violating human rights norms in various contexts, and by key pieces of *rhetoric* (e.g. in preambles, political discourse, judicial decisions) that publicly announce the purposes and values served by such rights, etc. These aspects of the practice contribute so much to our everyday understanding of what human rights are (and ought to be) that any purported theory of human rights that fails to *fit* with enough of them will inevitably strike us as "off topic" or as "changing the subject"—as confusing apples with oranges.[30]

(b) The Focus-Based Argument

The focus-based argument is motivated by a different set of considerations. Here, the main thought is that *focus* (in just the sense described by Nickel) matters when it comes to making normative claims about human rights. For example, if one wants to think about what human rights should be incorporated into law, then one has to

---

[29] There are other arguments worth discussing, to be sure [*See*, for instance: Gilabert 2012, pp. 458–60 (on "feasibility") and Sangiovanni 2007, pp. 20–7 (on "political realism")], but for reasons of space and efficiency I will only focus on (a) and (b) here.

[30] Beitz says something along these lines: "If the focus of critical interest is the idea of human rights as it arises in public reflection and argument about global political life, then it seems self evident that we should take instruction from the public practice in conceptualizing its central terms. This does not mean that there is no point in investigating other conceptions of human rights such as those that might be inspired by various ideas found in the history of thought; only that we ought not to assume that this would be an investigation of human rights in the sense in which they occur in contemporary public discourse" (Beitz 2009, p. 11). *Also see:* Gilabert 2012, pp. 5–6, for a similar point about "semantic continuity."

consider the implications of *legal* incorporation. In part, this requires thinking about the nature and functions of law in general, including the fact that legal norms are administered by public institutions (courts, bureaus, commissions, etc.) and are (typically) enforced by means of coercive power. These basic facts about the law *as it is* shape our understanding of what particular laws there *ought to be.* Consider: they may well counsel against the legal recognition of some morally compelling (but importantly "private" and/or institutionally impractical) human rights, such as the right amongst spouses to an equal say in important family decisions.[31]

What the argument claims is that something like this is true of the evaluation of human rights practice as a whole. That is, just as we take certain basic functions of *law* into account when we consider what laws there ought to be, we should also take the basic functions of human rights *practice* into account when we consider what rights the practice ought to recognize as genuinely "human." Theorists might have different views about what the basic functions of human rights practice are (limiting national sovereignty, focusing international concern, setting standards of political legitimacy, etc.), but the logic of the argument remains the same: focus *on* the practice requires fidelity *to* the practice. We cannot responsibly decide the ideal content of the practice without understanding the implications of recognizing rights in that environment, which requires a *faithful* appreciation of what the practice is really like.[32] Otherwise, our theory will be "so remote from the practice of human rights as to be irrelevant to it."[33]

VI

What should we make of these arguments? Let me conclude by offering some half-sceptical thoughts about each in turn. With respect to (a), it is certainly true that there are semantic constraints that govern the construction of a theory of human rights. There is no way around this. Whatever its aim, such a theory must achieve some degree of fit with the ordinary concept of human rights—with the ordinary *meaning* of the term. And this includes achieving some fit with elements of the practice: standard lists of human rights, standard roles, and pervasive rhetoric, etc. A theory that fails to do this—one that, say, invests such rights with content radically different from standard lists accepted by the practice—[34] is unlikely to strike us as a theory of human rights at all.

---

[31] The example is borrowed from John Tasioulas. *See:* Tasioulas 2012, p. 2.

[32] For a *version* of this kind of argument, *see:* Raz in this volume: "...my reflections on the practice of international human rights were partly aimed at identifying features of the practice that affect the considerations by which it should be judged" (p. 143).

[33] Raz 2010, p. 323. It is worth noting that this argument applies most naturally to the Political theories of Raz and Beitz. Orthodox theorists like Griffin and Tasioulas aim to develop an account of human rights that can guide legal and political practice but, as Nickel notes, that is not their *only* aim. Both theorists offer a sort of all-purpose account that is also meant to apply to interpersonal morality. This means that (at least at the initial stage of conceptual elaboration) there is less *focus*-based pressure on such theories to be faithfully attuned to the realities of human rights politics and law in particular, although there remain *semantic* reasons to do so.

[34] Rawls's theory (1999b, pp. 78–81) is an example of this.

That said, it is important not to exaggerate the amount of guidance the practice can offer us here. The practice provides us with some provisional "fixed points" for theoretical reflection about human rights, to be sure.[35] But it provides us with no real principled understanding of what it is that makes a right human—no real *theory*. In this sense, as Griffin notes, "the term 'human right' is nearly criterionless."[36] It almost certainly lacks the kind of disciplined use one would need to arbitrate a debate as fine-grained as the Orthodox–Political dispute. After all, none of the theories offered under these headings can be written off strictly on semantic grounds. They all possess *some* degree of semantic plausibility, particularly once we see them as focusing on different aspects or applications of human rights, as Nickel suggests we should.

Perhaps there are theories that fit with *more* of the practice than others do—that is, not just standard lists, but also standard roles, influential judicial decisions, and established rhetoric, etc. Some theories may have a semantic edge in that respect. But two points are worth raising here.

First, semantic fit is not the only virtue of a theory of human rights. And given the conceptual nebulousness of the practice itself, it seems best to think of semantic fit as something a theory of human rights should have an *adequate* or *sufficient* amount of, but not necessarily something it ought to *maximize*. This is particularly true for theories, like those at issue in the Orthodox–Political debate, that aim to articulate an account of human rights that can be used to evaluate and guide the practice, not just to describe it. For such theories, once basic conditions of semantic plausibility are met, the crucial thing, it would seem, is to develop a *normatively* plausible picture of human rights.[37]

Second, there are (unsurprisingly) various ways in which a theory of human rights might "fit" with the practice thereof. One general kind of fit is *substantive*, and occurs when a theory validates the same (or roughly the same) set of human rights as the practice does. Another general kind of fit is *interpretative*, and occurs when a theory accurately captures the normative considerations that *underlie* or *justify* the various rights proclaimed by the practice.

A theory can achieve *interpretative* fit in several different ways, some of which are identified by Nickel above.[38] These include modelling, in theoretical terms: (a) the *international consequences* of compliance or non-compliance with the norms of human rights practice, as Beitz, Rawls, and Raz do; (b) the various *ends* secured by these norms when they are complied with; (c) the *important ends* secured by them,

---

[35] The term is from Rawls 1999a, p. 18 (on his discussion of "reflective equilibrium").

[36] Griffin 2008, p. 14.

[37] Tasioulas and Griffin are helpfully explicit about this. Tasioulas, for instance, understands fidelity to be only one of three methodological desiderata that bear on the construction of a theory of human rights. These include: *fidelity*, *normative plausibility*, and *ecumenicism* (Tasioulas 2009; Tasioulas in this volume). And Griffin wants his theory to be not only faithful to the "discourse" but also *determinate* and *ethically plausible*. In his own words, he is looking "for the notion of human rights that fits into the best ethics that we can establish" (Griffin 2008, p. 2).

[38] Nickel in this volume.

such as human welfare, dignity, freedom, etc.;[39] and/or (d) any *shared ends* that they all secure, such as protecting universal human interests (Tasioulas) or normative agency (Griffin).

Some theorists may go for an all-of-the-above approach here, others may be more selective. And in diagnosing these ends and/or consequences, theorists might look at how the practice (i) *actually* operates, (ii) was *originally intended* to operate, and/or (iii) is *"officially" meant* to operate.

These options mark out different *objects* of fidelity—various aspects of the practice that a theory might be faithful *to*. But there are also questions about how to gauge the conceptual or semantic relevance of any one of these objects. After all, if we accept Nickel's plausibly broad understanding of human rights, the practice (understood principally as a legal and political phenomenon) is but *one* environment in which human rights can operate and find expression. And if that's correct, the objects highlighted above are useful but nonetheless *idiosyncratic* sources for theoretical reflection about human rights.

For instance, the human rights affirmed in contemporary international law are notably statist in substance: they generally impose duties on states rather than individuals. But this can easily be read as a consequence of the statist orientation of the *medium* in which these rights are affirmed—international legal conventions—rather than as a conceptually basic feature of the rights themselves, as Political theorists would have it. In this instance (and probably in others too) it may be more conceptually illuminating to "see through" some pervasive aspect of the practice, and read it as a contingent or local result of the application of some deeper idea.

All of this makes it rather difficult, barring certain extremes, to determine which theory of human rights has the semantic "edge," if any. The concept of human rights perpetuated by the practice is not only ambiguous; it can also be approached in myriad ways.

VII

There is nothing wrong with argument (b) as such. Focus or context plainly matters when we make normative judgements about human rights. Any theory interested in determining what rights should be recognized by human rights practice will have to consider the real-world implications of recognition in *that* domain. And this can't be done without a faithful or accurate understanding of the domain itself.

It is how theorists fill in the blanks—that is, how they characterize the practice and its implications for normative theory—that merits scrutiny. Consider, for example, Raz's account. According to Raz, the "distinctive element" of the practice is that it treats human rights violations as grounds for international actions (e.g. military intervention,

---

[39] For a version of this approach, *see:* Nickel and his discussion of "four secure claims" in Nickel 2007, ch. 4.

political and economic sanctions, etc.) that would ordinarily be considered infringements of national sovereignty.[40] Moreover, this real-world fact, in his view, should fundamentally structure our understanding of what the practice ought to be like. In particular, the practice should only recognize individual rights that genuinely merit such international protections—that can *justifiably* fulfil its distinctive political role.[41]

But there are a few reasons to be sceptical about these claims. First, it is not at all obvious that the practice is mainly or "distinctively" concerned with foreign intervention. In his contribution to this volume, Raz defends this claim by noting that the biggest historical change brought about by modern human rights practice is its transformation of our normative understanding of international relations and, in particular, the scope of national sovereignty.[42] But this observation runs up against an opposing one. Whatever theorists might say, human rights practice is in fact *highly* respectful of national sovereignty.

The norms of international human rights law are not drawn from natural law but from positive customs or treaties created by states themselves. And the practice is chock-full of rights—such as the right to the highest attainable standard of health,[43] to free higher education,[44] and to rest, leisure, and periodic holidays with pay[45]—for which sovereignty-overriding protection is clearly out of the question (unless one thinks of international criticism as a violation of national sovereignty: a highly unusual view).[46] Moreover, as Beth Simmons has persuasively argued, it is very often *domestic* pressure that incentivizes compliance with international human rights law.[47]

In its current state, the practice is probably best described as a vehicle for things like: articulating human rights standards, making public commitments to them, litigating, adjudicating, monitoring compliance, sharing information, and guiding domestic implementation. Much to the chagrin of some (and to the great relief of others), *enforcing* human rights standards via threat of international sanction, admonition, or intervention is simply not a prominent part of what the practice does. And this is true regardless of whether we think in terms of how the practice (i) actually operates, (ii) was originally intended to operate, or (iii) is "officially" meant to operate.[48]

Even if Raz's interventionist understanding of the practice were correct, however, this still wouldn't settle the question of its *normative* significance. For one, the practice might well have *other* features or functions that should affect our thoughts about what rights it ought to recognize. Along with its sovereignty-limiting dimension, for example, we might also (quite reasonably) think of the practice as fundamentally concerned

---

[40] The quote is from Raz's chapter in this volume; *also see:* Raz 2010, p. 328.
[41] Raz 2010, pp. 334–6.   [42] Raz in this volume, p. 143.
[43] ICESCR, Article 13.2 (c).   [44] ICESCR, Article 12.1.
[45] ICESCR, Article 7 (d).   [46] Tasioulas 2012, p. 24; Waldron in this volume (p. 132).
[47] Simmons 2009.
[48] There is very little, for example, in the International Bill of Human Rights itself that can plausibly be construed as threatening to national sovereignty. The prospect of punitive sanctions or international intervention in the case of human rights violations is never mentioned once. For more support on this general point, *see:* Alston 2013, p. 2072.

with the promotion of human dignity, as well as the freedom and well-being of all persons everywhere. And whatever else we think the practice does, there is no way of getting around its basic legal and political nature: a nature that makes it unsuitable for recognizing rights that we are uncomfortable placing in the hands of public institutions and officials, or to which we would rather not devote public resources.

A deeper concern is that the practice's interventionist or sovereignty-limiting dimension (whether dominant or not) seems like something that a *normative* theory of the practice should be able to critically evaluate, rather than simply take for granted. Some elements of the practice are fixed: its political and legal nature, for example. But others are more plausibly seen as open to revision. The practice's handling of human rights violations, or the particular consequences it assigns to such violations, seem best placed in this latter category, as a *revisable* element. It was certainly treated this way by those in favour of (and those against) the UN's 2005 endorsement of the *Responsibility to Protect*, a doctrine that attempts to make intervention in the case of extraordinarily grave human rights violations (i.e. genocide, war crimes, ethnic cleansing, and crimes against humanity) a recognized international responsibility.[49]

One of the odd things about Raz's theory of the practice, and this is true of Beitz's and Rawls's theories as well, is that they transform its (ultimately tentative) interventionist element into something fixed or axiomatic rather than revisable. This prevents them (or at least prevents their *theories*) from being able to question, critique, and reimagine the practice in ways that so many practitioners regularly do.

This may be no great loss in the end. There are surely other ways of taking on this critical or big-picture work. Still, it does seem like a mistake given the nature of the subject matter. Despite Nickel's interesting analogy, the practice is in fact quite *unlike* its strange bedfellow: the saw. Saws have perfectly well-established uses. Human rights practice, on the other hand, is a tool still in the process of being created and imagined. Philosophers should help.

References

Alston, Philip (2013), "Does the Past Matter? On The Origins of Human Rights" in *Harvard Law Review*, Vol. 126, No. 1, pp. 2043–81.

Beitz, Charles (2009), *The Idea of Human Rights* (Oxford: Oxford University Press).

Buchanan, Allen (2013), *The Heart of Human Rights* (Oxford: Oxford University Press).

Gilabert, Pablo (2012), "Is There a Human Right to Democracy? A Response to Joshua Cohen" in *Revista Latinoamericana de Filosofía Política*, Vol. 1, No. 2, pp. 1–37.

Griffin, James (2008), *On Human Rights* (Oxford: Oxford University Press).

Liao, S. M. & Etinson, A. (2012), "Political and Naturalistic Conceptions of Human Rights: A False Polemic?" in *The Journal of Moral Philosophy*, Vol. 9, No. 3, pp. 327–52.

Nickel, James (2007), *Making Sense of Human Rights: Second Edition* (Oxford: Blackwell Publishing).

---

[49] *See:* The General Assembly, "2005 World Summit Outcome" (available online).

Nickel, James (2014a), "Human Rights" in *The Stanford Encyclopedia of Philosophy*, ed. Edward Zalta (Stanford, Calif.: The Metaphysics Research Lab).

Nickel, James W. (2014b), "What Future for Human Rights?" in *Ethics & International Affairs*, Vol. 28, No. 2, pp. 213–23.

O'Neill, Onora (2005), "The Dark Side of Human Rights" in *International Affairs*, Vol. 81, No. 2, pp. 427–39.

Rawls, John (1999a), *A Theory of Justice: Revised Edition* (Cambridge, Mass.: Harvard University Press).

Rawls, John (1999b), *The Law of Peoples: With "The Idea of Public Reason Revisited"* (Cambridge, Mass.: Harvard University Press).

Raz, Joseph (2010), "Human Rights without Foundations" in *The Philosophy of International Law* (Oxford: Oxford University Press), ed. John Tasioulas & Samantha Besson, pp. 321–39.

Sangiovanni, Andrea (2007), "Justice and the Priority of Politics to Morality" in *The Journal of Political Philosophy*, Vol. 16, No. 2, pp. 2–28.

Simmons, Beth (2009), *Mobilizing for Human Rights: International Law in Domestic Politics* (Cambridge: Cambridge University Press).

Tasioulas, John (2009), "Are Human Rights Essentially Triggers for Intervention?" in *Philosophy Compass*, Vol. 4, No. 6, pp. 938–50.

Tasioulas, John (2012), "Towards a Philosophy of Human Rights" in *Current Legal Problems*, Vol. 65, No. 1, pp. 1–30.

5

Beyond the Political–Orthodox Divide

The Broad View

Andrea Sangiovanni

The current debate in philosophy about the concept of (moral)[1] human rights is split between two camps.[2] Orthodox theorists claim that human rights are those individual moral rights that we possess merely in virtue of our humanity.[3] Political views contend that human rights are those individual moral rights (or morally urgent interests)[4] whose violation (primarily) by states makes sovereignty-overriding interference or

---

[1] In this chapter, I focus on the question of what *moral* rather than *legal* human rights are. It is a further question what the relation between legal and moral human rights ought to be. See A. Buchanan, *The Heart of Human Rights* (Oxford: Oxford University Press, 2013) for the importance of drawing this distinction, and A. Sangiovanni, *Humanity without Dignity: Moral Equality, Respect, and Human Rights* (Cambridge, Mass.: Harvard University Press, 2017), ch. 5, and A. Sangiovanni, 'Are Moral Rights Necessary for the Justification of International Legal Human Rights?', *Ethics & International Affairs* 30 (2016): 471–81 for an evaluation.

[2] This chapter is reprinted, with permission, from Sangiovanni 2017, Ch. 4.

[3] J. Tasioulas, 'The Moral Reality of Human Rights', in *Freedom from Poverty as a Human Right*, ed. T. Pogge (Oxford: Oxford University Press, 2007); J. Griffin, *On Human Rights* (Oxford: Oxford University Press, 2008).

[4] This is Beitz's preferred formulation. See C. Beitz, *The Idea of Human Rights* (Oxford: Oxford University Press, 2009), esp. ch. 6. The distance between a morally urgent interest and a moral right seems, however, less wide than we might otherwise believe if we assume that what makes an interest 'morally urgent' is not (merely) how important it is for the agent but how stringent the third-party duties required for its satisfaction are. We should assume the latter for the following reason. Someone might have, say, a very pressing and morally urgent interest (in the former sense) in a medical treatment that costs millions. But the mere fact of its urgency would not be enough to ground obligations for states to satisfy it (and generate reasons for the international community to be concerned when the state fails to satisfy it); the interest would not therefore provide a ground for a human right on Beitz's view. Interests must therefore be morally urgent in the different sense that they generate stringent third-party duties—falling on states and owed to the individuals whose interests they are—to protect or satisfy those interests. But if this is true, then 'morally urgent interests' would entail the existence of a moral right (at least according to the Razian notion of a right). As Beitz himself recognizes, 'not every threat to an important interest is best made the subject of a [human] right' (p. 139). From now on, in the text, I therefore drop the parenthetical reference. I thank John Tasioulas for discussion on this point.

other forms of international action (including kinds of action that are *not* sovereignty-overriding, such as international assistance) permissible or required.[5]

In this chapter, I will argue that both views face insurmountable challenges and that, even if we overlook these challenges, the debate between the two camps risks dissolving into a mere verbal disagreement. I will suggest a path for moving beyond this stalemate by defending what I will call the 'Broad View' about the concept of human rights. Along the way, I will also reject a central assumption that is shared by both views (and that in part explains how the debate has ended up). This assumption is that there is a *single* overarching practice of human rights. The primary task of a philosophical theory of human rights should therefore be to reconstruct its moral core, derive a 'master list' of human rights from that core, and then to use that list as a critical standard to reform and improve the practice. Tasioulas (who defends an Orthodox view) is a good representative of this assumption: '[Our aim is] to identify the core or focal concept, the basic normative idea that enables us to make the best sense of what we pre-reflectively identify as the... practice of human rights.'[6] Similarly, according to Raz (who defends a Political view), 'The ethical doctrine of human rights should articulate standards by which the practice of human rights can be judged, standards which will indicate what human rights we have.'[7] Call this the Single Practice Assumption.

Once we adopt the Broad View and abandon the Single Practice Assumption, we will be in a position to conclude that we also ought to reject the search for a philosophically grounded master list of moral human rights by which the practice as a whole can be judged. The search for a master list of human rights that will both reveal the moral unity underlying *all* of human rights practice and serve as a standard for its criticism is chimerical. But this is not to say that more contextually focused *conceptions* of moral human rights cannot be developed. The chapter ends by showing how context can matter in developing particular conceptions of human rights.

Desiderata

All Political and Orthodox views begin in the same way, namely by drawing a distinction between the *concept* (or idea or nature) of human rights and their *content, scope,* and *grounds.* Roughly, the *concept* of human rights is meant to identify what human rights are, and an account of their *content, scope,* and *grounds* is meant to tell us what rights we have, who has them, and why we have them. For both of the going approaches, the

---

[5] J. Rawls, *The Law of Peoples* (Cambridge, Mass.: Harvard University Press, 1999); Beitz, *The Idea of Human Rights*; J. Raz, 'Human Rights without Foundations', in *The Philosophy of International Law*, eds. S. Besson and J. Tasioulas (Oxford: Oxford University Press, 2010).

[6] J. Tasioulas, 'On the Nature of Human Rights', in *The Philosophy of Human Rights: Contemporary Controversies*, eds. G. Ernst and J.-C. Heilinger (Berlin: Walter de Gruyter, 2011), at p. 39.

[7] Raz, 'Human Rights without Foundations', at p. 321. See also Griffin, *On Human Rights*, p. 25; Beitz, *The Idea of Human Rights*, p. 8.

task of identifying the concept is taken to be primary. To specify what human rights we *have,* we need to know what human rights *are* first.

How do we decide who has the better view? There are four desiderata that any theory of moral human rights should satisfy.[8] First, human rights theories must demarcate and explain the sense in which human rights are a proper subset of the set of all moral rights *simpliciter.* If they are unable to do so, then talk of human rights is redundant; one might just as well talk about moral rights. (Call this the Subclass Desideratum.) Second, human rights theories must be sufficiently faithful to the human rights culture that has emerged since 1945 and that is captured in the main human rights instruments, such as the Universal Declaration of Human Rights (UDHR) and the International Covenant on Civil and Political Rights (ICCPR). By 'sufficiently faithful,' I mean that human rights theories must not interpret human rights to be something so alien to the dominant practices that it would count as changing the subject. The desideratum is explained by our goal: in interpreting what human rights are, philosophers take themselves to be engaged in a collective project of identification, critique, and defence that is shared with practitioners.[9] (Call this the Fidelity Desideratum.) Third, human rights theories must be able to explain why we have *good normative reason* to be *un*faithful to human rights practices in cases in which the human rights theory diverges from the culture's self-understanding. The rationale for this desideratum should be clear: the ultimate goal of a human rights theory is not descriptive and explanatory but normative and critical. Our human rights theory should therefore give us good (though not necessarily exhaustive) reasons to depart from current practices where it would improve things to do so. (Call this the Normativity Desideratum.) Fourth, human rights theories should be reasonably determinate. They should, that is, provide a set of standards that are informative enough to aid us in evaluating and improving human rights practices (including, but not limited to, the system of international human rights law). This desideratum follows directly from a general worry that human rights talk is excessively loose and free-flowing. (Call this the Determinacy Desideratum.) As I will now seek to argue, I do not believe that either the Orthodox or Political view alone can successfully meet all four. To meet all four, we must adopt the Broad View, which subsumes both as distinct applications of a broader concept adapted for different contexts.

Against Orthodox Views

There are many and diverse criticisms of Orthodox views. In this section, I will focus on two that I believe to be decisive, the first one directed at James Griffin's theory of

---

[8] The Subclass, Fidelity, and Determinacy Desiderata are commonly recognized. See e.g. Tasioulas, 'On the Nature of Human Rights', at pp. 18–19. The Normativity Desideratum is surprisingly overlooked, with important consequences that I discuss in more detail in the sections 'Against Orthodox Views' and 'Against Political Views'.

[9] Cf. R. Dworkin, *Justice for Hedgehogs* (Cambridge, Mass.: Harvard University Press, 2011), p. 158.

human rights and the second at John Tasioulas's. Although I cannot show that any Orthodox view must fail in the same way, I hope to provide some progress to that conclusion by directing my criticism at two of the foremost Orthodox theories currently available.

Recall that for all Orthodox theorists, human rights are those moral rights that we possess merely in virtue of our humanity. To meet the Subclass Desideratum, therefore, Orthodox views must explain what it means to possess a moral right 'solely in virtue of our humanity.' Griffin attempts to solve the subclass problem by appealing to those moral rights that are *necessary for the protection of normative agency.* But what counts as 'normative agency' in the relevant sense? There is a danger here. If Griffin identifies 'normative agency' as a fully realized capacity 'to choose one's own path through life,' as he sometimes seems to, then *all* moral rights could be construed as contributing to such a life.[10] For example, do we have a human right that others' promises to us are kept (given that promise-keeping is important to one's capacity to pursue our conception of a worthwhile life)? A human right that others not cheat on their taxes (given how important tax-paying is to the functioning of the public services on which we depend)?[11] A human right that others not steal from us (given how important the stability of external property relations is to our 'path through life')? A human right to a proportionate prison sentence (given how important the curtailment of our freedom of movement is to one's exercise of agency)?[12] Interpreted in such an expansive manner, the account would fail the Subclass Desideratum.

As a result, Griffin often emphasizes that the moral rights must be *necessary* to the protection of agency.[13] But what does 'necessary' mean in this context? Suppose we take 'necessary' as delimiting those moral rights such that, without them, we could not live a worthwhile life as agents. But then the resulting human rights theory would be implausibly narrow; even slaves, or those who have been tortured, can still live worthwhile lives as agents. Simply being tortured or enslaved doesn't render one's life worthless. Similarly, being tortured or enslaved doesn't (in most cases) make us incapable of exercising *any* agency; it just makes it much harder.[14]

Griffin is alive to these concerns and tries to address them by appealing instead to the idea of a 'minimum.' He writes: '[Human rights] are protections of that somewhat austere state, a characteristically human life, not of a good or happy or perfected or flourishing human life.... There is a minimalist character to human rights.... The element of austerity, that reference to a minimum, must not be lost.'[15] Welfare rights,

[10] Griffin, *On Human Rights*, p. 45. See also pp. 32–3.

[11] Cf. Griffin, *On Human Rights*, p. 273: 'We do not say that a man who free-rides when filling out his income tax return violates his fellow citizens' human rights; he is a cheat, clearly, but not a human rights violator.'

[12] Cf. Griffin, *On Human Rights*, p. 273: 'Nor do we say, of a woman given an unjust prison sentence, either too little or too much, that her human rights have been violated; she has, though, not been fairly treated.'

[13] See e.g. Griffin, *On Human Rights*, p. 263.

[14] Raz makes a similar point in Raz, 'Human Rights without Foundations'.

[15] Griffin, *On Human Rights*, pp. 34, 53, 263; see also p. 41.

for example, secure 'minimum provision'; other rights secure a 'minimum' of health, education, information. As we have already noted, agency is not, however, an intrinsically 'minimalist' concept, especially if one includes, as Griffin does, protections for its realization and exercise. So from what normative source does Griffin draw the standard for how 'minimal' the protection afforded by a given right should be? What, in other words, determines the threshold above which a protection of agency ceases to be a human right? Griffin writes: 'For one thing, it seems that the more austere notion is what the tradition of human rights supports. For another, it seems to be the proper stipulation to make. If we had rights to all that is needed for a good or happy life, then the language of rights would become redundant.'[16] Griffin appeals here to both what we have called the Fidelity and Subclass Desiderata: we ought to append a 'minimalist' rider to the demand to protect the exercise and realization of agency because it tracks the way human rights are conceived by practitioners and solves the Subclass Desideratum. Although arguable—consider how 'maximalist' the International Covenant on Economic, Social and Cultural Rights (ICESCR)[17] is, for example—let us grant the assumption. With the Normativity Desideratum in mind, we now wonder: Do we have *good normative reason* to tailor our human rights theory to practice in this way? Why are practitioners (or those in the longer human rights tradition) *correct* to think of human rights as 'minimal' protections? (Or, alternatively, if practitioners are not using the term properly, what normative reason do they have to reorient their uses of the term in ways suggested by Griffin?) Griffin's account, I am suggesting, does not have the resources to provide us with an answer. And it is doubtful, even if he were to explain why we have good normative reason to think of human rights as *minimal* protections, whether the theory would be able to meet the Determinacy Desideratum. What criteria should we use to draw the 'minimum' threshold in a determinate place?[18]

Perhaps Griffin could turn here to what he calls 'practicalities,' namely the requirement that for something to be a human right it must not only be grounded in some aspect of agency but also reflect a 'socially manageable claim[] on others.'[19] On this interpretation, human rights claims must be 'minimal' because otherwise they would impose an 'unmanageable' range of moral duties on third parties. And one might understand 'unmanageable' here as 'unfeasible.' If there were a human right to more than a minimum, then it would impose moral duties on others to secure the object of

---

[16] Griffin, *On Human Rights*, p. 34.

[17] See e.g. Article 12.1, which promises the 'right of everyone to the enjoyment of the highest attainable standard of physical and mental health.'

[18] Though I won't be able to make good on this claim here, I also believe that Orthodox accounts of human rights that try to ground human rights in some account of basic human needs, or basic capabilities, also will fall afoul of both the Normativity and Determinacy Desiderata. See e.g. A. Sen, 'Elements of a Theory of Human Rights', *Philosophy & Public Affairs* 32 (2004): 315–56; D. Miller, 'Grounding Human Rights', *Critical Review of International Social and Political Philosophy* 15 (2012): 407–27. Why can only *basic* needs ground human rights claims? Why only *basic* capabilities?

[19] Griffin, *On Human Rights*, p. 38.

the right so onerous that they would be unfeasible. The problem here is that Griffin accepts that we can have a range of 'manageable' or 'feasible' moral duties grounded in correlative rights that *don't* count as human rights. We have, for example, a range of promise-keeping duties, justice-based distributive duties to others to secure more than a minimum of welfare, and justice-based corrective duties to pass proportionate sentences. All of these duties, furthermore, are 'directed' to a respective rights-bearer, such that someone who has had a promise broken without excuse, someone who has been denied their fair share, and someone who has been unfairly sentenced can all properly say that they have been *wronged*. So why couldn't all of these rights plausibly count as *human* rights? In the response envisaged here, Griffin must be able to say that these can't be *human* rights because they are 'socially unmanageable' or 'infeasible.' But this doesn't seem to be the case with any of the moral duties correlating with the rights just mentioned. And, given that any genuine moral right correlates with some duties, the response will fail comprehensively for all moral rights. The 'practicalities' defence, in short, does not succeed in meeting the Subclass Desideratum.

As noted by Tasioulas, Griffin's account also fails to explain why *only* personhood interests should count in generating human rights claims. Why shouldn't interests in, for example, 'accomplishment, knowledge, friendship, and the avoidance of pain'[20] also be sufficient (under the right circumstances) to ground third-party duties? Put in our terms, the restriction to personhood interests cannot satisfy the Normativity Desideratum. Take, for example, Griffin's exclusion of the severely mentally disabled and children from the scope of human rights.[21] What normative reasons do we have to exclude children and the disabled? The potential gain in determinacy is purchased at the price of arbitrariness.

Tasioulas's Orthodox account attempts to go beyond Griffin in two main ways: first, his account appeals to a much wider array of interests as grounds for human rights claims; second, his account puts much more emphasis on the directed duties that are triggered by any purported human right. The former aids Tasioulas in meeting the Normativity and Fidelity Desiderata. The latter is necessary to specify more carefully what can count as a rights-grounding interest in the first place, and therefore helps Tasioulas to satisfy both the Determinacy and Subclass Desiderata. Tasioulas's account is therefore well placed to become the champion among Orthodox theories. Is it successful?

I will argue that Tasioulas's view does not satisfy the Subclass Desideratum. Recall that Griffin attempted to meet the Subclass Desideratum through a *content*-based restriction that was meant to qualify and explain which moral rights we have 'merely in virtue of our humanity.' Griffin claimed that those moral rights we have in virtue of our humanity are those we have in virtue of our agency. Given Tasioulas's more pluralistic account of the grounds for human rights, he cannot do this. Instead, he appeals to the

---

[20] J. Tasioulas, 'Taking Rights out of Human Rights', *Ethics* 120 (2010): 647–78 at p. 662.
[21] Griffin, *On Human Rights*, p. 92.

idea that human rights are *general* rather than *special* moral rights. According to Tasioulas, 'the possession of a human right cannot be conditional on some conduct or achievement of the right-holder, a relationship to which they belong, or their membership of a particular community or group.'[22] But what about justly convicted criminals? They lose the right to free movement and association, and in many cases, also the right to political participation, hold office, and so on in virtue of their previous conduct. Does that mean that their human rights have been violated? Or that rights to freedom of association, free movement, political participation, and so on don't count as human rights since they are held conditionally on the basis of things one has done (or not done)? On this restriction, the only human rights there would be are the rights that could not legitimately be stripped from justly convicted criminals. However short the list is, it is far shorter than the list envisaged by Tasioulas or by any human rights movement. The suggestion risks purchasing the Subclass Desideratum at the price of the Fidelity Desideratum. But there is also the problem of the Normativity Desideratum: What normative reason do we have for thinking that human rights are limited to those rights that prisoners[23] cannot lose?

There is also the problem that the right to a fair trial, the right to vote, and the right to education, for example, also seem conditional, not on what one has done, but on whether one is subject to the legal authority of a political community (in the first two cases) and on whether one can benefit from an education (in the other). One holds a right to a fair trial only if one is relevantly subject to a legal authority, just as one holds a right to vote only if one is a member, in some relevant sense, of a political community. Similarly, one has a right to education only if one can benefit from it. These rights, therefore, don't appear to be rights that we have 'merely in virtue of our humanity.'

Tasioulas's solution is to fold the condition into the statement of the right: one has a general right to [vote *only if* one is a member of the political community in question];[24] one has a general right to [an education *only if* one can benefit]. One could apply, of course, the same strategy to the right to freedom of movement: one has a general right to [free association *only if* one has not been justly convicted of a crime of kind *x*]. The conditionalized general rights are possessed by all human beings (even those who have committed crimes or do not belong to a political community or cannot benefit from education), and so can be human rights.

The trouble is that this manoeuvre won't satisfy the Subclass Desideratum. The reason is that *any* moral right can be converted into a general right, including any *special* right, by folding its factual precondition into the statement of the right. For example, the special right that others keep their noncontractual promises to us (barring exceptional circumstances) can also be stated as a general right: we have a general right that

---

[22] Tasioulas, 'On the Nature of Human Rights', at p. 37.

[23] It is revealing that Griffin claims that prisoners' human rights are indeed infringed, but that this is justified, all things considered, on the basis that they morally deserve to be punished. See Griffin, *On Human Rights*, p. 64. I thank Rowan Cruft for pointing me to this passage in Griffin.

[24] The brackets indicate the scope of the rights claim.

[others keep their noncontractual promises to us *only if* they have actually made a promise to us and *only if* exceptional circumstances do not hold]. When we include the conditions in the content of the right, the right becomes fully general: even people who have not had any promises made to them have the (general) right that [others keep their promises to them *should they ever make such a promise*]. The right is held by people who have no special relations or history. Similarly, any *derived* moral right, such as my right to vote in Italian elections, can also be restated as a fully general right, and hence, on this account, a human right: one has a (general) right to [vote in Italian elections only if one is an Italian citizen]. All (genuine) moral rights, using this strategy, can be converted into general rights. The advantage is that Tasioulas can then deal with the prisoner, fair trial, and education counterexamples. The disadvantage is that he then fails to meet the Subclass Desideratum.

A potential response is to impose conditions on the *kinds* of antecedents that can be folded into the statement of the right. In response to a similar objection by Nicholas Wolterstorff, Tasioulas does just that.[25] To deal with the objection from derived rights (such as the right to vote in Italian elections), Tasioulas bans the use of proper names. And to deal with the fair trial and education objections, he requires that 'the conditions specifying the duties [and hence the rights which are their basis] must refer to circumstances that are not unduly remote for all human beings given the sociohistorical conditions to which the existence of the right has been indexed.'[26] But what about the promising counterexample? What about the right to a proportionate sentence? And what about other moral rights that also look to be entirely general, such as the moral right not to be insulted? All of those rights could easily be conditionalized, none of them uses proper names, and their corresponding duties do not refer to circumstances that are unduly remote.

Tasioulas could say (as he seems tempted to say)[27] that these are indeed human rights on a correct understanding of what human rights are. But this would be a difficult bullet to bite. It would undermine at a stroke one of the main advantages of an Orthodox view, namely its fidelity to the human rights movement (especially when compared with Political views, to which we turn in a moment). No human rights practitioner takes such an expansive view. We might try to add further conditions on admissible conditionals until we have a view that looks about right. It is unclear to me, however, whether any such general criteria could *exclude* things like promises or taxes or insults but *include* fair trials and education. But there is another problem. How do the stipulated conditions on admissible conditionals meet the Normativity Desideratum? What *normative reason* do we have to accept them? The addition of further conditions would seem *ad hoc*.

---

[25] See N. Wolterstorff, *Justice: Rights and Wrongs* (Princeton: Princeton University Press, 2010), pp. 314–15. Tasioulas responds in Tasioulas, 'On the Nature of Human Rights' at pp. 38–41.

[26] Tasioulas, 'On the Nature of Human Rights', at p. 39.

[27] See Tasioulas, 'On the Nature of Human Rights', p. 39.

I conclude that the going Orthodox approaches to human rights are insufficient on their own to satisfy the four desiderata. While there may be other Orthodox views that can respond to these objections and meet all four desiderata, the two most promising ones, I have argued, cannot.

Against Political Views

Political views are tailor made to satisfy the Subclass Desideratum, and hence do well where Orthodox views do poorly. The way they do so is by jettisoning the idea that human rights are those moral rights human beings possess *in virtue of their humanity.* Instead, they say that human rights are those moral rights that *have a certain function in international affairs.* As we have seen, Political views vary in the kinds of functions believed to be definitive of human rights. In this section, I will press a criticism that affects all subvariants, namely that they fail the Fidelity and Normativity Desiderata. By making the conditions for the existence of a human right depend too much on shifting contingencies, they depart significantly from the aims and purposes of an important aspect of current human rights culture.[28] And they provide no good normative reasons to do so. What is gained by satisfying the Subclass Desideratum is lost with respect to the Fidelity and Normativity Desiderata.

Imagine someone is tortured in Pakistan. And imagine that any criticism or other international action (whether sovereignty-overriding or not) would severely destabilize the region such that it would not be justified. According to the Political view, while there is certainly a moral right that has been violated, it is not a *human* right. But now imagine that international circumstances change enough that international action (whether sovereignty-overriding or not) becomes justifiable. Has the person tortured acquired a human right in the process—a right that they previously lacked? Can we gain and lose our human rights in virtue of shifting international circumstances?[29]

Political views therefore are a far cry from the way claims are pursued within human rights organizations, which are mostly concerned with bringing to light severe abuses in other states *whatever* the international circumstances supporting a particular course

---

[28] I am indebted to discussion in Jeremy Waldron, 'Human Rights: A Critique of the Raz–Rawls Approach', in this volume, for the arguments I make in this section.

[29] This also strikes me as applying to Beitz's discussion of women's human rights. He claims that many of the concerns defended in the Convention on the Elimination of All Forms of Discrimination against Women cannot be bona fide human rights because it would be infeasible to pursue international action to change them: 'The inference is that a government's failure to comply with those elements of women's human rights doctrine that require efforts to bring about substantial cultural change does not supply a reason for action by outside agents because there is no plausibly effective strategy of action for which it could be a reason. But if this is correct, then these elements do not satisfy one of our schematic conditions for justifying human rights: they are not appropriately matters of international concern. . . . But human rights are supposed to be matters of international concern, and if there are no feasible means of expressing this concern in political action, then perhaps to this extent women's human rights doctrine overreaches' (Beitz, *The Idea of Human Rights*, p. 195). Whether women have human rights turns out to vary according to how feasible international efforts at social change in fact would be.

of action.[30] And they don't even seem to track the usage of human rights law within the UN system (where one might think a Political view would find the most traction). In human rights law, whether something counts as a human rights violation, and the kinds of remedies that are available for such violations, are two different things.[31]

Political theorists have a ready response to this objection.[32] They can claim that the existence conditions for a human right vary not with the *all-things-considered* reasons for undertaking international action, but only with *pro tanto* reasons for such action. On this clarification, there can be *pro tanto* reasons to take international action with respect to the torture victim even if current international circumstances make it all-things-considered unjustified to do so. The objection to this common move comes in the form of a dilemma. The dilemma is raised when we consider what kinds of considerations we need to take into account in determining whether there is in fact a *pro tanto* reason to take some specific form of international action. The point is easiest to see with an intervention-based variant (I will generalize the point immediately thereafter). On such a view, human rights are those moral rights whose violation would give third parties a *pro tanto* reason to intervene militarily. We face a number of questions: Holding constant the harm involved in the violation of a given moral right, under what circumstances do we have such a *pro tanto* reason to intervene? What kinds of countervailing considerations can override or outweigh the reason? How strong is the reason? We now confront a choice. Do we answer these questions by identifying what a 'normal' set of circumstances for such intervention would be? Or do we identify the strength, weight, and presence of the reasons with more idealized circumstances?

Suppose we take the former route (this is the first horn of our dilemma). On this route, we begin by listing the most common consequences of military intervention, given what we generally know about the current international situation, the degree of support that can be expected for intervention among general populations, and so on. In this way, we abstract from any particular situation that we may face here and now. And then we ask: Would we have an *all-things-considered* reason to intervene militarily in the typical situation envisaged in the first step, in light of the violation of some moral right (or set of moral rights) x? If we answer yes, then the moral right (or set of rights) in question is a human right. It is a human right because the moral right's violation would warrant an intervention *under normal circumstances*. While the warrant is only provisional—it could be overridden or outweighed by more specific knowledge of any actual conflict—it is sufficient to ground the existence of a human right.

The problem is that this line of response faces the same difficulty as the first-cut, all-things-considered variant. Why should the human rights we have vary with what count as 'normal' circumstances? For example, military interventions can become much

[30] See e.g. A. Neier, *The International Human Rights Movement: A History* (Princeton: Princeton University Press, 2012), ch. 3.

[31] See e.g. P. Alston and R. Goodman, *International Human Rights in Context* (Oxford: Oxford University Press, 2008).

[32] See e.g. Beitz, *The Idea of Human Rights*, p. 109.

more difficult with subtle shifts in the international balance of power (consider how different the prospects for military intervention seem after the 2003 invasion of Iraq, for example). Do we say that before the shift (before 2003), individuals in Pakistan had one set of human rights, and after 2003 they have another? Once again, such a move would be wildly at variance with practitioners' self-understanding. What normative reason could there be to accept it? What it gains in meeting the Determinacy and Subclass Desiderata, it loses with respect to the Fidelity and Normativity Desiderata.

This horn of the dilemma is just as difficult to surmount for an international-action (rather than military-intervention) version of the Political view. For there too we wonder: What are the 'normal' circumstances that would warrant international action of type x? And there too we worry that this leaves human rights too dependent on the shifting sands that determine what count as 'normal circumstances.'

There is pressure to take the second route, namely to idealize the circumstances against which we determine the presence, weight, and strength of the *pro tanto* reasons. And here the Political view faces the second horn of our dilemma. Rather than point to 'normal' circumstances, the idealizing interpretation abstracts further from the things that we know about military intervention. It claims: There is a *pro tanto* reason sufficient to ground the existence of a human right as long as there would be all-things-considered reason to intervene militarily in *ideal* circumstances. To avoid the charge of contingency, the interpretation imagines what we might call a *frictionless* case, namely a case in which, say, military intervention was both costless and sure to succeed. Would we intervene in that case (again, given some specified violation of a moral right)? If so, then there is *some* reason to intervene, and this is sufficient to say that there is a *pro tanto* reason to intervene, and hence that the moral right is a *human* right. The danger here is that the view would then fail the Subclass Desideratum. If it were really true that military intervention were both costless and sure to succeed, then, absent countervailing considerations, the violation of *any* moral right would warrant such intervention. The verdict seems to hinge on what, exactly, we mean by 'costless' and 'sure to succeed.' Notice that the more realistic we make the costs and prospects of military intervention, the more the contingency objection begins to bite. And the less realistic we make them, the more the Subclass Desideratum impinges. This is a set of simultaneous equations with no solution. Any amount of contingency will seem to make the existence of a human right depend on the wrong kind of thing, and any elimination of such contingency will make human rights indistinguishable from moral rights.

Notice further that the second horn of the dilemma impales international-action variants with greater force than intervention ones. Because the range of legitimate remedial actions that can ground a human rights claim will be much less costly and disruptive than a military intervention (converging, at the limit, to mere criticism), the international-action variant will fail the Subclass Desideratum much more quickly than its interventionist cousin. After all, one might reasonably think that *any* violation of a moral right would give us *pro tanto* reason to criticize the violation publicly *especially* if such criticism is sure to succeed in preventing or stopping the violation and has no other costs. And even if the Subclass Desideratum would be satisfied—by isolating, for example, only morally more significant rights—it would fail to satisfy the Normativity Desideratum: of what use would the (long) list of claims that give us *pro tanto* reason to subject violators to international criticism be, given the diversity of concerns that practitioners within human rights organizations, international institutions, and states have? I conclude that Political views also cannot, on their own, meet all four desiderata.

A Merely Verbal Disagreement

Even if we assume that my criticisms of both views do not succeed, there is a further problem: debates between Political and Orthodox views have a tendency to resolve into merely verbal disputes. In this section, I illustrate how this happens. In the rest of the chapter, I provide a solution.

Imagine a proponent of the Orthodox view argues that there is a human right to education. The Orthodox theorist claims that this is because a moral right to education is possessed by each human being in virtue of their humanity alone.[33] The proponent of the Political view joins the discussion, claiming that the Orthodox view says something false. There is *no* human right to education. This is because a violation of a moral right to education does not (even *pro tanto*) justify sovereignty-interfering action by third parties. Are they really disagreeing? Or is this just a verbal dispute?

We can use what Chalmers calls the 'method of elimination' to test whether this disagreement is merely verbal.[34] The idea is to eliminate use of the key term—'human right'—and see whether any substantive dispute remains. The Orthodox theorist, let us suppose, claims that (a) there is an individual moral right to education that generates third-party duties on modern states to supply a basic minimum of education to each citizen, (b) this right is ultimately grounded in universal human interests in being able to live one's life free from deceit and domination by others, and hence is held 'in virtue of our humanity,' and (c) violations of the moral right to education would not justify, in current circumstances, kind of foreign, sovereignty-overriding interference (or other international action) to secure it. It strikes me that the Political theorist could happily *agree* with propositions (a)–(c). The only thing that the two parties are disagreeing about, I conclude, is whether to *call* that moral right a human right. This suggests, therefore, that they are engaged in a merely verbal dispute.

The Broad View

Is there a way out of this impasse? To sketch a way out, I proceed in two steps. First, I provide an articulation of the concept that is broad and ecumenical and that captures what is best in both the Orthodox view (the focus on moral rights) and the Political

---

[33] I here imagine that we have answers to the criticisms made in the text above.

[34] D. J. Chalmers, 'Verbal Disputes', *Philosophical Review* 120 (2011): 515–66 at p. 526.

view (the focus on the moral and political significance of human rights claims) while avoiding the worst in each one (the Contingency and Subclass objections). Second, I will distinguish more clearly the *concept* of human rights and particular *interpretations* of that concept, and demonstrate how doing so allows us to abandon the Single Practice Assumption and to account for the broad and diverse range of usages in contemporary human rights practices. I end by arguing that the Broad View satisfies all four of the desiderata with which we started.

I. *The concept*

According to the Broad View, human rights are not those moral rights *possessed* in virtue of our humanity, but those moral rights whose systematic violation ought to be of universal moral, legal, and political *concern*. Any violation[35] of a moral right that ought to garner universal moral, legal, and political concern is a human right.

It is worth highlighting four main features of the Broad construal of the concept. First, the concept is intended to have very wide scope, encompassing most contemporary usage. On the Broad construal, it is enough for a protest group, for example, to sincerely believe that the systematic moral rights violations they raise and reforms they pursue under the banner of human rights ought to garner universal moral, political, and legal concern for their claims to count as a *conceptually correct*—though not necessarily substantively valid—use of the term. It is a further question whether the systematic moral rights violations they believe ought to garner such concern *really are* moral rights violations and *really do* merit universal, concern just as it is a further question what *counts* as the relevant kind of universal concern. And, with a sideways look toward Political views, it is also a further question whether any specific remedial or corrective action is warranted given some set of systematic violations.

Second, the Broad construal is not so broad as to be meaningless. The Broad View tries to capture the distinctiveness of human rights claims in all their diversity. On the Broad View, the most distinctive aspect of human rights is the idea that the morally most urgent claims of individuals and minorities are taken to be matters of *universal* rather than only of local moral, legal, and political concern. (As we will see in Section II, what counts as relevantly 'universal' and relevantly 'moral,' 'legal,' and 'political' and what count as the rights' correlated duties will vary by context.) This basic feature of human rights was central to the American and French revolutions and their accompanying declarations, and connects those revolutions with the spread of liberal constitutionalism throughout the globe (including its near obliteration in the years leading up to the end of the Second World War).

Third, notice that the Broad construal does not isolate the subclass of human rights from the class of moral rights *simpliciter* via a reference to a property shared (equally) by all human beings, such as their humanity, or dignity, or normative agency. For all

---

[35] The violation must be systematic. To determine whether the assassination of Archduke Franz Ferdinand was a human rights violation, we need to assess whether assassinations *qua* assassinations merit universal concern, rather than the particular fact that a single such assassination led to a chain of events with global significance. I thank Adam Etinson for stressing the need to clarify.

I have said, there could be moral rights that are possessed by nonhumans[36] (or, indeed, the severely handicapped or children[37]) or by collectives.[38] As long as the systematic violation of those moral rights ought to be of universal moral, legal, and political concern, then they are not conceptually disqualified before the discussion ever gets started. This feature, as I will discuss in more detail in Section III, prevents further useless verbal disagreements.

Fourth, the Broad View does not isolate human rights, as Political views do, in virtue of a unique political function or role they play in international affairs, such as 'human rights are moral rights whose systematic violation would *pro tanto* justify humanitarian intervention, or sanctions, or diplomatic intervention,' or some other remedial action. Rather, it isolates them by reference to their moral *significance* for some (yet to be specified) moral, legal, or political context. Because it does not yoke the existence of a human right to the justification for some remedial action *as a matter of conceptual necessity,* it does not fall prey to the contingency objection. Notice, for example, that the Broad View allows for someone to *specify* (as the relevant form of universal moral, legal, and political concern) that they are only interested in those human rights whose systematic violation would trigger some form of intervention; what it bars them from saying is that this is all there is to the concept of a human right, or that these are the only human rights that are genuinely human rights, or that people who focus on other types of universal moral, legal, and political concern are necessarily misguided. As a result, a Political view stated as a specification of the Broad View no longer faces the contingency objection; a proponent of such a view can always say, 'Just because the human rights I am interested in are those that trigger some form of intervention doesn't mean that we can't have human rights in other senses, too.'

The Broad View, furthermore, leaves entirely open, as a result, who the duty-bearers can be as well as the particular remedial actions that ought (normally) to follow particular violations. As a conceptual matter, the Broad View allows for the primary duty-bearers to be not only states but also transnational corporations, nongovernmental organizations, paramilitaries, guerrillas, and indeed even nonaligned individuals. As long as the systematic violations in which each of these duty-bearers are engaged (are perceived to) merit universal moral, legal, and political concern, then the use counts as conceptually correct.[39] So-called interactional accounts of human rights are therefore *not* excluded on conceptual grounds (as they are according to the Political view).[40]

---

[36] In 2007, Austrian animal rights activists fought to have a chimpanzee (named Matthew Hiasl Pan) declared a person. See also the Nonhuman Rights Project, on which see more here: <http://www.nonhumanrightsproject.org/>.

[37] Cf. Griffin, *On Human Rights*, p. 92, where he denies that children or the cognitively disabled have human rights.

[38] Therefore, if the right to self-determination is a moral right held by a collective, then it can be, on the Broad construal, a human right. It is a further, normative and substantive question whether, in a particular context, its violation *qua* collective right merits universal moral, legal, and political concern.

[39] Cf. Beitz, *The Idea of Human Rights*, p. 122.

[40] For the distinction between 'interactional' and 'institutional' accounts, see T. Pogge, *World Poverty and Human Rights* (Cambridge: Polity, 2002), ch. 2.

Similarly, the Broad View does not exclude Orthodox views as long as they allow for other specifications of universal concern to count as legitimate interpretations of the concept of human rights and as long as they specify both what type of universal concern they envision and how that particular kind of universal concern allows them to meet the four desiderata (especially the Subclass Desideratum). An Orthodox view developed as an interpretation of the Broad concept might, for example, say that the human rights are those *basic* moral rights that we possess in virtue of our humanity and whose enjoyment is a necessary precondition for the enjoyment of any other moral right and then argue why a right's being basic merits some specific kind of universal concern.

The Broad View therefore subsumes both Orthodox and Political views, explaining each as a special interpretation of the overarching concept. We now face two questions: How can a view as broad as this meet any of the desiderata mentioned here? And: How does the Broad View avoid merely verbal disagreements? I will spend the rest of this chapter answering these questions.

II. *The diversity that stands between concept and conception*

The key to the Broad View lies in the way it conceives of the *relation* between concept and conception.[41] One natural way to proceed would be to list all the moral rights and correlated duties whose systematic violation would merit universal moral, legal, and political concern. Call a list generated in this way the 'Extended List.' (For the moment, I will assume that such a list could, in fact, be drawn up, even though I will soon question that very assumption.) The Extended List would constitute the endpoint of a fully fledged human rights theory that accepts the Broad construal of the concept, and be a competitor to similar lists generated by Political and Orthodox views (in their fullest articulations). It would be an attempt to specify the list of human rights and their correlated duties that underlies and justifies human rights practice as a single, coherent whole. I will argue that is *not* the way in which a defender of the Broad View ought to articulate a conception of human rights. Seeing how it would fail will help motivate our rejection of the Single Practice Assumption, which, of course, the Extended List approach also accepts.

While the Extended List approach would satisfy the Subclass and Fidelity Desiderata, it would straightforwardly fail the Determinacy and Normativity Desiderata. The Extended List would satisfy the Fidelity Desideratum because it would capture a central feature of all human rights claims, namely their universal and peremptory status. And it would also satisfy the Subclass Desideratum by isolating a subclass of all moral rights and their correlated duties, namely those moral rights and correlated duties whose systematic violation merits universal moral, legal, and political concern. Take the

---

[41] I am indebted to Rainer Forst for how to conceive of this relation and to helpful discussion with Massimo Renzo. I note in particular the structural similarity between Forst's 'right to justification' and its articulation in a system of political *cum* human rights, and my appeal to higher-order moral rights and how they are construed in different contexts of justification. See R. Forst, *The Right to Justification: Elements of a Constructivist Theory of Justice* (New York: Columbia University Press, 2011), ch. 9.

violation of promissory rights. Barring exceptional circumstances, such violations are not morally significant enough to warrant universal moral, legal, and political concern (on any plausible construal of 'universal' and 'moral, political, and legal concern'). Systematic violations by states of individuals' right to bodily integrity, on the other hand, clearly do.

But there would be insurmountable problems with a conception developed along the lines of the Extended List. First, notice that the Extended List is severely indeterminate. What particular duties and duty-bearers, for example, ought to be associated with the List? Should, for example, the List be taken to correlate with duties owed by states, by public, nonstate actors, or by any individual anywhere? How stringent are the duties? To whom are they owed? In the absence of some more determinate conception of 'universal moral, political, and legal concern' that can help us to answer these questions, it will be impossible to know what follows from one's acceptance of the List, and so what, in practice, the List would commit us to.

The Extended List would also fail the Normativity Desideratum. Imagine one has in hand a determinate version of the Extended List. What normative relevance would it have? Suppose we were called to the House of Lords with a freshly printed copy of our List. Of what use would it be to judges deciding whether to allow the indefinite detainment of foreign nationals suspected of terrorism on national soil (or, alternatively, judges deciding whether the European Convention on Human Rights [ECHR] ought to be applied extraterritorially to those detained by UK forces in Afghanistan)? How would the List help them determine a morally informed reading of the content and scope of the right to a fair trial according to the Convention? What moral rights and correlated duties, that is, warrant the *specific kind* of universal moral, legal, and political concern triggered by a Law Lords' ruling under the Human Rights Act? Knowing that there are moral rights and correlated duties that ought to merit some kind of (unspecified) universal moral, legal, and political concern would be irrelevant to their decision.

Or imagine we went to Human Rights Watch with our list. Human Rights Watch wants to know whether to mount a monitoring effort to track homophobia in South Africa. Once again: What good would it do to know those are moral rights and correlated duties that merit some kind of (unspecified) universal concern? What Human Rights Watch wants to know is whether moral rights to engage in homosexual relations warrant a global monitoring campaign designed to pressure governments and individuals into action. This is the same sort of scepticism that motivated a (wrongheaded) move away from the Orthodox to the Political view.

As a way of deriving a conception of human rights, the Extended List is a nonstarter. How can we do better? The solution begins by abandoning the Single Practice Assumption. Both Political and Orthodox views (and the Extended List approach) assume that there is an underlying moral unity to human rights practice, such that one can derive a single, unified list of moral rights that can be used to criticize any particular human rights practice. But why assume that there is any such master list there to be discovered? And why assume that practitioners—including the UN High Commissioner, the Justice on the European Court of Human Rights, the South African or German judge, activists in Amnesty International, domestic movements across Latin America, sub-Saharan Africa, and Asia—must all be implicitly appealing to such a unified list by using the term 'human rights'? Why not instead be faithful to the multiplicity? That is what the Broad View tries to do.

The way it does so is by treating 'human rights' as a context-sensitive term such as 'tall,' or 'every bottle' in the expression 'every bottle was empty.' 'Tall' has a general linguistic meaning that doesn't vary across contexts, namely *having a maximal degree of height above some threshold*. But the *content* of particular uses of 'tall'—and hence the property picked out by a particular use of the term—will vary according to the context. So when I say that 'Michael Jordan [who is six feet, six inches tall] is short,' I might be saying something true. The expression is true when I am speaking *about basketball players*. It is false when speaking *about men in general*. The term 'tall' does not, that is, refer to any property until the parameter determining the specific threshold above which one counts as tall has been settled—either explicitly by interlocutors (for example, when one participant in a conversation clarifies the reference class they intend for their usage of 'tall,' say, *basketball players*) or implicitly by the conversational context (for example, when the participants are at a basketball game, discussing the players).[42] Similarly, the expression 'every bottle is empty' may be true in a conversation at a dinner party, but false in the cellars of Möet et Chandon. In the latter case, the parameter that sets the domain of the quantifier is set implicitly by either the conversational context (we are in the cellars) or explicitly by the interlocutors themselves ('no, no, I meant every bottle *in the cellar* not every bottle *in this room*'), just as in the case of 'tall.'

I want to say the same about the expression 'human rights.'[43] While the term has a general linguistic meaning that doesn't vary across contexts (i.e. 'moral rights whose violation merits universal moral, political, and legal concern'), the term's specific content varies with the context referred to by the speaker, which determines what *kind* of universal moral, legal, and political concern is at stake. Put another way, there is no single, master list of human rights and correlated duties against which one can evaluate

---

[42] For one interpretation of the context-sensitivity of gradable adjectives, see Christopher Kennedy, 'Vagueness and Grammar: The Semantics of Relative and Absolute Gradable Adjectives', *Linguistics and Philosophy* 30 (2007); on quantifier domain restrictions, see J. Stanley and Z. Gendler Szabó, 'On Quantifier Domain Restriction', Mind & Language 15 (2000): 219–61. I here remain neutral on how, among other things, the semantic and pragmatic aspects of an utterance in a context combine to establish and fix the parameter, and what the best account of the parameter itself is.

[43] Here I note in passing that although I am focusing in this chapter on *moral* human rights, the same thing could be said regarding *legal* human rights, i.e. legal human rights are those legal rights that ought to garner a particular kind of universal legal concern but where the type of 'legal concern' envisaged varies by context (ECHR, ICCPR, etc.). So when I mention legal contexts in this chapter, I refer to moral human rights that might provide reasons for the realization of a corresponding legal right or norm or some other legal right or norm that, though not the same in content, is necessary to protect or promote the realization of an underlying moral human right.

expressions of the general form 'y has a human right to x' just as there is no all-purpose threshold above which someone counts as tall. As we will see in a moment, this context-sensitivity enables the Broad View to meet both the Determinacy and Normativity Desiderata in a way that the Extended List approach alone could not. (Call this the Context-Sensitive way of developing conceptions of human rights within the Broad View—or CSBV for short.)

To determine which particular specification of universal moral, political, and legal concern is appropriate for a given context, the CSBV theorist begins by asking: given the uses to which human rights are put in a certain context x, what moral rights and correlated duties would warrant the *specific kind* of universal moral, legal, and political concern relevant for that context? To answer this question, the CSBV theorist needs to provide an interpretation of the kind of universal moral, legal, and political concern at stake in the particular context he or she is interested in. This lower-level, and hence *mediating*, concept of human rights *for context* x helps to give shape and determinacy to the overall account, and is equivalent to explicitly fixing the domain for the quantifier 'every' in 'every bottle' or fixing the reference class and threshold for a gradable adjective like 'tall.'

For example, imagine you are a philosophically minded human rights activist within Amnesty International. You want to know what human rights violations should define the main aims of Amnesty's advocacy. You resist the temptation to answer: 'Just the ones in the UDHR' since you want to be able to evaluate whether the UDHR lists all (and only) the human rights we actually have or otherwise contributes to their realization. It would be a mistake (as we have seen) to make this evaluation by trying to find only those moral rights and correlated duties that we possess merely in virtue of our humanity. Instead, we ask: 'Which systematic violations of moral rights ought to garner universal moral, legal, and political concern?' You realize, however, that there will be no determinate, truth-evaluable answer to this question until we have specified exactly what *kind* of universal concern we have in mind.

The CSBV then says: 'Don't look for a single, general-purpose type of universal moral, legal, and political concern that will be adequate for *all* contexts in which human rights are invoked (as the Extended List approach did). Rather, accept the great diversity in the kinds of universal concern relevant to different contexts. With this in mind, begin by asking yourself what the point and purpose of Amnesty is; begin, that is, by giving an account of the role that human rights claims are meant to play in the particular practice you are interested in. What uses does Amnesty's invocation of human rights serve?' To this question, we might then respond: 'Human rights advocacy of the type pursued by Amnesty aims to protect individuals against standard state-authorized (and often also state-enforced) threats to liberty, especially (but not exclusively) in civil and political domains.' A fuller interpretation would refer to the history of Amnesty, and in particular to Amnesty's aim to be 'nonaligned': human rights were meant to be 'above politics,' and hence not identified with the particular aims of any one liberal democracy or communist state, Islamic regime, or more straightforwardly authoritarian regime.[44] Amnesty aims therefore to protect all individuals against the abuse of political power, wherever it occurs; hence the importance to Amnesty of the 'prisoner of conscience.' This also explains why Amnesty makes a special effort to monitor human rights abuses in the West (e.g. prisoners' rights in the United States).[45] In turn, Amnesty uses a variety of methods in its official campaigns. The strategies deployed seek mainly to 'name and shame' governments via public forms of pressure (e.g. letter-writing), to provide a monitoring and informational function, and to extend and monitor international human rights law (e.g. via its support for treaty-making and revision).[46] And while Amnesty sometimes urges third-party governments to take (or continue) some form of international action[47]—e.g. the imposition of sanctions or trade embargoes, the establishment of post-conflict tribunals, or the maintenance and expansion of peace-keeping operations—it never urges outright military intervention.[48]

With this mediating concept in hand—the kind of universal moral, legal, and political concern relevant from the point of view of a human rights activist within a non-governmental organization like Amnesty—the CSBV theorist can now turn to the defence of a specific *conception* of human rights under the mediating concept. What moral rights and correlated duties warrant the specific types of universal moral, legal, and political concern called for by an actor within Amnesty? To answer this further question, we say that the CSBV theorist ought to deploy the best and most comprehensive theory of the moral rights and correlated duties we have. What they should not do is to search for a single, master list of human rights and correlated duties that we can then use as a template or standard for the evaluation of all human rights practices and

[44] Cf. Peter Benenson's 1961 *Observer* article, 'The Forgotten Prisoners', which founded Amnesty International: 'The force of opinion, to be effective, should be broadly based, international, non-sectarian and all-party. Campaigns in favour of freedom brought by one country, or party, against another, often achieve nothing but an intensification of persecution' <http://www.amnestyusa.org/about-us/amnesty-50-years/peter-benenson-remembered/the-forgotten-prisoners-by-peter-benenson>. See also S. Moyn, *The Last Utopia* (Cambridge, Mass.: Harvard University Press, 2010), and Neier, *The International Human Rights Movement*, on Amnesty's neutrality.

[45] See also its very first campaign, launched in Benenson's 'The Forgotten Prisoners', which focused on the rights of prisoners from Romania, the United States, Angola, Portugal, Czechoslovakia, Greece, and Hungary.

[46] The monitoring and informational function is predominant in an organization like Human Rights Watch.

[47] An example is its recent call for the United Kingdom to accept greater numbers of refugees from Syria. See also its 2007 calls to impose economic sanctions on Sudan in the Darfur conflict <http://www.globalpolicy.org/images/pdfs/sudanamnesty.pdf>: 'Amnesty International is urgently calling upon the international community to assert its authority and immediately adopt steps to strengthen the implementation of the UN arms embargo and stem the flow of arms to Darfur as part of a package of immediate measures to help protect civilians and uphold their human rights as is required by international law.' No *military* action, on the other hand, was called for in 1997 in Zaire or in 1999 in Kosovo.

[48] See P. Redfield, *Life in Crisis: The Ethical Journey of Doctors without Borders* (Berkeley: University of California Press, 2013), pp. 104–5. Médecins Sans Frontières' (MSF) 1994 calls for outright military intervention in Rwanda under the slogan 'You can't stop genocide with doctors.' The internal struggle over this decision was crucial in the development of MSF. And cf. the internal dispute between MSF and one of its founding members, Bernard Kouchner (later the head of a splinter group, the Médecins du Monde), on the right (and duty) to undertake (often coercive) interventions *in situ*. See D. R. Dechaine, *Global Humanitarianism: Ngos and the Crafting of Community* (Oxford: Lexington, 2005); Redfield, *Life in Crisis*, p. 12.

claims whatever their specific scope, origin, or aims. This is because, I have argued, there is none that can be faithful to the multiplicity of human rights practices.

Had we been the framers of the ECHR (or, indeed, the International Covenant on Civil and Political Rights [ICCPR]), we would have begun in a very different way. The ECHR governs a set of regional signatories and is a legal instrument created by treaty. The moral rights and correlated duties that ought to (partially) guide the formation of a list for the ECHR, as well as how they should be interpreted, will invoke a type of universal moral, legal, and political concern and a set of moral considerations of a different nature from the ones that went into the development of a human rights conception for Amnesty.[49] Therefore, we would have ended up with a different mediating concept and hence a different conception of human rights and their correlated duties. And it will be different again if we are statesmen and -women evaluating whether intervention would be justified (in part) in Syria or Libya or Egypt on the basis (partially) of moral human rights violations, determining how wide the scope of the right to self-determination in the ICCPR ought, as a moral matter, to be, or—to name a last example—deciding which legal human rights, if any, merit some recognition as *jus cogens* (or, alternatively, *erga omnes*).[50] In none of these cases would grasping for a master list of human rights be helpful.

III. Avoiding merely verbal disagreement

One of the main merits of the CSBV is that it helps us avoid verbal disagreement. In this section, I explain how. This will also help us to further motivate our rejection of the Single Practice Assumption.

Recall the apparent disagreement between our Political and Orthodox discussants regarding whether the moral right to education should be considered a human right. I have argued that the disagreement was only apparent since elimination of the term 'human rights' from the dispute would make no substantive difference to their normative conclusions regarding violations of the underlying moral rights. I suggested that, if this was the case, then they should simply agree that they were talking at cross-purposes. I now want to argue that there are two ways that we can reframe their disagreement such as to restore its meaningfulness. Doing so, however, requires us at the same time to recast their disagreement in terms of the CSBV.

The first way the two participants could restore real disagreement would be to accept the Broad View and then simply adopt, for the sake of argument, either a Political reading of the parameter 'universal moral, legal, and political concern,' or a

---

[49] On the ECHR, see G. Letsas, *A Theory of Interpretation of the European Convention on Human Rights* (Oxford: Oxford University Press, 2007).

[50] See e.g. K. Parker, 'Jus Cogens: Compelling the Law of Human Rights', *Hastings Int'l & Comp L Rev* 12 (1988): 411–63; B. Simma and P. Alston, 'The Sources of Human Rights Law: Custom, *Jus Cogens*, and General Principles', *Aust YBIL* 12 (1988): 82–108; A. Bianchi, 'Human Rights and the Magic of Jus Cogens', *European Journal of International Law* 19 (2008): 491–508; and, on the distinction between *erga omnes* norms and *jus cogens*, see e.g. Bianchi, 'Human Rights and the Magic of Jus Cogens' at pp. 501–3.

more Orthodox one. For example, they might continue in the following way: 'Assuming, for the sake of argument, that human rights are those moral rights whose systematic violation would merit some kind of sovereignty-overriding interference, ought we to consider the moral right to education a human right?' Or: 'Assuming that human rights are those moral rights whose systematic violation would be sufficiently urgent to justify an international advocacy campaign to stop them from occurring, ought we to consider the moral right to education a human right?' If they were to proceed in this way, they would be, in effect, converging on a single mediating concept and then exploring what follows regarding which moral rights we ought to count as human rights. Converging in this way on a mediating concept would mean that any disagreements about which moral rights can play the assigned roles would become *substantive, normative* disagreements rather than merely verbal ones. To continue our analogy, this would be equivalent to two interlocutors discussing Michael Jordan's height and agreeing to stipulate whether they are talking about Michael Jordan *as a basketball player* or *as a man* simpliciter, and then seeing what follows once they do so.

There is, however, a problem with this approach to restoring the possibility of disagreement. The problem is that the decision to use one or the other concept looks ad hoc. In particular, it is not clear what is normatively at stake in adopting one or the other (or some further concept under the Broad View). We can diagnose why the choice looks ad hoc using the CSBV. The choice looks ad hoc because neither party to the dispute has specified the particular context for which they are proposing their mediating concept of human rights. Are they wondering which human rights ought to govern the expansion of the legal rights protected by the ECHR? Are they trying to determine whether Amnesty should be more active in advocacy designed to prevent mass illiteracy in countries whose governments have the capacity to extend it to all? Are they trying to evaluate whether the moral right to education should have ever been part of the UDHR in the first place? Are they assessing to what degree the failure to educate children in US inner cities should be considered a human rights violation from the point of view of the American Convention on Human Rights (i.e. despite the fact that the United States has not signed or ratified the Additional Protocol protecting that right)? Are they doing the same as Black Lives Matter activists? And so on.

The CSBV claims that the most appropriate concept of human rights to deploy in each of these contexts should be allowed to vary depending on the interpretative specification of the role human rights claims are meant to play in that context. For example, if the context was the ECHR, then the relevant concept of 'human rights' to use might be the Political one, given that the rights protected by the ECHR *do* license sovereignty-interfering judgements by the Court.[51] In the context of the ECHR, it would be very

---

[51] As a particularly interesting example of a strategic adoption of a more Political approach, consider that nongovernmental organizations (NGOs) like Amnesty and Human Rights Watch often file amicus briefs in particularly high-profile cases. See, for example, the joint amicus filed by Interights and Human Rights Watch, among others, in *Al Skeini and Others v. UK* (2011), 55721/07 ECHR, or Amnesty's amicus

unclear what role the more Orthodox reading would have to play. But now let us say we are activists in the Black Lives Matter movement, who are considering whether it is appropriate to speak of the inadequate provision of education in US inner cities as a human rights violation. In *this* context, the Political view might seem an odd one to adopt: our primary concern is not (let us suppose) to get the international community or other states to interfere directly in the US government's policies in a sovereignty-overriding way. The Orthodox view, on the other hand, would be much more consonant with our aims. As activists, our use of the term 'human rights' is intended to signal the gravity of the violations in light of the very point and purpose of any liberal democracy, and, in light of that fact, to seek a higher, constitutional status to the right to education within the United States. Finally, imagine we are wondering whether the right to education should have ever been included in the UDHR. Here we might be much less clear about what to think, given that the UDHR doesn't sanction any sovereignty-interfering action, and given the much broader role it has played in all kinds of political advocacy across the globe. Whatever concept we adopt in each of these cases, it should be clear by now that it would be a mistake to think that any single concept could pick out a single master list of human rights and correlated duties that meaningfully applies across all these different contexts.

Once we reject the Single Practice Assumption and adopt the CSBV, a new possibility for meaningful disagreement opens up: two interlocutors could be disagreeing about which mediating concept to use in light of either (a) a disagreement about the particular uses to which human rights claims ought to be put within a particular context or (b) a disagreement about which concept we ought to use given an underlying agreement about the role human rights claims are meant to play in that context. To return to our examples, two interlocutors might (a) disagree about the particular role that the UDHR ought to play in the international system, and so about which mediating concept of human rights is best suited to determining what counts as human rights for the purposes of the UDHR, or (b) two interlocutors might disagree about which mediating concept is best suited to play a role on which they already agree. Accepting this way of proceeding—and hence the CSBV—allows the interlocutors' conceptual disagreement to make sense in a way that it otherwise wouldn't have.[52]

It is useful to refer again to our example about height. The type of meaningful conceptual disagreement I have identified between an advocate of a Political view and an advocate of an Orthodox view is like the conceptual disagreement between two

in *Cayara v. Peru* (1993), Series C No. 14 IACHR. In those cases, NGOs take on the perspective of the court in question and adopt a particular concept of human rights that fits that perspective (while seeking, simultaneously, to extend the reach and ambit of the court's jurisprudence). On the role of NGOs generally in filing such briefs, see L. Van den Eynde, 'An Empirical Look at the Amicus Curiae Practice of Human Rights Ngos before the European Court of Human Rights', *Netherlands Quarterly of Human Rights* 31 (2013): 271–313. I thank Matthias Mahlmann, Steve Ratner, and Chris McCrudden for helpful discussion.

[52] These two kinds of disagreement would be examples of what D. Plunkett and T. Sundell, 'Disagreement and the Semantics of Normative and Evaluative Terms', *Philosopher's Imprint* 13 (2013): 1–37 call 'metalinguistic negotiations.' I am grateful to Eliot Michaelson for discussion.

interlocutors advocating different thresholds for evaluating tallness. The disagreement makes little sense if it is construed as an attempt to derive a single threshold for tallness that will be valid in *all* contexts, but does make sense once we assume, for example, that they are basketball coaches selecting players to purchase in the draft. We now know *why* they are interested in tallness as a property of players, and so we have a background against which it makes sense to evaluate and disagree over the use of particular thresholds. In the same way, the conceptual disagreement between the Political and Orthodox theorists makes little sense if it is construed as an attempt to fix criteria for universal concern across all contexts, but does make sense if we assume they are, for example, activists in the Black Lives Matter movement (as opposed to, say, drafters of an international treaty).

IV.   How does the CSBV help to satisfy the four desiderata?

In this section, we review how the Broad View satisfies the four desiderata with which we began.

THE SUBCLASS DESIDERATUM

The Broad View meets the Subclass Desideratum at both the conceptual and substantive levels. At the conceptual level, the desideratum is satisfied by the qualifier that the systematic violation of the moral right must merit some specific kind of universal moral, legal, and political concern. But, more importantly, the Subclass Desideratum is also met at the substantive level. In moving from the general construal to a mediating concept, the Broad View qua CSBV isolates a particular *kind* of universal moral, legal, and political concern as relevant to a particular context. This further delimits the scope of 'universal moral, legal, and political concern' and thus further precisifies and bounds the subclass.

THE FIDELITY DESIDERATUM

As I have argued, the CSBV strikes me as faithful to the *diversity* of practices under the banner of human rights—indeed much more faithful than either the Political or Orthodox view, precisely because of the latitude it allows in identifying appropriate usage of the concept, and precisely because it allows us to explain the sense in which all the different practices in which human rights are invoked are referring to the *same* general concept (though with very different content). Again, the analogy to 'tall' is instructive. The concept of tallness picks out a distinctive property of objects with a vertical dimension, namely that they are of above some threshold in height, just as the concept of a human right picks out a distinctive kind of moral right, namely a moral right whose systematic violation merits universal concern. And, just as thresholds for tallness will vary with the contexts to which speakers intend to refer, what counts as the relevant kind of universal concern will vary with the contexts to which practitioners, advocates, and so on intend to refer.

But, at this point, someone might worry: 'The Broad View doesn't strike me as very faithful to practitioners—whether lawyers, politicians, activists, professors—who overwhelmingly believe they are engaged in a *single* project.'[53] Given the diversity of practitioners' motivations, aims, and cultural, institutional, political, and social backgrounds, there may be reason to doubt that practitioners in all these contexts really do conceive of themselves as engaged in a single project.[54] But let us assume, for the sake of responding to the objection, that human rights practitioners around the world really do conceive of themselves as engaged in a single overarching project. Even if we grant this assumption, it strikes me that abandoning the Single Practice Assumption does not require us to abandon the idea of a single project. An analogy: it seems clear that we can all be engaged in the project of building a vibrant city together, even though we have different ideas about what makes for a vibrant city, and even though we are each engaged in very different aspects of city-building (some of us are artists, others engineers, planners, restaurateurs). As long as we conceive of our activity as coordinated in the right kind of way, there is no need for us to conceive of ourselves as engaged in a single practice of 'vibrant city-building' or to share much in the way of agreement on the truth-conditions for 'vibrant city.' It is enough if there is some very broad understanding of 'vibrant city' that we can all be understood to be promoting, each in our own way, each in our own context. It is the same with the human rights project: we can each participate in a project that can loosely be described as securing the realization of moral rights that merit universal moral, legal, and political concern, but at the same time have very different, noncompeting ways of understanding what kind of universal concern we are interested in securing and how we conceive of ourselves as helping to secure it. On this reading, the Justice of the European Court of Human Rights and the Amnesty activist can both rightly conceive of themselves as participating in a single project but with different, noncompeting ideas of what that requires in the more specific, circumscribed contexts in which each of them work. Indeed, one might argue that the term's protean, yet still unifying, character is in fact part of what makes it such a powerful political ideal.

THE NORMATIVITY AND DETERMINACY DESIDERATA

The Normativity and Determinacy Desiderata can be discussed together. If one looked only at the conceptual component of the Broad View, then one might worry that it would have difficulty meeting the Normativity and Determinacy Desiderata. As we have seen, the Broad construal of the concept is so broad as to be *very* indeterminate. So indeterminate is it that one might wonder how one could have a normative reason to adopt it (other than that it permits us to encompass most contemporary usage). On the Broad View qua CSBV, however, the satisfaction of the Normativity and Determinacy

---

[53] I am grateful to Charles Beitz for helping me to see the need for responding to his objection.

[54] I thank Philip Alston for discussion on this assumption.

Desiderata are relocated to the contextual and *substantive* level. Determinacy is gained by specifying a mediating concept that fixes a particular context of action and makes it clear what kind of universal concern is mandated by that context. And normativity is achieved by specifying the substantive moral rights that would justify the specific kind of universal concern envisaged. The Normativity Desideratum is satisfied, that is, by pointing to the normative force of the set of moral rights that can play the required roles.

Conclusion

In this chapter, I have argued that we should reinterpret both of the dominant philosophical accounts of the concept of human rights, namely Political and Orthodox views, as special cases of the Broad concept. According to the Broad construal of a human right, something counts as a (putative) human right when it is a moral right whose systematic violation ought to garner universal moral, legal, and political concern. I then argued that the evaluation of the truth of a human rights claim (understood in these terms) requires us first to specify a context, then a role that human rights are meant to play in that context, and finally the type of universal moral, legal, and political concern that is envisaged given that role. There is therefore no master list that can serve as a unitary system for the evaluation of all human rights practices. If I am right, then we should abandon the search for an overarching, general-purpose philosophical conception of human rights and turn rather to the piecemeal evaluation of particular human rights practices.

References

Alston, P., and R. Goodman (2008), *International Human Rights in Context* (Oxford: Oxford University Press).

Beitz, C. (2009), *The Idea of Human Rights* (Oxford: Oxford University Press).

Benenson, P. (1961), 'The Forgotten Prisoners', *The Observer*, London, Sunday, 28 May. Print.

Bianchi, A. (2008), 'Human Rights and the Magic of Jus Cogens', *European Journal of International Law* 19: 491–508.

Buchanan, A. (2013), *The Heart of Human Rights* (Oxford: Oxford University Press).

Chalmers, D. J. (2011), 'Verbal Disputes', *Philosophical Review* 120: 515–66.

Dechaine, D. R. (2005), *Global Humanitarianism: Ngos and the Crafting of Community* (Oxford: Lexington).

Dworkin, R. (2011), *Justice for Hedgehogs* (Cambridge, Mass.: Harvard University Press).

Van den Eynde, L. (2013), 'An Empirical Look at the Amicus Curiae Practice of Human Rights Ngos before the European Court of Human Rights', *Netherlands Quarterly of Human Rights* 31: 271–313.

Forst, R. (2011), *The Right to Justification: Elements of a Constructivist Theory of Justice* (New York: Columbia University Press).

Griffin, J. (2008), *On Human Rights* (Oxford: Oxford University Press).

Kennedy, Christopher (2007), 'Vagueness and Grammar: The Semantics of Relative and Absolute Gradable Adjectives', *Linguistics and Philosophy* 30.

Letsas, G. (2007), *A Theory of Interpretation of the European Convention on Human Rights* (Oxford: Oxford University Press).

Miller, D. (2012), 'Grounding Human Rights', *Critical Review of International Social and Political Philosophy* 15: 407–27.

Moyn, S. (2010), *The Last Utopia* (Cambridge, Mass.: Harvard University Press).

Neier, A. (2012), *The International Human Rights Movement: A History* (Princeton: Princeton University Press).

Parker, K. (1988), 'Jus Cogens: Compelling the Law of Human Rights', *Hastings Int'l & Comp L Rev* 12: 411–63.

Plunkett, D., and T. Sundell (2013), 'Disagreement and the Semantics of Normative and Evaluative Terms', *Philosopher's Imprint* 13: 1–37.

Pogge, T. (2002), *World Poverty and Human Rights* (Cambridge: Polity).

Rawls, J. (1999), *The Law of Peoples* (Cambridge, Mass.: Harvard University Press).

Raz, J. (2010), 'Human Rights without Foundations', in *The Philosophy of International Law*, ed. S. Besson and J. Tasioulas (Oxford: Oxford University Press).

Redfield, P. (2013), *Life in Crisis: The Ethical Journey of Doctors without Borders* (Berkeley: University of California Press).

Sangiovanni, A. (2016), 'Are Moral Rights Necessary for the Justification of International Legal Human Rights?', *Ethics & International Affairs* 30: 471–81.

Sangiovanni, A. (2017), *Humanity without Dignity: Moral Equality, Respect, and Human Rights* (Cambridge, Mass.: Harvard University Press).

Sen, A. (2004), 'Elements of a Theory of Human Rights', *Philosophy & Public Affairs* 32: 315–56.

Simma, B., and P. Alston (1988), 'The Sources of Human Rights Law: Custom, *Jus Cogens*, and General Principles', *Aust YBIL* 12: 82–108.

Stanley, J., and Z. Gendler Szabó (2000), 'On Quantifier Domain Restriction', *Mind & Language* 15: 219–61.

Tasioulas, J. (2007), 'The Moral Reality of Human Rights', in *Freedom from Poverty as a Human Right*, ed. T. Pogge (Oxford: Oxford University Press).

Tasioulas, J. (2010), 'Taking Rights out of Human Rights', *Ethics* 120: 647–78.

Tasioulas, J. (2011), 'On the Nature of Human Rights', in *The Philosophy of Human Rights: Contemporary Controversies*, ed. G. Ernst and J.-C. Heilinger (Berlin: Walter de Gruyter).

Wolterstorff, N. (2010), *Justice: Rights and Wrongs* (Princeton: Princeton University Press).

5.1

Human Rights in Context
A Comment on Sangiovanni

Rainer Forst

1

Philosophy progresses dialectically, by identifying alternative, contrasting views and then constructing third ways that capture more parts of the truth than the alternatives do. Thus many of us join Andrea Sangiovanni in aiming at an *Aufhebung* of the debate between what he calls "orthodox" and "political" accounts of human rights. The way in which Sangiovanni (rightly) characterizes the debate already shows why this is necessary, as there is no clear opposition between a view that takes human rights to be "those individual moral rights that we possess merely in virtue of our humanity" (p. 174)[1] and one that contends "that human rights are those individual moral rights...whose violation...makes sovereignty-overriding interference or other forms of international action...permissible or required" (pp. 174–5). The one view focuses on the *grounds* of human rights and the other on a particular *function* they have.[2]

Sangiovanni suggests an alternative theory that preserves the truth of both approaches. In his view, the main problem to be overcome resides in their shared assumption that there is a "*single* overarching practice" of human rights for which we need a "master list" derived from a "moral core" (p. 175). In line with his general understanding, developed in other places,[3] that normative concepts arise out of and only apply to particular social practices, Sangiovanni rejects such a notion of one practice and one single master list and argues for a "broad view." This view does hold on to a core concept of human rights as moral rights, but leaves the determination of particular conceptions of human rights to different socio-political contexts and agents in their role as, so to speak, agents of the construction of human rights. This is an

---

[1] All references in brackets are to Sangiovanni's chapter "Beyond the Political–Orthodox Divide: The Broad View" in this volume.

[2] I analyse the (seeming) opposition between ethical and legal-political accounts of human rights in Forst 2010, republished in Forst 2013a, ch. 2.

[3] See especially Sangiovanni 2007 and, most recently, Sangiovanni 2017.

intriguing proposal, and in this commentary I will try to clarify its implications and highlight some of the problems it faces. Ultimately, I criticize the proposal as being *too broad*, so that it runs the risk of normative arbitrariness, and as lacking firmer guidelines as to how concept, contextual conceptions, and interpretations are connected.

2

Sangiovanni suggests that a theory of human rights ought to satisfy four criteria, a suggestion I find very enlightening—yet one which, I fear, haunts his own approach. According to these criteria, a proper theory has to identify human rights as a subset of general moral rights (the "subclass desideratum"). Furthermore, the theory has to be faithful to international human rights practice ("fidelity")—and at the same time allow for a normative critique of it where necessary (the "normativity desideratum"). These two criteria are in tension, which raises the question of how much bite they can have. Still, I think they can be useful, as we can ask ourselves whether the distance that Sangiovanni's approach generates to current practice is well founded. Finally, the theory should allow for a determinate and concrete conception of human rights ("determinacy").

I take it that the first, third and the fourth of these criteria in particular call for a non-arbitrary, moral justification of the concept and of all possible conceptions of human rights, and I suggest combining these into the general and overarching criterion of *non-arbitrary justification*. In light of this, the broad view Sangiovanni develops encounters problems, as I will try to explain.

I will not comment in detail on the challenge Sangiovanni mounts against the orthodox and political views, as I find most of his arguments convincing. When it comes to orthodox approaches, his main point is that their way of identifying the proper subset of moral rights is inadequate. Political views especially falter on the charge of "making the conditions for the existence of a human right depend too much on shifting contingencies," and thus of departing "significantly from the aims and purposes of an important aspect of current human rights culture" (p. 182). This affirms my point about non-arbitrary justification: human rights, according to Sangiovanni, are a subset of moral rights that cannot "vary" with political circumstances as a result of contingent "shifts in the international balance of power" (p. 184) that influence the prospects of a successful intervention. Yet will his broad view do better in avoiding contingent determinations of conceptions of human rights?

3

The broad view starts from the following concept of human rights: Human rights are "moral rights whose systematic violation ought to be of universal moral, legal, and political *concern*" (p. 186). Sangiovanni emphasizes the parallel to the orthodox view in that he regards these rights as "morally most urgent claims" or universal "moral rights" (p. 186), but he does not want to commit himself to the claim that they are "possessed in virtue of our humanity" (ibid.). Here I would like to raise the following question: If the concept of human rights is to say something about *why* that subset of moral rights should be of universal concern, some reference to a thicker moral language like that of dignity or normative status might be unavoidable—otherwise, it seems, the concept is rather empty. The concept has to provide normative *reasons* for the universal concern, I take it, and such reasons cannot come from another source. That would lead to the danger of arbitrariness and contingent determination Sangiovanni wanted to rule out in his critique of political views.

To avoid the contingency objection, Sangiovanni insists that human rights are isolated "by reference to their moral *significance*" (p. 187). But he leaves open what this significance consists in—that is, what makes these rights morally significant. At this point, Sangiovanni turns to the relation between the general concept and more particular conceptions of human rights, which must be determined in practical contexts. He argues against a general "extended list" based on the concept of human rights and he also affirms that practices of human rights lack "moral unity" (p. 189). Rather, different contexts of the correct use of the concept provide the practice-interpreting theorist with "mediating concepts" (p. 191) that specify which right should be of universal concern in which context—and why. The main idea behind this is formulated as follows: "While the term [human rights; RF] has a general linguistic meaning that doesn't vary across contexts [...], the term's specific content varies with the context referred to by the speaker, which determines what kind of universal moral, legal, and political concern is at stake. Put another way, there is no single, master list of human rights and correlated duties against which one can evaluate expressions of the general form 'y has a human right to x'" (pp. 190–1). Thus the criteria governing the evaluation of human rights claims vary according to the context in which they are made. This means that the expression "his human rights have been violated" might be true when said in the context of the practice of Amnesty International but false in the context of the European Convention on Human Rights, for example. The thought here is that we need to know more about the particular context and aims of an institution like AI in order to understand the reasons and the kind of universal concern it highlights. So an AI-activist works with a very "different conception" (p. 193) of human rights from someone who tries to frame a European Convention on Human Rights, or from "statesmen and women" (p. 193) who deliberate about the justification of an intervention prompted by human rights violations.

I consider an approach like this, which tries to connect the concept and practical contexts of human rights as contexts of justification, important and share many of its aims; yet I think Sangiovanni's particular proposal for linking the concept and conceptions of human rights is problematic, for a number of reasons. First, as I said, given how vague the general concept of human rights is, it leaves the normative realm, which specifies what is to be of universal concern as a matter of human rights, far too open. There has to be some moral unity if that term is to be used meaningfully *across* the range of contexts, and the moral significance of these rights requires more normative substance than Sangiovanni is willing to invest. What do these rights protect or express? What is the basis for evaluating a disagreement between different conceptions of human rights that is not merely a verbal one?

Secondly, the context-description aims to be in line with current practice—but is not. It seems to me, to take the example used, that an AI-activist does not understand his or her protest against a human rights violation in the way Sangiovanni suggests. Such an activist will presumably not believe that, from another standpoint than his or her own (such as that of a statesman or that of a framer of a rights convention or that of a judge of an international court), there could be reasonable disagreement about the human right in question in general and the violation of it he or she is criticizing in particular. To be an activist who appeals to universal moral concern means precisely that the rights you think are violated in a certain context are rights that belong to a conception of human rights that no one can reasonably reject, from whatever standpoint. Otherwise the activist would have to agree, for example, that the leaders of the state he or she criticizes may be guided by another "mediating conception" to specify *their* conception of human rights—such as a religious doctrine, an idea of gender asymmetry, or considerations of political stability. Human rights language has been invented to rule out such differences of interpretation in the first place—human rights are meant to cut across the contexts that Sangiovanni thinks divide different conceptions. On this reading, his suggestion seems to be out of tune with the core of any practice of human rights, whether that of critics or of persons or institutions exercising a political mandate.

I do not think that this problem is overcome by introducing the idea of a "single overarching project" (p. 197) that human rights practitioners share. For what kind of practical project would that be if those engaged in it shared no "single practice" of trying to realize and secure human rights? When it comes to such struggles and conflicts, a "very broad understanding" (ibid.) of human rights does not suffice; rather, what is needed is a conception that no one can reasonably reject.

Thirdly, Sangiovanni's idea of contextual justification treats as differences between *conceptions* of human rights what are really differences of *interpretation* and *application*. One may, for example, ask oneself which human rights violations justify an intervention of a certain kind; but it does not follow that the violations that one thinks do not justify such an intervention are not "really" human rights violations. That would be to repeat the mistake of political views criticized by Sangiovanni. It would be to interpret human rights as political in the wrong way, to use a phrase of Rawls.

The distinction between an interpretation that differs as to the right means of realizing a human right and the question of different conceptions of human rights also shows up in Sangiovanni's discussion of the right to education. We might differ as to how to enforce such a right by way of international law and prefer to insist on more ground-level activism, but that does not mean that those who disagree in this way are at odds over whether there is a human right to education. A disagreement over the proper way to enforce a right to X is not necessarily a conceptual disagreement about the right to X nor one about whether there is a human right to X to start with. We might differ as to what exactly the right implies, but that is not a disagreement about that right as a human right but a difference of interpretation of how to secure or realize it.

To sum up, I doubt that the broad view meets the subset desideratum, as it leaves the moral grounding and significance of human rights far too open.

I also do not think that it meets the fidelity desideratum, as it cannot capture the context-cutting and critical appeal of the language of human rights.

And likewise, I have some doubts about the normativity desideratum, as the mode of contextual interpretation is left open: What is it constrained or guided by? Thus, how does it become determinate in a non-arbitrary way?

4

Given how much Andrea Sangiovanni and I agree about the importance of situating normative concepts in social contexts, let me add a few remarks about an alternative way to think about the concept and conceptions of human rights that he might find congenial.[4]

The *concept* of human rights says that they are morally grounded, legally and politically guaranteed rights of free and equal persons who have a basic claim not to be socially or politically dominated or mistreated by states or other agents, and—what is of particular importance—to be the normative authorities of the regime of rights and duties they are subject to. Human rights reflect the insight that the status—or dignity, to use that term[5]—of being free and equal and not being subjected to the arbitrary power of others needs to be secured by law in a twofold sense: the persons in question must be both the authors and the addressees of the law. Thus these rights are justified *horizontally* as those rights that free and equal normative authorities (who possess what I call a basic right to justification) could not deny each other; moreover, they have a *vertical* justification as rights that no political or social agent or institution may violate and which the state must secure. Their moral core consists in the fact that they confer the status of being a justificatory equal who must not be subjected to others' domination; and their non-arbitrary justification lies in considering—and mutually justifying—those rights that are necessary to secure that egalitarian status in the social world. This implies rights to life, liberty, security, to social and material resources, and to the political co-determination of the rights and duties you have. Human rights not only protect personal autonomy and dignity, but also express it. They express the general right not to be subjected to a regime of rights and duties that cannot be properly justified to its members. This idea I take to be most in line with the historical experience of the struggles for such rights, beginning with the revolutions against feudal and monarchical orders in the seventeenth century.

---

[4] Here I follow my reflections in Forst 2016, based on 2010 (now in Forst 2013a, ch. 2) and Forst 1999 (now in Forst 2012, ch. 9).

[5] See Forst 2011 (now reprinted in Forst 2013a, ch. 4).

This approach stresses the moral core of mutual respect essential for human rights as well as their particular subset function, namely to include only those rights that are required for being secure as a non-dominated, free, and equal person in the social and political realm. Classical "liberal" rights protect this status as much as do political rights or social rights that provide protection against political or social domination. The notion of non-domination used here is a discourse-theoretical and not a neo-republican one: it does not stress the "robust" freedom of choice from arbitrary interference, but instead the status of an agent of justification or an equal normative authority within a social order who has all the means and normative powers to avoid being subject to arbitrary rule or domination (i.e. rule without proper justification and without procedures and rights of justification in place).[6]

This view addresses the moral core and purpose of human rights and also includes non-arbitrary guidelines for the way in which a specific *conception* of human rights has to be constructed, namely by way of a discursive construction in which all those subjected are involved as justificatory agents—in practice as well as in a critical coun-terfactual dimension. This means that any conception of human rights for a particular context needs to be justified in a discursive manner guided by the criteria of reciprocity and generality, where no one may make a claim he or she denies to others (reciprocity of content) and where no one may impose his or her interests, needs, perspective, or convictions on others who could reasonably reject these (reciprocity of reasons). Finally, no subjected person may be excluded from the relevant justification community (generality).

The first context in which a conception of human rights is to be justified by way of such a discursive construction is the general moral-political context of a basic list of general human rights (what Sangiovanni would call a "master list") which contains all the rights that, given human experience thus far, would be non-deniable between free and equal persons who share a political and legal order. This list is the product of a dis-cursive construction and is necessary as a major reference point for any dispute over whether a certain right is actually a human right. As much as these rights are required in particular, concrete contexts, they must have a moral basis, and if they do, there is a list of such core rights that substantiate the normative core concept just explained. This list is general and vague and needs to be discursively concretized through political constructions; yet at this general level a general moral-political conception of these rights is indispensable. A severe dispute over human rights always goes back to this level. *Pace* Sangiovanni and also Seyla Benhabib, I do not see how we can move directly from the general concept to more particular political conceptions in either the hermeneutic way Sangiovanni thinks correct or the discourse-theoretical view that Benhabib proposes with her notion of "democratic iterations".[7] The construction of such a basic

---

[6] I discuss the difference between my and Philip Pettit's approach in Forst 2013b and Forst 2015 (now in Forst 2017, ch. 10).

[7] Benhabib 2011, pp. 126–31.

conception of human rights is and remains a moral matter; in this form of constructivism we gather and test the best moral arguments for certain rights to secure the standing of persons who are free from domination and are equal normative political-legal authorities within their normative order. That much "moral unity" is necessary.

The second context of constructing a conception of human rights is the political context of a state that has the task of securing basic human rights and also of ensuring that the concrete determination and interpretation of these rights is justifiable to all those subject to it. This does not mean to merely "apply" or "mirror"[8] a fixed set of morally constructed human rights; rather, the political constructions of basic rights on this level determine and interpret what it means in a given political community to have freedom of speech, the right to political participation, to a decent social status, and so on. Human rights are determined by way of discursive political constructivism in this context, and it is important to note that this is a moral-political form of justification by the participants themselves in a critical, counterfactual, and at the same time very concrete political way. When it comes to basic rights, all must be involved in the determination of these rights as political equals and as critical participants who think reflexively about their own status and that of others, and who transcend given legal and political forms in order to improve them. So human rights are at the same time the ground for such constructions as they are their result: In abstract form, they are the ground for such constructions because the general moral conception provides the justificatory background for any determination, both in procedure and substance, such that a political community has to determine what it means to realize and secure rights no person can justifiably be denied (which includes the rights of non-members). The result is a concrete conception of human rights for a political community. However, this conception must be in tune with the general moral conception and must be criticizable from that standpoint. Non-deniable core human rights provide something like a discursive veto against unjustifiable constructions of basic rights: Persons or groups thus have the normative power to reject a determination of a basic right—say, of gender equality—when a majority in a political community believes that, for example, forced marriage is in line with this general right, or when a political community thinks that it can ban minarets and still respect the human right to religious liberty. In every such political context and conception, non-arbitrary forms of legal interpretation and adjudication of basic rights disputes have to be devised; this is implied by the human right to be protected as a person with equal legal standing.

While there are many such political contexts of discursive construction where participatory equals determine their normative order in a non-arbitrary and constructivist way, being open to reflexive improvement and critique, another moral-political construction is taking place on the international and supranational levels. Here the construction of conceptions of human rights is required that are laid down in international declarations, treaties, and covenants, where these legal norms—and possible

---

[8] This is the worry of Buchanan 2013, pp. 14–23.

sanctions for violating them—are understood to be legally binding. In these contexts, the agents of construction are states with particular conceptions of basic rights as well as persons who make particular claims, possibly dissenting from their states' conceptions. The conceptions to be found on this international level therefore reflect a thinner notion of human rights as compared to the political conceptions within states. Thus, for example, no particular model of democratic organization can be formulated here apart from the general right to democratic participation. Yet that there is such a right must be stressed within the general moral conception as well as all political conceptions and the international conceptions. Otherwise the point of human rights— namely, not to be forced to live in a normative order where you are not part of the relevant justification authority as a justificatory equal—would be lost. At this level, a reflection on which rights violations ought to lead to which sanctions and by which prior procedure and through which agent needs to be included. Yet it is a mistake to combine this reflection with the basic arguments for human rights on any of the other levels. That would include arbitrary justifications, as Sangiovanni rightly criticized in the case of political views.

5

I will stop here with my all-too-brief sketch of a discourse-theoretical account as an alternative to Sangiovanni's way of relating concept, conceptions, and interpretations of human rights. In my account, the idea of a non-arbitrary justification of human rights does a lot of work, because I spell out on all conceptual levels what it means to be respected as an agent with a right to such justification. I think a similar thought underlies Sangiovanni's view. However, his analysis of the core concept is normatively too thin to convey this, and his conception of the contextual justification and interpretation of human rights is too indeterminate with respect to both substance and procedure.

After all, the reflexive point of human rights needs to be kept in mind: If human rights are essentially founded on the basic right to be secure in the status of being a normative authority free from political and social domination and co-determining the normative order one is subject to, then they must be rights constructed by their bearers themselves. This has implications both for the concept and for the various conceptions (and how they are interpreted). It means that human rights protect *and* express the autonomy of free and equal law-givers and law-addressees.

References

Benhabib, S. (2011) *Dignity in Adversity: Human Rights in Troubled Times* (Cambridge: Polity).
Buchanan, A. (2013) *The Heart of Human Rights* (Oxford: Oxford University Press).
Forst, R. (1999) "The Basic Right to Justification: Toward a Constructivist Conception of Human Rights," in *Constellations* 6, pp. 35–60.

Forst, R. (2010) "The Justification of Human Rights and the Basic Right to Justification: A Reflexive Approach," in *Ethics* 120, pp. 711–40.

Forst, R. (2011) "The Grounds of Critique: On the Concept of Human Dignity in Social Orders of Justification," in *Philosophy and Social Criticism* 37, pp. 965–76.

Forst, R. (2012) *The Right to Justification: Elements of a Constructivist Theory of Justice* (New York: Columbia University Press).

Forst, R. (2013a) *Justification and Critique: Towards a Critical Theory of Politics* (Cambridge: Polity).

Forst, R. (2013b) "A Kantian Republican Conception of Justice as Non-Domination," in Andreas Niederberger and Philipp Schink, eds, *Republican Democracy* (Edinburgh: Edinburgh University Press), pp. 154–68.

Forst, R. (2015) "Transnational Justice and Non-Domination: A Discourse-Theoretical Approach," in Barbara Buckinx, Jonathan Trejo-Mathys, and Timothy Waligore, eds, *Domination Across Borders* (New York: Routledge), pp. 88–110.

Forst, R. (2016) "The Point and Ground of Human Rights: A Kantian Constructivist View," in David Held and Pietro Maffettone, eds., *Global Political Theory* (Cambridge: Polity), pp. 22–39.

Forst, R. (2017) *Normativity and Power: Analyzing Social Orders of Justification* (Oxford: Oxford University Press).

Sangiovanni, A. (2007) "Justice and the Priority of Politics to Morality," in *The Journal of Political Philosophy* 16, No. 2, pp. 2–28.

Sangiovanni, A. (2017) *Humanity Without Dignity: Moral Equality, Respect, and Human Rights* (Cambridge, MA: Harvard University Press).

PART III

Morality and Law

6

Taking International Legality Seriously

A Methodology for Human Rights

Allen Buchanan & Gopal Sreenivasan

The aim of this chapter is to direct attention to a strangely neglected problem: the moral justification of *international legal* human rights. Philosophical theories of human rights are proliferating, but they have tended not to focus on this question. Unlike *moral* human rights, international legal human rights uncontroversially exist.[1] However, it is a further question whether or how far this feature of international law is morally justified. We shall argue that this further question is worthy of serious philosophical attention.

In the first instance, we do so by arguing for a fairly specific claim, namely, that the existence of a moral human right (e.g. to physical security) is neither necessary nor sufficient for the corresponding international legal human right (to physical security) to be morally justified.[2] This demonstrates that our question is fully independent of the issue about whether moral human rights exist, which is the issue that has received the most attention in the philosophical literature. We then proceed to identify some of the healthy variety of justificatory tasks that need to be discharged if one is to establish that a particular international legal human right is morally justified. Our main aim here is to indicate just how much philosophical distance there is to traverse before one can reach conclusions of this kind, even if one begins by simply assuming that the corresponding moral human right exists. We shall let the interest of the terrain in need of traversing speak for itself.

Finally, we shall draw some consequences from our argument for the simmering methodological debate between 'political' and 'old-fashioned' approaches to human

---

[1] See two of the canonical documents of international human rights law, the International Covenant on Civil and Political Rights (ICCPR) and the International Covenant on Economic, Social, and Cultural Rights (ICESCR).

[2] Griffin (2008), for example, is naturally read as embracing the necessity claim we reject here; and Raz (2010) entails that claim. For the basis of these attributions, see Section 6 of this chapter.

rights.[3] We shall argue that one element of our position is sufficient to vindicate a central aspect of the political approach and that another is sufficient to refute a central aspect of the old-fashioned approach. In a sense, then, our position favours the political approach. However, there is also a sense in which the pluralism we favour for the ground-level enterprise of morally justifying international legal human rights applies on the methodological plane as well. In both cases, we are happy to let many flowers bloom.

1

We shall argue separately for the non-necessity and insufficiency components of our core claim about the justificatory relation between corresponding pairs of moral and international legal human rights. Before we do so, however, it will be useful to review the basic distinction that gives rise to this relation in the first place. Indeed, it is surprising how many discussions of human rights fail to indicate whether the expression 'human rights' is being used to mean 'moral human rights,' 'international legal human rights,' or something else.[4]

We shall take the very basic distinction between moral and legal rights for granted. The present question is therefore how (or where) each of these species of rights inter-sects the category of specifically 'human' rights. *Moral human* rights are, minimally, universal moral rights. That is, they are moral rights held by *every* living human being. Some hold that moral human rights are, furthermore, *timeless* universal moral rights. This definition entails that they are held in common by all human beings across history. For just that reason, it is a controversial definition. For example, timeless universal moral rights cannot be held primarily against the *state* because many human beings existed before any states existed. But some scholars (e.g. Tasioulas 2007) maintain that moral human rights can be held primarily against the state. To avoid controversies that we do not ourselves have to decide, we shall understand moral human rights to be merely universal moral rights.

How to understand 'international legal human' rights is itself a somewhat complex matter. This fact is already grist for our mill, but we shall save the complexities for later. To begin with, we shall simply focus on the existing international legal system.[5] We shall take recognition by a valid international treaty that describes itself as a human rights treaty (such as the ICCPR or the ICESCR) as sufficient to qualify a right as an international legal human right. For concreteness, we shall emphasize three features of

---

[3] While it is standard practice to use the label 'political' as we do, to refer to the approach to human rights taken (e.g.) by Beitz, Rawls, and Raz, there is no standard label to refer to their opponents (who include Griffin and Tasioulas, as well as adherents of traditional natural rights theory). We do not regard the label we have invented as pejorative.

[4] For a recent exception, see Besson (2011), who argues for a kind of amalgam.

[5] Although our analysis applies to any supra-national legal system, we shall not focus on regional legal systems here, such as that of the European Union. Domestic constitutional rights are beyond the scope of our analysis.

the individual rights that satisfy this sufficient condition.[6] *International legal human* rights, so defined, are legal rights that

(i) individuals hold primarily against their own state;[7]

(ii) are binding on particular states if and only if they have ratified a suitable international treaty;

(iii) function to limit the exercise of sovereignty even within a state's own borders.

The third feature is generally understood to be distinctive of international legal *human* rights, as compared to other international legal rights, though it is controversial how strong a limitation on sovereignty they actually entail. (We shall distinguish some of the options in Section 6.)

According to article 11 of the International Covenant on Civil and Political Rights, 'no one shall be imprisoned merely on the ground of inability to fulfill a contractual obligation.'[8] Hence, there is an international legal human right not to be imprisoned for debt (as we shall abbreviate it). Taking this international legal right as an illustration, the first half of our core claim is that the existence of a universal moral right not to be imprisoned for debt is not necessary to justify it (call this, our *denial of necessity*) and its second half is that the existence of a universal moral right not to be imprisoned for debt is not sufficient to justify it (call this, our *denial of sufficiency*).[9] We shall argue for each half in turn.

2

Let us begin with our denial of necessity, which is the more controversial half of our core claim. Our argument for this denial derives from the very general premise that the law is chiefly an instrument, one that serves a diversity of moral purposes. While individual legal rights are one of the most powerful legal instruments, the morally legitimate purposes they can serve are not limited to (though they certainly include) implementing individual moral rights or giving them better practical effect.

---

[6] Some of the rights that satisfy this condition are not individual rights (e.g. the right of self-determination). In focusing on individual rights here, we are therefore ignoring some international legal human rights. Of course, in focusing on treaty-based rights, we are already ignoring other international legal human rights, such as rights arising under customary international law. But 'ignoring' does not mean *denying*. We have chosen these foci simply in order to minimize unnecessary controversies while placing some clear and concrete content in view.

[7] This feature can be further analysed in terms of three distinguishable elements. First, the rights in question are held primarily against *states*. Second, the state against which an individual holds the rights in question is, in the basic and simplest case, the state of which he or she is a *citizen*. Third, when a state is unable or unwilling to fulfil the duties correlative to the rights in question, other states have some sort of 'responsibility' to achieve their fulfilment, but this responsibility does not rise to the level of a legal duty. It follows that no individual holds an international legal human right against a state of which she is neither a citizen nor a resident. For this analysis, see e.g. Henkin et al. (2009, pp. 211–14).

[8] http://www.ohchr.org/EN/ProfessionalInterest/Pages/CCPR.aspx.

[9] Throughout the chapter, 'justify' and its cognates refer exclusively to *moral* justification. However, we shall not repeat the qualification on every occasion.

However, if the instrumental contribution that establishing an international legal right not to be imprisoned for debt makes to any one of these other purposes (or to any combination of them) suffices to justify that right, it follows that the existence of a universal moral right is not necessary to justify it. That is, no universal moral right of any kind need exist for the international legal right not to be imprisoned for debt to be morally justified.

We can distinguish a more radical and a less radical version of this argument from instrumentality. According to the more radical version, there is no significant restriction on the purposes that can serve to justify a(n international) legal right. Any morally permissible (but otherwise optional) purpose or combination of purposes is eligible. We might call this 'nearly naked instrumentalism.' To illustrate how plausibly it can be applied to the moral justification of various prominent international legal human rights, consider two examples.

Take a legal right to health first. Whether as part of a domestic or international legal system, this right admits of a powerful pluralistic justification that does not include an appeal to an antecedently existing moral right to health (or to any other moral right, for that matter).[10] A legal entitlement to goods and conditions that are conducive to health, including but not limited to healthcare, can promote social utility, contribute to social solidarity, help to realize the ideal of a decent or a humane society, increase productivity, and provide an efficient and coordinated way for individuals to fulfil their imperfect duties of beneficence. Taken together, these distinct lines of moral justification, none of which appeals to a moral right to health (or to anything else), make a strong case for having a legal right to health.

Similarly, a legal right not to be subject to arbitrary arrest or detention serves a number of important moral values, including individual autonomy, peaceful and productive social cooperation, social utility, and the protection of minority groups. At no stage does the argument for establishing a legal right require reference to a moral right not to be subject to arbitrary arrest or detention (or to any other moral right).

According to what we might call 'subtle instrumentalism,' only morally *mandatory* purposes are eligible to ground moral justifications of legal rights. Subtle instrumentalism is less radical than nearly naked instrumentalism insofar as it is closer to the position that we reject. For convenience, let us dub that position the 'mirroring view.' The mirroring view holds that the existence of a corresponding universal moral right *is necessary* to justify any international legal human right.[11] Although both positions exclude the eligibility of morally optional purposes, subtle instrumentalism remains

---

[10] See Buchanan (1984) for a more detailed discussion.

[11] As we have formulated it, the mirroring view is more specific than the position we reject, since it is restricted to *corresponding* universal moral rights (i.e. ones with the same content as the legal right being justified). By contrast, nearly naked instrumentalism and subtle instrumentalism each actually establishes the stronger, unrestricted conclusion that no reference to *any* moral right is necessary to justify an international legal human right. However, since it is often convenient to focus more narrowly on the 'corresponding' universal moral right, we shall often include that qualification, even though we are always licensed to ignore the limitation it imports.

crucially distinct from the mirroring view, since there are at least *two* species of morally mandatory purposes, namely, moral duties and moral rights. Alternatively, there are at least two species of moral duty: duties that correlate with (individual) rights and duties that do not correlate with any rights.[12]

In a nutshell, the difference between the two positions is that, for the purpose of morally justifying a legal right, subtle instrumentalism treats the two species of (corresponding) moral duty as interchangeable (either will do), whereas the mirroring view insists that only a directed moral duty will do. To illustrate this difference, let us return to the international legal human right (against the state) not to be imprisoned for debt. The mirroring view entails that this legal right is only morally justified if there is a universal moral right (against the state) not to be imprisoned for debt—that is, *only if* the state has a directed moral duty not to imprison anyone under its jurisdiction for debt. By contrast, subtle instrumentalism allows the moral justification of the same legal right to be equally well grounded in the state's *non-directed* moral duty not to imprison anyone under its jurisdiction for debt.

Hence, to vindicate the mirroring view against subtle instrumentalism, one would have to show that the moral justification of a legal right against the state *hinges on* the difference between the state's (corresponding) moral duty being directed or not directed—that is, between its being morally owed to individual right-holders or not. Now, on its face, this is improbable. However, it becomes wholly untenable once one clearly appreciates the fact that whether a moral duty is directed or not makes absolutely no difference to its weight. It makes no difference because the direction of a moral duty is explained independently of the duty's having any particular weight.[13] So while the moral justification of a legal right against the state may well hinge on the state's (corresponding) moral duty's having some particular *weight*, that fact provides no reason for taking the moral justification of the legal right to hinge on that same moral duty's having a direction. We therefore reject the mirroring view.

3

Before we turn to our denial of sufficiency, let us entertain three objections to our argument so far. The first objection protests that the standard of proof governing our denial of necessity is appreciably higher than we have managed to satisfy. Specifically, it claims that to reject the necessity of a corresponding universal moral right, we have to prove that some international legal right is actually morally justified, as opposed to merely adumbrating the elements of such a proof, and to show that the

---

[12] The former duties are sometimes called 'directed duties.' They are duties that are *owed to* the correlative right-holder. So, when a directed duty is infringed, the correlative right-holder is wronged. By contrast, when a non-directed duty is infringed, no one is wronged. For more detailed discussion, see Sreenivasan (2010).

[13] This truth holds across various theories of how to explain the direction of a moral duty. For discussion, see Sreenivasan (2010).

conditions sufficient for this moral justification do not include the corresponding moral right.

However, while exhibiting an alternative set of sufficient conditions is indeed one way to refute a claim of necessity, it is hardly the only way. So no objector can insist on it. More to the rhetorical point, in the case of a given international legal human right, insistence on the objector's way *presupposes* that the legal right really is morally justified.[14] Unfortunately for the objector, this presupposition is vulnerable to a reductio. To see this, we need to consider a case in which there is no universal moral right corresponding to some existing international legal human right. Since cases of that kind leave it open whether the legal right in question is morally justified, the assumption that some such case exists is consistent with the mirroring view. Accordingly, we are entitled to help ourselves to it as a background assumption. For concreteness, let us stipulate that the international legal human right not to be imprisoned for debt fits this bill.

Now this legal right is either morally justified or it is not. If it is not justified, then the objection fails because it has a false presupposition (there is no set of conditions sufficient to justify the legal right). If the legal right *is* morally justified, the objection fails because we are thereby assured that an alternative set of sufficient conditions exists. Our assurance arises as follows: since the legal right not to be imprisoned for debt is morally justified, some set of sufficient conditions for its moral justification must exist. Moreover, that set *cannot* include any corresponding moral right, since ex hypothesi there is no universal moral right not to be imprisoned for debt.[15] The sufficient conditions for the moral justification of the legal right therefore qualify as an 'alternative' set. Either way, then, the first objection fails.

The second objection concedes that the mirroring view does not express a general truth about international legal rights. Nevertheless, it insists that *human* rights have distinctive features that other international legal rights lack and counters that it is these features that require corresponding universal moral rights for their moral justification. Since the generality of our arguments from instrumentality does leave room for this objection, it is important for us to engage it. Still, as we shall now see, fixing on the distinctive features of a human right in no way disables our denial of necessity.

The most plausible candidate for the feature that is most distinctive of international legal *human* rights is the function of limiting the exercise of sovereignty even within a state's own borders. Let us focus on this function under its strongest interpretation, namely, where the limitation serves to legitimize armed intervention on the part of

---

[14] If a given legal right is *not* justified, then there is no set of conditions that is sufficient to justify it. Hence it makes no sense to insist that some such set be produced.

[15] This instantiation of our background assumption can only be blocked if a corresponding universal moral right exists *whenever* some international legal human right is morally justified. (Otherwise, we could just change the example.) However, the objector cannot appeal to this 'fact' without begging the question, since it is equivalent to the mirroring view.

other states.[16] If a corresponding universal moral right is not necessary to justify an international legal human right with *this* feature, we may safely dismiss the second objection.

While a licence for armed intervention may be a distinctive entailment of the violation of (some) international legal human rights, that entailment loses its distinctiveness as soon as one turns from international legal rights to consider international law more generally. Indeed, there is an entire branch of international law that consists in nothing but such entailments, namely, the *jus ad bellum*.[17] Unfortunately, even passing acquaintance with the *jus ad bellum* makes it plain that no universal moral right need be invoked in order to justify a licence for armed intervention. For even in the stripped down modern version of the doctrine, self-defence is a sufficient condition for permission to intervene militarily in another state (and has always been so recognized).[18] Or perhaps, strictly speaking, self-defence plus the expiry of some 'last resort' proviso is the sufficient condition. Either way, it is clear that no violation of a universal moral right is necessary to justify a permission for armed intervention.[19] In which case, no such right need exist to justify a permission for armed intervention. But if it is not true in general, why should a universal moral right be necessary to justify the permission when it is entailed by the violation of an international legal human right?

Of course, one might reply that a universal moral right is still necessary because the aim here is not simply to justify (potential) licences for armed intervention, but rather to justify them specifically by reference to the interests of *individuals*, considered just for their own sakes. We accept that an expansion of the just causes of war—beyond the realm of states' interests alone, to include the interests of individuals—is plausibly seen as one of the signal contributions modern human rights doctrine has made to the development of international law. Witness the novel banner of 'humanitarian intervention.'

However, it remains a mistake to conflate the moral significance of individuals, even considered for their own sake, with the necessity of appealing to universal moral rights.[20] It is perfectly coherent, for example, to appeal to the moral significance of individuals *directly*, as opposed to indirectly via their status as moral right-holders. One advantage of making this appeal directly is that its justificatory force is not then limited by the moral significance that individuals have when taken one by one.

---

[16] Obviously, it will not be true of every international legal human right that its violation can serve to license armed intervention. But there would still be something to the objection if it were true of some international legal human rights *and* the mirroring view held for those rights.

[17] For a brief historical overview, see McMahan (2010).

[18] For the modern version, see Walzer (1992, ch. 4). It would be a mistake to reply that self-defence is a moral right. Even if this is true, and even if a state's right of self-defence decomposes cleanly into individual rights of self-defence held by its citizens (which may be doubted), the right of self-defence is a liberty right, rather than a claim right. So it does not correlate with any duties that would be enforced by the armed intervention in question.

[19] On this point, see also Waldron (in this volume, §III (1)).

[20] We have diagnosed this as a mistake once already, in the context of distinguishing subtle instrumentalism from the mirroring view. But it may be useful to recognize the mistake from a different angle.

By contrast, the justificatory force of appealing to an individual moral *right*, even a universal one, is limited to the moral significance an individual has all by herself.

While this advantage is particularly salient in the context of attempts to justify armed intervention on behalf of individuals,[21] that is really only a dialectical bonus. For the mere possibility of a direct appeal to the moral interests of individuals is enough to show that their intrinsic moral significance can be invoked independently of any universal moral rights they may have. Accordingly, even if the distinctive function of some international legal human rights is to trigger a licence for armed intervention by other states, and to do so for the sake of individuals themselves, the moral justification of such international legal rights requires no appeal to any universal moral right.

The third objection offers to explain why, contrary to what we have said, the directedness of a state's moral duty may be crucial to justifying legal rights against that state after all. The explanation rests on two assumptions: First, if something is to be a legal right, it must be justifiable for the state to enforce it; and second, only duties that also correlate with moral rights (i.e. only directed moral duties) may be justifiably enforced. For our purposes, it is not necessary to take a position on the first assumption; we can remain agnostic on whether there is such a tight connection between legality and enforceability. However, the objection still fails because its second assumption is clearly false. It can be morally justifiable to enforce legal duties even if there is no correlative moral right.

For example, it is sometimes morally justifiable to enforce legal duties the fulfilment of which is necessary for securing morally important public goods, but the moral justifiability of their enforcement does not depend on any individual's having a moral right to the public good. In particular, when collective action problems would otherwise hinder the provision of a morally important public good, the state is morally justified in compelling individuals to do their part in contributing to that provision (see e.g. Buchanan 1984). Moreover, the state is so justified even though no individual has a moral right to any public good.[22] Since no one has any such moral right, it follows that the duty to contribute that is justifiably enforced by the state does not correlate with any individual's moral right to the public good.

4

Let us turn now to our denial of sufficiency. Since this denial is not very controversial, our discussion can be brief. For the same reason, we should also emphasize that our main claim in this neighbourhood, to be taken up in Section 5, will be that there is actually a vast gulf between the fact that some universal moral right exists and the fact that the corresponding international legal human right is morally justified. Our main

---

[21] Waldron (in this volume, §III (3)) spells this advantage out.

[22] For this conclusion about individual rights to public goods, see Sreenivasan (2017).

claim thus goes well beyond the familiar point that some logical space exists between those two facts.

But we can begin by reviewing the grounds for the familiar point. As the literature on the relationship between law and morality has long acknowledged, not all moral rights are suitable candidates for even domestic legalization. Sometimes the attempt to enforce a moral right would require dangerously high levels of coercive capacity on the part of the state. In other cases, even if enforcement would not result in abuses of coercive capacity, the content of a particular moral right is such that enforcing it would be inappropriate. One might argue that this is so with the rights generated by promises (as opposed to contracts) or the right to be treated with respect. This is enough to show that the existence of a moral right does not suffice to justify the enactment of the corresponding domestic legal right.

The familiar argument can be strengthened for the international case. Recall that the distinctive feature of international legal human rights is that they function to limit the exercise of sovereignty even within a state's own borders.[23] One way to see this is that, in relation to outsiders, the arrangement of a state's domestic legal system ordinarily enjoys a special layer of moral protection, although that protection is open to being defeated in the case of international legal human rights. It follows, however, that the moral justification for an *ordinary* domestic legal right does not suffice to defeat this special layer of protection.[24] But then if a universal moral right is insufficient to justify the corresponding domestic legal right, it is a fortiori insufficient to justify the corresponding international legal human right.

5

As we have said, our main aim in this chapter is constructive. We wish to draw philosophical attention to the question of whether a system of *international legal* human rights is morally justified (or how this might be established). To exhibit the independence of this question from standard controversies about the existence of moral human rights, we began by arguing that the existence of a universal moral right is neither necessary nor sufficient to justify the corresponding international legal human right. We now proceed to articulate some of the daunting range of questions that a philosophical theory has to address in working out whether this or that international legal human right is morally justified.

We hope that our contribution to setting an agenda will serve two purposes: First, to make abundantly clear how mistaken it is to assume that the major philosophical work of a theory of human rights will have been done if a sound theory of *moral* human rights is produced; and, more importantly, to stimulate theorists to develop views that

---

[23] For present purposes, this function does not have to bear its strongest interpretation, on which it intersects the *jus ad bellum*. The argument goes through under any interpretation.

[24] This is entailed by the fact that the scope for defeating the special protection is perforce exceptional.

answer the questions we pose. In order to serve our first purpose, we shall conduct the remaining discussion against the background assumption that any specific international legal human rights under examination are ones for which the corresponding universal moral rights exist. As will emerge, this turns out to be something of a dangling assumption. But then, that is precisely the point.

We shall organize our survey of justificatory tasks in terms of two significant distinctions. In the first place, we should distinguish the character of the operative *system* of international legal human rights from the inclusion of any *particular right* within some such system.[25] They represent different 'objects' of moral justification, as we shall say. In the second place, we should also distinguish the *moral correctness* of a given arrangement of international legal rights from its *political legitimacy*. They represent different 'species' of moral justification, as we shall say. This second distinction is related to the distinction between substantive and procedural correctness, insofar as political legitimacy is largely a procedural notion. However, a full account of this relation would be complicated and we shall not pursue it.[26]

Let us begin with tasks that concern the objects of moral justification. We take it that the specification of a system of rights is in some sense *prior* to the inclusion of any particular right within a given system. For example, including the right not to be imprisoned for debt, say, in a particular system of international legal human rights entails that this legal right will have all of the specific features of rights in that particular legal system.[27] By contrast, specifying the character of a given system of international legal human rights (i.e. specifying which features the rights it contains will have) does *not* entail that that system will include any right with a particular content. At any rate, it will be perspicuous to start with the task of morally justifying the character of the operative *system* of international legal human rights.

Perhaps the most basic question in this connection is, Why should there be an international system of individual legal rights at all? A closely related question is, What moral purpose(s) should an international system of individual legal rights serve? To illustrate the issues at stake, consider some moral purpose that a system of international legal human rights might reasonably be thought to serve, such as protecting (some of) the basic interests of individuals. One way to grasp the fundamental question here is to ask, Why is this purpose not adequately served—why are the basic interests of individuals not well enough protected—in the absence of an *international* system of individual legal rights? Why are the relevant interests not well enough

---

[25] For elaboration on this first distinction, see Buchanan (2015).

[26] In principle, one should also distinguish different 'modalities' of moral justification. To say, for example, that it was *morally justified* to include the right not to be imprisoned for debt within the *ICCPR* may mean that it was morally permissible to include it *or* that it was morally required to include it *or* that the balance of moral reasons favoured including it (without strictly requiring as much). We shall omit this layer of complexity from our discussion.

[27] If the relevant system contains a *hierarchy* of rights, the legal right not to be imprisoned for debt will only have the features of rights on its assigned level of the hierarchy. We describe the hierarchy option later in this section (3 paragraphs after note 28).

protected, for example, by the constitutional entrenchment of individual rights in *domestic* legal systems, without recourse to international law or institutions? This particular question may or may not have a good answer. Yet if the very existence of a system of international legal human rights is to be morally justified, there must be at least one significant moral purpose for the achievement of which some such system is necessary.

Of course, there may be more than one such purpose; and besides a system of international legal human rights may also serve other moral purposes, quite apart from those for which its existence is strictly necessary. Hence, even given that its existence is morally justified, it remains to clarify more generally the various moral purposes a system of international legal human rights should serve. It remains, that is, both to catalogue what these purposes are and to elucidate the relations among them. Should a central purpose of the system, for example, be to affirm and protect equal basic status for all individuals, as distinct from protecting their basic interests? How much weight should be given, in the design of the system, to preserving peace among *states* as opposed to other moral values?

Another fundamental range of questions concerns the myriad specific features of rights that together define the character of a system of rights. Which specific features should the operative system of international legal human rights have? Which should it omit? By way of illustration, consider three candidate features (or kinds of feature) in no particular order. First, there is the question of how much *authority* the international system should have vis-à-vis domestic legal systems. Presumably, a system with an unqualified supremacy over domestic law—including the domestic constitutional law of reasonably democratic, rights-respecting states—would be decidedly harder to justify, other things being equal, than one lacking such supremacy. Although few philosophers have participated in it (and many seem unaware of its existence and importance for philosophical theorizing about human rights), there is a vigorous debate among international and constitutional lawyers about whether international human rights law either actually has or should anyhow enjoy supremacy over domestic law, including domestic constitutional law.[28]

Second, there is the question of who bears the primary legal duties correlative to human rights—in other words, of where the duties are assigned. In the actual international legal system, as we have seen, these duties are assigned to states (who only bear them toward their own citizens or residents). However, it is possible to assign these duties not only to states, but to other agents as well (e.g. to international organizations or global corporations). Furthermore, fully-fledged legal duties to secure human rights, rather than mere 'responsibilities' to do so, might be assigned to third-party states (or to regional alliances of states) when a state fails to fulfil its primary duties towards its own citizens. More radically, states might be assigned primary legal duties toward individuals who are not under their jurisdiction. Should they be?

---

[28] For an overview of this debate, see Buchanan and Powell (2008).

Third, there is the question of how far (the violation of) international legal human rights should play a significant role in the moral justification of humanitarian military intervention or of other interferences with what would otherwise be regarded as the proper domain of state sovereignty. As we have already observed, they do play some such role in the actual international legal system (or at least, some human rights do). But it remains an open question, belonging to the agenda we commend, how far such a role can be morally justified.

Before we turn to the other 'object' of moral justification, let us notice a final point about the operative *system* of international legal human rights. It is evidently possible that a given specific feature of rights may be attached to some of the rights a system of rights contains and not to others. Moreover, exploiting this possibility may enhance the prospects for morally justifying certain features. Thus, to take a salient case, even if there are some international legal human rights whose violation can justifiably serve to license military intervention by other states, there are many others for which such a claim is scarcely plausible. It is plainly false, for example, that violation of the international legal human right not to be imprisoned for debt morally justifies military intervention. Differentiating the scope within which various specific features of rights operate introduces one or more *hierarchies* within a system of rights. A further question, then, is whether a system of international legal human rights should recognize a hierarchy of human rights—and if so, how its levels should be defined and which particular rights should be assigned to which level.

The other 'object' of justification concerns the inclusion of particular rights within some system of rights. There are three quite different ways in which one might approach the moral justification of a particular international legal human right. To begin with, one could hold the distinctive features of the actual system of international legal human rights constant; and then argue, against this set of background assumptions, that a particular right should be included in the actual system. This way of proceeding does not engage the deeper question of whether having a system with that character is morally justified. More ambitiously, one could first argue in favour of an international legal system of individual human rights with a certain character—perhaps one that is quite different from the existing system—and then argue that some particular right should be included within one's favoured system. Both of these approaches require a prior specification of the character of the system of rights in which the particular right being morally justified is to be included.

The final approach aims to dispense with this prior specification of the system of rights. Here the idea would be to argue that a particular right should be included in the operative system of international legal human rights, no matter what its specific character may be. In one sense, this approach may be the most ambitious of all. However, its ambition could be diluted, while still retaining its distinctive aim, by assuming that the operative system of rights includes a hierarchy of rights and that the particular right in question may be assigned to the lowest level of its hierarchy.

In addition to distinguishing two different objects of moral justification, so far as international legal human rights are concerned, we also distinguished two different *species* of moral justification, namely, moral correctness and political legitimacy. Since these two distinctions are fully independent of one another, our previous discussion—about justifying both the character of a system of rights and the inclusion of particular rights—can be read (as it naturally reads) as having been conducted entirely on the plane of *moral correctness*.

It is a separate question, however, whether the institutions and processes through which a given system—even the morally correct system—of international legal human rights was actually created are *politically legitimate*. A morally correct outcome may nevertheless lack political legitimacy—for example, if it was produced via the wrong process. In part, then, this raises very general issues about the requirements of political legitimacy (e.g. which processes are 'wrong' and why?). Still, substantial questions remain that are specifically about the international legal system.

One way to see this is to compare that system with well-developed domestic legal systems in various respects. Among other things, the current international legal human rights system lacks some key features of well-developed domestic systems that are thought to be important for the rule of law, such as representative legislatures and a hierarchy of courts with compulsory jurisdiction. Should these absences be regarded as defects? Are they obstacles to the legitimacy of the system of international legal human rights?

Of course, some of the differences between the international legal system and domestic systems arise from the nature of the case. In themselves, these differences are evaluatively neutral. However, some of them raise issues of institutional design that also have implications for political legitimacy. For example, a philosophical theory of international legal human rights should include an account of the proper division of labour between domestic, regional, and international institutions with regard to the interpretation of international legal human rights norms. Other evaluatively neutral differences raise questions of a more squarely philosophical nature about political legitimacy. A central and difficult example, largely unexplored in the literature, is what the conditions are for the legitimacy of international legal *treaties*. Since many international legal human rights—indeed, on our working definition, all of them—have their basis in some international legal treaty, the answer to this question has implications of the first importance for their own political legitimacy.

We realize that we have barely scratched the surface here. Our main point is that a philosophical theory of the international legal human rights system must go beyond providing sound moral arguments for various rights norms and include an account of the legitimacy of the institutions in which the norms are formulated, interpreted, and implemented.

6

In closing, we should like to draw some of the consequences of our analysis for the methodological debate between political and old-fashioned approaches to theorizing about human rights. Our goal here will be to make certain key points clearly, rather than to provide a thorough exegetical guide to the debate.

The first thing to be said is that the debate has been unfortunately impaired by the failure to distinguish moral human rights from international legal human rights—or, more generally, by the failure to recognize that there is more than one bona fide sense to the expression 'human right.' This means that attempts to argue—usually involving more assertion than argument—for one's preferred side in the debate by reference to 'the' meaning of 'human rights' (or to its 'central' or 'focal' meaning) are simply idle, since there is no one such (central or focal) meaning.

For present purposes, the two standard approaches can be initially related to this neglected fundamental distinction by means of the following simple characterization: old-fashioned approaches focus their claims on *moral* human rights, whereas political approaches focus their claims on something else. We shall add detail to this formulation presently. However, even this minor (albeit, faithful) clarification already makes another important point clear: namely, that insofar as large swathes of their respective claims (so understood) simply concern different things, there is a sense in which the old-fashioned and the political approaches can *both* be correct, at least up to a point.

In a similar vein, the approach we recommend here is also consistent with a core component of old-fashioned approaches. For we do not deny that there are universal moral rights nor that some of them are very important nor, indeed, that they can be relevant to the enterprise of morally justifying international legal human rights.[29] We only maintain that that enterprise can proceed, and may succeed, without paying much attention to the existence of universal moral rights; and that, in any case, a lot of the work it requires would remain to be done even if their existence were established.

Our initial characterization of political approaches was purely negative—their claims do *not* focus on universal moral rights. At the most general level, the positive claims of political approaches share two features. First, they concern what may be called, somewhat vaguely, the 'modern practice of human rights.' Second, they include (and perhaps, highlight) the claim that the function of 'human rights,' as defined within that practice, is to limit the sovereignty of states.

Different proponents of the political approach interpret this sovereignty-limiting function differently. Their variations range from Beitz's interpretation, at the weak end, that human rights are 'standards for domestic institutions whose satisfaction is a matter of international concern' (2009, p. 128) to Rawls's interpretation, at the

---

[29] We can even concede that the *strongest* justification for some international legal human right(s) may rely on premises invoking some universal moral right or other.

strong end, that human rights 'restrict the justifying reasons for war and its conduct' (1999, p. 79). In between there is also Raz's subtle interpretation, for example, that human rights

set limits to the sovereignty of states, in that their actual or anticipated violation is a (defeasible) reason for taking action against the violator in the international arena, even when...the action would not [normally] be permissible...on the ground that it would infringe the sovereignty of the state   (2010, p. 328).

Proponents of the political approach owe their readers a reasonably clear account of the boundaries of 'the practice' of human rights, as well as of the bases on which competing descriptions of the practice are to be adjudicated. But we shall not attempt to assess the extent to which they have discharged this burden. Our point is rather to observe that, on the very plausible assumption that international human rights law belongs to this practice (e.g. the major human rights treaties do), the approach we recommend counts as an *example* of a political approach. To confirm this observation, one would have to defend the further claim that international legal human rights function to limit the sovereignty of states. As should already be clear, we take it that this claim is plainly defensible. For while it can be controversial, for different specific rights, how strong an interpretation of this function the right will bear, these controversies do not detract from the basic claim that international legal human rights do bear some such interpretation.

However, our approach also differs from familiar political approaches to human rights in three important respects. To begin with, the approach we recommend does not aspire to completeness. We recognize that on any plausible delimitation of 'the practice of human rights,' international human rights law will only constitute a part of it. (We are thereby relieved of the burden of explaining how to draw the boundaries of the practice.)

More importantly, the agenda we have proposed is unremittingly *evaluative*. By contrast, existing political approaches have not, for the most part, ventured very far beyond simply describing the practice. With respect to the part of the practice in which we are interested, this point is amply demonstrated by the fact that Beitz (2009), who offers the most developed political account, has surprisingly little to say about international legal human rights at all.[30] In any case, what we are calling for is not a description (or more description) of international legal human rights—though, of course, some description is clearly necessary and we have nothing against more—but explicit and sustained attention to the question of whether and how far rights of this kind can be morally justified.

Finally, our approach in no way prejudges the question of how far an adequate account of human rights can be revisionist with respect to existing practice. To a considerable extent, this is simply a consequence of our interest in the practice being an

---

[30] On this point, we concur with Besson (2010).

evaluative one. In principle, it may turn out that the most fully justified system of international legal human rights has nothing significant in common with the existing system.[31] Thus, while the attention political approaches pay to the practice of human rights seems to carry the implication that an adequate account of human rights cannot be too revisionist of existing practice,[32] we are happy to let the justificatory chips fall where they may.

Returning to old-fashioned approaches, we should acknowledge that they too claim to pay serious attention to the practice of human rights (or, at least, that some of them do).[33] For example, Griffin (2008) distinguishes 'top down' from 'bottom up' approaches and claims to follow the bottom up approach. A 'bottom up' approach, in his sense,

starts with human rights as used in our actual social life by politicians, lawyers, social campaigners, as well as theorists of various sorts, and then sees what higher principles one must resort to in order to explain their moral weight, when one thinks they have it, and to resolve conflicts between them.   (2008, p. 29)

At the same time, political approaches pointedly reject the adequacy of the attention old-fashioned approaches pay to the practice of human rights. According to Raz, for example, they 'fail either to illuminate or to criticize the existing human rights practice' (2010, p. 324). So here, at least, we certainly reach a point on which the two approaches are inconsistent.

We do not propose to diagnose this disagreement fully, still less to adjudicate it. But it is worth noticing the obvious role that the mirroring view can play for the old-fashioned approach in this context. The mirroring view, recall, is the claim that the existence of a corresponding universal moral right is a necessary condition of morally justifying any given international legal human right. If the mirroring view is correct, then the content of a theory of moral human rights is, *ipso facto*, a contribution to the evaluation of international legal human rights (and hence, to the evaluation of a part of 'the practice of human rights'). What is more, *no* evaluation of that practice can then be complete without reference to some theory of moral human rights. In other words, the mirroring view guarantees the relevance of theories of moral human rights to the practice of human rights; indeed, it makes them indispensable to the evaluation of that practice. It is therefore very natural to read old-fashioned approaches to human rights as being committed to the mirroring view,[34] since it serves as the perfect bridge

---

[31] At the limit, for example, it may turn out that no such system is morally justified.

[32] For example, see Beitz (2009, pp. 8–11 and 102–6).

[33] Other adherents of the old-fashioned approach make no such claim (e.g. Gewirth, 1982).

[34] This commitment is not restricted to old-fashioned approaches. For example, Raz (2010) actually entails the mirroring view, since he there defines 'human rights' as the *subset* of individual moral rights that limit state sovereignty as he describes (pp. 329 and 335). But no right can belong to this privileged subset without also belonging to the larger set of individual moral rights, i.e. without also *being* an individual moral right. Hence, an international legal right qualifies as a 'human right' only if there is a corresponding moral right. More recently, however, Raz appears to have changed his position on the mirroring view. Elsewhere in this volume, he affirms that an international legal human right to adequate housing may be

between their focus on moral human rights and their aspiration of relevance to the practice of human rights.

We have already refuted the mirroring view, by means of our arguments from instrumentality in Section 2. Here we simply draw a consequence of that refutation for old-fashioned approaches: their relevance to the practice of human rights *cannot* be defended in terms of the mirroring view. If they claim such relevance, it must be defended in some other way. Insofar as they assert or rely on the mirroring view, old-fashioned approaches are mistaken. To the same extent, our own approach is not fully consistent with old-fashioned approaches.

Of course, adherents of an old-fashioned approach may quarrel with our formulation of the mirroring view—specifically, with its restriction to 'corresponding' universal moral rights. Universal moral rights, they might object, can contribute to the evaluation of an international legal human right even if the two sorts of right have different contents (in which case, none of the moral rights count as 'corresponding'). For example, some arguments for a human right to democracy are instrumental arguments, grounding the human right in universal moral rights, none of which are moral rights 'to democracy'.[35] Why cannot an old-fashioned approach help itself to this path to relevance?

We should distinguish two ways in which this objection may be taken. In one way, it may be intended to rescue the relevance of old-fashioned approaches to the practice of human rights. So understood, the objection is otiose, since we have not ourselves sought either to deny or to affirm that old-fashioned approaches are relevant to the practice. On that dispute with political approaches, we remain neutral.

But, in another way, the objection may be intended to reject our more fundamental claim that the moral justification of international legal human rights can be examined independently of the existence of universal moral rights. Here the conclusion on offer must be that even if *corresponding* universal moral rights are not necessary to justify a given international legal human right, some reference to some universal moral right or other is nevertheless required to justify it. We agree that reference to non-corresponding universal moral rights may sometimes be relevant or helpful in that connection; and also that instrumental arguments provide one example of how. Yet the objection is still mistaken. It forgets that what our arguments from instrumentality actually established was the stronger conclusion that an international legal human right can be morally justified without reference to *any* universal moral right whatsoever (see note 11). In that case, no tweaking on 'correspondence' or other possible relations between universal moral rights and the legal right to be morally justified will establish that the moral justification of international legal human rights depends somehow on the existence of universal moral rights.

morally justified even if there is no universal moral right to adequate housing (Raz, in this volume, text at and in his footnote 2).

[35] For example, see Christiano (2011).

7

In this chapter, we have argued that moral and political philosophers interested in theorizing about human rights should take the *international legality* of human rights seriously. One thing this means is that the question of whether international legal human rights can be morally justified should be addressed as an important and worthy question in its own right, quite distinct from the traditional question of whether moral human rights exist. As part of our attempt to frame this agenda, we have sought to convey, in at least a preliminary fashion, how rich and complex the issues involved in morally justifying an international system of legal human rights really are.

We have also argued that the moral justification of a given international legal human right is *not* burdened by the necessity of establishing that any corresponding moral human right exists. We hope that abandoning the dogma that morally justified international legal human rights must mirror pre-existing moral human rights will prove liberating. Among other things, it frees us to consider the possibility that an international legal human rights system may properly serve other moral purposes, in addition to realizing moral rights. It also frees us to consider the possibility that the purposes the system serves may not be fixed, but subject to revision and perhaps even progressive development, as has sometimes been the case with domestic legal systems. To replace the mirroring view, we should like to recommend an open-minded, pluralistic approach to the moral justification of an international system of legal human rights.[36]

References

Beitz, C. (2009) *The Idea of Human Rights*. Oxford: Oxford University Press.

Besson, S. (2010) 'Human Rights *qua* Normative Practice: *Sui Generis* or Legal?', *Transnational Legal Theory* 1: 127–33.

Besson, S. (2011) 'Human Rights—Moral, Political… or Legal? First Steps in a Legal Theory of Human Rights.' In T. Childress (ed.), *The Role of Ethics in International Law*. Cambridge: Cambridge University Press: 211–45.

Besson, S. and Tasioulas, J., eds. (2010) *The Philosophy of International Law*. Oxford: Oxford University Press.

Buchanan, A. (1984) 'The Right to a Decent Minimum of Health Care', *Philosophy and Public Affairs* 13: 55–78.

Buchanan, A. (2015) 'Why International Legal Human Rights?' In R. Cruft, M. Liao, and M. Renzo (eds.), *Philosophical Foundations of Human Rights*. Oxford: Oxford University Press: 244–62.

Buchanan, A. and Powell, R. (2008) 'Constitutional Democracy and the Rule of International Law: Are They Compatible?', *Journal of Political Philosophy* 16: 326–49.

---

[36] For helpful comments on previous versions of the chapter, we are very grateful to Adam Etinson, Erasmus Mayr, James Nickel, and Miriam Ronzoni. Allen Buchanan also presented a version at the Goethe University in Frankfurt, and we are similarly grateful to his audience for stimulating discussion and criticism.

Christiano, T. (2011) 'An Instrumental Argument for a Human Right to Democracy,' *Philosophy and Public Affairs* 39: 142–76.

Gewirth, A. (1982) *Human Rights*. Chicago: University of Chicago Press.

Griffin, J. (2008) *On Human Rights*. Oxford: Oxford University Press.

Henkin, L., Cleveland, S., Helfer, L., Neuman, G., and Orentlicher, D., eds. (2009) *Human Rights*. Second edition. New York: Thomson Reuters/Foundation Press.

McMahan, J. (2010) 'Laws of War.' In Besson and Tasioulas (eds.), *Philosophy of International Law*: 493–509.

Rawls. J. (1999) *The Law of Peoples*. Cambridge, Mass.: Harvard University Press.

Raz, J. (2010) 'Human Rights without Foundations.' In Besson and Tasioulas (eds.), *Philosophy of International Law*: 321–38.

Sreenivasan, G. (2010) 'Duties and their Direction,' *Ethics* 120: 465–94.

Sreenivasan, G. (2017) 'Public Goods, Individual Rights, and Third Party Benefits.' In M. McBride (ed.), *New Essays on the Nature of Rights*. Oxford: Hart Publishing: 127–48.

Tasioulas, J. (2007) 'The Moral Reality of Human Rights.' In T. Pogge (ed.), *Freedom from Poverty as a Human Right*. Oxford: Oxford University Press: 75–102.

Walzer, M. (1992) *Just and Unjust Wars*. Second edition. New York: Basic Books.

6.1

Instrumentalism and Human Rights

A Response to Buchanan and Sreenivasan

Erasmus Mayr

One of the most striking features of Allen Buchanan and Gopal Sreenivasan's highly insightful chapter[1] is their rejection of the view that the moral justification of international legal human rights (for short: ILHRs) requires the existence of corresponding universal moral rights (for short: UMRs). Since this is the feature which seems to put them most starkly at odds with many established theories about the nature of human rights, it will be the one I will focus on here. What I want to discuss is the relevance of their rejection of the necessity of UMRs for justifying ILHRs for some of the more established competing theories of human rights. More specifically, I will be interested in the impact of their argument on 'political' accounts like Joseph Raz's, which want to both characterize human rights via their specific role in the current human rights practice and, at the same time, argue that human rights form a subclass of moral rights. Does their argument show that such views are fundamentally flawed?

Buchanan and Sreenivasan's rejection of the view that the existence of UMRs is necessary for the justification of ILHRs (the 'necessity claim', for short) is based on their 'instrumentalist' view of legal rights. Neither in domestic nor in international legal systems, they argue, is there any *single* purpose exclusively suited for justifying the acceptance of a legal right. In particular, implementing a pre-existing moral right is not the sole, nor even a specifically privileged such purpose, but appeal to any morally permissible purpose can, in principle, do the trick—a view Buchanan and Sreenivasan call 'nearly naked instrumentalism'. This would make the 'mirroring' view, according to which 'the existence of a corresponding universal moral right *is necessary* to justify any international legal human right' (p. 214), untenable.

At first glance, this denial of the 'mirroring' view and the espousal of the argument from instrumentalism appears to be a fairly radical move which sets Buchanan and

[1] For helpful comments on earlier drafts I am indebted to Erich Ammereller, Stefan Brandt, Adam Etinson, Franz Knappik, Yuuki Ohta, and Gopal Sreenivasan.

Sreenivasan firmly at odds not just with the 'old-fashioned' or 'moral' conception of human rights, which directly identifies human rights with (a subclass of) moral rights held by all human beings. For, if successful, the argument from instrumentality would show that the appeal to *any* pre-existing moral rights, *whether universal or not*, is not generally necessary to the justification of a corresponding legal right. (As Buchanan and Sreenivasan emphasize, p. 214, n. 11, this result would not be restricted to *corresponding* legal rights, i.e. rights with the same content as the supposed moral right, either.) In this way, the argument would also threaten to undermine many of those contemporary theories which are normally dubbed 'political', such as Joseph Raz's or Charles Beitz's, even when those theories (like Raz's) do not require that human rights are *universal* human rights.[2]

But this appearance of radicalism is somewhat deceptive, at least as far as the rejection of the necessity claim itself is concerned. For this rejection directly concerns only *international legal* human rights, which are based on international treaties. And, as Buchanan and Sreenivasan themselves seem to admit (pp. 224ff.), one can accept *this* rejection even if one subscribes to a 'moral' conception of human rights, which identifies such rights directly with UMRs. Even though my main concern here is 'political' conceptions rather than 'moral' ones, it will be useful to briefly consider how this would work, in order to have a foil for our later discussion of the 'political' conceptions.

There are two main ways an adherent of the 'moral conception' might come to reject the necessity claim. First, she can argue that, in focusing on UMRs, she is simply concerned with a different sense of 'human rights' from the one Buchanan and Sreenivasan are latching onto when talking about ILHRs. But second, even if she does not think that there are different senses of 'human rights' (as Buchanan and Sreenivasan propose, p. 224) and insists that the only legitimate sense of 'human rights' is the one used by her own version of the moral conception, she can still accept that the justification of an ILHR does not always require a UMR. For she might simply accept that inclusion of a right in a list sanctioned by an international human rights treaty does not always presuppose that the right in question really be a human right! And it seems extremely plausible that this possibility should be allowed (*whatever* your view on human rights is): even if you think that in this case the list in question is, strictly speaking, 'incorrect', in wrongly labelling something a human right which is not, surely 'correctness' is only *one* virtue of such treaties, and a minor fault in this respect can be remedied by other benefits which need not have anything to do with human rights themselves, when these benefits are substantial enough to reduce any insistence that the list should be 'correct' to mere pettifoggery.[3] (Just imagine a case where the false 'labelling' of a right as a 'human right' in an international human rights treaty and the consequent international legal protection of that right has highly beneficial consequences for international peace

---

[2] Raz suggests that human rights need not be universal, (2010), pp. 332ff., but takes them to be a subset of *moral* rights nonetheless.

[3] A similar point is pressed by Raz in his contribution to this volume.

or for increasing the democratic accountability of governments. Clearly such considerations should sometimes be capable of justifying a false labelling.)

Adherents of the 'moral conception' therefore need not be overly concerned with a failure of the necessity claim itself. And it is not overly surprising that even a philosopher like James Griffin, who is widely regarded as a paradigm proponent of the 'old-fashioned' approach, is willing to admit that there may well be a gap between what should be accepted as a legal human right, on the one hand, and moral human rights which are based on human personhood, on the other. As he accepts, not all rights of the former kind need corresponding rights of the latter.[4]

Nonetheless, Buchanan and Sreenivasan think that adherents of the moral conception can be naturally read as subscribing to the necessity claim, because it 'guarantees the relevance of theories of moral human rights to the practice of human rights' (p. 226). But it seems doubtful to me that these adherents—or most of them—had any such straight nexus in mind (*vide* Griffin, who does aspire to provide a theory which is relevant to the current practice). Their aim may rather have been to capture a meaning of 'human rights' that evolved in the historical tradition that also led to the current practice. This would establish a much looser connection between their own project and the current practice than anything as tight as the 'mirroring claim'.[5] But be that as it may: It is certainly clear that adherents of the moral conception are not *ipso facto* committed to the necessity claim. Let us now turn to the question what would follow for the 'political' conception(s) of human rights if the necessity claim were to be rejected.

For proponents of a political conception, Buchanan and Sreenivasan's arguments are much more directly relevant and harder to dodge. For given their characteristic aspiration to either make sense of the current human rights practice and capture central strands of it, or at least to provide a critical standard to assess this practice, and given that this practice is, to a significant degree, shaped by the international human rights treaties, they cannot argue that the sense of 'human rights' they are concerned with is simply quite a different one from the one in which ILHRs are 'human rights'. The sense of 'human rights' they are after may be *somewhat* different, since the relevant 'practice of human rights' as a whole is arguably more encompassing than the part of it which concerns the international treaties. But surely the latter part is crucial to the practice as a whole and the two senses of 'human rights' must therefore be closely related. Thus, if it turned out, as Buchanan and Sreenivasan argue, that justifying ILHRs does not require corresponding UMRs, or any corresponding moral rights, this would raise major worries for those theories which both characterize human rights by their function in the modern practice of human rights *and* maintain that they are a subset of moral rights.

While the first way to accommodate a rejection of the necessity claim that was open to adherents of the 'moral' conception is thus severely restricted for an adherent of the

---

[4] Griffin (2010), p. 351: 'not all human rights should, for good reasons, become legal human rights and *vice versa*'.

[5] See Griffin's remarks about his project in (2008), pp. 4f.

political conception, the second way still remains open to her. Even if you think that human rights are defined by the role they play in the current practice, or by the fact that they are considerations which can justifiably play a certain role in limiting sovereignty, it does not follow that *only* human rights so defined can justify an ILHR. For, in building your theory of human rights you are allowed to somewhat tidy up messy aspects of the practice and to introduce some 'streamlining'; as a result, you will only have to claim that concerns that can *generally*, or under *normal* circumstances, play this role will qualify as human rights. This is compatible with admitting that sometimes particular circumstances make it the case that introducing an ILHR is justified even if there is no genuine 'human right' of this kind (in the sense you are interested in) and the inclusion of an ILHR in the treaty is, strictly speaking, a mislabelling.

But while this is enough to reconcile those adherents of the political conception who, at the same time, regard human rights as a subclass of moral rights, to a rejection of the necessity claim itself, taken literally, it is not yet enough to get them completely off the hook with regard to Buchanan and Sreenivasan's arguments. For, if the latters' argument from instrumentality is successful, it will not just show that UMRs and moral rights are not strictly necessary, but even that they play no privileged role for the justification of ILHRs (even when those are meant to justify (*in extremis*) armed intervention, and to do so "specifically by reference to the interest of *individuals*" (p. 217). In this case, not only will an ILHR not always require a corresponding moral right for its justification, but it will not even *standardly* do so. And this would seem to create major difficulties for theories like Raz's, since it would mean that something can justifiably fulfil (at least most of) the function(s) of a human right without being (or being correlated to) a moral right.

How can an adherent of a political conception like Raz's respond to this challenge? Her response will crucially depend on what she takes to be the basis of her claim that human rights are moral rights and on the precise role she ascribes to the current human rights practice in establishing this claim. There are two fundamentally different options here, which are not usually kept apart (and are not clearly distinguished in Raz's own writings), but for which the relevance of Buchanan and Sreenivasan's arguments is crucially different.

(A) A defender of a political conception à la Raz might take the connection between human rights and moral rights to be simply part of the meaning of 'human rights' which every adequate theory must do justice to, and which is established by common usage and the historical tradition, *without* having to be independently validated by the current practice of human rights or by the practice of the international human rights treaties in particular. On such a view, reference to the specific role or function which is characteristic of human rights in the current practice is not meant to be the only criterion which determines what human rights are. Rather, this reference serves only to pick out a subclass of moral rights in general and to identify it as the class of human rights. Reference to the specific role is thus not meant to establish that human rights must be moral rights—*this* is already presupposed, and the connection between human rights and moral rights is taken to be definitional. (While he does not explicitly address this issue there, I take this to be a natural way to understand Raz's own procedure in 'Human Rights without Foundations.' For he does not attempt to develop any independent argument to the effect that human rights must be a subclass of moral rights from features of the practice, but seems to use reference to their specific 'political' function merely as a device for singling out human rights among moral rights in general.)[6]

If an adherent of the political conception takes the relationship between human rights and moral rights to be 'definitional' in this way, and not as something which has to be derived from the role played by human rights in the current practice, she will remain unaffected by Buchanan and Sreenivasan's argument. For she can then easily admit that other things than human rights as characterized by her can play the functional role that is characteristic for human rights (e.g. justify international concern and interventions), since her claim about the nature of human rights leaves it open whether things which are not moral rights, and for *this* reason fail to qualify as human rights, can play this role as well. Calling these other items 'human rights' by including them as ILHRs in an international document may be, strictly speaking, a mislabelling, but this mislabelling can be justified if it has sufficiently good consequences.

(B) However, an adherent of the political view may also take reference to the current practice of human rights to serve a different role in identifying human rights. For she may also hold that the role or function of human rights in the current practice is the only criterion which singles out considerations as human rights (*without* any presupposition that these considerations must be, or correspond to, moral rights). On such a view, any claim that human rights are a subclass of moral rights must be validated by the current practice or by an appeal to how human rights claims within this practice can be justified. One way to try to validate this claim would be to argue that it belongs to the function of human rights in the current practice that they limit state sovereignty not just for any reason whatsoever, but 'specifically by reference to the interests of *individuals*' (cf. Buchanan and Sreenivasan p. 217).

It is *this* version, and *only* this version, of the political conception which Buchanan's and Sreenivasan's argument threatens to undermine. For their argument does suggest that there are considerations that can play (a crucial part of) the role which the current practice ascribes to human rights, without being identical to or correlated with moral rights (let alone UMRs). But does their argument really succeed in establishing this result?

To defend herself against their argument, an adherent of this version of the political conception need not, for the reasons mentioned earlier, defend the necessity claim itself. But she will have to argue that at least *normally* there is a connection between the

---

[6] See especially his formulations in (2010), pp. 328f. Contrary to Buchanan and Sreenivasan, I therefore do not think that Raz's earlier theory implies the mirroring view or that his later rejection of this view involves a volte-face.

justification of an ILHR which plays the specific role in limiting state sovereignty ascribed to human rights, on the one hand, and the existence of a (universal) moral right, on the other hand. (Let us call this the 'normal case' claim.) And, as it happens, I think she may well be able to mount such a defence, since Buchanan and Sreenivasan's argument which would rule out this possibility is inconclusive.

Buchanan and Sreenivasan offer this argument in addressing the possibility that, while the mirroring view may be false for international legal rights in general, ILHRs in particular may have special features which require corresponding UMRs for their justification (pp. 216ff.). To exclude this possibility, Buchanan and Sreenivasan argue that even if we take ILHRs to justify international measures 'specifically by reference to the interests of *individuals*, considered just for their own sakes,' this does not mean that UMRs will be needed, since there is the 'possibility of a direct appeal to the moral interests of individuals.' In justifying an ILHR, we can directly point to the moral significance of the individuals and their interests, without having to take an argumentative 'detour' via the individuals' status as right-holders and their moral rights to having these interests safeguarded. Though Buchanan and Sreenivasan at this point explicitly argue against the necessity claim, rather than against the 'normal case' claim, their argument, if successful, would apply to the latter claim as well, and would establish that not even normally moral rights, let alone UMRs, are required for justifying ILHRs. But their argument at this point cannot be considered as conclusive— at least not once we distinguish two crucially different versions of the necessity claim, and, correspondingly, two different versions of the 'normal case' claim.

When the mirroring view claims 'that the existence of a corresponding universal moral right is necessary to justify any international legal human right,' this necessity claim can be read in two ways (and the same holds for the 'normal case' claim). First, as saying that any justification of an ILHR, if it is to be sufficient on its own, must in fact *appeal to* a corresponding UMR, which is *cited* in the justification. On this reading, the necessity claim concerns the *content* of the argument we have to put forward in order to justify an ILHR. But, second, we can also read the necessity claim as stating only that a corresponding UMR must *exist* whenever such a justification is possible, though it *need not be mentioned, or cited*, in every sufficient justification.

While Buchanan and Sreenivasan explicitly formulate the necessity claim as an existence claim, which suggests the second, weaker reading, their arguments are aimed at the first reading and try to establish that no appeal to a UMR is needed in every sufficient justification of an ILHR. And with regard to this first reading, these arguments are successful. Sometimes pointing to the moral weight of a basic human interest, e.g. to have one's life safeguarded, and the international community's capacity to efficiently safeguard this interest, is enough to establish that an ILHR is justified, without our having to show first that there is also a (universal) moral right to have one's life safeguarded.

But this does not rule out the possibility that the interests in question can de facto only justify an ILHR, if there also exists a corresponding UMR. For it may still be the case that, whenever the moral interests of individuals are of sufficient moral weight to justify those restrictions on state sovereignty that ILHRs do impose, these interests must also provide the grounds for a corresponding UMR.

Such a connection would obtain, if, e.g., the conditions of the existence of a UMR turned out to be a subset of the conditions for justifying a corresponding ILHR. When the conditions for A are a subset of the conditions for B, we do not always have to appeal to A in order to explain or justify B, but can directly refer to the conditions for A themselves. For illustration, take the relationship between the strict moral duty to help someone in dire need and what one may call the demands of generosity, i.e. the standard of behaviour connected to the virtue of generosity. Whenever facts are such as to give rise to a strict moral duty to help someone, they will presumably also give rise to a demand of generosity: i.e. you will necessarily fail to behave generously, if you don't help. However, it is not the other way round, because, plausibly, there are cases where it would be ungenerous not to help, but matters are not such (e.g. the other's need is not so great) that a strict moral duty to help would be justified. So, the conditions for the existence of demand of generosity to help are a subset of the conditions for the existence of a strict moral duty to help. But when it comes to justifying a strict moral duty to help we need not appeal to the fact that it would also be ungenerous not to help, but we can directly refer to those facts that make it morally obligatory to help—even though these facts, whenever they establish the strict moral duty, will also necessarily establish a demand of generosity.

If the conditions for the existence of a UMR turned out to be a subset of the conditions for justifying an ILHR, we may thus likewise not have to mention this UMR in our justification—but its existence will still be guaranteed whenever the corresponding ILHR can be successfully justified. So even if Buchanan and Sreevinasan's argument refutes the necessity claim on the first reading, it may still fail to refute it on the second.

How successful you take their argument to be with regard to the second reading will ultimately depend on the particular theory of rights you subscribe to (which is an issue I cannot go into in detail here). For ILHRs are meant to specifically impose duties or sanctions which are grounded 'in the interests of *individuals*, considered just for their own sakes' (as Buchanan and Sreenivasan seem willing to accept). And on some theories of rights it seems plausible to assume that when an ILHR can be justified on such grounds, there are normally sufficient grounds for a corresponding moral right, too. (For instance, on some interest-based theories of rights, when an individual's moral interest is of sufficient weight to justify the imposition of duties on states, this interest should *ipso facto* be capable of also providing the foundation of a moral right of this individual to have her interests safeguarded).[7] This moral right need not be appealed to in justifying the ILHR, but its existence would follow—as a 'by-product', so to speak—from those elements which provide the basis for this justification.

Furthermore, if the ILHR is to be a right that all individuals have, the moral interest in question will either have to be a universal interest—which will get us a *universal*

---

[7] See e.g. Raz's proposed definition of rights in (1986), p. 166.

moral right. Or, alternatively, there will be a set of different interests some member(s) of which will have to be possessed by each individual—which will give us a *universal* moral right, too.

In consequence, there remains some leeway even for proponents of the second version of the political view, who want to derive the character of human rights as moral rights from the role of human rights in the current practice, to dodge Buchanan and Sreenivasan's argument from instrumentality and maintain that human rights are moral rights or even UMRs. While defenders of such views should admit—for the reasons rightly pointed out by Buchanan and Sreenivasan—that justifications of ILHRs need not mention moral rights and UMRs, there are still ways for them to argue that the successful justification of an ILHR requires the existence of a corresponding UMR (whose existence could be established as a 'by-product' of the argument for the ILHR). And this latter indirect connection could well be enough to support the claim that human rights are moral rights.

The impact of Buchanan and Sreenivasan's arguments against the necessity claim on versions of the political conception which take human rights to be a subset of (universal) moral rights is therefore more limited than they think. Not only are these views less reliant on the necessity claim and the mirroring view than Buchanan and Sreenivasan assume. To the extent that they are committed to claims similar to those threatened by Buchanan and Sreenivasan's arguments, they have also more resources available for their defence than the latter credit them with.

References

Besson, Samantha and Tasioulas, John (eds) (2010), *The Philosophy of International Law*, Oxford (OUP).

Griffin, James (2008), *On Human Rights*, Oxford (OUP).

Griffin, James (2010), 'Human Rights and the Autonomy of the International Law', in: Besson and Tasioulas (eds) (2010), pp. 339ff.

Raz, Joseph (1986), *The Morality of Freedom*, Oxford and New York (Clarendon Press).

Raz, Joseph (2010), 'Human Rights without Foundations', in: Besson and Tasioulas (eds) (2010), pp. 321ff.

7

The Turn to Justification

On the Structure and Domain of Human Rights Practice

Mattias Kumm

There are three puzzling structural features of global human rights adjudication[1] that have fostered scepticism about its philosophical respectability. First, the scope of legally recognized human rights is not narrowly focused on things fundamental or basic to human existence, but extremely broad (call this the problem of rights inflation). Second, most rights may be limited by measures that meet the proportionality requirement, thereby appearing to undermine prominently made claims that rights are trumps or firewalls that have priority over competing policy concerns (call this the problem of casual override). And third, notwithstanding the claim that human rights are universal, the kind of things that can be found on lists in international, regional, or national human rights documents vary considerably between jurisdictions and

---

[1] The term "global" in global human rights adjudication here refers to the predominant structures present in international, regional, and national human rights practice. There are no plausible reasons to exclude national constitutional rights practice from the scope of this enquiry, even though none of the practice-based accounts of human rights, such as those defended by John Rawls, Charles Beitz, or Joseph Raz, has included it. First, the genealogical connection between national constitutional and international human rights instruments is typically very strong. Domestic constitutional provisions are typically iterations of international human rights norms and vice versa (see Benhabib 2006). Second, the moral structures of national constitutional rights and international human rights are generally identical. (Some argue that US Constitutional practice is an exception.) Third, even the nomenclature is uneven: Many national constitutions refer to constitutional rights as human rights and in the European Union human rights have long been protected by the European Court of Justice as "general principles of law as they result from the constitutional traditions common to the Member States". For a discussion of these issues see also Möller (2014).

If the focus here is on rights adjudication, rather than the claims of human rights groups, the UN Human Rights Council, or foreign offices of states, it is not only because rights adjudication has become a central feature of human rights practice in past decades. It is also because even philosophers interested in human rights practice have failed to pay attention to structural features of rights adjudication as an important point of focus. Given the judicial practice of explicitly giving reasons, adjudication is the natural focus for those interested in structural features of rights reasoning.

instruments. And even when provisions are worded similarly, they are often interpreted differently in different states (call this the problem of variance).

Yet, there is nothing pathological about a human rights practice that has such a structure. On the contrary, each of these structural features, I will argue, is connected to a distinctive moral point. Gaining a clearer understanding of each of these moral points and elucidating how they relate to one another is an important step towards the development of a more comprehensive theory of human rights. These three structural features work together to establish a practice, I will argue, that reflects a particular conception of law and politics: Politics is the practice of rights-based justice seeking among free and equals under conditions of reasonable disagreement. Law is the authoritative resolution of questions of justice by norms, which in terms of the procedures used to generate them and the outcomes produced are demonstrably justifiable to those addressed in terms that free and equals might reasonably accept. The structure of human rights adjudication is geared towards establishing whether or not a particular legal norm burdening an individual can be demonstrably justified to that individual under this standard. In this way human rights operationalize what Rainer Forst has called the right to justification,[2] and is at the heart of a non-domination-oriented liberal conception of law and justice. If an account along these lines provides the best justification for the practice we have, we have not only gained a deeper moral appreciation of human rights practice such as it happens to be. We are also in a better position to interpret, and progressively develop that practice in a way to help it better realize its moral point.

In many ways the following is something between the articulation of a research agenda and a fully developed argument.[3] The descriptive part as it stands is too Eurocentric and even as such would require further substantiation. At important junctures an argument is merely gestured towards, rather than carefully elaborated, and alternative interpretations and critical arguments are given short thrift. If such a contribution is nonetheless of value, it is because it opens up a perspective on contemporary human rights practice that is philosophically distinctive, potentially transformative, and deserving of further exploration.

I. From Rights Inflation to Total Rights: On the Constitutive Function of Rights

1. It is a widespread view among philosophers that human rights, if they are to be defensible, occupy a limited domain, protecting only against a special class of injustices (call this the "limited domain conception of human rights"). That class uncontroversially includes such things as torture, arbitrary killings or detention, religious coercion, and many other fundamental things, even though a great deal remains disputed.

---

[2] Rainer Forst (2012).   [3] Sect. I-III draws on Kumm (2017).

There may be considerable difficulties in determining either the nature[4] or the content of the delimiting principle[5] to be used to distinguish between human rights claims and other claims of justice. These may be hard questions, but whatever difficulties there might be need to be confronted. They must be confronted, because human rights could not plausibly be understood as the normative foundation of the whole of law and politics and the grounds for a comprehensive political programme for the realization of freedom, equality, and justice for all (call this "the constitutive or 'total' human rights conception").

There appear to be a closely related set of reasons why, if the idea of human rights is to be made sense of, some version of the limited domain conception of human rights must be correct and any version of the total rights conception must be wrong. First, if human rights are binding for public authorities across time and space and all issues of law and politics turn on the best understanding of competing rights claims, there would seem to be very little space for either legitimate difference among states or political disagreement within states. Human rights would define the highly constricting parameters of a Procrustean bed in which humanity would have to lie. On the one hand, it is not clear what space for sovereignty and national self-determination would be left, if human rights were the foundation of and provided a determinative standard for all of law and politics. On the other hand, from the perspective of domestic constitutionalism, the consequences would also appear to be unattractive and implausible. If constitutional rights are conceived as national concretizations of human rights, as they tend to be in most jurisdictions,[6] and if human rights cover the whole domain of law and politics, what space is there for the give and take of democratic politics and of disagreement between parties, social groups, and citizens? Would the judicial enforcement of human rights not inevitably lead to juristocracy?

2. The problem is that actual human rights practice generally does not fit very well any limited domain conception of rights. Human rights claims do not, in legal practice, occupy a narrow domain limited to things fundamental, however that threshold might be understood. In legal and political practice rights claims occupy a domain that includes what might appear to be mundane and even trivial things.

This is perhaps most evident with regard to the scope of *liberty* rights. It might just seem like conceptually misguided political posturing, when political actors and local

---

[4] Is the delimiting principle moral, as for example Griffin (2008) or Nickel (2007) propose, or is it political functional, as for example Rawls (1999) or Raz (2010) suggest? For a critique of political functional accounts see Jeremy Waldron in this volume. For a critique of both moral foundationalism and functionalism in favour of justificatory pluralism see Tasioulas (2012) and Buchanan (2013).

[5] Griffin (2008), for example, proposes that the delimiting principle is to secure personal agency, whereas for Nickel (2007) it is to ensure the prerequisites for a minimally good life.

[6] US contemporary constitutional practice possibly qualifies as an exception in this regard. The age of the US Constitution and its Bill of Rights, long preceding any international human rights law, as well as the historicist originalist preoccupations that characterize contemporary constitutional reasoning, tends to foster an inward-looking and self-sufficient constitutional culture in which engagement with the "outside", to the extent it takes place at all, is discussed as a problem, rather than an in-built feature of constitutional rights practice. See also Weinrib (2006), p. 84.

newspapers in affected cities in Bolivia, Ecuador, and Columbia decried FIFA's 2007 decision to ban all international football matches above 2,500 metres as a violation of the right of fans to watch their team play in their capital city.[7] But the position of many internationally renowned courts seems to be not so different. The Court of Justice of the European Union (CJEU) has recognized a general human right to liberty—the right to do or abstain from doing whatever you please—as an integral part of the common European constitutional tradition. The well-known major early cases decided by the Court like *Nold*[8] and *International Handelsgesellschaft*[9] concerned questions that are unlikely to be high on the list of priorities for human rights activists. *Internationale Handelsgesellschaft* was a case concerning the forfeiture of a deposit lodged in connection with the issue of export licences for maize meal. The plaintiff had failed to export the quantities of maize he had obtained a licence for, by all indications because it turned out to be more profitable to sell to a domestic buyer. Under EC rules failure to export after obtaining the licence meant forfeiture of the deposit, unless the failure to export was the result of force majeure. That regime, the plaintiff claimed, violated his human right to freedom of action and economic liberty. In *Nold* the issue was whether EC rules relating to the distribution of fuels could require companies to meet a certain volume of sales requirements in order for them to qualify as a direct wholesaler with a right to direct purchase from a selling agency. The plaintiff believed that the denial of that status based on reduced sales volume was a violation of its right to freely practise its trade and profession. The position of the German Federal Constitutional Court (GFCC) is similar. It has interpreted a provision guaranteeing "the free development of one´s personality"[10] as effectively guaranteeing a general right to liberty.[11] In practice it has recognized such activities as riding horses through public woods,[12] feeding pigeons in public squares,[13] or importing a particular breed of dog[14] as falling under the scope of a right.[15] Even when an international legal instrument does not have a provision easily construable as a general right to liberty, courts tend to interpret expansively the scope of whatever more specific clauses they are provided with. The European Court of Human Rights (ECtHR), for example, has the tendency to read the scope of the right to privacy guaranteed under Article 8 of the European Convention of Human Rights (ECHR) as something close to a catch-all right, also covering, for example, increased noise production for residents living near Heathrow airport, brought about by a policy scheme permitting night flights.[16] Effectively, a critic has suggested,[17] the ECtHR recognized a human right to sleep well.

---

[7] See <http://en.wikipedia.org/wiki/High-altitude_football_controversy>.

[8] Case 4/73, [1974] ECR 491.   [9] Case 11/70, [1970] ECR 1161.

[10] Art. 2 Sect. 1 German Basic Law.   [11] BVerfGE 6, 32 (Elfes).   [12] BVerfGE 80, 137.

[13] BVerfGE 54, 143.   [14] BVerfG 1 BvR 1778?01 (Mar. 16, 2004).

[15] Strikingly, whenever a German government official publicly starts considering a general speed limit on German Autobahns, the claim to a right to freely go as fast as your car can safely go will be invoked.

[16] *Hatton v. United Kingdom*, (2003) 37 EHRR 28.   [17] Letsas (2008), at p. 126.

Furthermore, both the CJEU and the GFCC are also examples of courts that have taken a similarly expansive approach to *equality*. On the one hand equality as a human right is interpreted in a formal sense as requiring that the law, whatever distinctions it may contain, be enforced on its own terms, irrespective of who the parties to the dispute happen to be. On the other hand, there is a substantive dimension to equality. The commitment to equality also means that the law may not make distinctions between different groups of persons that are not defensible. Here is the relevant point: This does not only mean that a human rights text or courts try to interpretatively define a limited list of suspect categories like race, gender, ethnicity, sexual orientation, etc. Debates about what categories to include as suspect—e.g. should age discrimination be included? what about disability?—are mainly of symbolic and expressive significance in these jurisdictions and play a role in focusing attention. The reason why in many contexts not much depends on these lists is that the principle of equality is understood by many courts, including the European Court of Justice (ECJ) and the GFCC, as a general principle of non-discrimination, potentially subjecting all distinctions made by the legislator to rights-based judicial review. Any distinction made by the legislator between different persons requires justification and can be challenged by invoking a right to equality. On these grounds, the FCC has held unconstitutional non-smoking laws that allow restaurants to establish separate smoking rooms, but exclude that possibility for discothèques.[18] The ECJ has struck down an EU Regulation on the ground that it provides subsidies for one kind of product, but not another, when both products were substitutable and used the same materials and production processes.[19] In this way, the language of human rights becomes a tool to potentially subject all acts of public authorities that affect individuals detrimentally to rights review.

Besides an expansive approach to defining the scope of a human right, with some courts recognizing a general right to liberty and a general right to equality along the lines described above, rights practice also has other structural features that further extend the range of questions that can be reached by invoking rights. These can only be briefly gestured towards here.

Human rights are not generally understood only as negative claims that individuals have against the state, restricting what the state can do to them, requiring the state to abstain from doing something. States are not just under a duty to *respect* rights. They are also under a positive duty to *protect and fulfil* human rights. Many human rights instruments from the UN Declaration of Human Rights to the International Covenant on Social, Economic, and Cultural Rights and many national constitutional codifications of human rights include social and economic rights, like the right to housing, to food, healthcare, or basic social security. These rights require positive state action to be fulfilled. Furthermore, even outside the domain of textually codified social and economic rights, courts often recognize duties of the state to protect interests falling under the scope of

---

[18] BVErfG, 1 BvR 3198/07 (Aug. 6, 2008).
[19] Case C-117/76 *Ruckdeschel & Co. v. Hauptzollamt Hamburg-St Annen*, ECR 1753.

a right against third parties or other threatening circumstances. The classical rights provisions relating to liberties are interpreted by many courts as grounding protective duties. The right to life is not only infringed when a police officer uses lethal force unjustifiably, but also when the police does not undertake reasonable measures to protect someone from concrete threats by third parties.

A particular subset of positive duties rarely concerns the state's duties to provide for particular forms of organization and procedure: due process rights in the widest sense. In this way *the basic institutional structure of the state itself is a central focus of human rights law*. Perhaps least surprisingly human rights instruments tend to address questions relating to *the judiciary*. Ignoring variations, qualifications, or additional requirements and focusing on the core point: An impartial and independent court or tribunal must be available to hear claims relating to individuals legally guaranteed rights and must be able to provide effective remedies. More surprising is perhaps the fact that for all intents and purposes international human rights law is plausibly interpreted as requiring the institutionalization of some form of liberal democracy.[20] The UDHR[21] requires "genuine and periodic elections which shall be by universal and equal suffrage and shall be held by secret vote or by equivalent free voting procedure" and the ICCPR[22] states that "Every citizen shall have the right and opportunity . . . without any unreasonable restrictions to vote and to be elected at genuine periodic elections which shall be by universal and equal suffrage and shall be held by secret ballot, guaranteeing the free expression of the will of the electors." Various constitutions have "due process" guarantees, which ground participatory rights in the context of administrative proceedings. Furthermore, and perhaps most audaciously, Article 28 of the UDHR even provides that "everyone is entitled to a social and international order in which the rights and freedoms set forth in this Declaration can be fully realized".[23]

Given the scope of rights, just about any claim of injustice—whether injustice is brought about by state action or inaction or by institutional structures cementing forms of domination—can plausibly be brought within the framework of human rights. Even though contingent features and limitations of any particular human rights instrument may present obstacles in specific instances, we should generally expect to be able to reframe any claim that injustice has been done to someone as a claim that human rights have been violated.

3. One way to make sense of the seemingly limitless scope of rights is to understand rights as having not just a constraining, but a constitutive function. The point of human rights, we might say, is not only to constrain law and politics in the name of

---

[20] For a more elaborate argument see T. Franck, "The Emerging Right to Democratic Governance", 86 AJIL 1992, 46; more recently, and more sceptically, see Marks (2011).

[21] Art. 21 Sect. 3 UDHR.   [22] Art. 25 b ICCPR.

[23] Here the issue is not only the level of abstraction (what exactly is this a right to?), but also the question of the addressee of the right claim: Is it a right against the state to engage in a particular foreign policy geared towards the establishment of some such order? Is it a claim against certain international institutions? For a discussion of problems relating to the allocation of duties among different potential addressees of anti-poverty human rights, see Besson (2013).

some fundamental human interests, however conceived. Instead we should think of *human rights constituting a particular conception of law and politics: a conception of law and politics as justice-seeking among free and equals.* If this is their moral point, we should expect the domain of human rights to be coextensive with the domain of political justice and that is indeed the tendency that the phenomenon of "rights inflation" points to.

Of course there is nothing new about the idea that all law and politics ought to be conceived as the concretization and specification of highly abstract rights of free and equals.[24] To the extent that contemporary rights practice reflects structural features of a total rights conception, this is not a historical novelty, but connects contemporary practice to its Enlightenment political roots in the eighteenth-century American and French revolutionary traditions. We see it when the French Declaration of Rights of Man and Citizens declares in the Preamble that "ignorance, neglect, or contempt of the rights of man *are the sole cause* of public calamities and of the corruption of governments" and "have determined to set forth in a solemn declaration the natural, unalienable, and sacred rights of man, in order ... that the acts of the legislative power, as well as those of the executive power, may be compared at any moment *with the objects and purposes of all political institutions* and may thus be more respected."[25] The core task of democratic legislation in a true republic was to delimit the respective spheres of liberty between individuals in a way that takes them seriously as equals, and does so in a way that best furthers the general interest and allows for the meaningful exercise of those liberties. Democratic self-government was conceived not only as human rights-based, but as having as its appropriate subject matter the delimitation and specification of rights. Legislation, such as the enactment of the *Code Civile*, was rights specification and implementation.

II. Not Casual Override: Justification in Terms of Public Reason! On the Point of the Proportionality Requirement

1. But saying that just about any issue of justice can be framed as a human rights issue does not yet say anything about what it means to have framed the issue in that way. What exactly follows from the fact that just about any state behaviour affecting a person falls under the scope of a human right? What exactly do you have in virtue of having a human right? When the behaviour of a state falls within the scope of a right—a prima facie infringement of a right has occurred—that does not imply that such behaviour is an actual violation of the right and therefore unjust. The fact that you have a right to do as you please does not mean that a law that prohibits you from

---

[24] For Kant there was only one fundamental right: The right to equal liberty; see Kant (1991).
[25] See Preamble, Universal Declaration of the Rights of Man and of the Citizen (1789).

murdering another person is violating your rights. Rights can be limited. Infringements of rights are susceptible to justification.[26] But how exactly should those limits be drawn?

Even though there are interesting and significant differences between conceptions of human rights in the liberal tradition, they generally share the idea that something protected as a matter of right may not be overridden by ordinary considerations of policy. Rights have been described as "trumps"[27] over competing considerations of policy, as having priority over "the good"[28] in some strong sense, and as "firewalls"[29] providing strong protections against demands made by the political community. Circumstantial all-things-considered judgements on what is in the general welfare are generally insufficient grounds to justify infringements of rights. Reasons justifying an infringement of rights, if they exist at all, have to be of a special strength.

Yet this claim of a special priority of rights sits uneasily with a prominent feature of human rights adjudication. A general feature of rights analysis all over the world is some version of a proportionality test.[30] An act of a public authority that infringes the scope of a protected right can still be justified, if it can be shown to pursue legitimate purposes in a proportional way. Only acts by public authorities that are disproportionate will be struck down on the grounds that they violate an individual's right.

True, there are human rights provisions such as "no one shall be subjected to torture",[31] "the death penalty shall be abolished",[32] "no one shall be imprisoned merely on the ground of inability to fulfil a contractual obligation",[33] etc. Such rights have a rule-like structure and can either be absolute rights or subject to certain rule-like exceptions. Specific rules of this kind are best understood as authoritative determinations made by the parties negotiating human rights treaties about how all the relevant first order considerations of morality and policy play out in the circumstances defined by the rule. Notwithstanding interpretative issues that may arise at the margins, clearly

---

[26] It is no solution to avoid these issues by insisting that rights properly so called are only fully specified rights, that is whatever is left after the justificatory process has established the priority of a rights claim against all countervailing considerations. First, we would still need to know how exactly we should go about the task of properly specifying rights and assess competing claims. Second, giving up on calling an infringement of a right a prima facie violation of a right would be deeply at odds with the dominant structure of practice. Third, the justificatory process itself is such an integral point of rights practice that a conception of rights which is only outcome focused (focused on what survives justification) would fail to capture one of its core moral points.

[27] Dworkin (1977).   [28] Rawls (1993).   [29] Habermas (1993).

[30] Huscroft, Miller, & Webber (2014); Barak (2012); Klatt & Meister 2012; Sweet & Mathews (2008); Beatty (2005).

[31] Art. 2 of the Convention against Torture and Other Cruel, Inhuman or Degrading Treatment or Punishment. states: "Each State Party shall take effective legislative, administrative, judicial or other measures to prevent acts of torture in any territory under its jurisdiction. No exceptional circumstances whatsoever, whether a state of war or a threat of war, internal political instability or any other public emergency, may be invoked as a justification of torture."

[32] Art. 1 of Protocol 13 of the ECHR states: "The death penalty shall be abolished. No one shall be condemned to such penalty or executed."

[33] Art. 11 ICCPR states: "No one shall be imprisoned merely on the ground of inability to fulfill a contractual obligation."

the judicial enforcement of such rules is not subject to proportionality analysis or any other meaningful engagement with moral considerations.

But at the heart of modern human rights practice are rights provisions that are not only more abstract, they exhibit a different structure. Take the right to freedom of speech, the right to freedom of assembly, or the right to privacy. Clearly these rights must have limitations. The right to freedom of speech does not mean you have a right to shout "fire" in a crowded cinema, the right to freedom of assembly does not mean you have a right to organize a spontaneous mass demonstration in the middle of Fifth Avenue during rush hour, nor does the right to freely manifest your religion mean that you have a right to fulfil your perceived religious duty to engage in a violent crusade against those whom you deem to be infidels, even if your church professes those obligations to exist for true believers. Furthermore, it is unlikely that the limits of these rights can be stated in the form of a set of neatly circumscribed rule-like exceptions. The question is how exactly those limits should be determined.

The architecture of rights provisions in modern human rights treaties and constitutions provides a good first indication. Characteristic of human rights treaties and constitutions enacted after the Second World War is a bifurcated structure: The first part of a provision defines the scope of the right. The second describes the limits of the rights by defining the conditions under which an infringement of the right is justified.

Article 8 of the European Convention of Human Rights (ECHR), for example, reads as follows:

1. Everyone has the right to respect for his private and family life, his home and his correspondence.
2. There shall be no interference by a public authority with the exercise of this right except such as is in accordance with the law and is necessary in a democratic society in the interests of national security, public safety or the economic well-being of the country, for the prevention of disorder or crime, for the protection of health or morals, or for the protection of the rights and freedoms of others.

The first part defines the scope of the interests to be protected—here: "respect for his private and family life, his home and correspondence". The second part establishes the conditions under which infringements of these interests can be justified: If the infringement is duly authorized by law and the infringement is substantively justifiable "as necessary in a democratic society in the interest of national security, public safety" etc.

The first step of human rights analysis typically consists in determining whether an act infringes the scope of a right. If it does a prima facie violation of a right has occurred. The second step consists in determining whether that infringement can be justified under the limitations clause. Only if it cannot is there a definitive violation of the right.

Even though the term proportionality is not generally used in limitation clauses immediately after the Second World War, over time courts have *practically uniformly interpreted these kinds of limitation clauses as requiring proportionality analysis.*

Besides the requirement of legality—any limitations suffered by the individual must be prescribed by law—the proportionality requirement lies at the heart of determining whether an infringement of the scope of a right is justified. Any law or legal measure restricting a right must meet the proportionality requirement. More recent rights codifications often recognize and embrace this development and have often substituted for the rights-specific limitation clauses a general default limitations clause. Chapter VII, Article 52 (1) of the European Charter of Fundamental Rights, for example, states: "Subject to the principle of proportionality, limitations may be made only if they are necessary and genuinely meet the objectives of general interest recognized by the Union or the need to protect the rights and freedoms of others."

Even though there is some variance in how the proportionality test is understood in judicial practice, the most widely used and defended version[34] asks the following set of sequential questions. First, did the infringement further a legitimate aim?[35] Second, was the measure necessary? A measure is necessary if and only if there are no alternative, less restrictive means. Of all equally effective means the one that is least restrictive has to be chosen. This part of the test thus establishes a pareto-optimality requirement. Third, there is the balancing test: Do the benefits of the measure outweigh the costs imposed on the rights-bearer.

The following example serves as an illustration of how the justification of rights infringements under such a framework operates. It concerns a recent case decided by the ECtHR that concerns the question of whether a provision criminalizing sexual intercourse among blood relations is compatible with a right to private life. In *Stübing*[36] the GFCC had upheld the law and the complainant challenged that decision before the ECtHR. The point of the following is not to either report on the decision or analyse and discuss in any depth all of the relevant arguments. It merely serves as an illustration of how the proportionality test helps structure human rights enquiry.

The case concerned biological siblings, who had grown up apart and only met each other on the occasion of their mother's funeral. They fell in love, lived together as a family and had four children before the man was convicted and incarcerated for violating the German criminal law prohibiting incest. Historically the point of incest regulation in many of the states where it exists was to reinforce and validate a widespread and deeply held moral belief that incest is wrong. As the court notes, citing cross-country surveys, the prohibition of incest continues to enjoy wide support among populations on moral grounds. But the first core issue is whether the validation of moral beliefs about how one should or should not live one's life is a legitimate purpose, when the public is not relevantly affected. Even though this is by no means uncontested in all

---

[34] Note 29.

[35] Strictly speaking there are two questions here, which is why the proportionality test is sometimes said to have four prongs: Was the aim legitimate (a normative question) and did the measure actually further that legitimate aim (an empirical question).

[36] See *Stübing v. Germany*, ECtHR Judgement of Apr. 12, 2012.

contexts, and may on occasion be the subject of direct controversy, the reinforcement of widely held moral norms relating to how one should conduct one's private life is typically not recognized as a legitimate purpose justifying the infringement of a right under the first prong of the proportionality test, and it wasn't recognized as such in this case, either by the ECtHR or the German FCC. Such beliefs generally do not qualify as a legitimate public purpose, unless they are connected to other plausible concerns of public policy.[37] In this way the first prong of the proportionality test implicitly functions to ferret out perfectionist purposes. Beyond the exclusion of widely held beliefs about how one should live one's life as a ground for limiting a right, the first prong of the proportionality test also excludes a number of other politically salient factors as irrelevant: It excludes as irrelevant the brute fact that a majority wants something, that something is conventionally done in a particular way, or that it has always been in a certain way. "We want this", "we don't do this kind of thing around here", and "we have a tradition of not tolerating that kind of thing" is never a sufficient argument, as powerful a factor as it might be in the political process. There is obviously nothing intrinsically wrong with moral beliefs, preferences, conventions, or traditions. But to serve as a valid justification for the infringement of a right, moral beliefs, preferences, conventions, and traditions have to be connected to plausible public policy concerns to be relevant. The widespread implicit endorsement of this position in human rights practice is apparent in the fact that courts insist on focusing on other concerns of public policy when they discuss the first prong. Although practically no measure ever fails the first prong, because it is practically nearly always possible to find some more plausible public policy concern, the first prong implicitly serves to categorically exclude a wide range of considerations that may well have been highly relevant to the political process but raise serious concerns from the point of view of a liberal political morality.

So both the ECtHR and the German Constitutional Court focused their discussion on other possible legitimate public purposes: Is the prohibition of incest justifiable on the grounds of protecting the roles and structures of the traditional family? But if the idea is to protect minors against adult family members (parents or older siblings), then other provisions of the criminal code—in particular statutory rape—have that covered. And to the extent that the statute applies also to adults, is it a legitimate purpose to

---

[37] Restricting rights on grounds of *public* morality is widely recognized, of course. But public morality is in play only when the public is affected by behaviour in the relevant way: Copulation in public or even running around naked in public can be prohibited on the grounds that people are seriously put off by it. Here a balance has to be struck between the competing concerns of those who seek to behave in a certain way in public and those who wish not to be confronted with such a behaviour when they are in public. The admonition to be tolerant is countered by the admonition to be respectful and some kind of balance will have to be struck. But these cases are to be distinguished from morality legislation in the strict sense where the issue is simply one of moral conviction as the ground for prohibitions, without any consideration of how the proposedly immoral behaviour affects others. The majority does not have the right to prevent you from doing what they think is morally wrong, simply because they think it morally wrong. Even though this is not uncontested, a more comprehensive survey of human rights jurisprudence would prove the pattern that rights adjudicating courts—certainly across Europe—tend to implicitly side with H. L. A Hart against Lord Devlin on this point.

criminalize the sexual practices of consenting adults to reinforce traditional family roles and structures? This, again, appears to be morality legislation.

But perhaps the legitimate purpose is the protection of the weaker, psychologically vulnerable member in such a potential relationship? Here there are two problems. First, it seems questionable to make the generalized paternalistic assumption that an adult's consent to incest relationships must be the result of weakness and psychological vulnerability (is this an empirical assumption driven by the belief that a morally upstanding person surely would not give her consent?). And if the concern is the exploitation of weakness and psychological vulnerability of one party, then that should be a condition for its criminalization. Otherwise the criminalization even of those whose consent does not suffer from any deficiencies is overbroad: It does not serve the purported purpose. It thus fails the second prong of the proportionality test: The law is not necessary, because a more restricted law would be equally effective in achieving the legitimate purpose without burdening those who have given their free consent.

The final purpose discussed is eugenic. Given the heightened probability of genetic defects of potential children between family members, they should abstain from acts that might lead to such children being born. But even if one were to accept this as a legitimate public health purpose (a disputed point among the judges), the general criminalization of sexual intercourse would probably fail the second and third prong of the proportionality test. To begin with the provision is overbroad and thus not necessary: It also covers situations where the issue of giving birth to a child with genetic disabilities is moot. In the case before the court the husband had already undertaken a vasectomy after the fourth child was born, thereby excluding any further procreation. And even in cases where there is a possibility of childbirth: Would it not be more appropriate to ensure that the parties are sufficiently informed of the relevant dangers? In the case of mature mothers beyond 40, or couples with blood group incompatibility issues or other defects, there is a comparable probability that any offspring produced will suffer from disabilities. It would appear to be obviously disproportionate in any of these contexts to criminalize a couple that, with full knowledge of the risks, decided to have a child anyway.[38] If that is so, it is not clear why it should be different in the context of incestuous relationships. The suspicion is that the moral opprobrium connected to incest, rather than any plausible policy concern, is doing the work.

A majority of judges on the German FCC had nonetheless upheld the law, ostensibly because they were persuaded by some combination of the various policy rationales. And the ECtHR let the court's decision stand invoking the state's "margin of appreciation".[39] But whatever you believe the right resolution of the issue to be, the

---

[38] The above presents a stylized and simplified version of the argument put forward by the dissenting opinion of Judge Hassemer of the German Constitutional Court.

[39] Given the remarkably unpersuasive arguments of the majority, probably the best way to make sense of these decisions is to assume that neither the German Constitutional Court nor the ECtHR was willing to invest a great deal of institutional legitimacy in striking down a law that apparently reflected widespread moral views, when the harm done by upholding it appeared to be limited. Notwithstanding the tragic

example illustrates two characteristic features of rights reasoning: First, the fact that a rights-holder has a prima facie right does not imply that he holds a position that gives him any kind of priority over countervailing considerations of policy. An infringement of the scope of a right merely serves as a trigger to initiate an assessment of whether the infringement is justified. The second characteristic feature of rights reasoning is the flipside of the first. Since comparatively little is decided by acknowledging that a measure infringes a right, the focus of rights adjudication is generally on the reasons that justify the infringement. Furthermore, the three-prong structure of proportionality analysis provides little more than a checklist for the individually necessary and collectively sufficient conditions that determine whether the reasons that can be marshalled to justify an infringement of a right are good reasons, all things considered. What should also have become clear is that the issues raised within such a structure can be complicated and may be subject to reasonable disagreement.

Note how there is a space within this structure to accommodate categorically structured commitments of political morality and liberal accounts of justice: Under the first prong of the proportionality test certain purposes—for example perfectionist purposes—can be categorically excluded as illegitimate. Furthermore, note that the idea of balancing does not imply the existence of a common matrix or some kind of technocratic calculus. Balancing is a metaphor that refers to the requirement that all relevant things need to be taken into account and that a balanced judgement has to be made, whether, under the circumstances, public authorities could reasonably give precedent to furthering a particular legitimate purpose.[40] When such a judgement is made, the public reasoning of judges tends to be constrained somewhat both by the gravitational pull of their own previous decision[41] as well as by the settled legislative or judicial judgements underlying other related areas of the law. Balancing is thus practically guided not just by the court's previous decisions, but also by ideas of reflective equilibrium or coherence as it applies to the relevant legal order.

Assessing the justification for rights infringements is to a large extent an exercise of an institutionally situated form of general practical reasoning. Given the modest role of authoritative texts and the centrality of assessing justifications within the framework of the proportionality test, it lacks the constraining features that otherwise characterize legal reasoning. Given the structure of human rights norms, there is something misleading in the idea that judges *interpret* rights. Judges do not interpret rights: they assess justifications. The apparent "casual override" that is reflected in the ubiquitous use of the proportionality test is connected to the distinctive contestatory

family involved in the case, there haven't been many cases relating to incest for years, nor is that expected to change. What cases such as these indicate is that even if moral convictions of the majority do not count as a legitimate purpose to restrict rights, socially widespread convictions nevertheless serve as an empirical constraint on what courts are willing to do.

[40] For a fuller discussion see Kumm (2007).

[41] This is true even in non-common law continental jurisdictions, where there is no official doctrine of precedent and earlier decisions are not formally accorded any authoritative weight nor regarded as sources of law.

and justificatory function of rights. The proportionality test, structured as it is, effectively establishes a test of public reason. Human rights norms empower rights-bearers to challenge existing power relationships by insisting that those relationships be suscep-tible to justification in terms of public reason.

But if everything that falls within the scope of a right must therefore be susceptible to proportionality based justification: What is the proper domain of sovereignty, national self-determination, and political democracy? The answer becomes clearer once we understand the sources of the third puzzling feature of human rights practice: Its variance.

III. Variance and Reasonable Disagreement: Levels of Specification and Legitimate Difference

Human rights claim to be universal. Human beings are claimed to have them simply in virtue of being human, not in virtue of being a member of this or that political community or region. Yet there are two complementary phenomena that appear to undermine the idea that human rights are truly universal. On the one hand there are differences between human rights treaties. International human rights treaties differ from regional human rights treaties, which in turn also differ from one another. And national constitutions rarely simply incorporate by reference global or regional human rights treaties. In the context of drafting their own Bill of Rights new lists are com-posed, differing again both with regard to the number of rights guarantees and, in part, in their content, from other instruments.[42] On the other hand, even when inter-national, regional, and national rights provisions appear to be textually similar, they may still be interpreted quite differently. Any general human rights instrument—global, regional, or national—will include a right to freedom of religion or freedom of speech, for example. But the practices that are deemed justifiable under that provision differ considerably across jurisdictions. What accounts for that difference? In this section I will distinguish between two kind of variances: Differences in the levels of specification, and substantive differences.

(a) Levels of specification

The length of human rights lists depends primarily on the level of abstraction at which human rights are specified.[43] It is futile to ask how many human rights there really are. To illustrate the point focusing only on classical negative liberty rights, we can imagine three kinds of approaches: Country A decides to list only one liberty right in

---

[42] The Israeli Supreme Court, for example, has developed a rich and expansive practice of rights protection grounded on a basic law mandating the protection of only "dignity and liberty". On the other side Brazil's constitution lists 77 negative rights in its Art. 5, followed by 34 social rights of urban and rural workers in Art. 7.

[43] See also Nickel's (2007) discussion of "the problem of lists" on p. 92.

its constitution: A general right to liberty. Country B, more conventionally, decides to add, say nine more specific liberty rights, such as a right to life and physical integrity, privacy, a right to freedom of speech, association, religion, as well as the right not to be subjected to unreasonable punishment. Country C, finally, has a list of 100 liberty rights. It has all the rights that state B has codified, but each of those rights is further specified in nine more concrete provisions. Instead of merely guaranteeing a right not to be subjected to unreasonable punishment, for example, it also includes: a right not to be sentenced to a prison term merely for being unable to pay your debt; a provision that prohibits the death penalty for all but a limited class of specifically listed particularly egregious crimes; a prohibition to sentence anyone to death who was not 18 at the time they committed the crime; a prohibition to subject anyone under the age of 14 to criminal punishment. And so on.

Note how there is no necessary correlation between a high level of protection of human rights and the level of specificity with which they are codified. It is not inconceivable, for example, that a court charged with interpreting the abstract provision prohibiting unreasonable punishment in state B might conclude that the death penalty is not just unreasonable to impose on minors or less than egregious crimes, as is established in state C. It might hold that the death penalty is unreasonable altogether and that the correct interpretation of the right means that capital punishment should be abolished entirely. Indeed, one of the reasons for greater specificity in a human rights instrument may well be the desire of the political drafters of the instrument to cabin in the power of other interpreters, in particular judiciaries. By spelling out in more concrete rule-like form legal guarantees of what a right amounts to, the drafters preclude more ambitious interpretations of the more abstract right.

So what accounts for the difference in the lengths of these lists and the chosen level of abstraction for human rights provisions? There are a number of factors in play. One of them is historical: Particular historical experiences of abuse tend to lead to specific provisions seeking to ensure and to expressively highlight the commitment that those specific forms of abuse do not happen again. In that sense Nietzsche's dictum that a people's laws reflect what they have overcome applies also to the issue of which human rights issues are more concretely highlighted by being explicitly expressed. Is it surprising that in the USA the First Amendment covers freedom of religion and freedom of speech, given what so many immigrants were fleeing from? Is it surprising that the German Basic Law enacted after the Second World War established an unqualified right to asylum after so many had been persecuted and were struggling to leave Fascist Germany and to be granted asylum elsewhere? Is it surprising that privacy and data protection concerns appear to be highlighted in Europe to a greater extent then elsewhere, after so many states had been captured by authoritarian or totalitarian governments for a considerable part of the twentieth century? Other considerations are political. They might concern the scope of political agreement among relevant actors. Given that human rights instruments, whether international law treaties or constitutions, require a great deal of consensus, the question is also what exactly the parties are able to agree on. Sometimes that will favour abstractions: The parties agree on an abstract principle, even if they disagree about how it should be specified. Sometimes, although in human rights practice much more rarely, that will favour concrete rules: Parties may agree on specific rules, where agreement on the more abstract principle justifying that rule is absent.[44] Furthermore, including a specific norm in a human rights instrument is an easy way to please constituents. The drafters take up their constituents' pet concern, include it in the list, thus symbolically acknowledging its importance, all the while not really giving anything away, if the provision does not take the form of a concrete rule, but remains a principle subject to proportionality analysis.[45] Finally the level of specification also depends on perceptions of what should be left in political play as part of the ordinary political give and take, as democratic majorities shift. Conversely an understudied form of abuse of power is the over-constitutionalization of rights: when present (qualified) majorities preclude future majorities from specifying rights differently by entrenching them in the form of concrete rules in the constitution, rather than just enacting ordinary legislation that can later be changed when majorities change.[46]

A second form of human rights overkill can also take the form of the judiciary effectively strangling the political process by leaving an increasingly small margin for genuine political decision, as constitutional doctrines develop in an ever finer web of doctrinal specifications over time. Call this the problem of juristocracy.[47] The perennial issue here is that of the appropriate degree of deference: What level of deference, "standard of review", what "margin of appreciation" should a human rights judiciary

---

[44] In that sense Cass Sunstein's (1995) account of under-theorized agreements is one-sided. Under-theorized agreements do not only lead to decisions one step at a time. They may sometimes push decision-makers, including judges, to announce bold principles, even when there is a great deal of disagreement on how that principle ought to be specified across a wide range of issues. In this way decision-makers can guide other actors, encouraging them to settle issues within the defined framework of principle, weighing in only as they see fit under the circumstances.

[45] Imagine, for example a constitution containing only a right to privacy. It is not unlikely, that a court interpreting that provision will read a right to data protection as a more specific form of privacy protection into that right and develop its own data protection jurisprudence on that basis, as the ECtHR and the German FCC has done. Now imagine a politician seeking to establish his data-protection credentials to gain favour with a powerful data protection focused group. He puts forward a proposal to include a right to data protection in the constitution. Perhaps the kind of high-profile political debates associated with constitutional amendments are well suited to focus attention on the issue of data protection. And perhaps it would serve a political community concerned about data protection well to have that concern articulated and symbolically validated in the form of a right in their constitution. But legally the specific inclusion in the constitution would change nothing: The courts already recognize such a right, deriving it from a more abstract right. Perhaps its explicit codification may embolden the judiciary to be less deferential to political actors when adjudicating questions concerning data protection. But we should not exclude the possibility that the symbolic validation of the right might function primarily as a distraction. Instead of discussing more concrete issues, such as the more effective control of the intelligence services or the demands to be made on companies relating to data management, progress takes place and political profiles are sharpened in the domain of the symbolic only.

[46] This appears to be a core strategy of Fidesz and Viktor Orban in Hungary. See Scheppele (2011).

[47] See Hirschl (2004).

concede to national political institutions and the democratic process when it applies the proportionality test and assesses the reasons put forward by the parties?

Here it must suffice to propose a basic conceptual distinction to help illuminate the issue.[48] As I have argued, the proportionality test, structured as it is, effectively establishes a test of public reason. But this test of public reason, as it is applied by courts, does not generally track the requirement that justice be done. The proportionality test itself may indeed track justice. But courts insist on applying that test in a deferential way, using doctrines such as "the margin of appreciation", "standards of scrutiny", or comparable doctrines. The point of these doctrines is to fix the difference between what justice requires (a question to be determined by other, more participatory processes) and what is reasonable. Reasonableness here refers to the idea of justifiability in terms of public reason—that is, justifiability in terms that free and equals might reasonably accept. Debates about the proper level of deference and the scope of the margin of appreciation in specific contexts ought to be understood as debates about the epistemic contours of the distinction between rights-based justice and reasonableness.

This means that human rights adjudicating courts are best understood as *policing the boundaries of the reasonable, not the boundaries of justice*. Participants of the democratic process should aspire to justice, but human rights courts do not review whether they succeed in that endeavour. The bar is set lower, by focusing merely on reasonableness understood as the justifiability in terms of public reason. The job of courts is not to govern and generally tell public authorities what justice and good policy requires. But it is their task to detect and strike down as instances of legislated injustice measures that, whether supported by majorities or not, impose burdens on some people, when no sufficiently plausible defence in terms of public reasons can be mounted for doing so. This is what it means for courts to apply the law in the context of human rights adjudication.

This understanding of the role of courts acknowledges the circumstances of politics: there is often reasonable disagreement about what justice requires and that reasonable disagreement can only be legitimately settled by an appropriately participatory political process involving democratically accountable representatives. But it also insists that not all winners of political battles and not all disagreements, even in mature democracies, are reasonable. Often they are not. Political battles might be won by playing to thoughtless perpetuation of traditions or endorsement of prejudicial other-regarding preferences, ideology, fear mongering, or straightforward interest-group politics falling below the radar screen of high-profile politics. The point of the practice of rights based justification is to determine whether the settlement burdening the rights claimant is in fact reasonable.

The implicit claim is that acts by public authorities that are unreasonable in the sense of lacking justifiability in terms of public reason can make no plausible claim to

---

[48] For an extended argument along those lines see Kumm (2010), p. 169.

legitimate authority in a world committed to human rights. For those acts the question is not what justifies the "countermajoritarian" imposition of outcomes by non-elected judges. The question is what justifies an act, when it can be ascertained with sufficient certainty in an impartial procedure involving independent judges that it imposes burdens on individuals for which there are no reasonable justifications.

(b) Substantive differences

A great deal of variance can be accounted for by pointing to different levels of speci-fication, along the lines analysed in this chapter. But other differences are substantive. A substantive position protected as a right in one human rights instrument, or under one court's interpretation, is simply rejected in another. To mention some well-known examples, limited to the transatlantic context:[49] The death penalty is now categorically prohibited in Europe, but not in the USA. A great deal of hate speech that enjoys pro-tection under the First Amendment of the US Constitution can be and is prohibited in Europe. Freedom of religion in Europe has been held to be compatible with a wide range of public practices that the US Constitution prohibits. Here I can only very briefly discuss two kinds of factors that account for such differences and what they imply for our understanding of universal human rights.

The first factor is the *differences in context* across jurisdictions. Some of the differ-ences in what is recognized as a human right might be attributable to differences in context that justify and account for that difference. Just to gesture at possible arguments, leaving open the question of whether any particular one can ultimately be sustained: Might it not matter for the purpose of justifying the exclusion of reli-gious symbols from public schools in the USA that the USA is a deeply diverse and religiously vibrant country? And as a corollary, might it not be relevant to the claim that crosses in classrooms do not violate the rights of non-Christian pupils in Italy,[50] not only that Italy is relatively homogeneously Catholic, but also that religious symbols and art have acquired a secular, cultural meaning for many and appear to be devoid of any kind of missionary zeal? Might the establishment of a national Church in places like the UK or Scandinavian countries be tolerable exactly because of widespread religious lack of interest and the cultural relativization of religion, thereby making it easier for those who really want to have nothing to do with a faith that is not theirs not to feel excluded or threatened? Might there be a difference between a Holocaust survivor being subjected to Nazi demonstrations on the streets of Berlin or in Skokie, Illinois? Might the experience of the Weimar Republic, which saw a liberal constitu-tional democracy fail because it lacked democratic support both among ordinary citizens and among its elites, justify prohibitions of parties seeking to abuse the demo-cratic process to abolish democracy and establish a communist or Fascist dictatorship? Different circumstances across communities may justify different specifications of

---

[49] For an illuminating set of contributions examining these questions across issue areas, see Nolte (2005).
[50] See *ECHR Lautsi v. Italy*, Judgement of Mar. 18, 2011.

human rights, thus justifying variance within a universalist framework. The concrete and local norm has to be justifiable in terms of universal human rights norms, but the human rights norms are only properly specified locally if they take account of the relevant local contexts. The tension between the universal and the local is thus internalized in the process of human rights concretization and specification.

The second factor to explain variance is *genuine disagreement* about human rights. Human rights concretization and specification is an activity that is subject to the general circumstances of politics: It is burdened by reasonable disagreement. In the context of norm concretization and specification that disagreement is addressed in what Seyla Benhabib has called iterative democratic processes.[51] These are participatory processes of contestation and deliberation leading to a more concrete constitutional settlement. It should not be surprising that different iterative democratic processes—whether the process of constitution-giving or gradual further norm-concretization by way of human rights litigation—can lead to slightly different settlements. The idea of human rights is connected to a universalist understanding of its core commitments to freedom, equality, and democratic self-government. But it is a mistake to think of human rights concretization and specification as a task that does not involve a participatory process of contestation and deliberation at the end of which different settlements about rights might well be reached.

IV. The Promise of Human Rights

It turns out that the seemingly limitless scope of rights that gives rise to the challenge of "rights inflation" is connected to the constitutive function of rights. Very much true to their roots in the eighteenth-century American and French revolutionary traditions, the point of human rights is not only to constrain law and politics in the name of some fundamental human interests, however conceived. Instead human rights constitute a particular kind of law and politics: a conception of law and politics as justice-seeking among free and equals. If this is their moral point, we should expect the domain of human rights to be coextensive with the domain of political justice and that is indeed a tendency that the phenomenon of "rights inflation" points to.

Furthermore, the apparent "casual override" that is reflected in the ubiquitous use of the proportionality test is connected to the distinctive contestatory and justificatory function of rights. The proportionality test, structured as it is, effectively establishes a test of public reason. Human rights norms empower rights-bearers to challenge existing power relationships by insisting that those relationships be susceptible to justification in terms of public reason. That test is met only if the behaviour of public authorities is demonstrably susceptible to a plausible justification in terms of reasons that the addressee(s) might reasonably accept.

---

[51] Benhabib (2006).

Finally, variance between global, regional, and national human rights instruments and different interpretations of rights by courts and political actors across jurisdictions also has an important moral point: Variance is best understood to reflect the requirement internal to universalist human rights practice itself to respect the values of democratic self-government and sovereign self-determination. Variance can be the result of one of three things: Differences in the level of abstraction/specification, the existence of relevant differences across local contexts that justify different specifications, or reasonable disagreement about how a right is best specified under given circumstances. The more human rights are specified, the more space there is likely to be for legitimate difference across time and across jurisdictions. The concrete and local norm has to be justifiable in terms of universal human rights norms, but the human rights norms are only properly specified locally if they take account of relevant and potentially variant local contexts and reflect respect for democratic procedures used to specify rights. In this way the tension between the universal and the local is internalized in the structure of human rights discourse and generates legitimate difference.

For a better understanding of the conception of human rights that emerges from the analysis here, it may be helpful to relate it to some recent critical writing.[52] Critical historical and practice focused authors have claimed that human rights reflect a chastened kind of minimalist idealism, replacing more ambitious ideals (1), that human rights focus is ameliorative, not transformative (2), and that human rights are imagined to be apolitical by those who invoke them (3). In the following I will seek to briefly discuss what is right and what is wrong about each of these claims.

(1) The demands made by human rights are in an important sense not minimalist. Human rights are certainly not a limited set of particularly urgent rights, as many have claimed.[53] Instead I have argued here that they are inextricably connected to the idea of politics as the process of establishing justice among free and equals under conditions of reasonable disagreement and conceptions of law that limit it to norms that are justifiable to those they address in terms that they might reasonably accept as free and equals. In this way human rights establish principles for the design of the basic institutional structure of just political orders and define the limits of legitimate authority.

Yet there is some truth in the claim that human rights are fundamentally more modest than competing political ideals. Human rights do not claim to provide an answer to the questions of ultimate orientation, meaning, and purpose of a human life; they have nothing to say about the historical origins and teleology of human society or the world. They do not preach "the new man". They do not come with an existentially perfectionist formula. They offer no redemptive relief for those committed to the right kinds of collective or individual action. That is one of reasons why it is misleading to claim that human rights are a modern distillation of the ethical core

---

[52] Moyn (2010); Brown (2004); Marks (2013).   [53] Rawls (1999); Ignatieff (2001).

of Christian teachings. The latter speak of love and redemption. Human rights speak of preventing injustice and seeking to institutionalize rights-based justice. Loving your neighbour as you love yourself is clearly not the same thing as respecting in others the rights you claim for yourself. Instead of offering a teleology of a life well lived and the promise of redemption, human rights merely insist on respecting the rights of others as side-constraints to any such life. It is possible to imagine a human rights utopia where everyone's rights are respected and yet all other features usually associated with utopias are absent. Deep suffering caused by unrequited love, disappointing friendships, lack of appreciation, failed aspirations, accidents, the misery and burdens of illness (even when available treatments are exhausted), the grief of fortuitous early death, anxieties, boredom, experiences of meaninglessness and alienation would remain a common feature of human existence, even in a world where human rights were fully realized. Of course a world in which human rights were effectively guaranteed would be a world in which a range of historically and socially powerful causes for devastation, unhappiness, anxiety, and wasted lives would be removed. And perhaps one way to live a life well is to make the cause of human rights and fighting injustices in their name central to it. But human rights lack the redemptive promise that theocratic, Marxist, Fascist and many other nationalist political ideologies come with. That does not mean that the triumph of the language of human rights signals the beginning of the reign of Nietzsche's last man.[54] It just promises the end of idolatrous politics.[55]

(2) Human rights have been claimed to be *ameliorative* in how they operate, compared to the transformative nature of other ideologies. But human rights are not inherently transformative or ameliorative. What they are in a particular context depends on that context. Human rights can be and have historically been transformative and ameliorative. They were transformative in the American and French Revolutions in the eighteenth century. In many countries today they remain potentially transformative. True, in most liberal democracies they routinely serve as ameliorative mechanisms. But even in liberal democracies they again and again help bring about a fundamental transformation. They may help shift the public culture of a political community from a "culture of authority" to a "culture of justification".[56] Or they may be the cause for the transformation of a particular domain of law and politics, such as the law governing prisoners and psychiatric ward inmates, or race and gender relations and how we legally regulate sex. We do not know what transformative potential they might prove to have in the future. But an understanding of how rights operate structurally and how they have been used historically suggests that there is no reason to presume that the future struggles for rights-based justice will be any less transformative than they have been in the past.

---

[54] The link between the triumph of liberal democracy and Nietzsche's evocative description of the "last man" in *Thus Spoke Zarathustra* is, of course, a central theme in Fukuyama (1992).

[55] Ignatieff (2001) is right that human rights can themselves become idolatrous, but that is an idolatry easily remedied by critiques drawing on the resources of the human rights tradition itself.

[56] Cohen-Eliya & Porrat (2013).

(3) As the discussion has already indicated, human rights are obviously not apolitical. They may have been understood in that way by Amnesty International and 1970s and 1980s activist groups at Columbia Law School, but they are not thought of that way either by those who drafted the Declaration of Human Rights and Citizens in 1789 France or those Chinese citizens who drafted the Charter 08 on the occasion of the 100th anniversary of the Chinese Constitution and the 60th anniversary of the UN Declaration of Human Rights. Human rights, like other political ideologies, have given and continue to give rise to revolutionary struggles, political movements, as well as nonviolent forms of dissident behaviour. Constitutional documents, reflecting a commitment to that tradition, sometimes explicitly authorize resistance, against those who seek to abolish a rights-based liberal democratic constitutional order. And authoritarian regimes, rightly fearing the revolutionary impetus of human rights, pay great attention to intimidating and, if need be, locking away those who advocate them.

But human rights are apolitical in one sense. Abstract propositions contained in human rights treaties or national constitutional charters *claim* to articulate propositions that should reasonably be endorsed as correct by persons of otherwise different political persuasions. Similarly, when judges adjudicate rights, they claim to be enforcing a standard that should be embraced by all, declaring a violation of rights only what does not meet the test of public reason. Rights provisions in human rights treaties and national constitutions and courts adjudicating human rights seek to articulate an overlapping consensus among reasonable persons who might disagree about much else in law and politics. That does not mean, of course, that they are beyond challenge or will not appear to be controversial to some. But wherever human rights are codified, be it in global international treaties, regional treaties, or national constitutions, human rights provisions are conceived as the foundation and a framework for a particular conception of law and politics. That conception of law and politics never loses focus of the fact that what public authorities impose on others in the name of good policy, justice, or legality has to be justifiable to them as a free and equal partner in the practice of collective self-government. But it is also very aware of the fact that persons—even well-informed and motivationally appropriately disposed persons—will disagree about what justice and good policy will require in concrete circumstances. As I have argued, from a normative point of view the practice of ordinary politics is best understood as the participatory struggle for the best specification and concretization of our human rights as free and equals under conditions of reasonable disagreement. Once we specify a right in the context of an ordinary political process, we no longer call the concrete specification a human right, but a statutory or administrative right. We recognize the possibility that other political majorities or administrative decision-makers may legitimately conclude that the right is better specified differently. We use the language of human rights only to challenge a particular specification as falling outside the domain of reasonable specifications. Unreasonable specifications of a right are by definition specifications that can't be demonstratively justified to those burdened by them as free and equals.

The language of human rights, then, does not refer to a domain outside of politics, it constitutes the basic grammar of liberal democratic politics. The rights of free and equals constitute the foundation and the framework of politics, but the political process itself is an iterative participatory process of contestatory human rights concretization and specification. Rights-based justice is not to be deduced from first principles by philosopher kings, avant-garde party leaders, or religious scholars or prophets but politically fought over and positively enacted as law in participatory processes among free and equals, subject only to the judicially enforceable constraint of plausible justifiability. Human rights simultaneously stand above politics and are at the heart of the political process.

References

Barak, Aaron, *Proportionality* (CUP 2012).

Beatty, David, *The Ultimate Rule of Law* (OUP 2005).

Benhabib, Seyla, *Another Cosmopolitanism* (OUP 2006).

Besson, Samantha, "The Allocation of Anti-Poverty Rights Duties: Our Rights, but Whose Duties?", in K. N. Schefer (ed.), *Poverty and the International Economic System: Duties to the World's Poor* (CUP 2013), 408.

Brown, Wendy, "'The Most We Can Hope For': Human Rights and the Politics of Fatalism", 103 *South Atlantic Quarterly* (2004), 451.

Buchanan, Allan, *The Heart of Human Rights* (OUP 2013).

Cohen-Eliya, Moshe, & Iddo Porrat, *Proportionality and Constitutional Culture* (CUP 2013).

Dworkin, Ronald, *Taking Rights Seriously* (Harvard University Press 1977).

Forst, Rainer, *The Right to Justification* (Columbia University Press 2012).

Franck, Thomas, "The Emerging Right to Democratic Governance", 86 *AJIL* (1992), 46.

Fukuyama, Francis, *The End of History and the Last Man* (Avon Books 1992).

Griffin, James, *On Human Rights* (OUP 2008).

Habermas, Jürgen, *Between Facts and Norms* (Polity Press, 1993).

Hirschl, Ran, *Towards Juristocracy: The Origins and Consequences of the New Constitutionalism* (Harvard UP 2004).

Huscroft, G., B. Miller, and G. Webber, *Proportionality and the Rule of Law* (CUP 2014).

Ignatieff, Michael, *Human Rights as Politics and Idolatry* (Princeton UP 2001).

Kant, Immanuel, *The Metaphysics of Morals* (CUP 1991).

Klatt, M., & M. Meister, *The Constitutional Structure of Proportionality* (OUP 2012).

Kumm, Mattias, "Political Liberalism and the Structures of Rights: On the Place and Limits of the Proportionality Requirement", in George Pavlakos (ed.), *Law, Rights and Discourse: Themes from the Legal Philosophy of Robert Alexy* (Hart 2007), 131–66.

Kumm, Mattias, "The Idea of Socratic Contestation and the Right to Justification: The Point of Rights-Based Proportionality Review", 4(2) *Law & Ethics of Human Rights* (2010), 142–75.

Kumm, Mattias, "Is the Structure of Rights Practice Defensible? Three Puzzles and Their Resolution", in V. Jackson and M. Tiushnet (ed.), *Proportionality: New Frontiers, New Challenges* (CUP 2017), 51-74.

Letsas, George, *A Theory of Interpretation of the European Convention on Human Rights* (OUP 2008).

Marks, Susan, "Four Human Rights Myths", in David Kinley, Wojciech Sadurski, and Kevin Walton (eds), *Human Rights: Old Problems, New Possibilities* (Elgar 2013).

Marks, Susan, "What has Become of the Emerging Right to Democratic Governance?", 22 *EJIL* (2011), 507–24.

Möller, Kai, "From Constitutional to Human Rights: On the Moral Structure of International Human Rights", 3 *Global Constitutionalism* (2014), 373–403.

Moyn, Samuel, *The Last Utopia: Human Rights in History* (Harvard UP 2010).

Nickel, James, *Making Sense of Human Rights*. Second Edition (Blackwell 2007).

Nolte, Georg (ed.), *US and European Constitutionalism* (CUP 2005).

Rawls, John, *Political Liberalism* (Columbia UP 1993).

Rawls, John, *Law of Peoples* (Harvard UP 1999).

Raz, Joseph, "Human Rights without Foundations", in Samantha Besson and John Tasioulas (ed.), *The Philosophy of International Law* (OUP 2010).

Scheppele, Kim Lane, "Hungary's Constitutional Revolution", NYTimes OpEd Dec. 19, 2011.

Stone Sweet, Alec, and Jud Mathews, "Proportionality Balancing and Global Constitutionalism", 47 *Columbia Journal of Transnational Law* (2008), 73–165.

Sunstein, Cass, "Incompletely Theorized Agreements", 108 (7) *Harvard Law Review* (May 1995), 1733–72.

Tasioulas, John, "Towards a Philosophy of Human Rights", 65 (1) *Current Legal Problems* (2012), 1–30.

Weinrib, Lorraine, "The Postwar Paradigm and American Exceptionality", in Soujit Choudhry (ed.), *The Migration of Constitutional Ideas* (CUP 2006).

7.1

Human Rights and Justification
A Reply to Mattias Kumm

Samantha Besson

In his interesting and elegant piece "The Turn to Justification", Mattias Kumm claims that the current global human rights (legal) practice has three structural features: it is inflationary; it allows for routine overrides; and it is variable.[1] While those features may at first be perceived as problematic, and have actually been deemed as such by some human rights theorists in the past,[2] Kumm claims that they are not. Not only are they morally justified, but they actually correspond to what he refers to as "a non-domination-oriented liberal conception of law and justice" (p. 239).

What underpins the chapter's argument is the claim that human rights have an inherently justificatory structure (e.g. pp. 239, 251, and 256) and that such rights are, as a result, "constitutive" of law and "liberal democratic politics" qua processes of mutual justification (p. 260, Section IV). Because human rights reasoning is justificatory in itself, human rights are to be found everywhere in the legal order (hence their seeming inflation; Section I); they trigger constant justified restrictions (hence the seeming casualty of their override; Section II); and their specifications can only occur in a specific context (hence their seeming variance; Section III).

In this short commentary, I would like to argue that this claim about the justificatory structure of human rights is not only quite common, but that it is trickier than it is made to seem in Chapter 7. Moreover, as I plan to explain, it does not account for any of the three features identified by the author, both because it simply does not and because those features cannot be observed in the practice of human rights in the first place. I will first address the main justificatory claim (Section 1), and will then turn to each of the three structural features of human rights identified in the chapter (Sections 2, 3, and 4).

---

[1] Numbers in brackets refer to the respective pages in Mattias Kumm's chapter.

[2] On human rights inflation, see e.g. the discussion in Nickel 2007, ch. 6; on casual override, see e.g. the discussion in Griffin 2008, ch. 3; and on variance, see e.g. the discussion in Buchanan 2013, chs. 6 and 7.

1. Human Rights as Justification and the Justification of Human Rights

Like Kumm, I understand legal human rights as moral rights and, as such, as grounds for moral duties. Rights protect interests that are recognized as sufficiently important to give rise to duties. In other words, they are grounds for reasons for action and are in themselves justifications as a result. Every time a right gives rise to specific duties in concrete circumstances, a ground and hence a justification for those specific duties is provided. As I have argued elsewhere, this turns human rights law, and human rights reasoning and adjudication in particular, into a (legally formalized and constrained) forum of justification for human rights duties and, in turn, of justification for potential restrictions to those duties.[3]

To this extent, Kumm is right about the inherently justificatory structure of human rights. Where he errs is the extent to which this accounts for the three structural features he identifies in the practice of human rights, as I will explain next.

What the author also underestimates is the extent to which this inherent justificatory structure of human rights is at odds with many of the distinct moral justifications *of* human rights (albeit pluralistic ones) proposed by current human rights theorists.[4] Although Kumm is careful not to articulate what his exact position is with respect to those distinct moral justification(s) of human rights (e.g. note 4), and rightly so given that those justifications are not what his chapter is about, his argument about the justificatory structure of human rights itself may be problematic for the proposed account of politics and justice he defends. Indeed, the latter seems to be Rawlsian in inspiration (e.g. p. 257) and relies on some test of substantive reasonableness. At places, moreover, the author even reads as endorsing some form of moral foundationalism (e.g. p. 251). Provided they are applied to human rights, both features of Kumm's argument are in tension, however, with the more procedural and democratic approach to justification at play in Rainer Forst or Seyla Benhabib's accounts of human rights that are also used in the chapter (e.g. pp. 239 or 256).

To alleviate this tension between claiming that human rights are justificatory and providing distinct justifications for them, I have argued elsewhere that we should not look for justifications of human rights outside the political-moral equal status they are constitutive of.[5] On this approach, equality does not amount to a founding value of human rights, but to a status they are constitutive of. Importantly, this justification of human rights through their own justificatory function or self-justification is not in tension with an independent justification of the interests protected by human rights or

---

[3] For a full argument, see Besson 2013, pp. 38–40.

[4] For a discussion of the various proposals, and in particular of moral (i) or legal (ii) justifications of moral (i.a) and/or legal (i.b) rights, and the distinction from the discussion of their legitimate authority as grounds of legal duties, see Besson 2013, pp. 39ff. See also Waldron 2013; Buchanan 2013, chs. 3 and 4.

[5] See Besson 2013, pp. 44–6.

of the content of human rights themselves (i.e. their corresponding duties), provided such justifications are needed or provided.

2. Human Rights' Limited Object and Unlimited Scope

In Section I of Chapter 7, Kumm argues that the practice of human rights is inflationary. By this, he does not mean what is usually meant by human rights theorists (i.e. their object and/or content are/is unlimited), but that human rights are found everywhere in legal reasoning (i.e. their material scope is unlimited). His two examples are the right to liberty and the principle of non-discrimination—not only but mostly in EU legal reasoning, and this is telling because EU law is not only or merely about the protection of human rights. He then accounts for this feature of the practice by reference to the inherently justificatory nature of rights that itself matches what Kumm understands to be the nature of law in a liberal democracy. This reading of human rights practice is what the author refers to as "total rights".

This is not only a mischaracterization of the legal practice, but it misses the truly perplexing inflation of human rights in practice.

True, rights and duties are common elements in legal reasoning. Not all rights are human rights, however. And the two examples given are clearly not human rights and, importantly, are not even considered as such legally. The free movement of persons under EU law has not developed as a fundamental right and the Court of Justice of the European Union does not apply fundamental rights reasoning when interpreting and applying it. The non-discrimination principle is more complex, but its auxiliary position in fundamental rights reasoning, be it under EU law or ECHR law, shows how it is not treated as another fundamental right by human rights courts. Evidence for this may actually be found in the kind of proportionality test used by those courts when assessing restrictions to the freedom of movement or to the principle of non-discrimination: it is very different from the one used in the human rights context, thus strengthening my argument in Section 3. As to Kumm's point about the mere possibility of "reframing" any claim of injustice into a human rights claim (p. 243), it is moot: mere reframing does not turn that claim into a practice—and even less a justified one. As a matter of fact, it is hard to understand why Kumm insists on identifying the whole domain of justice with that of human rights (p. 256). Human rights may be constitutive of some political justice and, to that extent, be constitutive of one's equal political status,[6] as I have argued elsewhere, but without being conflated with the whole of (political or other) justice. Democracy is a case in point or, less controversially, distributive equality.

A related feature of human rights practice that is more intriguing for the purposes of human rights theory, but is not addressed in the chapter, is not the scope, but the object and/or content of human rights. The difficulty lies, in other words, in the many

---

[6] See Besson 2012b; Besson 2014b.

international legal rights referred to as "human rights" that do not correspond to what can be reasonably understood as (moral) human rights (e.g. the right to paid holidays, Article 7 ICESCR). Here, the solution may be to provide a careful account of the relationship between law and morality, between moral and legal rights, and, finally, between moral and legal human rights, on the other.[7] Then, moral justifications for legal rights that are not "human rights" may be articulated.[8] It is unclear, however, what the position of the author of the chapter is on those relationships—he refers at times to the legal "recognition" of human rights (p. 255) and to their "codification" (p. 247), but those terms may be understood either way. Moreover, the question of the delineation between the object and/or content of human rights and that of other moral and legal rights is not addressed. A key feature in a constitutive account of human rights of the kind proposed in the chapter, where human rights constitute one's political-moral equal status,[9] could be, as I have argued elsewhere, to identify what makes people fundamentally equal morally.[10] However, this relational feature cannot be unlimited and could certainly not cover all interests protected by rights other than human rights. Nor could Kumm's concurrent reference to freedom. Nor can this relational feature and the status it constitutes actually be the object of human rights and a distinct object has to be articulated. Regrettably, these crucial questions are not addressed in the chapter.

3. Absolute and Non-Absolute Human Rights

In Section II of the chapter, Kumm argues that human rights are rarely protected in an absolute fashion and that restrictions are a central feature of reasoning about human rights. He takes the widespread use of the proportionality test as evidence of this feature. He then accounts for this feature of the practice by reference to the inherently justificatory nature of human rights by unpacking the connection between human rights reasoning and public reason.

Again, this is not only a mischaracterization of the practice, but it also blinds us to a more complex feature of human rights practice: to quote James Griffin, "human rights are resistant to trade-offs, but not completely so".[11]

To start with, the section mischaracterizes the practice to the extent that, while it is true that human rights are prone to trade-offs, those restrictions are not justified according to the proportionality test Kumm describes. Not only is proportionality not used by human rights courts in the widespread fashion the author implies (p. 246),[12] but when it is, it is not used as an instrumental rationality or "pareto-optimality" test (p. 247) contrary to many accounts of some of the prongs of the proportionality test. On the contrary, one may argue that it is used to sustain an egalitarian interpretation of

---

[7] See Besson 2011; Besson 2015. See also Buchanan 2013.

[8] See e.g. Buchanan 2013, chs. 3 and 4.   [9] See Besson 2012a; Besson 2012b.

[10] See Besson 2015; Besson 2013.   [11] Griffin 2008, p. 76.

[12] Of course, this is not to say that scholarly interest in proportionality is not widespread. It is quite the contrary, actually. It is interesting, however, to find mostly *scholarly* references in footnotes relating to an argument pertaining to proportionality reasoning in *practice*.

conflicting human rights' duties.[13] In any case, upholding a cost and benefit approach to proportionality (p. 247) is in tension with the kind of moral justification Kumm's chapter endorses by reference to Rainer Forst's right to justification (p. 239).

More importantly, the feature of human rights practice that is most intriguing in this context is the coexistence of those common restrictions to human rights, on the one hand, with the absolute stringency of some of them or, at least, of some of their duties, on the other. One may mention so-called "absolute rights" (e.g. Article 3 ECHR)[14] or some of their minimal "core duties" (e.g. the right to know one's biological origins under Article 8 ECHR).[15] It is not enough to hint at the rule-like structure of certain human rights or at abstract specifications here, as the author does (pp. 245–6 and 251ff.). The latter cannot account for the absolute stringency of the human rights duties one encounters in judicial reasoning itself. Nor does the identification of alleged rules account for how this stringency may be justified from the perspective of the equality and indivisibility of human rights. Regrettably, the chapter does not explain how this works and what we should make of the coexistence of absolute and non-absolute human rights duties in any given human rights theory.

4. Universal and Local Human Rights

In Section III of the chapter, Kumm argues that human rights have to be specified in context and that this accounts for their variation from one domestic or regional context to the next. He accounts for this in terms of actual contextual differences both in the degree of abstract specification of the rights or in the consecutive interpretation of those rights, but also of reasonable disagreements about the right interpretation of those rights. Another source of variation pertains to the level of specification of human rights chosen by various international legal instruments for the protection of human rights. This variance in human rights practice reflects the "values of democratic self-government and sovereign self-determination", says Kumm (p. 257).

Again, this is not only a mischaracterization of human rights practice, albeit a slight one this time, but it also eludes a more complex feature of that practice: the minimal level of universal protection guaranteed by international human rights law.

To start with, the author slightly mischaracterizes the practice to the extent that he equates variations in the interpretation of human rights by domestic courts or in domestic human rights catalogues with variations within international human rights law and interpretations; the latter do not diverge that much overall, as a matter of fact. So doing, actually, Kumm also straddles too quickly issues of human rights-based judicial review arising in domestic liberal democracies (pp. 253ff.) with those arising out of

---

[13]   See Letsas 2015; Besson 2017b.

[14]   See e.g. ECtHR, *Ilaşcu v Moldova and Russia* 2004-VII, 40 EHRR 46, par. 334.

[15]   See e.g. Joint Dissenting Opinion of Judges Wildhaber et al., in ECtHR, *Odièvre v France* 2003-III, (2004) 38 EHRR 43, par. 11. See Besson 2017b.

supranational judicial review exercised by international human rights courts. A related source of puzzlement is that his argument about democratic sovereignty and the domestic contextualization of human rights in this section of the chapter seems to provide the answer to the critique he discusses of his "total rights" position in the first section: someone may disagree with the total rights approach, but endorse the democratic sovereignty and contextualization argument.[16]

More importantly, the really difficult issue with human rights is precisely to situate the minimal level of protection that is guaranteed universally despite contextual differences, and how it is to be identified legitimately. While Kumm is right that human rights are to be both universal and local at the same time (p. 256), and I have argued elsewhere that they can and should be so,[17] a minimum needs to be set and this should be done so as to be legitimate, and democratically legitimate in particular. This could be done through the progressive consolidation of transnational human rights law in particular.[18] However, it is important that the democratic qualities of those means of consolidation at the international and universal level are considered and provided for.[19] Regrettably, this question goes amiss in the chapter, which only vaguely gestures at the tension between the universal and the local, and at the need to "justify" local interpretations by reference to "universal human rights norms" (p. 256).

So, to conclude, the three features of the global human rights practice identified in the chapter are more ambivalent and therefore more difficult to account for in one single theory of human rights than the chapter seems to argue. Human rights are both limited in content and object as well as potentially unlimited in scope; they are at the same time prone and resistant to trade-offs; and they are both universal and local in justification. While it is true that human rights are justificatory through and through, this is only one of their many specificities in terms of judicial reasoning and does not help much in understanding these three dual features of human rights.

References

Benhabib, S., *Dignity in Adversity: Human Rights in Troubled Times*, Cambridge and Malden, Mass.: Polity Press 2011.

Besson, S., "Human Rights and Democracy in a Global Context: Decoupling and Recoupling", (2011) 4:1 *Ethics & Global Politics* 19–50.

Besson, S., "The Egalitarian Dimension of Human Rights", (2012a) *Archiv für Sozial- und Rechtsphilosophie Beiheft* 19–52.

Besson, S., "The Right to Have Rights—From Human Rights to Citizens' Rights and Back", in M. Goldoni & C. McCorkindale (eds), *Arendt and the Law*, Oxford: Hart Publishing 2012b, 335–55.

---

[16] See e.g. Tasioulas 2013a and 2013b.
[17] See Besson 2012a; Besson 2012b; Besson 2015. See also the essays in Benhabib 2011.
[18] See Besson 2015; Besson 2014a; Besson 2016; Besson 2017a; Besson 2018.
[19] See Besson 2013.

Besson, S., "Justifications of Human Rights", in D. Moeckli and S. Shah (eds), *International Human Rights Law*, 2nd edn, Oxford: Oxford University Press 2013, 34–52.

Besson, S., "European Human Rights Pluralism: Notion and Justification", in M. Maduro, K. Tuori, and S. Sankari (eds), *Transnational Law—Rethinking European Law and Legal Thinking*, Cambridge: Cambridge University Press 2014a, 170–205.

Besson, S., "International Human Rights and Political Equality—Implications for Global Democracy", in E. Erman & S. Näsström (eds), *Equality in Transnational and Global Democracy*, London: Palgrave 2014b, 89–123.

Besson, S., "Human Rights and Constitutional Law: Mutual Validation and Legitimation", in R. Cruft, M. Liao, and M. Renzo (eds), *Philosophical Foundations of Human Rights*, Oxford: Oxford University Press 2015, 279–99.

Besson, S., "Human Rights' Adjudication as Transnational Adjudication—Putting Domestic Courts as International Law Adjudicators in Perspective", in M. Footer and A. Reinisch (eds), *International Law and…ESIL Proceedings of the 10th Anniversary Conference*, Oxford: Oxford University Press 2016, 43–65.

Besson, S., "Human Rights as Transnational Constitutional Law", in A. Lang and A. Wiener (eds), *Handbook on Global Constitutionalism*, London: Edward Elgar 2017a, in press.

Besson, S., "Human Rights in Relation", in S. Smet (ed.), *Human Rights Conflicts*, Oxford: Oxford University Press 2017b, 23–37.

Besson, S., "Comparative Human Rights Law—Human Rights as a Comparative Project", in M. Reimann (ed.), *Oxford Handbook on Comparative Law*, 2nd edn, Oxford: Oxford University Press 2018, forthcoming.

Buchanan, A., *The Heart of Human Rights*, Oxford: Oxford University Press 2013.

Griffin, J., *On Human Rights*, Oxford: Oxford University Press 2008.

Letsas, G., "Rescuing Proportionality", in R. Cruft, M. Liao, and M. Renzo (eds), *Philosophical Foundations of Human Rights*, Oxford: Oxford University Press 2015, 316–40.

Nickel, J. W., *Making Sense of Human Rights*, 2nd edn, Oxford: Blackwell 2007.

Tasioulas, J., "Human Rights, Legitimacy, and International Law", (2013a) 58 *American Journal of Jurisprudence* 1–25.

Tasioulas, J., "Justice, Equality, and Rights", in R. Crisp (ed.), *Oxford Handbook of the History of Ethics*, Oxford: Oxford University Press 2013b, 768–92.

Waldron, J., "Is Dignity the Foundation of Human Rights?", (2013) *NYU School of Law, Public Law Research Paper No.* 12–73.

8

Appreciating the Margin of Appreciation

Andreas Follesdal

I. Introduction

'Sovereign is he who decides on the exception.'

(Schmitt 1985, p. 5)

International courts and tribunals are often hailed as harbingers of the rule of law to the anarchy among states.[1] Such hopes are sometimes tempered by worries about the power of the ever increasing number of such courts, their origins in the consent of sovereign states notwithstanding. Politicians and scholars alike perceive tensions between such self-binding and states' and citizens' claims to self-governance. How should an international court or tribunal best 'balance the sovereignty of Contracting Parties with their obligations under the Convention' (Macdonald 1993, p. 123)—so as to pay due respect to both the treaty and to its sovereign creators?

The European Court of Human Rights (ECtHR, 'the Court') is a prime suspect. It reviews whether states uphold their obligations under the European Convention on Human Rights (ECHR), a convention under the Council of Europe. The Court is also authorized to rule on whether states may violate certain of their citizens' rights—as the Convention permits—in order to protect morals, the conflicting rights of others, national security, or other considerations (e.g. Art. 8, Art. 15).

One mechanism that arguably serves to reduce the risk that the ECtHR will abuse its power is the margin of appreciation (MA) doctrine that the Court has developed. The Court grants states the authority to decide, in some cases, whether they are in

[1] This chapter was written under the auspices of MultiRights, an ERC Advanced Grant agreement n° 269841; the Research Council of Norway through its Centres of Excellence Funding Scheme, project number 223274—PluriCourts; and the research project 'Justice in Conflict', The Arctic University Norway. I am very grateful for comments from Adam Etinson, George Letsas, and Geir Ulfstein.

compliance with their treaty obligations—typically whether states are justified in violating some individuals' rights because the violations are proportionate to acceptable social objectives or other rights.

The room for discretion is especially important with several partly conflicting objectives, ranging from conflicts among human rights to conflicts between human rights and other important objectives.

Some may hold that such a MA is not enough, and instead claim that international or regional courts and treaty bodies should not review the legislation of well-functioning democracies, out of respect for their citizens' autonomy. Indeed, the rampant value pluralism and variations in natural and social conditions across states counsels some deference by international courts concerning how states should best respect and promote various objectives—including human rights. The abstraction of such rights may thus be amongst their virtues, since they can—and must be—specified in different ways to reflect such differing circumstances (Etinson 2013).

Is the MA doctrine a sound response to this perceived dilemma between majoritarian democracy and the protection of human rights? To answer that question several issues must be made more clear, in particular details about the scope of the MA, and the conditions under which the Court in this way defers to the judgement of national authorities. The normative assessment of the doctrine requires elaboration of these issues.[2]

The present chapter presents and defends some form of the MA doctrine precisely as a contribution by the Court both to protect human rights *and* to promote domestic democracies. I shall also suggest reforms to render it more legitimate. Section II provides a somewhat charitable explanation of what the current MA doctrine is.[3] Section III considers various arguments that have been presented in its favour, and seeks to bring them to bear on various aspects of the doctrine. Section IV looks in greater depth at the tensions between democratic self-governance and the authority of the ECtHR, and interprets the MA doctrine as promoting the same values as does democratic rule. Section V considers several objections. Section 6 draws some conclusions, including about whether the MA doctrine should be emulated by other international courts and tribunals—a trend noted by some observers (Shany 2005). The focus is on two central contentious issues: the policy that an emerging 'European consensus' should limit the scope of the MA, and ways to reduce the risk of domination by the ECtHR judges.

II. What is the Margin of Appreciation?

The MA doctrine is a principle of interpretation and adjudication that the European Court of Human Rights sometimes uses. It grants a state the authority, within some limits, to determine whether they have violated Convention rights in a particular case.

---

[2] I owe this clarification to Letsas.

[3] For more comprehensive accounts of the doctrine, cf. Brems 1996, Mahoney 1998, del Moral 2006, Letsas 2007, Kratochvil 2011.

The doctrine is not found in the Convention text proper, but is a long standing practice that the Court itself established. Protocol 15, which is not yet in effect, includes provisions that will incorporate the MA into the Preamble of the Convention.

Many trace the doctrine back to the 1958 *Cyprus case*. The government of Cyprus, then under UK rule, imposed emergency measures to curtail an insurrection, including legislation that permitted flogging and collective fines (Bates 2010, 195; Simpson 2004, chs. 18–19). Greece brought the case to the then European Commission of Human Rights, which noted that under Article 15, the UK authorities 'should be able to exercise a certain measure of discretion in assessing the extent strictly required by the exigencies of the situation.' Art. 15 states that:

1. In time of war or other public emergency threatening the life of the nation any High Contracting Party may take measures derogating from its obligations under this Convention to the extent strictly required by the exigencies of the situation, provided that such measures are not inconsistent with its other obligations under international law.
2. No derogation from Article 2 [The right to life], except in respect of deaths resulting from lawful acts of war, or from Articles 3 [Prohibition of torture], 4 (paragraph 1) [Prohibition of slavery] and 7 [No punishment without law] shall be made under this provision....

In this case the Commission maintained both that it was competent to decide whether a derogation from the Convention was justified, and whether the state's measures were indeed 'strictly required by the exigencies of the situation.' These competences notwithstanding, it granted national authorities 'a certain measure of discretion' in deciding on these issues—but hardly ever with regard to the non-derogable Art. 2, 3, or 4 (cf. Greer 2006, p. 10).

Note that what is at stake here is not how to interpret which rights individuals have.[4] Instead, the state is granted the authority, within some limits, to determine whether these rights are violated in a particular case. The ECtHR thus applies a MA when it decides not to review or challenge a state's decision (Letsas 2006, p. 706; Letsas 2007, pp. 80–1).

The Court elaborated the doctrine in the *Lawless v. Ireland* case, concerning measures to counter the IRA:

The concept of the margin of appreciation is that a government's discharge of [its] responsibilities is essentially a delicate problem of appreciating complex factors and of balancing conflicting considerations of the public interest; and that, once the Commission or the Court is satisfied that the Government's appreciation is at least on the margin of the powers conferred by Article 15, then the interest which the public itself has in effective government and in the maintenance of order justifies and requires a decision in favour of the legality of the Government's appreciation. (*Lawless v. Ireland* 1961, series B p. 408)

---

[4] This is sometimes referred to as a MA as regards the state's *interpretation* of norms (cf. Shany 2005, p. 910). Letsas calls this a 'substantive' concept of MA (Letsas 2006, p. 706; Letsas 2007, pp. 80–1).

The MA typically applies to trade-offs between one Convention right and other rights, or some social goal or emergency situation. Art. 15 cases are not typical: later cases often concern sensitive and contested moral issues and established national traditions. There may also be cases where a state maintains a certain substantive interpretation of a right rather than the interpretation favoured by the Court, while there is no such conflict at stake. Some scholars also call another phenomenon the 'margin of appreciation', namely when the Court respects states' discretion to choose the means by which to ensure their obligations (*Fadeyeva v. Russia* 2005; cf. Kratochvil 2011; Shany 2005, p. 935).

1 Scope of application: which rights?

The MA originated with regard to the emergency situations that allow limitations of certain rights, such as Art. 15. It has been used for articles that include limitation clauses, namely Arts 8–11 (the right to private and family life, freedom of thought and religion, of expression, and of assembly, respectively), each of which include require-ments akin to the proportionality requirements listed above. It is also used concerning prohibitions of unequal treatment or non-discrimination (Art. 14); and Art. 6 (right to a fair trial)—including access to courts.

Some claim that the MA may apply to all articles of the ECHR (del Moral 2006), but the ECtHR has rarely allowed an MA with regard to the non-derogable rights: Arts 2 (the right to life), 3 (prohibition against torture), and 4 (1) (prohibition of slavery and forced labour) (cf. Greer 2006, p. 10; Schokkenbroek 1998).

When it comes to how 'wide' an MA the ECtHR grants states, several authors have identified various elements that affect this decision (Brems 1996, del Moral 2006, Mahoney 1998).

2 The importance of the right

The 'limitation clauses' in the ECHR all require that the restrictions are 'necessary in a democratic society'. Consistent with this stress on democratic institutions, the Court only reluctantly grants an MA to any restriction of rights that is central to the democratic functions of a state, such as freedom of expression for political debates; and freedom of association and free elections (Brems 1996, pp. 266, 268). Such restrictions may occur, but must satisfy high standards of justification.

3 The importance of the social interests

The nature of the social objectives also appears to affect the scope of the MA. When the objectives are the human rights of others, the ECtHR seems to grant states a *wider* MA (Del Moral 2006, p. 617; *Klass and Others v. Germany* 1978; Leander v. Sweden 1987). In such cases a broad MA may seem defensible, yet not without limits, since there is still a risk that a state will place too little weight on certain rights of some subjects, relative to others.

The limitations clauses of Arts 8–11 ECtHR indicate some weighty social interests that permit restrictions on the rights:

There shall be no interference by a public authority with the exercise of this right except such as is in accordance with the law and is necessary in a democratic society in the interests of national security, public safety or the economic well-being of the country, for the prevention of disorder or crime, for the protection of health or morals, or for the protection of the rights and freedoms of others.   (Art. 8 (respect for private and family life))

There are some variations among the articles: Art. 9 (freedom of thought) and Art. 10 (freedom of expression) do not mention 'national security', 'economic well-being of the country', or 'prevention of disorder or crime'). Art. 9 includes 'public order'. Art. 10 includes territorial integrity, the protection of the reputation or rights of others; to prevent the disclosure of confidential information, or to maintain the authority and impartiality of the judiciary.

Such potentially countervailing interests have been considered by the ECtHR: The protection of morals, including sexual morality (*Handyside v. the United Kingdom* 1976) and blasphemy (*Wingrove v. the United Kingdom* 1996); maintaining the authority and impartiality of the judiciary (*Skalcka v. Poland* 2003); and national security (*Observer and Guardian v. UK* 1991). On the latter, the ECtHR has granted a wide MA to states when the objective is to fight terrorism (*Klass and Others v. Germany* 1978), but not on to prevent crime in general (Brems 1996, p. 263).

4 Evidence of domestic good faith reasoning and balancing

One interesting aspect of the MA practice is that the ECtHR often, if not always, requires that the state must actually have stated reasons for its position. The state authorities must give evidence that they have performed the requisite 'balancing' or reasoning about the rights sacrificed for the social objectives. One reason is that 'it is only in the event that the national authorities offer grounds for justification that the Court can be satisfied ... that they are better placed than it is to deal effectively with the matter' (*Schalk and Kopf v. Austria* 2010, dissenting opinion; cf. Kratochvil 2011, p. 333).

Such cases indicate that the Court does not grant a state an MA unless it is convinced that the state authorities have actually carried out such 'balancing'. Note also that the Court does not leave it completely to the state to set the standard for sufficient quality of the deliberation, or to determine and specify its main interests. The Court has sometimes found such a review unsatisfactory, because it did not find a 'reasonable relationship of proportionality ... notwithstanding the wide margin of appreciation available to the national authorities' (*A v. Norway* 2009, p. 74).

5 'Balancing'—the proportionality test

The Court has specified the sort of reasoning the state must give evidence of, in order to be granted an MA, in the form of a 'proportionality test'.

Courts in several jurisdictions apply various tests to determine whether there is 'proportionality' or 'fair balance' between the means and the aim sought. There has also been a certain debate among scholars, much of it centred on an account presented and defended by the legal scholar Robert Alexy (Alexy 2002):

1. The infringing measure has to a) further a legitimate aim, and b) the measure must further that aim
2. 'Necessity': There must be no more effective but less intrusive measure
3. 'Balancing': the promotion of the legitimate aim must outweigh the extent of rights infringement. Thus his 'Law of Balancing' holds that 'The greater the degree of non-satisfaction of, or detriment to, one principle, the greater must be the importance of satisfying the other' (p. 102).

ECtHR has drawn on several of these practices in developing its own test (*Handyside v. the United Kingdom* 1976, *James and Others v. the United Kingdom* 1986, p. 50). A charitable account based on cases and various statements by the Court may run thus: Discretion might be granted with regard to at least five different elements. As part of the decision whether to grant an MA, the Court assesses:

1. The legitimacy of the social objective pursued
2. How important the restricted/derogated right is, e.g. as a foundation of a democratic society (*Handyside* para. 49)
3. How invasive the proposed interference will be
4. Whether the restriction of the right is necessary (para. 4)
5. Whether the reasons offered by the national authorities are relevant and sufficient (para. 50).

For each of these, the Court may grant the state more or less leniency. For instance, the Court appears to seldom override a state's stated claims about the social objective pursued. Note that some of these factors may well change over time in light of experiences about what rights are necessary for a 'democratic society' (Arts 8–19) (del Moral 2006, p. 613), or concerning realistic alternative policies.

6 Consensus among the member states

A final, puzzling aspect of the MA doctrine concerns 'the existence or non-existence of common ground between the laws of the Contracting States' (*Rasmussen v. Denmark* 1984, para. 40); *X, Y and Z v. the United Kingdom* 1997, 13; cf. Brems 1996, pp. 248, 276). The ECtHR may restrict the MA when a consensus emerges, or increase the burdens of argument.

The Court's attention to emerging consensus may be a plausible way to regulate its dynamic (often called 'evolutive' or 'evolving') interpretation of the ECHR. For instance, in *Tyrer v. the United Kingdom* the Court found that corporal punishment by birching over time had become degrading and thus unacceptable.

Other examples include the death penalty (*Soering v. the United Kingdom* 1989) and distinctions between 'legitimate' and 'illegitimate' children (*Marckx v. Belgium* 1979). Note that violations of rights 'of fundamental importance' are not permitted even where there is a lack of consensus. Thus in the Hirst case concerning convicted prisoners' voting rights (*Hirst v. UK* 2005), the Court maintained that 'even if no common European approach to the problem can be discerned, this cannot in itself be determinative of the issue'.

George Letsas argues that the consensus practice has evolved beyond determining an actual 'shared approach' among the states, but simply relies on 'some abstract sense of common standards'— sometimes garnered from non-binding international documents (Letsas 2013, p. 115). This development grants even more discretion to the Court.

We now turn to consider reasons for and against this MA doctrine as outlined.

III. Why Apply a Margin of Appreciation?

Several arguments have been offered to justify versions of the MA doctrine. I submit that some of these proposals are only placeholders for more complex arguments.

1 Subsidiarity

Some authors hold that a principle of subsidiary supports the MA doctrine (Spielman 2012; Kratochvil 2011; del Moral 2006, p. 614; Sweeney 2005). However, I would argue that such appeals to subsidiarity rather indicate the sorts of arguments that will need to be made.

In the history of political thought a principle of subsidiarity regulates how to allocate or use authority within a political or legal order, typically in those orders that disperse authority between a centre and various member units. A principle of subsidiarity thus expresses a commitment to leave as much authority to the more local authorities as possible, consistent with achieving the stated objectives. The principle holds that the burden of argument lies with attempts to centralize authority (Follesdal 1998). Defensible conceptions of subsidiarity will not support a broad MA in general: that would be contrary to the objectives of the ECHR (Kratochvil 2011, p. 332). Instead, the arguments for the MA doctrine must show that certain interests of individuals require centralized authority above the state, e.g. human rights protected and promoted by the ECHR. But individuals' interests will also require that such international judicial review be constrained by an MA. Why should that be? We turn to some such proposed arguments now.

2 Epistemic

The Court referred to an epistemic reason for an MA in some early cases. I shall suggest that there is something to this argument, but not concerning all relevant facts. National authorities are said to be in a better position to grasp the relevant details and the necessary restrictions of rights stemming from the 'requirements of morals' (*Handyside v. the United Kingdom* 1976, para. 48). The Court maintained that

[b]y reason of their direct and continuous contact with the pressing needs of the moment, the national authorities are in principle in a better position than the international judge to decide *both on the presence of such an emergency and on the nature and scope of derogations necessary to avert it.*

> (*Ireland v. theUnited Kingdom* 1978; my emphasis; cf. *Frette v. France* 2002; Greer 2006, p. 34; Kratochvil 2011, p. 326; del Moral 2006)

What are we to make of this argument? It seems correct that local observers familiar with the culture, values, and norms are in a better position to register and understand the conflicts and tensions that arise in particular cases, and which modifications of domestic policies and laws can alleviate the rights violations. This is crucial, for instance when specifying fairly 'abstract' human rights for particular institutions (Etinson 2013, pp. 485–6).

However, it is not obvious that the national authorities are well placed to specify the damage done to minorities' interests, claims about a shared 'national' morality notwithstanding. Likewise, domestic authorities are not always the best judges as to whether their conceptions of morality are indeed at risk. Furthermore, not all components of majority morality can claim complete protection. For instance, in *Handyside* para. 49 the Court insisted that freedom of expression also protects information and ideas that

.... offend, shock or disturb the State or any sector of the population. Such are the demands of that pluralism, tolerance and broadmindedness without which there is no 'democratic society'.

The domestic government may well understand some of the means used to uphold majority norms and values—for instance that crucifixes or religious instruction in school aid a Christian majority in bringing their children up in their faith (*Folgero and others v. Norway* 2007; *Lautsi v. Italy Ii* 2011). But national authorities are not obviously better equipped to assess whether such means are necessary. And proximity to the public debates may also mislead national authorities to overstate threats and overlook human rights violations against less visible groups. Assessments of whether particular restrictions of rights are necessary may require comparisons across relevantly similar states. For this international courts may in fact be better placed. I therefore find the epistemic argument unconvincing as a general support for the MA doctrine as a whole—at least there would seem to have to be convincing evidence that the domestic authorities have assessed alternatives in good faith.

3 'Hard cases' where there are several 'not wrong' answers

A more philosophical argument for an MA doctrine is based on the relationship between human rights norms and institutional design. Many normative theories of political justice recognize that normative standards underdetermine the assessment of institutions. That is, several different institutions and sets of rules may satisfy such standards. In particular, consider the complex philosophical issues that arise when there are 'hard cases' that are difficult to assess. Consider Dworkin's theory of interpretation, which concerns 'hard cases' where it seems that several different assessments may be morally and legally 'not wrong.' He has argued that the correct assessment is made on the basis of that unique interpretation of the legal rules that is consistent with a normative theory that best fits and justifies the law as a whole, as an ideal judge—Hercules—would decide (Dworkin 1977, p. 83; Dworkin 1986a; cf. Arai-Takahashi 2013). An MA doctrine may be appropriate in cases where the ECtHR recognizes that there is reasonable disagreement about what even a Hercules would say, or if the ECtHR questions whether there is only one unique assessment that can be ranked as 'best.' Such disagreements may occur about which normative theory best justifies the existing domestic laws and the ECHR—and where such disagreements lead to different judgements by the domestic court and by the ECtHR about whether limitations of rights are necessary. A defence of an MA may also draw on Michelman's argument from 'the fact of reasonable interpretive pluralism' (Michelman 2000). He defines this as

the fact of irresolvable uncertainty and, in real political time, irreparable reasonable disagreement among inhabitants of a modern country about the set of entrenchments and interpretations of human rights . . . that would truly satisfy justice in the country's historical circumstances.   (p. 70)

He holds that

Reasonable interpretive pluralism thus opens a gap between the question of true justice in politics and the question of what it would be morally right or justifiable for anyone to be doing about the matter of political coercion.   (p. 71)

This form of pluralism may ground some deference for domestic courts' judgements in 'hard cases,' and this may be particularly appropriate for an international court. Note that this point also applies to cases of the MA doctrine where no 'balancing' between Convention rights and other social objectives is at stake, but where instead the question is how to specify a particular right.

I find the philosophical point behind this argument convincing. However, the implications are difficult to discern, and seem to open a Pandora's box with regard to how the ECtHR can bring this argument to bear in sufficiently clear rules about 'hard cases' in an MA doctrine. A specification of this argument in terms of which cases are philosophically irresolvable, and the limits of *reasonable* pluralism, seems impossible. The ECtHR can easily become vulnerable to charges that judges are left free to decide what counts as a hard case completely unchecked—and that powerful states will be granted a wide MA on this basis. So while this is an argument in favour of the MA, the implications for MA practice remain unclear. This concern returns in the context of another argument just below.

4 Reduce the risk of domination by judges

A further plausible argument in support of the MA doctrine stems from the need to reduce the risk of domination by judges, e.g. as explored by neo-republicanism: that we have an interest in protection against the arbitrary use of political power—in this case, the power of unchecked judges (Pettit 1997, Pettit 2010). The MA doctrine, *if* suitably specified, may be defended as a restraint on courts' discretion, if in its absence states would be more vulnerable to the preferences of judges. I return to this proviso below, in V.2, because when it is not satisfied the risk of domination looms large.

On this line of argument the design challenge is to prevent domination over citizens both from their own domestic authorities, and from international judges. I submit that one way to limit the risk of domination is to specify the doctrine, e.g. along the five elements of the proportionality test. A second check is to prevent the Court from addressing excessively minute violations where few if any important interests are at stake. The judges may still use their discretion in unacceptable ways, but such developments limit the risk of 'arbitrary' or unjustified discretion.

5 The reputation, impact, and legitimacy of the ECtHR

A further argument in favour of the doctrine is that a policy of self-restraint may help international judges maintain their reputation in the eyes of domestic authorities and other members of the 'global community of law' (cf. Helfer 2006). Several authors argue that the ECtHR should focus only on 'important' issues (Kratochvil 2011, p. 357; referring to Koskenniemi 2009, p. 14). This concern supports strategic decisions by the ECtHR about which cases to take on, and how to do so.

These thoughts might appear to favour a wide MA, whereby the ECtHR increases apparent compliance by states, and thus boosts its legitimacy indirectly, by reducing states' burdens. In particular, it should not challenge a state which will blatantly denounce the Court, since such noncompliance may reduce other states' compliance in the longer term (Arai-Takahashi 2013, cf. Alter 2008a, p. 41). Thus Macdonald underscores that

> ... The margin of appreciation gives the flexibility needed to avoid damaging confrontations between the Court and Contracting States over their respective spheres of authority and enables the Court to balance the sovereignty of Contracting Parties with their obligations under the Convention.   (Macdonald 1993, p. 123)

However, the concern about reputation and legitimacy goes both ways: it also supports a *narrow* MA. The ECtHR risks a loss of credibility in the eyes of many states and NGOs if it *fails* to call blatant violations of the ECHR when they occur, or if the legal analysis used to grant a wide MA fails to satisfy standards of good judicial practice (cf. Helfer 1993, p. 98). To conclude: The argument in support of the MA doctrine as legitimacy boosting seems plausible, as does the implication that 'unimportant' violations should be left to the discretion of member states. But the argument does not support a wide margin, since that would threaten the perceived legitimacy of the Court as a protector of human rights.

6 Deference to democratic self-governance

Finally, let us consider the argument for the MA doctrine introduced at the beginning of this chapter: Deference to democratic decision-making. Judges of the Court often refer to this argument:

> ...the democratic legitimacy of measures taken by democratically elected governments commands a degree of judicial self-restraint.
>
> (*Karatas v. Turkey* 1999, dissenting opinion; Benvenisti 1999, p. 843;
> Christoffersen 2011, Mahoney 1998, p. 81).

Such respect for majoritarian decisions based on deliberation is presumably based on respect for individuals' interest in self-determination and non-domination. Indeed, one of the shared beliefs of the signatories of the European Convention on Human Rights was an instrumental claim about democratic governance: that

> those fundamental freedoms which are the foundation of justice and peace in the world...are best maintained on the one hand by an effective political democracy.
>
> (Council of Europe 1950, Preamble)

Thus the Court claims that

> The national authorities have direct democratic legitimation and are, as the Court has held on many occasions, in principle better placed than an international court to evaluate local needs and conditions. (*Hatton v. UK* 2003, p. 634)

What are we to make of this argument?

The obvious objection is of course that the ECHR and the Court binds democratic states because they have voluntarily consented to constrain the scope of their majoritarian rule, precisely by subjecting themselves to such international judicial review. If they were concerned to exempt democratic decisions from such review, they should have ensured such clauses in the Convention. Indeed, as long as contracting states do not withdraw, the conflict seems overblown.[5]

How, then, can we move forward to understand the relationship between democracy and such human rights review as the Court performs—limited by an MA? I shall suggest that the Court's use of an MA provides a helpful way to respect and promote the values both of democratic self-governance and of human rights protections.

IV. Rethinking the Relationship between Deference to Democratic Self-Governance and the MA

Without delving deeply into democratic theory, assume for our purposes that democracy is a set of institutionally established procedures that regulate

---

[5] I owe some of these formulations to Letsas.

1) competition for control over political authority,
2) on the basis of deliberation,
3) where all or almost all adult citizens may participate in an electoral mechanism
4) whereby their expressed preferences over alternative candidates determine the outcome
5) in such a way that the government is accountable to, and thereby responsive to, all or as many as possible.
(cf. Dahl 1998, Follesdal and Hix 2006, pp. 547–9)

The best argument for such democratic decision-making is that—compared to the alternatives—democratic rule is over time more reliably responsive to the best interests of all members of the political order (cf. Beitz 1989, p. 113; Levi 1998, pp. 94–6). I submit that the value of such responsiveness can in turn be justified on the basis of a variety of normative traditions, including such liberal versions as Dworkin' commitment to *equal respect and concern* (Dworkin 1986b), or Rawls's theory of justice as fairness (Rawls 1971)—but also according to other normative traditions (Sen 1999).

These 'best interests' include basic needs and fair shares of benefits and burdens. Among these goods is non-domination in the form of a share of political influence. This brief definition and defence of majoritarian decision-making has at least three implications for the scope of a defensible MA, with regard to both the set of states and the human rights supported. The argument proceeds in two steps. First we ask why the interests of individuals are better secured by engaging a body such as the ECtHR than by leaving domestic democratic authorities alone. Secondly, we ask why these interests are even better served by constraining the ECtHR by an MA.

1 Why international human rights judicial review?

The Preamble of the ECHR states that the aim of the convention is to help secure 'the universal and effective recognition and observance of the Rights therein declared' and 'to take the first steps for the collective enforcement of certain of the rights stated in the Universal Declaration', on the basis of a

profound belief in those fundamental freedoms which are the foundation of justice and peace in the world and are best maintained on the one hand by an effective political democracy and on the other by a common understanding and observance of the human rights upon which they depend.

These objectives seem unobjectionable, and presumably ones that individuals in Europe can share. On this basis, what are then the contributions of the ECtHR, and what authority does it need? Which interests are better served by centralizing the adjudication of human rights violations to a regional court at all? This requires that we recall the role that the ECtHR (originally the Commission) is authorized to serve: to 'ensure the observance of the engagements undertaken by the High Contracting Parties' (Art. 19 ECHR). The role of the ECtHR is thus explicitly supplementary to the—democratic—states, with regard to protecting human rights. There are at least three reasons to be wary of the normative case for democratic rule as it applies to states within the Council of Europe.

A) The democracy argument only holds for well-functioning democracies that generally secure both deliberative preference formation, and majoritarian aggregation of votes based on free and fair elections. However, not all Council of Europe states are well functioning in this sense. The 'European Commission for Democracy through Law'—the 'Venice Commission' of the Council of Europe—regularly reports the need for constitutional and legislative reforms to improve the 'Functioning of democratic institutions and the protection of fundamental rights' (Venice Commission 2012). Democracy Audit, the Polity scale and other analyses score the signatory states from 'top ten' to 'low' on various indicators of democratic quality.[6] This has implications for the Court's procedures.

More democratic states—however defined—have a stronger claim to deference from the ECtHR than do less democratic states. However, the ECtHR must apply its procedures to all states, rather than create conflicts about listing some states as not democratic enough to merit deference.

B) Deliberation under conditions of freedom of speech and association may surely be better than authoritarian alternatives at promoting the best interests of all citizens. But majoritarian democratic mechanisms provide no automatic safeguard in this respect. This is one reason for John Hart Ely's argument for judicial review, to safeguard the rights necessary for a democratic process in a broad sense (Ely 1980). This is one reason why the ECtHR should be particularly attentive to ensure these rights; and judicial review to protect these rights does not seem to raise a 'democratic' objection.

C) Even when democratic procedures work quite well, there is no guarantee that they will always yield a sufficiently fair and responsive decision—the more plausible claim in their favour is that they are more likely than authoritarian alternative procedures to do so. So there may be miscarriages of democratic deliberation and majority votes even when democracies function as well as it is reasonable to expect. In particular, majoritarian democracies are prone to subject persistent minorities to several risks. The majority that decides on legislation and policies may easily overlook the consequences on some individuals, or discount their plight unreasonably, or even deliberately set out to hurt them. Such risks are higher for individuals with unusual needs or policy preferences (Barry 1991). Again, there are good reasons for the ECtHR to check domestic legislation—even democratic—to ensure that the rights of minorities are protected; and the claims to deference toward majoritarian democratic self-governance are less strong in these cases.

To conclude, respect for majoritarian democratic decision-making is generally merited, but this does not seem to hold with much force against the review of decisions that

---

[6] Cf. <http://www.worldaudit.org/democracy.htm>, <http//:www.systemicpeace.org/polity/polity4.htm>, <http://www.democracyranking.org>.

violate the rights of minorities or the rights necessary for a well-functioning democracy. Note that I do not spell out in detail which rights these are, but only hold that the general case for respecting democratic decision-making does not hold up for decisions that put such rights at risk.

2 Why constrain the ECtHR by an MA?

So far I have sketched a case for why the ECtHR should be authorized to serve: to 'ensure the observance of the engagements undertaken by the High Contracting Parties' (Art. 19 ECHR). The role of ECtHR is thus explicitly supplementary to the states, in protecting the human rights of individuals on their territory.

But if this is the general role of the ECtHR, why should such a supplementary role be *reduced* by introducing the MA doctrine, which essentially seems to return adjudication of the ECHR to the domestic courts of the very same member state accused of a violation?

I submit that the state organs should retain the final authority when the ECtHR *cannot* or is *unlikely* to provide extra protection of individuals' rights. This helps justify an MA, which should apply insofar, and under those conditions, where the domestic courts and other authorities are at least as well suited to determine whether there is a breach of human rights. When might this be?

Recall that the MA is claimed by the court to be appropriate for at least two main issue areas where the domestic authorities are better suited than the ECtHR to judge, subject to the state having performed a proportionality assessment:

- 'Balancing' against other urgent issues such as emergencies, public safety, the economic well-being of the country etc., as often permitted (Art. 8 private life, Art. 9 religion, Art. 10 expression).
- Applying the norms to the specific circumstances of a state—the shared values, traditions, perceived threats, and culture.

The MA should, however, only apply sparingly or not at all to rights central to the functioning of democratic mechanisms or to the rights of minorities that are likely to be overruled by majorities. Do these two cases, duly specified, exhaust the limits of the MA?—indeed, is this an exhaustive list of the rights of the ECHR?[7] I believe not: there are several rights that majorities also enjoy, which are thus not systematically at risk in majoritarian decisions—yet which are not central to democratic procedures. Cases include freedom of expression on non-political matters which do not involve racism etc., but that may challenge rights to privacy. On this line of argument, such conflicts may not obviously be better judged by an international court. This indeed seems to fit the practice of the Court.

Also note in passing that the Courts' MA practice provides a shrewd way to avoid a 'two-tier' system of treating more democratic states more leniently than other states. The doctrine does not mention the democratic quality of the state. However, the

---

[7] I am grateful to Letsas for raising this issue.

list of check points of the proportionality test would tend to be necessary areas for any state—democratic or not—to be sufficiently responsive to individuals' interests as protected by human rights. And the absence of such a test, in a democratic state and others, should suffice for the Court to not grant a MA. If there thus is no evidence of democratic deliberation worthy of the name, there is no reason for the Court to grant an MA: the risk is then clearly present that the domestic majoritarian decisions are not sufficiently responsive and respectful of each individuals' equal status and interests.

To conclude: I have sketched some reasons why an international court such as the ECtHR may review decisions of a formally democratic majoritarian state. Such review is based on the same values—the interests of individuals—that form one of several reasons to value democratic self-governance itself. I have also indicated some reasons why, for certain rights, under certain conditions, the ECtHR's authority should be restrained in favour of national authorities. Leaving aside exactly which rights an MA may apply to—beyond the non-derogable—the MA requires actual evidence of democratic deliberation, as tested by a proportionality test—in which case the domestic authorities also have given evidence that they do indeed have the relevant knowledge about alternative policies and their effects which make the 'epistemic' argument apply.

V. Arguments against the Margin of Appreciation Doctrine

I now consider five criticisms of the present MA doctrine.

1 Vagueness creates legal uncertainty

A main objection to the current MA doctrine is that it is too vague: it is hardly even a 'doctrine' in the sense of a principle or position that forms part of a legal system. There are at least three kinds of concern. First, the MA creates legal uncertainty, because states are unable to predict and hence cannot avoid violations of the ECHR (Lester 2009; cf. Brauch 2005, p. 125; Macklem 2006; Arai-Takahashi 2013). Indeed, even the judges of the Court disagree about the MA to such an extent that legal certainty seems at risk. To some extent the uncertainty is due to the legal norms, rather than the MA doctrine itself. Consider Art. 10 which protects freedom of expression—but

subject to such formalities, conditions, restrictions or penalties as are prescribed by law and are necessary in a democratic society, in the interests of national security, territorial integrity or public safety, for the prevention of disorder or crime, for the protection of health or morals, for the protection of the reputation or rights of others, for preventing the disclosure of information received in confidence, or for maintaining the authority and impartiality of the judiciary.

(Art. 10, para. 2)

The Court has often but not always granted states an MA in determining whether such interests override the right. Thus in the *Sunday Times* case, a majority of eleven judges found against the UK that Art. 10 protected newspapers reporting on a case. But nine dissenting judges held that this should have been left to the domestic judiciary:

The difference of opinion separating us from our colleagues concerns above all the necessity of the interference and the margin of appreciation which, in this connection, is to be allowed to the national authorities.   (*The Sunday Times v. the United Kingdom* 1979)

Similar disagreements among judges arose in *Observer and Guardian v. UK* 1991 as well as *Wingrove v. the United Kingdom* 1996.

One upshot of this criticism is that the MA doctrine should be made more precise, and more consistently applied, than is at present the case.

2   Vagueness increases the risk of domination

A second concern is that the vague MA doctrine leaves too much discretion to judges (cf. Section III.5). In particular, the procedure to determine an 'emerging common practice'—or 'some abstract sense of common standards' is exceedingly opaque— sometimes also contested by the participating judges (*Rasmussen v. Denmark* 1984, para. 40), *X, Y and Z v. the United Kingdom* 1997, p. 13; cf. Brems 1996, p. 248).

the Court leaves itself vulnerable to the charge that it manipulates the consensus inquiry to achieve an interpretation of the Convention that it finds ideologically pleasing.

(Helfer 1993, p. 154; cf. Brems 1996, p. 282)

I return to discuss the rationale for this consensus policy in V.5. One main response is to make the rules of the doctrine—including the consensus test—more precise.

3   The MA fails to secure the ECHR's objective: promoting human rights

A more precise MA doctrine would not necessarily assuage concerns that such discretion prevents the ECtHR from protecting human rights in the short and long run. The Court thereby 'side-step[s] its responsibility as the ultimate interpretative authority in the Convention system' (Yourow 1996, p. 181). Indeed, '[t]he essence of the international control mechanism may evaporate if there is in fact no effective check upon national power' (Yourow 1996, p. 181; cf. *Z v. Finland* 1998).

Is this a legitimate criticism? Consider Benvenisti's claim that:

By resorting to this device, the court eschews responsibility for its decisions. But the court also relinquishes its duty to set universal standards from its unique position as a collective supranational voice of reason and morality. Its decisions reflect a respect of sovereignty, of the notion of subsidiarity, and of national democracy. It stops short of fulfilling the crucial task of becoming the external guardian against the tyranny by majorities.   (Benvenisti 1999, p. 852)

I grant that if the MA becomes very wide, the value added of the ECtHR diminishes: it leaves each state to be judge in its own case. However, note five limits to this concern.

First, the MA does not apply to the important non-derogable rights such as the right against torture, slavery, or forced labour. Secondly, the criticism seems misguided in the cases of MA that concern a 'balancing' among rights in the ECHR. When the ECtHR grants states an MA with regard to such reasoned trade-offs among rights, the MA doctrine does not automatically lead to less stringent human rights protection. The worry is then rather that the government resolves the conflict among rights in a substantively wrong way. However, as part of the MA procedure the Court does check that domestic authorities have considered a variety of ways to secure the conflicting rights as much as possible, and so as to ensure some of the more important rights. Other remaining worries concern cases that do not concern balancing or trade-offs among human rights, but between rights and other political objectives.

Thirdly, the practice of concern here is not that domestic courts are given full discretion with regard to the adjudication of rights claims, but rather: that national courts enjoy some, albeit limited discretion. In particular, according to the doctrine as laid out here, national courts enjoy such an MA only when the ECtHR is satisfied that a national court has duly considered the various conditions as to whether the limitations to the rights are permitted under the ECHR.

Fourthly, such domestic review is a necessary but insufficient condition: the ECtHR not only checks that national courts do perform a good faith test of the five requirements. It can also find weaknesses in the arguments or in the balancing. Thus in *Rasmussen v. Denmark* 1988 the ECtHR held that the state had overlooked alternative means to secure its objectives, alternatives that would have avoided the restrictions of rights (cf. Helfer 1993, p. 161).

Finally, even though the states have subjected themselves to the ECtHR, whose task is to promote human rights, the ECtHR is not authorized to promote and protect human rights by all means. Neither the function, the composition, nor the mode of operation of the ECtHR are set up to provide a 'collective supranational voice of reason and morality' as Benvenisti claims. Rather, the express task of the ECtHR is more limited: to 'ensure the observance of the engagements undertaken by the High Contracting Parties' (Art. 19 ECHR). The role of the ECtHR is really a 'subsidiary' or supportive and supplementary role in the promotion of human rights. Thus, the question we should ask is whether the MA doctrine accomplishes this supportive task.

To conclude, I submit that a well-specified MA, one guided by the various considerations that speak in its favour, can reduce several of the concerns stemming from vagueness, as well as achieve its core objective.

4 The MA fails to recognize and promote the universality of human rights

Benvenisti notes that

The judicial output of the ECHR and the other international bodies carries the promise of setting universal standards for the protection and promotion of human rights.

These universal aspirations are, to a large extent, compromised by the doctrine of margin of appreciation. (Benvenisti 1999, p. 843)

This challenge merits more attention than space allows here, though some comments may alleviate the concern. The worry seems to be that individuals in different states may enjoy different sets of human rights, dependent on whether their state is accorded an MA that permits the rights violation, or not. How could this possibly be compatible with the 'universal' aspirations of human rights standards?

In response, first recall that the MA does not apply to non-derogable rights. Furthermore, I suggest that Charles Beitz's general account may be helpful: that human rights are not invariant across time and space, but still 'universal' in the sense that they may be claimed by 'all members of contemporary societies' (Beitz 2009, p. 112). Moreover, such rights may be understood to be universal in that they are 'matters of international concern whose violation by governments can justify international protective and restorative action.' For our purposes, the rights of the ECHR are standards that 'The international [in this setting: the Council of Europe] community may through its political institutions [such as the ECtHR] *hold states accountable for*' (Beitz 2009, p. 109; my additions).

On this account, in what way does the MA doctrine challenge the universality of human rights? One point may cause unease from some philosophical perspectives: the MA doctrine as laid out here assumes and responds to claims that there are unavoidable tensions between human rights, at least among the rights of the ECHR. These rights cannot all be secured 'universally' in the sense of maximally or without conflicts.

In one significant sense the MA doctrine provides no such challenge. Consider that the ECtHR holds *all* state parties to the Convention to account, requiring a reasoned, public justification for such trade-offs. Another aspect of universality may seem lost insofar as the MA doctrine allows for abrogations of some rights in some circumstances in some states, but not necessarily in other cases. In response, recall first that the issue is not the authority to interpret the substantive contents of the right, but rather the authority to determine cases in which the right may be justifiably limited. Secondly, several of the rights of the ECHR explicitly allow for such limitations—forcing us to reconsider how legal human rights can be both universal and given high normative rank, yet fit to differing particular circumstances.

5 Concerns about the consensus test

A consensus test may make sense as a constraint on 'evolutive interpretation' by judges, thus reducing the risk of domination. However, there are several problems with this consensus condition as currently used to regulate the MA.

First, the consensus practice is vague, leading to contested applications. Sometimes claims about an emerging consensus seem overdrawn. Indeed, one may suspect that judges are not constrained in their discretion at all by a requirement that they observe an emerging consensus. One example concerns the distinction states have made between 'legitimate' and 'illegitimate' children. The Court in *Marckx v. Belgium* 1979 claimed there was an emerging European consensus to this effect, citing conventions with such wording. However, the majority of European states had not signed these conventions at the time (Letsas 2013, p. 115; Merrills 1988, p. 74). Sometimes the Court refers—arguably haphazardly—to non-European states such as New Zealand and Australia (*Christine Goodwin v. the United Kingdom*; cf. del Moral 2006). In some cases the judges disagree amongst themselves whether there *is* a development among the states toward shared grounds (*Cossey v. the United Kingdom* ECtHR 1990, Appl. No. 10843/84, 21). Indeed, the ECtHR does not seem to have an established procedure to determine whether there is a requisite consensus (Benvenisti 1999; Yourow 1996, p. 158; cf. Helfer 1993).

Critics moreover claim that the weight of the consensus factor remains unclear, both in principle and in practice. Why, for instance, should a consensus among other states reduce the MA, in areas where a state faces particular dilemmas among rights, and has established its own methods of handling them? And in practice, it turns out that a consensus—or lack thereof—is not decisive, especially when 'important' rights are at stake, such as rights central to democratic governance. Sometimes the perceived consensus only leads the Court to require the accused state to provide an even more convincing argument for its policies (Helfer and Slaughter 1997, p. 314).

A third challenge to the consensus practice arises when new states join the ECHR (del Moral 2006). If their established practices or values count, the ECtHR may be forced to broaden the MA in cases where the newcomers destroy the previous consensus. Such may be the case for states who lack an established domestic tradition of human rights jurisprudence, or who have adopted other ways of securing human rights than those adopted by long standing members of the Council of Europe. If these practices should not prevent the Court from maintaining that there is a consensus, we must ask how the Court should determine which consensus matters, and which does not.

These concerns give rise to a more fundamental question: why should a European consensus, when it exists, lead the ECtHR to limit the MA? This practice—even when consistent—would seem to violate three long standing claims concerning the ECHR and the ECtHR.

A) The ECHR purports to be an agreement between 'governments of European countries which are like-minded and *have a common heritage of political traditions*, ideals, freedom and the rule of law' (Preamble). But the practice under debate underscores that in many areas such a 'shared heritage' does not exist—at least not yet. This normative source of the ECtHR's authority itself is thus questioned when the lack of consensus is so openly acknowledged. In response, defenders of the consensus practice may counter that this practice precisely underscores this normative basis: it is exactly when there is a perceived broad consensus about a shared 'heritage of political traditions' that the Court is and should be authorized to seek to correct an individual domestic law, regulation, or application thereof that deviates from this consensus (cf. Helfer 1993, p. 135).

B) Many have held that the objective of the ECtHR should not be to harmonize European states, but rather only to establish high minimum levels of human rights protection. Uniform moral standards is not a goal of the Court (Merrills 1988, pp. 282–3; Carozza 1998, p. 1228). This is a different, less Procrustean—and perhaps less controversial—objective than that of the European

Court of Justice, which must explicitly harmonize several policy areas among the member states. However, the consensus policy serves precisely such a harmonizing effect, even if this is not the intended objective: The ECtHR explicitly narrows the space for institutional variation when the majority of judges agree that they observe an emerging European consensus.

C) One important aim of the ECHR is to protect those who find themselves in the minority against majorities' abuse of power, intentional or not. Indeed, a standard weakness of majoritarian democratic decision-making is to ignore a minority's interests. Thus, there would seem to be little reason to limit the human rights protections of a minority based on a consensus of majorities. In this vein, George Letsas notes that 'if human rights are distinctively counter-majoritarian then it makes no sense conditioning their scope and meaning on what the majority itself believes' (Letsas 2013, p. 123; Letsas 2007). A central concern is that there is no reason to believe that an 'emerging consensus' among *majorities* in Europe ensures that certain minority rights will be protected. To the contrary, it may in principle be a minority of European states that continue to ensure better human rights protection, while a majority of statesconverge on a less optimal set of policies—be it concerning counter-terrorist measures, or concerning the Roma–Sinti minority. An emerging consensus does not guarantee that the consensus provides better human rights protection. Thus, the domain of application of such a consensus test must be carefully delineated.

I submit that the upshot of this discussion about the consensus policy is that its scope of application and methodology are now too vague. Currently the Court is vulnerable to understandable suspicion that it abuses its discretion under the guise of the present consensus doctrine. As it stands, the practice carries a high risk of 'manipulative relativity' (del Moral 2006). This is not to deny that it may become defensible as a way to regulate Court discretion concerning its dynamic interpretation, and hence reduce the understandable fears of domination by judges.

A more developed procedure to determine consensus may thus help the Court's task to combine sufficient respect for state sovereignty whilst performing its obligations of international human rights judicial review. Such reforms must also seek to reduce the general vagueness of the MA doctrine to enhance legal certainty and bolster domestic democratic deliberation. The review of reasons for the MA in Section 2 indicates how the MA should be specified further.

VI. Some Conclusions

This chapter's discussion yields several conclusions concerning how well the MA doctrine combines protection of human rights and due respect for democratically accountable legislation, governance and adjudication.

First, worries that the MA doctrine eviscerates the Court's ability to protect human rights are overdrawn. The domain of rights violations where the MA may apply is limited. Indeed, the Court seems to refuse states an MA with regards to rights that are necessary for well-functioning democratic rule, or where the decisions do not reflect democratic deliberation and will formation—i.e. when the state fails the 'proportionality test'. Such a test may even entice states to improve their democratic deliberations.

As to the various arguments marshalled in favour of the MA doctrine, I have granted that the MA doctrine may be especially appropriate in cases where the ECtHR recognizes that there is reasonable disagreement about whether the state violates the ECHR, e.g. due to conflicting views of which normative theory best justifies the existing domestic laws and human rights, or due to domestic courts' somewhat better understanding of some relevant circumstances. Deference to domestic (and democratic) courts about such 'hard cases' is especially appropriate for an international court that is less democratically accountable than are national courts. The Court may still serve an important role in such cases, e.g. by applying a proportionality test to ensure that the domestic decision procedures have indeed been conducive to deliberative processes. Indeed, such a test can be seen as motivated by the epistemic argument in favour of the MA doctrine, because it may help ensure that domestic authorities are aware of the harms done and available alternatives.

The role accorded alleged sightings of a 'consensus' seems overdrawn. Claims about an 'emerging' 'consensus' may be important to regulate the Court's discretion in evolutive interpretation, and may be appropriate as a reason to restrict the scope of the MA. But the current methods for ascertaining such a consensus seems instead to increase the risk of domination by the Court.

A third conclusion concerns what to make of recent proposals to formalize the MA doctrine. When should the Court grant states a MA? In particular, who should have the final say in determining whether a violation has occurred, and on what grounds? This seems part of recent UK proposals to limit the role of the ECtHR:

17.... The margin of appreciation implies, among other things, that it is the responsibility of democratically-elected national parliaments to decide how to implement the Convention in reasoned judgments. The role of the Court is to review decisions taken by national authorities to ensure that they are within the margin of appreciation.

(UK Government 2012, p. 5)

This chapter's discussion argues that such a proposal should be interpreted to allow the ECtHR to not only check whether the case is substantively within the MA, but that the Court should also be authorized to perform a proportionality test of the arguments offered by the state—which I have argued should often be a necessary condition for granting states an MA at all. Similarly, mere evidence of domestic reasoning or balancing should not stop the ECtHR from striking down legislation or a practice. Indeed, the UK proposed that

23. c)... Article 35 of the Convention should further be amended to make clear that an application is inadmissible if it is the same in substance as a matter that has been examined by

a national court taking into account the rights guaranteed by the Convention, unless the Court considers that:

i) The national court clearly erred in its interpretation or application of the Convention rights; or

ii) The application raises a serious question affecting the interpretation or application of the Convention;...   (UK Government 2012)

I submit that the decision as to what counts as 'examined by', 'clear error', and 'serious question' should remain for the Court to decide, rather than national authorities. Note that Protocol 14, which entered into force in 2010 (Council of Europe 2010), includes a requirement that cases are only admissible if an applicant has suffered a 'significant disadvantage'—and when a national court has considered the subject matter of the case (Art. 35, new para. 3b). Even then, I submit that it seems sound to grant the Court the authority to perform a proportionality test, and not only check the substantive alleged breach of the Convention.

I conclude that the Margin of Appreciation doctrine of the European Court of Human Rights merits respect, but also friendly amendments. Only if the proportionality test is strictly maintained, and the consensus practice seriously reconsidered and specified, is it plausible to maintain that the Margin of Appreciation doctrine succeeds in combining protection of human rights with the respect democratic states in Europe deserve.

Does this conclusion entail tighter supervision of national policies by the Court, and hence increased risk of domination by them? Not quite. First, the more specific standards and procedures need not reduce the scope of states' opportunity set, but may sometimes increase their options. Secondly, specification of the MA 'doctrine' should help limit the Court's discretion, and make its decisions more predictable—and thereby render states less vulnerable to the discretion of ECtHR judges.

Finally, do these reflections have implications for whether other international courts and tribunals should endorse an MA doctrine? There are several considerations worth mentioning, if only in passing. First, human rights courts have peculiar mandates as compared to many other international courts: States established them not only in order to bind other states and thus obtain collective benefits otherwise out of reach, but also to restrict their own sovereign authority for the benefit of their own citizens (Alter 2008b). The former 'other-binding' objectives of international courts may sit less easily with a large MA granted to each state.

Secondly, the respect for domestic democratic decision-making is less salient for many international courts and tribunals—concerning human rights or other topics, as compared to the signatories of the ECHR. The dilemma between pursuing treaty objectives and respect for *democratic* sovereignty may thus not be as common and central for such international courts. This may mean that a 'proportionality test' may be even more appropriate, rather than an explicit 'democratic quality' test.

Thirdly, the damages wrought by domination may loom larger in other sectors and for other international courts than the ECtHR. Consider that in issue areas other than human rights, such as trade or investment, each state has more to risk if other states defect from the agreements. Such relative or absolute externalities are arguably smaller for many violations of human rights (though the majoritarian decision rules of the EU render citizens vulnerable to human rights violating member states, thus blurring this difference, cf. Follesdal 2009). The selection process of judges is thus also sometimes more politicized for international courts in other sectors than in human rights. This may foster reticence in regard to whether other international courts and tribunals should adopt an MA doctrine. At the very least such doctrines should be far more precisely defined than the doctrine of concern in this article, namely that of the ECtHR.

To conclude, a more specified MA doctrine, informed by the best reasons in favour of such a doctrine, can protect human rights and reduce the risk of domination by an international court, yet cannot remove that risk completely. But then individuals face other risks too, not only in undemocratic states but also in fairly well-functioning democracies. Violation of their human rights by their own state is surely one such risk—which states acknowledged when they ratified the ECHR. The democracies subject to the ECtHR may no longer be sovereign in Schmitt's sense—but no less worthy of respect for that reason. On the contrary: closer supervision need not entail domination, especially if the judges are not free to let their discretion run loose but serve to promote decisions based on democratic deliberation, and help reduce risks of miscarriages of democratic decision-making. In such cases the Margin of Appreciation doctrine of the ECtHR can engender trust in the population that indeed their government merits obedience and respect.

References

Alexy, Robert 2002. *A Theory of Constitutional Rights*. Translated by Julian Rivers. Oxford: Oxford University Press.

Alter, Karen 2008a. 'Agents or Trustees? International Courts in their Political Context.' *European Journal of International Relations* 14: 33–64.

Alter, Karen 2008b. 'Delegating to International Courts.' *Law and Contemporary Problems* 71: 37–6.

Arai-Takahashi, Yutaka 2013. 'The Margin of Appreciation Doctrine: A Theoretical Analysis of Strasbourg's Variable Geometry.' In *The European Court of Human Rights*, ed. Andreas Follesdal, Birgit Peters, and Geir Ulfstein, 62–105. Cambridge: Cambridge University Press.

Barry, Brian 1991. 'Is Democracy Special?' In *Democracy and Power*, ed. Brian Barry, 24–60. Oxford: Oxford University Press.

Bates, Ed 2010. *The Evolution of the European Convention on Human Rights: From its Inception to the Creation of a Permanent Court of Human Rights*. Oxford: Oxford University Press.

Beitz, Charles R. 1989. *Political Equality*. Princeton: Princeton University Press.

Beitz, Charles R. 2009. *The Idea of Human Rights*. Oxford: Oxford University Press.

Benvenisti, Eyal 1999. 'Margin of Appreciation, Consensus, and Universal Standards.' *International Law and Politics* 31: 843–54.

Brauch, Jeffrey A. 2005. 'The Margin of Appreciation and the Jurisprudence of the European Court of Human Rights: Threat to the Rule of Law.' *Columbia Journal of European Law* 11: 113–50.

Brems, Eva 1996. 'The Margin of Appreciation Doctrine in the Case-Law of the European Court of Human Rights.' *Heidelberg Journal of International Law* 56: 240.

Carozza, Paulo G. 1998. 'Uses and Misuses of Comparative Law in International Human Rights: Some Reflections on the Jurisprudence of the European Court of Human Rights.' *Notre Dame Law Review* 73: 1217–37.

Christoffersen, Jonas. 2011. 'Individual and Constitutional Justice: Can the Power Balance of Adjudication Be Reversed?' In *The European Court of Human Rights between Law and Politics*, ed. Jonas Christoffersen and Mikael Rask Madsen. Oxford: Oxford University Press.

Council of Europe 1950. 'European Convention for the Protection of Human Rights and Fundamental Freedoms, as Amended by Protocols Nos. 11 and 14. Entry into Force 3 September 1953.' In ETS 5; 213 UNTS 221.

Council of Europe 2010. 'Protocol 14 to the European Convention on Human Rights.' In *Treaty Series No.* 194, ed. Council of Europe.

Dahl, Robert A. 1998. *On Democracy*. New Haven: Yale University Press.

del Moral, Ignacio de la Rasilla 2006. 'The Increasingly Marginal Appreciation of the Margin-of-Appreciation Doctrine.' *German Law Journal* 7, no. 6: 611–24.

Dworkin, Ronald 1977. *Taking Rights Seriously*. London: Duckworth.

Dworkin, Ronald 1986a. *Law's Empire*. Cambridge, Mass.: Harvard University Press.

Dworkin, Ronald 1986b. 'Liberalism.' In *A Matter of Principle*, 181–204. Oxford: Clarendon Press.

Ely, John Hart 1980. *Democracy and Distrust: A Theory of Judicial Review*. Cambridge, Mass.: Harvard University Press.

Etinson, Adam 2013. 'Human Rights, Claimability and the Uses of Abstraction.' *Utilitas* 25, no. 4: 463–86.

Fadeyeva v. Russia (2005). ECtHR Application No. 55723/00, 9 June 2005.

Folgero and Others v. Norway, EHHR (2007). ECtHR Application No 15472/02, 29 June 2007.

Follesdal, Andreas 1998. 'Subsidiarity.' *Journal of Political Philosophy* 6, no. 2: 231–59.

Follesdal, Andreas 2009. 'Universal Human Rights as a Shared Political Identity: Impossible? Necessary? Sufficient?' *Metaphilosophy* 40, no. 1: 65–76.

Follesdal, Andreas, and Simon Hix 2006. 'Why There is a Democratic Deficit in the EU: A Response to Majone and Moravcsik.' *Journal of Common Market Studies* 44, no. 3: 533–62.

Greer, Steven 2006. *The European Convention on Human Rights: Achievements, Problems and Prospects*. Cambridge: Cambridge University Press.

Handyside v. the United Kingdom, ECtHR 24 5493/72 523 (1976), 7 December 1976.

Hatton v. the United Kingdom, ECtHR (2003). 36022/97, 8 July 2003.

Helfer, Laurence 1993. 'Consensus, Coherence and the European Convention on Human Rights.' *Cornell International Law Journal* 133–65.

Helfer, Laurence 2006. 'Why States Create International Tribunals: A Theory of Constrained Independence.' In *International Conflict Resolution*, ed. Stefan Voigt et al. Tübingen: Mohr Siebeck.

Helfer, Laurence, and Anne-Marie Slaughter 1997. 'Toward a Theory of Effective Supranational Adjudication.' *Yale Law Review* 107: 273–392.

Hirst v. UK, Reports of Judgments and Decisions 2005-IX (2005).

Ireland v. the United Kingdom ECtHR (1978). Application no 5310/71.

James and Others v. the United Kingdom, ECtHR, 8 EHRR 123 Application no 8793/79 (1986).

Karatas v. Turkey (1999). ECtHR Application no. 23168/94, 8 July 1999.

Klass and Others v. Germany ECtHR (1978). 2 EHRR 214.

Koskenniemi, Martti 2009. 'The Politics of International Law—20 Years Later.' *European Journal of International Law* 20, no. 1: 7–19.

Kratochvil, Jan 2011. 'The Inflation of the Margin of Appreciation by the European Court of Human Rights.' *Netherlands Quarterly of Human Rights* 29, no. 3: 324–57.

Lautsi v. Italy II, ECtHR, EHRR (2011). Application no 30814/06.

Lawless v. Ireland, Eur Commission for the Convention on Human Rights 1 EHRR 15, (1961). Application no 332/57.

Lester, Anthony 2009. 'The European Court of Human Rights after 50 Years.' *European Human Rights Law Review* 4: 461–78.

Letsas, George 2006. 'Two Concepts of the Margin of Appreciation.' *Oxford Journal of Legal Studies*, 26: 705.

Letsas, George 2007. *A Theory of Interpretation of the European Convention on Human Rights* Oxford: Oxford University Press.

Letsas, George 2013. 'The ECHR as a Living Instrument: Its Meaning and Legitimacy.' In *The European Court of Human Rights*, ed. Andreas Follesdal, Birgit Peters, and Geir Ulfstein, 106–41. Cambridge: Cambridge University Press.

Levi, Margaret 1998. 'A State of Trust.' In *Trust and Governance*, ed. Margaret Levi and Valerie Braithwaite. New York: Russell Sage.

Macdonald, Ronald St J. 1993. 'The Margin of Appreciation.' In *The European System for the Protection of Human Rights*, ed. Ronald St. J. Macdonald and F. Matcher. Berlin: Springer.

Macklem, Patrick 2006. 'Militant Democracy, Legal Pluralism, and the Paradox of Self-Determination.' *International Journal of Constitutional Law* 4: 488–516.

Mahoney, Paul 1998. 'Marvelous Richness of Diversity or Invidious Cultural Relativism?' *Human Rights Law Journal* 19, no. 1.

Marckx v. Belgium, ECtHR (1979). Application no 6833/74.

Merrills, John G. 'The Development of International Law by the European Court of Human Rights.' Manchester: Manchester University Press, 1988.

Michelman, Frank 2000. 'Human Rights and the Limits of Constitutional Theory.' *Ratio Juris* 13: 63–76.

Observer and Guardian v. the United Kingdom, ECtHR 1991, 14 EHRR 153, Application no. 13585/88 (1991).

Pettit, Philip 1997. *Republicanism: A Theory of Freedom and Government*. Oxford: Clarendon Press.

Pettit, Philip 2010. 'Legitimate International Institutions: A Neo-Republican Perspective.' In *The Philosophy of International Law*, ed. Samantha Besson and John Tasioulas, 139–60. Oxford: Oxford University Press.

Rasmussen v. Denmark, 71 European Court HR ser B (1988).

Rasmussen v. Denmark, 87 (1984). 28 Nov. 1984, 7 EHRR 371 at, Application no. 8777/79 (ECtHR).

Rawls, John 1971. *A Theory of Justice*. Cambridge, Mass.: Harvard University Press.

Schalk and Kopf v. Austria (2010). Judgement 24 June 2010, 53 EHRR 20, Application no. 30141/04 (ECHR).

Schmitt, Carl 1985. *Political Theology*. Chicago: The University of Chicago Press.

Schokkenbroek, Jeroen 1998. 'The Basis, Nature and Application of the Margin-of-Appreciation Doctrine in the Case-Law of the European Court—General Report.' *Human Rights Law Journal* 19, no. 1: 30–4.

Sen, Amartya K. 1999. 'Democracy as a Universal Value.' *Journal of Democracy* 10, no. 3: 3–17.

Shany, Yuval 2005. 'Toward a General Margin of Appreciation Doctrine in International Law?' *European Journal of International Law* 16, no. 5: 907–40.

Simpson, Alfred William Brian 2004. *Human Rights and the End of Empire: Britain and the Genesis of the European Convention*. Oxford: Oxford University Press.

Skalcka v. Poland (2003). ECtHR, Application No 43425/98, decided 27 May 2003.

Soering v. the United Kingdom (1989). ECtHR, Application no. 14038/88, Judgement 7 July 1989.

Spielman, Dean 2012. 'Allowing the Right Margin. The European Court of Human Rights and the National Margin of Appreciation Doctrine: Waiver or Subsidiarity of European Review?' *Working Paper Series of the Centre for European Legal Studies, University of Cambridge*.

The Sunday Times v. the United Kingdom (1979). ECtHR, Series A No. 30. 2 EHRR 245, Judgement 26 April 1979.

Sweeney, J. 2005. 'Margins of Appreciation: Cultural Relativity and the European Court of Human Rights in the Post-Cold War Era.' *International and Comparative Law Quarterly* 54, no. 2: 459–74.

UK Government. 'Draft Brighton Declaration on the Future of the European Court of Human Rights—Second Version.' (2012), <http://adam1cor.files.wordpress.com/2012/02/2012dd220e.pdf>.

Venice Commission 2012. *Annual Report* 2011, Cdl-Ra(2011)001 Council of Europe.

Wingrove v. the United Kingdom ECtHR (1996), 24 EHRR 1, 25 November 1996.

X, Y and Z v. United Kingdom, Judgement 22 April 1997, 24 EHRR 143, Application no. 21830/93 (European Court of Human Rights).

Yourow, Howard Charles 1996. *The Margin of Appreciation Doctrine in the Dynamics of European Human Rights Jurisprudence*: Leiden: Brill.

Z v. Finland, 25 European Human Rights Reporter 371 (1998) Application no. 22009/93.

8.1

The Margin of Appreciation Revisited

A Response to Follesdal

George Letsas

The Margin of Appreciation (MA) is a legal doctrine developed by the European Court of Human Rights in the course of interpreting and applying an international treaty, the European Convention of Human Rights (ECHR). Like any other legal doctrine, its soundness depends on whether it is justified by normative principles that bear on the justifiability of institutional practices. Some legal doctrines may lack any normative support, or be directly condemned by sound moral principles. Recall, for example, the old common law doctrine that a woman cannot in law be raped by her spouse, because she has given her consent upon getting married.[1] That doctrine not only contravened women's right to sexual autonomy but also lacked any normative basis (such as privacy, or the protection of the institution of marriage) in its defence. Other legal doctrines may compromise a moral principle but, on balance, be justified by more weighty moral considerations. A philosophical account of the MA must therefore enquire into whether the doctrine stands on a sound normative basis, and whether that basis overrides other normative reasons, with which it may conflict. Given that the MA is a doctrine of international human rights, such enquiry will naturally draw on normative considerations to do with the morality of human rights, the value of state sovereignty, and the practice of international courts.

Andreas Follesdal's insightful contribution to this volume engages in precisely this enquiry. His conclusion is that the MA is defensible, subject to certain conditions being met. In this commentary, I explore Follesdal's account, and take issue with part of his argument. I begin with setting up the normative enquiry in a slightly different way than he does.

---

[1] This was fully abolished by the House of Lords in 1991 in *R v. R* [1992] 1 AC 599, recognizing marital rape as a criminal offence.

The Margin of Appreciation as Discretion

It is common for the law to use doctrinal labels, often called 'fictions', whose meaning is technical and has no direct analogue outside the domain of law. The law defines such concepts in terms of a set of legal consequences (i.e. enforceable rights, duties, liabilities, powers) that follow upon the obtaining of certain facts. Think of the legal concepts of a contract or a trust. A contract is not merely an exchange of promises. To know what a contract is, is to know the legal consequences that will be enforceable in court (e.g. getting the other party to perform, or to pay damages) when certain factual conditions are met, such as offer and acceptance, consideration, intention to create legal relations, etc. Once we know what facts a legal doctrine takes as relevant, and what consequences it attaches to them with respect to enforceability, we can move on to the philosophical task of assessing its justifiability. One may challenge the justifiability of the institutional *consequence* a legal doctrine draws, or one may challenge the *factual conditions* the doctrine imposes for the ensuing of these institutional consequences.

The Margin of Appreciation is one such doctrinal concept. Outside its legal use, the meaning of the doctrine is unhelpfully vague. All that is clear is that it is something enjoyed by contracting states in the sphere of complying with their treaty obligations, with respect to so-called 'qualified' rights.[2] But what that something is, is not clear. Follesdal mentions two definitions. According to the first, it is the states' degree of *discretion* in choosing the means by which to ensure their obligations. This definition is widely used in the literature and it reveals the origins of the doctrinal label in French administrative law, and the discretion enjoyed by the executive in carrying out its functions. But the problem with defining the Margin of Appreciation as a 'degree of *discretion*' is that the latter is semantically too close to the former to be illuminating as a definition. The concept of discretion is itself unhelpfully vague. So the definition advances our understanding of the doctrine no further. But more importantly, the definition is an insufficient basis for engaging in the philosophical task of normative assessment. What would it mean to say that one is against contracting states' having discretion as to how they comply with their human rights obligations under the ECHR? What normative proposition would that person be denying?

One way to further specify the claim that contracting states have discretion in complying with their legal obligation to respect qualified human rights is this: what counts as respecting qualified rights, i.e. what counts as following the legal standard the ECHR imposes, is a matter of following *principles* rather than *rules*. The distinction between rules and principles is very well known from Ronald Dworkin's critique of H. L. A. Hart.[3] In the case of rules, the standard is known automatically, in virtue of the clear and widely shared linguistic meaning of a text or utterance. By contrast, in the case of principles, we have to exercise evaluative judgement in order to discover what

---

[2] Private and family life, freedom of thought and religion, freedom of expression, freedom of association, and right to property.

[3] Dworkin 1967.

that standard is. Dworkin's argument is that the need to exercise judgement in applying principles does not entail the absence of a legal standard, what he calls discretion in the 'strong' sense. To be sure, the wording of the qualified rights of the ECHR is abstract and does not make specific the moral principles that constitute the relevant legal standard. But that does not mean that there is no legal standard governing what they ought to do; it does not mean that states are free to choose any course of action. It simply means that what the ECHR rights require in each given case is a matter of evaluative judgement to do with the moral principles underlying each human right.

Thus understood, the idea that states enjoy discretion in carrying out their legal obligation to respect the qualified rights of the ECHR makes more sense. It explains why the margin of appreciation figures in the interpretation of 'qualified' rights. For in the case of absolute rights, such as the right not to be tortured, it is normally[4] easy to identify what the legal standard is. Not only do we have a pretty clear idea of what torture is, but also *all* types of torture are prohibited. If we find out that some contracting state has tortured someone, then we know immediately that it has violated the ECHR, without us having to exercise any evaluative judgement. By contrast, it is not normally easy to identify what the legal standard is in the case of qualified rights, such as freedom of expression. Not all state intrusions on free expression are prohibited by the ECHR. For example, the prohibition of defamation, libel, or incitement to violence does not violate the ECHR. We need to exercise an evaluative judgement about the principles justifying freedom of expression, in order to identify which state intrusions on expression are human rights violations. And assuming that evaluative judgements about rights are *truth-apt*, then the legal restrictions that freedom of expression (article 10 ECHR) imposes on states are no less stringent, and no less objective, than those imposed by the right not to be tortured.[5] In other words, to say that states enjoy discretion when it comes to qualified rights is to say that not all intrusions on these freedoms make contracting states liable under the ECHR. It is *not* to say that there is no right answer as to what limits the right imposes on states and to suggest that states have strong discretion when limiting the right. We have, yet, no reason to abandon the premise that the primary duty of courts is to comply with legal standards imposed by human rights law and that, when these standards require evaluative judgement, courts (and states) have to exercise it.[6]

---

[4] Normally, but not always, as the—dubious—claim made by US officials that waterboarding does not amount to torture indicates.

[5] By truth-aptness, I do not mean to assume any robust metaphysical view about evaluative judgements, such as moral realism, but only a modest moral cognitivism.

[6] To say that rights, because of their abstract character, 'underdetermine' what states are obligated to do under human rights law seems to me misleading (see Follesdal p. 276 and Etinson 2013). It fails to distinguish between uncertainty and indeterminacy. It is *uncertain* what duties the abstract right to freedom of expression imposes on states. We have to assess the weight of normative principles that bear on the justifiability of the right. But once we have done that, the right is *determinate* in the sense that there is a right answer to the question of whether the state acted in contravention of these normative principles. We should not infer indeterminacy from uncertainty.

I should here note a confusion that is frequently made. From the claim that there is a right answer to what obligations human rights impose on states, it does not follow that each state must follow uniform rules. It does not follow that all states must adopt the *same* legislative or other measures.[7] This is precisely because human rights are principles, and not rules. Principles have a dimension of weight and their applicability in each case takes into account contextual and contingent factors that vary across states. Here is an example. Consider the principle that consent (say to medical treatment or sexual acts) is valid only if someone is competent to give it. Suppose further that someone is competent only if he has sufficient intelligence and maturity to understand what he is consenting to. At what age children acquire this competence will vary from place to place, person to person, and time to time. The maturity and intelligence of the average 15-year-old child living in a metropolitan city today is greater than that of the average 15-year-old living in rural parts of the country in the eighteenth century. It follows that the principle may be satisfied by different legislative rules on the age of consent, depending on the circumstances of each state. In other words, diversity of practice is perfectly compatible with the idea that there is a right answer to what the abstract moral principle requires. The right answer is that the age of consent should be relative to a threshold of mental conpetence. The relevant abstract principle (i.e. that one must be sufficiently mature in order to be competent to consent) is universal, even though its application allows for diversity.[8]

The idea that the qualified rights of the ECHR are principles, rather than rules, inviting the exercise of an evaluative judgement, gives more specific content to the notion of the margin of appreciation. But it still falls short of forming an adequate basis for the normative assessment of the doctrine. This is for two reasons. First, it is uncontroversial. Few would argue that *every* state intrusion on the interests protected by the qualified rights, such as expression and privacy, is a human rights violation. Few would argue that the application of universal human rights principles necessarily entails uniformity of state practice. And few would deny that, in order to determine which intrusions on those interests constitute a violation of the ECHR, we need to exercise an evaluative judgement about the value of free speech or privacy. Second, it has the wrong shape to be the object of normative assessment. Recall that legal doctrines take certain facts as a condition for the enforceability of some normative claim (i.e. rights, duties, liabilities, and powers). To ask whether a legal doctrine is normatively defensible is to ask whether it is justified for the law to condition the enforceability of a claim on that fact. Yet the idea that we need to exercise an evaluative judgement

---

[7] See Legg 2012. Legg draws this inference from my defence of right answers in human rights and then criticizes my position on the basis of value pluralism. But the inference is mistaken and I do not hold the position that right answers in human rights require uniformity of state practice. The right answer may be that more than one legislative or executive scheme is compatible with the ECHR.

[8] It is not an accident that early discussions of the MA present it as an instance of cultural relativism. See Mahoney 1998. But the term 'cultural relativism' is unfortunate if it is meant as the negation of the existence of universal moral principles.

in order to identify what the qualified rights of the ECHR require says nothing about the factual conditions under which these rights are enforceable.

So, understood as 'discretion', the MA is normatively inert. One cannot agree or disagree with it.[9] In previous work, I called this understanding of the concept of the margin of appreciation '*substantive*'.[10] The reason was that the Strasbourg Court would often state the conclusion reached, following the exercise of its evaluative judgement about the substance of the right, in terms of whether the state has 'acted within its margin of appreciation' or whether it has 'overstepped' it. My aim was to capture that big part of the case law in which the Court uses the doctrinal label. But I stressed that such mention of the doctrinal label plays no role in the substantive judgement of what the right is. It is conclusory and redundant and should be abandoned. Similar points have been made by judges of the Court in their separate opinions.[11] For it is the right that determines the state's margin, understood as discretion, not the other way around. To say therefore that some state action is not a violation of the ECHR, because it falls within the state's margin of appreciation, is to beg the question about what the ECHR required in that case. Though there are cases where the Strasbourg Court has begged the question in that way, the problem in those cases is not the invocation of the margin of appreciation, but the failure to provide adequate reasons for the conclusion reached.

In sum, the idea that states enjoy discretion in respecting the qualified rights of the ECHR should be uncontroversial. This idea says nothing about how the Strasbourg Court, or other international courts, should decide cases. It is moreover compatible both with the universality of human rights and with allowing a degree of diversity between states in pursuing their goals. It is difficult to see how one can be for or against the MA, if by that doctrinal label we simply mean to express the proposition that identifying the obligations that qualified rights impose on states requires an evaluative judgement. So we have to be charitable and entertain another definition for what the margin of appreciation is, if it is to have any normative purchase.

The Margin of Appreciation as Deference

A second suggestion is to define the margin to be not about the discretion of contracting states, but about the power of review of the European Court. In particular, the suggestion is to define the margin as referring to the conditions under which the European Court will not rely on its own evaluative judgement about qualified rights,

---

[9] It could be argued that human rights are not principles—calling for judgement in determining their content—but categorical rules that allow for no exception. It would then follow that states should enjoy no discretion in interfering with human rights. This absolutist position however does not fit human rights law, which contains many rights that do not operate as categorical rules, such as the right to free speech, private life, and freedom of religion. States can interfere with such rights without necessarily violating them. Even the right not to be tortured, hailed as an absolute right in international law, calls for evaluative judgement in deciphering its scope. See Mavronicola 2012. I am grateful to Adam Etinson for drawing my attention to the objection from moral absolutism.

[10] Letsas 2006.   [11] See Rozakis's separate opinions.

but rather will *defer* to the judgement of national authorities. I called this concept of the MA '*structural*' as it speaks to the institutional structure that exists between Strasbourg and national authorities: when a case goes to Strasbourg there has normally been a judgement on it on the part of national courts, because of the requirement to exhaust domestic remedies.[12] Follesdal follows this definition when he says that the MA 'grants the state the authority, within some limits, to determine whether the Convention rights are violated'. The problem however is that this definition, though an improvement on its discretion-based alternative, is still incomplete as a legal doctrine which we can normatively assess. It does not state the conditions under which international human rights courts should defer to the judgement of national authorities. A full normative assessment of the doctrine of the MA requires supplementing the definition with the conditions under which the Court is to defer to the judgement of national authorities.

Having said that, the definition based on judicial deference towards national authorities has some normative bite. First, it appears to rule out the proposition that international courts must always exercise their own judgement as to what human rights litigants before them have. And second, it appears to allow for the possibility that contracting states will be the sole judge of what human rights people have under the ECHR. Without further qualifications, the above two propositions are rather extreme. The first is in direct tension with the value of legality. Normally, the role of courts is to decide themselves what legal rights litigants before them have, rather than follow the decisions of some other body. And it is clear that the ECHR has authorized the Strasbourg Court to decide what human rights people have as a matter of international law. The second threatens to make the purpose of having international human rights review redundant. If a contracting state is the sole judge of whether it has violated someone's human rights as matter of law, to whose judgement the Strasbourg Court ought to defer, then that state becomes judge in its own cause. There would then be little point in having judicial review of state action by an international court. The judicial outcome before Strasbourg in all cases where a margin of appreciation is granted would be that there is no violation, since if the state thought there was a violation, then it would have remedied it, rendering the case inadmissible. The role of the Court would then be the very limited one of ensuring that domestic authorities have properly addressed the substantive rights issue in question and of determining what their decision was.

The preceding remarks suggest that the deference-based definition is too coarse-grained. They suggest that deference to contracting states should not only be exceptional, subject to limited conditions, but also that it should be inconclusive. By 'inconclusive', I mean the possibility that when the Strasbourg Court defers to the judgement of national authorities, it should assign some weight to it but not conclusive weight.

---

[12] The requirement to exhaust domestic remedies is the norm in international human rights law. See article 35 para. 1 ECHR and article 2 of the First Optional Protocol to the ICCPR.

The Court is still to exercise its own judgement as to whether there was a violation and possibly override the weight it assigned to the judgement of the respondent state. This idea of deference as 'inconclusive weight' diminishes the risk of international human rights review becoming redundant. It is also echoed in Strasbourg's motto that the states' margin of appreciation 'goes hand in hand with European supervision'.

So I propose to modify the deference-based definition of the Margin of Appreciation as follows. The MA refers to the conditions under which the Strasbourg Court is to assign substantial (albeit not conclusive) weight to the judgement of national authorities as to whether the abstract moral principle underlying a qualified ECHR right has been violated. This definition is the one that requires serious normative scrutiny. It is incomplete in that it fails to state what these conditions are. We can distinguish four such conditions: (a) The fact that there has been 'democratic deliberation and will formation', within the respondent state, as to whether the applicant's qualified right has been violated; (b) the fact that there is no consensus amongst contracting states on whether the complained form of state interference amounts to a human rights violation; (c) the fact that there is reasonable and good-faith disagreement about whether there is a violation across states; and (d) the fact that the European Court has epistemic limitations relative to national authorities. Follesdal's defence[13] of the MA, as I understand it, is in support of conditions (a), (b), and (c).[14] His argument is largely based on the values of democracy, sovereignty, and accountability. Though I agree with Follesdal that these are important values, I am sceptical that they provide normative support for conditions (a), (b), and (c). My argument places greater emphasis than his does on the values of the Rule of Law and human rights.

Sovereignty, Democracy, and Consensus

Follesdal remarks that international human rights courts have a dual commitment. On the one hand they have to respect the treaty and uphold its human rights values and on the other hand they have to show respect for state sovereignty.[15] But it is not clear to me why the two are in tension and why respect for sovereignty supports deference to democratic decisions of national authorities. This is because contracting states have opted to restrict their sovereignty by creating legally binding obligations under international law and by authorizing the European Court of Human Rights (and the Committee of Ministers) to enforce these obligations. These obligations may consist in

---

[13] Since the normative arguments for or against each of these conditions for deference are separate, requiring separate normative assessment, it is somewhat misleading to speak in general in terms of being for or against the doctrine of the MA. For the purposes of normative assessment, there is no such thing as a single doctrine of the MA. There are as many doctrines as the proposed conditions for deferring to the judgement of national authorities.

[14] It is not clear whether Follesdal takes these conditions conjunctively or disjunctively. Pages 275–83 suggest the latter. My criticism stands in either case.

[15] Follesdal pp. 269, 278, and 288.

abstract principles, requiring the Court to exercise evaluative judgement in order to discover them, but as I noted earlier this does not mean that these obligations are loose or indeterminate. States authorized the European Court to exercise this judgement as a matter of international law. More precisely, the obligation to comply with Strasbourg's judgements is the *result* of an exercise of the sovereign will of contracting states, through the power to make treaties under international law, rather than a *threat* to it. Unlike the case of other international human rights treaties (e.g. the ICCPR), European states decided to create a fully judicial body with direct access (since the reform of Protocol 11) for all individuals within their jurisdiction. The will of contracting states to give the Court's judgements legally binding force is very clear in the text of article 46 of the ECHR.

It may be objected to the argument above that some (or most) contracting states may not have intended to bind themselves to comply with Strasbourg's judgement in cases covered by conditions (a), (b), and (c) above. And it is true that old members, like the United Kingdom, may have never envisaged that the Strasbourg Court would make controversial decisions on human rights, such as on prisoners' right to vote,[16] with which the democratic legislature of the respondent state disagrees, and as to which there is no consensus amongst contracting states. I find this objection unconvincing on two grounds. First, because—as with any contract—one is bound by the objective meaning of the terms used in the agreement rather than by the subjective will of the parties.[17] Second, because contracting states may at any point withdraw from the ECHR, should they choose to do so. Unlike judicial review under most constitutional bills of rights, the obligation to abide by Strasbourg's judgements is not entrenched. To be sure, there may be political costs involved in withdrawing (e.g. diminishing prospects of joining other international organizations or increasing reputation costs), but these are not substantial enough to make membership to the ECHR coercive. Besides, not only have contracting states continued to be parties to the ECHR after Protocol 11,[18] but also they have reaffirmed their commitment in subsequent Protocols, none of which introduces any 'exemptions clauses' for conditions (a), (b), and (c) above. States could have easily introduced a 'democratic override' clause within the ECHR, and made it explicit, through the use of an additional Protocol. But they haven't.

Sometimes the argument from sovereignty takes a different shape. It is coupled with an appeal to the democratic process within the respondent state.[19] What if the

---

[16] *Hirst v. United Kingdom, MT and Greens v. United Kingdom.*

[17] On the so-called objective theory of interpretation see Charles Fried, *The Ambitions of Contract as Promise: Thirty Years On*, available at: <http://www.ucl.ac.uk/laws/jurisprudence/docs/2013/charles_fried_paper.pdf>. Fried cites Learned Hand's defence of the objective theory of interpretation, even 'were it proved by twenty bishops that either party, when he used the words, intended something else than the usual meaning which the law imposes upon them'. *Hotchkiss v. Nat'l City Bank of N.Y.*, 200 F. 287, 293 (SDNY 1911). On the view that intentionalism and originalism are ill suited for the interpretation of international human rights treaties see Letsas 2010.

[18] The reform of Protocol 11 allowed individuals to apply directly to the European Court of Human Rights and gave it compulsory jurisdiction. See article 34 ECHR.

[19] Follesdal speaks of 'democratic sovereignty' (p. 290).

representatives of the people have deliberated, in good faith, upon the applicant's case and concluded that there is no human rights violation? Shouldn't the Strasbourg Court defer to that judgement? Follesdal's answer is yes, on condition that the state is genuinely democratic and that the judgement in question does not violate rights that are preconditions for democracy (e.g. freedom of political expression) and the rights of persistent minorities.[20]

It seems to me that the argument from democracy is separate from the argument from sovereignty. A state does not have to be democratic in order to be sovereign. In fact, if I am right, the two here are pulling towards opposite directions. So long as a state remains a party to the ECHR, sovereignty requires government officials to respect their state's decision to be bound by Strasbourg's judgements. Democracy on the other hand requires government officials to respect the decisions of elected representatives. This might seem to pose a dilemma for national governments in cases where Strasbourg is minded to take a different view from national legislatures on whether the ECHR has been violated. But this is not a dilemma that arises for the Strasbourg Court because the Court, being international, is primarily bound by *international law*, for the following reason. The *Rule of Law* requires international courts to respect decisions of national authorities only if they become relevant in virtue of one of the sources of international law (treaty, custom, and general principles). The mere fact that some decision is democratic is not sufficient to produce normative effects in international law, unless the decision takes the appropriate form so as to bind the state in its external relations (e.g. denouncing a treaty). Nor is it necessary for a state decision to be democratic in order to produce legal effects in international law. Non-democratic states or emerging democracies can validly bind themselves under international treaty law, including binding themselves to respect human rights. So, in the absence of an explicit 'democratic override' in the ECHR, and so long as contracting states do not withdraw their membership, it is not clear why national decisions on what counts as a human rights violation should be relevant for the Strasbourg Court.

Some may find the above argument too quick. It is based entirely on the value of the Rule of Law and the Court's legal duty to respect the will of sovereign states, but only as it is expressed in the objective terms of the treaty. Even if the argument is correct, it fails to explain why states should not amend the ECHR and add a 'democratic override' clause. It also ignores references to democracy made in the text of the ECHR itself. It might be objected: If commitment to democracy is a value shared between members of the Council of Europe, shouldn't the Court try not to undermine it?

It is here worth elaborating on the implications of judicial deference on the part of Strasbourg towards democratic decisions within the respondent state. Democratic deliberation need not guarantee that the outcome will be justifiable as a matter of principle. This is not only because democratic decisions might be prejudiced towards minorities, but also because they are routinely ill informed, influenced by the prevailing

---

[20] Follesdal, p. 281.

political climate of the day and the swinging moods of the electorate. Parliament may accept the application of a particular principle in one domain but, out of neglect, ignorance, or prejudice, refuse it in another. It is also important to note here that the mere existence of legislation against which an ECHR challenge is launched does not mean that there has been proper deliberation on whether it violates human rights. Legislatures routinely pass laws without proper deliberation, let alone deliberation on whether the bill going through violates human rights standards. Not all states moreover have pre-enactment check of compatibility with human rights, and even for those that do, it is often more of a formality than an opportunity for careful consideration of human rights issues. In other words, there is often no proper democratic deliberation, of the kind that Follesdal's argument requires, to which the Strasbourg Court can assign weight, even if it wants to.

So a systematic deference towards contracting states will result in a patchy and unprincipled case law on the relevant Convention rights. One state will decide that some indiscriminate measure (e.g. prisoners' voting) is not in breach of the ECHR, another (or the same) state will accept that some other indiscriminate measure (e.g. collection of DNA evidence from suspects)[21] breaches the ECHR, and a third one will take no decision either way. Is the Court supposed to find no violation in the first case and a violation in the other two? Or is it supposed to say that indiscriminate measures do not violate the ECHR?

The worry here is that courts have a fundamental duty of legality to make decisions based on appropriate moral principles that they should apply consistently across the individual cases that reach them.[22] If the primary aim of international human rights courts is to develop principled human rights standards for all member states, then systematic deference to democratic deliberation will seriously undermine it. This is for the additional reason that the Strasbourg Court will have to defer to the decisions of forty-seven different legislatures. Deference by domestic courts to one and the same legislature might result in some degree of principled consistency, particularly if they belong to a well-functioning democracy that has good-faith commitment to human rights. But deference to forty-seven different legislatures, many of which belong to far from well-functioning democracies, will inevitably result in an incoherent patchwork of judicial outcomes. So the fact that a human rights court is international provides reason for less deference, not more.

To be sure, Follesdal's argument does not support unqualified and systematic judicial deference because of the two conditions he imposes: respect for rights that are necessary to the democratic process and protection of what he calls 'persistent' minorities. And even when these two conditions are met, he seems willing to allow the Court to override the decision of national legislature, in cases of 'clear error'. He also reminds us

---

[21]   S and Marper v. United Kingdom.
[22]   Dworkin calls this conception of the value of the Rule of Law 'integrity'. See Dworkin 1988.

that the MA applies only to qualified rights, and not to all Convention rights. So it is important at this stage to explore in greater detail Follesdal's two conditions.

Theories of Rights and the Counter-Majoritarian Objection

Follesdal's first condition echoes John Hart Ely's[23] well-known minimalist conception of judicial review, as safeguarding procedural rights essential to the democratic process. But the second condition goes further, recognizing as the aim of judicial review to protect rights of minorities. My question is whether these two conditions, properly interpreted, cover all of the human rights that we have. If they do, then it would follow that the Court should never grant a margin of appreciation when it believes that an ECHR has been violated. It would follow, in other words, that when these two conditions are met, the reason why the Court should not find a breach of the ECHR violation is the absence of a rights-violation, rather than the need to defer to democratic deliberation. The point I am making here is that one's conception of the Margin of Appreciation, understood as judicial deference, depends—as a prior issue—on one's theory of the content of rights. This is because the idea of judicial deference makes sense only if it applies to questions that the Court is meant to be deciding. If one's theory of deference applies solely to matters outside the scope of human rights (e.g. the distribution of economic resources) then it is not really a theory of deference, as a human rights court is not meant to decide these matters anyway. If Follesdal's two conditions capture all there is to the scope of the qualified ECHR rights, properly understood, then his argument would in effect be against the Margin of Appreciation.[24] So we need first an account of the nature of human rights, before we can answer the question of whether the Court should ever defer on the question of what these rights are.

On this point, it seems to me that Follesdal's second condition (the protection of minorities) is more expansive than he makes it out to be. The condition echoes a widely held view about constitutional rights and judicial review, according to which they aim to protect unpopular minorities against the risk of the tyranny of the majority. The idea is that the government in a democracy is prone to pander to the preferences of the majority in order to get re-elected. If these preferences are prejudiced towards the conception of the good life of particular minorities (e.g. homosexuals or religious minorities), as they often are, then their interests will unjustly suffer. Entrusting the government to filter illicit majoritarian motives out of its policies would make it a

---

[23] Ely 1981.

[24] Dworkin's 'political' theory of human rights for example (as distinct from his theory of rights) limits their scope to protection against contempt for one's dignity, as a condition for the internal legitimacy of the state. If that were the correct theory of human rights, then the Strasbourg Court would have to uphold state decisions that do not show contempt for one's dignity. And it would have to do so because these decisions do not violate human rights, and not because they are democratic. For a critique of Dworkin's theory of human rights see Letsas 2014.

judge in its own case and is unlikely to succeed. Courts by contrast are less vulnerable to majoritarian pressures and are more likely to 'smoke out' policies based on illicit motives, which is an argument in favour of strong judicial review of legislative action.[25] This is why judicial deference to democratic decisions that are likely to contain majoritarian prejudices makes little sense. It defeats the whole point of judicial review and makes electoral majorities judges in their own cause. Call this the counter-majoritarian argument.

The counter-majoritarian argument provides support to a number of judgements in which the Strasbourg Court upheld claims of unpopular groups again the preju-dices of the majority: children born out of wedlock (*Marckx*), homosexuals (*Dudgeon, Frette, EB, Schalk and Kopf*), transsexuals (*Rees, Sheffield and Horsham, Goodwin*), foreign immigrants (*Saadi v. United Kingdom,*[26] *Siliadin v. France*[27]), religious minorities (*Kokkinakis v. Greece*[28]), people with HIV (*I.B. v. Greece*). Such cases form a substantial part of Strasbourg's case law on qualified rights. But Follesdal must think that there is more to rights than this blocking of majoritarian prejudices, since he takes deference to democratic deliberation to be in principle justified outside the domain of vulnerable minorities. Though I agree that the smoking out of majoritarian prejudices towards vulnerable minority groups is not the only aim of human rights, it is crucial to ask what else falls within the scope of human rights and whether the rationale for the counter-majoritarian argument applies there as well. So what other aims are human rights meant to protect?

Follesdal refers to the serving of individual interests and the need to accept trade-offs between rights and social interests, as well as between different rights. He alludes in other words to an interest-based theory of rights. And he takes the proportionality test, as applied by courts, to be a check on the way in which democratic institutions have balanced the various interests involved. Now, if the point of human rights were to shield individual interests against the pursuit of public goals, then there would be little reason to give courts the task of deciding what the correct balance should be between the various competing interests. Their task would be limited to supervising the outer limits of the balancing made by the legislature. Deference to the balancing made by democratic institutions would then make perfect sense. But the interest-based theory is not the only available theory of rights.[29] I have argued elsewhere[30] that the limita-tion clauses in the qualified ECHR rights, and the related test of proportionality, are best seen as a reference to the abstract right to what Dworkin calls *equal respect and*

---

[25] The idea of smoking out illicit motives figures in US constitutional theory. Richard Fallon has argued that it is not only what underlies the test of strict scrutiny of the US Supreme Court but also the test of proportionality as applied in Europe and elsewhere, arguing in effect that the test is the same. See Fallon 2007.

[26] *Saadi v. United Kingdom* (Appl No. 13229/03) Judgement of 29 January 2008.

[27] *Siliadin v. France* (Appl No. 73316/01) Judgement of 26 July 2005.

[28] *Kokkinakis v. Greece* (Appl No. 14307/88) Judgement of 25 May 1993.

[29] On the constrast between interest-based and reason-blocking theory see Letsas 2009.

[30] Letsas 2015.

concern.[31] This is not the right to have any particular interest promoted or protected by one's government; rather, it is the right to be treated with equal respect and concern in the way the government deploys its coercive force.

If we understand human rights as founded on this abstract right to equal respect and concern, then their aim would not be limited to the blocking of illicit majoritarian prejudices. It would also apply to cases where the government has employed blanket or indiscriminate measures that prevent it from taking into account morally relevant differences between different classes of individuals. And it would apply to indiscriminate measures as well, even if they are not motivated by prejudice towards some 'persistent' minority. Consider for example the case of *S and Marper*, which had to do with the UK's blanket policy of collecting and storing the DNA of all criminal suspects, regardless of whether they had subsequently been acquitted. The Court found that the government's failure to distinguish between those suspects that have been acquitted and those that have been convicted was disproportionate. The rationale was that it is unfair to treat those who have been acquitted as if they have committed the crime for which they were charged. It is unfair to treat acquitted suspects in the same way as convicted ones. Here, it is the fairness of the scheme of DNA retention that the Court took to be a human rights violation, not the way in which the state had balanced the interests involved (i.e. the privacy of the suspects and the prevention of crime). Finding such indiscriminate measures in breach of the ECHR is a big part of Strasbourg's case law.[32]

I see no reason why a human rights court should show deference towards indiscriminate measures, particularly since they are most often the product of democratic neglect, rather than of proper democratic deliberation.[33] And such neglect is often the result of imperfections in the democratic process, in that the people who suffer from indiscriminate measures (such as prisoners, immigrants, juveniles, children) do not have sufficient representation to influence the legislative process. Even if the legislature specifically applies itself to the human rights issue, as the UK Parliament did on prisoners' right to vote,[34] there is little guarantee that there will be proper regard for the interests of underrepresented groups. So it seems to me that the same counter-majoritarian argument against deference that applies in the case of unpopular minorities, also applies in the case of indiscriminate measures. And it also applies to cases where the problem is not the presence of indiscriminate measures but the *absence* of any measure,

---

[31] See Dworkin 1997.

[32] The *Hirst* case on prisoners' right to vote for instance was decided on the basis that the UK ban is indiscriminate. The Court did not say that all prisoners should have the right to vote.

[33] It should also be observed here that in a large number of cases that go before the Court the violation consists in the actions of the executive and the judiciary rather then in democratically enacted legislation. In such cases, it makes little sense to say that democracy requires deferring to the judgement of national judiciary or the national executive, unless their actions are subsequently endorsed by the national legislature.

[34] In February 2011, Members of Parliament backed a backbench cross-party motion supporting the blanket ban by a vote of 234 to 22.

despite wide knowledge that some vulnerable group is the victim of exploitation.[35] These are cases in which the Strasbourg Court imposes a so-called 'positive obligation' on states to take action.

In sum, the rationale against granting a margin of appreciation to democratic decisions that conceal majoritarian contempt towards minorities, *also* applies to democratic decisions (or lack thereof) that are based on neglect towards vulnerable groups. This rationale flows out of the abstract right to be treated with equal concern and respect. Put together, cases where the applicant's status as an equal has been offended by majoritarian contempt and cases where it has been offended by neglect, account for the majority of the cases where the Strasbourg Court has found a violation. And if rights are based on some dimension of the value of moral equality, then the ruling of these violations exhausts the legal duty of a human rights court. Follesdal's second condition, expanded in the way I suggest, ends up making the margin of appreciation redundant. For if a democratic decision does not show contempt or neglect, in the sense discussed herein, then it falls outside the domain of human rights and the Court should let it stand for that reason alone.[36]

Conclusion

The doctrinal label of the MA is used in different contexts with different meanings. Understood as the idea that qualified rights are abstract principles whose application requires evaluative judgement, and may allow for diversity, it is uncontroversial. Understood as the idea that human rights courts should defer on the view of legislatures as to what counts as a violation, it is objectionable. Deference undermines the egalitarian dimension of human rights whose role is to protect individuals against both contempt and neglect by the governing majority of the day. It also undermines the value of the Rule of Law and courts' duty to decide cases under principled consistency. That's not to say that judicial review by international human rights courts does not raise any special normative challenges, to do with the fact that they are international. It is morally relevant for example if the ruling of a human rights violation will result in one or several contracting states withdrawing from the Court's jurisdiction, a risk that domestic human rights courts do not face. But such political considerations—which can also be labelled as cases for granting a margin of appreciation—have little to do with the values of democracy, human rights, and the rule of law. They raise valid concerns, but they are exceptional and do not occupy the Court's main role, particularly

---

[35] Consider for instance the case of *Siliadin v. France*, which concerned the absence of legislation in France making domestic slavery a criminal offence. See Mantouvalou 2006.

[36] In the end, the practical implications of my view may not be very different from Follesdal's. Many cases that he would describe as meriting a margin of appreciation, I would describe as raising no human rights issue. But the difference between his account and mine is not terminological, particularly since I have a more expansive view of the 'margin-free' zone imposed by his two conditions.

since it started feeling confident in its own legitimacy.[37] Nor do we have to deny that international courts should be interested to know what national authorities have said on the human rights issue before them. Like looking at foreign jurisdictions and reading academic articles, judges have epistemic reasons to enrich their understanding of human rights. But enriching one's understanding hardly qualifies as deference.

In the end, the doctrinal label of the MA is shorthand for all the normative challenges that an international human rights court, like Strasbourg, faces. It invites us to think harder about the foundations of human rights, the value of the rule of law, and the kind of commitment that contracting states undertook by setting up the European Court of Human Rights. In taking up this invitation, we should move away from the unhelpful idea of discretion and the dangerous idea of deference. We do better to focus on the normative issues that a particular human rights case raises and to demand that those who favour granting a margin of appreciation explain why. We should then hope that their argument is not based solely on the fact that national authorities think that the applicant's human rights have not been violated. No authority, however democratic, is worthy of deference if it has shown contempt or neglect for the applicant's status as an equal.

References

Dworkin, Ronald (1967) 'The Model of Rules', in *Faculty Scholarship Series*. Paper 3609 (available online).

Dworkin, Ronald (1988) *Law's Empire* (Cambridge, Mass.: Harvard University Press).

Dworkin, Ronald (1997) *Freedom's Law: The Moral Reading of the American Constitution* (Cambridge, Mass.: Harvard University Press).

Ely, John Hart (1981) *Democracy and Distrust: A Theory of Judicial Review* (Cambridge, Mass.: Harvard University Press).

Etinson, Adam (2013) 'Human Rights, Claimability and the Uses of Abstraction', in *Utilitas*, Vol. 25, No. 4, pp. 463–86.

Fallon, Richard (2007) 'Strict Judicial Scrutiny', *UCLA Law Review*, Vol. 54, pp. 1267–337.

Legg, Andrew (2012) *The Margin of Appreciation* (Oxford: Oxford University Press).

Letsas, George (2006) 'Two Concepts of the Margin of Appreciation', in *Oxford Journal of Legal Studies*, Vol. 26, No. 4, pp. 705–32.

Letsas, George (2009) 'Rights and Duties on Pitcairn Island', in Dawn Oliver (ed.), *Justice, Legality and the Rule of Law* (Oxford: Oxford University Press), pp. 157–82.

Letsas, George (2010) 'Strasbourg's Interpretive Ethic: Lessons for the International Lawyer', *European Journal of International Law*, Vol. 21, No. 3, pp. 509–41.

Letsas, George (2013) 'The ECHR as a Living Instrument: Its Meaning and Legitimacy', in Geir Ulfstein, Andreas Follesdal, and Birgit Peters (eds), *Constituting Europe: The European Court of Human Rights in a National, European and Global Context* (Cambridge: Cambridge University Press), pp. 106–41.

---

[37] See Letsas 2013.

Letsas, George (2014) 'Dworkin on Human Rights', in *Jurisprudence: An International Journal of Legal and Political Thought*, Vol. 6, No. 2, pp. 327–40.

Letsas, George (2015) 'Rescuing Proportionality', in R. Cruft and M. Renzo (eds), *Philosophical Foundations of Human Rights* (Oxford: Oxford University Press), pp. 316–41.

Mahoney, Paul (1998) 'Marvellous Richness of Diversity or Invidious Cultural Relativism', in *Human Rights Law Journal*, Vol. 19, No. 1, pp. 1–6.

Mantouvalou, Virginia (2006) 'Servitude and Forced Labour in the 21st Century: The Human Rights of Domestic Workers', in *Industrial Law Journal*, Vol. 35, No. 4, pp. 396–414.

Mavronicola, Natasa (2012) 'What is an "Absolute Right"? Deciphering Absoluteness in the Context of Article 3 of the European Convention on Human Rights', *Human Rights Law Review*, Vol. 12, No. 4, pp. 723–58.

PART IV

Ideals and their Limits

9

Dwelling in Possibility
Ideals, Aspirations, and Human Rights

Kimberley Brownlee

> I dwell in Possibility—
> A fairer House than Prose—
> More numerous of Windows—
> Superior—for Doors—
>
> Of Chambers as the Cedars—
> Impregnable of Eye—
> And for an Everlasting Roof
> The Gambrels of the Sky—
>
> Of Visitors—the fairest—
> For Occupation—This—
> The spreading wide my narrow Hands
> To gather Paradise—
>
> Emily Dickinson[1]

Introduction

Most moral and political philosophers think that for human rights to play the important practical roles we need them to play in policymaking, regulation, and accountability they must be feasible.[2] This feasibility constraint on human rights comes in different strengths. Some of the best-known varieties of it in the literature are:

1. a *remediability test* that the right in question can be practically addressed and its violation remedied;[3]

---

[1] Dickinson, Emily, 'I Dwell in Possibility' in, *The Poems of Emily Dickinson*, ed. Ralph W. Franklin (Cambridge, Mass.: Harvard University Press, [1951] 1998). Reprinted electronically by the Poetry Foundation: <http://www.poetryfoundation.org/poem/182904>.

[2] I am very grateful to Rowan Cruft, Adam Etinson, Pablo Gilabert, and Thomas Parr for helpful comments on this chapter. I also thank Thomas Parr and Kartik Upadhyaya for their research assistance on this paper.

[3] Henry Shue states that human rights provide social guarantees against common, serious, and remediable threats. He says that the measure of successful prevention of threats is not utopian; people are not

2. an *enforceability test* that there is some specifiable and more or less effective mechanism for enforcing the right;[4]
3. a *social influenceability test* that other people could make a material difference through taking an interest in what that right protects;[5]
4. a *reasonable burdens test* that the right does not impose overly heavy burdens that render its implementation infeasible or unduly costly when other equally important concerns are taken into account;[6]
5. an *implementability test* that the duties imposed by the right are ones that can be successfully implemented in a majority of countries today.[7]

Most theories of human rights do not demand absolute, universal feasibility as an existence condition for human rights, but instead temper the feasibility constraint with some aspirational elements. For instance, Amartya Sen, who advances the *social influenceability test*, denies that rights must be feasible in any straightforward sense. He asks: 'Why should complete feasibility be a condition of cogency of human rights when the objective is to work towards enhancing their actual realization, if necessary through expanding their feasibility?'[8] The fact that some rights are not at present completely feasible does not in itself entail that they are not rights at all. Rather, 'that understanding suggests the need to work towards changing the prevailing circumstances to make the unrealized rights realizable, and ultimately, realized.' Pablo Gilabert develops this idea with the notion of *dynamic duties*, which are duties to expand the range of what is feasible by changing prevailing conditions.[9]

---

entitled to protection against ineradicable threats such as eventual serious illness, accident, or death. Shue notes, though, that what is eradicable changes as conditions, resources, and technologies change; we have little excuse today in letting people die from malaria, but more excuse in letting people die from cancer. Shue 1996, pp. 32–3.

[4] Raymond Geuss argues, bluntly, that there either are or are not mechanisms for enforcing human rights. If there are not, then 'it would seem that calling them "rights" simply means that we think it would (morally) be a good idea if they were enforced, though, of course, they are not. A "human right" is an inherently vacuous conception, and to speak of "human rights" is a kind of puffery or white magic.' See Geuss 2001, p. 144.

[5] See Sen 2004. Sen introduces a weak feasibility test, which he calls the *social influenceability test*, as one condition for the plausibility that a given right is a human right. He states that a human right 'has to satisfy a condition of plausibility that others could make a material difference through taking...an interest [in what that right protects]' (329). This condition of social influenceability excludes, for example, things like a right to tranquillity from qualifying as a human right. As a feasibility test, it is less demanding than others since all it asks is that it be possible in practice for people to make some difference by paying attention to a putative right.

[6] Nickel 2007, p. 78.

[7] Nickel 2007, pp. 78–81. This test can be understood, at least partly, as specifying the framing of human rights, rather than as a strict condition on the existence of certain rights. Nickel says that human rights need to be selected and formulated so that they can be effectively implemented. He says that 'Neither morality nor law is advanced by rights that are stated so idealistically that most of their addressees will be excused most of the time on grounds of inability' (81).

[8] Sen 2004, p. 348.

[9] Gilabert 2009, pp. 559–81; and Gilabert 2012, chs. 4 and 7.

Similarly, James Nickel says that human rights can exist and be high-priority goals even when there are considerable barriers to their (legal) implementation. He notes that affirming a given human right 'does not imply that we must immediately implement that right at the cost of sacrificing things that are of higher priority.'[10] Nor does it follow from the fact that a claim cannot be immediately implemented as a legal right that it should not be respected as a moral right. Taking the example of a right to assistance during disability or illness, Nickel argues that, even if it cannot at present be implemented as a legal right, 'it can be implemented as a moral right in the sense that people recognize as part of their morality the legitimacy of calling upon government and other people to assist one during illness and disability.'[11] Acknowledging such a right even in the absence of legal implementation brings with it, Nickel says, duties for both government and citizens to promote the growth of opportunities that will make full implementation possible as well as duties of charity and benevolence.

But, not all defences of the feasibility constraint are tempered by aspirations to expand what is feasible. In its strongest form defended by Raymond Geuss, the feasibility constraint says that human rights, particularly socio-economic rights, are simply liberal ideals. They are expressions of moral belief about what we would like to see enforced, but as such they are things to which we can only aspire. They are not things to which we can appeal to regulate conduct.[12]

Moreover, even among the more tempered defences of the feasibility constraint, there seems to be an assumption that it is regrettable that there are aspirational elements to human rights practice, that somehow this feature, by nature, shakes the foundations of what human rights are and what they can do. In what follows, I show that feasibility as such is irrelevant to human rights.[13] Even if a right were to fail all of the feasibility-related tests noted above, this would not threaten its status as a human right with all its positive connotations of practical importance, action-guidingness, and accountability.

My argument turns, in part, on properly understanding the nature of ideals and aspirations.[14] Let me lay down some terminology. An *ideal* is a conception of perfection or model of excellence around which we can shape our thoughts and actions and through which we can seek to effect significant changes in perspectives and practices. Ideals differ from ordinary goals along several dimensions. The most notable differences for present purposes are that ideals are comprehensive, aspirational, and at present

---

[10] Nickel 1982, p. 261.   [11] Nickel 1982, p. 262.   [12] Geuss 2001, pp. 138–46.

[13] In this chapter, I use the terms *realizable* and *feasible* interchangeably and the terms *unrealizable* and *infeasible* interchangeably. *Unrealizability* is perhaps a broader notion than *infeasibility*; the latter has specific connotations in human rights debates of implementation, enforcement, and workability. But, even so, the term *infeasible* is synonymous with *unattainable* and *unachievable*, which are synonymous with *unrealizable* as I am using it.

[14] For a defence of my account of ideals and aspirations, see Brownlee 2010a and Brownlee 2010b. For an application of this account to the concept of *conscience*, see Brownlee 2012, ch. 2.

unrealizable and, by contrast, ordinary goals are specific, non-aspirational, and at present realizable.

Briefly, concerning comprehensiveness, our sincerely chosen ideals have a comprehensive effect on our thoughts, actions, and feelings in key domains of our lives.[15] Ideals can be the animating objects of a life that is perceived as meaningful both by the one who lives it and by others. By contrast, ordinary goals need not be comprehensive, all-consuming, or meaning-giving. A gardener's ideal of cultivating a beautiful paradise has a deeper and more comprehensive effect on the shape of her life than do her specific, mundane goals of weeding regularly, watering regularly, and learning about flora, fauna, and gardening techniques, even though, of course, these specific, mundane goals contribute to the cultivation of her grand ideal.

Concerning aspirationality, an *aspiration* is an attitude of steadfast commitment to, longing for, and striving for something that is at present beyond us and may ultimately remain beyond us, namely, an ideal. The attitude of aspiration distinguishes our relation to our ideals from our relation to our ordinary goals, which do not require the emotional commitment, longing, and striving that ideals require. A gardener may have an ordinary desire to achieve her ordinary goal of pruning her roses this week, which is very different from the deep longing she has to realize her horticultural heaven, a longing she must have if she is to make any progress toward attaining such a grand ambition.

Note that neither our ideals nor our aspirations to realize them have to be genuinely valuable. We can be mistaken about our conceptions of excellence and about our aspirations to achieve them. But, within the category of ideals, there are ideals that are genuinely valuable, and, as I shall show, a subset of those ideals includes human rights as moral rights.[16]

Concerning unrealizability, ideals are presently unrealizable. I use the term 'presently unrealizable' in a technical sense to highlight that ideals are a distinct conceptual category from deep impossibilities such as living forever, travelling back in time, or giving birth to oneself, which defy the imaginative contemplation of how to seek with appropriate focus to realize them. Deep impossibilities are necessarily unrealizable. Ideals, by contrast, originate in our imaginations as models of advanced states, excellence, or perfection that can animate us to achieve more significant things than we believed possible. Ideals are by nature possible to realize in principle, but not at present and perhaps not even, ultimately, in the future.[17] In my hands, *present unrealizability* is a broad notion that includes unrealizable events that will, in all probability, remain forever out of reach, such as the philosopher's own ideal of truth. As C. A. J. Coady puts it, it is possible in principle for the philosopher always to make only true assertions

---

[15] Coady 2008, pp. 51–2.

[16] In what follows, I take a commonsense view of what counts as a human right, including both civil and political rights and social and economic rights.

[17] In other writing, I have rejected a straightforward notion of 'ought implies can'. See Brownlee 2010b.

and sound arguments, but most likely doing so will forever elude her.[18] There is no condition of future realizability built into the notion of *present unrealizability*.

There are at least two dimensions to the present unrealizability of an ideal. The first is the *kind* of unrealizability: What are the reasons for the unrealizability? The second is the *degree* of unrealizability: How likely is it that the unrealizability will lift? Or, alternatively, to what extent are different aspects of the ideal realizable even though the ideal itself is presently unrealizable?[19] In recent work, I distinguished three kinds of ideals, which I call *sustainability ideals, significant moment ideals*, and *ongoing progress ideals*.[20] In this chapter, I add a fourth kind of idea to this list, which I call *just out of reach ideals*. Both of the dimensions of unrealizability—the reasons and the degree—vary across the four kinds of ideals that I discuss in what follows.

Once we understand the nature of these four different kinds of ideals, and once we appreciate that even the most uncontentious human rights are ideals of one or more of these kinds, then we will understand why feasibility is not a condition for human rights status and, hence, is irrelevant to their practical importance and action-guidingness. In short, we will see that, between the narrow hands of practicable human-rights norms, there is the paradise of genuine moral aspiration.

1. Sustainability Ideals

The first kind of ideal that I will isolate is a *sustainability ideal*, which makes the clearest case that ideals can be eminently practical and action-guiding despite their present unrealizability.

A sustainability ideal requires us to sustain indefinitely a particular attitude, disposition, mode of conduct, state of affairs, or combination of those things. What makes a sustainability ideal an ideal is not its *content*, but its *maintenance* over time. In brief, even if, at this moment, the requisite attitude, disposition, conduct, or state is readily realizable, it comprises an ideal if, in all probability, its ongoing maintenance is unsustainable and that maintenance is key to its full realization. For example, for ordinary adults, being a good parent is a sustainability ideal. Although it is feasible for ordinary adults to be good parents today and perhaps tomorrow and the day after that, nevertheless being *a good parent* in a comprehensive, ongoing sense is an ideal for ordinary adults because, in all probability, ordinary adults cannot sustain indefinitely the requisite attitudes and conduct necessary to be good parents in the comprehensive sense. We cannot say that we are good parents in this sense if we are good parents this afternoon and then horrible parents this evening or mediocre parents from now on.

---

[18] Coady 2008, pp. 59–61.

[19] For a discussion of distinctions between types, domains, and degrees of feasibility, see Gilabert 2009.

[20] See note 14. In that work, I used the term *great moment ideals* to describe *significant moment ideals*. I have changed my terminology to avoid the evaluative connotations of the qualifier 'great'. Ideals are not necessarily genuinely valuable, and therefore significant moment ideals are not necessarily great moments.

(Ordinary adults can be 'good enough parents' where that does not require the sustained maintenance of any particular standard of good parenting across time.)

Like good parenting and many other ordinary values and norms, human rights are, by nature, sustainability ideals. This is because, on the one hand, it is part of a human-rights norm to require the ongoing protection of the fundamental interest that it identifies, and yet, on the other hand, the ongoing protection of a human right is, in all probability, unsustainable no matter how modest its content. The reason it is unsustainable is that, to honour a human right fully, it is not enough to secure it momentarily as a one-off, or to fluctuate between securing it for all people and failing to secure it for anyone, or to secure it continuously for some people and not for others. Ongoing protection requires continuously satisfying an appropriate standard of protection for all, and this is probably unsustainable in any society. For example, a government might succeed for a time in meaningfully securing its people's human rights to political participation and due process. But, no government can sustain indefinitely the combination of attitudes and practices necessary to ensure that those rights are always fully respected. There will inevitably be circumstances in which some people are either denied due process or illegitimately disenfranchised due to errors or prejudices.[21]

That said, the demands of *ongoing protection* vary across human rights, and they are not as demanding for rights to participation and due process as they are for rights such as protection against torture. Undoubtedly, ongoing protection of the right against torture requires an absolute guarantee. Protection against torture is a baseline, and anything below that baseline is a human rights failure. By contrast, for other human rights, such as political participation and due process, ongoing protection does not require an absolute guarantee, but a reasonable level of protection for all people that is broadly sensitive to circumstances, crises, and other constraints on an absolute, universal guarantee. A government's protection of the rights to political participation and due process does not fall below an adequate standard of ongoing protection when that government temporarily imposes martial law in a time of war or when rare, isolated cases of mismanagement result in the momentary breach of a person's political human rights.

When it comes to the *degree* of unrealizability, sustainability ideals have a high degree of unrealizability since they require *ongoing* maintenance. As noted, the ongoing maintenance of anything of value is most likely unsustainable. This is true even for very modest projects such as being a *decent* parent (rather than a good parent) or meeting a *modest* level of protection of a human right (rather a reasonable or absolute level of protection). The vagaries of circumstance and ability make ongoing maintenance of these things unrealizable, in all probability, even for those people who are well placed to carry out these projects.

Sustainability ideals have a potentially low degree of unrealizability (and sometimes have no degree of unrealizability) in the *content* to be sustained since what sustainability

---

[21] This observation does not invite a discussion of timelessness. We can focus on the synchronic universality of human rights and still see that the ongoing protection of human rights is a sustainability ideal.

ideals require at any one moment need not be demanding. Typically, for ordinary adults, being a good parent at any one moment is readily realizable, as it is not very demanding. And, for most people, being a merely *decent* parent at any one moment is readily realizable, as it is even less demanding. The same goes for most, if not all, human rights in our age of globalization, communication, and technological advancement. Human rights are not grand images of human flourishing, but norms that pick out the brute moral minimum necessary to treat human beings as human beings.[22] As such, what they require is (comparatively) undemanding. For most societies, honouring a given human right at a given moment is readily realizable.

A critic might object that not every society has the resources and political structures to honour in a given moment the basic demands of either a single human right or the full set of human rights (whatever that may be). Protecting a human right at a given moment may be readily realizable in an affluent, stable, well-run society, but not in an impoverished, unstable, poorly run society. For instance, the human right to health may be readily realizable at any one moment in western democracies, but not in developing countries, or at least not without sacrificing other equally valuable human rights and societal goals.

Moreover, a critic might continue that, in general, there is a disanalogy between societies seeking to honour human rights norms and ordinary adults seeking to be good parents because societies' task is much more demanding than parents' task even though human rights norms pick out only the conditions for a *minimally* decent human life. In other words, *most* societies, be they affluent or not, are not like ordinary adults when it comes to honouring human rights norms. As such, human rights norms have a high degree of unrealizability both in their content and in their ongoing protection, so the argument goes.

A proper reply would need to marshal empirical evidence to determine whether it is indeed very demanding for *most* societies to protect some or all human rights in a given moment. But, even if the evidence were to show that, in a given moment, most states cannot honour human rights on their own, this would not entail that human rights set very demanding moment-to-moment standards. Both the global community and the most affluent, stable nations bear some responsibility for securing human rights for all, and, more often than not, they can ensure in a given moment that human rights are generally protected. This is true at least for those human rights whose protection depends largely on certain economic resources rather than on, additionally, the establishment and maintenance of certain political structures, institutions, and legal processes.[23]

Amongst the societies that have the requisite resources and political structures to honour all human rights, there will inevitably be variation in the degree and quality of

---

[22] This is the standard view of the nature of human rights. However, it is not universally endorsed. See, for example, Tasioulas 2012.

[23] For a defence of a similar claim, see Gilabert 2009.

their ongoing maintenance of human rights. Just as some ordinary adults will be good parents more often than not, and some will be good parents more often than others are, so too some societies will organize their structures and resources so that they secure human rights more often than not, and will honour their human rights obligations more often than other societies do. Consequently, the fact that human rights are sustainability ideals does not preclude us from judging the degree of success that a person, society, or government has in sustaining them. We can fault the aspirations of the sufficiently affluent society that fails to embrace human rights norms as a central concern and we can forgive the failings of the society that lacks the resources to meet an adequate level of human rights protection.

A critic might then say that, regardless of the demandingness of human-rights content, the unsustainability of their ongoing protection shows that they are implausible practical guides. But this does not follow. As indicated above, all ordinary values and norms are sustainability ideals if their value lies partly in their ongoing maintenance rather than in a one-off instantiation.[24] Dispositions such as love, compassion, kindness, care, generosity, and gratitude are valuable in part as sustained displays of commitment, and as such they are sustainability ideals.[25] But, their ideality does not affect their practicability or action-guidingness. They can still inform our decisions, infuse many of our actions, and be benchmarks against which we assess our efforts even though we cannot sustain them at all times. The same can be said of human rights.

Finally, a critic might argue from the other side that human rights, in particular, and sustainability ideals, in general, are actually not at present unrealizable at all, and hence are not really ideals. This is because, as sustainability ideals, human rights do not obviously fail any of the feasibility tests noted at the beginning of this chapter. Instead, as sustainability ideals, they seem to be remediable, implementable, enforceable to some degree, socially influenceable, and reasonable. They simply are not consistently so.[26]

In reply, this objection misidentifies the location of the ideality in sustainability ideals. Their ideality does not lie in their content. It lies in their *ongoing* maintenance. Consequently, it is irrelevant to the sustainable-ideality of a human right that a given threat to it may be remediable in this moment or that it may be implementable in the majority of countries in this moment, or that it may be enforceable or socially influenceable in this moment. What is relevant is the very fact that the consistent ongoing maintenance of the protection, implementation, enforcement, social influence, and reasonableness of the human right is, in all probability, unsustainable. Human rights protection is like the philosopher's ideal of constant truth noted above, which Coady observes will in all likelihood forever elude her.

---

[24] Valuable acts such as altruistic acts are valuable as one-off events.

[25] This is not to say that a single burst of loving feeling or compassion has no value. It does. But, next to it there is the much greater value of sustained love and compassion.

[26] I thank Adam Etinson for highlighting this objection.

In sum, as sustainability ideals, human rights retain their practical relevance and action-guidingness, on the one hand, while being legitimate objects of our aspirations, on the other.

2. Significant Moment Ideals

The second kind of ideal that I will isolate is what I call a *significant moment ideal*. This kind of ideal raises no problem of ongoing maintenance. The reason for its present unrealizability lies in its content. This kind of ideal picks out a significant, broadly specifiable event, objective, or experience that is at present unrealizable and is viewed by those who strive for it as highly valuable. For example, for a committed white supremacist living in the USA, some significant moment ideals would be white people achieving racial purification and domination over a sufficiently large territory.

In the case of human rights, the significant moment ideals tend to relate to universal recognition and implementation either of specific rights or of human rights in general. Common-sense examples include ending all war, eradicating poverty, eradicating torture, slavery, and human trafficking, and achieving democracy in states that currently lack it.

Most, if not all, commonly recognized human rights might seem to be significant moment ideals since there is no human right (on the standard lists at least) of which we can say uncontroversially that, at present, it is adequately universally recognized and implemented.[27] But, actually, this fact about current conditions does not show that every commonly recognized human right is at present unrealizable and, hence, a significant moment ideal. This is because there is a difference between something's being presently *realized* or *unrealized* and something's being presently *realizable* or *unrealizable*. The fact that something is not presently realized does not mean that it is not presently realizable. Therefore, the lack of universal recognition of any given human right does not show that every human right is a significant moment ideal.

For example, the human right against torture *might* be presently realizable but simply not respected and protected as it should be. Of course, showing that the right against torture is presently realizable but unrealized would be difficult since the argument must rely on the counterfactual claim that, were we to do certain things that are feasible for us to do, we would achieve universal protection of this human right. To show that this counterfactual claim is credible, we might try to see, first, if the right against torture has ever previously been realized universally under conditions similar to our present conditions; second, if similar things to the right against torture, such as the right to physical security or the right to life, are presently realized; and third, if the kinds of conditions necessary to realize the right against torture,

---

[27] I thank Tom Parr for noting that we can speak of a human right to breathable air, and such a right, at present, would seem to be universally respected (albeit only by accident).

such as functioning legal mechanisms, political will, and respect for persons, are either in place or easy to achieve.

On all of these fronts, the current situation is bleak. But even that does not show that the human right against torture is not at present realizable. Sometimes only a small shift in attitudes is needed to radically alter moral practices in a short space of time. As Kwame Anthony Appiah points out in his discussion of moral revolutions, long-standing honour-driven practices such as duelling in Britain and foot-binding in China ended quite rapidly, but not through legal prohibition. (Duelling had been banned for two centuries before the English nobility finally abandoned it.) Rather, these practices ended within a generation or two once notions of honour changed so that these practices came to be seen as ridiculous or shameful.[28] Similarly, once the South African Apartheid regime finally dissolved, it apparently became difficult afterward to find anyone who would admit to having supported it. In similar fashion, it may be that, with small shifts in societies' perceptions of their honour, societies can achieve radical changes in attitudes toward fundamental human rights such as the right against torture.

Now, a critic might argue that, if certain human rights are indeed significant moment ideals, then this shows that they are not mundane, moral minima as the discussion in Section 1 of sustainability ideals implies they are. Rather, they are *significant* in the sense that their momentary realization would be highly demanding.

In reply, the significance of an event depends on its context. Even if all human rights are significant moment ideals for us as a human community, they are not all significant moment ideals for every society within the human community. For example, in some societies, human rights to democratic participation are not significant moment ideals, and we know this because those rights have been realized. Democracy is a mundane, realized system of government (however imperfect) in the societies where it now is practised. Those societies contrast with societies like Myanmar/Burma or South Africa under Apartheid where democracy seemed enduringly a significant moment ideal. Aung San Suu Kyi and the National League for Democracy struggled to achieve the significant moment of realizing a democracy in Burma until a glimmer of possibility began to shine in Aung San Suu Kyi's release in 2010, her election as an MP in 2012, and her election as State Councillor in 2016. Similarly, Nelson Mandela and the African National Congress (ANC) strove for decades without success to realize democracy in South Africa and only finally achieved the significant moment of a democratic election in 1994. Once such a significant human-rights moment was realized, then the issue of maintenance arose. The democracy in South Africa was not, and is not, perfect and never will be, but it may be judged by how well it satisfies a reasonable standard of democratic governance even though sustaining the requisite elements of that kind of governance at all times is most likely impossible.

---

[28] Appiah 2010.

In cases where a human rights objective is a significant moment ideal for some societies and a practical reality for others, that ideal can be action-guiding for the former since those societies can have some confidence that the objective is indeed possible for them to realize in principle even though it is not presently realizable. In cases where a human rights objective is a significant moment ideal for all of us, the ideal may still be action-guiding in a regulative sense as a benchmark against which we measure our efforts.

3. Limitlessly Progressive Ideals

A third, richer kind of ideal is a *limitlessly progressive ideal*. This kind of ideal is what it says on the box—it's limitlessly progressive. It is an ideal of potentially never-ending progress in the cultivation of its requisite elements. A limitlessly progressive ideal can take one of two forms. The first is analogous to a sustainability ideal in that both require ongoing engagement. But, whereas a sustainability ideal requires simply ongoing *maintenance* of the requisite elements, a limitlessly progressive ideal requires ongoing *development* of those elements (up to the point where no further development is possible in principle). A person's progress in cultivating a limitlessly progressive ideal can be measured along a continuum. The question to ask is: In general, does she continue to get better at the thing in question?

The content of such a limitlessly progressive ideal can start out as something objectively modest and undemanding, such as an ordinary adult's ambition to be a decent parent or a music student's ambition to play the violin competently. But, the content of the ideal necessarily increases in its objective demandingness over time as its pursuer improves in her performance. That said, from her subjective point of view, the demandingness of the ideal need not increase since it moves in lockstep with her development of its elements. In adopting a limitlessly progressive ideal of parenting, the ordinary adult not only aspires to sustain the ideal of being a decent parent, but also aspires to *improve* (continuously) to become, first, a good parent, then a very good parent, then a great parent, and then an exemplary parent, and so on. This continuum of parenting virtuosity might be boundless. An ordinary adult could presumably always be a slightly better parent than she is now being or has been before. She could always be a slightly better parent *in this moment* and she could be a slightly better parent *in general* across time than she is being now or has been.[29]

The second form of a limitlessly progressive ideal is analogous to a significant moment ideal. It may be understood as a succession of significant moment ideals, ascending like steps on a ladder. A parent can aspire to realize the one-off success of being a *very* good parent in a particular moment, just as a society can aspire to realize the significant moment of a democratic election. And, if the parent should happen to

---

[29] Even if there were an upper bound, it may lie beyond the present abilities and understanding of any actual parent.

succeed, then she can aspire to realize the one-off success of being a *great* parent, just as the society can aspire not only to have a democratic election, but also to set up one or two additional democratic institutions. Each of these latter ideals of one-off achievement is an improvement on what preceded it. The focus here is not on sustaining or *continuously* improving in the realization of the requisite elements, but on ensuring that each new realization of the elements is a degree better than the realization that preceded it.

Limitlessly progressive ideals do not apply to human rights without qualification. This is because human rights are not about either continuously improving the quality of people's lives or about step-by-step improvements without end. Human rights are not about human flourishing. Rather, they are about brute, basic suffering. They are about protecting us from the worst kinds of suffering, such as starvation, malnutrition, degrading treatment, torture, physical insecurity, abject poverty, crushing ignorance, and denial of legal and political recognition.

That said, we can talk about human rights in terms of *ongoing progress ideals* to realize minimal moral standards. In the case of human rights, such ongoing progress ideals are derivative of the significant moment ideals discussed in Section 2. They pick out the kinds of progress that we have to make to achieve the significant moments of realizing and implementing human rights. For example, in Myanmar/Burma, Aung San Suu Kyi and the NLD have been trying to continue to progress, little by little, in their efforts to expand the possibility for the realization of genuine democracy in their state, free from the influence of the military forces. At some points, progress has been possible; at others not. Similarly, the eradication of world poverty is a significant moment ideal that requires striving for ongoing progress, step by step, to improve the conditions of people who live in abject poverty. It also requires striving for ongoing progress in cultivating global political will to make poverty a central concern, and this includes changing the attitudes of well-off members of affluent societies toward the abject suffering of people in poverty around the world.

The action-guidingness of ongoing progress ideals of human rights tracks the action-guidingness of the significant moment ideals of human rights from which they derive. If a significant moment ideal is sufficiently well specified, then the steps needed to continue to strive to improve the conditions for its realization should be fairly transparent and, as such, able to guide us in our efforts to bring it closer to the realm of the realizable.

4. Just out of Reach Ideals

The final kind of ideal I will isolate is what I call *just out of reach ideals*. This kind of ideal does not pick out a grand project or event. Instead, it picks out something that is *just* beyond our present abilities. A just out of reach ideal is like the apple on the tree branch a metre above our head. It is like the First Class mark on the exam that we miss by two points, or tossing the basketball for a three-pointer and having it routinely bounce off the rim. In each case, success is in sight, but just beyond our present abilities.

In terms of their degree of unrealizability, just out of reach ideals have a low degree of unrealizability. Their content may be quite mundane in objective terms, such as scoring one of the baskets that we keep missing by an inch or being just a little more forgiving of someone who has harmed us than we are at present able to be. And, their content is also mundane in subjective terms, as it is 'just' out of reach. Being just a little more forgiving than we are at present able to be is not much more forgiving than we are now, and hence may well become realizable if we try hard enough.

When it comes to human rights, the momentary realization of many particular rights is a just out of reach ideal in many societies. Here, just out of reach ideals represent the final pushes to achieve genuine respect, protection, and fulfilment of given rights or sets of rights. In a society struggling to achieve democracy, the 'significant moment' of a genuine democratic election seems at present to be a just out of reach ideal. In South Africa, following Nelson Mandela's release from prison in 1990, the significant moment of a genuine democratic election became a just out of reach ideal for over three years as the ANC worked things through with the de Klerk government in what finally resulted in the democratic election of 1994. As this example suggests, a single event can be an ideal of more than one kind.

Similarly, a human right such as the right to health may be just out of reach for many developing countries when we look at those countries' abilities without the global community because those countries do not have the resources to realize that right for all of their people, but they are close to doing so. Or, rather, they do have the resources to realize the right to health for their population, but not while, at the same time, giving sufficient resources to education, security, corrective justice, and other valuable political, legal, and social commitments.

Since just out of reach ideals have a low degree of unrealizability, they are unproblematically action-guiding. We can strive to bring into the realm of the readily realizable that which is presently just beyond our reach. If our striving proves fruitless, then we were probably mistaken in thinking that the ideal was *just* out of reach.

5. Conclusion

This discussion has shown that, like most ordinary things of value, human rights have an inescapably ideal dimension. First, human rights are all, by nature, sustainability ideals. Their ongoing maintenance will probably forever elude us no matter how affluent, well-structured, and well-run our societies are. Second, many human rights are significant moment ideals in many places. The examples of a human right to democratic participation and a human right to health are the most obvious. As such, third, these rights have component parts that are ongoing progress ideals, such as the effort to continue to improve the chances to achieve democracy in a state that currently lacks it. Fourth, many human rights are just out of reach ideals for many societies given both those societies' present resource constraints and their political and economic weaknesses relative to the dominant societies on the world stage.

But, as this discussion has shown, all of these necessarily ideal elements of human rights do not show that they are impracticable. Despite their ideality, they retain their action-guidingness and their capacity to put pressure on governments and other bodies in virtue of, first, their modest, basic content as norms that pick out the brute moral minimum in decent treatment of human beings and consequently, second, the duties they generate to expand the feasibility of human rights protection.

References

Appiah, Kwame Anthony (2010), *The Honor Code: How Moral Revolutions Happen*. New York: Norton.

Brownlee, Kimberley (2010a), 'Moral Aspirations and Ideals', *Utilitas* 22: 3, 241–57.

Brownlee, Kimberley (2010b), 'Reasons and Ideals', *Philosophical Studies* 151: 3, 433–44.

Brownlee, Kimberley (2012), *Conscience and Conviction: The Case for Civil Disobedience*. Oxford: Oxford University Press.

Coady, C. A. J. (2008), *Messy Morality*. Oxford: Oxford University Press.

Geuss, Raymond (2001), *History and Illusion in Politics*. Cambridge: Cambridge University Press.

Gilabert, Pablo (2009), 'The Feasibility of Basic Socioeconomic Human Rights: A Conceptual Exploration', *Philosophical Quarterly* 59: 237, 559–81.

Gilabert, Pablo (2012), *From Global Poverty to Global Equality: A Conceptual Exploration*. Oxford: Oxford University Press.

Nickel, James (1982), 'Are Human Rights Utopian?', *Philosophy & Public Affairs* 11, 246–64.

Nickel, James (2007), *Making Sense of Human Rights*. Second edition. Oxford: Blackwell.

Sen, Amartya (2004), 'Elements of a Theory of Human Rights', *Philosophy & Public Affairs* 32, 315–56.

Shue, Henry (1996), *Basic Rights: Subsistence, Affluence, and US Foreign Policy*. Second edition. Princeton: Princeton University Press.

Tasioulas, John (2012), 'Towards a Philosophy of Human Rights', *Current Legal Problems* 65, 1–30.

9.1

In What Sense Should Respect for Human Rights Be Attainable?

A Response to Brownlee

Rowan Cruft

I

In her insightful and illuminating chapter, Kimberley Brownlee outlines four ways in which human rights are 'comprehensive, aspirational and presently unrealizable' *ideals*, rather than ordinary goals: human rights are 'sustainability ideals', 'significant moment ideals', 'ongoing progress ideals', and 'just out of reach ideals'.[1] Brownlee argues that because 'even the most uncontentious human rights are ideals of one or more of these kinds', it follows that 'feasibility is not a condition for human rights status'.[2] Instead, human rights can exist, and indeed guide action, even if they are not *feasible* or *realizable*: 'Even if a right were to fail all of the feasibility-related tests noted above'—namely, Shue's remediability requirement, Geuss's enforcement requirement, Sen's social influenceability requirement, and Nickel's reasonable burdens and implementability tests—'this would not threaten its status as a human right'.[3]

I begin by arguing that Brownlee's inference seems incorrect when construed simply as the claim that *because* human rights are ideals, they *cannot* be subject to feasibility conditions. Even though we should agree that human rights are ideals of the types outlined by Brownlee, this does not in itself entail that there can be no feasibility conditions on human rights. Feasibility conditions are compatible with the ideality of human rights as outlined by Brownlee.

I go on to consider an alternative, more complex interpretation of Brownlee's claim, an interpretation perhaps better supported by her chapter: that because human rights' ideality, as outlined by Brownlee, is compatible with human rights guiding action and bearing practical importance, there is *no reason* for the theorist to commit herself to

---

[1] Brownlee, pp. 315–17.   [2] Brownlee, p. 317.
[3] Brownlee, p. 315. Note that I follow Brownlee in using 'feasible' and 'realizable' interchangeably (Brownlee, note 13).

feasibility conditions on human rights. Assessing the plausibility of this claim will draw me into methodological debates relevant to the evaluation of the rival 'political' and 'orthodox' views of human rights: should the conceptual analysis of human rights closely reflect the legal and political practice? I will not take a stance on this question, but will show that a negative answer best supports Brownlee's complex argument against feasibility conditions.

In Section IV I introduce a suggested further argument of the simple form rejected at the start: because human rights are—I will propose—'ideals' in the specific sense of being natural rights held by all modern humans, their existence cannot be subject to feasibility conditions requiring that they be actually recognized or responded to (as advocated by 'rights externalists').[4] This simple argument can supplement Brownlee's complex one.

I end with a brief comment on Brownlee's analogy between human rights and parenthood.

II

First, I consider Brownlee's inference taken in an (uncharitably) simple way. Brownlee argues persuasively that human rights are 'sustainability ideals', by which she means that they require duty-bearers 'to sustain indefinitely a particular attitude, disposition, mode of conduct, state of affairs, or combination of those things'.[5] And she notes, again persuasively, that 'no government can sustain indefinitely the requisite combination of attitudes and practices necessary to ensure that those rights are always fully respected. There will inevitably be circumstances in which some people are either denied due process or illegitimately disenfranchised due to errors or prejudices'.[6] It is worth noting that for human rights, unlike some other ideals and ends with this 'sustainability' or 'infinite' aspect, the duties or requirements have a range of statuses: some are requirements of *non-violation* (e.g. duties not to create a secret police force to assassinate members of the opposition), others are requirements whose non-fulfilment would qualify as a *deficit* but perhaps not a *violation* (e.g. duties to set up open democratic systems that make it hard to create a secret police force), some are requirements on *individuals* and others on *states*.[7] Brownlee seems correct to note that many of these

---

[4] Darby 2004. My point will also undermine Geuss's 'enforcement' condition (Geuss 2001, p. 144).

[5] Brownlee, p. 317. Compare Sebastian Roedl's notion of an 'infinite end': 'Examples are: living healthy, honouring one's parents, and being true to one's word. In the representation of these ends there is no opposition of progressive and perfective aspect: as I am living healthy, I have lived healthy; as I am honouring my parents, I have honoured them; as I am being true to my word, I have been true to my word. Hence, these ends do not come to a limit. It is not that, at some time, I am done with living healthy, or honouring my parents, or being true to my word. My wanting to live healthy does not expire. I may give up on it, and so my wanting to live healthy may come to an end; I may no longer want that. But that it comes to this is not internal to its logical character. Therefore we may call such an end an infinite end' (Roedl 2010, pp. 147–8).

[6] Brownlee, p. 318.   [7] For discussion of the violation/deficit distinction, see Brems 2009.

requirements—of each type—will be 'sustainability' requirements that agents will, predictably, fail to fulfil sometimes. She also seems correct to note that 'all ordinary values and norms are sustainability ideals if their value lies at least partly in their ongoing maintenance rather than in a one-off instantiation'.[8] I think we can add that even one-off instantiation requirements (perhaps: to look after my neighbour's parcel on the one occasion it is left with me) will predictably go unfulfilled when considered as a global set (*someone* will fail to care for the parcel for *their* neighbour).

But human rights' status as sustainability ideals is compatible with their meeting feasibility requirements. For example, human rights can be remediable in Shue's sense—that is, they can protect people only against harms for which protection is possible, rather than protecting against 'ineradicable threats like eventual serious illness, accident, or death'[9]—yet nonetheless be ideals which duty-bearers will predictably fail to fulfil sometimes. Similarly, the predictability of occasional failures to meet the duties entailed by human rights is compatible with conceptual requirements demanding that human rights be protected by enforcement mechanisms (as Geuss implausibly demands), or be 'socially influenceable' in Sen's sense.[10] It is also compatible with requirements that human rights impose only 'reasonable burdens' and be 'implementable'.[11]

In response to this point, Brownlee writes: 'the consistent ongoing maintenance of the protection, implementation, enforcement, social influence, and reasonableness of the human right is, in all probability, unsustainable. Human rights protection is like the philosopher's ideal of truth and sound reasoning, which Coady observes will in all likelihood forever elude her.'[12] But it is surely a very strong feasibility requirement which requires that for something to be a human right, it must be possible for it to be implemented, enforced, and so on *across time without exception*, contrary to the predictability of occasional lapses. I do not think the feasibility requirements should be read in this way.[13]

Another way to put this point is that what it is 'possible' for me to do, as encapsulated in feasibility requirements like Shue's, should not be taken as limited by what I predictably will not do. There is a sense in which it *is* possible to be '*a good parent* in a comprehensive, ongoing sense', precisely because, as Brownlee notes, 'for ordinary adults, being a good parent at any one moment is readily realizable, as it is not very

---

[8] Brownlee, p. 320. One might try to argue that human rights are not 'sustainability ideals' because human rights demand, for example, merely that the risk of unfair trials be *mitigated* rather than that there be *no* unfair trials. But even on this weak interpretation, I would say that human rights are still 'sustainability ideals' because even mere mitigation involves 'ongoing maintenance' and hence will, predictably, not be pursued in some places at some times. Thanks to Adam Etinson for raising this issue.

[9] Shue 1996, p. 32.   [10] Geuss 2001, p. 144; Sen 2004, p. 329.

[11] Brownlee, p. 314, drawing on Nickel 2007, pp. 78–81.   [12] Brownlee, p. 320.

[13] It is worth noting, in response to Brownlee's reference to Coady, that if there are (as seems likely) some feasibility requirements on epistemic norms of sound reasoning and the pursuit of truth, they will not require that I be superhumanly capable of adhering to such norms across time without exception, contrary to the predictability of irrational moments.

demanding'.[14] Because it is possible at any one moment to do what the ideal good parent would do, it is in the relevant sense 'possible' to achieve the ideal of ongoing good parenthood, even though predictably nobody will achieve this across time. I suggest that feasibility requirements—whether on parenthood or human rights—demand the 'possibility' of achieving such ideals only in this sense. They do not require that attainment of the ideal across time without exception be a realistic, live option.

Thus for example Nickel's feasibility test maintains that '[a] necessary condition for the justification of a specific human right is the possibility of successfully implementing it in an ample majority of countries today'.[15] This, I suggest, does not require implementability now in a majority of countries *across time with no lapses*. A right could meet Nickel's feasibility requirement even if there will unavoidably be occasional lapses in its implementation within a majority of countries.

The same point can be made regarding the other forms of ideal Brownlee outlines: many human rights are 'significant moment ideals' picking out 'a significant, broadly specifiable event, objective, or experience that is presently unrealizable';[16] many are 'ongoing progress ideals' picking out 'the kinds of progress that we have to make to achieve the significant moments of realizing and implementing human rights';[17] and many are 'just out of reach ideals' picking out 'something that is *just* beyond our present abilities'.[18] But human rights' ideality in these senses is, I think, perfectly compatible with their being subject to feasibility requirements of the kinds outlined. This is partly because the kind of unrealizability referred to by Brownlee in describing the ideality of human rights is fairly weak: in Brownlee's sense of unrealizability, the achievement of democracy in Burma was unrealizable before 2010, and has begun to become realizable since Aung San Suu Kyi's release and then election in 2012.[19] By contrast, the kind of unrealizability that would make a human right fail Shue's remediability test is much stronger: under Shue's conception, a right would be unrealizable if it required 'social guarantees against every conceivable threat' or 'guarantees against ineradicable threats like eventual serious illness, accident, or death'.[20] Similarly, Nickel's implementability test involves a moderately strong conception of what it would be for a human right to be unrealizable (though not as strong as Shue's): an unrealizable right in Nickel's sense could not be successfully implemented in a majority of countries today.[21] When we focus on these different conceptions of unrealizability, we see that a human right could be unrealizable in Brownlee's sense while being realizable in Nickel's or Shue's. In general, it appears that the ideality of human rights to which Brownlee correctly draws attention is consistent with feasibility requirements on human rights.

---

[14] Brownlee, pp. 317 and 319.   [15] Nickel 2007, pp. 78–9.   [16] Brownlee, p. 321.
[17] Brownlee, p. 324.   [18] Brownlee, p. 324.
[19] Brownlee, p. 324. Note that this was written before more recent (2017) developments.
[20] Shue 1996, p. 32.   [21] Nickel 2007, pp. 78–9.

III

As I mentioned at the start, there is a different way to read Brownlee's argument. This is as the claim that because human rights can be action-guiding and practically important even while being ideals of the kinds outlined, there is no reason to add feasibility requirements on human rights' existence.

There are of course some kinds of infeasibility which would make human rights incapable of guiding action. For example, they cannot require the logically, metaphysically, or physically impossible. This seems to be part of Shue's point (human rights cannot guarantee against death), and can also be found in Miller and Tasioulas.[22]

But Brownlee seems correct to point out that human rights can be action-guiding even if what they require is impossible in weaker senses: even if, for example, we know that no state or individual will be able to fulfil human rights across time (because they are 'sustainability ideals'), or even if under current conditions human rights are unachievable although as conditions change they could become achievable (because they are 'just out of reach ideals'). Brownlee is persuasive in her claim that such ideality is compatible with human rights providing a practical guide to action. This, I venture, is due to the weakness of the conceptions of impossibility involved in such ideality. We can have no idea how to pursue the logically, metaphysically, or physically impossible, because we cannot form a practical idea of what such a goal would be.[23] (Or it might be that what it is to be impossible in one of these strong senses is precisely to be unpursuable.) In contrast, as Brownlee shows, we *can* pursue what we predictably will fail to attain, and what we cannot attain at the moment. Such 'ideal' goals can shape our intentions and plans—including concrete institutional plans such as the 'human rights action plans' found in many states.[24]

As I am interpreting her here, Brownlee's point seems in part to be that because human rights' ideality is compatible with their guiding action, there is no need for further feasibility requirements on human rights. We can imagine thinking the same thing about personal ideals: as a pianist, my ideal of pianistic achievement might be out of my reach but not physically impossible for me. The fact that I will, predictably, fall short of my ideal does not undermine its capacity to guide my action in terms of practising, exercises, attending lessons and masterclasses. Given its practicality, why should I limit this ideal by imposing further feasibility constraints? Why, for example, should I downgrade my conception of what I am trying to achieve to the kind of performance compatible with a 'reasonable' practising regime which allows time for

---

[22] See Miller 2015, p. 233 and Tasioulas 2015, p. 59. Tasioulas interestingly argues that a human right to romantic love would require something which is impossible in a broadly 'conceptual' sense: love motivated by *duty* (a duty correlative to a human right) cannot be romantic love (Tasioulas 2015, p. 59).

[23] A perfectly competitive market is physically impossible, I suspect; those who think we should aim to 'approximate' such a thing should take note.

[24] See the national action plans listed at: <http://www.ohchr.org/EN/Issues/PlansActions/Pages/PlansofActionIndex.aspx>.

other aspects of my life? This might leave me uninspired and under-motivated, while the more demanding 'infeasible' ideal works better.

But, as I hope this example shows, in certain circumstances there can be good reasons to introduce feasibility requirements on ideals, requirements that go beyond the requirements of logical-physical possibility needed for the ideal to be action-guiding. For instance, the importance of family or career commitments might give me good reason to limit my pianistic ideal. Similarly, there could be grounds to introduce feasibility constraints on human rights, even though absent such requirements their ideality in Brownlee's sense would still leave them as practical guides to action. For example, a theorist's methodology might legitimately ground extra feasibility constraints.

Suppose we follow Beitz in 'tak[ing] the doctrine and practice of human rights as we find them in international political life as the source materials for constructing a conception of human rights'.[25] If this doctrine and practice invokes feasibility constraints as part of the concept of human rights, then we have reason to accept such constraints. This, I suggest, is one way to understand Nickel's feasibility constraint: the international practice of human rights simply incorporates the requirement that it be possible to implement a human right in a majority of countries now; it incorporates a requirement that human rights not be 'mere showcase rights'.[26] By contrast, it is less clear that *natural rights* (as opposed to *human rights*) must be implementable in a majority of countries, because the discourses in which the concept 'natural rights' appears do not presuppose this—while discourses involving 'human rights' do.[27]

One way to challenge this is to reject the methodological commitment to fidelity to the way 'human rights' is used in the dominant international practice. One might reject this commitment because one is not interested in the concept found in international practice, perhaps because one prefers to focus on the face-value intension of the concept as 'the rights we have in virtue of being human'.[28] Or one might reject the commitment on the ground that it cannot be honoured, as Tadros suggests: 'the question "what is a human right?" has a non-stipulative answer only if there is a dominant discourse of human rights with a certain degree of coherence in its use of the concept of a human right. I suspect that there is no single dominant discourse.'[29] Alternatively, one might reject the commitment even though one thinks it *could* be honoured, on the grounds that the discourse does not pick out a normatively important concept—as Tadros also suggests: 'even if [philosophers could identify a dominant discourse of human rights, and identify what features of a right make it a human right in that

---

[25] Beitz 2009, p. 102.   [26] Nickel 2007, p. 81.

[27] My claim about natural rights is debatable. Some, such as Tasioulas, add feasibility constraints on human rights conceived as natural rights (Tasioulas 2015, pp. 50–1—see condition (iii) in the schema in this section), and one might see Locke's 'provisos' as constraints that prevent our natural property rights from being excessively burdensome on their correlative duty-bearers. But such constraints do not seem essential to natural rights theory. Thanks again to Adam Etinson for discussion.

[28] Griffin 2008, p. 2.   [29] Tadros 2015, p. 443.

discourse], there would be little point in doing it. For the way in which we draw the distinction between human rights and other rights lacks normative implications.'[30]

The latter claim can be questioned. If Rawls is correct and human rights are grounded in international public reason in a way that other rights are not, then the distinction between human rights and other rights will be relevant to the acceptability, legitimacy, or enforceability of complaints about a state's treatment of its citizens. Complaints framed in terms of human rights will be legitimate, and enforcement to support such complaints might be legitimate, given the fact that human rights are matters of public reason, accessible to any reasonable peoples. Complaints framed in other terms—e.g. in the Lockean terms of rights conferred by a Christian god—will not be legitimate or enforceable internationally in the same way.[31] Similarly, if Raz is correct then a right's being a human right entails that its violation is a legitimate matter of international concern, where its being some other type of right would not.[32] Each 'political' approach has normative implications. Further, either approach might well bring with it some feasibility constraints beyond the most minimal. For example, rights whose violation 'is equally condemned by both reasonable liberal peoples and decent hierarchical peoples' should not normally, I think, place unreasonable burdens on correlative duty-bearers.[33] Such excessively demanding rights would be unlikely to be matters of public reason.

I have outlined two routes taking us to additional feasibility constraints on human rights. First, one might simply observe usage in the dominant practices of human rights and note that such constraints exist. Secondly, one might infer from the special normative role of human rights within such practices that, to play this role, human rights must be subject to some feasibility constraints. There is a range of ways to challenge the second approach (e.g. by questioning the alleged role etc., as Tadros outlines). The simplest challenge—and it applies to both approaches—is methodological: why should we take our conception of human rights from the practice? Why trust 'ordinary usage' in this way? Of course, a deeply radical departure from usage (e.g. one on which 'human rights' had the same referent as 'aeroplane') would just involve changing the subject. But for 'human rights' there seems to be a range of usages, including the historical link to natural rights, and it is unclear why we should prioritize that which is currently dominant.

I suggest that to support her rejection of feasibility requirements, Brownlee would benefit from some such a methodological move. The international practice does seem to involve certain feasibility requirements, and this is not surprising given its genesis in the compromises of international treaty-making: often, states will not want to sign up to rights which are not in some sense readily feasible. To reject such requirements, Brownlee would do well, I think, to explain why we are better off with a conception of human rights that is not specially tied to the international practice and its limitations.

---

[30] Tadros 2015, pp. 443–4.   [31] Or at least this is my reading of Rawls 1999.
[32] Raz 2010.   [33] Rawls 1999, p. 79.

I cannot develop this argument myself here, but I think such an approach can be made to work—especially given, as Tadros notes, our unclarity about whether international law and politics constitute the dominant discourse here (what about national human rights laws? what about the 'ordinary person' and their conception of human rights as important rights borne by humans?).

In itself, a defence of something other than the 'political' conception of human rights will not be enough to deliver Brownlee's conclusion that human rights need not be subject to demanding feasibility conditions. For within, say, an 'orthodox' or natural rights approach there might seem to be moral reasons to introduce some extra feasibility requirements (e.g. in order to limit human rights' demandingness)[34] or there might seem to be conceptual reasons to do this (e.g. if human rights must be suitable for legalization). Nonetheless, in my view Brownlee's argument, under the interpretation developed in this section, has some force if human rights are natural rights. It has force in that it makes it unclear how to answer the following question: given that human rights can be action-guiding even though they are ideals of the kind Brownlee outlines, why should we take human rights to be subject to additional feasibility requirements beyond the minimum requirements necessary for them to be action-guiding?[35] 'Political' conceptions give some persuasive answers to this question (appealing to conditions built into human rights' political role), but if human rights are simply natural moral rights, it is less clear how to answer it. Perhaps it can be answered—e.g. by appealing to the moral costs of burdensome duties—but Brownlee's argument shows us that it needs an answer, and simply to claim the existence of such extra feasibility requirements is not to answer it.

IV

There is one type of feasibility requirement on human rights which I am sure we should reject: the strong 'rights externalist' view that to qualify as a human right, such a right has to be recognized by members of the society in which it exists.[36] Geuss's requirement that human rights be actually enforced entails fulfilment of the rights externalist's requirement, for a right cannot be enforced if it is not recognized. Or at least it cannot be enforced *as a right* if it is not recognized. Therefore, in rejecting the view that human rights must be recognized if they are to exist, I reject Geuss's actual enforcement requirement.[37]

Why do I reject this? In this case, I do not think we need an argument against it. Rather, simply asserting its negation is persuasive: one of the distinctive features of human rights is that one holds them if one is a human (or at least if one is a contemporary

---

[34] See note 27.
[35] See also the related debate about whether incompatible rights are logically possible (Waldron 1989).
[36] See e.g. Darby 2004.   [37] See Geuss 2001, pp. 144–5.

human),[38] whether or not they are recognized within one's society. Thus political prisoners in contemporary North Korea hold human rights not to be imprisoned even if nobody in North Korea believes this—not even the prisoners themselves following 're-education' programmes. If human rights are those we hold 'in virtue of being human', then we will hold them as all other humans do, even if our particular branch of humanity denies this.

There is a sense in which human rights' recognition-independence involves a form of ideality, but not the form Brownlee highlights. It is the ideality of normative phenomena whose existence is in some respect distinct from their place on concrete legal lists or from their embodiment in legal judgements. We can infer directly from this kind of ideality to a rejection of Geuss's actual enforcement requirement and the rights externalism it entails.

V

I want to end by discussing parenthood and human rights as different forms of ideal. Brownlee's notion of good parenthood as a 'sustainability ideal' and a 'limitlessly progressive ideal' initially struck me as implausible. A parent who aimed at faultlessly good parenting, or who kept aiming at being a better parent, struck me as unattractive in rather the same manner as Wolf's moral saints.[39] Doesn't a child benefit by seeing their parents' faults and weaknesses, or at least by seeing that their parents have some faults and weaknesses even if the full extent of these are hidden? In response, Brownlee might counter that if a child benefits from parenting that reveals frailties, then the best parents will reveal such frailties. But if so, good parenting no longer looks like such a hard ideal to attain.

This line of reasoning worried me at first, but I am not sure how problematic it is for Brownlee. The kind of ideal parenting that avoids the costs of saintliness is still very hard to attain invariably over time, and so even this 'frailty-revealing' parenthood might fit Brownlee's conception of parenthood as an ideal.

In any case, no such qualms seem relevant to human rights as an ideal. There is no sense, I suggest, in which partial violation of human rights is valuable in the same way that a parent's revealing their faults can be valuable.

It follows that respect for human rights really can qualify as an ideal in the ways Brownlee outlined. I argued in Section IV that we should reject social recognition or actual enforcement as conditions on human rights. But, as outlined in Sections II and III, whether to reject further feasibility conditions depends—among other things[40]—on methodological questions about the aim of our theory.[41]

---

[38] See debates about whether human rights are held universally across time, or simply 'synchronically' under modern conditions universality' (Tasioulas 2010, pp. 31–6).

[39] Wolf 1982.   [40] See notes 27 and 34, and accompanying main text.

[41] Many thanks to Kimberley Brownlee and Adam Etinson for helpful discussion.

References

Beitz, Charles R. 2009. *The Idea of Human Rights* (Oxford: Oxford University Press).

Brems, Eva 2009. 'Human Rights: Minimum and Maximum Perspectives', *Human Rights Law Review* 9, 349–72.

Darby, Derrick 2004. 'Rights Externalism', *Philosophy and Phenomenological Affairs* 68, 620–34.

Geuss, Raymond 2001. *History and Illusion in Politics* (Cambridge: Cambridge University Press).

Griffin, James 2008. *On Human Rights* (Oxford: Oxford University Press).

Miller, David 2015. 'Joseph Raz on Human Rights: A Critical Appraisal', pp. 232–44 in Rowan Cruft, S. Matthew Liao, and Massimo Renzo (eds), *Philosophical Foundations of Human Rights* (Oxford: Oxford University Press).

Nickel, James 2007. *Making Sense of Human Rights*. Second edition (Oxford: Blackwell).

Rawls, John 1999. *The Law of Peoples* (Cambridge, Mass.: Harvard University Press).

Raz, Joseph 2010. 'Human Rights in the Emerging World Order', *Transnational Legal Theory* 1, 31–47.

Roedl, Sebastian 2010. 'The Form of the Will', pp. 138–60 in Sergio Tenenbaum (ed.), *Desire, Good, and Practical Reason: Classical and Contemporary Perspectives* (Oxford: Oxford University Press).

Sen, Amartya 2004. 'Elements of a Theory of Human Rights', *Philosophy & Public Affairs* 32, 315–56.

Shue, Henry 1996. *Basic Rights: Subsistence, Affluence, and U.S. Foreign Policy*. Second edition (Princeton: Princeton University Press).

Tadros, Victor 2015. 'Rights and Security for Human Rights Sceptics', pp. 442–58 in Rowan Cruft, S. Matthew Liao, and Massimo Renzo (eds), *Philosophical Foundations of Human Rights* (Oxford: Oxford University Press).

Tasioulas, John 2010. 'On the Nature of Human Rights', pp. 17–60 in Gerhard Ernst and Jan-Christoph Heilinger (eds), *The Philosophy of Human Rights* (Berlin: de Gruyter).

Tasioulas, John 2015. 'On the Foundations of Human Rights', pp. 45–70 in Rowan Cruft, S. Matthew Liao, and Massimo Renzo (eds), *Philosophical Foundations of Human Rights* (Oxford: Oxford University Press).

Waldron, Jeremy 1989. 'Rights in Conflict', *Ethics* 99, 503–19.

Wolf, Susan 1982. 'Moral Saints', *Journal of Philosophy* 79, 419–39.

10

The Nature of Violations of the Human Right to Subsistence

Elizabeth Ashford

There are two centrally important but divergent aspects of human rights discourse. The first is the concept of a human rights violation, as marking out a boundary that must not be crossed. Human rights violations constitute treatment that is morally intolerable, both in the sense that it is completely morally unacceptable and in the sense that it ought not be tolerated; people ought to have extraordinarily strong protection against human rights violations, and a ban on them is rightfully juridically enforced. Thus, the duty not to violate human rights is held to have a peremptory, "sacred" moral force.[1]

As Eva Brems argues, while this concept of a violation has a central juridical role, it is also a deep feature of prevalent thinking about human rights:

...the concept of violation does not only appeal to lawyers. Likewise, in ethical and political human rights discourse, the need is felt to determine a borderline. Whoever crosses that line will be labeled a human rights violator. It seems that the legal concept of a human rights violation reflects the essence of our mental image of human rights: they express what is most valuable, most sacred and should not be touched upon.[2]

In addition to the concept of a human rights violation, there is an important aspirational and progressive aspect to human rights discourse; while the concept of a violation marks out a borderline that must not be crossed, the aspirational aspect views the achievement of human rights as a horizon line to which to aspire and towards which to gradually progress.[3] This second aspect of human rights discourse is particularly associated with socio-economic rights, which are described in international human rights documents as progressively realizable.

The strictly mandatory and the aspirational aspects of human rights discourse are often held to be in deep tension with one another. The proliferation worry about the introduction of socio-economic human rights into the corpus of human rights has

---

[1] The term "sacred" is used by both Brems and Cranston, in the passages cited herein.
[2] Brems 2009, p. 350.   [3] Ibid., pp. 354–6.

tended to be motivated by the concern that socio-economic rights are really goals, since they lack the peremptory moral force of genuine human rights. Accordingly, it is argued, the effect of their acknowledgement as human rights is to dilute the currency of human rights. Maurice Cranston, for example, in his classic critique of social and economic rights, argues that these so-called "rights" actually constitute ideals, and therefore belong to a fundamentally different moral category from moral rights: "However else one might choose to define moral rights, they are plainly not ideals or aspirations."[4] He infers that by including social and economic "rights" into the corpus of human rights, the "effect may even be to bring the whole concept of human rights into disrepute". Cranston's account of genuine human rights appeals to the concept of them as marking out a "sacred" moral threshold, which must not be crossed: "There are certain deeds which should never be done, certain freedoms which should never be invaded, some things which are supremely sacred." This language echoes Brems's account of the notion of a human rights violation as constituting a "borderline" which marks out "what is...most sacred and should not be touched upon".[5]

In fact, the aspirational aspect of human rights can be accommodated without diluting the force of the notion of a human rights violation, as long as these two aspects of international human rights discourse are carefully distinguished. This requires being clear about when the label of "violation" is applicable and when it is not, and identifying human rights violations in such a way as to ensure that the notion retains its urgent moral force. By clearly differentiating the concept of a human rights violation from that of a horizon line to which to aspire we can combine both concepts within human rights discourse without conflating the two.

Accordingly, even if various socio-economic rights are goals, as long as their status as goals is clear they can be accommodated into the corpus of human rights without undermining the force of those human rights that mark out a moral threshold that must not be crossed. On the other hand, if some socio-economic human rights are taken to be on a par with classic negative human rights, such as the right against torture, it is important to show that there is a duty not to violate these socio-economic rights that has an urgent and peremptory moral force comparable to the duty not to violate classic negative rights.

As Allen Buchanan has argued, the *term* "human rights" is not univocal. In particular, it can refer either to fundamentally important moral rights held by every person simply in virtue of their universal moral status, or to those rights that are recognized in the international practice of human rights and conferred by international law.[6] It would be an unwarranted philosophical prejudice to assume that the latter must always be grounded on and mirror the former. The latter may have a range of justifications, including the propagation of ideals and the promotion of morally important goals. In the preamble to the United Nations Charter, its stated purpose is *both* "to reaffirm faith in fundamental human rights" and to promote "social progress and better standards

---

[4] Cranston 1973, p. 68.   [5] Brems 2009, p. 350.   [6] Buchanan 2010, pp. 680–1.

of life in larger freedom".[7] As Beitz argues, insisting that international human rights declarations ought to limit themselves to affirming fundamental moral human rights would both diminish and misrepresent the aspirations of international human rights doctrine.[8]

Nevertheless, there is a widely held assumption that there are *some* fundamentally important universal moral rights that impose binding obligations that are owed to every person, non-fulfilment of which constitutes a human rights violation and is *ipso facto* morally intolerable. For ease of exposition, I refer to these as "fundamental human rights". It is also accepted by most jurists that these fundamental moral rights play a central role in the grounding of at least some of the human rights recognized in international law, such as the right against torture.

When fundamental moral rights do underpin certain of the human rights conferred in international law, it is indeed the case that the latter ought to be analogues of the former such that, insofar as the practice fails to adequately recognize and implement the duties not to violate those fundamental human rights, it fails to be minimally just. This is a key aspect of the role played by fundamental moral human rights in critiquing the existing practice of human rights.

The question this chapter addresses is whether or not the human right to subsistence, which is widely internationally recognized, is underpinned by a fundamental human right, which has a peremptory moral force parallel to that of classic negative human rights such that the persistence of severe poverty should be classified as a human rights violation. While it is uncontroversial that torture or genocide, for example, constitute human rights violations, the claim that the persistence of severe poverty constitutes a human rights violation is much more controversial.

A central argument against taking the right to subsistence to be a fundamental human right, on a par with classic "negative" human rights such as the right against torture, is that it does indeed fail to impose peremptory, binding obligations. Accordingly, it is argued, it is more plausibly taken to constitute a goal, or perhaps a "right–goal hybrid",[9] than a fundamental human right. Moreover, as I contend, many defences of the claim that the right to subsistence is a fundamental human right, on a par with classic negative human rights such as the right against torture, have failed to offer an account of the duties not to violate it according to which they have the same kind of mandatory force as that of duties not to violate classic negative human rights. It is striking that even defenders of a basic human right to subsistence do not in fact tend to apply the term "violation" to the persistence of severe poverty.

I argue here that there is a fundamental moral human right to subsistence, and that the ongoing allowing and infliction of severe poverty constitutes a human rights violation that demands abolition. Thus, while I agree with Cranston's emphasis on the importance of clearly distinguishing mandatory human rights from goals, I disagree

---

[7] Preamble to the United Nations Charter, 1945.   [8] Beitz 2003, pp. 40 and 44; Beitz 2009.
[9] Nickel 2010.

with his analysis of the status of the right to subsistence. I also argue that the existing international practice of human rights fails to adequately recognize some of the duties not to violate this right, and some of the respects in which the right is being violated.

Section 1 briefly analyses the content of duties to respect the right to subsistence. I then turn in Section 2 to an analysis of some central features of the notion of a human rights violation. As I argue, one conceptual strait-jacket that should be avoided is that of understanding the concept of a human rights violation in such a way as to rule out *ex ante* the possibility that it could be applicable to contemporary social contexts involving hugely complicated large-scale social interaction. We should allow for the possibility of structural human rights violations, which consist not in discrete harmful actions or omissions perpetrated by specific agents against specific victims, but in ongoing patterns of behaviour of a vast number of agents that avoidably and unjustifiably inflict or allow extremely severe harms to a large number of victims. I call these "structural human rights violations", where the term "structure" refers to patterned interactions. The challenge, then, is to specify an account of human rights violations that retains their special moral force while avoiding arbitrarily restricting them to small-scale social contexts. Accordingly, I defend some core criteria by which to determine whether the notion of a human rights violation is applicable, and show how these criteria apply to structural human rights violations that arise in large-scale social contexts. In the case of each of these criteria, I discuss their implications for how the duty not to violate the right to subsistence should be understood, if it is to constitute an fundamental human right to which the notion of "violation" is genuinely applicable.

Section 3 defends Cranston's claim that a constraint on fundamental human rights is that the universal fulfilment of duties to respect the rights is a practicable demand (at least under standard circumstances). Following Cranston's terminology, I call this "the practicability constraint". As I argue, however, one important complexity is that in order to allow for the possibility of structural human rights violations, the practicability constraint should not be interpreted as requiring that the universal respecting of the right is immediately achievable. I illustrate this with the example of the ending of slavery.

Section 4 argues that in order for the right to subsistence to meet the practicability constraint, responsibility for fulfilling the primary duties to respect it cannot be confined to the right-holders' own government. I contend, then, that in order for the right to subsistence to constitute a fundamental human right, to which the notion of a human rights violation is genuinely applicable—with a peremptory moral force parallel to that of classic "negative" human rights—the primary addressees must include members of the international community: affluent nations, multinational corporations and global social institutions, and individual agents in affluent countries. This account of the right to subsistence diverges from the way it is understood in international law, according to which the primary addressees of the right are the right-holders' own governments, and the role of the international community is to fulfil secondary, back-up duties "to step in when states default".

Section 5 defends the claim that the ongoing allowing and infliction of severe poverty should be classified as a human rights violation, and that members of the international community should indeed be taken to share responsibility for this violation. Section 5.i offers a morally minimal substantive account of the kind of treatment of persons that has all the features of a human rights violation outlined in part 1. And Section 5.ii argues that the ongoing allowance and infliction of severe poverty, by members of the international community as well as by right-holders' own governments, constitutes just such treatment.

I aim to show, then, that while Cranston is right that fundamental human rights must meet the practicability constraint, we should not infer from this that the right to subsistence is a goal or aspiration rather than a fundamental human right. Rather, we should take it to belong to the class of fundamental human rights that constitute "everyone's minimum reasonable demand *against the rest of humanity*" (my italics). The ongoing shared failure by the international community as well as right-holders' own governments to implement the institutional reforms needed to end the allowing and infliction of severe poverty constitutes a structural human rights violation that demands abolition.

1. The Content of Duties to Respect the Human Right to Subsistence

I take the substance of the right to subsistence to be an adequate opportunity to obtain the means of subsistence. This is a claim to an opportunity to earn a subsistence income, or, if one is unable to do so (because of factors such as disability or natural disasters, or because opportunities to earn a subsistence income are currently unavailable), to be provided with the means of subsistence.

I take the duties to respect the right to subsistence to comprise the negative correlative duty not to actively deprive persons of their means of subsistence, and two positive duties: the duty to ensure that persons have the opportunity to earn a subsistence income in the first place (to a reasonable degree of security), and the duty to provide the means of subsistence to those who are unable to earn for themselves a subsistence income. Universal compliance with these duties would end severe poverty, understood as lacking a realistic opportunity to obtain the means of subsistence.

The duties to respect a human right, non-fulfilment of which in itself constitutes a human rights violation, can be termed "primary duties". By contrast, secondary duties are duties to protect against, or remedy the effect of, violations of these primary duties. (I offer a fuller analysis of this distinction in Section 2.) In the case of the right to subsistence, it imposes secondary duties to enforce a prohibition on violations of the negative duty not to deprive people of their means of subsistence, and duties to aid those who have been deprived of the means of subsistence by other agents. However, unless we assume that all instances in which persons lack the opportunity to obtain the means of subsistence are a result of their having been actively deprived of it by other agents, then (on the assumption that the substance of the right is an opportunity to obtain the means of subsistence) it has to impose among its *primary* duties the positive duty to provide people with the means of subsistence. Otherwise, it cannot meaningfully be held to be a right *to subsistence*. The duty to provide the means of subsistence to those unable to earn for themselves a subsistence income because of severe disability, for example, is a primary duty.

In this respect, my analysis of the duties differs from Shue's tripartite analysis of the duties imposed by human rights. Shue takes the duty to respect human rights to be the duty to avoid depriving right-holders of the substance of the right; in subsequent writing, he explicitly affirms that such duties can be termed duties "to respect" the right.[10] The other duties are back-up positive duties, to protect persons against such deprivations, and "to aid the deprived". In the case of classic "negative" human rights such as the right against assault, the duty to aid the deprived is always a back-up duty to aid those who have been deprived of the substance of the right (such as freedom from assault) by other agents—in this case, assault victims. However, in the case of the right to subsistence, those deprived of the means of subsistence includes both those who have been deprived of their means of subsistence by other agents, and those who lack the means of subsistence without having been wrongfully deprived of it by other agents (such as those unable to earn a subsistence income because of severe disability). On my analysis, while the former duty of aid is a back-up duty, the duty to aid those who lack the means of subsistence as a result of natural factors is a *primary* positive duty. I contend, then, there is one important respect in which the right to subsistence differs from classic so-called "negative" human rights such as the right against torture: it imposes positive duties among its primary duties.

Of course, the extent to which deprivations of subsistence are to be attributed to the failure (principally by social institutions) to fulfil positive duties to supply adequate opportunities to obtain the means of subsistence, and the extent to which they are to be attributed to social institutions' (and transnational corporations' etc.) actively depriving persons of such opportunities, is hotly debated. It is certainly plausible that a great deal of existing severe poverty does result from persons' having been actively deprived of the means of subsistence by other agents. However, the assumption that *all* existing deprivations of subsistence result from violations of the negative duty not to deprive persons of the means of subsistence relies either on contentious empirical assumptions, or on a philosophically contentious analysis of the content of the negative duty. Thomas Pogge's argument that the global institutional order is responsible for actively inflicting most existing severe poverty[11] has been criticized on both these fronts.[12] In order to avoid contentious assumptions, I take the right to

---

[10] "I am delighted to accept the re-naming of the first, most negative duty as the duty to respect" (Shue 1984, p. 84).
[11] Pogge 2002.   [12] For example, Patten 2005; Tan 2010; Hayward 2008.

subsistence to impose positive duties among its primary duties, and assume that achieving the ending of severe poverty (understood as lacking the opportunity to obtain the means of subsistence) requires the fulfilment of non-derivative positive duties as well as negative duties.

2. Features of Duties not to Violate Human Rights

i. The corresponding rights constitute rock-bottom moral claims

The peremptory force of the notion of human rights violations principally belongs with a conception of human rights as, in Cranston's words, "of paramount moral importance". As Henry Shue puts it, basic human rights constitute "the morality of the depths" and "everyone's minimum reasonable demand against the rest of humanity".[13] Shue's account of these rights as "the lower limits of tolerable human conduct" evokes a minimal moral threshold that must not be crossed, and echoes Brems's account of human rights as constituting a "borderline" that expresses "what is most valuable, most sacred, and should not be touched upon".

One central aspect of the paramount moral importance of many (on some accounts, of all) fundamental human rights is the significance of the interests they protect; such rights are widely held to protect interests essential to a minimally decent human life. Conversely, violations of them constitute the kind of treatment that is liable to mar or altogether destroy persons' lives. However, it should be emphasized that it is not the magnitude of the harms alone that marks out human rights violations, but the fact that the inflicting or allowing of these harms constitutes *treatment* of individuals that is morally intolerable.

As Griffin points out, protecting someone's most basic interest in staying alive, or in not suffering severe brain damage, could require mounting a hugely expensive crash programme to find a cure for a very rare disease from which the person is suffering.[14] A society's refusal to fund such a programme would not plausibly constitute morally intolerable treatment of the person concerned, even though it would predictably result in the person's death or brain damage.

In order to justify the claim that a form of treatment constitutes a human rights violation, we need to show that the allowing or infliction of an extremely severe harm is fundamentally morally unjustifiable. Indeed, the proliferation objection is often

---

[13] Shue 1996, p. 19. My use of the term "fundamental human rights" closely resembles Shue's term "basic rights", but my focus in this chapter is slightly different. Shue defines basic rights as those rights enjoyment of which is essential to the enjoyment of any other human right, and argues that the right to subsistence is indeed a basic right. (I have defended a development of this argument, in Ashford 2009). My focus here, by contrast, is on showing that the positive and negative duties to respect the right to subsistence have a moral force parallel to that of duties to respect the right against torture. As I argued in Section 1, the category of positive duties to respect the right to subsistence, non-fulfilment of which violates the right, does not easily fit with Shue's tripartite division of duties.

[14] Griffin 2008, p. 98.

directed at defences of economic and social rights that focus on the importance of the interests or capabilities that would be protected by recognition of such rights, and fail to give sufficient weight to justifying the duties the rights would impose.

ii. Duties not to violate human rights constitute a minimum core of obligations

Even when we limit our focus to fundamentally important human rights, a further central aspect of marking out the concept of a violation is to draw a distinction between the duty to respect such rights, non-fulfilment of which in itself constitutes a violation, and the other duties the rights impose. Following Nickel's useful terminology, these other duties can be called duties to *realize* human rights. As he argues, the fulfilment of these duties is needed to "make the right real", by making "the protection or remedy effectively available to the right-holders".[15]

As Brems points out, the duty not to violate a human right is binary: either a right is violated, or it is not. The duty not to violate a human right constitutes a bottom line (in Shue's phrase, "the lower limits of tolerable human conduct"), which must not be crossed. By contrast, the duty to realize a human right is progressively achievable. As Nickel argues, the full realization of a right is an idealized level of realization. It thus functions as a horizon line to which to aspire.

Nickel suggests that the right to subsistence might be best understood as a "right–goal hybrid", that imposes both progressively realizable obligations and a minimum core set of peremptory obligations. It may have enough mandatory elements for the concept of "right" to be applicable.[16] This nicely fits the move in international law to integrate the injunction to achieve the progressive realization of the right to subsistence with a violations approach that identifies a "minimum core [of] obligations to ensure the satisfaction of, at the very least, minimum essential levels of [for example] . . . essential foodstuffs, of essential primary health care, of basic shelter and housing, or of the most basic forms of education" (Brems 2009, p. 355).

Currently, the concept of progressive realization is only applied in the realm of socio-economic rights. It should be emphasized, though, that classic negative human rights also impose duties that are progressively achievable, in addition to the duties not to violate the right. For example, while the duty not to violate the right against torture is a peremptory duty that can and should always be complied with,[17] the duty to realize the right against torture is progressively achievable; there are always further measures that could be taken to improve the degree of security against torture enjoyed by right-holders. There is thus an important respect in which classic negative rights are "progressively realizable". This implies that the label "right–goal hybrid" could also be applied to these rights. Conversely, insofar as socio-economic rights are held to impose a minimum core set of obligations that constitute a bottom line, the discourse of

---

[15] James Nickel, paper presented at Festschrift Conference for James Nickel, Duke University.
[16] Nickel 2010.
[17] At very least barring exceptional circumstances; I discuss this further in Section 2.iv.

violations can be applied to such rights.[18] In comparing the deontic force of these rights with that of the right to subsistence, the central question is whether or not there is a minimum core of obligations imposed by the human right to subsistence with the same peremptory moral force as that of duties not to violate classic human rights.

iii. Duties not to violate human rights constitute primary obligations

A key aspect of the distinction between the duty to respect human rights and the other duties human rights impose is that the former are primary duties, whereas the latter are secondary duties. Primary duties are duties the fulfilment of which constitutes the right's being respected, and non-fulfilment of which constitutes the right's violation. Those who violate the primary duties imposed by rights are responsible for the actual violation of the right, and can be identified as the perpetrators of the violation. Secondary duties are duties to implement a range of measures to protect against or remedy the effects of non-fulfilment of the primary duties.

Thus, responsibility for actually violating human rights is confined to the agents who violate the right's primary duties. Only these agents are appropriately labelled as the violators of the right. Other agents may be held responsible for failing to adequately fulfil secondary duties to protect against such violations and so on, but they do not share responsibility for actually violating the right, and so the label of human rights violator is not applicable to them.

Secondary duties can be understood as back-up duties, which arise because other agents are liable to fail to fulfil a right's primary duties. This is depicted by the image of "successive waves of duties" imposed by human rights, to which Waldron and Shue appeal.[19] If all the primary duties were fulfilled, the right would be universally respected. Secondary duties are back-up duties to protect right-holders against violations perpetrated by other agents, or to aid those who have already suffered them. Thus, primary duties are tied to first-order assignments of responsibility. If the primary duties were fully complied with, no other duties would arise.

As Shue points out, unless the duty to respect human rights is enforced, it is entirely predictable that rights violations will occur. Simply reminding people of their duty not to violate human rights, without actually enforcing such a duty, would be irresponsibly utopian. An adequate account of human rights must therefore also recognize a duty to protect persons against being deprived of the substance of their rights by other agents, by enforcing the duty to respect the right. This is a back-up duty, to protect right-holders against violations of the right. It arises because agents cannot simply be trusted and relied on to comply with their duties not to violate human rights.

The third type of duty is the duty to aid those who have been deprived of the substance of their right by other agents. While this duty belongs to the third wave of

---

[18] As Brems argues, a violations approach to socio-economic rights is increasingly being used: "First promoted in academic circles, the violations approach to economic, social and cultural rights has been backed by the CESCR" (Brems 2009, p. 357).

[19] Shue 1996, p. 166; Waldron 1993, p. 25.

back-up duties, from the point of view of the right-holders it is of the utmost urgency, since the fulfilment of this duty is all that stands between them and death or some other drastic and irremediable harm. As Shue's analysis makes clear, then, duties that come under each of the three categories are of enormous moral significance.

Nevertheless, the question of whether a duty is classified as a primary duty not to violate a human right, or as a back-up duty, remains a centrally important issue. With respect to the right to subsistence, it makes a significant difference whether the duties it imposes on affluent countries are taken to be back-up duties to facilitate or enforce the primary duties, or whether affluent nations are held to share responsibility for fulfilling the primary duties themselves.

Agents who violate the primary duties have primary moral responsibility for the victims' plight, and primary remedial responsibility to aid the victims, where this is possible. By contrast, secondary duties are duties to protect against or remedy the effects of violations perpetrated by other agents.

Primary duties not to violate human rights have a special moral stringency. Indeed, David Miller argues that the secondary duty to secure the right to subsistence when the agents assigned responsibility for fulfilling the primary duties have defaulted on those duties should be seen as a humanitarian duty, rather than a duty of justice. He argues that an additional duty of *justice* cannot be imposed on an agent merely because other agents fail to discharge their duties of justice (Miller 2011, pp. 241–4).

One reason why back-up duties are considered less stringent than primary duties is the view that it is unreasonable to take agents to be under demanding duties as a result of the wrongful behaviour of others; primary duties have a particular urgency in part because they correspond to a first-order assignment of responsibility. There is indeed a widespread perception among agents in affluent countries that it would be unreasonable to undertake demanding duties to remedy the plight of those suffering severe poverty when the primary responsibility for their plight lies with their own government.

If, by contrast, citizens in affluent countries are held to share responsibility for non-fulfilment of the primary duties imposed by the right to subsistence then, in Pogge's words, "the buck stops with us". Pogge's approach is to argue that there is a coercively imposed global institutional order the operation of which is responsible for actively inflicting most existing severe poverty. A further way of showing that "the buck stops with us" is to show that we share responsibility for fulfilling the primary positive duties imposed by the right to subsistence.

Violations of the primary duties carry a special moral opprobrium. Agents who have violated primary duties are the actual violators of the right. As Brems notes in the passage with which this chapter began, the concept of violation is grounded in the need to "determine a borderline", such that "Whoever crosses that line will be labelled a human rights violator"; labelling agents as human rights violators implies that their treatment of persons has transgressed the threshold of minimally decent treatment—it is beyond the pale.

I now turn to one important aspect of the special moral stringency of primary duties.

iv. Duties not to violate human rights are not appropriately standardly subject to countervailing moral considerations

A central aspect of the special moral force of duties not to violate human rights is that, at the very least under standard circumstances, they are not appropriately weighed up against competing moral duties and considerations. Rather, they should simply be fulfilled. This is central to our mental image of human rights as expressing what is "most sacred and should not be touched upon".[20]

A paradigmatic example of this is the duty not to torture. While there is debate over whether or not this duty might be outweighed in an extreme situation, by, say, the duty to save a large number of lives, there is widespread agreement that it is not appropriately standardly subject to trade-offs.

Jeremy Waldron, in an influential article, rejects the view that rights are not appropriately standardly subject to trade-offs. Waldron argues that if we take rights to be grounded in important human interests and to impose positive duties to protect those interests then they are liable to be subject to trade-offs whenever conflicts of interest are unavoidable. He points out that even the right against torture can be seen to be subject to trade-offs, when we consider that it imposes duties to protect persons against torture, and that it can be reasonably debated how much should be spent on protecting people against torture given limited resources and other important expenditures.[21]

While Waldron offers powerful objections to accounts of rights that take them to impose only negative duties, it is, I contend, an essential aspect of the force of human rights that the *primary* duties they impose standardly outweigh or trump countervailing moral considerations. In the case of the right against torture, it can be argued that while the duty to protect the right is unavoidably subject to certain resource constraints and trade-offs, the primary duty not to *violate* the right is not appropriately subject to trade-offs at the very least in all but exceptional circumstances, let alone standardly so. We can therefore acknowledge that it can be reasonably debated just how much money should be spent on protecting people against torture given limited resources and other important expenditures, while nevertheless holding that the primary duty imposed by this right, not to torture, under all standard circumstances outweighs or trumps opposing moral considerations and other *pro tanto* moral duties.

This is an important aspect of the moral force of the notion of a human rights violation, as marking out treatment of persons that (at very least under standard circumstances) is morally intolerable, and thus lacking any adequate moral justification; if, conversely, we held that the primary duties to respect a certain human right were standardly justifiably outweighed by countervailing moral considerations, it would

---

[20] Brems 2009, p. 350.   [21] Waldron 1993, p. 216.

follow that there would standardly be a justification for failure to fulfil those duties. This would indeed dilute the moral force of the notion of a human rights violation.

Waldron argues that if we take human rights to be grounded on core human interests, then whenever different persons' interests conflict, we should expect there to be conflicts between human rights. However, as has been widely argued, persons' most important interests can be set back without this constituting a directed wrong; for illustration of this we can return to Griffin's example of the persons suffering from very rare life-threatening illnesses that would be enormously and unreasonably expensive to treat. As Saladin Meckled-Garcia argues, a directed wrong constitutes an unreasonable trade-off between the duty-bearers' interests or aims, and the interests of the right-holder that are set back as a result of non-fulfilment of the duty to respect the right.[22] In this example, the failure to give the treatment does not constitute an unreasonable trade-off, given the limited resources and the number of comparably urgent competing claims to those resources.

I contend, then, that if the moral force of the notion of 'violation' is to be retained, the strength of all the relevant moral considerations that standardly obtain should be taken into consideration prior to identifying what constitute fundamental human rights. The duties to respect such rights are not themselves standardly appropriately subject to trade-offs. Rather, they standardly constitute overriding duties. We can thereby take it to be built into the notion of a human rights violation that it constitutes treatment of persons that (at very least under all standard circumstances) cannot be justified by appeal to countervailing moral considerations. Rather, it constitutes an unjustifiable trade-off.

Accordingly, there is no fundamental human right to advanced expensive medical care; given the overall level of resources, it is standardly the case that the failure to provide advanced medical care to a particular individual may be justifiable. (I should emphasize, once more, that this is compatible with also acknowledging rights to health that are indeed progressive and aspirational, and a prime candidate is the right to the "highest attainable degree of health".) By contrast, if the right to minimum preventive health care is classified as a fundamental human right, this contains the judgement that given the overall level of resources, the failure to provide such care constitutes a trade-off between the duty-bearers' aims and interests, and the right-holder's interest in the health care, that is morally intolerable.

I contend, therefore, that if the right to subsistence is to have a peremptory moral force parallel to that of classic negative human rights, then the primary duties it imposes should not be taken to be standardly subject to balancing and trade-offs. One aspect of the moral significance of the question of whether or not the right to subsistence is held to impose on governments and citizens of affluent countries *primary* duties towards those in poor countries who are not under their jurisdiction is that such duties simply trump considerations of the domestic economic interest of affluent

---

[22] Meckled-Garcia 2013.

countries. The claim that these agents are under primary duties *contains* the judgement that the failure to respect them would constitute an unacceptable trade-off between their own aims and interests and the interests of those whose lives are blighted or altogether destroyed by severe poverty. The primary duties themselves are not appropriately weighed up against considerations of domestic economic interest.

By contrast, if the responsibility of the international community is thought to be primarily that of fulfilling back-up duties "to step in when states default", then this responsibility is much more likely to be seen as appropriately weighed up against considerations of domestic economic interest.

It should be noted, though, that in order to avoid ruling out *ex ante* the category of structural human rights violations, we should allow that the unjustifiable trade-off may be constituted by certain aspects of background social institutions and mores. As I argue in Section 5, if the ongoing patterns of behaviour that emerge from the way in which features of social institutions and mores structure agents' behaviour result in extremely severe harms—liable to blight or destroy persons' lives—and those harms could be avoided at modest economic cost under feasible and feasibly achievable alternative social institutions and mores, this constitutes a flagrantly unjustified trade-off and a structural human rights violation.

v. Duties not to violate core human rights are correlative duties

An essential aspect of the moral force of fundamental human rights is that they entail corresponding duties. According to the canonical Hohfeldian analysis of this, there must be a one-to-one relation between rights with a certain content, and correlative directed duties, owed to the right-holder, with the same content. A core feature of primary duties to respect human rights, then, is that such duties define the content of the right.[23]

One of the most important objections to the claim that the right to subsistence is a fundamental general human right is that the primary duties that would correspond to such a right have in large part not been specified and allocated. Accordingly, it is argued, it is indeterminate what would constitute a violation of the right to subsistence and who could be held to account for such a violation.[24]

This is a powerful objection. In order to offer an adequate defence of the claim that the notion of a 'human rights violation' is genuinely applicable to the persistence of severe poverty, we do need to retain a broadly Hohfeldian conception of the right to

---

[23] It should be emphasized that a Hohfeldian account of the primary duties, according to which the content of such duties conceptually follows from the content of the right, is compatible with holding that empirical and strategic reasoning is needed to determine the content of the secondary duties to protect persons against violations of the right. As Shue puts it, while empirical investigation is needed to decide the content of secondary duties to "to protect the right against violation, or to restore the right after violation", the content of the primary duties not to violate the right is given by "the conception of the right and what the right is to" (Shue 1996, p. 161).

[24] This objection has been powerfully pressed by Onora O'Neill (2000, p. 105).

subsistence as constituting a claim–duty pair, such that the affirmation of the right entails affirming that certain agents are actually under corresponding duties.[25]

However, in order to accommodate structural human rights violations, we should avoid assuming that human rights constitute claims against the behaviour of each, considered one by one. In our contemporary social context, the ongoing patterns of the behaviour of a vast number of agents round the globe can have a devastating impact on persons they never encounter; and, conversely, agents' capacity to prevent persons from suffering drastic and irrevocable harm, at small personal cost, is not limited to those they directly encounter in small-scale emergency situations. In this complex social context, avoiding the unjustifiable allowing or infliction of some of the most severe and prevalent harms is likely to require a coordinated division of moral labour of a level of complexity such that it can only be achieved by the institutional specification, allocation, and enforcement of a schema of duties compliance with which would avoid the harms. In order to avoid ruling out *ex ante* the possibility that such harms could constitute a human rights violation, we need to allow that a human right might be a claim against a group of agents to fulfil a shared general duty of justice to implement such a schema, rather than being restricted to constituting claims against each, *seriatim*.

It should be emphasized that while there is likely to be a multiplicity of schemas of regulations and duties compliance with which would end the allowing and infliction of the harms, it does not follow from this that the right is indeterminate. Each such schema would supply each right-holder with, and avoid depriving them of, the object of their right. The content of the shared duty is therefore given by the content of the right. In the case of the right to subsistence, it can be seen as a claim against the addressees of the right to fulfil a shared general duty of justice to implement a schema of duties compliance with which would supply each right-holder with, and avoid depriving them of, the object of their right: an adequate opportunity to obtain the means of subsistence.

3. The Practicability Constraint

Maurice Cranston argues that a constraint on fundamental human rights is that the universal fulfilment of the primary duties to respect such rights must be a practicable demand. Following Cranston's terminology, I term this "the practicability constraint".[26]

---

[25] This contrasts with Tasioulas's analysis of rights, as constituting *grounds* for imposing corresponding duties. His response to O'Neill's worry about the status of the right to subsistence as a general human right is that we can affirm the existence of a human right to subsistence before its corresponding duties exist, because they have not yet been imposed on anyone, by showing that each individual's interest in subsistence is sufficient grounds for imposing such duties. However, the worry remains that if no one is actually yet under a duty to aid particular severely poor right-holders, because such duties have not yet been specified and allocated, then severe poverty persists without its being possible to identify any agents as responsible for a human rights violation.

[26] Cranston 1973.

A common objection to welfare rights is that since they are rights to certain goods, respecting these rights requires the fulfilment of positive duties; and since fulfilling positive duties requires the expenditure of resources, then, given scarcity of resources, these positive duties are liable not to be universally fulfillable even under standard circumstances. Accordingly, an objection to the claim that the right to subsistence is a fundamental human right is that, given the limited resources internal to many poor countries, the universal fulfilment of the positive duties correlative to this right is not a practicable demand. But this objection assumes that the only agent responsible for fulfilling the primary duties to respect the right is the right-holders' own government.

Maurice Cranston, in a classic formulation of this objection, argues that taking the right-holders' government to be under a duty to supply the objects of welfare rights for all its citizens, when it lacks the resources to do so, violates the requirement that "ought implies can". He concludes that welfare rights should be seen as ideals and aspirations, rather than fundamental human rights.

Jeremy Waldron responds to Cranston's objection by arguing that since a hallmark of human rights is that they are "attributed to individuals one by one, not collectively or in the aggregate", the constraint that "ought implies can" should be applied to the duty to meet each right-holder's claim, considered separately.[27] Even if a state cannot afford to supply the object of certain welfare right (such as education) for all of its citizens, it is the case that for each citizen, considered separately, the government could afford to provide the good to that individual. Therefore it is the case that the positive duty to meet the claim of each individual right-holder, considered separately, can be fulfilled. He concludes that it is not logically inconsistent to take rights to impose jointly unfulfillable duties.

While this position is indeed logically consistent, it does undermine the special moral force of duties to respect fundamental human rights. As I argued in Section 2.iv, in order to retain the special moral force of the notion of a human rights violation we should take it to be built into the notion that it constitutes treatment of persons that is morally intolerable. On Meckled's analysis, it constitutes an unreasonable trade-off between the right-holder's interest in the object of the right and the aims or interests of the duty-bearer. But if the practicability constraint is not met, then trade-offs between duties to respect different persons' rights simply cannot be avoided, even under standard circumstances. It follows that it must standardly be justifiable to violate persons' rights.

Suppose that a right-holder's own government is taken to be the addressee of a right to a certain resource, and the scarcity of the resource is such that the government is in a position to distribute it to some of its citizens, but not to all of them who need it. On Waldron's account, since the government could supply the resource to each of these citizens, considered one by one, they can each be held to have a right to the resource. However, once the government has distributed all the available resource to some of the

---

[27] Waldron 1993, p. 208.

citizens, and there is none left over, then the government is not now in a position to distribute the resource to the remaining citizens who still need it. It is indeed now the case that the government is unable to distribute the resources to those other citizens, and therefore cannot be under a duty to do so.[28]

One implication of this is that the government has an excuse for failing to achieve for all its citizens the respecting of the welfare right. The government did not act wrongly in distributing the resource to some of the citizens until it ran out of the resource, on the assumption that each of those citizens had a right to it; and having run out of the resource, the government now has a legitimate excuse for failing to distribute the resource to all the citizens, because this failure by the government is simply unavoidable, even under standard circumstances. The notion of a human rights violation, as constituting treatment of persons that is morally intolerable, is not applicable in this context, without diluting the moral force of the term. Whereas tragic trade-offs between different persons' basic interests that are simply unavoidable call for regret, human rights violations call for moral outrage.

Indeed, the ICESCR does not designate any state that fails to provide the means of subsistence for all its citizens as 'a human rights violator'. This is precisely in virtue of the acknowledgement of the limited economic and social resources and infrastructures internal to many poor countries, in virtue of which governments are unable to achieve the universal respecting of the right to subsistence.

Beitz argues that "a 'violation' may be said to occur when a protected interest is set back as a result of a government's failure to satisfy these requirements, whether through *lack of capacity* or of will" (my italics).[29] However, if a government lacks the capacity to achieve the universal respecting of its people's right to subsistence, the notion of "violation", as denoting conduct that is morally intolerable, is not applicable. As Beitz concedes, "This clearly stretches the ordinary idea of a 'violation.'"[30]

A further problem with rejecting the practicability constraint on fundamental human rights is that it undermines the universality of such rights. As Beitz points out, the chief hallmark of human rights is that they are claimable by all.[31] But in order for a right to be claimable by all, it must be the case that for *every* right-holder (i.e. every human being) the fulfilment of the duty to respect that person's right must be a practicable demand. Thus, an implication of taking rights to be the claims *of each*, considered one by one, without considering the number of other persons with claims on the resource and the overall level of that resource that is available, is that they are not genuinely universal claims *of all*.

I contend, then, that the constraint that 'ought implies can' should be applied to the primary duties corresponding to the fundamental human rights of every right-holder, rather than of each right-holder considered *seriatim*. Cranston is right that we should take it to be a constraint on fundamental human rights that the universal respecting of

---

[28] For a similar concern, see Eddy 2006.   [29] Beitz 2015, p. 540.   [30] Ibid., p. 540.
[31] Beitz 2009, pp. 71–2.

the rights is a practicable moral demand. It follows that the level of available resources and number of claims on those resources should be taken into consideration in deciding whether a claim to the resource constitutes a fundamental human right.

(I should emphasize that I am only taking the practicability constraint to apply to fundamental human rights. As Beitz points out, what O'Neill labels as "aspirational human rights" do have genuine normative force. In particular, they impose a duty on a government to implement measures that will "help establish conditions in which those deprived could enjoy the substance of the right in the future".[32] Since, as we have seen, the concept of human rights is not univocal, and since there is an important aspirational aspect to the international practice of human rights, aspirational human rights should not be disqualified as genuine human rights. Nevertheless, they do, I contend, lack the moral force of fundamental human rights. It is certainly plausible that many socio-economic rights are aspirational human rights, rather than fundamental human rights. My focus here is simply on the question of whether one particular socio-economic right, the right to subsistence, is a fundamental human right.)

Once more, however, accommodating a category of structural human rights violations raises another very important complexity in how the practicability constraint ought to be interpreted. Paradigmatic duties not to violate human rights (duties not to torture, and so on) are fully defined and delimited requirements that each agent (or addressee) can individually completely discharge to all. By contrast, structural human rights violations consist in ongoing patterns of behaviour of a large number of agents that unjustifiably inflict or allow extremely severe harms to a large number of victims. Ending structural violations requires changing those patterns of behaviour, by challenging and overhauling those aspects of prevalent social institutions and mores that lead to the harms.

There is a complex interdependence between social institutions and mores; social mores both underpin and are reinforced by social institutions, and vice versa. A change in prevalent moral beliefs and norms grounds support for institutional reforms. In particular, widespread recognition that a certain kind of behaviour or pattern of behaviour constitutes a human rights violation plays a central role in underpinning support for reform of the laws that allow that behaviour. Conversely, official recognition of a right against the harms that result from such behaviour, and the institutional enforcement of the duties and regulations compliance with which would avoid such harms, helps entrench this change in the prevalent social mores.

On my analysis, the agents who participate in structural human rights violations are under a shared general duty of justice, owed to all the victims, to bring about this reform of social mores and institutions. Fulfilment of this shared duty is a practicable demand, in the sense that if each agent—and indeed plausibly even a fairly small subset of them—took reasonable steps towards achieving it, it would be accomplished. However, fulfilling it cannot be accomplished immediately. An essential step in achieving

---

[32] Beitz 2015, p. 543.

it is the official recognition of a fundamental human right against the harms, and the institutional specification and implementation of a schema of regulations and duties compliance with which would end the harms. This is needed to solve the coordinated action problem, to entrench the reform of the social mores that underpin adequate compliance with the regulations and duties, and to ensure a reasonably equitable distribution of the burden of avoiding the harms.

This can be illustrated with the example of nineteenth-century American slavery, which was a paradigmatic human rights violation. A centrally important aspect of the violation consisted in the operation of a set of social institutions and norms. This aspect of slavery constituted a structural human rights violation, and ending it required reform of those social institutions, which in turn required solving numerous complex and difficult collective action problems (to the point that Lincoln argued that achieving its abolition would take several generations).

Slavery was not purely a structural human rights violation. It was also constituted by the individual actions of slave-owners. Each of these agents was under a duty not to own slaves, and this duty was one they could each individually completely discharge. Nevertheless, there was a respect in which the practicability of even this duty was affected by the institutional aspect of slavery. Given that slavery underpinned the entire economy and way of life, a small-hold farmer, prior to abolition, might have been dependent on slaves for a subsistence income for himself and his family. If so then the burden on him of *individually* taking the necessary steps to withdraw from the practice, in the absence of coordinated reform of the social institutions based on slavery, would have been enormous, and exceeded the limits of the cost that nearly all human beings are willing to undertake. This of course did not mean that it would have been psychologically impossible for him to undertake this burden, and it by no means excused his owning the slaves. However, it does imply that in an important sense of the word "practicable", it was not practicable to expect every agent to take these individual steps to withdraw from the practice of slavery in the absence of a coordinated institutional abolition of the practice. This provides an illustration of Shue's emphasis on the importance of the design of institutions that do not leave individuals with duties to avoid, the fulfilment of which would necessitate superhuman qualities.[33] In this respect too, then, reform of the social institutions and mores that had previously been based on slavery was central to making fully practicable the individual duty to avoid owning slaves. Official recognition of a fundamental human right against slavery played a crucial role in achieving its abolition.

This suggests that the practicability constraint should not be interpreted as requiring that the duty to refrain from violating a human right is immediately individually fully enactable by every addressee. It requires, rather, that there are feasible and feasibly achievable institutionalized schemas of duties compliance with which would constitute the universal respecting of the right.

---

[33] Shue 1996, p. 59.

This suggests that a central test in determining whether a certain right is a fundamental human right or an aspirational goal is whether the term "abolition" is applicable. Although the ending of slavery could not be accomplished overnight, it would have been grossly morally inadequate to take the reduction of slavery to be a goal towards which to progress. Rather, the complete abolition of slavery in the shortest possible time-frame was an urgent demand of basic justice. Prior to its achievement, the social institutions and mores constituted a structural human rights violation, and were morally intolerable.

Similarly, if the persistence of severe poverty does constitute a human rights violation, then it calls for complete abolition in the shortest possible time-frame. It is not morally adequate to take the right to subsistence to impose duties to take steps towards reduction of severe poverty (any more than it would have been adequate to set as a goal the reduction of slavery to a certain degree within a certain extended period).

4. The Implications of the Practicability Constraint on the Right to Subsistence

A crucial question, then, in determining whether or not the right to subsistence is a fundamental human right, on a par with classic "negative" human rights, is whether there are indeed enough natural, social, and technological resources to provide each person with an adequate opportunity to obtain the means of subsistence.

There is in fact fairly widespread consensus that while many poor countries currently lack the resources, infrastructures, and governing capacity to secure the means of subsistence for all their citizens, the eradication of severe poverty is a feasible demand relative to level of *global* resources, technology, and feasible social institutions. It follows that whereas if we do take the relevant level of available resources to be the level internal to poor countries themselves, then the practicability constraint is not met, if, by contrast, the international community is taken to share responsibility for fulfilling the *primary* positive (and negative) duties, then the practicability constraint is met. Indeed, it can be argued that it is precisely because of the cheapness of eradicating severe poverty, relative to the overall level of global resources, that the ongoing failure to have done so is morally intolerable.

It should be noted that to establish that there is a fundamental human right to subsistence, it is not enough to show that the universal respecting of the right is a feasible demand in the majority of countries today, which is how Nickel interprets the practicability constraint. (Indeed, it is in virtue of the limited resources internal to certain poor countries, in conjunction with his assumption that the right-holders' own governments are the primary duty-bearers, that Nickel suggests classifying socio-economic rights—including the right to subsistence—as goals, or right–goal hybrids, rather than rights "in the strict sense".[34]) It would follow from that interpretation that

----

[34] Nickel 2010.

those who belong to the very poorest countries do not have a genuinely claimable right to subsistence. Yet one of the most important roles of fundamental human rights is to protect every human being, without exception, against treatment that is morally intolerable. This role is particularly important for the most vulnerable human beings, and citizens of the poorest countries who are not members of the political elite.

Nevertheless, a striking feature of current international law, accepted by many theorists, is that the primary addressees of the right to subsistence are the right-holders' own governments. The international community is held to be under a default responsibility to offer assistance, but it is not held to be under a primary duty to do so. As Beitz argues, according to the international practice of human rights, states are the bearers of the primary duties to respect their people's human rights, and the principal role of the international community is "to hold states accountable for respecting their people's human rights".[35] Thus the international community is under a back-up responsibility "to act when states default".[36] Even if a government lacks the resources and infrastructure to secure the means of subsistence for all its citizens and the international community fails to offer the emergency aid needed to remedy the subsistence shortfalls (and to assist the country's longer-term development), the international community is not thereby held to be perpetrating a human rights violation.

On this conception, the right to subsistence is indeed treated as a goal rather than a fundamental human right. Indeed, it is in virtue of the limited resources internal to many poor countries, in conjunction with the assumption that right-holders' own governments are the primary addressees of their right to subsistence, that the right to subsistence is viewed as progressively realizable, "in accordance with the resources internal to each state". The governments of many poor countries have an excuse for failing to secure the means of subsistence to all their citizens, and therefore cannot reasonably be (and are not) labelled as human rights violators. And if the responsibility of the international community is confined to that of fulfilling back-up duties "to step in when states default", then it too cannot be labelled a human rights violator, in allowing the persistence of severe poverty. Thus, severe poverty persists without its being possible to hold anyone to account for perpetrating a human rights violation.

I contend, then, that if the right to subsistence is to be taken to constitute a fundamental human right, members of the international community must share responsibility for fulfilling the primary positive duties correlative to the right to subsistence, in addition to secondary, back-up duties. At very least, in circumstances in which the right-holders' own government currently lacks the capacity to secure the means of subsistence for each of its citizens, the international community must be held to be under a primary positive duty to offer enough assistance to enable it to do so. The right to subsistence must impose "on the rest of humanity" an overarching shared general duty of justice to acknowledge an allocation of duties under which the universal respecting of the right is a practicable demand.

---

[35] Beitz 2015, p. 540.   [36] Ibid., p. 539.

If the right to subsistence is taken to impose on agents in affluent countries *primary duties* (rather than only default responsibilities) at the very least to offer enough assistance to enable every government to secure the means of subsistence for all their citizens, the notion of "violation" can be applied to the persistence of severe poverty. Insofar as affluent countries and citizens fail to implement measures that would enable poor countries to secure the means of subsistence for all their citizens, they thereby share responsibility for a human rights violation. And insofar as affluent countries have implemented this duty, so that right-holders' own governments do have the capacity to respect the right to subsistence of all their citizens, then these governments can indeed now be held accountable for a human rights violation if they fail to do so.

It should be emphasized that if responsibility for respecting the right is taken to be confined to right-holders' own governments (and the role of the international community is limited to that of discharging a back-up responsibility to step in "when states default"[37]), the practicability constraint is also not met for the primary negative duty imposed by the right to subsistence, to avoid depriving persons of their means of subsistence. As Adam McBeth argues, "The modern global economy poses challenges to a conception of human rights that channels all responsibility through the state, since much of the economic activity and the entities that drive it are themselves disconnected from the state and beyond the regulatory control of the state."[38] Certain features of the global basic structure, and of the operations of powerful transnational corporations, make a hugely significant contribution to the complex causal chains that culminate in persons' coming to be actively deprived of the means of subsistence.

The two-level model takes the primary role of human rights to be that of protecting persons against the very worst abuses perpetrated against them by their own government, to which they would otherwise be vulnerable. In the contemporary social context, however, many of the most severe and prevalent threats to persons' basic interests, including the threat of deprivations of the means of subsistence, result from hugely complex causal chains resulting from the ongoing patterns of the behaviour of a vast number of agents and agencies round the globe. The two-level model assumed in the international practice of human rights needs to be modified to reflect this.[39]

On modest empirical assumptions, given the overall level of global resources, technology, and feasible institutional infrastructures, there are feasible and feasibly achievable global and domestic social institutions that could specify (a multiplicity of) schemas of positive and negative duties compliance with which would end severe poverty (at modest cost to the individual duty-bearer). If the right to subsistence is to be taken to constitute a fundamental human right, it must impose on the rest of humanity an overarching general primary duty of justice to implement one such institutionalized schema.

---

[37] Ibid., p. 539.   [38] McBeth 2013, p. 153.
[39] Beitz suggests that the practice may need to be modified in light of the huge power of multinational corporations (Beitz 2015, p. 550).

5. The Persistence of Severe Poverty as a Structural Human Rights Violation

I take fundamental human rights to be claims by each person not to be treated in ways that are completely incompatible with minimally adequate recognition of persons' universal moral status. Accordingly, human rights violations constitute treatment that is fundamentally incompatible with such recognition. Thus, the only moral assumption underlying the affirmation of basic human rights is that every person has basic moral worth and can therefore justifiably demand not to be treated in ways that are fundamentally incompatible with that moral worth. This is a morally minimal assumption, held by any acceptable moral theory.

My account of human rights violations appeals to two further assumptions, both of which I take to be uncontentious. The first is that treatment that unjustifiably allows or inflicts extremely severe harms—liable to blight or destroy persons' lives—is fundamentally incompatible with minimally adequate recognition of the moral value of those persons' lives. The second is that the allowing or infliction of such harms is unjustifiable if the harms are foreseeable, could be avoided at small cost to every duty-bearer, and are not justified by any countervailing moral considerations.

This account of human rights appeals only to minimal and uncontentious moral premises, and meets all the criteria I have offered for what constitutes a human rights violation. First, the duty not to treat persons in this way is of paramount moral importance. Second, since the harms are avoidable, it is built into this duty that it is practicable. Third, since the infliction or allowing of the harm is unjustifiable, then it is also built into the duty not to treat persons in this way that the treatment cannot be justified by appeal to countervailing moral considerations; the force of all the relevant moral considerations has already been taken into consideration in arriving at the judgement that the allowing or infliction of the harm is unjustifiable. Therefore, the duty not to violate a human right is not itself appropriately standardly subject to being balanced and weighed up against opposing moral considerations.

It should be emphasized, though, that one restriction that is not built into this account is that treatment of persons that constitutes a human rights violation must consist in discrete harmful actions or omissions perpetrated by a specific agent against a specific victim. If the ongoing patterns of the behaviour of a vast number of agents cause or allow extremely severe harms—liable to blight or destroy persons' lives—to a vast number of victims, and the infliction or allowing of the harms is avoidable and unjustifiable, then this constitutes a human rights violation. I refer to violations of this kind as "structural human rights violations".

As I now briefly argue, the ongoing allowing and infliction of severe poverty conforms to this account of a human rights violation.

i. The infliction of severe poverty as a structural human rights violation

One of the principal barriers to adequate recognition that the persistence of severe poverty constitutes a human rights violation is the huge complexity of the causal chains that lead to particular persons' coming to be deprived of the means of subsistence. The principal causes of severe poverty, and the most effective solutions to it, are hugely contested empirical questions. For this reason, Pogge's strong claim that there is a coercively imposed "global institutional order", the operation of which is responsible for actively inflicting most existing severe poverty, is extremely controversial.

At the same time, however, it is widely agreed that much severe poverty does result from persons' coming to be actively deprived of the means of subsistence, and that *certain features* of the operation of global social institutions and transnational corporations, and of agents' conformity with certain social mores prevalent in rich (as well as poor) countries, make a significant contribution to this. (These norms are exemplified by the resistance from the agricultural lobby to removing protectionist trade policies, and by certain business organizations to reforming of tax laws that divert revenues from poor countries. These norms are also exemplified by the political culture in affluent countries under which governments feel constrained by the electoral imperative of maximizing economic growth.) There is a complex interdependence between the features of social mores and social institutions; the former both underpin and are reinforced by the latter.

Thus, even on a philosophically uncontentious account of the negative duty correlative to the right to subsistence (as the duty not to deprive persons of the means of subsistence), and on modest empirical assumptions, the infliction of severe poverty is endemic to the operation of certain features of global as well as domestic social institutions, and to agents' conformity with certain social mores prevalent in both affluent and poor countries.

It is uncontroversial that severe poverty blights or altogether destroys the lives of millions of people each year. Since the harms are on a vast scale, extremely severe, and endemic to the normal operation of domestic and global social institutions and mores, they are entirely foreseeable.

Moreover, there is reasonably widespread acceptance of the empirical assumption that there is a plurality of feasible domestic and global social institutions under which severe poverty (understood as lacking a realistic opportunity to earn or obtain a subsistence income) could be avoided, at small cost to every right-holder. (The debate generally focuses on how responsibility for achieving this should be divided up among various agents.) I am making the further assumption that the achievement of the needed institutional reform is itself a practicable demand that could be achieved at small cost to every duty-bearer. (As with the abolition of slavery, the juridical recognition that the ongoing persistence of severe poverty constitutes a human rights violation, and the specification and enforcement of a set of regulations fulfilment of which would avoid it, would play a crucial role in achieving its abolition.) On these assumptions, the harms are avoidable under alternative social institutions at small cost to every duty-bearer.

This brings us to the question of whether or not the infliction of the harms is unjustifiable. The proposals that have been put forward concerning the reforms needed to avoid the infliction of the harms could be achieved simply at the cost of moderately reduced profit for affluent businesses and nations. This economic cost does not countervail against the duty to avoid inflicting a harm that blights or destroys millions of persons' lives. Agents' ongoing failure to undertake the economic cost of implementing the reforms constitutes a trade-off between the interests of affluent agents and the interests of those suffering severe poverty that is flagrantly incompatible with minimally adequate recognition of the moral value of the lives that continue to be marred by severe poverty. It thereby constitutes a structural human rights violation.

I contend, then, that the agents who participate in the social institutions and mores under which the infliction of severe poverty is endemic are under a shared general duty of justice to reform them. This is a duty to specify, allocate, and enforce a schema of obligations and regulations compliance with which would avoid the harms. Agents' ongoing failure to have implemented these reforms and changed the patterns of behaviour that systemically lead to deprivations of the means of subsistence constitutes a structural human rights violation.

ii. The allowing of severe poverty as a structural human rights violation

There is in fact a widely held intuition that there are certain circumstances in which the duty of aid can constitute a general duty of justice, non-fulfilment of which constitutes a human rights violation. There is, for example, widespread recognition of a general positive duty of justice to administer emergency medical care to illegal immigrants; while such immigrants are denied many welfare rights, the right to emergency health care is held to be a general human right, rather than a special right grounded in reciprocal relationships with fellow citizens.[40]

The underlying rationale for this duty, I suggest, is that in circumstances in which an agent could at small personal cost prevent a drastic and irrevocable threat to a person's basic interests, liable to blight or altogether destroy his life, then the failure to do so would be incompatible with minimally adequate recognition of the moral value of that person's life. As Griffin puts it, failing to toss out a life preserver to stop someone drowning would constitute the "discarding" of that person's life; it would amount to allowing the person's life to be thrown away.

---

[40] James Griffin discusses the example of the statutes regarding the welfare rights of illegal immigrants in the State of California (Griffin 2008, p. 182).

The duty of easy rescue is geared to small-scale social contexts, in which one agent directly encounters another person in dire straits. Once more, though, it is important to avoid arbitrarily limiting our conception of duties of justice so that they are not applicable to contemporary large-scale social contexts.

The most salient difference between easy rescue scenarios and preventing the threat to basic interests posed by severe poverty is the scale and complexity of the threat and of the means of addressing it. Adequately addressing severe poverty requires a division of moral labour of a level of complexity such that it can only be achieved by institutional coordination; it requires institutionally specifying and allocating a schema of duties compliance with which would prevent severe poverty. However, given the overall level of global economic resources, on modest empirical assumptions there is a plurality of feasible and feasibly achievable schemas of duties that would achieve this at small cost to the individual duty-bearer. I suggest, then, that the underlying rationale for taking agents to be under general duties of justice to perform easy rescues also constitutes a rationale for taking affluent agents to be under a shared general duty of justice to implement one such schema. The abstract general duty of justice not to allow persons' lives to be thrown away, that imposes on bystanders in emergencies a general duty of easy rescue, also imposes on affluent agents a shared general duty of justice to achieve the institutionally coordinated response needed to prevent severe poverty.

On this account, although social institutions play an essential role in the efficient and effective discharging of the duties imposed by the right to subsistence, the fundamental duty-bearers are individual relatively affluent agents. The positive and negative duties to prevent severe poverty are derived from the abstract general duty of justice not to discard persons' lives. Although social institutions are responsible for specifying and allocating a schema of duties, they are not thereby creating duties, but are enabling agents to implement a duty they are already under, not to discard persons' lives.

Our ongoing shared failure to have implemented an institutionalized schema of duties that would prevent severe poverty is incompatible with minimally adequate recognition of the moral value of the lives that continue to be blighted or altogether destroyed by severe poverty. It constitutes a trade-off between the interests of the affluent and the interests of those whose lives are blighted or destroyed by severe poverty that is morally intolerable.

A full analysis and defence of this argument is beyond the scope of this chapter, but I hope to have indicated the plausibility of taking the right to subsistence to be a core human right, to which the notion of a human rights violation is indeed applicable.

References

Ashford, Elizabeth. 2009. "The Alleged Dichotomy Between Positive and Negative Rights and Duties", in Beitz and Goodin 2009.

Beitz, Charles. 2003. "What Human Rights Mean", *Daedalus* 132: 36–46.

Beitz, Charles. 2009. *The Idea of Human Rights*. Oxford: Oxford University Press.

Beitz, Charles. 2015. "The Force of Subsistence Rights", in Rowan Cruft, Matthew Liao, and Massimo Renzo (eds), *Philosophical Foundations of Human Rights*. Oxford: Oxford University Press.

Beitz, Charles and Goodin, Robert. 2009. *Global Basic Rights*. Oxford: Oxford University Press.

Brems, Eva. 2009. "Human Rights: Minimum and Maximum Perspectives", *Human Rights Law Review* 9: 349–72.

Buchanan, Allen. 2010. "The Egalitarianism of Human Rights", *Ethics* 120: 679–710.

Cranston, Maurice. 1973. *What Are Human Rights?* New York: Taplinger.

Eddy, Katherine. 2006. "Welfare Rights and Conflicts of Rights", *Res Publica* 12: 337–56.

Griffin, James. 2008. *On Human Rights*. Oxford: Oxford University Press.

Hayward, Tim. 2008. "On the Nature of our Debt to the Global Poor", *Journal of Social Philosophy* 39.

McBeth, Adam. 2013. "What Do Human Rights Require of the Global Economy? Beyond a Narrow Legal View", in Cindy Holder and David Reidy (eds), *Human Rights: The Hard Questions*. Cambridge: Cambridge University Press.

Meckled-Garcia, Marcia. 2013. "Is There Really a 'Global Human Rights Deficit'? Consequentialist Liability and Cosmopolitan Alternatives", in Gillian Brock (ed.), *Cosmopolitanism Versus Non-Cosmopolitanism*. Oxford: Oxford University Press.

Miller, David. 2011. "Taking Up the Slack? Responsibility and Justice in Situations of Partial Compliance 1", in Carl Knight and Zofia Stemplowska (eds), *Responsibility and Distributive Justice*. Oxford: Oxford University Press.

Nickel, James. 2010. "Human Rights", in Edward N. Zalta (ed.), *The Stanford Encyclopedia of Philosophy*, Fall 2010 Edition: <http://plato.stanford.edu/arhives/fall2010/entries/rights-human/>.

O'Neill, Onora. 2000. *Bounds of Justice*. Cambridge: Cambridge University Press.

Patten, Alan. 2005. "Should We Stop Thinking about Poverty in Terms of Helping the Poor?", *Ethics and International Affairs* 19:19–27.

Pogge, Thomas. 2002. *World Poverty and Human Rights: Cosmopolitan Responsibilities and Reforms*. Cambridge: Polity.

Shue, Henry. 1984. "The Interdependence of Duties", in Philip Alston and K. Tomasevski (eds), *The Right to Food*. Dordrecht: Martinus Nijhoff.

Shue, Henry. 1996. *Basic Rights: Subsistence, Affluence, and U.S. Foreign Policy*, 2nd edn. Princeton: Princeton University Press.

Tan, Kok-Chor. 2010. "Rights, Harm, and Institutions", in Alison Jaggar (ed.), *Pogge and his Critics*. Cambridge: Polity.

United Nations, "Charter of the United Nations", 26 June 1945. In *Yearbook of the United Nations*, 1946–7, 831–50.

Waldron, Jeremy. 1993. *Liberal Rights: Collected Papers*. Cambridge: Cambridge University Press.

10.1

Remarks on Elizabeth Ashford's "The Nature of Violations of the Human Right to Subsistence"

Daniel Weinstock

In this excellent, thought-provoking chapter, Elizabeth Ashford takes her bearings from two aspects of human rights discourse that seem to pull in different directions. On the one hand, to say that someone has a human right to x means that her failure to obtain x is a matter of the utmost moral urgency, and in particular that those who fail to provide her with x are guilty of a very grave moral violation. On the other, we view human rights discourse as pointing the way forward toward as yet unachieved moral goals. According to this more aspirational use of the term, we should work toward a world in which failure to provide all persons with a good comes to be seen as a moral scandal, though its violation does not now constitute the violation of a right in the full sense, because we do not yet possess the wherewithal with which to provide all persons with the good in question. Ashford argues that, *pace* rights theorists such as Maurice Cranston, this tension does not point to any fundamental incoherence at the heart of rights discourse. Rather, on Ashford's view, the coherence of rights discourse "requires being clear about when the label of 'violation' is applicable, and when it is not, and identifying human rights violations in such a way as to ensure that the notion retains its urgent moral force" (p. 338). The aim of her chapter is, first, to show what human rights violations consist in, and second, to show that the human right to subsistence is an instance of a right the violation of which is a moral scandal, rather than simply pointing in the direction that moral progress ought to take.

I will argue that Ashford's argument ultimately doesn't work, but that its failure is instructive. It points toward a poverty in our moral vocabulary, one which we would do well to address. To put it very simply, that poverty consists in the fact that unless we can find a way of saying that someone has a right to x, the fact that they do not have access to x appears to be a matter of lesser moral import. I will proceed as follows. First, I will briefly summarize Ashford's argument. Second, I will show why I believe that the argument doesn't work. Briefly stated, I will show that the claim that members of affluent societies have an obligation to combat severe poverty, an obligation on a moral par with their obligation not to torture or not to violate other core negative rights, downplays, in a way that Ashford's argument ultimately tacitly recognizes, the institutional dimension of the moral task of seeing to the subsistence needs of the world's less fortunate populations. Third, I will argue that even if it turned out that we could not make good the case for a fundamental moral right to subsistence, this would not relegate the fact of abject poverty to the status of a lesser moral goal.

I

The part of Ashford's argument upon which I wish to focus has to do with the claim that the right to subsistence imposes primary duties upon all members of the global community. Primary duties, to quote Ashford, "are duties the fulfilment of which constitutes the right's being respected, and non-fulfilment of which constitutes the right's violation" (p. 345). By contrast, secondary duties "are duties to implement a range of measures to protect against or remedy the effects of non-fulfilment of the primary duties" (p. 345). This distinction can be cashed out by noting that only the holder of a primary duty actually violates a human right.

Making good the claim that we all have primary duties not to violate the right to subsistence of other humans requires establishing a number of other controversial propositions. Again, considerations of space require that I focus on a subset (though an important subset) of these propositions. First, it requires showing that by not acting to alleviate the subsistence needs of our fellow humans, we are violating their rights. This distinguishes her claim, subtly but importantly, from Thomas Pogge's much-discussed claim according to which our duty is the negative one to abstain from imposing upon the citizens of poor countries an economic and political system that predictably visits hardship upon them.[1]

Second, it requires showing that the account of the right to subsistence satisfies a feasibility constraint. Actually, there are two distinct feasibility constraints pointed to by Ashford. First, on the grounds that "ought implies can", it must be the case that the resources required in order to satisfy our obligation to see to the subsistence rights of others actually exist. And second, it requires showing that there is something *we* can do in order to satisfy our obligations.

Now, it might seem that I have just denoted the same constraint in two slightly different ways. After all, if the resources exist to satisfy the right, and if they are at our disposal, then it follows that the satisfaction of the second constraint is trivial, once the first has been established. Part of the burden of my argument will be to show that these two constraints are, in fact, distinct, and that we cannot simply read the content of our obligation off the mere fact that the resources exist to satisfy the obligation.

---

[1] Pogge 2008.

How does Ashford establish that there is in fact a positive duty to take steps to remedy the lack of subsistence of vast segments of the world's population? Following many other theorists, she claims, plausibly, that "in circumstances in which an agent could at small personal cost prevent a drastic and irrevocable threat to a person's basic interests, liable to blight or altogether destroy his life, then the failure to do so would be incompatible with minimally adequate recognition of the moral value of that person's life" (p. 360). In the same way that I act in an indecent manner, one that can be taken to violate a moral obligation, if I walk past a child drowning in a shallow pool of water for fear of missing an appointment or dirtying my new shoes, I act equally indecently if I merely stand by and watch people starve at great distances when I can do something to remedy their plight.[2]

An obvious objection is that the analogy ignores the fact that distance is not just a factor, say, that might make us less likely to empathize with others. Rather, it is evidence for the fact that it is not clear, as it is in the case of the drowning child, what I must do to remedy the bad situation, and indeed, whether I am the person who must do something to remedy it. Thus, the problem of whether there exist ethical grounds to hold that I have a primary moral obligation to satisfy the right to subsistence of others shades into an aspect of the feasibility problem. The grounds exist (the non-subsistence of distant others constitutes, *ceteris paribus*, as much of a ground to hold me to a duty as does the drowning of the child), and so the only question is to determine whether all things are in fact equal, which in the present circumstances means, *inter alia*, whether there exists an identifiable, feasible and effective action I can pursue in the subsistence case.

Following Charles Beitz, Ashford rejects the idea that the problems that distance poses should be a reason to reject the claim that I am possessed a moral obligation to act.[3] We limit the scope of human rights to an implausible degree if we assume that only face-to-face cases as simple as that of the drowning child can be sources of human rights. Quoting Ashford: "In our contemporary social context, the ongoing patterns of the behaviour of a vast number of agents round the globe can have a devastating impact on persons they never encounter; and, conversely, agents' capacity to prevent persons from suffering drastic and irrevocable harm, at small personal cost, is not limited to those they directly encounter in small-scale emergency situations" (p. 350).

In order not to straitjacket ourselves in this manner, Ashford argues that we have to identify ways in which we must act in order to alleviate the suffering of others that take into account the fact that this is not something that we can do individually, through individual, uncoordinated actions. Rather, we must coordinate with others so as to achieve the satisfaction of the right to subsistence.

Ashford's insistence on coordination means that she does not fall prey to the critique of the simple, redistributionist scheme that can arguably be found in the work of Peter Singer, according to which we satisfy our obligations simply by transferring resources.

---

[2] The *locus classicus* for this kind of argument is Singer (1972).   [3] Beitz 2009.

This redistributionist conception of our obligations has been ably critiqued by Andrew Kuper.[4] Though she does not at the end of the day agree with Pogge that our obligation consists merely in the negative one of not imposing institutions upon the poor that will predictably cause their inability to satisfy their subsistence needs, she *is* like Pogge keenly aware of the institutional dimension of the problem of world poverty. It is not just a question, for Ashford as for Pogge, to determine that there are enough material resources in the world to satisfy the subsistence needs of all, and simply to transfer them. Rather, we must also establish that there are feasible institutional schemes that can regulate, for example, the production and trade of material resources in a manner likely to sustainably meet the substinence needs of the world's poor.

It is thus important that in her discussion of the material feasibility constraint upon the determination of a human right to subsistence, Ashford includes what for lack of a better term we might call "institutional resources". She writes: "On modest empirical assumptions, given the overall level of global resources, technology, and *feasible institutional infrastructures*, there are feasible and feasibly achievable global and domestic social institutions that could specify (a multiplicity of) schemas of positive and negative duties compliance with which would end severe poverty (at modest cost to the individual duty-bearer)" (p. 357, my emphasis).

Thus, there is a right to subsistence, and therefore a primary obligation on all our parts to contribute to the subsistence of needy people, because (1) the interests at stake are fundamental to people being able to lead minimally decent lives, (2) it is not just the governments of the countries most affected by want that violate the right to subsistence, and because (3) the ascription of an obligation to all agents lying beyond the borders of the afflicted state does not fall foul of feasibility constraints because the resources exist to satisfy all subsistence needs, and people can coordinate so as to make use of those resources in a way that will satisfy said needs.

II

In what follows, I want to put pressure on the third claim. To begin with, it is important to delve a little deeper into what Ashford means when she says that the obligation to assist those whose subsistence needs are not met falls on all of us. There are three ways in which this could be understood. First, it could mean that each one of us, taken one by one, should act in a way that contributes to that end. Second, it could mean that the obligation falls on our representative governmental institutions, and thus that the obligations are ours only in a derivative sense.

Ashford intends neither of these two first meanings, it seems. She writes that the right to subsistence is "a claim against the addressees of the right to fulfil a shared general duty of justice to implement a schema of duties compliance with which would

---

[4] For the debate between Kuper and Singer see Kuper 2006, and Singer 2006.

supply each right-holder with, and avoid depriving them of, the object of their right: an adequate opportunity to obtain the means of subsistence" (p. 350). This passage rules out the possibility of interpreting the collective nature of the global responsibility to alleviate human suffering as one that each individual can satisfy, simply on their own. But she also writes of primary duties of subsistence being held against "governments *and citizens* of affluent countries" (p. 348), which rules out an interpretation that would make the satisfaction of the right simply a governmental affair.

Thus, on Ashford's account, we have an obligation to act not singly, but in concert, to satisfy subsistence rights. Now, as we have seen, that concerted action is aimed at making use of the goods already available to humankind in order to satisfy subsistence rights. Those goods, recall, include "global resources, technology, and feasible institutional infrastructures". Now again, there are two ways in which the items listed in this set can be construed as relating to one another. First, they can be understood as constituting discrete, unrelated goods, each one of which can be brought to bear upon the alleviation of global want. Second, they can be understood in a manner that makes the setting up of institutions whose rules specify the way in which resources and technologies are utilized the crucial step. What is needed is a scheme that regulates the global economy in a manner that reliably conduces to the sustainable satisfaction of basic human needs.

In keeping with her rejection of the distributivist paradigm exemplified (at least according to a dominant interpretation) in the work of Peter Singer, Ashford is clearly to be read the second way. Putting these two interpretative choices together, we get the result that, on Ashford's view, we have an obligation that is on the same order and level of stringency as is the obligation to abstain from torture to coordinate in such a way as to give rise to these institutional schemes.

I want to say two things about this conclusion. The first is that it is probably the correct way in which to think about what is morally required in order to respond to the problem of unmet basic needs in the world today. The second, however, is that it is more difficult than Ashford allows to shoehorn this requirement into the human rights framework, especially if, as she insists, these rights are seen as giving rise to primary obligations. This is the case for at least the following three, ultimately interrelated reasons.

First, there is much controversy among scholars and among practitioners as to the institutional scheme that will sustainably achieve the goal of putting an end to need. Proposals span a wide gamut, and include market-oriented approaches that excoriate the countries of the global North for their imposition of barriers to entry to the market for developing nations that prevent them from competing on equal terms on global markets. According to these views, what is needed is to complete globalization's work by turning the world into a real global market.[5] Others go the opposite route and insist that "developing nations" should be allowed to follow their own economic and political

---

[5] For a version of this view see Bhagwati 2007.

paths, something that is impossible if globalization is allowed to proceed apace.[6] Still further debates have to do with the priority between setting poorer nations on a course that will allow them to avoid need sustainably over time, and approaches that emphasize the need to respond to urgent need now.[7]

These debates should not be taken as pretexts for complacency or quietism. There is urgency in arriving at a consensus on what model will best allow the world's poor to be governed in ways that conduce to the realization of their most basic interest in subsistence. The point I want to make here is that there is an epistemic and a temporal obstacle to construing the establishment of a scheme of institutions that will allow for the sustainable meeting of basic needs as a right giving rise to the same kind of obligation as the obligation, say, not to torture represents. The epistemic and temporal hurdles that must be cleared are of a kind that makes the claim that we have an obligation to put an end to need, here and now, more difficult to sustain.

The problem can be seen from a second angle when we consider what the primary obligation to put an end to urgent need requires of the individual. Now, as we have seen, Ashford does not believe that the obligation should be thought of as one that can be captured by considering each individual agent taken singly. What is required, in her view, is coordination.

But consider what is required of the individual agent in order to effectively coordinate with others to achieve the required end. For simplicity's sake, let's consider the issue from the point of view of citizens of a single nation (putting aside the fact, acknowledged by Ashford, that putting an end to want is, ultimately, a global problem). What should an individual citizen of an affluent nation do in order to coordinate with her fellow citizens? Consider: there are three main actions through which the citizens of large-scale democracies act politically in a manner that has impacts on a global scale: they vote, they donate, and they consume. Imagine a person who sincerely wants to do all three of these things in a manner that will optimize her contribution to the goal of ending global need.

Begin with voting: imagine she believes that party A has the best policy as far as coming to the aid of the global poor is concerned, but that the likelihood of that party being elected is small. Party B, which is much more likely to win, has a policy that she believes will only be 50 per cent as effective in coming to the aid of the global poor, though it is likely, if implemented, to put an end to the most abject poverty. Should she vote for Party B, knowing that further reforms that might take the global poor from mere subsistence to flourishing might be made less likely over time, given the path-dependency of further institutional reform? I don't know the answer to these questions. The point I want to make for present purposes is that either path seems defensible from a moral point of view. Coordination between a large number of agents on a single feasible scheme of institutional reform will be made more difficult by the

---

[6] See the essays collected in Mander and Goldsmith 2014.
[7] Some of these issues are discussed in Rubenstein 2015.

fact that there is no single way of using the vote that is likely to be seen as an especially salient point around which to coordinate.

An analogous point can be made about consumer boycotts, which is a standard way in which citizens-as-consumers can strive for political and economic change. The coordination required in order to place the right amount of pressure on economic rogues is considerable, and the concern is always present that it will end up representing more of a salve on the conscience of the individual agent than an effective way in which to combat poverty. Finally, the effectiveness of donation in durably giving rise to significant improvement in the absence of substantial institutional reform is likely to be limited, on Ashford's own plausible assumption about the systemic nature of the causes of extreme need.

The epistemic hurdles to effective coordination among individuals are thus daunting when seen from the perspective of the individual citizen of an affluent nation trying to figure out how to coordinate effectively with others in order to bring about meaningful change in the circumstances of the global poor.

Third, if it is the case that "institutional infrastructures" have priority among the various kinds of resources of which it is said that they are in sufficiently abundant supply to ensure the subsistence of the world's population, in the sense that such infrastructures are required to ensure that the other resources will be produced, regulated, traded, etc., in a manner that will ensure subsistence, then it is in fact unclear that Ashford's argument establishes a right to subsistence at all. Rather, it establishes something like a right to just institutions. If this is the case, then it is also unclear that she has actually defended a *primary* obligation to contribute to the subsistence of the world's population, that is, an obligation the very satisfaction of which constitutes the satisfaction of the right to subsistence of the needy. Rather, it begins to seem more like a secondary obligation, that is, an obligation "to implement a range of measures to protect against or remedy the effects of non-fulfilment of the primary duties" (p. 345). Imagine a system whereby all affluent states constitute a fund that can be drawn upon to provide material resources to populations whose governments are unable or unwilling to see to their material needs. Presumably, it would count as one of the possible institutional infrastructures the setting up of which would contribute to people in poorer countries being able to satisfy their most urgent material needs. And yet, it seems the very image of a "back-up" set of institutions, that is, an institutional set-up whereby we make other institutions more likely to satisfy the subsistence rights of people, rather than satisfying them oneself.

I should emphasize that I do not consider this to be a substantive criticism of Ashford's position. Rather, it aims to question the way in which she herself understands the implications of her argument. If indeed, the best way in which to contribute to the subsistence needs of the world's needy is to set up appropriate institutions, then for that very reason it seems difficult to assimilate the resulting obligations to the kind of unmediated primary obligations we have, say, not to torture people. Now, that admission would only seem a downgrading of the moral urgency of these obligations if we assume that the only way to express moral urgency is in terms of immediately actionable rights. But that would be to be complicit in an unnecessary restriction of the conceptual repertoire through which we express the very many kinds of obligations that we have. In Section III of this commentary I want to elaborate on this point very briefly.

III

There are, to simplify only slightly, three families of positions that have been taken by philosophers with respect to the issue of the nature of the distributive obligations that link the affluent and the poorer peoples of the world. According to a first position, which we might call the indifference position, there is no morally significant difference between the duties we have toward fellow nationals and those that connect us to people beyond our borders. This position is held both by those who, like Peter Singer, believe that distributive obligations are unmediated by institutions and those who feel that the institutions that allow us to speak of primary obligations of distributive justice are already in place—that there is, so to speak, a global basic structure.[8]

At the other end of the spectrum are those, like Rawls and Miller, who believe that true justice can only obtain within the confines of the nation state.[9] Though they hold that fortunate states have an obligation to come to the rescue of states that find themselves temporarily afflicted with the aftermaths of civil wars and natural catastrophes, the kinds of institutional connection that need to be in place in order for people to have an obligation to see to the stable and sustainable satisfaction of the subsistence needs in their view don't obtain, nor ought they to obtain.

There is a third position, one that finds its first articulation in Kant's philosophy of the *Rechtstaat*, according to which people have a right not to be subjected to "lawless" interactions with others. By that he meant that when people are in any kind of regular interrelation, then they risk exploiting one another unless their interactions are subjected to a social contract that establishes rules acceptable to all. What people in the state of nature have a right to is not directly to the provision of goods by other individuals. Rather, they have a right to an institutional framework that will allow them to avail themselves of rights. They have a right, one might say, to justice, understood not just as an abstract principle but as an institutionally grounded reality.[10]

I believe that Ashford's argument is best understood as belonging to this third, institutionally more demanding category of moral requirement. It also seems clear that this requirement—that we urgently pursue the work of completing those institutions in a manner that is fair to all concerned—places obligations upon those states that benefit from an imperfectly realized set of institutions that are difficult to assimilate to the logic of primary obligations. But again, this is not to deflate the urgency of engaging

---

[8] Singer 2004; Pogge 2008.   [9] Rawls 2001, Miller 2008.   [10] Kant 1996.

in institutional reform, but merely to suggest that the logic of primary obligation is ill suited to express that requirement. We need more concepts with which to express the very many kinds of moral requirements that are ours in virtue of our location in the web of relations obtaining between the world's states and populations. Among those concepts are ones that denote the urgency of contributing to the establishment of just institutional schemes.

References

Beitz, Charles (2009), *The Idea of Human Rights*, Oxford: Oxford University Press.

Bhagwati, Jagdeesh (2007), *In Defense of Globalization*, Oxford: Oxford University Press.

Kant, Immanuel (1996), *The Metaphysics of Morals* (edited and translated by Mary Gregor), Cambridge: Cambridge University Press.

Kuper, Andrew (2006), "More than Charity: Cosmopolitan Alternatives to the 'Singer Solution'", in *Ethics and International Affairs*, vol. 16, no. 1, pp. 107–28.

Mander, Jerry, and Edward Goldsmith (eds) (2014), *The Case Against the Global Economy*, 2nd edition, London: Routledge.

Miller, David (2008), *National Responsibility and Global Justice*, Oxford: Oxford University Press.

Pogge, Thomas (2008), *World Poverty and Human Rights*, 2nd edition, Oxford: Polity Press.

Rawls, John (2001), *The Law of Peoples*, Cambridge, Mass.: Harvard University Press.

Rubenstein, Jennifer (2015), *Between Samaritans and States: The Political Ethics of Humanitarian INGOs*, Oxford: Oxford University Press.

Singer, Peter (1972), "Famine and Affluence", in *Philosophy and Public Affairs*, vol. 1, no. 3, pp. 229–43.

Singer, Peter (2004), *One World: The Ethics of Globalization*, New Haven: Yale University Press.

Singer, Peter (2006), "Poverty, Facts, and Political Philosophies: A Reply to 'More than Charity'", in *Ethics and International Affairs*, vol. 16, no. 1, pp. 121–4.

PART V

The Challenges of Politics

11

Reflections on Human Rights and Power

Pablo Gilabert

1. Introduction

Human rights are particularly relevant in contexts in which there are significant asymmetries of power, but where these asymmetries exist the human rights project turns out to be especially difficult to realize. The stronger can use their disproportionate power both to threaten others' human rights and to frustrate attempts to secure their fulfilment. They may even monopolize the international discussion as to what human rights are and how they should be implemented. This chapter explores this tension between the normative ideal of human rights and the facts of asymmetric power. It has two objectives. The first, pursued in Section 2, is to reconstruct and assess a set of important power-related worries about human rights. These worries are sometimes presented as falsifying the view that human rights exist, or at least as warranting the abandonment of human rights practice. The chapter argues that the worries do not support such conclusions. Instead, they motivate the identification of certain desiderata for the amelioration of human rights practice. The chapter proceeds to articulate twelve such desiderata. The second objective, pursued in Section 3, is to propose a strategy for satisfying the desiderata identified in the previous section. In particular, the chapter suggests some ways to build empowerment into the human rights project that reduce the absolute and relative powerlessness of human rights holders, while also identifying an ethics of responsibility and solidarity for contexts in which power deficits will not dissolve. Power analysis does not debunk the human rights project. Properly articulated, it is an important tool for those pursuing it.

Philosophical work about human rights has not systematically addressed issues of power. This is in part understandable because such issues involve empirical questions that philosophers are not best equipped to answer. However, given the tension mentioned in the previous paragraph, a full account of human rights must include considerations about power. More generally, a full account of human rights should include such considerations because human rights are to be pursued through political practice, and political practice often involves asymmetric power relations. Philosophers can in fact make a contribution when it comes to the conceptual and normative articulation of how power matters for our understanding and pursuit of human rights. This philosophical work may proceed at a relatively high level of abstraction and be primarily concerned not with the empirical description of power structures or with specific policy recommendations but with the general concepts and substantive principles that shape the human rights project. Philosophers should not apologize for working at that level if they clarify how their enquiry connects to more specific descriptions and recommendations. Philosophical proposals help organize and orient our practical reasoning. And this is particularly needed in the case of the relation between human rights and power, on which conceptual clarity and normative articulation is largely lacking.

Before proceeding, let me provide some characterizations of *power* and the *human rights project*. These characterizations are general, broadly shareable, and allow for making thematic the relevant issues to be discussed in the chapter. I start with power. In certain circumstances C, an agent A has power with respect to whether some outcome or state of affairs O occurs to the extent that A can voluntary determine whether O occurs. More specifically: In certain circumstances C, an agent A has power over subject S (where S is either a thing or an agent, be it agent A or some other) with respect to whether some final outcome or state of affairs O occurs to the extent that A can voluntarily determine whether S exists or behaves in such a way as to generate O.[1] The general idea is simply that an agent's power is their ability to shape aspects of the world as they choose. Regarding human rights, there is some agreement that they are moral entitlements that have special moral urgency, hold universally at least in modern times, are primarily critical rather than positive standards, and should often at least in part be pursued through political action and institutions. The political project of human rights, at least since the end of the Second World War, comprises several forms of domestic and global action and institutions geared to the fulfilment of a set of basic civil, political, and socioeconomic rights. The key international documents of the human rights movement, the Universal Declaration of Human Rights (UDHR), the International Covenant on Economic, Social and Cultural Rights (ICESCR), and the International Covenant on Civil and Political Rights (ICCPR), include a general statement of such rights. The practice is emergent.[2] It rallies around a project that is itself in the making. There is dispute about what claims should be recognized as human rights

---

[1] This characterization is very open and does not pre-empt substantive debates: it allows for degrees of power; it includes power over oneself and over others; it can apply to both individual and collective agents; it includes "good" and "bad" ways of exercising power (e.g. through rationally convincing someone to do something or through force, coercion, or manipulation); it includes power over things besides persons (e.g. technological power to transform material environments); it includes various possible subjects of power: not just someone's action, but also the formation of their beliefs, desires, and other features and circumstances. For a survey see Lukes 2005.

[2] Beitz 2009, pp. 42–4.

and how they should be justified and implemented. We need an account of how power is significant for each of these areas of discussion, and the rest of the chapter provides some reflections and proposals meant to contribute to such an account.

2. Exploring Power-Related Worries about Human Rights

2.1. What might the upshot of the worries be?

Many scholars have voiced power-related worries about human rights. In this section I survey some of them. This is not an easy task because for the most part the authors presenting such worries are not clear about what their upshot is supposed to be. There are at least three quite different possible judgements that might result from power-related worries:

Inexistence: there are no human rights.[3]
Abandonment: the human rights project should be abandoned.
Shaping: the human rights project should be (re)shaped in certain ways.

In this subsection I present a preliminary argument for the claim that the most appealing practical judgement to entertain is Shaping. In subsection 2.2 I discuss several power-related worries and identify what I take to be their strengths and mistakes, with a particular focus on unearthing desiderata for the shaping of the human rights project.

A common difficulty in the literature on human rights and power is the lack of careful distinction between descriptive and normative talk. The former comprises reports, explanations, and predictions about what some people think, say, or do. The latter, by contrast, comprises claims as to what some people *ought to* think, say, or do. This difference should apply in human rights discourse. In this context, normative claims are about what human rights there are. They purport to refer to normative facts about what treatment individuals are entitled to in their social life. Descriptive claims, on the other hand, purport to refer to empirical (psychological, social, etc.) facts about what people believe they are entitled to in their social life, and they report, explain, or predict how people act with respect to some putative entitlements. Normative claims address such putative entitlements directly, affirming their existence or inexistence, and make judgements about the duties that correlate with them.[4]

---

[3] The claim may be less sweeping, saying that *some* human rights do not exist. I assume here that human rights have the four features identified in Section 1. In particular, I assume that human rights are primarily *moral* rights, and as such they are independent of legal or institutional recognition.

[4] Let me make two remarks to prevent misunderstanding. A source of confusion may be that normative talk, in purporting to refer to certain facts (in claiming their existence), seems to engage in a kind of description. But what is purportedly referred to is characterized in directly normative phrases (as what some agents are *entitled* to, have a *duty* to, etc.). The "normative facts" referred to concern what ought to be the case, not what is the case. Second, normative claims may be either *evaluative* or *prescriptive* (they are evaluative when they focus on what some agents ought to do if they could, and prescriptive when they

To illustrate, consider the following utterances:

(a) "[P]ower and interests define the dominant conception of human rights in any historic period"
(b) "[R]ights should be understood as a process that reflects particular historic configurations of power relations".[5]

(a) is a descriptive claim. (b) is somewhat ambiguous, and the text in which it appears sometimes hints at a normative and sometimes at a descriptive interpretation. The normative version could be mistaken. We want to be able to distinguish between rights that are *taken as* existing and rights that *actually* exist. This distinction helps us make sense of a typical role of rights talk, which is to *challenge* dominant conceptions of rights. It could be problematic to say, in the normative mode, that a right to freedom of religion exists in a social setting in which the majority accepts it and enforces it institutionally but did not exist a generation earlier when only a minority accepted it or when it was not institutionally implemented. It is indeed important to ascertain whether a certain putative right is backed by a particular historical configuration of power relations. But such configurations do not settle the normative issue of whether people have the putative right. In other places the author of the text in which (a) and (b) appear insists that he is not contesting the ideal of human rights, but providing an analysis of power relations that would in fact support action geared to its fulfilment.[6] This kind of disclaimer is common in power-based critical discussions of human rights. Thus, Mutua speaks about the "basic nobility and majesty that drive the human rights project," and Kennedy recommends that we think pragmatically so that "the purposes of human rights are achieved".[7] But notice that the disclaimer makes sense precisely because there is a difference between descriptive and normative talk about power and human rights. As we will see it is of course also important to properly combine descriptive and normative claims in political reasoning. But their conflation frustrates clear thinking about how to achieve it.

Power-related worries often involve the claim that human rights practice fails to fulfil, or even sets back, its own aims. What is the normative significance of this descriptive point if true? Does it warrant Inexistence, Abandonment, or Shaping? It seems to me that it normally fails to warrant Inexistence. First, as we saw, those making the descriptive point sometimes presuppose the existence of the rights about whose fulfilment they puzzle. They embrace the aim of the practice that power relations allegedly set back, which is the fulfilment of human rights. They cannot say that we do not have the rights they think we should realize. More importantly, the truth of the descriptive claim does not by itself affect the existence of human rights. The existence of a human right is a normative fact about what people owe to each other. As such, it is

focus on what agents ought to do given actual feasibility constraints). When the term "normative" is used in this text, the context will make clear which of the two senses is assumed.

[5] Evans 2005, pp. 26, 34.   [6] Ibid., p. 8.   [7] Mutua 2002, p. 10. Kennedy 2004, p. 4.

independent from other facts about whether people pursue, or succeed at fulfilling, human rights. People may fail to seek (or achieve) what they ought to seek (or achieve). If the dominant powers successfully frustrate the pursuit of some rights, this does not entail that the rights do not exist. Saying the contrary would imply the absurd conclusion that human rights do not exist when the power asymmetries are maximal and the top dogs are systematically able to set back the urgent interests of the underdogs. It would actually generate a perverse incentive for human rights violators to become as asymmetrically powerful and dominating as possible as the best way to respond to the criticism that they violate human rights.

So power-related worries do not yield Inexistence.[8] What is really at stake is not the truth of human rights principles, but the practice of seeking their fulfilment. Do the worries yield Abandonment? Abandonment is a normative recommendation. It may of course be simply based on the normative claim that there are no human rights. But we are considering the more circuitous (and prima facie more appealing) challenge based on the view that overall it is more desirable (taking the fulfilment of human rights themselves as our evaluative yardstick) to drop human rights practice than to

[8] There is an association between some power-critiques and the Inexistence claim. I have addressed a version of these critiques that stands at odds with its own moral character, i.e. its (explicit or implicit) commitment to basic norms of respect and concern which it regards as being violated by the practice of human rights as it stands. But I acknowledge that there could be other sceptical, relativistic, or nihilistic versions of power-critique. I believe that we must distinguish between human rights as moral entitlements and as conventionally articulated statuses. Normative argument is based on the former, not the latter. Conventions can be morally mistaken. My view of this distinction assumes a form of cognitivism about moral human rights. There are some irreducibly normative truths referring to what we have moral reason to do, and moral human rights are among them. (For a discussion of how this kind of cognitivism does not entail unsavoury metaphysical assumptions that reason-involving properties exist as natural properties in the spatio-temporal world or in some non-spatio-temporal part of reality, Parfit 2011, sect. 113). Given space constraints, I cannot address other power-related worries about the existence of moral human rights that challenge this view. One possible such worry surmises that human rights exist only where there are specific institutional articulations and effective mechanisms of enforcement of them and that since these are absent in the current world human rights do not exist in it. This view is counterintuitive because one of the roles of human rights talk is precisely to justify the introduction of enforcement mechanisms where they do not exist, are feasible to introduce, and are needed to protect human rights. But a defender of this challenge could reply that my response is merely a move in "power politics", an attempt to impose the satisfaction of my moral beliefs on others. On this view, the existence of human rights is a subjective matter of what we invent and establish through power politics, not an objective matter of independent normative facts that we can discover. This nihilism is at odds with my intuitions that our moral beliefs about human rights track objective normative reasons, and that they need not be linked with a will to impose our moral attitudes on others. But I acknowledge that this challenge deserves further discussion. For exploration of the challenge just mentioned see Geuss 2001, pp. 143–6.

A second challenge is perhaps inspired by Carl Schmitt's account of "the political" as a domain of radical antagonism (Schmitt 1996). It says that human rights talk is either at odds with political practice (which is fundamentally about how to fight our enemies, not about how to fraternize with every human being) or a tactical device within it. Human rights talk is either hopelessly naive or it displays rhetorical manipulation. Although I believe that conflict is a common feature of politics, and that universalist discourse is often used hypocritically, I disagree that radical antagonism is in every case a necessary or desirable feature of politics, and that we cannot or should not disentangle universalist commitments from their manipulation. But again I acknowledge that this challenge deserves further discussion. I thank Adam Etinson and Elizabeth Frazer for their comments about the issues addressed in this footnote.

engage in it. This might seem to be so if the practice aimed at fulfilling human rights principles were systematically self-defeating. Perhaps trying to fulfil human rights is like trying to fall asleep. Perhaps we should abandon the practice in the hope of disabling mechanisms that set back its purpose. If this were the case, then although human rights principles would not be false, they would be deficient as action-guiding propositions. This is worrisome because we intuitively see normative principles as having the two roles of helping us determine whether certain practical outcomes are morally desirable and of helping us decide what to do. If pursuing the fulfilment of human rights principles were bound to be self-defeating, then those principles would not be action-guiding.

But these considerations need not yield Abandonment. If a principle does fulfil the role of determining the moral desirability of certain final outcomes of action, then even if it were to be self-defeating as a direct guide to action it could be orienting in an indirect way. If the final outcome that is morally desirable according to the principle is not likely to be achieved by directly aiming at it, then we could aim at bringing about other outcomes that will cause the final outcome as a by-product. When we engage in this planning, it is the final outcome that guides us in the selection of intermediate outcomes. Returning to the example of sleep: we can decide to solve mathematical puzzles, read a novel, etc., which in turn will tire us out and make us fall asleep. We should not simply close our eyes and tell ourselves "Fall asleep now!" Something similar could be the case with human rights. Perhaps we could pursue changes in the international economic and political order that would create incentives for powerful agents to act in ways that would prevent human rights violations. We are familiar with indirect mechanisms at the domestic level. A state can motivate agents to do what is right by engaging their greed (through economic incentives) and fear (through threats of penalties).

The previous response to Abandonment accepts, for the sake of argument, that the direct pursuit of human rights is overall self-defeating. But I have not found in the relevant literature evidence for that overall claim. To support it, the defender of Abandonment would have to show that a global political environment in which we engage in human rights advocacy would probably be worse than another in which we do not. To show this it is not enough to mention a set of appalling examples about power-relations subverting human rights purposes. Abandonment is a sweeping proposal, and it requires comprehensive evidence. In fact, one of the most comprehensive recent empirical studies of contemporary human rights practice suggests that on balance the international practice has been positive.[9] Given the absence of comprehensive

---

[9] Simmons 2009, ch. 9. Simmons says that the common sentiment that "international law has done very little to improve the rights chances of people around the world...has largely developed in an evidenciary vacuum" (p. 350). Kennedy acknowledges the difficulty of justifying sweeping comparative claims about the consequences of engaging and not engaging in the human rights project (Kennedy 2004, pp. 32–3). Beitz shows that general sceptics about the human rights practice cannot avoid defending a general claim about its relative undesirability (Beitz 2009, p. 207).

support backing its claim about the systematically self-defeating nature of human rights practice, the presence of important empirical support for the opposite claim, and the inherent moral desirability of human rights, we should be reluctant to embrace Abandonment.

But even if it were true (against the existing evidence) that human rights practice has been overall self-defeating, this would not yield Abandonment. The relevant comparison in the assessment of the practice should be broader, including not only (i) what has happened in the human rights practice so far and (ii) what would have happened had human rights practice not been pursued, but also (iii) what could have happened, or could happen in the future, if human rights practice had been, or were shaped in other ways.[10] This leaves us with Shaping, the most plausible upshot of power-related worries about human rights. The idea here is that the worries provide us with reasons to arrange the human rights practice in certain ways. The rest of this chapter explores Shaping. Before proceeding, it is important to highlight the fact that the human rights project involves many possible patterns of domestic and global action,[11] and that the same power-related worries that warrant rejection of some forms of action in some circumstances may not defeat others. For example, even if unilateral foreign coercive intervention is likely to be a bad response to human rights violations in the overwhelming majority of cases, other forms of action, including international diplomatic criticism, campaigns by grass-roots international human rights movements, or domestic resistance, may be appropriate.

2.2. Specific power-related worries and desiderata for shaping human rights practice

2.2.1. PAROCHIALISM AND IMPOSITION

A typical power-related worry about human rights practice is that it involves an imposition of particular values by stronger Western societies on weaker, non-Western ones.[12] This worry relies on two claims. The first, empirical claim is that the origin and content of human rights doctrine reflect parochial values that are not widely accepted amongst people in non-Western societies. The second, normative claim is that it is wrong to disregard the will or opinions of others by externally imposing the implementation of human rights principles on them.[13]

---

[10] The comparison could be complicated further by including (iv) what could have happened, or could happen in the future, if a normative ideal different from human rights had been, or were pursued in its place.

[11] Nickel 2007, p. 101; Beitz 2009, pp. 33–40.

[12] Brown claims that "[t]he contemporary human rights regime is, in general, and for the most part, in detail, simply a contemporary, institutionalized and universalized version of the liberal position on rights" (Brown 1997, p. 43). Žižek claims that '"human rights' are, as such, a false ideological universality, which masks and legitimizes a concrete politics of Western imperialism, military interventions and neo-colonialism" (Žižek 2005, pp. 128–9). Kennedy argues that the human rights project is "tainted" by its parochial origins: it is less effective as a result, and its generalization of Western liberal ideas and political frameworks "impoverished local political discourse" in countries where other viable and potentially effective ideas were marginalized (Kennedy 2004, pp. 18–21).

[13] Beitz 2009, p. 203 (Beitz construes the second claim differently).

These claims are problematic, especially if they are used to support Inexistence and Abandonment. The use of the empirical claim faces four familiar challenges. First, the origins of contemporary human rights doctrine were not so parochial. The drafters of the UDHR included members of different world cultures, and they consulted a variety of intellectuals across the world to develop an account that would resonate widely.[14] Second, the development of an international legal framework for the pursuit of human rights was primarily pushed not by representatives of the strongest Western countries (they in fact often blocked or delayed it), but by leaders of relatively weak democratic and Third World countries and by NGOs, public intellectuals, and activists.[15] Third, the content of most human rights stated in the UDHR protect interests that are widely recognized. For example, the interests in not being tortured, having enough to eat, being educated, having housing, accessing employment, and avoiding unfair trial are clearly not merely "Western". There are of course other claims in human rights documents that are controversial, such as those concerning more demanding social rights, strong political rights, and non-discrimination on the basis of gender. (Notice that some of these rights are disputed by some people in the West.) However, fourth, we should avoid a conventionalist view according to which a right exists only if those possibly affected by its implementation already accept that it exists. Normative claims about human rights are not reports of public opinion. We should avoid the fallacy of moving from the empirical claim that there is disagreement about a right to the normative claim that there is no such right. Women had rights against discrimination before the belief that they do became an item in mainstream political agendas. Another common fallacy that operates in the neighbourhood is the genetic fallacy, according to which we should judge the plausibility of an idea by considering its origins. The truth value of the normative claim that there is a human right to democracy is not threatened by the truth (if it is a truth)[16] of an empirical historical report saying that the belief in the value of democracy is Western in origin.

The normative claim seems plausible. But it should be qualified. It is not necessarily always true that the disvalue of external imposition outweighs the value of the outcomes that could only be reached through it. Serious emergencies can warrant exceptions. But in any case we must see that the current practice of human rights is not one in which coercive international action is widespread. In fact, the two Covenants include (in their Article 1) strong clauses affirming peoples' right to self-determination, and their implementation is normally led by domestic political actors.[17] On the other hand, we should not only worry about international imposition. We should also worry about domestic imposition. It is not uncommon for worries about foreign interference to be voiced by agents who want to maintain domestic practices of oppression and

---

[14] Glendon 2002, ch. 5.   [15] Simmons 2009, pp. 40–1, 46–9, 352–3.

[16] Sen argues that democratic values also sprang up independently in many Asian societies (Sen 2009, ch. 15). "Like fire, or painting or writing, democracy seems to have been invented more than once, and in more than one place" (Dahl 1998, p. 9).

[17] Simmons 2009, pp. 365–73.

domination. This is not only the case when it comes to some "non-Western" leaders challenging strong political human rights whose fulfilment would threaten their authoritarian rule. It was common for example in the United States, when many political leaders worried about official recognition of international human rights law that could be used to challenge the oppression of African-Americans in the American south.[18] Certain forms of imposition might (with the usual caveats regarding likely effectiveness and avoidance of unacceptable consequences) be justifiable *in extremis* to protect some from severe impositions by others. This need not be a form of paternalism, as those protected may already resent their condition.[19]

But the empirical and normative claims involve genuine concerns for Shaping. The history of colonialism and the contemporary global imbalances in economic, military, and cultural power must put us on guard. It is indeed problematic when the articulation of the content and implementation of human rights is in the hands of disproportionately powerful agents and does not seriously include all those to whom they would apply. It is also a problem when some powerful agents act in self-righteous ways, without proper acknowledgement of their own deficits. For example, Americans proselytizing for democratic governance around the world should also pay attention to the serious pathologies facing their domestic politics, shaped as it largely is by the influence of people with large sums of money to fund campaigns, control the media, and offer lucrative jobs to public servants after they leave office. In response, human rights practice should accept the following desiderata:

(D1)   *Epistemic openness*: We should have a fallibilistic attitude towards the correctness and completeness of the set of human rights we currently accept. We should pay attention to the voice and point of view of people from diverse social settings.

(D2)   *Presumption against external imposition*: Absent strong countervailing considerations, the implementation of human rights in a social context should be such that the agents in that context have effective opportunities to control it.

(D3)   *Humility*: When criticizing others, those pursuing human rights should not be condescending and arrogant, and they should be open to criticism.

2.2.2. HEGEMONIC MANIPULATION

Antonio Gramsci argued that "the supremacy of a social group manifests itself in two ways, as 'domination' (*dominio*) and as 'intellectual and moral leadership' (*direzioni*)".[20] Whereas the former exacts compliance through force or coercion, the latter recruits the willing consent of the members of subordinated groups through persuasion. The achievement of the second kind of supremacy is what Gramsci called "hegemony". Hegemonic mechanisms involve (*inter alia*) normative discourses that capture some of the interests of the members of subordinated groups while being on balance tilted in

[18] Simmons 2009, pp. 40, 43.   [19] Beitz 2009, pp. 84–5.
[20] Gramsci 2000, p. 249 (see also pp. 195, 205–6, 211–12, 306–7, 333–4, 345).

favour of the interests of the members of the group shaping the discourses, thus cementing the power of the latter over the former.

Might human rights discourse work as a hegemonic device? Some believe that it does. Each contender in the Cold War used human rights discourse to bleed support from the other: the USSR emphasized the underperformance of the USA regarding the civil rights of African-Americans and the social rights of workers, and the USA criticized the violations of freedom of speech, association, and political participation in the countries under Soviet control.[21] Each funded purportedly nongovernmental human rights organizations that articulated these criticisms.[22] Some characterize human rights discourse as a tool wielded by capitalists to cement their power in the contemporary global economy. According to Evans, "[h]uman rights are conceptualized as the freedoms necessary to maintain and legitimize particular forms of production and exchange," they focus on a "set of values delimited by an assumed normative consensus that legitimizes activities associated with market discipline, specifically, negative rights and those associated with property".[23] There is also the general suspicion that the "enforcement of human rights by the international community is determined, in practice, by the foreign-policy imperatives of the major powers".[24] At the limit, human rights are invoked as part of the justification of coercive interventions that in the eyes of many are primarily motivated by economic or geopolitical interests rather than by human rights concerns. For example, many think that the American invasion of Iraq was about control of oil rather than about responding to international terrorism or promoting democracy.

Finally, there is the widespread phenomenon of inconsistent implementation. The USA ratified the ICCPR but not the ICESCR. While it criticized the Soviets for trampling on civil and political rights, it supported the dictatorship of Pinochet in Chile, which violated both in egregious ways. It is common for foreign aid to be focused on countries with which the donor country has extensive trade links, disregarding other countries even if they need more help.[25] International prosecution and criticism for war crimes commonly targets leaders of poor countries, but very rarely if at all leaders of powerful countries.[26] These phenomena seem to support the view that human rights discourse surfaces in strong ways only when it is likely to serve the strategic interest of powerful agents.

---

[21] Glendon 2002, ch. 11.   [22] Simmons 2009, pp. 47–8.

[23] Evans 2005, pp. 43, 44. Evans also stresses how socioeconomic (and even political) rights are ignored and undermined to create attractive conditions for investment and intensive exploitation of labour by multinational corporations. Such corporations have extensive influence on governments and international decision-making agencies (such as international trade organisms) (pp. 44–5, 50).

[24] Brown 1997, pp. 53–4. See Žižek 2005.

[25] In 2012, the Canadian government decided to end its aid efforts toward several countries, alleging that the "operation costs" are too high. Many of those countries are among the poorest in the world. On the other hand, Canada will continue its support to countries with which it has ongoing trade agreements or in which it is carrying out significant business activity, even though several of them are significantly less poor (Sheikh 2012).

[26] Evans 2005, p. 31.

The foregoing considerations obviously do not warrant Inexistence. The instrumental use of human rights talk does not disprove the existence of the human rights talked about. In fact, it exploits the widespread, and independent conviction that those rights exist. What about Abandonment? Would the relatively powerless be better off if human rights were not part of the domestic and international political vocabulary? As I have said, this is hard to ascertain. But there are reasons to think that the use of human rights discourse has very important positive effects. To begin with, human rights are not only invoked by the powerful. Appeal to them was, and is, a common normative resource in the struggle of subaltern groups such as women under patriarchal regimes, the working poor in wealthy and developing countries, and mistreated prisoners across the world. Second, hegemonic manipulations can be unmasked and criticized by referring to human rights. For example, contemporary international and domestic economic arrangements can be faulted for their violation of the human rights of workers in sweatshops and their association with political regimes that flout the civil and political rights of protesters. Third, although human rights discourse can be coupled with different wider normative conceptions of social organization (such as capitalism and socialism), it imposes constraints on them by identifying a minimum of decency and dignity for any agent subject to their rules. Even if human rights discourse is subject to hegemonic articulations, it involves recognition of a form of minimal justice that should be welcomed rather than dismissed. It would be worse if such a minimum moral core were not on the table as something to reckon with (even through manipulation). Finally, as Koskenniemi points out, the hegemonic pattern of discourse has the pragmatic consequence of helping build an international political community in which general rights and duties are routinely invoked and discussed, and this forces players of the hegemonic game to be more inclusive of the interests of others.[27] I would go further: the moral language game of human rights has a tendency to subvert merely strategic reasoning. It does so by invoking constraints of symmetric regard and impartial concern between human beings. These are never reducible to the search for strategic advantage: although they might at times coincide with it, they may also be used to challenge its tendency to select norms that downplay the needs of the weak, or to apply appropriate norms inconsistently. The moral component of hegemonic devices has independent significance.

So we probably should not abandon the human rights project. But the worries about hegemonic manipulation are of course very serious. They give rise to the following desiderata regarding Shaping:

(D4)   *Multilateral authorization*: Responding to the problem of corruption of human rights discourse by unilateral international interventions, we should pursue "an international regime combining a mechanism for approval of unilateral protective efforts with a capacity to apply incentives to encourage fidelity to the efforts' purposes".[28]

---

[27] Koskenniemi 2004.   [28] Beitz 2009, p. 207. Buchanan and Keohane 2004.

(D5)   *Prioritizing the worst off*: In proposing and assessing the desirability of international actions to promote human rights, we should primarily focus on those whose human rights situation is the worst.[29]

(D6)   *Encouraging imagination of multiple articulations*: Human rights can be components in different wider conceptions of social justice. We should be open to these different articulations, both to respond to discursive manipulation and to foster wider support for the human rights project.

(D7)   *Public reasoning*: In proposing and assessing invocations of human rights in domestic and global politics, we should promote practices of public reasoning in which we can impartially test their fairness and consistency.[30]

2.2.3. HUMILIATION AND SOLIDARITY

Another power-related worry about human rights practice is that it encourages a pattern of social relations in which some people's agency is downplayed while others' is unduly exalted. Those undergoing human rights deprivations are seen as helpless victims, and those stepping in to help are seen as active saviours.[31] What is wrong with this pattern? Although critics are not fully explicit on this question, it seems that there are two worries, one factual and the other normative. The factual objection is that the description of processes of human rights deprivation and amelioration by reference to victims and saviours is inaccurate. Those undergoing human rights deprivations may have been causally involved in their own deprivation. Perhaps they are partly responsible for their current situation because of their not having taken available steps to protect themselves (for example by engaging in political collective action more often to fight dictators, politicians' corruption, etc.). And perhaps they are, or could be, much more active in the process of amelioration. The "saviours", on the other hand, may not really be able to do much unless they engage the active agency of those undergoing deprivations. They cannot on their own reorganize the social life of the "victims". A normative consideration operating in this worry is this:

(D8)   *Non-humiliation*: When some agents help others to overcome situations of human rights deprivation, the former should acknowledge, and engage, the initiative and active agency of the latter.

---

[29] This is a *pro tanto* consideration, which might be outweighed. One example concerns effectiveness: the situation in country A may be worse than in country B, but those in country C (the ones undertaking human rights supportive action) may be significantly more able to affect B than A. Another case concerns responsibility to compensate for harm: those in C may have to prioritize action regarding B if they have been complicit in bringing about the human rights deficit in B (but not in A, or less so).

[30] D7 is wider than D4, including domestic and international public debate that shapes opinion but not directly decision-making in specific institutions.

[31] Mutua 2002, ch.1. See also Kennedy 2004, p. 29. Žižek claims that "[t]oday's 'new reign of ethics'... [invoked by human rights advocates] relies on a violent gesture of depoliticization, depriving the victimized other of any political subjectivation" (Žižek 2005, p. 128).

This is an important desideratum for the shaping of the human rights project.[32] We should respect other people's agency by seeing them as active shapers of their own social life—at least so far as the fulfilment of their human rights is concerned. This point can indeed be used to criticize some forms of humanitarian intervention that see those whose human rights are violated as mere victims to be saved by other, powerful agents. Sometimes the "victims" bear some responsibility for their condition; and sometimes they can, and should, be among the key political players in the struggle for improving their condition. We disrespect people if we fail to recognize the extent to which they are active agents.

However, we should not exaggerate the concern about independent agency. Another important point is that we should take reasonable steps to help other human beings in need. It is a pervasive fact of human existence that people need help from others to avoid the bad and achieve the good. This of course also applies to the most urgent forms of the bad and the good, which human rights track. Sometimes others simply cannot successfully defend their rights on their own. Sometimes dictators will crush their dissent and systematically torture and kill them. Sometimes their hunger can end but is not terminated in the near future because the needed and reasonably available external help is not provided.[33] As a matter of fact, human beings can achieve little in the way of satisfaction of their most urgent interests without the active help of others. An ideal of radical independence or self-sufficiency is infeasible. It seems also unappealing because it misses the significance of cooperation and community in social life. We thus have reason to accept:

(D9)   *Solidarity*: We should help others achieve conditions in which their human rights are fulfilled.

In fact, the value underlying this desideratum is among the key ones animating the human rights project. Article 2 of the UDHR calls all human persons to act in a "spirit of brotherhood". Solidaristic support to achieve the fulfilment of human rights is owed both domestically and internationally. To fully express and elaborate this value, the human rights practice needs to avoid a narrow emphasis on independence. Such emphasis undermines the application of D9: it fosters feelings of shame in those seeking help, and of guilt in those helping. This is unfortunate: rights can, and should

---

[32] Its disregard of course does not warrant the claim that there are no human rights, and it has not in fact been so widespread as to support Abandonment. Simmons responds thus to Mutua's worry that the human rights movement is framed by a narrative of "saviours" rescuing "victims" from "savages": "*Treaty commitments are directly available to groups and individuals whom I view as active agents as part of a political strategy of mobilizing to formulate and demand their own liberation.* Rather than viewing international law as reinforcing patriarchal and other power structures, the evidence suggests that it works against these structures in sometimes surprising ways" (Simmons 2009, p. 7). When governments explicitly commit to human rights international law, they raise the expectations of domestic and foreign political actors, who then press for the fulfilment of those commitments with various means (litigation being just one of them).

[33] Ironically, those who emphasize the worry about "victimization" risk embracing the bourgeois ideology they claim to combat: *they* may fail to attend to the phenomena of social dependency and solidarity that render the ideal of radical individual independence both infeasible and undesirable.

be seen, as a way of marking our need for and commitment to support each other in the search for a decent or dignified life.[34] Human rights practice should be shaped by a form of *respectful solidarity* that combines D8 and D9.

2.2.4. BOURGEOIS IDEOLOGY AND DEEP CHANGE

Although it was not focused on contemporary human rights but on the "natural rights" claimed in the modern bourgeois revolutions, Karl Marx's critical remarks on rights (especially in his early text "On the Jewish Question") have been extremely influential. Given this influence and the insights they involve, I will discuss four of them:

(A)   Modern bourgeois revolutions involve "political" but not full "human emancipation". They introduce a package comprising "the rights of the citizen" (i.e. political rights to assemble, vote, etc.) and the "rights of man" (rights to free speech, personal security, private property, etc.) that achieves the dissolution of feudal society. But this package involves a dualism that is multiply problematic. The division between the political community or the state, and the private sphere or civil society, functions in such a way that the former (and its abstract forms of equality, freedom, and brotherhood) masks, permits, affirms, depoliticizes, and is a means to preserving the latter (with its pervasive egoism and inequalities of social power).[35]

(B)   The specific "rights of man" invoked in the French and American Revolutions are the claims of "egoistic man, of man separated from other men and from the community".[36]

(C)   Rights discourse neglects the differences among individuals, condoning problematic inequalities. For example, in the first stage of a communist society in which distribution is based on a right of each to receive according to their productive contribution, those with greater native productive talents will be better off than others who exert the same amount of effort in their productive activities. The best society will be one in which we move beyond this inherent limitation. Thus, the final stage of communist society would instantiate the slogan "From each according to his ability, to each according to his needs".[37] This society lies beyond the realm of rights.

A general claim underlying much in Marx's (and many Marxists') challenges is this:

(D)   The "rights of man" are presented as universal, but often they articulate the specific interests of specific groups of people in specific societies (such as the interest of the bourgeoisie in private property over productive assets).

Each of these points involves important and true insights but also mistakes and exaggerations. I will briefly discuss them. I will also consider how they might apply to

---

[34] The human rights project can involve a recognition and valuation of mutual dependency. The UDHR can indeed be seen, in Glendon's apt phrase, as a "Declaration of Interdependence" (Glendon 2002, ch. 10). On the relation between human dignity, empowerment, and solidarity see Gilabert 2015a.

[35] Marx 1978a, pp. 34–43. An insightful characterization of (A) can be found in Brown 1995, ch. 5.

[36] Marx 1978, pp. 42–3.   [37] Ibid., pp. 530–1.

contemporary human rights. This is not the context Marx had in mind, of course. But some contemporary writers extend these points to human rights, and it is in any case a worthy exercise to consider the plausibility of such extension.[38]

(A) involves two important insights. First, rights talk emerges in specific historical circumstances. To understand the former we do well to attend to the latter, which include certain power dynamics. This point is relevant for understanding contemporary human rights talk, and is indeed a key motivation for this chapter. Marx is also correct to think that what he calls "political emancipation" is not enough: without important changes in the economy, the "freedom", "equality", and "brotherhood" announced in the political sphere will be compromised.

There are, however, two problems with (A). First, it seems to ignore that political rights can be exercised to reshape the egoistic economy Marx says they are bound to presuppose. In fact, they have been exercised in that way in the development of welfare states. Welfare states stop short of socialism, of course, but they go well beyond laissez-faire capitalism. Political power and socioeconomic power interact in complex ways that do not always fit the functionalist picture involved in (A).[39] Second, it is true that the distinction between the public and the private can be, and has been, used to obscure the problematic power relations operating in the latter (such as the exploitation of labour in factories, or the physical abuse of women in households). But the idea that there should be areas of personal life that are relatively free from public monitoring is in fact an achievement of modern liberalism that should be retained. I think that Marx would have agreed with this given that his socialism had significant libertarian components and was explicitly opposed to forms of communitarianism (or what he called "primitive communism") that obliterate individuals' self-differentiation and liberty. But for as long as conflicts between personal and collective autonomy are likely (I think this likelihood is inescapable, but Marx disagreed), some distinction between the public and the private, and some rights protecting the latter from abuses by majorities capturing the former, will make good normative sense. These personal freedoms are not *capitalist* liberties to own means of production and exploit workers, but entitlements (qualified by whatever important constraints of fairness are appropriate) to some levels of non-interference in our personal affairs and relationships.

(B) also involves important insights. It is true that some of the alleged rights advocated in bourgeois revolutions protected egoistic, instrumentalist, or exploitative forms of economic interaction, and this seems problematic from the point of view of human emancipation. It is also true that rights talk sometimes presents some capitalist liberties as if they protected universalizable interests. Marx is correct to worry about the tendency to make modern, capitalist, "egoistic man" into the "natural" or "authentic" one.[40] However, Marx's discussion of the "rights of man" of the French (and American)

---

[38] For example, Douzinas 2010 invokes versions of (B), (C), and (D). Žižek 2005 invokes versions of (A) and (D).

[39] For exploration of the debates on this issue within the socialist tradition see Wright 2010.

[40] Marx 1978a, p. 46.

revolution is too narrow, and his sweeping dismissal of them is unacceptable. We simply cannot accept that liberal individual liberty rights are just shields for bourgeois egoism. Liberty of conscience and freedom of the press (both mentioned in the French Declaration) are extremely important rights that any social system that recognizes the significance of people's capacities to shape their own life from within would have to include. Marx is also mistaken to assume that "equality" is of no political significance. It is not true that it only means the "equal right to liberty... [for every man as a] self-sufficient monad".[41] The recognition of formal equality and equal liberty are (even if insufficient) enormous achievements. They were denied people in feudalism, and they would become templates to be filled in in substantive ways through the identification of various new specific liberties and through their extension to larger sets of persons (such as slaves, workers, and women).[42] The idea that all persons should have equal legal entitlements is an undeniable triumph against the earlier assumption that some deserve more rights than others, or are inherently more worthy of respect and concern. Second, Marx's criticisms definitely do not apply to standard contemporary lists of human rights (such as the UDHR). These do not entail capitalist property rights. And they include numerous socioeconomic rights (see UDHR, Articles 22-6, which include social security, appropriate remuneration for workers, rest and leisure, health care, educational opportunities, etc.). They also state domestic and global duties to cooperate with the fulfilment of socioeconomic (and other) rights. So even if Marx is correct to criticize the narrow emphasis on independence and separateness in early liberal individualism, current human rights discourse and practice is explicitly attuned to the need for, and obligation to give, solidaristic support.

Turning to (C), Marx seems to me correct to criticize the so-called "contribution principle" (captured in the slogan "To each according to their contribution") in that its application is consistent with inequalities of outcome that arise from morally arbitrary differences in individuals' natural endowments. I also find the slogan "From each according to their abilities, to each according to their needs" appealing as it involves a more desirable view of social cooperation that captures both the importance of recip-rocal contribution and sensitivity to difference.[43] More generally, it is true that the application (and even the formulation) of rights often fails to capture the relevant differences among individuals. We can derive important desiderata from these points. The emphasis on responsibility towards others was captured in D9. We can add:

(D10)   *Sensitivity to diversity*: In formulating, justifying, and implementing human rights, we should be sensitive to important differences among individuals.

Clearly, even if two individuals have the same rights, they may need different specific policies to attend to their fulfilment given relevant differences between them. This is

---

[41]   Marx 1978a, p. 42.
[42]   Hunt 2007, chs. 3–4. On the need for socialists not to dismiss human rights see Blackburn 2011.
[43]   Gilabert 2015b.

already expressed in the human rights movement, for example through the generation of instruments identifying specific needs and claims on the part of certain groups (such as the Convention on the Elimination of All Forms of Discrimination Against Women and the Convention on the Rights of the Child).

Marx's dismissal of the idea of rights is however too sweeping. As we saw, differences *can* and *should* be incorporated in rights discourse and practice. Even if people have equal rights to a decent standard of living, they may need different things to achieve it: some cannot walk and need wheel chairs or ramps to access buildings, others need special medicines, some are very young and need special nutrition, some are very old and need special care. Rights talk need not be abstract in ways that obscure important differences. Even though relatively abstract, rights claims can be framed to protect individuals against likely threats and problems that arise in their social life. Their formulation could address types of social circumstances to be avoided or promoted. This can happen at different levels of generality.[44] On the other hand, some amount of abstraction is unavoidable in lumping cases under common headings (as any set of rules must). Some of the problems might be solved by breaking types into important subtypes either in the formulation of specific rights or at the level of the policies that implement them (this is what D10 would demand). But the tension between standardization and singularity is likely to remain. We can only seek to navigate it through lucid contextual judgement. Of course, this would not be necessary in a society of superabundance and dissolution of serious conflict of interests (which Marx seems to envisage for the higher phase of communism in "Critique of the Gotha Program" (Marx 1978b)). This society would be one in which rights talk is no longer necessary: everyone would as a matter of course get what they need. But such a prospect seems wildly infeasible. In any case, for as long as it is not achievable, we will encounter scarcity, conflict, and power differentials. We will need normative guidelines for addressing such circumstances. And the rights idiom (properly understood) is suited to that important task.

Finally, regarding human rights, it is important to notice that they mostly are basic sufficientarian demands. Thus, socioeconomic human rights fall well short of socialist

---

[44] Thus, we may identify specific human rights in the contemporary world as specific urgent claims that people have against their own government and fellow citizens and against international organizations, foreign governments, and foreign citizens. These may be based on more abstract rights or general claims based in extremely important interests shared by all human beings, and whose protection involves responsibilities for anyone who can affect their fulfilment. As stated, this distinction is of course too sharp. We could think of a spectrum going from more to less abstract rights. We could then identify, for example, (1) fairly abstract rights that hold in any social context, (2) the rights mentioned in the UDHR and the Covenants, Conventions, and Treaties, (3) the rights stated in national constitutions, (4) the specific rights as construed by governments' laws and policies, and (5) individuals' claims in specific circumstances. Even this sequence is somewhat artificial; for example, some of the rights mentioned in the UDHR clearly belong to (1) (e.g. the right to life identified in Article 3). The main point, however, should be clear. Rights can be more or less abstract, and these differences are significant for our reasoning about the content, justification, and implementation of different rights. Differences among individuals can be articulated at any of these levels, depending on their practical relevance. See Gilabert 2011 and 2013.

demands of equality. But there is no necessary conflict here. Socialist rights can be seen as including human rights as a proper subset. One can campaign for both. Still, the distinction is morally and politically important. Human rights are far more morally urgent than their complement in the socialist ideal. And one should be willing to achieve broader political alliances with those who endorse human rights but not socialist rights if this is necessary to immediately stop the evils of human rights violations (such as torture, starvation, and political oppression). On the other hand, the Marxian suspicion about just focusing on human rights is in order. If inequalities outside the domain of human rights are too wide, then perhaps not even the most basic human rights will be secure. For example, if inequalities of wealth and economic power are very wide, they may corrupt the political system, making it unlikely to impose the regulations needed to keep people out of severe poverty. Many contemporary capitalist societies exhibit this problem. Thus, broader, even if not distinctly socialist, economic reforms may be necessary to secure human rights themselves.

I will not comment on (D) because I have already covered the relevant issues when introducing desiderata D4–D7. D4–D7 can also be seen as responses to the threat of ideological manipulation. Their fulfilment would help disrupt the presentation of the contingent as necessary, the particular as universal, and the temporary as invariant. Marx's concern is clearly worth taking on board. I will return to this issue in Section 3.

Another important issue inspired by critical considerations of the kind Marx introduced is the issue of "structural change". Many power-related discussions about human rights worry that human rights discourse is superficial because it does not address the causes of human rights deprivations. To do so, we should focus on the economic and political structures that frame domestic and international relations. Mutua, for example, says that we should critically discuss capitalism, imperialism, and the market economy besides merely regulating their worst outcomes.[45] Others worry that the human rights movement is narrowly focused on developing legal frameworks for holding individuals responsible, without addressing the circumstances that enable or encourage them to undermine human rights. The underlying desideratum seems to be this:

(D11)   *Deep change*: In pursuing the fulfilment of human rights, we should seek to change economic and political structures and other deep factors that make human rights deprivations likely.

This desideratum is appealing. In fact, even many of those who focus on international human rights law accept it.[46] But this does not show that legal instruments are not

[45] Mutua 2008, p. 1027. See Kennedy 2004, p. 11. It is true that socioeconomic rights have been down-played by Western governments and many international NGOs. But this has started to change. The UN Millennium Goals include targets regarding poverty eradication, and NGOs such as Oxfam and (recently) Amnesty International have been focusing on economic deprivation. Still, more focus on "economic tyranny" and "economic powerlessness" is necessary if "asymmetries of power" are to be seriously addressed (Mutua 2008, pp. 1029, 1033).

[46] Simmons 2009, p. 366.

important. They have enabled citizens to effectively force their government to act to protect their rights (as is the case, for example, with Colombian women fighting for their reproductive rights by pressing their government to honour its ratification of CEDAW).[47] Furthermore, some human rights directly capture deep structural dimensions, as is the case with the strong political rights envisioned in UDHR (e.g. Art. 21) and ICCPR (e.g. Art. 25). The practice can, and should, go further by addressing features of the international order. Thus, Thomas Pogge has discussed the need to change features of that order that enable and incentivize the formation of authoritarian governments that violate their citizens' rights (such as the international privilege to sell the natural resources they seize, and to purchase weapons they use to suppress dissent).[48] Others have emphasized the need to change trade regimes and the governance structures of international institutions such as the World Trade Organization in order to facilitate fair trade, which could help millions to escape severe poverty.[49] These efforts reflect (D11), and are in tune with the important, framing Article 28 of the UDHR, according to which "Everyone is entitled to a social and international order in which the rights and freedoms set forth in this Declaration can be fully realized." More efforts of this kind are obligatory.

2.2.5. POLITICAL ACTION IN NONIDEAL CIRCUMSTANCES

A final desideratum I want to identify is this:

(D12)   *Nonideal ethical reasoning*: In pursuing the fulfilment of human rights we may encounter situations in which sufficiently many others act in ways that thwart that fulfilment, or do not act in ways that support it. In such nonideal circumstances we may follow special guidelines for action that would not apply in different, ideal circumstances.

The need for distinguishing between ideal and nonideal normative reasoning, and the significance of the latter for politics, are important issues that are becoming salient in debates in political philosophy.[50] I have defended elsewhere the need to engage in nonideal theorizing when it comes to the pursuit of global justice and human rights.[51] I have emphasized the need for acknowledging what I call *dynamic duties*. These duties are focused on expanding agents' capacities for political action so that more extensive implementations of human rights become more realistic. In the present context of discussion, this requires a hard look at power relations: the power of those blocking human rights pursuits must be limited, the power of those seeking their fulfilment must be expanded, and choices involved in such processes will include tradeoffs that would not be necessary in ideal circumstances in which the implementation of human

---

[47] Simmons 2009, pp. 245–53.   [48] Pogge 2008, chs. 4 and 6.
[49] Stiglitz 2006, ch. 3. For a philosophical account of global justice centered on the responsibilities of powerful agents shaping international relations see Miller 2010.
[50] Valentini 2012.   [51] Gilabert 2012a, chs. 4 and 7.

rights is more feasible and more systematically embraced by influential actors. I thus agree with Kennedy that we need to adopt a pragmatic approach that is sensitive to both desirable and undesirable consequences, including costs, risks, and uncertainty—the "darks sides" of human rights practice—in order to better realize its goals.[52] This requires from political actors an ethical sense of responsibility: they have to weigh the moral significance of alternative forms of action (and inaction), and choose those that are, in their best judgement and overall, no worse than the alternatives.

3. Building Empowerment into the Human Rights Project

3.1. Power as an obstacle and as a resource for human rights

In 2.1 I emphasized the distinction between descriptive and normative claims about human rights and power. In 2.2 I identified some desiderata for shaping the human rights project to attend to important issues regarding power. Such desiderata combine descriptive and normative considerations without conflating them. Their full exploration would of course require the identification of specific agents, institutions, and modes of action. But such an exploration is beyond the scope of this chapter. In what follows I will instead focus on a more general and framing issue about how to design a strategy that responds to the desiderata regarding power and human rights. The strategy I propose suggests that we build empowerment into our view of human rights. The first step in developing this view is that we notice that the moral valence of power for human rights is not always negative.

A way to get to this point is by considering the insightful account of the relation between power and human rights provided by Stammers.[53] At the level of description, Stammers claims that rights talk has been used in history both to "challenge" and to "sustain" certain relations of asymmetric power. Thus, in some forms of liberalism, some "innate" rights to liberty were invoked to challenge state power, but they were also used to sustain capitalists' economic power in the private sphere. In some forms of socialism, the socioeconomic rights of workers and others were invoked to challenge the economic power of capitalists, but they were also used to sustain state power in societies that denied civil and political rights to its citizens. Finally, peoples' right to self-determination was invoked to challenge imperialism and colonialism, but was used by some elites within Third World countries to sustain their privileges and control of state power. Similar claims might hold for forms of power concerning gender, sexual orientation,, and race. At the normative level, Stammers suggests that we see human rights as justified challenges to certain existing forms of power. We can see them as responding to "standard threats of power" (a notion he coins by modifying

---

[52] Kennedy 2004, pp. 3–8, 327–57.   [53] Stammers 1993.

Henry Shue's notion of "standard threats"). Human rights can thus be seen as a "set of protection rights".

I find Stammers's descriptive and normative accounts illuminating and sound as far as they go. But they are insufficient and potentially misleading. First, the normative proposal is too narrow. Power is not only something human rights relate to by identifying forms of protection, as an *obstacle or threat*. Power can also be enabling for human rights, i.e. a *resource*. To capture both possibilities, we should focus on the significance of power for people's ability to access objects that satisfy important or urgent interests. *Protection rights* are rights that people have against others using power in ways that undermine access to those objects. *Enablement rights* are rights to have power *to* access those objects. Noticing this distinction (and the plausibility of both elements in it) suggests another problem with Stammers's normative proposal. Since what grounds human rights is not just the presence of power threats, but also the importance of the interests that are threatened (or whose fulfilment is not enabled), the content of human rights cannot simply be identified by looking at power relations. We also need to look more broadly at forms of social action that would facilitate access to the objects of urgent human interests. (There is a counterpart at the descriptive level: we need to explore *enabling* besides *disabling* forms of power relations.) Preventing undesirable power disparities, or blocking their undesirable consequences, should not be the only animating concerns. Human rights are about securing a decent or minimally dignified life for all. This includes, but goes beyond, avoiding or protecting people from power threats. Our understanding of human rights should be power-sensitive but not narrowly power-centred.

3.2. An expressive-elaboration model

In a way, normative talk about human rights and descriptive talk about power are like oil and water: they always come apart. Might doesn't make right (as Rousseau famously said),[54] and rights don't make might (as the history of rights violations amply shows). But descriptions of power in human rights practice are relevant for a full picture of normative reasoning about human rights. We can incorporate power analysis *within* the normative framework to identify the feasibility and contents of various human rights.

We can develop an *expressive-elaboration model* of empowerment within the human rights project. We can, first, elaborate the content of specific rights as requiring that the right-holders have power to access certain goods. To properly respond to an agent's right to a certain object O is to take reasonable and feasible steps to respect, protect, and promote the agent's capability to get O if they choose to do so. Second, when we engage in this elaboration we can express our commitment to agents' empowerment by recognizing their right to participate in it as equal partners. We can see the meta-level practices of discovery, justification, and implementation of various ground-level

---

[54] "[F]orce does not make right." Rousseau 1997, p. 44.

human rights as themselves areas of empowerment that we should take reasonable and feasible steps to respect, protect, and promote. Both of these points would incorporate the dimension of power as a resource mentioned in 3.1.

Given space constraints I cannot here develop this approach fully, and I present it as a hypothesis for future exploration. But let me note two important potential consequences of pursuing it. First, this approach has consequences for what human rights we should accept. The second point, for example, demands that we see strong political rights (including democratic rights) as part of the human rights package. Political rights are important in themselves because they involve the recognition of agents' capacity for political judgement and self-determination. They are also instrumentally significant because they enhance agents' power to identify, implement, and defend their other rights. (Notice that this includes both the protection and enablement considerations mentioned in 3.1.) This is an important result given the scepticism that some philosophers have recently voiced as to whether there is a human right to democracy.[55]

Second, this approach would help us cater for the desiderata identified in this chapter. The kind of empowerment envisaged in the first (ground-level) point would cater for D2, D5, D8, D10, and D11. If we construe human rights as demanding capabilities to achieve their objects, then we foster right-holders' ability to determine whether they get the objects of their rights (D2), we can focus on bolstering the capacities of the worse-off to do so (D5), we activate the initiative of rights-holders to shape their own condition (D8), we enable ourselves to focus on what they need to have the power to get the objects of their rights given their diverse circumstances (which affect their power) (D10), and we are moved to explore deep changes that give them abilities besides formal opportunities to achieve a decent or minimally dignified life (D11). If we also incorporate the second (meta-level) point, then we will also be well positioned to cater for D1, D2, D3, D4, D6, D7, D8, and D10. If we construe the human rights project as fostering robust and cooperative practices of political self-determination, then we can foster multiple arenas of formal and informal, domestic and international political participation in which agents can engage in public reasoning (D7) and decision-making, revise their beliefs about what various agents do, can, and should do to fulfil rights (D1 and D3), minimize unilateral coercive imposition (D2 and D4), engage others as equal cooperators in the project of fulfilling human rights (D8), and envisage multiple possible ways of fulfilling human rights that are appropriate for different individuals in different circumstances (D6 and D10).

---

[55] Cohen 2010, ch. 10; Beitz 2009, sect. 26. For a defence of the human right to democracy see Gilabert 2012b. I should emphasize that political empowerment involves many possible expressions, from democratic decision-making, to public reasoning, to protest and rebellion. The full panoply must be considered, especially when facing nonideal circumstances as desideratum D12 demands. See Gilabert 2012a, ch. 4. For an earlier discussion of the idea of an expression-elaboration model see Gilabert 2005.

3.3. The limits of empowerment

The remarks made in 3.1 and 3.2 emphasize the need to build empowerment into the theory and practice of human rights. We should seek to reduce asymmetries of power, and bolster the absolute power of all to access the objects of their rights. Although these moves would help us cater for most of the desiderata identified in Section 2, they are not sufficient for as long as significant levels of relative or absolute powerlessness (relevant for the fulfilment of human rights) persist. In fact, their complete elimination may not be feasible. But even if the elimination of relative and absolute powerlessness were feasible in the long term, in the immediate future they will exist. We will then have to think about proper ways of acting in the face of such circumstances of power. Our response should include the acknowledgement of dynamic duties to reduce relative and absolute powerlessness over time, and to immediately respond to human rights deficits in the present. But the agents of those duties here and now will often be unequal in their power, and will not always be able to thoroughly respond to existing human rights deficits. In facing these circumstances, we will be thinking about how to cater for desiderata D12 and D9. This will take us beyond the demand for empowerment, forcing us to articulate an ethics of power wielding in nonideal circumstances. The relatively powerful will have to wield their superior power responsibly. And the relatively powerless will have to accept the solidaristic help of others. So we will need to develop ethical standards for the use of unequal power, and envisage ways to recalibrate our sense of the importance of having power for living decent or minimally dignified lives.[56]

References

Beitz, Charles, 2009. *The Idea of Human Rights*. Oxford: Oxford University Press.

Blackburn, Robin, 2011. "Reclaiming Human Rights." *New Left Review* 69, 126–38.

Brown, Chris, 1997. "Universal Human Rights: A Critique." *International Journal of Human Rights* 1, 41–65.

Brown, Wendy, 1995. *States of Injury*. Princeton: Princeton University Press.

Buchanan, Allen and Keohane, Robert, 2004. "The Preventive Use of Force: A Cosmopolitan Institutional Proposal." *Ethics and International Affairs* 18, 1–22.

Cohen, Joshua, 2010. *The Arc of the Moral Universe*. Cambridge, Mass.: Harvard University Press.

Dahl, Robert, 1998. *On Democracy*. New Haven: Yale University Press.

Douzinas, Costas, 2010. "*Adikia*: On Communism and Rights." In C. Douzinas and S. Žižek, eds, *The Idea of Communism*. London: Verso.

Evans, Tony, 2005. *The Politics of Human Rights. A Global Perspective*, 2nd edn. London: Pluto.

[56] For helpful comments or conversations, I thank Charles Beitz, Adam Etinson, Elizabeth Frazer, Stephen Macedo, Julio Montero, and participants in a colloquium at the University of Toronto. My research was supported by a grant from the Social Sciences and Humanities Research Council of Canada and by a fellowship from the Princeton University Center for Human Values.

Geuss, Raymond, 2001. *History and Illusion in Politics*. Cambridge: Cambridge University Press.

Gilabert, Pablo, 2005. "A Substantivist Construal of Discourse Ethics." *International Journal of Philosophical Studies* 13, 405–37.

Gilabert, Pablo, 2011. "Humanist and Political Perspectives on Human Rights." *Political Theory* 39, 439–67.

Gilabert, Pablo, 2012a. *From Global Poverty to Global Equality: A Philosophical Exploration*. Oxford: Oxford University Press.

Gilabert, Pablo, 2012b. "Is There a Human Right to Democracy? A Response to Joshua Cohen." *Revista Latinoamericana de Filosofía Política/Latin American Journal of Political Philosophy* 1, 1–37.

Gilabert, Pablo, 2013. "The Capability Approach and the Debate between Humanist and Political Perspectives on Human Rights. A Critical Survey." *Human Rights Review* 14, 299–325.

Gilabert, Pablo, 2015a. "Human Rights, Human Dignity, and Power." In R. Cruft, M. Liao, and M. Renzo, eds, *The Philosophical Foundations of Human Rights*. Oxford: Oxford University Press.

Gilabert, Pablo, 2015b. "The Socialist Principle 'From Each According to Their Abilities, to Each According to Their Needs'." *Journal of Social Philosophy* 46, No. 2, 197–225.

Glendon, Mary Ann, 2002. *A World Made New*. New York: Random House.

Gramsci, Antonio, 2000. *The Antonio Gramsci Reader*. Ed. D. Forgacs. New York: NYU Press.

Hunt, Lynn, 2007. *Inventing Human Rights: A History*. New York: Norton.

Kennedy, David, 2004. *The Dark Sides of Virtue: Reassessing International Humanitarianism*. Princeton: Princeton University Press.

Koskenniemi, Martti, 2004. "International Law and Hegemony: A Reconfiguration." *Cambridge Review of International Affairs* 17, 197–218.

Lukes, Steven, 2005. *Power: A Radical View*, 2nd edn. New York: Palgrave.

Marx, Karl, 1978a. "On the Jewish Question." In R. Tucker, ed., *The Marx–Engels Reader*, 2nd edn. New York: Norton.

Marx, Karl, 1978b. "Critique of the Gotha Program." In R. Tucker, ed., *The Marx–Engels Reader*, 2nd edn. New York: Norton.

Miller, Richard, 2010. *Global Justice: The Ethics of Poverty and Power*. Oxford: Oxford University Press.

Mutua, Makau, 2002. *Human Rights: A Political and Cultural Critique*. Philadelphia: University of Pennsylvania Press.

Mutua, Makau, 2008. "Human Rights and Powerlessness: Pathologies of Choice and Substance." *Buffalo Law Review* 56, 1027–34.

Nickel, James, 2007. *Making Sense of Human Rights*, 2nd edn. Oxford: Blackwell.

Parfit, Derek, 2011. *On What Matters* (2 vols). Oxford: Oxford University Press.

Pogge, Thomas, 2008. *World Poverty and Human Rights*, 2nd edn. Cambridge: Polity.

Rousseau, Jean-Jacques, 1997. *The Social Contract*. In *The Social Contract and Other Later Political Writings*. Cambridge: Cambridge University Press.

Schmitt, Carl, 1996. *The Concept of the Political*. Chicago: The University of Chicago Press.

Sen, Amartya, 2009. *The Idea of Justice*. Cambridge, Mass.: Harvard University Press.

Sheikh, Fawzia, 2012. "Canada Cuts Aid Budget but Middle-Income Trade Partners Unaffected." *The Guardian* (Wednesday 2 May 2012).

Simmons, Beth, 2009. *Mobilizing for Human Rights: International Law and Domestic Politics.* Cambridge: Cambridge University Press.

Stammers, Neil, 1993. "Human Rights and Power." *Political Studies* 51, 70–82.

Stiglitz, Joseph, 2006. *Making Globalization Work.* New York: Norton.

Valentini, Laura, 2012. "Ideal vs. Non-Ideal Theory: A Conceptual Map." *Philosophical Compass* 7, 654–64.

Wright, Erik, 2010. *Envisioning Real Utopias.* London: Verso.

Žižek, Slavoj, 2005. "Against Human Rights." *New Left Review* 34, 115–31.

11.1

Reflections on Human Rights and Power
A Commentary

Elizabeth Frazer

Pablo Gilabert argues that the concerns of theorists who understand the phenomenon, and the institution, of human rights primarily in terms of 'power' can be met by building practices of 'empowerment' into human rights practice. In the course of his analysis he is also concerned to address some of the ways power theorists attack human rights theory, in particular their arguments (a) that human rights do not (really) exist, (b) that human rights practices should be abandoned, and/or (c) that human rights practice should be shaped, or organized, in certain ways. Gilabert rejects (a) and (b), and endorses (c). He argues that when we articulate, seek to defend or enforce, or to make judgements about, individuals' human rights, we should ensure that we meet twelve criteria, or desiderata. These are: epistemic openness, a presumption against coercive imposition, humility, multilateral authorization, prioritization of the worst-off, encouragement of imagination of multiple articulations, the use of public reason, non-humiliation, solidarity, sensitivity to diversity, deep change of social and political structures, and non-ideal ethical reasoning.

According to Gilabert these empowerment practices would be sufficient to head off the power related worries that are voiced by theorists who are critical of contemporary human rights theory and doctrine. These worries are that human rights doctrine has a parochial (European, seventeenth- and eighteenth-century) origin, that it is imposed on people with quite different ethical and political inheritances, that this imposition relies on hegemonic manipulation, that it involves humiliation, that human rights practice is non-solidaristic, and that human rights are based on a competitive (bourgeois) model of social relations. Gilabert's position can thus incorporate, in part anyway, the critical theses that human rights institutions are the upshot of a power process, that the attribution of human rights to all humans as such is a move in a domination game, that such attribution is in the interests of some individuals and groups more than it is in the interests of others, and that human rights practice institutionalizes the domination of some by others. He argues that, if any of these theses are true, redress can be ensured by practices of empowerment. In any case, the prescription of practices of empowerment as part of human rights practice is valid, so would apply even if the theses are not true. An upshot of all this, in Gilabert's analysis, is that power critique does not undermine human rights practice; rather, it endorses it.

In this commentary I want to focus on two elements of Gilabert's argument. These are, first, the account of and treatment of the question of the 'existence' or otherwise of human rights, and second, the use of an intentionalist analysis of power. In both of these cases, matters seem to me to be more complicated than the argument (presented here in a necessarily compressed way, of course) fully acknowledges. In particular, one of the twelve proposed ways of mitigating power effects in human rights practice is 'deep change:... we should seek to change economic and political structures and other deep factors making human rights deprivations likely'. Now, I definitely concur that structural change is called for. However, two thoughts are prompted. First, 'deep change' is pretty challenging, as the history of inequality in settings modern and traditional, industrial and agricultural, in welfare states and other kinds, tells us. We need then to consider very carefully what kind of project this deep structural change must be, who might be able to take it forward, and under what conditions. Second, what, exactly, is the place of human rights practice in such an empowerment project? We want to make such structural changes because existing structures deprive persons of appropriate welfare, leaving needs unmet. They also, to be sure, make human rights deprivations likely. But it seems to me that it is needs and welfare that drive a restructuring project, not the rights as such. Rights, on the other hand, may well be instrumental for the securing of welfare and the meeting of needs. Further, the kind of knowledge, and social and organizational capacity, that is required if we are to have any hope of meeting anything like Gilabert's twelve desiderata is a specifically political knowledge and capacity. The realization of rights requires knowledge and understanding of power structures. In my analysis, this makes of human rights practice a specifically political practice.

I also want to consider the way this focus on power structures suggests an analysis of power different from the one that Gilabert deploys in order to explicate the power critique of rights. He presumes, for the sake of his argument, an intentionalist model of power.[1] There is, I believe, a tension between this model or theory of power, and the desideratum of 'deep change', which implicitly turns our attention more in the direction of a stucturalist analysis. Intentionalist models conceptualize power as a property or capacity of an individual, and in terms of the individual's agency and action. Powerful agents have capacities that they can intentionally deploy in order to bring about states of affairs that they desire, or to get others to act in such a way as to bring about that state of affairs. Agents who have power exerted over them, in turn, experience (among

---

[1] Intentionalist models are frequently taken as basic, or paradigmatic, in political theories of power: see Lukes 1974; Lukes 1986. For detailed analysis of various versions of intentionalism: Barry 1989.

other things) the diminution of their own independent agency, the thwarting of their own desires, and the nonsatisfaction of their own preferences.[2]

The intentionalist picture of power is strikingly congruent with a standard theory of rights, in which individuals' moral rights are identified (and justified, perhaps) by reference to a basic value like autonomy, or by reference to interests of a particular quality. A moral right, such as that to education, supports or generates a prescription that the right should be endorsed culturally, institutionalized legally, and protected by government and state or, at least, by international organizations, preferably all of the above. When women and girls are denied education, for instance, someone else's preferences—about how they should live, conduct themselves, what they should do, etc.—are satisfied, not their own. The framework of rights means that a girl's preference for or interest in education can be expressed as a right to education, which in turn means that any denial of education is not just a deprivation of something that she needs, or a thwarting of her preference, but is also a violation of her rights.

Rights disempower some individuals (rights violators) and they empower rights holders. This is one element of the congruence between intentionalist theories of power and traditional theories of rights. That a person has a right to be educated does not ensure education, any more than a right not to be assaulted assuredly prevents assault. But resistance to deprivation or violation is justified, as are claims and actions in pursuit of education, even where significant others do not believe that education is right. Further, over time, and in a context of the institutionalization and wider social endorsement of a right to education, moral prescription might act as a constraint on the conduct of would-be violators or deprivers—either because they partly internalize the right and concede it, or because as a publicly articulated norm any violation cannot, will not, go uncontested.

How should we think of these 'rights' that play this role in a process of power distribution? In this framework, rights also are properties of individuals. At least they are properties that are ascribed to individuals. We can treat individuals' rights like variables—a person will have more or less depending on their social and material relationships; and human rights doctrine holds that there is a range of rights that all persons have irrespective of their relationships. At any rate, we treat persons as if they have such rights. As we have seen, the model is one of rights augmenting, or diminishing, the power of individuals—they redistribute power. Grammatically, these ideas are underscored by the doctrine of power and rights as things that we have, or don't.

Gilabert argues that positions that hold that human rights do not exist fail. They fail, at least, as arguments against human rights practice and institutions, and as arguments against propositions regarding how human beings ought to treat one another. Girls ought to be educated, so the argument goes, and that is so irrespective of the merits of philosophical analysis of the existence of human rights in general, of the existence of a

---

[2] Barry 1989, pp. 222–69 for an account of the measurement of power in terms of the distance between the preference satisfaction of the powerful and that of the sufferer of power.

universal right to education, or of a particular girl's right to education. According to this line, then, locutions like 'this girl has a right to education' need not make any metaphysical claim for the existence of an entity. Rather, it is simply short, without remainder, for something like 'it is the case that all girls should be educated', or 'we should ensure that all girls are educated'. This certainly does seem to turn our focus away from rights as properties, to standards of conduct and norms of treatment of persons.

In her particular version of the 'action frame of reference' Arendt's political theory seeks to move away from ontology—the philosophical focus on the ground of being—and instead focus on action. For her, declarations are irrelevant unless they are accompanied by transformations in relationships and by the construction of institutions. The force of politics lies in what we do, not in what we say. What is important is people's position vis-à-vis power—how are people positioned in relation to states? How are they positioned in relation to each other and to the potential for creative action in concert? This, in my interpretation, is the point of her critical repudiation of twentieth-century human rights theory.[3] Now all of this seems to be consistent with Gilabert's emphasis on the practice of human rights, and on empowerment as a desideratum of that practice. But I wonder whether the idea of power as a property really helps that focus.[4]

Here is another way of understanding power. As much as, even more than, the exercise of a capacity to change the world and to affect other people's conduct, power—a power structure—should be thought of as a pattern of opportunities for, barriers to, and resources for, individuals' own action and conduct. These opportunities, barriers, and resources are comprised of material, psychological, and symbolic goods and bads, time, physical capacity and force, and also norms and laws. Depending on one's position in such a structure, depending on one's holdings of goods and bads, physical capacities, time, and one's relations to others (for example, dependency or having dependents on one), one is more or less able to act, to cooperate with, or to resist pressure from others.[5]

It's important not to fall into any trap of seeing the agency and the structure theories of power as dichotomous or mutually exclusive. The account here does emphasize capacities, so is to that extent agent-centred. But the emphasis on position and relationality decentres agency. It means that the 'properties' or capacities of an agent come after that agent's relation with others, after their position vis-à-vis a distribution. Some versions of social theory put this very strongly: subjects are the outcomes of structures. Sometimes, it seems that autonomous dynamics are attributed to power, as though it were completely independent of human agency. I don't want to endorse such models. But I also want to take issue with any strong emphasis on intention, on individual

---

[3] Arendt 1951, esp. pp. 291–301; Arendt 1973, esp. pp. 148–9.

[4] For a different set of complications of the power as capacity or ability view: Morriss 2002, esp. pp. 156ff.

[5] This position follows Foucault 1980. However, Foucault dissented from the theoretical connotations of the term structure which I here use in its relatively weak sociological sense. And the implications of Foucault's theory for understanding political agency are controversial: for instance, see McNay 1992.

agents' properties and capacities. Rather, I want to focus on the way structures explain the possibilities and limits of human action, including, critically, actions such as opposing violations of rights that are ascribed to one by legal authorities, or by political actors, or by moral judges.

Structures are held in place in part normatively. They are endorsed as necessary, or desirable, or inevitable, or sanctified by time, as the rightful state of affairs, as prescribing or necessitating the right thing to do. People act, prescriptively, out of deference to them, sometimes because they have internalized and endorsed the distribution, sometimes because it is publicly articulated and conduct in accordance with it is sanctioned positively or negatively. Norms are not uncontested; we should expect that they are variously complied with, and we should even expect to find subcultures in which dominant norms are subverted or violated, or where alternatives are articulated.[6] If it is socially endorsed, justified, and normal, that all individuals should be educated to a threshold level, individuals will tend to endorse that judgement in their daily conduct; however, they will not be surprised to meet alternative views, and that can be the basis of social conflict. If it is socially endorsed and normal that girls, say, should be educated differently, or to a different threshold, or not at all, then that norm will be enacted, or at least, there will be efforts, competition, in that direction. People who attempt to challenge or overturn norms, at the level of society, to have new norms institutionalized in law, find it relatively difficult to do so. But norms do, of course, change over time, and sometimes they change as a result of concerted political effort. The point with regard to a theory of power, though, is that individuals benefit to varying degrees from the structure, and from their particular position in it.[7]

Structures are held stable in part normatively, and in part by the concerted effort of those who benefit from them. In the face of efforts to redistribute material goods, people who stand to lose materially resist politically, physically, socially. The histories of girls' rights to education, whether at home, or in school, are stories of claims, counterclaims, proscription, resistance, and sometimes coercion and violence. Sometimes, of course, members of dominant groups may endorse and support redistributions from which they will not directly benefit materially, because they are convinced that it is morally right, or that the all-round effects will benefit them overall or in the long run. Women's education has had male champions, from particular fathers, to financial benefactors, and progressive legislators.

But the critical point is that the relatively powerful can be material in the oppression of the relatively powerless without doing anything particular to anyone in particular— just by living a daily life. When an individual endorses, complies with, and hence contributes to the reproduction of a norm, that reproduction, the macro outcome, does not have to have any place in the individual's intention or even awareness. Casualties of the power structure need not be deliberately targeted, oppressed, or exploited; and

---

[6] For emphasis on social actors' negotiated relationship with norms: Barnes 1988.
[7] See Barry 1991.

powerful people might not even be aware of their existence, let alone the relationship between their respective situations. Oppressed people need not know, exactly, that they are being oppressed.

What difference does such a theory of power make to our understanding of human rights doctrine? To be cognizant of power is to be cognizant of domination—the way some agents' (whether individuals, groups, or institutionalized formations like 'the west' or 'Europe') understandings of the world structure distributions of goods and resources. Of course, power often takes the form of imposition, and coercion. Individuals are arrested and subject to trial on the basis of human rights law; or compliance with human rights doctrine is used as a counter in a trade for membership, recognition, or exchange of other goods. But this capacity for domination, or susceptibility to oppression, is itself the upshot of position in an established structure. People who are positioned centrally, with a rich endowment of resources, bequeath their positions to their chosen descendants. Without meaning to, just by conducting themselves according to norms and reasonable expectations, they can prevent those who occupy relatively marginal, disadvantaged positions, from moving to the centre, from accumulating more. They can effectively prevent efforts to restructure the distribution without lifting a finger.

This approach to power has been argued by critics to delete responsibility.[8] In my judgement such a deletion does not follow at all. I have argued that the intentionalist theory of power is insufficient for understanding how unequal structures of disadvantage are established and maintained. When I buy a t-shirt I don't intend to deprive a child of education; but my purchase might be one move in a set of market interactions that effectively does just that. This is the point of political critiques of market interactions. We might argue that as well as having the right to education, for instance, individuals have responsibilities to understand the world in which and from which they live, and to gain a serious understanding of the structures that govern their lives and that position individuals such that they are susceptible, or not, to exclusion, to deprivation. We can see that the stability of a structure, or the prevention of its transformation, is explicable by reference to the acts and omissions of those with more goods and resources, more capacities, in interaction with the efforts of those who have less. Girls who are not allowed to go to school may have a moral duty to protest. Individuals who are in a position to protect them, to provide schooling, to prevent violations, have a responsibility to deploy their power in order to change the distribution of that power. If the structure should be transformed, and we think of that proposition as prescriptive, then those who can are the ones who should act.[9]

Now it may be that the promoters, defenders, and guardians of human rights—governments, legal authorities, campaigning organizations—are, indeed, the kind

[8] See Dowding 2003, p. 305.
[9] For complications in the prescriptive vs normative distinction, see: Estlund 2008, pp. 259–75; Valentini 2009.

of focal points of potential action in concert that might act in such a structurally transformative way. The empowerment desiderata that Gilabert recommends are a tall order by any account, but organizations like these will be in the forefront of any possible effort in that direction. Whatever the final prescription in this regard, I want to emphasize that this amounts to an argument for a political, not a legal, nor simply moral, nor any kind of naturalistic laissez-faire, approach to rights. It takes political consciousness to see power where others see (or purport to see) natural facts about how the world works, or where they see only moral principles. Any understanding of a power structure shows us a range of mechanisms that prevent people from acting morally or bringing about a morally required state of affairs. It shows the limits and the deleterious consequences of market exchanges, of certain traditional cultures and divisions of labour and privilege.

Political power and action are denigrated in many quarters. Politics, its logic, the conduct of politicians, and the constraints of possibility, have all been identified as threats to morality. In political philosophy, morality is commonly thought of as a necessary constraint on politics. It is for this reason that assertions of the politically constructed nature of human rights are taken by some political philosophers to be, on the face of it, subversive of rights' truly moral nature, and to be treated with analytic caution.[10] Politics is denigrated as antithetical to morality—it compromises truth and principle, it engages in instrumental reasoning—and there is no point denying that in some constructions of political thought, so it is.[11]

But in another version of political power—one which emphasizes our capacity to see the structural upshots of individual interactions, which emphasizes our capacity to remake structures, and our capacity not just to decide, but to decide how we collectively are going to decide—we attempt to understand the structure that constrains us now, and to act, to take the risk of attempting to transform it. In political action we necessarily (seek to) go beyond the constraints of the present.[12] Political power enjoins re-visioning of the world. It allows for the realization that things are other than they seem—that, for instance, girls are humans and might be engineers, that we (human beings) can organize the structures that govern us. We can bring them into view, we can argue about them, we can concoct schemes for restructuring them, and sometimes, just sometimes, we can embark on a programme of restructuring. Which works. But not smoothly, not without friction; and not without unforeseen consequences. All of this uncertainty and ambiguity generates a further raft of reasons why in many quarters politics has a bad name as such. For, as well as re-visioning, politics has to face

---

[10]   Valentini 2012.

[11]   For example, in a common construction of politics as 'machiavellian' and centred on dissimulation, means–end reasoning, and domination; in the Weberian insistence that politics and ethics are completely separate domains; and in the liberal idea that politics is just what it is, and hence must be constrained by morality. Frazer 2006.

[12]   This account of political action, capability, and openness owes a good deal to Arendt 1958.

up to, embrace, uncertainty, and many commentators and critics are exceedingly intolerant of uncertainty.

I argue that understanding of the structure of power—of the mechanisms that hold it stable, and of the possibilities for restructuring it—is a critical form of political knowledge. This kind of political knowledge, in turn, seems to be a critical resource in any strategy of empowerment guided by the complex twelve desiderata of human rights practice that Gilabert recommends. He argues that power critiques of human rights doctrine and practice don't undermine the practice but rather endorse it. I think this focus on the good and bad consequences of the reproduction without transformation of power structures, and on the good and bad consequences of efforts to transform them, certainly do not undermine human rights practice. But it does seem to have implications for our understanding of the place of human rights in ethics and political philosophy, and the appropriate place of human rights practice in political life and action.

We certainly may have good reasons for thinking that the issue of girls' education, and other issues like it, are well formulated in the language of rights, and that struggles for rights have effectively served causes like that of girls' education well. But efforts in empowerment—the empowerment of some, the disempowerment of others—seek justice in power itself. The point is a restructuring of power, of resources, so that needs are met, and welfare secured. Rights, moral and legal, and rights that are universal, might well be strategically significant, even the best, way of pursuing the reconstruction of power structures so that individuals can flourish, and so that wrongful violence cannot be engaged in with impunity. But on this account rights are a political means to a just end, rather than being ends themselves.

References

Arendt, Hannah (1951). *The Origins of Totalitarianism* (new edition with added prefaces). San Diego: Harcourt Inc.

Arendt, Hannah (1958). *The Human Condition* (Chicago: University of Chicago Press).

Arendt, Hannah (1973). *On Revolution* (Harmondsworth: Penguin).

Barnes, Barry (1988). *The Nature of Power* (Cambridge: Polity Press).

Barry, Brian (1989). *Democracy, Power and Justice: Essays in Political Theory* (Oxford: Oxford University Press).

Barry, Brian (1991). 'Is It Better to Be Powerful or Lucky?', in Barry, *Democracy and Power: Essays in Political Theory I* (Oxford: Oxford University Press), pp. 270–302.

Dowding, Keith (2003). 'Resources, Power and Systematic Luck: A Response to Barry', *Politics, Philosophy and Economics*, Vol. 2, No. 3, pp. 305–22.

Estlund, David M. (2008). *Democratic Authority: A Philosophical Framework* (Princeton: Princeton University Press).

Foucault, Michel (1980). 'Disciplinary Power and Subjection', in Colin Gordon (ed.), *Power/Knowledge: Selected Interviews and Other Writings 1972–77* (Brighton: Harvester). Reprinted in Lukes (1986).

Frazer, Elizabeth (2006). 'Max Weber on Ethics and Politics', *Politics and Ethics Review,* Vol. 2, no. 1, pp. 19–37.

Lukes, Steven (1974). *Power: A Radical View* (Basingstoke: Macmillan Education Limited).

Lukes, Steven (ed.) (1986). *Power* (Oxford: Basil Blackwell).

McNay, Lois. (1992). *Foucault and Feminism* (Cambridge: Polity Press).

Morriss, Peter (2002). *Power: A Philosophical Analysis* (Manchester: Manchester University Press).

Valentini, Laura (2009). 'On the Apparent Paradox of Ideal Theory', *The Journal of Political Philosophy* Vol. 17, no. 3, pp. 332–55.

Valentini, Laura (2012). 'In What Sense are Human Rights Political? A Preliminary Exploration', *Political Studies,* Vol. 660, no. 1, p. 180.

12

The Hazards of Rescue

C. A. J. Coady

The human rights movement has been one of the striking features, indeed in many respects one of the most successful features, of international relations in the second half of the twentieth century on into the twenty-first century. Its success has been to use the powerful vocabulary of rights, with both the moral and legal overtones that vocabulary carries, to highlight gross abuses of power by institutions, groups, and individuals across the spectrum of local and international communities. These powerful institutions have included, most notably, states and their armed forces, but also revolutionary groups and cultural or religious groups that have committed such crimes as murder, rape, torture, major dispossession, and deliberate starvation.

It is of course one thing to notice and applaud this heightened consciousness of the wrongs inflicted on human beings worldwide by powerful forces, both state and non-state, it is another to believe that this awareness and rhetorical discourse has unequivocally improved the plight of the afflicted millions of victims of human rights violations or reduced the scale of such violations. Here, I think, the record is more mixed than one might hope, especially for the efforts of well-intentioned foreigners attempting to rescue suffering people abroad or to redress their wrongs. In what follows, I will explore some ambiguities and problems that often beset efforts to implement human rights by rescue.

Key Concepts: Human Rights, Humanitarianism, Realism, and Moralism

(a) Human rights

The advocates of the universal claims of the doctrine of human rights have striven to move the attention of citizens beyond their own borders to see and respond to the plight of others in 'the international community', the widespread use of the latter term itself being, in part, an acknowledgement of the demands of universal human rights. Human rights have been incorporated into international law, both in what is called Human Rights Law and in Humanitarian Law. The former is directed primarily at the preservation of human rights in peaceful societies whereas the latter is concerned with protecting specified human rights in war and other armed conflicts. Even so, there are significant overlaps, such as the prohibition on torture. The normative force of human rights is also part of what motivates humanitarian law, and it is a significant factor in the rise of all those NGO groups that seek to dispense humanitarian aid to suffering people in all parts of the world, since the urgency of rescue is often correlated with the scale and nature of human rights violations. And as I shall explain in this chapter, human rights have accompanied and reinforced, though with some ambiguity, the earlier institutional embodiments of the humanitarian spirit in the form of International Red Cross and similar movements.

Philosophers and other theorists have been greatly exercised in recent years exploring the exact nature of human rights, seeking to answer such questions as: Are human rights genuinely universal or do they legitimately vary across different cultures and eras? Are the commonly accepted lists of human rights sufficiently cohesive to admit of one single explanation or justification? How are human rights different, if at all, from such universal rights as natural rights? What is the relation between individual and group human rights? Can human rights be overridden, and if so by what?[1]

In what follows I am going to side-step full discussion of most of these questions, important as they are, since my concern is less with them than with something slightly different though related. My problems are those concerned with responses to human rights violations and for the purposes of this discussion I will assume (what in any case I believe to be true) that human rights are universal in application, morally based though they have both a political and legal dimension, and that—despite whatever difficulties there may be in deciding the content and interpretation of such rights (e.g. do political rights of participation extend to children and prisoners?)—there is a central, widely acknowledged group of them that it is of great importance to have protected. Granted that much, I want to test some common assumptions about the mode of protection and support that outsiders can offer for such rights. These include common assumptions about armed humanitarian intervention to rescue people from crisis situations, but I will journey to that topic by way of examining what appear to be less contentious unarmed interventions first. Ultimately, I will try to show that the practice of humanitarianism, in both these forms, is much more precarious and contestable than often envisaged.

(b) Humanitarianism

In his play *Murder in the Cathedral*, T. S. Eliot famously put into the mouth of Thomas Becket the self-cautioning words: 'The last temptation is the greatest treason, to do the right deed for the wrong reason.' This certainly resonates with the moral problems posed by the arguments for armed humanitarian intervention, since the presence and influence of reasons inimical to declared humanitarian motives may often jeopardize

---

[1] For one important extended discussion of these issues see Griffin (2008).

the morality and the actual operation of an intervention; this has been raised as a problem for the humanitarian aspects of the 2003 intervention in Iraq with respect to both US commercial and political motives regarding the acquisition of Iraq's oil supplies and the grand motive of 'democratizing' the Middle East. Many also criticized Vietnam's military intervention in Cambodia because the desire for political control of its neighbour allegedly dominated the declared humanitarian motive of removing Pol Pot. I shall, however, be more concerned in what follows with another 'treason' or dangerous failing, namely what might be called 'doing the wrong deed for the right reason' which tracks the old saying that 'the road to hell is paved with good intentions'.

The 'right reason' of course in connection with the advocacy of violent or non-violent humanitarian intervention is that of compassion for suffering, persecuted victims and the associated moral imperative to do something to aid or rescue such victims. This compassionate concern is clearly part of what has fuelled the modern success of the human rights movement, and is prominent in the various NGOs that offer aid, support, and selfless care to people in desperate need in all parts of the world. It is also an obvious factor in the United Nations' adoption of a Responsibility to Protect (RtoP) programme as a guiding principle for its membership and its operations.

In some respects, the term 'humanitarianism' is an odd one for this concern since much of it would have been covered in the past by virtue expressions such as 'justice' or 'charity', but the point of it is to express a certain solidarity with all human beings wherever they live and so to import a type of cosmopolitanism into the attitudes and virtues with which we confront severe harms and deprivations wherever they occur. There is also a hint in the emphasis on humanity of a secular disengagement from earlier forms of religiously inspired charitable activities on the international stage, mostly connected with missionary activity. Many organizations like the Red Cross, Oxfam, or Médecins Sans Frontières, insofar as they can be said to have an ideology, are inspired by what might be called humanism rather than religion. This is not to deny that a number of modern humanitarian organizations remain religiously inspired, though they are less directly linked to missionary activity. Nor is it to deny that it is possible for a form of humanism to have itself a religious dimension as the various advocates of Christian humanism, for instance, would maintain.

Though now closely bound up with the idea of human rights, the expression 'humanitarian' had a rather different origin and historical development from the discourse of 'human rights' though their eventual merging is very natural.[2] It is plausible to see 'humanitarianism' in its recognizably modern form as arising from the shock experienced by the Swiss banker Henry Dunant on visiting the battlefield of Solferino in 1859 (during the Second Italian War of Independence) and discovering the ghastly carnage of death and severe wounding and mutilation wrought upon soldiers by warfare. Profoundly moved by the sight of such suffering, he then organized

---

[2] Tom Farer discusses the history in Farer (2012). He cites Michael Barnett (2011). Samuel Moyn discusses some other interesting aspects of the history in Moyn (2010).

locals to provide limited aid and succour to the dying and wounded on both sides. His impartial compassion for the dead and wounded, and his realization of the inadequacy of ad hoc measures, resulted in a self-published, ultimately influential book, *Un souvenir de Solferino* (*A Memory of Solferino*), which led to the creation of the International Committee of the Red Cross. Initially, the Red Cross was concerned solely with humane treatment of wounded and sick soldiers with a later extension to the treatment of captured soldiers, which may have accounted for the rapid and widespread acknowledgement of its concerns in international legal instruments such as the first Geneva Convention of 1864. The momentum of the humanitarian movement quickly developed concerns regarding warfare that were wider than the welfare of soldiers, which is evidenced by contemporary international humanitarian law's concern for civilians affected by war. Later, the humanitarian impulse was inevitably incorporated into the discourse of human rights and the UN's Universal Declaration of Human Rights. While bearing in mind the differences to be discussed below in origin and emphasis of both movements (humanitarianism and human rights) I will use the designation 'humanitarian' to refer to aid that is provided to relieve an existing situation of desperate need that may or may not have resulted from deliberate human rights violations, though, as we shall see, the latter raise problems about what to do about the threat of further actual or potential human rights violations brought about by the provision of aid itself.

So a movement that began in reactions of compassion and mercy, and might well have been conceived as an expression of charity, quickly moved via covenants and laws into the territory of justice. The terms 'charity' and 'justice' are open to a variety of interpretations, of course, and charity in particular has in recent times come to be seen as a dubious disposition since it can have an air of condescension about it in that recipients of charitable aid are thought to be demeaned by being objects of such charity.[3] This is not the place for a detailed analysis of the difference between the virtues of charity and justice, but the discourse of human rights (and perhaps of rights more generally) puts pressure on the idea of good dispositions that are not the recognition of a strict obligation to acknowledge the rights of others. This pressure is especially acute when the plight of those others results from severe maltreatment rather than natural disaster. In cases of murder, torture, unjust imprisonment, rape, forcible relocation, and much else, it is plausible to speak of injustice and rights violations whereas an earthquake or a flood does not violate rights or wreak injustice. Moreover, acts of murder, torture, etc. are more egregious as rights violations when perpetrated by those in positions of power and trust such as governments and their agencies.

So when the new humanitarians respond to such violations, they do not see themselves as merely dispensing charity since they reject accounts of justice that localize its

---

[3] Interestingly, in more recent times, this allegation has morphed into a critique of human rights themselves, which have been criticized by Alain Badiou, for instance, as presenting a demeaning picture of the victims of rights violations. See Badiou (2001), pp. 10–16.

application to particular national or cultural contexts, or make such application primary in what they see as objectionable ways. Consequently, in addition to the motivation of compassion mentioned above, we should cite moral indignation as a reason driving the advocates of aid organizations in those cases where suffering is not the outcome of natural disaster but of human intent or gross negligence.[4] For such cases, the new humanitarians will also think it insufficient to say that these are indeed injustices, but that only the local authorities (or other local groups) are under an obligation to refrain from violations or to remedy them when they occur. Justice and injustice have a much wider reach and the idea of human rights is an attempt to characterize that reach. This outlook is supported in theoretical terms by the philosophical movement called 'cosmopolitanism' which seeks to ground a political ethic in universal moral imperatives. Cultural relativism is a primary target of this cosmopolitanism, but contract theories and other forms of 'partiality' also come under fire. Of course, cosmopolitanism is not unique in seeking such universality since natural law, intuitionism, utilitarianism, and Kantianism also seek something similar. I will not examine the differences in emphasis or grounding between such approaches here, since that is not essential to my purposes; I merely mention this as background. A further point about the emphasis on justice and injustice is that it stands in some tension with a criterion of political 'neutrality' that developed early in the practices of the humanitarian aid movements since they were anxious to avoid taking sides in the situations of armed conflict or persecutions into which they hoped to bring relief or rescue. This is a point to be discussed in the section dealing with difficulties created by the requirements of 'neutral aid'.

(c) Realism and moralism

One further background point is that the concept and theory of political realism is often invoked at this point as a caution on, and often a rejection of, human rights impulses. The realist position associated with such theorists as Hans Morgenthau, George Kennan, and Reinhold Neibuhr, amongst many others, is a somewhat pluralist and even amorphous outlook which is often interpreted, and indeed often proposed by its adherents, as rejecting any role for morality in international politics and sometimes even in politics at all. As I have argued elsewhere, the genuine insights of realism are better understood as rejecting what can be seen as distortions of morality rather than morality itself; these distortions I have grouped under the heading of moralism in recognition of the ways in which such terms as 'moralistic' have become increasingly pejorative expressions since, roughly, the middle of the nineteenth century.[5]

---

[4] In themselves, natural disasters evoke compassion and not moral indignation. Such indignation is only appropriate for the acts or omissions of moral agents, though sometimes moral indignation is appropriate where human agency, but for culpable negligence, could have prevented the natural disaster or mitigated its effects.

[5] For fuller discussion of moralism and the link with realism see Coady (2008a), chs. 1 and 2.

Although much of the application of terms like 'moralistic' is beset by vague and even confused understanding, there are moralistic attitudes and judgements that deserve condemnation on moral grounds. I have elsewhere attempted a loose catalogue of the different sorts of thing that could figure in a proper account of moralism as a sort of vice.[6] I will advert to some of them in the detailed discussions of intervention, but here I will simply generalize over them, at the risk of some simplification, to say that they tend to be violations of prudence where I understand prudence to be itself part of morality. Many philosophers, by contrast, treat prudence as antithetical to morality in being solely a concern for one's own interests, but I prefer the more ancient tradition of viewing prudence as the virtue that helps us implement moral concerns realistically.[7] Our own individual interests are part of the material with which prudence is concerned but only part of it; it is clearly possible to exercise prudence on behalf of others, when, for example, one is in a position of care for others, either formally or by chance, and certain forms of apparently helpful response would not be in the overall or longer-term interests of those others. This requires a developed sense of how best to implement moral principles and virtues in situations of complexity, and the contexts of foreign aid provide such complexity in abundance.

There have undoubtedly been significant achievements of humanitarianism as a movement of ideas and practices and I have no desire to belittle them nor to adopt an attitude of cynicism or amoralism towards the concern for universal justice and the desire to protect the numerous victims of injustice in various parts of the world. So I would distance myself from some of the harsher realist criticisms of aid, such as those levelled by Alex de Waal who tends (amongst other criticisms) to see the institutional and public relations interests of aid agencies as always dominating their humane concerns. This is not to deny the genuine points made by de Waal about the pressures of such interests.[8] Indeed, the harsh critics have a point in as much as the assertion of moral indignation as a counterweight to indifference, cynicism, or realpolitik carries its own temptations and costs that need to be confronted if morally motivated protest and action is to be fully serious and effective. In what follows, I will explore this issue, in part by deploying the concept of moralism.

The Hazards of Humanitarian Aid

I shall begin with the morality of non-violent humanitarian aid, in particular with the various non-governmental agencies who view themselves as principally or significantly concerned with bringing the resources of the richer nations to bear upon conspicuous

---

[6] Coady (2008a), chs. 1 and 2.

[7] For an influential treatment in that tradition that echoes Aristotle's discussion of 'phronesis' see Aquinas (2007), 2a2ae.47.

[8] de Waal (1997). See pp. 204–12 for an account of the wildly exaggerated claims made by aid agencies about the impending disasters in the externally displaced persons' (EDP's) camps in eastern Zaire in 1996. (This is also cited in Vaux (2001), pp. 207–8.)

suffering in countries that are unable or unwilling to cope with that suffering on their own. I have in mind such agencies as Oxfam, Médecins Sans Frontières, and the International Red Cross, to name only a few. Similar considerations will apply to some extent to various United Nations or governmental agencies, like Australia's AusAID, that share this sort of concern. But governmental agencies and often enough other agencies deal not only with what we might call crisis aid but also (and sometimes principally) developmental aid. The latter is geared to long-term objectives of lifting people out of poverty or other disadvantages principally by improving their nation's economies or those aspects of them to do with such matters as health and education, whereas crisis aid is geared more to interventions to meet immediate and damaging emergencies, such as those created by armed conflict, brutal persecution, or natural disasters. Of course, the distinction is rough, but it is useful for my purposes since the problems of crisis aid more obviously translate into problems for military intervention even though they may contain some lessons for development aid as well. My discussion will therefore focus on crisis aid.

There is now a striking literature on the problems facing aid organizations, much of it written by members of such groups or close observers of them in 'the field', and a great deal of it impressively self-critical. Although the debate began earlier, it was given stimulus by Mary B. Anderson's, *Do No Harm: How Aid Can Support Peace—or War*, and it has been followed by numerous books and articles, perhaps the most impressive of which is Fiona Terry's *Condemned to Repeat? The Paradox of Humanitarian Action*.[9] Although the various writers are by no means unanimous in their analyses, there is convergence on a number of points that mostly fit into the framework that I have tried to articulate elsewhere when discussing the problem of moralism in international affairs. It should also be noted that there is a growing sceptical literature on the failings of developmental aid and again a good deal of it involves criticism from within the aid community itself. Jonathan Glennie, for instance, himself an aid activist and a key player in the 2005 'Make Poverty History' campaign, has argued persuasively that increased governmental aid in Africa has often increased poverty and distress. As he says: 'In reality, in many African countries aid has meant more poverty, more hungry people, worse basic services for poor people and damage to already precarious democratic institutions.'[10] Glennie does not decry governmental financial aid entirely; he thinks it can have an important subsidiary role. He argues that its serious deficiencies relate to structural social and political conditions in the countries receiving aid and in global economic and trade arrangements that contribute to the ineffectiveness of the aid. These deficiencies include corrupt local leadership, international debt arrangements that require countries to repay debts accumulated irresponsibly by

---

[9] Anderson (1999); Terry (2002). There is a good account of some of the other books in the area by Tom Farer in Farer (2012).

[10] Glennie (2008), p. 2.

deposed dictators, and unreasonable conditions imposed by global finance organizations like the International Monetary Fund.

Before examining the issue of crisis aid in detail it is worth remarking that an overarching consideration regarding it is captured by the old tag, itself one of the lessons in Aesop's fables (especially the fable of the fox and the goat in the well), that you should always look before you leap. The imperative of rescue is augmented by the capacity of modern communication technology to present heart-rending images and information about suffering which can generate responses that are inappropriate in various ways to the reality of what is happening in the target nation. Moral sympathy uninformed by complete, or at least thorough, understanding can lead to bad out-comes from good motives. Moreover, the fable's lesson is incomplete since you also need to look after you leap, even when you've had a good look in advance: after the goat jumped into the well at the fox's enticing invitation about the quality of the drinking water (the fox having accidentally fallen in before) he should have thought more carefully about the consequences of giving so selfish a creature as the fox a helping hoist out of the well. As a result the goat was left haplessly in the well while the fox went on his way, disregarding any promise to help. Of course, humanitarian crises often call for swift responses, but a swift response that is uninformed can merely speed further misfortune.

(a) Moral indignation and the distorting influence of certain forms of moralism

So the first specific pitfall in aid efforts is the way that moral outrage at suffering, especially that caused by human rights violations, can cloud judgement about the situation in which the suffering takes place. This response exhibits what I have called the moralism of deluded power and also the moralism of unbalanced focus.[11] The former produces the delusion that moral stands and utterances by themselves can produce more effects for good than they really can, but it can also encourage the belief that one's conscientious reaction to the wrongdoing of others, or even the harmful effects of nature, provides comprehensive insights into how best to respond to the crises and acquits one of the need to understand the precise contexts of the wrongdoing or the natural events. Indeed, human rights discourse itself can produce the comfort-ing belief that declarations, manifestos, and appeals to human rights have much more power to change the world than in reality they do.

The moralism of unbalanced focus implicitly recognizes a variety of goods and evils but explicitly concentrates upon one to the exclusion or illegitimate down-grading of relevant others. So, to take an example from another area, it has been plausibly argued that some Christian moralists in their attitude to public policy have allowed an excessive focus on sexual morality to blind them to the import-ance of other values, such as social justice and health care rights. This is a criticism

---

[11] See Coady (2008a).

levelled, for instance, at American Catholic bishops for their interventions in the debates about the Obama health care reforms.

A third category of moralism is moralism of abstraction in which damage can be done by concentration on abstract principles to the exclusion of the ways in which such principles (duties, virtues, or prohibitions) need to be sensitively interpreted, implemented, or refined in concrete circumstances. And a fourth kind of moralism is what I have called a moralism of imposition or interference, which is a type of illegitimate paternalism whereby an outsider's assessment of the needs and desires of a target community is imposed, often without recognition of dissonance, upon the members of that community. There is of course a certain degree of interaction and sometimes overlap between these categories, as when dedication to the abstract principle of the responsibility to protect encourages external impositions that insufficiently respect local autonomies, which imposition, in turn, promotes (or constitutes) a moralism of unbalanced focus. The slogan 'the white man's burden' that helped disguise many of the grave injustices of old-style colonialism was partly a product of self-deception and racist fantasy, but also sometimes expressed a genuine concern for the improvement of the colonized people by way of the benefits of 'Western civilization'. These benefits were often understood in a lofty and abstract way that helped promote imposition and lack of focus.

As for the moralism of deluded power, David Rieff's passionate book *A Bed for the Night* illustrates its effects nicely in its detailing of the many ways in which the human rights movement, and humanitarianism more generally, have often contributed to the suffering of the poorest by creating a sense (and promise) of achievement that is largely delusory in practice. Rieff ridicules constant appeals to 'the international community' as invocations of an imaginary entity that invites complacent belief in the success of processes that are largely ineffective. He claims that the basis for optimism about human rights is often 'not an improvement in human lives but an improvement in human rights norms. And to me it remains not just an open question, but a question that desperately needs to be asked, what this has actually accomplished for people in need of justice, or aid, or mercy, or bread, and whether it has actually kept a single jackboot out of a single human face.'[12] His own answer to this question is largely pessimistic. But although his criticism highlights the moralism of deluded power, he probably underestimates the effect of non-delusional resort to human rights and other moral vocabularies and legal pronouncements. Amnesty, for example, has achieved some degree of success by marshalling condemnations of human rights violations, as suggested by numerous letters from victims of abuse who credit their deliverance to the intercession of Amnesty.[13] Legitimate suspicion of the dangers of deluded moralism should not lead us to ignore cases in which moral declamation does produce results however subtly and slowly.

[12] David Rieff (2002), p. 15.
[13] See, for instance, the information provided online by Amnesty International (accessed 30 July 2013).

Rieff and other pessimists with experience in the field tend to highlight the following problems: Confusion and misdescription of the crisis to which intervention is addressed; profound ambiguities in the mode of delivering aid such that the aid contributes to compounding the crisis; uncertainties about the relevance or interpretation of 'impartiality' or 'neutrality' as a canon of aid delivery; unclarity about the purposes and scope of the delivery of aid, ranging from the narrow perspective of Rieff's 'a bed for the night' to the ambitious objective of helping institute political reform that will provide for a regime respecting human rights.

An interesting example of misdescription was the aid organizations' response to what they characterized as a severe famine in Cambodia in 1979. Although the topic is contentious there is evidence that seems to suggest that these famine claims were considerably exaggerated. Alex de Waal cites John Pilger and William Shawcross, hardly ideological allies, as agreed that aid agencies exaggerated the scale of famine and underestimated the resourcefulness of rural Cambodians in recovering from the Khmer Rouge depredations. As he puts it: 'The fund-raising machine developed its own momentum regardless of realities in the country.'[14] Here, as elsewhere, agencies relied upon dramatic pictures and powerful rhetoric in the media to raise consciousness and money, but it is possible, indeed likely, that some of the mistaken claims were not only due to the agencies' desire to raise funds by presenting the situation in the most dramatic and appealing fashion, but stemmed from a blurred focus induced by their own sympathetic reactions to real suffering.

(b) Is saving one life enough?

A similar confusion embodying these sorts of moralisms can be seen in the defences offered against criticisms of misguided or problematic aid efforts. The former head of Médecins Sans Frontières, Bernard Kouchner, said in response to criticisms of failings in rescue efforts by aid agencies: 'If we can only save one life that is enough.'[15] This is a classic case of the effects of a moralism of unbalanced focus, since palpably it is not always enough, though Kouchner's words capture a common sentiment aroused by the confronting of humanitarian disasters. The fact is that saving one innocent life at the cost, for instance, of dooming a thousand other innocents by your actions is never going to be 'enough'. One need not be any sort of utilitarian to realize that cost/benefit calculations must come into the equation when considering how to implement a well-intentioned policy of rescue. This is a clear dictate of the prudence mentioned earlier, and, to reiterate the point made there, it is no dictate of selfishness since not only is it legitimate to place some weight upon potential costs to the rescuers themselves, but it is equally, if not more important to count the potential costs to all those on the receiving end of 'rescue'.

In the simple example of 'one is enough' it is easy to see the flaws in the approach, but there are many considerations other than numbers directly saved by an aid

---

[14] de Waal (1997), p. 78.   [15] See BBC 4 (2012).

intervention, or lost for the lack of it, that are relevant to the wisdom of rescue attempts. One that was implicit in the beginnings of humanitarianism at Solferino, and has been a continuing source of concern, is the fact that the sympathetic act of repairing wounded soldiers may merely return them to the battlefield and aid the continuance of violent conflict. There are also situations in which the delivery of medical supplies is going to save lives threatened by an epidemic, but add substantially to widespread misery and persecution because the bulk of the valuable supplies will be expropriated by villainous political thugs who will sell the medicines for arms or otherwise misuse them in order to continue programmes of violent or coercive oppression. It may well be that such aid should not go ahead, even at the cost of those lives, though the weighing of competing costs is a difficult matter.

Moreover, this is not a fanciful philosophers' scenario. Alain Destexhe, onetime secretary-general of Médecins Sans Frontières said of humanitarian aid to Cambodia in the 1980s that 'it revived and boosted the Khmer Rouge war effort…'[16] and a similar problem confronted MSF in the 1990s in the Rwandan refugee camps in Zaire, where the provision of medical and other humanitarian aid was so misused by Hutu genocidists in positions of power in the camps that MSF (and also the International Rescue Committee) made the agonizing decision to withdraw altogether from the camps.[17] They did this in full awareness that some people in the camps would die or suffer badly as a result of that withdrawal. Other NGO aid agencies weighed the competing costs differently and decided to stay. I am not arguing for either decision, but merely pointing out that imperatives like 'it is enough if one life is saved' ignore the moral complexities in favour of a simplistic moralism: in this case mostly a moralism of unbalanced focus that blots out the wider complexities in its concentration on saving a single life. Similar caveats need to be made about the mantra '*something* must be done' which tends to ignore the fact that not everything well intentioned can count as a genuine solution or even part solution to the wise relief of suffering.

(c) Moral ambiguity

The Rwandan case is one in which a choice to continue aid would significantly benefit people whose political agenda was broadly recognizable as deplorable, but there will be other cases where the 'good guys'/'bad guys' dichotomy so beloved of many politicians is far less clear. The need for medical and food relief often arises in situations of political and frequently violent disruption and conflict. The rights and wrongs of such conflict are bound to be complex and debatable, laden with historical intricacies and personal and communal animosities. Indeed, even the bad political agenda of one side in an ongoing conflict does not clear the policies of the opposing side of all taint, as some have argued in the case of the Rwandan massacres and their aftermath. The predominantly Tutsi insurgents not only contributed a cause for the massacres but their organization, the Rwandan Patriotic Front, was itself guilty of atrocities, though the

---

[16] Terry (2002), p. 196.   [17] Terry (2002), pp. 196ff.

exact extent remains unclear. Nor is their former leader and now President, Paul Kagame, free of the taint of autocratic rule, persecution of opponents, and promoting war in neighbouring Democratic Republic of the Congo: just such allegations by Human Rights Watch and other significant organizations have been growing in recent years.[18]

Sometimes these ambiguities are true of the agenda of aid agencies themselves. Consider, for instance, how such agencies can be prone to what I have called the moralism of imposition. This is a form of paternalism whereby an outsider's assessment of the needs and desires of a target community is imposed, often without recognition of dissonance, upon the members of that community. Ignorance of unfamiliar cultures, misunderstanding of local conditions, and feelings of superiority can combine with political considerations, themselves sometimes unrecognized or unacknowledged, to override local knowledge and will with negative, even disastrous consequences.[19] These political considerations can encompass many different things, from the global national or ideological interests of a particular country or region with which the intervening agency is particularly associated (or believed to be aligned), to the promotional interests of the agency itself. It will be particularly acute in those increasingly common cases where humanitarian aid is allied to military interventions; in cases like Afghanistan or Iraq, the aid agencies may themselves become targets of military attack from groups who view them as allied to the military interveners and this has led to the removal of crucial aid agencies from such theatres of conflict. Médecins Sans Frontières, for example, was withdrawn from Afghanistan in such circumstances and UN Aid agencies have had similar problems in a variety of places. Some of the attacks on aid agencies have had more criminal than political motives since there is a considerable cash value in the supplies and equipment they carry, but the political factor is significant.

(d) The difficulty of neutral aid

The issue of human rights also plays into the political dimensions of aid work. From the beginnings of the humanitarian movement there have been tensions in the objectives of relief or rescue. A criterion of 'neutrality' was early established as an index of legitimate aid; the idea was partly pragmatic in that the relief of severe suffering with medical, sheltering, and nutritional assistance was more likely to work when its providers were seen to be independent of foreign state sources, local opposed belligerents, and even the state power of the country or region in which the suffering was occurring. It was also partly moral in itself in as much as the aid providers did not think it appropriate to their role to be enmeshed in the local causes of strife that were often opaque to them and 'none of their business'.

---

[18] For a summary of allegations and some attempted refutations see *Afro-American Network*, 13 May 2013. (Accessed online 18 May 2013.)

[19] In connection with development aid, the many criticisms of the role of the IMF in developing countries highlight flaws that bespeak moralism of imposition in that an alien ideology of neo-liberal economics has been imposed with little understanding of local circumstances and sensitivities.

There are, however, two factors that militate against this impartiality. The first is the fact that, in many cases, the sufferings are the direct result of atrocious behaviour that the increasing acknowledgement of the concept of human rights makes it difficult, if not unconscionable, to ignore. After all, the humanitarian response is often, at least in part as discussed earlier, a response to injustice. Once such behaviour is recognized there is inevitably a question about how to deal responsibly with it and its agents when you are on the spot. The second is the fact that politics is implicit in much of the normal activities of aid groups and this in two ways:

The first such way consists in the facts that some aid groups are actually agencies of their governments or of some international political authority such as the United Nations and hence subject to charters and pressures that have some political character, and NGOs (though less bound in this way) are inevitably involved in political dealings with the organized groups that govern or struggle for control of the nations or regions into which the aid must come; in addition, these organizations are subject to pressures from supporters, including governments, in their various home bases. As mentioned above, belligerents in civil conflicts can easily view aid agencies as aligned with interests hostile to their cause and this can result in attacks upon aid workers. Moreover, this perception is often all too legitimate, at least to a degree, since invading armies and incumbent governments will inevitably seek to co-opt NGOs and other agencies for their own purposes. At the beginning of the Afghanistan invasion in October 2001, then Secretary of State Colin Powell described NGOs as 'force multipliers' and 'an important part of our combat team'. In April 2009, Richard Holbrooke, the US special envoy for Pakistan and Afghanistan, estimated that 90 per cent of US knowledge about Afghanistan comes from aid groups. Holbrooke's claim seems to make it clear that information valuable to US political and military operations might be made available (wittingly or not) to US government sources by aid workers.[20]

Second, even without such direct involvement, the work of aid groups can give, or at least appear to give, legitimacy to the military activities of invaders or other warrior groups. Such groups can see their identification with humanitarian support as helping them to 'win hearts and minds' and as giving credence to political and social reconstruction of structures they have contributed to destroying. Aid can easily be co-opted by such agents, especially when the co-option comes bearing advantages to the aid groups in terms of facilitating the delivery of genuinely needed assistance. So if the aid groups are of value to 'their' governments and military the reverse is also a disturbing reality since aid groups sometimes need the support of a sympathetic military to provide them with protection and often logistical support. This is disturbing precisely because it tends to negate the practical advantages of neutrality.

The topic of neutrality raises another very different type of issue concerning the criteria for distribution of aid between countries and areas. This is a complex matter

---

[20] Whitelaw (2009). This cites Colin Powell and Holbrooke and gives an overview of the problems. (Accessed 18 May 2013.)

that I cannot treat properly here, but it is worth noting. The idea is that aid agencies have a duty to distribute their aid with maximum efficiency not only in the choice of means but in the selection of goals. It has been argued that they should prioritize certain needs above others and concentrate their efforts on just a few countries where the aid can be most effective. So they should set primary, strategic objectives that are perhaps less immediately dramatic but more significant for the long run rather than choosing on the basis of direst immediate need and should avoid spreading themselves more even-handedly to numerous trouble-spots around the globe. Thomas Pogge has argued a version of this case, insisting that NGOs should concentrate on what he sees as the primary problem of poverty and should do so in countries selected for their capacity to deliver the aid efficiently. He regards widespread poverty in the under-developed world as itself a sort of systemic crisis causing far worse effects than the intermittent disasters to which aid organizations usually respond. His views provoked controversy, and mostly strong disagreement, amongst the aid representatives present at the conference at which they were presented.[21]

(e) Summary

What we see from this résumé of difficulties is that the perfectly commendable impulse to aid the distant suffering victims of oppression is much more difficult to translate into effective help than it seems when viewed in simple, indeed simplistic moral terms. The ignoring or minimizing of these difficulties is compounded by moralistic outlooks such as the moralism of abstraction, which ignores or insufficiently attends to the cir-cumstances that surround, qualify, and make fully understandable the crises to which aid is deemed necessary. It is moralism of imposition to impose one's own impera-tives and plans without sufficient attention to how the victims themselves view their needs and prospects. It is moralism of deluded power to imagine that loudly voiced and legitimate moral indignation at suffering and oppression and good intentions aimed at remedying it will by themselves do a great deal to effect a remedy. And it is moralism of unbalanced focus to think that common responses such as Bernard Kouchner's 'sav-ing one life is enough' or the plea 'we must do *something*' are contributions to a realistic implementation of moral concern.

I am not arguing that these moralistic distortions are inevitable; only that they are traps that the aid impulse is prone to. Indeed, as I have mentioned, there are many in aid agencies themselves, and among close observers of the responses to global emergencies, who have lamented the failure to consider some or all of these pitfalls (though they do not describe them in my terms). Even one of the most pessimistic of critics, David Rieff, pays a heartfelt, if complex and hesitant, tribute to what successes the aid community has achieved when he says: 'they are the last of the just, these humanitarians.'[22] Rieff, indeed, has some trouble making up his mind about what can

---

[21] See Pogge (2007). Joseph Carens's response (2007) is in the same book.
[22] Rieff (2002), p. 333.

be achieved, opting usually for the prospects of minimal objectives—'a bed for the night'—but it is at least unclear that more cannot occasionally be achieved, and indeed the extent of the awareness of the problems is a token of hope for better performance in implementing humanitarian ideals.

Humanitarianism and War

The cases for both crisis aid and humanitarian military intervention as rescue from persecution are underpinned by commendable public moral indignation at the atrocities being committed and the suffering they cause. As demonstrated in this chapter, these reactions frequently result in wholehearted endorsements of both forms of aid that need careful scrutiny. We must now examine the difficulties with these endorsements in the case of military intervention.

At the other extreme from enthusiastic support for humanitarian military intervention, there has often been strong resistance to interventions that violate or trespass upon the national sovereignty of states, a sovereignty that was a crucial element in the constitution of the United Nations and a precautionary principle during the Cold War. The moral indignation mentioned brought this outlook under increasing fire during the 1990s when much debate about the legality of humanitarian military interventions took place under the stimulus of the human tragedies played out in that decade in Bosnia, Kosovo, Rwanda, and other parts of Africa. One result of that debate was the UN declaration of the Responsibility to Protect that swung at least the rhetorical victory decisively towards intervention, and helped move supporters of humanitarian military intervention from advocacy of a right or permission to intervene to advocacy of a duty to do so.[23] In the twenty-first century, however, the invasions of Iraq and Afghanistan, which had humanitarian pretensions, if not primary motivations, are widely perceived to have been disastrous, and this has at least posed new questions for the enthusiastic proponents of war for humanity.

Elsewhere, I have argued that such military intervention should satisfy stringent conditions of just war theory as well as the primary condition of 'just cause'.[24] I did so partly in the hope that attention to this would help to better orient debate about military intervention for humanitarian purpose. The justice of one's cause is primary to what is often called the 'jus ad bellum' that specifies the moral conditions that must be met in order to resort legitimately to war. Absent satisfaction of 'just cause', a consideration of the other conditions does not arise. Nevertheless, it is not enough to have a 'just cause' for intervening: the 'prudential' conditions (as I have called them) of the jus ad bellum should also be met. Such conditions specify that the proposed violence

---

[23] For philosophers arguing the case for a duty to intervene see Lefkowitz (2011); Bagnoli, and also Tan, both in Nardin and Williams (2006); for a more complex view of the relation between right and duty to intervene, with some restrictive qualification on the duty, see Fabre (2012).

[24] Coady (2003) and (2002). See also Coady (2008b), pp. 73–87.

should be a last resort, that there should be reasonable prospects of success, that the war should begin with and be sustained by a right intention, that it should be under the control of a legitimate authority, and that it should be a proportional response to the injustice. Stemming, in part, from the condition of right intention are the conditions on the conduct of war, often referred to as the *jus in bello*, in contrast to the *jus ad bellum*. More recently, there has been much attention paid to, and much controversy about, what is called the *jus post bellum*, and sometimes the *jus ex bello*, which seek to specify the moral and legal considerations that should apply to efforts to end a war and to the post-war treatment of the defeated enemy and matters related to the implications of cessation of hostilities.[25] All of these are relevant to military intervention on behalf of humanitarian ideals including the defence of human rights but in what follows, I will consider mostly the *jus ad bellum*.

(a) Pressures to neglect or dilute the prudential conditions of the jus ad bellum

In the case of interventions, there are two pressures that tend to diminish the role of the prudential considerations in our practical reasoning. The first is the widespread habit of minimizing or ignoring the relevance of the prudential conditions altogether, and the second is the attempt to create a new category of political violence (at least for states) that makes the satisfaction of the prudential conditions less demanding. The former was very notably exhibited, for example, in the justifications offered by Israel and its many supporters for the invasion of Lebanon in 2006; when attacks by Hezbollah and the capture of two Israeli soldiers were trumpeted as a justification for the war with scarcely a nod towards the purposes that the onslaught could reasonably be expected to achieve, nor consideration of the available resorts other than violence, or the proportionality of the response. It is also palpable in responses to critics of the Iraq or Afghanistan invasion that ask indignantly 'So, you wanted Saddam Hussein/ the Taliban to stay in power?' The same style of objection was often made to critics of the Vietnam War: 'So you want the Viet Cong to win?' Similarly, those who cautioned against outside military intervention on the side of the insurgents in the complex civil war in Syria faced the accusation of wanting the horrible dictator Assad to win. But most critics of such interventions do not object to them because they ignore or underestimate the wrongs the interventions hope to remedy, but because they think that the interventions will fail to remedy them, or will remedy them at too great a cost in lives, disruption, and flow-on effects or that there are non-violent ways of dealing with the wrongs. They may be mistaken, but misrepresenting their attitude to the just cause rather than facing the prudential considerations is no way to deal with them.[26]

---

[25] For discussions of the *jus post bellum* see Orend (2002); Coady (2011).

[26] The prudential considerations may also be overwhelmed by exaggeration of the threat posed by the injustice the remedying of which satisfies the condition of just cause. It can be argued that the proportionality condition in particular has become a victim of neglect because of the excessive and sometimes hysterical

The latter pressure for watering down the strength of the prudential conditions has gained particular currency in some theoretical circles as the escalating costs and commitments of forays into large-scale military interventions during the new century—particularly the staggering financial, social, and personal costs of the lengthy wars in Afghanistan and Iraq—have created hopes for less damaging ways of advancing political, and sometimes humanitarian, projects in foreign parts. One of the most influential sallies into this sort of territory has been Michael Walzer's conceptualization of what he has called *jus ad vim* or force-short-of-war. I have criticized Walzer's treatment elsewhere and will here be brief with it, though its gathering of momentum recently probably means that it needs fuller discussion at a later date, particularly in view of the development of techniques of warfare such as drones that reduce costs of life and limb to the attacker.[27] The basic idea of *jus ad vim* is that we are wrong to think of war as all of a piece since there are some exercises of military power that are less damaging, more 'surgical', and less problematic than all-out warfare. For such exercises of violence (though its proponents prefer to use the less confronting term 'force') the standard of proof for the *jus ad bellum*, especially for its prudential conditions, will be less stringent than in the case of full-scale war. Hence, the talk of intervention rather than of war. There are two major difficulties for the *jus ad vim* story in so much as it seeks to weaken the prudential constraints (some or all) of the just war tradition.

The first is that force-short-of-war sounds much more "'surgical' and constrained than it usually turns out to be, at least from the point of view of those to whom the force is applied. Swift and decisive interventions have a tendency to turn into long and costly bloodbaths, witness the history of embattled occupation in Iraq after the prompt declaration of early victory and the similar, even more protracted conflict in Afghanistan. Walzer's own example of the American no-fly zones over Iraq through the years 1991–2003 hardly illustrates his thesis, as I argued in *Morality and Political Violence*.[28] The second point is that there is a difference between a condition being weakened or relaxed and its applying fully but with different outcomes in different circumstances. Walzer is anxious to weaken the condition of last resort, though his argument seems to apply more broadly, but conditions like prospect of success and last resort are simply specifications of widely accepted prudential constraints applying to the realm of moral and rational action that has negative costs. Last resort basically advises caution in the resort to violence even in a good cause; if there are other feasible ways of efficiently achieving the good result that don't entail killing and maiming then

---

reactions to contemporary terrorist threats. This is a serious problem for the military and even civil security responses embodied in the 'war on terror'. My thanks to Adam Etinson for this suggestion.

[27] My criticism of Walzer is contained in Coady (2008b), pp. 92–3. I here set aside the possibility of military humanitarian interventions that do not amount to war in as much as the deliberate bloodshed is non-existent (where perhaps the presence of foreign troops simply deters the continuation of the abuses that triggered the intervention) or where the bloodshed by foreigners is so minimal as not to warrant so grand a term as war. It is enough to say that the vast majority of interventions are not like that.

[28] See Coady (2008b), pp. 7, 91–3.

they must be explored and will generally be preferable. This point applies to deliberately killing two people just as it applies to killing 200,000, but killing 200,000 is a vaster crime than killing two, so last resort will have more impact in the latter case than the former.

(b) Comparisons between humanitarian war and aid

These theoretical or casual erosions of the prudential conditions serve to remind us that the moralism discussed earlier concerning non-lethal aid applies even more emphatically to the delivery of humanitarian violence. The Iraq and Afghanistan incursions were at most peripherally humanitarian in impulse or design, though the removal of Saddam Hussein and the destruction of the Taliban government were often produced as humanitarian justifications post facto for the invasions when their primary public justifications (removal of weapons of mass destruction in the former case and combating a terrorist threat to the United States or the 'free world' in both cases) proved absurdly unviable or insufficiently convincing. Yet the move to treating them as humanitarian exercises shows again the way that a genuine moral objective can assume the power to eclipse the prudential concerns about implementation that are just as morally relevant as the primary humane impulse they should accompany. The removal of a vicious regime engaged in widespread human rights violations is a 'genuine moral objective' even if those who plead it are less than fully sincere, as many leaders of the 'coalitions of the willing' may have been when invoking humanitarianism.

Nonetheless, its genuine status can easily lead to moralism. It can induce the blindness to concrete circumstances (moralism of abstraction) that commonly produces negative outcomes for an armed intervention such as exacerbating conflict and furthering human rights disasters. It can override the relevance of other significant values such as national self-determination, respect for life, and the need to honour and support the building of that fragile entity, international law (moralism of unbalanced focus). It can make for the sort of domination of the local scene that rightly gave colonialism a bad name since the foreign military invaders inevitably bring overwhelming and often intrusive political power along with their superior armaments (moralism of imposition). Moreover, the loftiness of the language and thinking of humanitarianism—rescue from oppression, tyranny, and even genocide—can so infect the minds of the invaders that a fog of righteousness prevents their seeing the negative realities involved in their violent intervention, and hence the constant overestimation of successes that have been familiar in Iraq and Afghanistan, and, so notably, much earlier in Vietnam (moralism of deluded power).

The parallel with the problems of aid agencies is instructive, but of course inexact, principally because the aid agencies are not in the business of killing and physically injuring as means to their ends. Nonetheless, the problems involving insufficient understanding of local history, culture, and politics that can plague aid groups frequently beset militaries and foreign governments to an even greater degree. Similarly, the siphoning off of medical and food supplies to rival insurgent groups or to governments for their own often dangerous purposes afflicts both aid and military interventions. And just as aid groups can often exacerbate the fighting by providing resources that can be turned into cash or by having to pay bribes to continue their work, so military invaders on a humanitarian mission will often find themselves embroiled willy-nilly or by deliberate plan in supporting local forces who are corrupt or who have vested interests in prolonging conflict and suffering.

As noted, humanitarian military interventions also compound the problems of non-lethal humanitarian aid by connecting such aid, directly or indirectly, with the military project. The miseries attendant upon even well-intentioned invasions and occupations mean that aid groups are often viewed as allied with intervening militaries and then are placed in the problematic positions discussed earlier.

(c) Summary

In the face of all these difficulties it is tempting to conclude that humanitarian rescue, of either the military or non-military kind, is doomed to failure. I do not advocate so drastic a conclusion, if only because the failures and costs discussed here may be avoidable in specific situations, and even where they are not, the positive benefits of aid and rescue may in certain circumstances be sufficient to offset the costs. After all, there are always costs and compromises to any complex activity, especially those involving politics. The slogan 'do no harm' can be misleading if it goes beyond the prohibition of intentional or negligent harming to rule out all actions that produce some incidental harm (even though foreseen) along with considerable good. The moral I would draw instead is that the moralistic high ground so often involved in discourse about rescue frequently obscures the likely risks, costs, and failures. These negatives when realistically confronted should especially inhibit the rush to military intervention on behalf of human rights and rescue and should shape and inform the call for humanitarian rescue and remedy of a non-military kind.

References

Afro-American Network, 'Rwanda Under International Pressure: General Kagame Increases Budget for External Intelligence' 13 May 2013. Accessed 18 May 2013 at: <http://www.afroamerica.net>.

Amnesty International at <http://www.amnesty.org.uk/> (accessed 30 July 2013).

Anderson, Mary B., *Do No Harm: How Aid Can Support Peace or War* (Boulder, Colo.: Rienner, 1999).

Aquinas, Thomas, *Summa Theologiae* (Cambridge: Cambridge University Press, 2007).

Badiou, Alain, *Ethics: An Essay on the Understanding of Evil*, trans. Peter Hallward (London: Verso, 2001).

Bagnoli, C., 'Humanitarian Intervention as a Perfect Duty', in Terry Nardin and Melissa S. Williams (eds), *Humanitarian Intervention* (New York: New York University Press, 2006).

Barnett, Michael, *Empire of Humanity: A History of Humanitarianism* (Ithaca, NY: Cornell University Press, 2011).

BBC 4 television programme 'The Trouble with Aid' broadcast on 9 December 2012.

Carens, Joseph, 'The Problem of Doing Good in a World That Isn't: Reflections on the Ethical Challenges Facing NGOs', in Daniel A. Bell and Jean-Marc Coicaud (eds), *Ethics in Action: The Ethical Challenges of International Human Rights Non-governmental Organizations* (Cambridge: Cambridge University Press, 2007).

Coady, C. A. J., 'The Ethics of Armed Humanitarian Intervention', in *Peaceworks, No. 45* (Washington DC: United States Institute of Peace, 2002).

Coady, C. A. J., 'War for Humanity: A Critique' in Deen K. Chatterjee and Don Scheid (eds), *Ethics and Foreign Intervention* (Cambridge: Cambridge University Press, 2003).

Coady, C. A. J., *Messy Morality* (Oxford: Oxford University Press, 2008a).

Coady, C. A. J., *Morality and Political Violence* (Cambridge: Cambridge University Press, 2008b).

Coady, C. A. J., 'The Jus Post Bellum', in Paolo Tripodi and Jessica Wolfendale (eds), *New Wars and New Soldiers: Military Ethics in the Contemporary World* (Farnham: Ashgate, 2011).

Fabre, Cecile, *Cosmopolitan War* (Oxford: Oxford University Press, 2012).

Farer, Tom, 'Two Cheers, for Humanitarianism', *Ethics and International Affairs*, 25/3 (2012).

Glennie, Jonathan, *The Trouble with Aid: Why Less could Mean More for Africa* (London and New York: Zed Books, 2008).

Griffin, James, *On Human Rights* (Oxford: Oxford University Press, 2008).

Lefkowitz, David, 'On a Duty of Humanitarian Intervention', in Paolo Tripodi and Jessica Wolfendale (eds), *New Wars and New Soldiers: Military Ethics in the Contemporary World* (Farnham: Ashgate, 2011).

Moyn, Samuel, *The Last Utopia: Human Rights in History* (Cambridge, Mass.: Belknap Press, 2010).

Orend, Brian, 'Justice After War', *Ethics and International Affairs* 16/2 (2002).

Pogge, Thomas, 'Moral Priorities for International Human Rights NGOs', in Daniel A. Bell and Jean-Marc Coicaud (eds), *Ethics in Action: The Ethical Challenges of International Human Rights Non-governmental Organizations* (Cambridge: Cambridge University Press, 2007).

Rieff, David, *A Bed for the Night: Humanitarianism in Crisis* (New York: Simon and Schuster, 2002).

Tan, K., 'The Duty to Protest', in Terry Nardin and Melissa S. Williams (eds), *Humanitarian Intervention* (New York: New York University Press 2006).

Terry, Fiona, *Condemned to Repeat? The Paradox of Humanitarian Action* (Ithaca, NY: Cornell University Press, 2002).

Vaux, Tony, *The Selfish Altruist: Relief Work in Famine and War* (London: Earthscan publications, 2001).

de Waal, Alex, *Famine Crimes: Politics and the Disaster Relief Industry in Africa* (Bloomington, Ind.: Indiana University Press, 1997).

Whitelaw, Kevin, 'As Risks Rise, Aid Agencies Struggle to Adapt', *National Public Radio*, 17 November 2009. See also: <http://www.npr.org/> (accessed 18 May 2013).

12.1

The Politics of Humanitarian Morality
Reflections on "The Hazards of Rescue"

Vasuki Nesiah

C. A. J. Coady argues that human rights have their foundations in morality and that there is "a central, widely acknowledged group of them that it is of great importance to have protected".[1] That said, he also cautions that moral arguments for human rights do not have an unequivocally positive record and the core analytic thrust of his chapter is to identify the different ways in which moral arguments for human rights can distort our vision, and lead us to problematic actions. Focusing on human rights as "rescue" ethics, Coady claims that the moral imperative to rescue is central to the normative force of human rights, and moreover that it is this normative force that informs humanitarianism—both military and non-military humanitarian intervention. He identifies and analyses a range of ways in which moral arguments can run aground and become undesirable forms of "moralism": these include what he terms the problems of "unbalanced focus", "imposition", "abstraction" and "deluded power". For instance, the problem of deluded power can make one mistake the moral critique of a problem for a way of actually doing something about it; in this way it can substitute for action rather than motivate action. The problem of imposition conveys how moralism can engender a hubris that legitimizes actions that are undesired by local populations. The problem of unbalanced focus is about how the moral critique of a problem can overstate its scale and intensity in ways that monopolize our energies and crowd out attending to other pressing problems. Coady sees these hazards of moralism as not just hypothetical problems but ones that can have, and have had, adverse consequences leading to "bad outcomes from good motives". Thus his elaboration of the drawbacks of moralism draws on historical examples that range from the US intervention in

---

[1] My thanks are due to Prof. Coady and Adam Etinson for their helpful comments on a first draft of this intervention; it is much improved as a result of their input.

Iraq and Afghanistan, to the work of humanitarian organizations such as MSF in contexts such as Rwanda and Cambodia.

Coady situates his focus on the potential pitfalls of moralism in a larger debate with realism. While realists may argue that there is no space for morality, including human rights norms, in international relations, Coady claims a place for moral reasoning that survives the realist arithmetic of interest/power maximization. Thus the distinction between moralism and morality is crucial to Coady; he argues that the realists have compelling objections to moralism but not morality, and indeed that some of their arguments about moralism are compatible with and instructive for anyone who also has an investment in the role of hazard conscious morality. Coady's elaboration of the common traps of moralism in humanitarian work seeks to develop a case for humanitarian morality that gives adequate weight to assessments of the consequences of our moral convictions and how these translate into action. Indeed, he argues that this prudence is not a counterweight to morality but internal to morality properly elaborated. Coady's account of the various pitfalls of moralism is compelling. The distinction he makes between moralism and morality takes him a significant distance in his engagement with realism. It also makes a persuasive case that those invested in human rights morality can strengthen their case by challenging the distortions of human rights moralism.

Realists are often seen to analyse international relations as a domain of self-interest and power.[2] Accordingly, realist approaches may look at human rights interventions as efforts to instrumentalize human rights in advancing self-interest. It is an approach that pays little attention to the background conditions that shape political interests (including our perceptions of self, be it individual, local or national), and which dimensions of structure we experience as normalized and which we experience as open to contestation or entailing political power. In this vein, the realist approach is uninterested in the material and ideational structures that shape and constrain interest and agency, including those shaping humanitarian actors. Thus, on one account of the political, the realists could be seen as depoliticizing the landscape, while on another account of the political, the realists could be seen as politicizing everything—for instance, in explaining all action through an analysis of self-interest and power and rejecting any role for morality.

The dominant field of humanitarian morality can also be situated in relation to two approaches to the political. On one account, the political context of humanitarian action is something that humanitarian morality should take into account to avoid the distortions of moralism. Citing American humanitarian agencies in Afghanistan as an example, Coady notes that aid agencies may have a link (or be perceived to have a link) with the policies of "donor" countries, and/or "recipient" countries. Coady suggests that prudent attention to these political contexts should inform humanitarian morality and the actions of humanitarian actors. A related but distinct conception of the

---

[2] See also Morgenthau 1978.

relationship between politics and humanitarian morality attends to the historical context of the humanitarian field itself, and the technologies of knowledge and power that it employs and deploys. Here probing the politics of morality involves critical analysis of why particular notions of humanitarian morality gain traction at particular historical moments—examining what work humanitarian morality is activating not just in terms of the local contexts of particular humanitarian actions but in terms of humanitarianisms' historical role. Paying attention to the politics of humanitarian morality in this sense requires a genealogical analysis of the field of humanitarianism at any given moment. For instance, in the current moment, is there a story about capitalism or empire (not just of the local contexts where humanitarian agencies originate and operate) that tells a tale about humanitarian morality (not just moralism)? In this vein, Michelle Barnett argues that there are three different moral claims that can be associated with the three different eras of humanitarianism that she identifies— imperial, postcolonial, and liberal.[3] This is but one of many recent efforts to better understand the politics of humanitarianism as such. Focus on the political context within which humanitarianism functions is critical but that in itself is just one step in grappling with the multiple contested notions of humanitarian morality and their continuities and discontinuities with different regimes of global governance—i.e. what Antonio Donini describes as "the meta functions of humanitarianism".[4]

Coady's advocacy of a chastened space for humanitarianism valuably highlights the importance of being prudent about the political environment of humanitarian morality, i.e. political context in the first sense. Yet this marrying of morality and prudence may be inadequate to understanding the politics of humanitarian engagements if arguing in the key of morality is itself part of the problem that warrants scrutiny. Politics is not just external to humanitarian morality as a feature of the landscape that humanitarianism engages. We need to interrogate the politics of humanitarian morality, not just the distortions of moralism, if we are to not miss the forest for the trees.

I

In the remainder of this commentary I make a case for critically probing the politics of humanitarian morality by briefly highlighting the contours of its particular significance in our current context. The field of human rights has long included the domain of both ethics and politics, but in recent years the ethical turn has crowded out the political in ways that are significant. Central to this depoliticizing shift has been the fact that the focus on human rights in the context of humanitarian crisis has gained unprecedented prominence in the global public sphere in ways that have dominated the field of human rights more generally.

---

[3] Barnett 2011.   [4] Donini 2011.

Coady claims that human rights and humanitarianism have merged and that, not-withstanding their distinct origins, this was an inevitable and natural trajectory for both fields. On this basis he then goes on to focus on human rights in the context of humanitarianism to make claims about human rights as such. I would argue that there continue to be important distinctions in the philosophical, legal, and institutional architecture of human rights and humanitarianism; moreover, there are important tensions between them and between the cultures and debates that shape scholarship and practice in both fields. However, it is clear that post-Kosovo, human rights and humanitarianism have more (and more visible) meeting points. These intersections and convergences extend from the work of the Security Council to the work of grass-roots advocates, from international legal developments to reflections in international moral and political philosophy. This has meant that the dominant strands of scholar-ship and practice regarding human rights in the context of humanitarian crisis has been inflected with some defining dimensions of humanitarianism.

I highlight three distorting effects of these inflections on how we understand the politics of human rights. First, the merger thesis brings to the fore a depoliticizing thrust where humanitarian morality works to crowd out politics within the human rights field. Historically, humanitarianism has seen politics as a "moral pollutant". For the hundred plus years since Henry Dunant's walk on the battlefields of Solferino, the ICRC (and the humanitarian field at large) has claimed political neutrality as critical to humanitarianism. Over the last couple of decades scepticism about the possibility or desirability of political neutrality has catalysed significant debate amongst scholars, practitioners, and observers. Yet even the most prominent critics of the current state of the humanitarian field often call for a return to political neutrality and urge that a clean moral compass is the solution.[5] Thus deep hostility to politics remains an influential feature of the field and apolitical humanitarianism persists as the avowed goal of humanitarian organizations like the ICRC. This hostility has crept into human rights in the context of humanitarian crisis. Increasingly apolitical, and in some cases anti-political, a focus on what is often described as basic moral concerns has come to dominate human rights scholarship, policy making, and practice addressing humani-tarian crisis. This is the idea that there is a core set of human rights principles that are "central, widely acknowledged" and, by implication, reflect a common consensus, beyond meaningful political contestation. For instance, Michael Ignatieff's call for "putting cruelty first" exemplifies humanitarian morality's ambition of a cosmopolitan human-ism that simplifies the political stakes in engaging with human rights issues. Ignatieff is not arguing against attention to the political context of intervention—presumably in "putting cruelty first" he would endorse advancing that moral sentiment in ways that are prudent and politically sensitive as Coady recommends. Thus this is not just a problem of moralism's hazards; yet it is depoliticizing in the deeper sense that we have described. In turning to humanitarian morality as the field's fundamental priority,

[5] Rieff 2002.

"putting cruelty first" is advanced as if this were a claim innocent of power. Yet human rights work is itself always deploying and negotiating power—not only engaging with or being sensitive to a political context external to it.

A second and related distortion effect of focusing on human rights in the humanitarian context is that it lends itself to treating human rights engagements as ones that are episodic and epic injections in moments of disaster, rather than routine and structural dimensions of political subjectivity and global governance. Yet, the laws and norms of the international human rights framework engage with claims in both extraordinary and ordinary circumstances. They deal with questions of humanitarian crisis, war, and genocide, but they also deal with the structures and policies that govern the everyday. Arguably the majority of provisions in human rights instruments deal with political contestations that shape the quotidian contexts of our daily lives, be it as citizens of particular nations or citizens of the world. This everyday reach of human rights extends from international trade to constitutional development, from shaping the terms of civil society audibility to impacting how justice and accountability get institutionalized in local contexts. In other words, there are important stakes that attend "routine" human rights interventions that a depoliticized morality focusing on the terrain of catastrophe and exceptionality is inadequate to address.

Indeed, if we move away from humanitarian contexts to human rights in the everyday, human rights engagements are less likely to be described in terms of epic moral choices. Arguably, it was the "ordinary" rights of national citizenship—of political participation, freedom of speech, due process, freedom of religion, equal treatment, and such—that are central to the traditions of the French and American revolutions that scholars such as Lynn Hunt link to the birthing of the human rights tradition.[6] Alternative birth stories such as Samuel Moyn's focus on 1970s Soviet dissidents and Jimmy Carter's human rights legacy (now most familiar in the Carter Center's role conducting routine election monitoring) also locate human rights as a struggle for civil liberties through issues that were central to the East European dissident movements such as freedom of expression and the fight against censorship—routinized "peace time" atrocities rather than humanitarian emergencies.[7] In addition, and significantly, human rights "solidarities" that have become institutionalized in the quotidian work of the United Nations implicate not only humanitarian responses but also, and significantly, everyday issues such as the right to education, health care, development, and similar claims that speak to the relational dimension of rights claims—relational claims that foreground the politics of trade and aid, cosmopolitanism and sovereignty; claims that do not reflect a common consensus about human rights priorities or strategies. These human rights claims implicate morality but morality is not a central vector through which these issues are adjudicated. Certainly, in contrast to human rights in the context of extraordinary humanitarian crisis, the substance and tone of morality plays a much less significant tone in discussions of human rights in the

---

[6] Hunt 2008.   [7] Moyn 2010.

context of the ordinary. The right to education or the fight against censorship are not the rights of others (alone) but rights that implicate all of us and the distribution of resources and meanings struggled over in our local and trans-local public spheres. In other words, these are basic civil rights that are central to our political lives. A discussion of the human rights field that focuses only on contexts of extraordinary crisis will distort our analysis of the promises and hazards that attend the field; it narrows the human rights conversation to a ground where politics is displaced by the moral urgency of dealing with catastrophe.

Finally, the focus on humanitarian crisis also distorts who emerges as the subject of rights. In particular, human rights are translated into an export product with engagements activated not by our rights but "theirs", not violations at home but violations elsewhere. As Rancière notes, in the context of ethnic conflict and slaughter, the rights of man become "the rights of those who were unable to enact any rights or even any claim in their name".[8] Human rights are rendered irrelevant at home but relevant in far off lands needing rescue—"you do the same as charitable persons do with their old clothes. You give them to the poor. Those rights that appear to be useless in their place are sent abroad, along with medicine and clothes, to people deprived of medicine, clothes, and rights." Rescue ethics helps reinforce the assumptions and hubris of privilege in ways that evoke the enabling ideologies of empire. It not only disregards or marginalizes the claims, priorities, and interests of local populations but it does so in their name. These populations are framed as always already victimized so they have no rights to be deprived of—politics has already been evacuated by humanitarian crisis; indeed, it is intervention that will restore their human rights.

Part of the logic of human rights in humanitarian crisis is that these are about the rights of "others"; catalysing not just the possibility of engagement but (according to this logic) a moral duty to intervene, a "responsibility to protect".[9] If we begin with human rights in humanitarian crisis and begin connecting the dots, we can be led to intervention, military and non-military, as a human rights project. For instance, as Samuel Moyn[10] has described, the millennium brought us "America pursuing low-minded imperial ambitions in high-minded humanitarian tones." With invocations of humanitarian concerns as the backdrop, the dawn of a new era of human rights becomes part of the promise of humanitarian morality at every stage of framing and responding to humanitarian crisis. Yet these are not problems solely of unbalanced moral focus or exaggeration (to cite some of the hazards of moralism) but also part of what is enabled by the rescue ethics of cosmopolitan humanism that crowded out a political discussion of intervention and contributed to its legitimization. For instance,

---

[8] Rancière 2004.

[9] If Kosovo emerged as a certain marker at the intersection of human rights and humanitarianism, it was also a historical marker for when human rights began to do significant work in the production of legitimacy for intervention. Significantly it was the report that was produced in response to Kosovo and Rwanda that then generated the doctrine of responsibility to protect. Evans 2001.

[10] Moyn 2007.

the "responsibility to protect" was the ground of Michael Ignatieff's defence of the US intervention in Iraq as a human rights project. Significantly, however, humanitarians scarred by the Bush administration's manipulation of the language of humanitarian moralism have argued even more vociferously for political neutrality and a de-politicized approach to humanitarianism as a shield against the hazards of moralism in contexts of "catastrophe". Moreover, political neutrality, this humanitarianization of politics, becomes part of the knowledge apparatus and institutional thrust of humanitarian morality not only in the particular contexts of Iraq and Afghanistan but in the field at large. Thus as Didier Fassin has recently argued, "humanitarian reason" translates political issues such as social inequality, dissidence, and political violence into need, victimhood, and trauma.[11]

II

As Section I has outlined, the focus on humanitarian contexts of human rights exerts a distortion effect where moralism crowds out politics, treats human rights engagements as episodic rather than structural, and channels our gaze onto the rights of distant victims who by definition warrant intervention in their name.

Coady doesn't say explicitly that rescue ethics speaks to what he sees as the most critical domain of human rights work. However, he notes that "the urgency of rescue is often correlated with the scale and nature of human rights violations", suggesting, in effect, that rescue ethics deals with the most momentous human rights violations. Moreover, while Coady draws attention to these hazards of moralism, this recognition comes in lieu of a genealogical analysis of the rise of human rights moralism in the current moment. Thus, against those critics who launch a more wholesale critique, Coady advocates for the positive impact of the "non-delusional resort to human rights and other moral vocabularies and legal pronouncements". Thus his own project in cataloguing the hazards of moralism is also in effect a project of cabining those hazards for targeted troubleshooting while saving the larger enterprise of human rights morality. Coady urges that "Legitimate suspicion of the dangers of deluded moralism should not lead us to ignore cases in which moral declamation does produce results however subtly and slowly." His larger project is to encourage a more nuanced and mindful moral engagement with human rights that is attentive to the complexity of the issues and the context on the theory that "the extent of the awareness of the problems is a token of hope for better performance in implementing humanitarian ideals".

Yet with rescue ethics dominating human rights, even the nuanced and mindful accounting of "the potential costs to all those on the receiving end of rescue" has a depoliticizing thrust. Indeed, here the prudence that modifies moralism may be better understood as the twin of moralism rather than its counter. Today ethics and expertise

---

[11] Fassin 2011.

go hand in hand in a professionalized human rights field that couples moralism and prudence to rescue better.

What would be the dominant inflection of human rights if the ordinary is foregrounded? One answer to that question may be the reciprocity of political community. For instance, in his discussion of the politics of human rights, Balibar cites Arendt's focus on "dissidence—in the specifically modern form of 'civil disobedience'— (as) the touchstone of the founding *reciprocity* of rights".[12] Balibar and Arendt's discussion of dissidence warrant a more extensive discussion than this commentary permits so at this point I just invoke reciprocity as a shorthand counterpoint to rescue ethics. The contrast between reciprocity and rescue offers a window into the domain of the political that gets translated into morality in contemporary discussions of empire, but also in relation to the broader structural effects of humanitarian reason that we referenced earlier. We get a sense of the political reach that these terms gesture to if we layer the opposition between rescue vs. reciprocity onto our earlier discussion of the dichotomies that animated human rights in the context of the extraordinary vs the ordinary, of the global vs the trans-local, of the epic and episodic vs the structural and routine. It suggests also that rather than applaud the "heightened consciousness of the wrongs inflicted on human beings worldwide", we may need to probe the ascent of humanitarian ideals within the human rights field at this particular historical conjuncture. There has already been some scholarship on how the human rights field was shaped by the ideological ballast of the end of the cold war and the role of this newly reshaped human rights field in the contours of the new world order.[13] Significantly, however, the specific catalogue of moralism's drawbacks that Coady develops is compatible with a more robust political and historical analysis of rescue ethics. Fully understanding the hazards of moralism would also require historicizing the increased significance of the ethical turn within human rights. Indeed, the alternative political and historical interrogation of human rights morality that we gesture to here may provide the critical scaffolding that most powerfully supports and extends Coady's "cataloguing" project.

References

Barnett, Michelle (2011), *Empire of Humanitarianism* (Ithaca, NY: Cornell University Press).

Bot, Micheil (2014), *Etienne Balibar's Reading of Hannah Arendt's Politics of Human Rights* (see <http://www.hannaharendtcenter.org/?p=12607>).

Donini, Antonio (2011), "The Far Side: The Meta Functions of Humanitarianism in a Globalized World", *Disasters*, Vol. 34, No. S2, pp. 220–37.

Evans, Gareth et al. (2001), *The Responsibility to Protect: Report of the International Commission on Intervention and State Sovereignty*, IDRC, Canada.

Fassin, Didier (2011), *Humanitarian Reason: A Moral History of the Present* (Berkeley: University of California Press).

---

[12] Bot (2014).   [13] See Rancière 2004; Moyn 2010.

Hunt, Lynn (2008), *Inventing Human Rights: A History* (New York: W.W. Norton & Co.).

Morgenthau, Hans J. (1978), "Six Principles of Political Realism", in *Politics Among Nations: The Struggle for Power and Peace*, 5th edition, revised (New York: Alfred A. Knopf), pp. 4–15.

Moyn, Samuel (2007), "On the Genealogy of Morals", *The Nation*, 16 April 2007.

Moyn, Samuel (2010), *The Last Utopia: Human Rights in History* (Cambridge, Mass.: Harvard University Press).

Rancière, Jacques (2004), "Who is the Subject of the Rights of Man?", *South Atlantic Quarterly*, Vol. 103, No. 2/3, pp. 297–310.

Rieff, David (2002), *A Bed for the Night* (New York: Simon and Schuster).

PART VI

Individuals, Borders, and Groups

13

Human Rights and Collective Self-Determination

Peter Jones

Introduction

The ideas of human rights and of peoples' rights of self-determination have long been closely associated.[1] Both have a pedigree stretching back before 1945, but both have received more formal international recognition in the post-1945 world. In 1948, the United Nations promulgated its Universal Declaration of Human Rights (UDHR) and that has been followed by a plethora of UN declarations, covenants, and conventions giving more detailed statements of human rights. The right of self-determination figured in the first article of the first chapter of the UN's Charter, where one of the UN's purposes was said to be the development of friendly relations among nations 'based on respect for the principle of equal rights and self-determination of peoples'. That right has also received frequent reaffirmation in subsequent UN documentation.

These two categories of right were brought together in the common first clauses of The International Covenant on Civil and Political Rights (ICCPR) and The International Covenant on Economic, Social and Cultural Rights (ICESCR), both of which were adopted by the UN in 1966. The preambles of both covenants present the rights they contain as human rights that 'derive from the dignity of the human person'. Yet the first clause of the first Article of each Covenant runs as follows:

All peoples have the right of self-determination. By virtue of that right they freely determine their political status and freely pursue their economic, social and cultural development.[2]

The inclusion of this clause in covenants that were ostensibly human rights covenants usefully encapsulates the question I want to examine in this chapter. Was the UN right

[1] I am grateful to Derek Bell, Adam Etinson, Pietro Maffetone, and Ian O'Flynn for their helpful comments on an earlier draft of this chapter.

[2] The article's second clause also asserts rights of peoples: 'All peoples may, for their own ends, freely dispose of their natural wealth and resources without prejudice to any obligations arising out of international economic co-operation, based upon the principle of mutual benefit and international law. In no case may a people be deprived of its own means of subsistence.'

to include peoples' rights to self-determination in a human rights document, with the implication that those rights could and should be absorbed by the idea of human rights? Or are these two categories of right quite separate and perhaps antagonistic, one asserting the rights of groups and the other asserting rights held by individual human beings that are designed, in part, to protect them from various sorts of power, including the power of groups?

The right of peoples to self-determination as a right in international law has a tortuous history.[3] While I shall make occasional reference to it as an internationally recognized legal right, I shall treat it mainly as a moral right that international law ought to recognize; I shall treat human rights in the same way. However, I do not mean to imply that either sort of right is 'moral' in a way that precludes its being also 'political' in the special sense in which John Rawls, Charles Beitz, and Joseph Raz have proposed 'political' conceptions of human rights.[4] My main argument will be that we can conceive a people's right of self-determination as a collective human right, provided we understand a people as a 'political' entity in a sense that I shall explain in due course.

Self-Determination: An Individual Right?

If there is a right to self-determination, whose right is it? Since we are here concerned with *collective* self-determination, the answer may seem obvious: the collectivity whose self-determination is at stake. Even so, some commentators suggest that we should conceive the right to collective self-determination as an individual right. Jeremy Waldron insists that a people's right to self-determination is 'an individual right, albeit an individual right necessarily exercised in common with the similar rights of millions of other persons.... It is not the right of a group; instead it comprises the rights of millions of individuals participating in a common exercise of collective decision, under conditions of equality and fairness.'[5] Similarly, Daniel Philpott holds that 'self-determination is an individual right because it is the individual who chooses to live under a certain government', even though that right 'must be exercised in a group'.[6]

A possible way of understanding Waldron's and Philpott's claims is that rights of collective self-determination are rights that individuals *exercise* together, but that are *possessed* by individuals as separate individuals.[7] There can indeed be cases that conform to that model. For example, a group of individuals, each of whom possesses an individual right to freedom of worship, may each opt to pray with the rest of the group so that their individual rights to pray are exercised together rather than separately. However, it is difficult to assimilate the right to collective self-determination to that case. The praying individuals pool their individual rights to engage in a shared act of prayer.

---

[3] Cassese 1995.   [4] Rawls 1999; Beitz 2009; Raz 2010.
[5] Waldron 2010, p. 408.   [6] Philpott 1995, p. 369.
[7] This may also be the model that Jack Donnelly has in mind when he suggests that peoples' rights 'are best seen as rights of individuals acting as members of social groups' (2003, p. 222).

Analogously, we might suppose that individuals, each of whom possesses a right of individual self-determination, can pool their individual rights to engage in an act of collective self-determination. But an act of collective self-determination is not the same as so many simultaneous acts of individual self-determination. It is an act that determines the collective life of a group and that act is not reducible to a set of conjoint individual acts of individual self-determination. Even in the case of the individuals who pray together, the individual rights model remains satisfactory only so long as we conceive the shared act as a set of individual acts of prayer that the praying individuals perform in one another's company. Suppose that their shared act takes the form of an integrated act of worship in which people assume different roles and perform different rituals so that the act becomes essentially rather than contingently collective in character. It then becomes implausible to represent a right to the collective act of worship as no more than the pooling together of rights to acts that individuals possess separately as individuals. If there is a right that there shall be an integrated act of worship it must be a right that the worshipping individuals possess collectively rather than severally. I say more to substantiate that claim below.

In conceiving a right as a collective right, we need not exclude the possibility that there may be individual rights that relate to the collective right. For example, a collective right to a collective act of worship may be accompanied by a right of each individual to participate in the collective act; but that individual right of participation is not the same as a right to collective worship as a collective act. Similarly, each individual member of a people may have, qua individual, the right to participate in its collective self-determination; but all of those individual rights taken together do not equate with the right of collective self-determination. Rather they are individual rights to participate in the exercise of a (separate) collective right.

Self-Determination as a Collective Right

Unsurprisingly, therefore, we seem obliged to conceive a people's right to collective self-determination as a right that belongs to a people as a people rather than to its members severally. We have, in other words, to conceive it as a group right. But how are we to understand a group right? By common consent, a group right is a right possessed by a group as a group rather than by its members taken severally. Beyond that, however, there is much disagreement about what we should understand a group right to be. Frequently it has been thought of as the right of a group conceived as a corporate entity.[8] It has been supposed that, if groups, like natural persons, are to hold rights, those groups must possess a unity of being that is in some way analogous to the unity of a natural person. They must be conceivable as group-individuals or group-persons. The group must also possess a being that is not reducible to that of its members; that

---

[8] For three different versions of this 'corporate' conception of group rights, see French 1984; McDonald 1991; Newman 2011.

property is often thought essential if a group is to hold its rights as a group rather than as rights that are reducible to those of its members. Perhaps most importantly of all, this 'corporate' conception of group rights ascribes moral standing to the group as such, a moral standing that is separate from and independent of the moral standing of the individuals whom the group encompasses. Moral standing is a precondition of right-holding, which leads easily to the thought that a group can possess moral rights only if it enjoys moral standing as a group.

Scepticism about group rights is most commonly directed at this corporate model.[9] The sceptics doubt that we should ascribe to groups the unity of being that we ascribe to natural human persons. They also reject the ascription of moral standing to groups as groups. They do not usually object to the ascription of legal standing, legal person-hood and legal rights to groups, but they reject efforts to attribute to groups the moral analogues of those legal ascriptions. Here I shall not pause to comment critically on the corporate conception of group rights. I observe only that, if we conceive a people's right to self-determination according to that conception, we shall understand it to be categorically different from human rights, understood as the rights of natural human persons. A people as a right-holder will be a different kind of being from a natural human person, and that difference will stand in the way of absorbing its right of self-determination within the category of human rights.

We can, however, conceive group rights in a quite different way and one that is altogether more consonant with human rights thinking. We can conceive them as rights that a group's members hold together rather than separately, that is, jointly rather than severally. In previous work I have described this conception of group rights as 'collective' rather than 'corporate'.[10] Proponents of the corporate conception commonly use the adjective 'collective' to describe group rights as they conceive them, but, arguably, that usage is inappropriate.[11] The adjective 'collective' makes an implicit reference to a plurality of beings; hence the etymological link between 'collective' and 'collection'. If we conceive a group right as the right of a single integral entity—the right of a corporate individual—we misdescribe it as 'collective'. A collective right properly so called is the shared right of a plurality of beings; it has a plurality of holders rather than only one. It is in that sense that I shall use the term 'collective right'.

A collective right is, then, a right that a group of individuals holds collectively rather than severally, jointly rather than separately. On this collective conception, there is no right-holding group that has a being and a moral standing separately from the individuals who make it up. The right-holding group is simply the set of individuals who constitute the group and the moral standing that underwrites their group right is the moral standing of the several individuals who make up the group. But their collective right remains an authentic group right since it is a right that the members of the group hold only together and not separately. The conception here is not therefore one in which

---

[9] e.g. Graff 1994; Hartney 1991; Narveson 1991.   [10] Jones 1999, 2009.

[11] In the works listed in note 8, French, McDonald, and Newman all use the adjective 'collective'.

individuals hold rights as individuals and in which their individual rights are some-how aggregated to yield a collective right. Quite the contrary, a collective right is a right that the right-holding members of the group hold jointly and *only* jointly. Understood according to this conception, the right of a people to collective self-determination will be the jointly held right of the flesh-and-blood individuals who make up the people to determine their collective destiny. No individual member of the people as a discrete individual will have the right to collective self-determination; rather it will be the set of all individuals constituting the people that jointly hold the collective right to be collectively self-determining.

a. Raz on collective rights

I have objected that it is implausible to interpret the right to collective self-determination as a right possessed by individuals individually; but what makes that interpretation implausible? What justifies the claim that the right to collective self-determination must be a collective right? Joseph Raz has offered an answer. His version of the interest theory of rights is well known and widely used: X has a right 'if and only if X can have rights, and, other things being equal, an aspect of X's well-being (his interest) is a sufficient reason for holding some other person(s) to be under a duty'.[12] Working from that basic definition, Raz lays down the conditions in which a right will be a collective right.

First, it exists because an aspect of the interest of human beings justifies holding some person(s) to be subject to a duty. Second, the interests in question are the interests of individuals as members of a group in a public good and the right is a right to that public good because it serves their interest as members of the group. Thirdly, the interest of no single member of that group in that public good is sufficient by itself to justify holding another person to be subject to a duty.[13]

The fundamental thought here is that there can be cases in which a group of individuals share an interest in a good; the interest of any one individual taken singly does not suffice to justify subjecting another or others to the duty that a right to the good would entail; but the interests of all individuals in the group may suffice to justify the duty. If they do, the group of individuals will possess a right collectively that none of them possesses individually. Raz uses the case of self-determination to exemplify his conception of collective rights.[14] Yasser Arafat had an interest in Palestinian self-determination but Arafat's interest alone did not give him a right that the Palestinian people should be self-determining. It did not justify imposing the 'far-reaching demands' that self-determination would make on the lives of whole communities. But the interests of the Palestinians taken as a whole do yield the necessary justification. Thus the Palestinian people collectively possess a right to self-determination that none of them possesses individually.

---

[12] Raz 1986, p. 166.   [13] Ibid., p. 208.
[14] Ibid., pp. 207–9; see also Margalit and Raz 1990.

Raz's conception of a collective right has attracted much criticism, often from commentators who believe that his notion that interests can accumulate across individuals, until they reach a threshold that brings into being a collective right, is too aggregative and utilitarian in character to be consistent with rights-thinking.[15] But despite the unease of the critics, there are cases in which the relevance of numbers is hard to deny. For example, if we think there can be language rights and if we think that in some circumstances a linguistic minority (e.g. French-speakers in Canada) can have a right against the larger society that its language should be usable in the public domain, the size of the linguistic minority seems inescapably relevant to the case for that right. Given the costs and inconvenience involved in a society's making public provision for a second language, the interest of a single individual in that public provision is not going to provide the necessary justification; but the interests of many such individuals (perhaps, as in the case of French-speaking Canadians, numbered in millions) may very well do the job. Other things being equal, the case for similar provision for a much smaller linguistic group will be harder to make. That is not to say that numbers are the only relevant consideration; for example, the speakers of an indigenous minority language may have a claim to special treatment that the speakers of a migrant language do not. It is to say only that the size of a group may make a difference to the collective rights it can claim.

That said, Raz's route to collective rights is not the only route available to us. Moreover, his cumulative case for collective rights does not provide the most compelling case for a collective right of self-determination. For one thing, in the case of a people with a well-established state, the duties imposed by the right may be entirely negative—duties only to refrain from acts, either external or internal, that obstruct or frustrate the people's self-determination; since those duties impose little or no burden upon their bearers, it may take little to justify them. For another, we do not think that peoples with large populations have rights of self-determination more readily than those that have small populations, or that the moral weight we should give to peoples' rights of self-determination should vary according to the size of their populations.[16]

b. Collective rights and collective goods

In the case of self-determination, we do better to focus on the nature of the good that is the object of a right. If a good is the object of a right, it can be its collective nature as a good that makes it necessarily the object of a collective right. Raz himself distinguishes between contingent public goods and inherent public goods and, in a usage that I shall follow here, describes inherent public goods as 'collective goods'.[17] A contingent public good is a good that people happen to enjoy publicly, that is with others, but

---

[15] e.g. Preda 2013; Réaume 1988, p. 25, 1994, pp. 126–7; Tamir 1999.

[16] Cf. Raz's remark: 'The right [of a community to self-determination] rests on the cumulative interests of many individuals. (This explains why though the interest does not depend on the size of the group, the existence of the right and its strength does.)' (1986, p. 209.)

[17] Ibid., pp. 198–9.

contingently rather than necessarily; it is only contingently non-excludable and non-rival in consumption. Clean air and clean water are examples. Communities typically enjoy these as goods public to each community, but their delivery as public goods is a contingent matter. We have the technology to provide clean water to individuals or households privately. Delivering unpolluted air to people privately is technologically more complex, but the publicness of unpolluted air is still a contingent matter. More significantly for our purpose, it is not essential to the goodness of clean air and clean water that they should be public goods. It is not essential to the very goodness of my breathing clean air that you should be breathing it too, nor to the goodness of your drinking clean water that I should be drinking it too.

Some goods are, however, inherently public. Their being enjoyed with others is essential to their being the goods that they are. Raz gives the examples of living in a tolerant society, in an educated society, and in a society infused with a sense of respect for human beings.[18] His notion of a collective good as inherently public is close to, though not identical with, Denise Réaume's notion of a participatory good.[19] For Réaume, a participatory good is a public good of a particular type. It is a good that, by its very nature, requires the participation of others. Raz and Leslie Green describe this sort of good as a 'shared' good, Waldron as a 'communal' good, and Andrei Marmor as a 'common' good.[20] I shall follow Réaume in using the term 'participatory' good, although I shall suggest that we have reason to use the term more generously than she does. Some commonly cited examples of participatory goods are friendship, a team game, and a convivial party. I cannot enjoy friendship on my own; I can play a team game only if others play it too; and only a plurality of people can generate and experience conviviality. Some other goods that Réaume argues are participatory, at least in some of their aspects, are living in a cultured society, sharing in a common language, and being a member of a religious community.

Réaume's main purpose in isolating participatory goods as a particular type of public good is to argue that rights to those goods must be group rights. Since a participatory good necessarily involves the participation of others, a right to the good must be a right possessed by the group who participate in the good; it cannot be a right possessed by one participant only or by each participant individually. That is not necessarily true of rights to non-participatory, or contingent, public goods. Consider clean air and clean water again. If a factory owner pollutes a community's air in a significantly harmful way, or if someone causes death or disease by polluting a community's water supply, we can reasonably hold that the polluter violates rights possessed individually by each member of the community rather than a collective right possessed by the community as whole. The members of the community may be harmed by a single act of pollution, but the fact that they are harmed simultaneously need not entail that they are wronged collectively rather than individually.

---

[18] Ibid., p. 199.   [19] Réaume 1988.
[20] Raz 1995, pp. 35–6; Green 1988, pp. 207–9; Waldron 1993, pp. 339–69; Marmor 2001.

Even if rights to participatory goods can only be collective rights, it does not follow of course that participatory goods must be the objects of collective rights since some may not be the objects of rights as all. Normally a group will have no claim-right against outsiders that they should participate in the group's activities in order to facilitate and sustain the group's enjoyment of its participatory good; such a right would impose an undue burden upon others.

Raz identifies a tolerant society, an educated society, and a society infused with respect for human beings as collective goods, only to argue that they are not the sort of goods to which there can be rights, individual or collective.[21] On the other hand, a group, such as a choir or a religious community, might plausibly possess a collective right against outsiders that they should not be prevented from enjoying their participatory good. Or a group may have a collective right to external support for its participatory good, such as an orchestra's right to a public subsidy or a linguistic minority's right to public measures designed to safeguard its language.

If we return to the case of collective self-determination, it matches Réaume's idea of a participatory good in that collective self-determination is an intrinsically collective good. It is a good that can be enjoyed only along with others who make up the collectivity. I said a moment ago that Réaume's idea of a participatory good was close to, but not identical with, the idea of a collective, or inherently public, good. The reason is that she implies that participatory goods are goods that involve participation understood as the active engagement of participants with one another. In particular, she holds that the participants in a participatory good produce together the good that they consume together and that 'the publicity of production is a part of what is valued—the good *is* the participation,'[22] as, for instance, in the cases of friendship, a square dance, and a game of football. However, active participation is not necessarily a feature of a collective good. For example, the self-determination to which a people has a right may be understood as requiring its population actively to engage with one another in shaping their collective future; but it might also be understood, and has often been understood, as requiring no more than a people's non-subjection to external rule. If we understand it in the latter, more parsimonious, way, the good of self-determination will be entirely passive consisting in an absence—the absence of external rule; but it will remain a collective good since it will be the good of not being collectively subject to external rule. Thus collective goods will be coextensive with participatory goods only if we relax the meaning of 'participatory' so that it describes all goods that must be enjoyed with others if they are to be enjoyed at all and not only goods that require positive engagement in a participatory act.[23]

c. Collective rights and equal moral standing

From all of the above, we might conclude that the right to collective self-determination must be a collective right, since collective self-determination is a collective good and

---

[21] Raz 1986, pp. 199–209.   [22] Réaume 1988, p. 10 (her emphasis).
[23] I consider the relationship between collective rights and participatory goods more fully in Jones 2014.

rights to collective goods must be collective rights. However, the structural features of a collective good alone are not enough to deliver that conclusion. James Morauta has pointed out that there is nothing *logically* wrong with an individual's having a right to a participatory good, even though we might find that possibility morally unappealing.[24] Take the case of a team game. I and I alone may have a right that others shall play a team game with me so that they are duty-bound to turn out and play the game with me whenever I so demand. If a third party prevents our playing the game, the party that will be wronged is not the entire group of players but me, since I alone possess the right that we shall play the game.[25] There is nothing logically amiss with that state of affairs. We might, under these circumstances, question whether the team game remains a collective good but, for the sake of the point at issue here, we can assume that the other players always positively enjoy the games I require them to play, so that the game continues to be a collective good for all of its participants.

It is not easy to replicate this possibility in a convincing fashion for the collective good of collective self-determination. If I alone, rather than the people themselves, were to have the right to determine a people's collective future, my right would not be a right to *collective* self-determination; it would be a right that *I* should determine the collective life of the people. To parallel the case of the team game, the example would have to be one in which I, rather than the people themselves, had the right that the people should be collectively self-determining. They should be self-determining if and because I require that they should and, as before, a third party that prevented their being self-determining would violate a right that I possess rather than one that belongs to the people themselves. Nevertheless, this state of affairs would be no less morally monstrous than a single person's being entitled to determine the collective life of a people, since it too would imply that the right-holding individual had a right over the lives of his fellow citizens; for collective purposes, their lives would be at his disposal.

How can we see off this morally implausible, if logically possible, individual right? The obvious answer is by adding the assumption that each member of the self-determining people enjoys equal moral standing. None of them will then possess the extraordinary moral standing necessary for the people's collective self-determination to be an object of his or her individual right. We need to add two qualifying comments. First, equal standing is an unnecessarily strong assumption to remove the possibility that one individual could possess the right that a people should be collectively self-determining; all we require is that no individual has sufficiently unequal standing to be the sole possessor of that right. However, there is no obvious reason why we should relax the assumption of equal standing. Secondly, individuals of equal standing can possess unequal interests in a good and it is logically possible that one individual's interest in a collective good could so exceed the interests of all others that he uniquely had a right to

[24] Morauta 2002.
[25] I set aside the logical possibility that the teams themselves could have a collective right against third parties to be unprevented from playing the games I require them to play.

the good. However, contingencies aside,[26] it is difficult to see why individuals' interests in their society's being self-determining should be unequal. More generally, special arrangements aside,[27] it will be difficult for an individual's peculiar interest in a collective good to justify his having an individual right to the collective good, given the claim that such a right would make upon the lives of others.[28]

Collective Self-Determination as a Collective Human Right

How then do the ideas of collective rights in general and the right to collective self-determination in particular, as I have presented them here, comport with the idea of human rights? A common objection to claiming group rights as human rights is that the holders of human rights are human beings, and human beings are individual beings; hence, even if groups do have rights, their rights will not be human rights.[29] As I previously indicated, if we conceive group rights according to the corporate model, that objection would seem to hold. Group rights will be the rights of entities that are categorically different from human beings, and that possess moral standing independently of the human beings they house. A 'people' corporately conceived will be a different sort of being from the individual human beings who make up its population and who possess human rights. But insofar as we conceive group rights according to the collective model, that will not be so. Group rights so conceived *will be* rights held by individual human beings; they will differ from individually held rights only in being rights that are held by individuals jointly rather than severally. The collective right of a people to collective self-determination will be a right held jointly by the individuals who together constitute that people. Thus, insofar as we conceive group rights as collective rights, it becomes possible to conceive them as human rights. Of course, not all collective rights will be human rights, just as not all individual rights are human rights. But the mere fact that a right is possessed collectively rather than individually will not, of itself, preclude its being a human right.

Some basic human rights have both individual and collective dimensions and that helps to expose the arbitrariness of insisting that rights can be human rights only if

---

[26] By 'contingencies' I mean possibilities such as a particular individual's being especially liable to gain or lose economically from breaches of his people's self-determination.

[27] If, for example, I have entered into a contractual arrangement with the other team-players according to which, in return for generous payment, they have undertaken to play the team game with me whenever I so wish, and if the contract was unsullied by duress, exploitation, and the like, there need be nothing morally objectionable in my having an individual right to their playing the team game.

[28] In fairness to Raz, I should note that his formal definition of a collective right could accommodate my reasoning in this section. Although, in elaborating on that definition, he focuses on the different 'weights' of individual and combined interests, the reason why 'the interest of no single member of that group in that public good is sufficient by itself to justify holding another person to be subject to a duty' (1986, p. 208) could be the reason I give here: the collective nature of the good combined with the equal standing of its claimants.

[29] e.g. Donnelly 2003, pp. 23–7; Galenkamp 1993, pp. 64–73; Nordenfelt 1987.

they are held individually. Consider the right to freedom of religion. That freedom would normally be understood to include the freedom of a Sikh to participate in a nagar kirtan (a public religious procession) and the freedom of a Muslim to attend a mosque. It would also be taken to encompass the freedom of a Sikh community to stage a nagar kirtan and the freedom of a Muslim community to construct a mosque. Are we to say that, while the first two cases are matters of human right, the second two are not, simply because the rights at stake in those second cases would be held collectively?[30]

If the collective nature of the right to collective self-determination is not an obstacle to its being a human right, how does the right fare when judged against features that *are* necessary for a human right? In responding to that question, I shall avoid giving a definition of human rights of my own, since I do not want my argument to turn on the peculiarities of a definition of my own devising. Rather I shall comment on some generally accepted features of human rights.

Since human rights are the rights of human beings, one obvious such feature is universality. In fact, some qualifications to universality as a necessary condition of human rights are reasonable and generally accepted. We can, for example, limit some human rights to adult human beings rather than insist that all must be possessed at every age. We can also limit universality to the present, so that human rights have to fit the world in which we live now, without also having to make sense for the medieval era or the Stone Age.[31] The universality of the right of collective self-determination needs no special pleading. In our world, all human beings find themselves encompassed by political units of one form or another and each unit's population can be the joint bearers of its collective right of self-determination.

A second generally required feature of a human right is the significance and seriousness of its moral content. Perhaps the easiest way to make that case for collective self-determination is to point to the way that it connects to the liberty and equality provided for by individual human rights. The liberty of peoples to shape their own collective futures is the collective equivalent of their members' individual freedom to chart the course of their own lives; the idea of non-domination applies with equal facility to both.[32] The equality of status written into the idea of human rights is reproduced both in the equality enjoyed by individuals as joint holders of the right of collective self-determination and in the equality enjoyed by different collective bearers of that right, i.e. peoples, in relation to one another. It is difficult to see what political order of things, other than collective self-determination, could be consistent with the human rights values of liberty and equality.

What then of the more contentious claim that their political role should be a defining feature of human rights, rather than only a practical consequence of their moral

---

[30] That the human right to freedom of religion can take a collective form has been recognized both in international human rights law and in judgements of the European Court of Human Rights; see Rivers 2010, pp. 33–71. I defend the idea of collective human rights in more general terms in Jones 2013.

[31] Cf. Raz 2010, pp. 332–4; Tasioulas 2010, pp. 666–72.   [32] Cf. Pettit 2010.

significance? The right of peoples to be self-determining is an organizing principle of the contemporary political world and violations of that right are manifestly deemed of proper concern to the international community. Of course, proponents of the 'political' conception do not judge rights to be human only with reference to the actual practice of the international world; they also require that, morally, violations of those rights would justify international intervention, at least in principle. But that morally necessary justification is not difficult to deliver for collective self-determination. Neither of two of the best-known proponents of the 'political' view, John Rawls and Joseph Raz, shows any inclination to incorporate the right of collective self-determination within human rights, but that is because each remains wedded to a conception of human rights as individually held, not because the right fails to match their political conception.[33] By contrast, another prominent exponent of the political conception, Charles Beitz, does argue for the inclusion of the right of collective self-determination in human rights doctrine.[34]

If we do conceive the right to self-determination as a collective human right, it cannot be a right that is fundamentally at odds with other human rights. It cannot be a right that challenges or threatens individually held human rights, but there is no reason why it should. After all, on the conception I have proposed, the individuals who jointly hold collective human rights are the same individuals who singly hold individual human rights.[35]

Can we say, then, that a people's right to be self-determining is a collective human right? Unfortunately, not without some further skirmishing since the assertion that a people has a right to be self-determining can be made to affirm either or both of two different claims. One is the claim that there should be a one-to-one match between the people whose collective lives are determined and those who do the determining. I shall call this 'the determination principle'. It holds that, however humanity is divided into units for political purposes, each unit of population is entitled to determine the course of its own life.

The other is the claim that a particular population constitutes a collective self that has, or ought to have, a right of self-determination. Here the focus shifts to the identity of the 'self' that is entitled to be self-determining. Which units of population should we recognize as the 'selves' that are entitled to self-determination? I shall describe that question as 'the issue of selfhood'.

My general claim is that the determination principle can be brought within the compass of human rights thinking, but that the issue of selfhood cannot. The match there should be between determined and determining populations can be a human rights matter, while the division of humanity into self-determining units cannot. Even so, the inability of human rights to resolve the issue of selfhood is no reason for not

---

[33] Rawls 1999; Raz 2010.   [34] Beitz 2009, pp. 181–6.

[35] I comment more fully on the fear that collective human rights will threaten individual human rights in Jones 2013, pp. 109–12.

holding that each people, suitably understood, possesses a collective human right to be collectively self-determining.

The Determination Principle

The determination principle has been particularly associated with the right to independent statehood, but there is no reason why it should be realized only in that form. It is quite consistent, for example, with multi-level governance, whether the levels additional to state governance fall above or below it. All the determination principle requires is that there should be a match between the population that is subject to a particular level of governance and the population that has ultimate control over that level. Advocacy of increased autonomy for groups within states, as an option that is preferable to and more feasible than independent statehood, has been a conspicuous feature of recent writing on self-determination.[36] I endorse that tendency but, for the sake of simplicity, I shall continue to consider self-determination mainly in relation to statehood.

The determination principle is now very widely accepted. For most of the twentieth century, its worldwide application was controversial; imperial powers such as Britain and France were happy to invoke it for themselves but not for the peoples who made up their empires. But, following the era of decolonization, challenges to the principle have largely disappeared. Disputes concerning self-determination nowadays are much more likely to concern the identity of the selves that should be self-determining. Even so, a number of issues and uncertainties still surround the determination principle.

Self-determination is usually held to have external and internal dimensions. Externally, it requires outside powers not to interfere in a people's internal affairs, while internally it vests ultimate authority in the people and serves notice to its members that none should usurp that authority.

In an increasingly globalized world, the feasibility of self-determination's external dimension is often questioned. Even if we set aside that empirical issue, we confront normative questions concerning the type or degree of external impact that is compatible with self-determination. At the very least, self-determination requires that a people should not be formally subject to, and legally obligated by, decisions that are made externally to itself, unless those decisions fall within the jurisdiction of a global or international body, such as the United Nations, of which the people is a member. Does self-determination demand more than that? A people's collective life can be radically affected by external decisions, such as decisions on economic, environmental, or military matters, even though that people is not formally subject to those decisions. On the other hand, if self-determination were to veto every form of external affecting, it would become impossibly demanding. So one major uncertainty concerning the determination principle is just what kind or degree of external affecting it can find acceptable.

[36]   e.g. Buchanan 2004, pp. 401–24; Kymlicka 2001, 2010; Miller 2000, pp. 125–41; Moltchanova 2009.

Issues and uncertainties also surround the internal dimension of self-determination. A people may have ultimate authority over its own affairs, but what does that imply for its governmental arrangements? One answer, frequently given, in both the past and present, is that a people is entitled to determine its own form of government, democratic or undemocratic.[37] But another is that self-determination requires democracy.[38] The issue is further complicated by assertions of an individual human right to democracy. There cannot be both that right and a collective human right (or any other kind of right) of a people to determine its own form of government; so which should it be? The claim that there is a *human* right to democracy is controversial.[39] The idea of an *individual* right to democracy is also problematic. Democracy must count as a collective good and we have already seen the difficulties we encounter if we make collective goods the objects of individual rights. Should we then substitute a collective right to democracy? That would still be a strange right if it afforded peoples no moral option but to organize themselves democratically. My own inclination is to interpret the right to internal self-determination more generously as the right of a people to decide on its own form of government, which I take to be consistent with requiring governments, whatever their form, to respect human rights; but I cannot defend that inclination here.

Do these issues and ambiguities discredit the claim of collective self-determination to be a human right? Controversy over the precise content and implications of a human right is the rule rather than the exception, even when the human right is widely accepted. The right to collective self-determination is not unusual for the differences of interpretation it attracts. Moreover, the debate here is not really over its status as a *human* right but over its precise content whatever sort of right it is.

The Issue of Selfhood

Who should be the peoples who enjoy self-determination? Can human rights provide the answer? If we identify peoples with the populations of established states, the implausibility of claiming the right to peoplehood as a human right is readily apparent. The borders that demarcate peoples in the current world are the products of all sorts of historical accidents and contingencies. There is no way in which we could, through the application of a general principle that might form part of a theory of human rights, show that the current division of the world's population into peoples is a uniquely right division. That is not to say that we have no reason to continue with it. There is no natural or quasi-natural way of dividing humanity into peoples and, given that absence, we have reason, at least *pro tanto*, to keep the borders we have. They may be the contingent products of a complex series of historical occurrences, many of which we may now

---

[37] e.g. Altman and Wellman 2009, pp. 11–42; Waldron 2010, p. 408.   [38] e.g. Philpott 1995.

[39] For a range of arguments on this issue, see Altman and Wellman 2009, pp. 11–42; Beitz 2009, pp. 174–86; Christiano 2011, 2013; Cohen 2006; Rawls 1999; Reidy 2012.

reckon to be of doubtful moral probity, but at least they exist and, if all trace and consequence of them were erased, we would be at a loss to know how they might be replaced. So their mere existence may be a reason for their continuance. It is significant, for example, that during the period of African decolonization of the 1960s and 1970s, the principle of *uti possidetis* (existing borders should remain intact, unless adjusted by the mutual consent of contiguous former colonies) was followed and was subsequently affirmed by the Organization of African Unity, in spite of the 'artificiality' of the borders that defined former African colonies. *Uti possidetis* was also prominent in decolonizations in Asia and South America and in the fragmentation of the Soviet Union and Yugoslavia.

We cannot, however, dispose of this issue merely by inspecting the status quo, since the legitimacy or desirability of existing political divisions is frequently challenged, often with good reason. The relevant issue here is whether those challenges might find a plausible foundation in human rights thinking. Some theorists justify secession on voluntarist grounds, so that justified secession approximates to an exercise of the human right to freedom of (dis)association.[40] In truth, however, the need for a seceding population to be a territorial group, to be large enough to be a viable political unit, and to meet various criteria relating to its impact upon others, together with the unlikelihood of unanimity, add up to a very imperfect form of voluntary association. And if voluntary association really were to be the ground of legitimate peoplehood, we would have to find that plausible for all populations, not only those who had opted for secession.

Nationalists have sometimes claimed that it should be nationhood that determines statehood. If nationhood existed as a uniform, comprehensive, and well-demarcated socio-cultural feature of humanity, we might be able to claim that all human beings belonged, pre-politically, to nations and that each body of nationals had a collective human right to be politically self-determining. But nationhood does not assume that even and inclusive form, and generally contemporary writers who are sympathetic to the claims of national identity do not seek to translate them into universal human rights.[41]

My commonplace observations here do not deny that there can be good reasons for constituting a particular population as a people or that those reasons might sometimes justify the assertion of a collective right to peoplehood. Rather, they aim to recognize that the content and weight of reasons relating to each case will vary and are likely to be too heavily dependent on the particularities of history, context, and circumstance to be accommodated by human rights thinking.

That conclusion may seem at odds with the claim I have been defending in this chapter. If a particular population has no human right to be a people, how can it possess

---

[40] For examples of voluntarist theories of secession, see Altman and Wellman 2009, pp. 43–68; Beran 1998; Copp 1998; Lefkowitz 2008; Philpott 1995. For sceptical commentary, see Buchanan 2004, pp. 373–9; Norman 1998; Weimer 2013.

[41] e.g. Miller 1995; Kymlicka 2001, 2010.

a collective human right to be collectively self-determining? The answer is by being a 'people' in a particular sense. My claim is that, insofar as a population is constituted as a people for political purposes, that people has a right to be self-determining. So 'people' here has a specifically political meaning. It does not refer to a people as an entity distinguished by a pre-political or non-political characteristic, such as its culture, ethnicity, religion, or indigeneity. Rather it refers to a population that is, as a matter of fact, constructed as a political unit, whether that unit be a state or a sub-state or supra-state unit. Whether that population should be so constructed—whether it ought to be a political people—is a different matter and not one that can be settled by invoking the collective human right to collective self-determination. The collective human right demands that political arrangements should comply with the determination principle—the principle that requires there to be a one-to-one match between those whose lives are determined and those who do the determining. But, as I have indicated, that principle does not address the question of how the world should be divided into self-determining peoples.

Critics frequently berate the UN for attributing the right of self-determination to peoples, while failing to address the controversial question of who should be a people. But if we understand 'peoples' in the political sense I have proposed, it makes perfect sense to assert the right of peoples to be collectively self-determining while remaining agnostic on the issue of whether peoples, as currently constituted, are as they should be. Even if populations are currently constructed as peoples sub-optimally and we can contemplate a superior arrangement, existing peoples will possess the human right of collective self-determination so long as they remain constructed politically as peoples. If and when they are reconstructed politically as peoples, those reconstructed peoples will have the same collective human right to be self-determining.

Conclusion

I have argued that a people's right to self-determination is a collective right in the specific sense in which I use that term—a right held jointly by the individuals who make up the right-holding collectivity. The right is necessarily a collective right because its object is a collective good, in respect of which each member of a people enjoys equal standing.[42] Understood in that way, its collective nature is no barrier to its being a human right. It also possesses the universality and moral significance that are normally required of human rights, so that we have good reason to deem it a human right. However, as a human right, it is possessed only by populations who are constituted politically as peoples. It is not possessed by populations who are not, but who possess a good claim to be, political peoples, which is not to deny that such populations can have

---

[42] That argument does not imply that a collective right can be a right *only* to a collective good, or that individuals can be the joint holders of a collective right *only* if they enjoy equal standing and are equally interested in the object of the right. See further Jones 1999, 2014.

rights of other sorts to be constituted as peoples. If all that is correct, the right of peoples to collective self-determination will not have been mislocated in the ICCPR and the ICESCR, whatever the historical reasons for its being included in those human rights covenants.

References

Altman, Andrew, and Christopher Heath Wellman (2009), *A Liberal Theory of International Justice* (Oxford: Oxford University Press).

Beitz, Charles (2009), *The Idea of Human Rights* (Oxford: Oxford University Press).

Beran, Harry (1998), 'A Democratic Theory of Political Self-Determination for a New World Order', in Percy Lehning (ed.), *Theories of Secession* (London: Routledge), pp. 32–59.

Buchanan, Allen (2004), *Justice, Legitimacy, and Self-Determination: Moral Foundations for International Law* (Oxford: Oxford University Press).

Cassese, Antonio (1995), *Self-Determination of Peoples: A Legal Reappraisal* (Cambridge: Cambridge University Press).

Christiano, Thomas (2011), 'An Instrumental Argument for a Human Right to Democracy', *Philosophy and Public Affairs*, 39 (2), 142–76.

Christiano, Thomas (2013), 'An Egalitarian Argument for a Human Right to Democracy', in Cindy Holder and David Reidy (eds), *Human Rights: The Hard Questions* (Cambridge: Cambridge University Press), pp. 301–25.

Cohen, Joshua (2006), 'Is There a Human Right to Democracy?', in Christine Sypnowich (ed.), *The Egalitarian Conscience: Essays in Honour of G. A. Cohen* (Oxford: Oxford University Press), pp. 226–48.

Copp, David (1998), 'International Law and Morality in the Theory of Secession', *Journal of Ethics*, 2 (3), 219–45.

Donnelly, Jack (2003), *Universal Human Rights in Theory and Practice*, 2nd edition (Ithaca, NY: Cornell University Press).

French, Peter (1984), *Collective and Corporate Responsibility* (New York: Columbia University Press).

Galenkamp, Marlies (1993), *Individualism and Collectivism: The Concept of Collective Rights* (Rotterdam: Rotterdamse Filosofische Studies).

Graff, James A. (1994), 'Human Rights, Peoples, and the Right to Self-Determination', in Judith Baker (ed.), *Group Rights* (Toronto: University of Toronto Press), pp. 186–214.

Green, Leslie (1988), *The Authority of the State* (Oxford: Clarendon Press).

Hartney, Michael (1991), 'Some Confusions Concerning Collective Rights', *Canadian Journal of Law and Jurisprudence*, 4 (2), 292–314.

Jones, Peter (1999), 'Group Rights and Group Oppression', *Journal of Political Philosophy*, 7 (4), 353–77.

Jones, Peter (2009), 'Cultures, Group Rights and Group-Differentiated Rights', in Maria Dimova-Cookson and Peter Stirk (eds), *Multiculturalism and Moral Conflict* (London: Routledge), pp. 38–57.

Jones, Peter (2013), 'Groups and Human Rights', in Cindy Holder and David Reidy (eds), *Human Rights: The Hard Questions* (Cambridge: Cambridge University Press), pp. 100–14.

Jones, Peter (2014), 'Collective Rights, Public Goods and Participatory Goods', in Magali Bessone, Gideon Calder, and Federico Zuolo (eds), *How Groups Matter* (London: Routledge), pp. 52–72.

Kymlicka, Will (2001), *Politics in the Vernacular: Nationalism, Multiculturalism and Citizenship* (Oxford: Oxford University Press).

Kymlicka, Will (2010), 'Minority Rights in Political Philosophy and International Law', in Samantha Besson and John Tasioulas (eds), *The Philosophy of International Law* (Oxford: Oxford University Press), pp. 377–96.

Lefkowitz, David (2008), 'On the Foundation of Rights to Political Self-Determination: Secession, Nonintervention, and Democratic Governance', *Journal of Social Philosophy*, 39 (4), 492–511.

McDonald, Michael (1991), 'Should Communities Have Rights? Reflections on Liberal Individualism', *Canadian Journal of Law and Jurisprudence*, 4 (2), 217–37.

Margalit, Avishai, and Joseph Raz (1990), 'National Self-Determination', *Journal of Philosophy*, 87 (9), 439–61.

Marmor, Andrei (2001), 'Do we Have a Right to Common Goods?', *Canadian Journal of Law and Jurisprudence*, 14 (2), 213–25.

Miller, David (1995), *On Nationality* (Oxford: Oxford University Press).

Miller, David (2000), *Citizenship and National Identity* (Cambridge: Polity).

Moltchanova, Anna (2009), *National Self-Determination and Justice in Multinational States* (Dordrecht: Springer).

Morauta, James (2002), 'Rights and Participatory Goods', *Oxford Journal of Legal Studies*, 22 (2), 91–113.

Narveson, Jan (1991), 'Collective Rights?', *Canadian Journal of Law and Jurisprudence*, 4 (2), 329–45.

Newman, Dwight (2011), *Community and Collective Rights: A Theoretical Framework for Rights held by Groups* (Oxford: Hart Publishing).

Nordenfelt, Johan (1987), 'Human Rights: What They are, and What They are not', *Nordic Journal of International Law*, 56 (1), 1–8.

Norman, Wayne (1998), 'The Ethics of Secession as the Regulation of Secessionist Politics', in Margaret Moore (ed.), *National Self-Determination and Secession* (Oxford: Oxford University Press), pp. 34–61.

Pettit, Philip (2010), 'A Republican Law of Peoples', *European Journal of Political Theory*, 9 (1), 70–94.

Philpott, Daniel (1995), 'In Defense of Self-Determination', *Ethics*, 105 (2), 352–85.

Preda, Adina (2013), 'Group Rights and Shared Interests', *Political Studies*, 61 (2), 250–66.

Rawls, John (1999), *The Law of Peoples* (Cambridge, Mass.: Harvard University Press).

Raz, J. (1995), 'Rights and Politics', *Indiana Law Journal*, 71 (1), 27–44.

Raz, J. (2010), 'Human Rights without Foundation', in Samantha Besson and John Tasioulas (eds), *The Philosophy of International Law* (Oxford: Oxford University Press), pp. 321–37.

Raz, Joseph (1986), *The Morality of Freedom* (Oxford: Clarendon Press).

Réaume, Denise (1988), 'Individuals, Groups, and Rights to Public Goods', *University of Toronto Law Review*, 38 (1), 1–27.

Réaume, Denise G. (1994), 'The Group Right to Linguistic Security: Whose Right, What Duties?', in Judith Baker (ed.), *Group Rights* (Toronto: University of Toronto Press), pp. 118–41.

Reidy, David (2012), 'On the Human Right to Democracy: Searching for Sense without Stilts', *Journal of Social Philosophy*, 43 (2), 177–203.

Rivers, Julian (2010), *The Law of Organized Religions: Between Establishment and Secularism* (Oxford: Oxford University Press).

Tamir, Yael (1999), 'Against Collective Rights', in Christian Joppke and Steven Lukes (eds), *Multicultural Questions* (Oxford: Oxford University Press), pp. 158–80.

Tasioulas, John (2010), 'Taking Rights out of Human Rights', *Ethics*, 120 (4), 647–78.

Waldron, Jeremy (1993), *Liberal Rights* (Cambridge: Cambridge University Press).

Waldron, Jeremy (2010), 'Two Conceptions of Self-Determination', in Samantha Besson and John Tasioulas (eds), *The Philosophy of Interational Law* (Oxford: Oxford University Press), pp. 397–413.

Weimer, Steven (2013), 'Autonomy-Based Accounts of the Right to Secede', *Social Theory and Practice*, 39 (4), 625–43.

13.1

Linking Self-Determination and Human Rights
Comment on Peter Jones

Will Kymlicka

Introduction

Peter Jones has provided a characteristically lucid conceptual analysis of the various ways in which rights to collective self-determination can be connected to, but also distinguished from, human rights. The conclusion of his analysis is that "the determination principle can be brought within the compass of human rights thinking, but that the issue of selfhood cannot". I agree that these two principles can be analytically distinguished in the way Jones describes, but I see no reason why both are not appropriate parts of the international human rights regime. On the contrary, there are powerful philosophical and political reasons why both should be so included.

Part of our disagreement concerns how best to understand or to characterize the injustice that occurs when the collective selfhood principle is violated. But I suspect we may also disagree at a more fundamental level about the sorts of injustices which should be the particular focus of the international human rights regime. I will suggest that the international order may have a particular obligation to protect against violations of the selfhood principle precisely because the international order is itself so deeply complicit in these violations. While international human rights law undoubtedly serves many different moral functions, this is one of its most important: to remedy the injustices that international law itself has helped to create. This feature is missing in Jones's analysis, which tends to view international human rights law as an attempt to implement an ahistorical theory of universalizable rights, rather than as an attempt at the moral reform, indeed moral rescue, of international law itself.

In this short commentary, I will first lay out my view of the sorts of injustices that are involved in the denial of self-determination, and then consider why the international community might have an obligation to protect against violations of both the determination principle and the selfhood principle, and why international human rights norms are the appropriate vehicle to provide this protection.

Four Violations of Self-Determination

As Jones notes, the international community has repeatedly affirmed the principle of self-determination as a key component of international human rights. But what exactly is the problem to which rights of self-determination are supposed to provide an answer? I think it's worth distinguishing four different contexts in which self-determination can be unjustly violated, and in which rights of self-determination can serve as a shield:

1. Imperial Occupation: one context where self-determination is violated is when an imperial power coercively asserts imperial rule over the people and territory of another society. European colonial rule in Africa and Asia is the paradigm case. Note that imperial rule in this context does not involve large-scale settlement in the colonized territory—the British never numbered more than a few thousand in most of their Asian and African colonies. This is military occupation but not settlement, or "imperium" but not "dominium" to use the classical terms.

In today's world, this sort of old-fashioned imperial occupation is deeply illegitimate, and deeply unstable, and in most cases in Asia and Africa it has given way to decolonization, independence, and self-determination by the native population. But sometimes, the imperial power, or at least some of its members, do not want give up control over the colonized territory, and so adopt various strategies to make their rule seem less "foreign" and "imperial", and more like acceptable forms of domestic rule. There are at least three possible avenues here:

2. Postcolonial Minority Rule and Majority Disenfranchisement: in contexts where there is large-scale colonial settlement, the settlers may over time seek to establish their own independent state, even though they form a minority in the colonized territory. White rule in South Africa is the paradigm case of such postcolonial minority rule. In order to maintain their rule in an independent South Africa, they needed to disenfranchise the native African population through apartheid.

3. Annexation: another option is for the imperial society to annex part or all of the colonized territory to the metropole, so that it is no longer legally an occupied or colonized territory but rather becomes an integral part of the imperial homeland. The American annexation of Hawaii is a paradigm case; France's annexation of Algeria is an interesting failed example. While France was willing to give up most of its African colonies, and to allow them to become independent, it viewed Algeria as a special case, marked by its annexation to France proper. Annexation may go along with disenfranchisement of the native population,

who are likely to oppose annexation, but over time, may allow for the native population to become citizens, at least under certain conditions, as with the Algerian Muslims who could choose to become French citizens if they opted for French civil law over Muslim personal law.

4. Mass Settlement and Majority Rule: Finally, the most complete way of ensuring the perpetuation of imperial rule is to promote mass settlement so that the settlers and their descendants eventually outnumber the native population. The British settler states of the United States, Canada, and Australia are paradigm examples. In all of these cases, the indigenous peoples are now a very small percentage of the population, and so here again there is no need to disenfranchise them, since they are subject to majority rule of a predominantly settler population.

These are the paradigmatic ways in which imperial powers deny self-determination to those they colonize: imperial occupation; postcolonial minority rule; annexation; and mass settlement.

These four strategies of imperial rule are continuous in the underlying ideologies used to justify the violation of self-determination, and in their underlying effects on those whose self-determination is denied. They are all underpinned by the same racist and supremacist ideologies—they all rest on the assertion that the hegemonic society is fit to rule while denying the same to native peoples. And the choice between these strategies is largely tactical. If whites in Canada had not outnumbered indigenous peoples at the time of independence in 1867, they too would have adopted the South African apartheid strategy for maintaining minority white rule. Conversely, if whites in South Africa had formed a demographic majority, then they might have been happy to include natives as citizens. In fact, most real world cases involved a mixing and matching of these strategies, with various combinations or sequences of imperial rule, disenfranchisement, annexation, and mass settlement. Think about the history of Hawaii, which involved all of these tactics at different stages, all equally premised on the denial of the self-determination of the indigenous population.

Since all of these violations of self-determination are continuous in their ideological sources and unjust effects, there would appear to be a strong prima facie case for including all of them under international norms of self-determination. All else being equal, we should seek to formulate a norm of self-determination that can cover all of these contexts, and that can protect against all of these different strategies and tactics for denying self-determination.

Determination versus Selfhood

Jones, however, argues that all else is not equal, and that we can and should draw a sharp distinction between the first two tactics (imperial occupation; postcolonial minority rule) and the second two tactics (annexation; mass settlement). The first two,

Jones argues, involve a denial of the determination principle: the principle "that there should be a one-to-one match between the people whose collective lives are determined and those who do the determining". The second two, by contrast, do not (or need not) disenfranchise anyone on the territory over which government is exercised, and so comply with the determination principle. When Algeria was annexed to France, the native Algerians could (in principle) choose to be included in "the people" who govern France. Similarly, when massive European settlement in Canada outnumbered indigenous peoples, the indigenous peoples could, in principle, choose to be included in "the people" who govern Canada.[1] The problem, in these latter cases, is not the denial of the determination principle, but the failure to correctly identify the relevant "self" that should have rights of self-determination in the first place. While native Algerians and native Canadians were eligible to be included in the French or Canadian people who exercise a right of determination, they were not recognized as forming their own people, with their own rights to govern their own territory.

As I have said, I agree with Jones that we can analytically distinguish the cases along these lines. Excluding certain people from the collective self that governs a territory is different, conceptually, from denying that certain people form their own collective self. I do not understand, however, why this analytic distinction should be thought to have the moral and legal consequences that Jones attaches to it. Why should we suppose that international human rights norms should only address violations of determination, and not failures of selfhood? After all, Jones makes no attempt to show that violations of determination are inherently or typically more unjust than violations of selfhood, either in their effects or their motivations. As I noted, the motivations behind denials of determination and denials of selfhood are often identical, rooted in the same political projects of consolidating rule over the territory of native populations, administered by the same political actors, and justified by the same supremacist ideologies, differing only in their tactical assessments of how best to achieve this goal. Insofar as international human rights norms should function to delegitimize and prevent such unjust political projects, it seems odd to preclude some strategies but not others.

In fact, there is a sense in which the latter two strategies involve an intensification of the injustice of the denial of self-determination. To be sure, all of these four strategies are devastating in their own ways to those denied self-determination, and moreover they all tend to be accompanied by further violations of fundamental rights. We can find all too many examples of genocide, ethnic cleansing, mass rape, enslavement, and torture across all four of these contexts, incited by the supremacist ideologies that justify the denial of self-determination, combined with fears that the native populations will resist their imperial overlords. But there is a sense in which annexation and mass settlement involve an intensification of the denial of self-determination. Annexation and mass settlement means that this denial pervades more deeply into everyday life,

[1] As with the case of Algerian Muslims, Canada's Aboriginal peoples could choose to become Canadian citizens if they showed that they had assimilated.

reworking the fabric of social and political life in a way that makes both the collective self and its aspirations for self-determination more invisible and out of reach. Indeed, we might say that annexation and mass settlement can be fatally unjust, in a way that imperial rule and postcolonial minority rule often are not. Indigenous peoples subjected to imperial rule and/or postcolonial minority rule can often survive this ordeal, and live to see the day when they can reassert their rights to self-determination. This indeed is the clear pattern, as both imperial rule and apartheid-like disenfranchisement have gradually given way to self-determination. The self that is denied self-determination in these two strategies persists as a viable collectivity, waiting in the wings to regain their rightful self-determination when inherently unstable projects of imperial occupation and postcolonial minority rule collapse.

By contrast, annexation and mass settlement is often much more disruptive and destructive of indigenous societies, displacing them from their homelands to accommodate new settlers, undermining their traditional economies, stripping them of institutions of self-rule, and turning them into small dispersed enclaves at the margins of settler society. As a result, it becomes increasingly difficult for them to assert rights of self-determination, since they have been stripped of their territory, and are often a small minority even in their historic homeland. This is indeed precisely why political projects of imperial rule often have as their ultimate objective annexation and mass settlement: this represents the ultimate defeat of indigenous self-determination. Imperial powers are always worried that there is a viable collective self waiting in the wings to reassert self-determination, and so often seek to crush this collective self in ways that are facilitated by annexation and mass settlement. These latter strategies change the "facts on the ground" in ways that are potentially fatal to aspirations for self-determination (and indeed in ways that are intended to be fatal to these aspirations).

So it seems puzzling to suggest that international human rights norms should forbid provisional denials of self-determination, through imperial occupation and postcolonial minority rule, but remain "agnostic" on the ultimate denials of self-determination through annexation and mass settlement. I cannot see any plausible argument of justice for this proposal.

I should also note that there is no evidence that denials of selfhood are any less likely to trigger instability or violence or humanitarian crises than denials of determination. Even if we thought that international human rights norms should be particularly attentive to those injustices that are likely to trigger international conflict and instability, the social science evidence shows clearly that "demographic engineering"—the redrawing of boundaries and encouraging of settlement to turn indigenous peoples and other ethnonational groups into a minority in their historic territory—is a major source of violence and humanitarian crises.[2] And this is what we should expect, precisely because mass settlement is potentially fatal to aspirations for self-determination.

---

[2] For the empirical evidence, see Gurr 2000; Toft 2005.

Native populations can often outwait imperial occupiers, but they cannot outwait annexation and mass settlement.

So why then does Jones seek to exclude denials of selfhood from international human rights norms? The answer, I gather, is that the principle of selfhood, unlike the principle of determination, is "too heavily dependent on the particularities of history, context, and circumstance" to meet the test of "universality". I'm not entirely sure how to interpret this requirement of universality, and how it applies to other areas of human rights, such as the rights of women, children, or people with disabilities. It seems to me that the principle of selfhood is no more or less universalizable than many other areas of human rights which address vulnerable groups.[3]

But even if we can make sense of the idea that the principle of selfhood is somehow distinctly non-universalizable, I would still question why this should matter. Why suppose that international human rights norms should only address those injustices that are independent of the "particularities of history, context and circumstance"? After all, as I've already mentioned, there's no reason to believe that such injustices are any worse in their motivations or effects than injustices that arise from the denial of selfhood. Why privilege one category of injustices as the focus of international human rights norms?

The Moral Purposes of International Human Rights Norms

One possible response here would be a purely semantic one: the Universal Declaration of Human Rights (UDHR) is, by its title, limited to "universal" rights. But we can't settle normative disputes with semantic arguments, and if anyone thought that it was semantically inappropriate to add non-universal rights to the UDHR, then we could simply relabel it as, say, the Global Declaration of Human Rights, or the International Declaration of Human Rights.

To address the substantive issue about the merits of including a principle of collective selfhood, we need to dig deeper to explore the moral purposes of international human rights norms. What is it we hope to achieve by formulating international human rights norms? What is the moral work these norms are intended to do?

Jones does not pursue these questions in depth in his chapter—since they obviously would require a paper on their own—but he implicitly endorses a very traditional and long-standing view amongst philosophers, which is that the UDHR is intended to embody a philosophical theory about universalizable moral claims. I find this traditional view implausible, not least because it is divorced from any credible story about the nature of international law as an institution, and from any plausible theory about the justice of the international order.

---

[3] For arguments that the principle of selfhood meets relevant tests of universalizability, see Tamir 1991; Anaya 1996, 2004.

Along with several other theorists, such as Patrick Macklem and Charles Beitz, I would argue that we should start from the premise that international human rights norms are one part of a larger international order, and must therefore be evaluated in light of, and as part of, a larger theory about the justice of such an international order.[4] There is nothing wrong with moral philosophers developing a theory about what kinds of moral claims meet different tests of universalizability, but there is no a priori reason why we should think that this is the relevant moral yardstick for evaluating the goals and purposes of the international order.

We would do better, I think, by asking what are the specific kinds of pathologies that tend to afflict the international order—what are the most familiar or characteristic forms of injustice within the international order—and then asking how international human rights norms can help redress these characteristic injustices. What are the standard threats to international justice, and how can we address them?

Viewed this way, the focus on self-determination, in both its determination and selfhood dimensions, becomes not only understandable but even inevitable. The obvious fact is that international law, far from protecting native populations against foreign rule, has historically served as a handmaiden of European imperialism. International law has not only historically supported the colonization of indigenous peoples, it largely emerged precisely *in order* to facilitate European imperialism.[5] Europeans in effect started a worldwide race war with their imperial projects, and developed international law as a weapon in this war.

International law was, therefore, in great danger of being discredited in the post-war period, and its very legitimacy—and the legitimacy of the international order more generally—depended on its ability to reform itself. In particular, it needed to show that it could address *the injustices that it itself created*, not least the massively unjust distribution of sovereignty that resulted from the way international law denied self-determination to indigenous peoples while awarding it to European colonizers.

This struggle for legitimacy has taken many forms, including support for decolonization and condemnations of apartheid (i.e. support for Jones's "principle of determination"), but also support for the rights to self-determination of indigenous peoples, and the right to contest unjust annexation, as in the case of East Timor or Western Sahara (i.e. support for Jones's "principle of selfhood"). And just as the original injustices were continuous in their motivations and effects, so too are these remedies. The normative principles that underpin condemnations of colonial occupation and apartheid also underpin the expressions of support for indigenous rights and for the reversal of wrongful annexations, and the jurisprudence on the former cases informs and supports the jurisprudence on the latter cases, and vice versa. There is one evolving jurisprudence on the right of self-determination that integrates both determination and selfhood, focusing on how to protect vulnerable groups from all of the strategies and tactics for violating self-determination.

---

[4] Macklem 2008b, 2015; Beitz 2009.   [5] Keal 2003; Anghie 2004.

This is clearly a different way of thinking about international human rights norms than is presupposed in Jones's article. On both views, international human rights norms are intended to protect against fundamental injustices. But on my view, these are first and foremost injustices that the international order itself creates. International human rights norms have a "civilizing" function,[6] but it is not backward cultures that need to be civilized—rather, it is the international order itself that needs moral reform.

This is particularly clear in the emerging analysis and jurisprudence surrounding the UN's Declaration of the Rights of Indigenous Peoples of 2007, which includes recognition of rights of self-determination. As James Anaya puts it, "international law, although once an instrument of colonialism, has developed and continues to develop, however grudgingly and imperfectly, to support indigenous peoples' demands".[7] Similarly, Patrick Macklem argues that the Declaration can best be understood, not as responding to some exogenous injustice out in the world, but rather as rectifying injustices that international law itself created: "international indigenous rights mitigate some of the adverse consequences of how international law validates morally suspect colonization projects that participated in the production of the existing distribution of sovereign power."[8] In this sense, if the UN Declaration helps to legitimize indigenous demands, it is equally true that the Declaration helps to re-legitimize international law itself in a postcolonial era.[9]

This re-legitimization of international law is an unfinished project, and there will be many bumps along the way. I have elsewhere discussed some of the immense challenges in formulating international norms of self-determination, and in particular the problem that international norms are currently committed to an unworkable distinction between "minorities" and "indigenous peoples". Addressing the selfhood issue, I believe, will ultimately require replacing the crude minority/indigenous dichotomy with a more sophisticated categorization that better tracks the morally significant dimensions of self-determination.[10] And to be honest, I am not particularly optimistic that the necessary reforms will emerge. In that sense, I agree with Jones that formulating international norms to address problems of determination is often easier than formulating norms to address problems of selfhood.

However, I would strongly deny that problems of selfhood do not fit "within the compass of human rights thinking". On the contrary, I would insist that we have no option but to try to formulate norms of self-determination that address both dimensions. The legitimacy of the international order depends upon it. And we can only make progress on this task if we resist attempts to confine international human rights norms to an abstract theory of moral universalizability that is largely disconnected from the pressing issues of injustice that the international order has not only inherited, but itself helped to create.[11]

---

[6] Koskenniemi 2001.   [7] Anaya 1996, p. 4.   [8] Macklem 2008a.
[9] Xanthaki 2007, pp. 6, 285.   [10] Kymlicka 2007; 2011.
[11] Far from compromising the universality of human rights, one could argue that highlighting colonialism would help to make human rights more universal. As Barreto (2012) notes, the standard genealogy of human

References

Anaya, S. James (1996) *Indigenous Peoples in International Law* (New York: Oxford University Press).

Anaya, S. James (2004) "International Human Rights and Indigenous Peoples: The Move towards the Multicultural State", *Arizona Journal of International and Comparative Law* 21/1: 13–61.

Anghie, Antony (2004) *Imperialism, Sovereignty and the Making of International Law* (Cambridge: Cambridge University Press).

Barreto, José-Manuel (2012) "Decolonial Strategies and Dialogue in the Field of Human Rights: A Manifesto", *Transnational Legal Theory* 3/1: 1–29.

Barreto, José-Manuel (2014) "A Universal History of Infamy: Human Rights, Eurocentrism and Modernity as Crisis", in P. Singh and B. Mayer (eds), *Critical International Law: Postrealism, Postcolonialism, and Transnationalism* (Oxford: Oxford University Press).

Beitz, Charles (2009) *The Idea of Human Rights* (Oxford: Oxford University Press).

Gurr, Ted Robert (2000) *Peoples Versus States: Minorities at Risk in the New Century* (Washington: US Institute of Peace Press).

Keal, Paul (2003) *European Conquest and the Rights of Indigenous Peoples: The Moral Backwardness of International Society* (Cambridge: Cambridge University Press).

Koskenniemi, Martti (2001) *The Gentle Civilizer of Nations: The Rise and Fall of International Law 1870–1960* (Cambridge: Cambridge University Press).

Kymlicka, Will (2007) *Multicultural Odysseys: Navigating the New International Politics of Diversity* (Oxford: Oxford University Press).

Kymlicka, Will (2011) "Beyond the Indigenous/Minority Dichotomy?", in Stephen Allen and Alexandra Xanthaki (eds), *Reflections on the UN Declaration on the Rights of Indigenous Peoples* (Oxford: Hart Publishing).

Macklem, Patrick (2008a) "Indigenous Recognition in International Law: Theoretical Observations", *Michigan Journal of International Law* 30/1: 177–210.

Macklem, Patrick (2008b) "Minority Rights in International Law", *International Journal of Constitutional Law* 6/3: 531–2.

Macklem, Patrick (2015) *The Sovereignty of Human Rights* (Oxford: Oxford University Press).

Tamir, Yael (1991) "The Right to National Self-Determination", *Social Research* 58: 565–90.

Toft, Monica Duffy (2005) *The Geography of Ethnic Violence: Identity, Interests and the Indivisibility of Territory* (Princeton: Princeton University Press).

Xanthaki, Alexandra (2007) *Indigenous Rights and United Nations Standards, Self-Determination, Culture and Land* (New York: Cambridge University Press).

rights ties them to a specifically European history of key events that focus on relations between states and citizens (e.g. Magna Carta, French and American Revolutions, the Holocaust), ignoring that the key human rights events for the rest of the world have often involved relations between empires and the colonized. Building the latter into the heart of our conception of human rights would enhance "the universal appeal of human rights" since it would better reflect "the ecumenical jurisdiction of the victims of modernity" (Barreto 2014, p. 166).

14

Human Rights, Membership, and Moral Responsibility in an Unjust World

The Case of Immigration Restrictions

Alex Levitov & Stephen Macedo

International human rights instruments establish both a fundamental right to collective self-determination and a right of individuals to free movement. What principles and priorities should guide us when these two sets of claims come into conflict? When and under what conditions are political communities morally entitled to exclude those who wish to enter? And when, on the other side, do the rights of individuals seeking entry take priority? These issues are both philosophically contested and of great practical import, and this chapter seeks to illuminate them.

Article 1 of the International Covenant on Civil and Political Rights (ICCPR) describes collective self-determination as the right of peoples to "freely determine their political status and freely pursue their economic, social and cultural development." On the other hand, Article 12 of the ICCPR establishes that "Everyone shall be free to leave any country, including his own," and the Universal Declaration of Human Rights (UDHR) contains similar language.[1] The force of this right may be greatest in the case of refugees and asylum seekers fleeing persecution; and indeed the UDHR establishes the "right to seek and to enjoy in other countries asylum from persecution."[2]

What is the scope of the right to collective self-determination, and how can it be reconciled with various rights to free movement? In these twin commitments and in other ways, international human rights law seems to reflect the tension between what have come to be known as broadly "statist" and "cosmopolitan" conceptions of global justice. Statist or "membership-based" theories maintain that we have special duties of justice to our fellow citizens and that the full demands of social justice, however one

---

[1] See UDHR, Article 12.   [2] UDHR, Article 14.

conceives them, apply only within well-defined political societies.[3] Cosmopolitan or "globalist" conceptions of global justice, on the other hand, hold that in the most important respects all human beings are citizens of one world: members of one community of mankind, and that demanding and extensive duties of justice, such as Rawls's difference principle, apply to all individuals on a global scale. With respect to immigration policy specifically, "statists" tend to emphasize that political communities are entitled to a fair range of discretion in determining their entry policies, whereas cosmopolitans emphasize a right to free movement.

Those on the statist or membership side include John Rawls, David Miller, Joshua Cohen, and many others, including the present authors.[4] Rawls has emphasized that one important role of legitimate states is to act as the agent of particular peoples, politically organized, in regulating the use of the land and other resources and the population so that "the people's territory" can support them "in perpetuity": "People must recognize that they cannot make up for failing to regulate their numbers or to care for their land by...migrating into another people's territory without their consent."[5] David Miller has argued that the basic right of movement is limited: people have a right to live within a territory with an adequate range of options, and to move around in that territory. But there is, he emphasizes, no basic right to live wherever one wants.[6] These and other considerations have suggested to defenders of the statist or membership view that political communities have considerable discretion in shaping their immigration policies, at least (as Rawls is keen to emphasize) in an ideal international society of internally "well-ordered" peoples.[7]

On the cosmopolitan or globalist side, Joseph Carens has argued for decades that "borders should generally be open and that people should normally be free to leave their country of origin and settle in another," constrained only by the requirements of public order. We should insist on a right to migrate across borders, Carens suggests, for precisely the same reasons we insist on religious freedom and other familiar individual liberties (including freedom of movement *within* a political society): namely, because "it might prove essential to one's life plan." Restrictive citizenship laws, by contrast, are like "feudal birthright privileges," restricting the freedom of some individuals on the basis of factors that are arbitrary from a moral point of view.[8]

Other theorists argue from specifically democratic premises to the conclusion that political communities should not have the unilateral right, as Arash Abizadeh

---

[3] As Thomas Nagel puts it, it is only from political institutions "under strong centralized control" that we can claim "a right to democracy, equal citizenship, nondiscrimination, equal opportunity, and the amelioration through public policy of unfairness in the distribution of social and economic goods" (Nagel 2005, at p. 127); even if some of these demands can be pressed, in some form, against various transnational institutions, statists maintain that sharing membership in a state is necessary to trigger all of them.

[4] See, for example, Rawls 1999a; Blake 2001; Macedo 2004; Cohen 2006; Freeman 2007; and Miller 2010. Precursors of the cosmopolitan statist view we develop below include Miller 2005a; Julius 2006, at pp. 191–2; Sangiovanni 2007, at p. 35, and Scheffler 2010.

[5] Rawls 1999a, p. 8.   [6] Miller 2007, ch. 8.   [7] Rawls 1999a, pp. 38–9.

[8] Carens 1987, at pp. 251, 258, 252. See also Carens 2013.

puts it, "to control and close the state's boundaries."[9] He criticizes national border controls on the grounds that they are decided by only a subset of those affected by them. The reason, he says, is that "the demos of democratic theory is in principle unbounded, and the regime of boundary control must consequently be democratically justified to foreigners as well as to citizens": what we need, then, are "cosmopolitan democratic institutions" to shape countries' border control policies.[10] Robert Goodin has similarly argued that "[t]he democratic ideal ought ideally to enfranchise 'all affected interests.'" Since virtually everyone in the world is affected by the actual or possible policies and actions of powerful states such as the United States of America, including by its immigration policies, the principle suggests that "virtually everyone everywhere" should "vote on virtually everything" via a system of world government.[11] These theorists raise doubts about the familiar idea that a right of collective self-determination includes the right to control one's borders, even if a suitably organized global demos might be expected to endorse such a right.

Mathias Risse offers an interestingly mixed view, according to which states' rights of self-determination are constrained by considerations flowing from what he asserts is mankind's common ownership of the earth. He asserts that each person has a claim to an equal share of the earth's resources, regardless of national membership. States, on his view, are justified in excluding others from their territory "*only if* that space is populated by sufficiently many people," taking the average population-to-space ratio across existing states as a rough threshold of sufficiency.[12]

This chapter will examine the scope of the right to self-determination by focusing on this tangled question of border controls. We join those scholars, including Rawls, Miller, Cohen, and others, who argue that legitimate forms of collective self-governance are of considerable moral significance. We espouse, therefore, the generally "statist" or "membership" perspective outlined above, according to which the content of what we owe to fellow citizens and what we owe to outsiders is different. This broad perspective admits of strong and weak variants. Strong statists hold that we have no obligations to non-members beyond certain minimal duties of non-aggression and mutual aid. Few people actually espouse that view,[13] and certainly we do not. We defend a "weaker" version of statism that holds that our obligations to non-members extend, for a variety of reasons, beyond the humanitarian minimum.[14] Indeed, in treating individual persons as the ultimate units of moral concern, in attaching this status to every living person equally, and in according this status global force, our view can be

---

[9] Abizadeh 2008, at p. 38. He insists that "democracy may require boundaries, but not closed boundaries under unilateral domestic control."

[10] Abizadeh 2008, at p. 38.   [11] Goodin 2007, at p. 68.

[12] Risse 2008, at p. 29. See also Risse 2012, ch. 9.

[13] A much-discussed exception is Nagel 2005.

[14] This distinction between strong and weak statism follows Cohen & Sabel 2006, at p. 150, responding to Nagel's strong statist view.

described, fairly and without contradiction, as a *cosmopolitan* variant of the statist approach, as per Thomas Pogge's well-known definition of cosmopolitanism.[15]

While the full demands of justice are properly associated with membership in a political community, it is a grave mistake to hold that outside the state there is only minimal humanitarian concern. Confusion has been created by running together the idea that *full obligations of justice apply only domestically*, with the very different idea that *beyond the state our moral relations, duties, and obligations to others are minimal*. We argue that fairly extensive moral duties and obligations extend across state borders, and for easily discernible reasons. As our interactions with foreign populations and institutions deepen and broaden, our obligation to deal fairly with outsiders operate across a wider field. As our own society grows in wealth while others remain desperately poor, we acquire a more extensive duty to alleviate preventable deprivation and suffering wherever it occurs. So too, as our own political institutions stabilize, and we learn something about the foundations and prerequisites of stable and legitimate political order, we acquire a duty to do what we reasonably can to assist others to develop their own decent institutions of self-government. And finally, as our extensive interactions with outsiders make us prone to committing acts of injustice and domination in the absence of effective multilateral institutions, we acquire a duty to strengthen global institutions. These seem to us common-sense observations, and we develop them in this chapter. We also argue that our duties to outsiders may be more urgent than our domestic obligations, and may take priority over them, at least sometimes.

One other preliminary observation. Confusion has been introduced into these discussions by failing to note that the sorts of principles that Rawls has developed to govern the foreign policies of liberal states are avowedly aspects of ideal theory. As such, it seems to us that Rawls's normative picture, while useful and illuminating, is importantly incomplete and even inadequate to the *non-ideal* world in which we live.[16] In our non-ideal world, it seems obvious that wealthy political communities such as the USA ought to be doing more to promote greater distributive justice at home and also to address dire poverty abroad. And yet, there are also serious controversies concerning whether, for example, government-to-government foreign aid does more harm than good. The upshot, we think, is that there are no simple answers to the practical question of how we should prioritize the various moral imperatives that confront us from inside and outside the political community. Theory provides

---

[15] Pogge 1992, at pp. 48–9.

[16] Of course, statists in the Rawlsian tradition have not neglected the matter of non-ideal theory altogether, for it has been a central concern of that project to specify how "the foreign policy of a reasonably just liberal people" ought to adapt to *others'* unwillingness or inability to comply with the norms of a justifiable international order (Rawls 1999a, p. 10, emphasis omitted); what this tradition has not addressed is the question of how a given political community ought to prioritize its moral responsibilities in the face of *domestic* noncompliance: that is, where its own institutions and policies are less than "reasonably just." For a helpful discussion of the Rawlsian distinction between ideal and non-ideal theory more generally, see Simmons 2010.

only limited guidance in real-world decisions about how to fairly balance our duties to outsiders and fellow citizens in cases of conflict. However, we are not ultimately sceptics about the possibility of normative guidance in this domain and, keeping in mind the limitations of ideal theory, we offer some proposals about directions for institutional reforms at the end.

To move from ideal theory to the real world, we will focus on US immigration policy. Many scholars, politicians, and pundits argue that immigration policies that are "generous" to poor persons abroad will worsen the relative well-being of the least well-off Americans, thus presenting us with a possible conflict between the demands of domestic distributive justice and the duty of assistance to outsiders. Indeed, recent empirical work emphasizing the general ineffectiveness, or even counter-productiveness, of government-to-government foreign aid makes all the more pressing the question of whether freer migration of labour is the most promising "Plan B" for international development assistance.[17]

The argument of the chapter proceeds in three steps. Section 1 characterizes our version of the statist or membership account of political justice, emphasizing the wide range of moral responsibilities that statist theories standardly take us to have to those residing outside our borders. The membership view we defend makes extensive demands on individuals and public institutions in the developed world. In Section 2, we explore one way in which our membership-based obligations may come into conflict with our duties to outsiders by taking up the problem of large-scale migration from low-income countries into wealthy, yet substantially unjust, liberal-democratic states. Having earlier acknowledged the variety and stringency of our duties to non-members, we here introduce a further complication: when faced with an array of potentially competing moral demands, states have independent and, we suggest, normatively compelling interests in determining how to balance and prioritize their unmet responsibilities for themselves, free from the interference of agents outside their particular political community. Because distinct political societies may reasonably disagree about how best to prioritize their competing moral responsibilities, and should at times be left free to make policy choices that are in fact less than fully reasonable, we must afford states a modicum of discretionary authority over matters, such as national immigration policy, where divergent interests and duties may be at stake. At the same time, we acknowledge that unbridled state-level discretion may lead citizens and public officials to systematically neglect their outstanding moral duties altogether, and even to use the alleviation of domestic injustice as a false pretext for evading their moral responsibilities internationally. We therefore propose, by way of conclusion, a set of standards for holding states accountable for fulfilling their unmet moral responsibilities and suggest how these standards might guide the design and reform of global governance institutions and practices.

---

[17] See Easterly 2006; Deaton 2015; Collier 2013, which emphasizes various risks of a shift toward unconstrained migration. And see Kapur & McHale 2006, pp. 137–72, 175. For a contrary take, see Pritchett 2006.

1. The Circumstances of Justice: Domestic and Global

All persons have natural duties to respect the equal basic freedom or agency of others, and to promote and support institutions that help secure our basic interests as agents. In conditions of mutual interdependence, these duties can be fulfilled, and our freedom secured, only by state institutions capable of making legitimate law. Following in the social contract tradition of Rousseau and Kant, we hold that humans are obliged when they can to remove themselves from the "state of nature"—the natural condition of lawless anarchy—and to form or support a legitimate state. That duty holds most powerfully and urgently, at least initially, with respect to those with whom we live in close proximity and with whom we regularly interact. In the absence of a common public authority capable of making authoritative law, and resolving disputes in a way that fairly represents the interests of all contending parties, individuals will be prone to disagree about their competing claims and the shape and borders of their rights vis-à-vis one another. Without a public authority in common we will find ourselves all too vulnerable to unjust treatment by others, and too tempted to use force in our defence that others cannot regard as fully authoritative. So, we have a duty to found a legitimate and effective public authority or to support one where it exists and work toward its improvement. We can live together with others in peace and security, cooperating on fair terms and respecting one another's rights, only when we all submit our competing claims to legitimate political institutions.[18]

Legitimate states formed by and acting on behalf of particular political communities secure members' agency interests (or basic freedoms) as individuals and as members of political communities with distinctive cultures, languages, and traditions. Legitimate states give definiteness to the rights and obligations of citizens, as well as assurance that these will be secured in practice, thereby facilitating their trustful interactions and allowing them to engage in complex forms of cooperation with one another. States also promote a wide variety of public goods, from national defence and domestic security to economic cooperation and excellence in education and the arts. Long-standing states typically promote and gain support from the existence of a common language and culture, which are public goods for the community in question. A shared language and culture may also be instrumentally important in helping build social capital and in supporting the trustful interactions that make political, social, and economic cooperation possible.[19] Genuinely legitimate states—those that deserve to be and, for this reason are generally regarded as, legitimate—fulfil a variety of important moral and practical functions.

---

[18] Here we follow Rousseau, Kant, and more recent "natural duty" theorists, such as John Rawls, Jeremy Waldron, and Anna Stilz. This paragraph and the next are indebted, in particular, to Stilz 2009, chs. 2–4 and Levitov 2013, ch. 1. A useful contrast is with John Locke, who argues that it is rational to leave the state of nature, but does not argue that we have an unchosen obligation to do so.

[19] See Putnam 2007, and, more generally, Miller 1995, chs. 5–6. On our view, a purely public or civic culture can serve these important functions, and so need not be incompatible (at least in principle) with the presence of multiple national or ethnic cultures, as on the view of some nationalist theorists.

Following others, and our own past writings, we hold that the uniquely extensive burdens and benefits generated within the bounds of a political society, together with the unmatched power of states to regulate the incidence and distribution of these burdens and benefits, give members of political communities uniquely extensive justificatory obligations to one another. Domestic principles of justice regulate and shape the major social, political, and economic institutions that form the context and background of our endeavours and interactions, our strivings, successes, and failures. From cradle to grave (and beyond) our interests, identities, relationships, and opportunities are pervasively shaped by the political system that we collectively create and within which we live. As members of a political community we are joined in a collective enterprise across generations, and our individual prospects depend deeply on the opportunities we secure through these shared institutions.[20] The "basic structure" of institutions in successful political societies furnishes a set of enabling capacities for doing justice under law and for deliberating about and promoting a wide variety of public goods. And so, the *fullest* moral demands associated with justice hold among members of political communities.[21]

Legitimate states give shape and substance to their members' rights and other entitlements in a way that is, as Walzer would put it, to some significant degree local and particular, reflecting their own distinctive culture and traditions. Rawls too in his later writings gave more weight to a respectable range of diversity among decent, "well-ordered" peoples.[22] Local institutional discretion is bounded by an account of human rights understood as those common standards that ought to be recognized by the international community, whose violation by domestic governments is a matter of global concern.[23] Human rights standards ought also to include moral criteria for legitimacy in law-making: adequate voice and inclusion for all of a society's members in deliberative processes, such that governments can be justifiably regarded by the international community as the authoritative representative of all its people.[24] Within

[20] The basic institutions and laws of society—the "basic structure," in Rawls's parlance—which include the constitutional and political systems, the laws governing family life, inheritance, property, commerce, and taxation, pervasively shape people's relations and life chances. The discussion that follows draws on a more extended explication and defence of the Rawlsian position in Macedo 2004. Others have developed versions of this approach, including David Miller, Michael I. Blake, Donald Moon, Joshua Cohen, Leif Wenar, and Andrea Sangiovanni.

[21] In Rawls's justice as fairness, these requirements include not only the provision of a fully adequate scheme of equal basic liberties, but also a guarantee that all socioeconomic inequalities are consistent with the principle of fair equality of opportunity (ensuring citizens roughly equal chances of success in a chosen field of endeavour, given similar natural abilities) and the difference principle (requiring that income and wealth be distributed so as to maximize the position of the least advantaged group). For a more general statement of the "full" requirements of social justice, see Nagel's remarks, cited in footnote 3.

[22] Rawls 1999a; and also among politically liberal communities that realize one among a family of reasonable liberal conceptions of justice. Samuel Freeman has a useful account of the increasing acknowledgment of diversity and reasonable disagreement concerning principles of justice in Rawls's later work; see also Freeman 2003, pp. 37–44.

[23] Here we follow Scanlon 2003 and Beitz 2009.

[24] One of us says more about this in Macedo 2004, which interprets Rawls's account of consultation hierarchies in decent political communities more robustly than some others. See also Wenar 2002.

these important bounds, the authoritative conception of justice for us is the one we have actually resolved upon as the law of our community: the constitution or fundamental political charter of our society. Different political communities will arrive at somewhat different conceptions of justice and the public good through their own deliberative and representative mechanisms, but those differing conceptions have local authority only where political institutions are and are seen to be legitimate. Legitimate law generates, as Waldron emphasizes, a "special kind of 'ought.'"[25]

The natural duty of justice directs us to create and uphold a particular kind of uniform institutional scheme, since it is only through such a shared system of authoritative and enforceable legal rules that we can secure the essential demands of justice in our relations with others. But if the duty of justice directs us in the first instance to establish a state with those with whom we interact most regularly, it points outward beyond the bounds of political communities as well. We call our view "cosmopolitan statism" because it both acknowledges the existence of special obligations among citizens, but also affirms that members of well-functioning and prosperous states owe a range of further duties to those who are not. The natural duty of justice enjoins us, in Rawls's formulation, "to support and to comply with just institutions that exist and apply to us ... [and] to further just arrangements not yet established, at least when this can be done without too much cost to ourselves."[26]

What, then, do we owe to outsiders—those who are not members of our political community—on the membership view?

We have, first, general humanitarian duties to relieve those in distress, and to intervene in the event of gross and systematic violations of human rights. In the absence of some form of direct connection to or responsibility for a humanitarian crisis, this is a duty of *beneficence*: to help secure the basic interests of other persons who are in need, or who lack minimally adequate access to basic human needs, such as security and subsistence and the institutions needed to secure these basic interests, at least where this can be done without incurring undue costs to ourselves.[27] Reasons of this sort become increasingly weighty as the urgency of the interests at stake increases and as the cost of action to the relevant agents—including the opportunity costs of neglecting their own valuable projects, relationships, and independent responsibilities—declines. Considerations of beneficence are sufficient, at the very least, to ground a duty of easy rescue, requiring that we make small or even moderate sacrifices to our own interests in order to prevent or alleviate the great suffering or misfortune of others.[28] These

---

[25] Waldron 2003, p. 47, quoting Hart & Sacks 1994, p. 5. A particular political community might choose to enact a system of law that is thoroughly cosmopolitan in spirit, but societies are not required to do so.

[26] Rawls 1999b, p. 99.

[27] See Henry Shue's account of basic rights to security and subsistence, Shue 1996, chs. 1 and 2.

[28] Here we adapt the Principle of Rescue from Scanlon 1998, pp. 223–9. We leave open the question of whether considerations of this kind would also ground what Scanlon terms a duty of "helpfulness" to those at any level of need; in the face of reasonable pluralism about the good, it is at least not obvious to us that we must help advance the interests of well-off individuals, for example, even if this can be done at no (or only trivial) cost to ourselves.

duties hold irrespective of any historical or ongoing relationship or common institutional affiliation among persons.[29]

Second, as noted, we have a natural duty "to further just arrangements not yet established, at least when this can be done without too much cost to ourselves."[30] This duty requires that those living in reasonably just and prosperous states help those burdened by unfavourable conditions to establish well-ordered institutions in their own societies. Following Rawls, we shall refer to this aspect of our natural duty of justice as the "duty of assistance."[31] Our duty of assistance (unlike the demands of social justice domestically) has a "target and cutoff point," instead of operating "continuously without end."[32] It does not require that we replicate state institutions on a global scale, or that we stand in the same relations to all humans that we do with respect to our fellow citizens. It does not require ongoing efforts to regulate inequalities (on the basis of, for example, the difference principle or some other principle of distributive justice) among all persons regardless of political membership. As we shall see, however, this duty does not exhaust the moral principles that apply to wealthy and powerful societies in their interactions with others.

Thus whereas critics of Rawls have tended to assume that the target is bare sufficiency, designed to ensure a minimum "threshold of subsistence" for all,[33] we agree with Caleb Yong that the duty of assistance is best thought of as "a duty of transitional justice, grounded in the natural duty to support and further just institutions."[34] Unlike the duty of beneficence, then, the duty of assistance directs us to help others not simply to advance their urgent interests as individuals but to achieve the specifically *institutional* and *collective* goal of establishing a well-ordered regime of their own. (Indeed, as Rawls points out, although poverty and other conditions of great need may be among the unfavourable circumstances, "not all [burdened] societies are poor, any more than all well-ordered societies are wealthy."[35] It is therefore at least conceivable that some societies owed the duty of assistance would not require aid on grounds of beneficence alone.) The important point is that there is a target, and after it is achieved societies should be in a position to support and sustain their own domestic institutions for social provision, to arrive at their own legitimate law based on their own shared

---

[29] See also Miller 2010, ch. 1, as well as the discussion of "strong beneficence" in Beitz 2009, pp. 167–8.
[30] Rawls 1999b, p. 99.
[31] See Rawls 1999a, pp. 106–7, noting that, like the duty of just savings in the domestic case, the aim of the duty of assistance "is to realize and preserve just (or decent) institutions, and not simply to increase, much less to maximize indefinitely, the average level of wealth, or the wealth of any particular class in society. In these respects the duty of assistance and the duty of just savings express the same underlying idea" (p. 107). Again following Rawls, we shall assume that the duty of assistance applies to "decent" non-liberal regimes that are well ordered under a conception of justice of this sort, and not simply to those organized under a ("fully reasonable") liberal conception (see p. 106).
[32] Rawls 1999a, pp. 119, 117.
[33] Tan 2004, p. 166; see also Caney 2002, at p. 102 and Ypi 2012, p. 108.
[34] Yong 2012, accessed online at: <http://www.nuff.ox.ac.uk/politics/papers/2012/Yong_working%20paper_2012_05.pdf>.
[35] Rawls 1999a, p. 106.

understandings. Domestic constitutions will reflect different societies' differing choices and their differing interpretations of justice and democracy, or, as Walzer emphasizes, the particular "social meanings" that are prevalent.[36] The range of such differing interpretations of basic political morality is constrained by universal standards, as already mentioned, especially human rights, which include standards for decent domestic governance.[37]

The importance of living with others under an effective and legitimate political authority supports the idea that citizens have special obligations to one another. It also provides guidance concerning our duties to outsiders who do not live under their own effective institutions: we ought to assist them to do so. The major difficulty with the second agenda is practical: it is often not easy to help others secure effective institutions of their own.

When individuals anywhere face grave risks to their most urgent interests, or when they lack the social preconditions of a decent political community, we have a duty to do our part in alleviating their plight and helping them build and maintain well-ordered institutions of their own. Our duties of beneficence and assistance thus comprise the cosmopolitan side of our statist view; these are "natural duties" owed to all human beings as such. Insofar as the most urgent problem of the global poor is persistent absolute poverty, and the common root of that problem lies in the difficulty that many peoples have experienced in establishing decent and effective governance institutions, these duties work in tandem to advance the basic well-being of all persons and to strengthen and improve the institutions under which they live.

Yet while beneficence and assistance are matters of natural duty—binding regardless of our past actions or ongoing relationships with others—we may incur a further range of moral responsibilities by choosing to interact with individuals and institutions beyond our borders. These obligations, too, the cosmopolitan statist account readily accepts.

Among these "duties of reciprocity," as we might call them, are general duties of fair dealing with one another: duties of non-exploitation and non-domination, including the duty of political communities to curb the capacity of their citizens or corporations to exploit others. In addition, fair dealing would seem to include a duty not to be a free rider on the efforts of others to address common problems, including environmental issues such as global warming, disaster relief, and humanitarian assistance.

A second aspect of these duties of reciprocity grows out of the fact that particular relations of exploitation or domination give rise to specific obligations of rectification, redress, and reform. If our government has engaged in abusive relations with other states to their detriment, or if we have allowed our corporations to exploit or oppress

---

[36] See Walzer 1983.

[37] We should emphasize that on the Rawlsian view, "decent" societies that are fully respectable members of international society not only have a sufficient level of material resources, but also respect their members' human rights and sustain governing practices which, if not fully democratic, really do represent and take seriously the interests and views of all groups in society. For a fuller exploration of these issues, see Macedo 2004.

poorer and weaker societies, then we acquire debts to these other societies. An account of rectification for past injustices across societies depends on the nature and extent of the injustices, so there is no general story to be told. Very likely, the USA has acquired substantial unpaid debts of this sort, though aggrieved parties lack authoritative impartial institutions to adjudicate claims against us and to specify the forms of redress and rectification.

Finally, these two general aspects of reciprocity argue for an important third, derivative duty that grows out of the fact of ongoing and fairly extensive interactions with others: if current institutional arrangements in the international realm permit or even facilitate the domination of weaker states by stronger states, then we have a duty to improve those institutions or to create new institutions (insofar as we can) that curb the abuses of the current state system, and that facilitate the development of the poorest regions, so that relations across states are reciprocally justifiable. In addition to righting various historical wrongs and creating the conditions for fair exchange and cooperation, these reforms would also seem to be aspects and implications of the "natural duty of justice": the duty to foster the conditions within which just relations can be established and sustained.

2. Competing Duties under Non-ideal Conditions: The Case of Immigration

As we have seen, the statist account of social justice holds that, while we have more extensive moral obligations to the members of our political community than we do to non-members, we nevertheless have significant responsibilities to those living outside the boundaries of our state. But how should we balance or prioritize competing duties when both our domestic institutions and our global relations and institutions fall short of the ideal: under conditions, that is to say, in which our membership-based duties of justice are at least partly unfulfilled *and* in which we could and should do more to assist non-members whose basic needs are going unmet? If, in many cases, there is no strict order of priority or precedence, and instead a range of reasonable ways of balancing these competing moral demands, should countries have *total discretion* over how to prioritize their competing moral demands—in deciding, for example, whether to give greater weight to their unmet duties to members or to non-members—or are such choices governed by some further set of normative principles or guidelines?

To give some concreteness to this enquiry, we will focus our attention on the question of how the United States, and other countries similarly situated, should balance the claims of insiders and outsiders in the context of setting national immigration policy. Over the past half-century, American immigration policies and practices have become in some respects more accommodating to the less well-off abroad.[38]

---

[38] The next several paragraphs draw on Macedo 2007 and especially Macedo 2011.

Yet evidence also suggests that increased migration of low-skill workers to the USA has exacted costs in terms of social justice at home. We can briefly note three ways—economic, political, and cultural—in which increased immigration appears to have had deleterious effects on the position of the worst-off Americans. First, the influx of low-skill workers into the American labour market has contributed to the substantial decline in the wages of less well-educated natives, especially high school dropouts (roughly the bottom 10 per cent of the workforce). Labour economist George Borjas has estimated that perhaps as much as half of the widening wage gap between more and less well-educated workers over the last few decades has been due to the increase in low-skill labour caused by immigration.[39] Since the 1960s, the skills levels and earnings of immigrants have declined considerably relative to the native US population. Much of the growth in immigration since 1960 has been among people entering at the bottom 20 per cent of the income scale. As Borjas observes, "Since the immigration reforms of 1965, U.S. immigration law has encouraged family reunification and discouraged the arrival of skilled immigrants."[40] Whereas in 1960, the average immigrant man living in the USA earned 4 per cent more than the average native-born American, by 1998 the average immigrant earned 23 per cent less. The ethnic makeup of immigration has also changed with the percentage arriving from Europe and Canada falling sharply and the percentage from Latin America and Asia rising.

We can add one other element to this labour market story. As Borjas again observes, nations with notably more progressive domestic policies than the USA also often have immigration laws that are quite different. Canada's immigration policy favours better-educated and high-skilled workers and this seems likely to have distributive effects that are the opposite of US policy. By increasing the pool of skilled workers relative to the unskilled, Canadian policy tends to lower the wages of the better off and to raise the relative level of the worse off.[41]

Other economists, such as David Card, disagree with Borjas's estimates of the magnitude of the effects and argue that immigration's contribution to the widening wage gap is much smaller than Borjas's original estimate.[42] Nevertheless, it is notable that it seems widely agreed among labour economists that there is some negative effect on the poorest US workers, and the debate concerns the magnitude of this negative effect.[43]

One response to the foregoing argument is that if immigration increases our collective wealth while worsening income disparities, why not welcome immigration and redistribute the surplus via tax and spending policies? This brings us to a second

---

[39] Borjas 1999, pp. 11, 22–38, 82–6, 103–4.

[40] Borjas 1990; the quote continues, "75% of legal immigrants in 1987 were granted entry because they were related to an American citizen or resident, while only 4% were admitted because they possessed useful skills."

[41] Borjas 1999, pp. 176–7. Australia and Ireland have introduced similar education- and skills-based quota systems; see Malanga 2006.

[42] For further discussion, see Macedo 2011.

[43] It is now generally accepted that immigration has negative economic consequences for low-wage workers in general and for African Americans in particular. See Johannssons and Shulman 2003, p. 95.

possible negative effect of immigration on social justice in the USA. Recent patterns of immigration may help explain why increasing inequality has come about without a corresponding increase in political pressure for redistribution; because immigration to the USA has made the median *voter* better off relative to the median *resident*, it may have both worsened the relative standing of the least well-off Americans and made it less likely that pivotal (or median) voters would support redistributive programmes.[44] Recent patterns of immigration to the USA may, thus, worsen the relative lot of the least well-off Americans while also making redistributive policies less politically popular. That is one more way in which recent immigration may worsen the lot of the least well-off.

Third, there is some evidence that the feelings of solidarity and mutual identification that help support social justice can be undermined by the increased racial and ethnic heterogeneity associated with immigration; increasing diversity can, in the short to medium term, diminish support for the provision of public goods, including programmes aimed at helping the poor,[45] and may over time contribute to a slower rate of growth in the overall size of the welfare state.[46]

It should be emphasized, of course, that all of these empirical claims are controversial. Just how immigration and increased ethnic and racial diversity inhibits social spending is unclear, for example: the rise of New Right political parties in Europe is associated with controversies over immigration, and mainstream parties may need to shift to the right in response.[47]

The available evidence would thus seem to suggest that high levels of immigration from low-skilled non-members—while no doubt advancing the interests of the migrants themselves and (by way of often extensive remittances) their families and associates in their country of origin[48]—nevertheless serves to weaken (somewhat) the position of the worst-off Americans, under conditions that already fall well short of the requirements of social justice.

If particular patterns of immigration to the USA are likely to worsen the position of the domestically least advantaged while at the same time advancing the urgent interests of non-members, how should citizens and policy makers in the USA respond? In effect, we might think of an American voter confronting two sets of opposed

---

[44] See, for example, McCarty, Poole, and Rosenthal 2006, ch. 4.   [45] Putnam 2007.

[46] Soroka, Banting, and Johnston 2007.

[47] Soroka, Banting, and Johnston argue that the "effect seems wholly political and wholly through its direct impact on mainstream governing parties," and reflects the influence of "perceived cultural threat and economic cost," pp. 278–9. The challenge is to devise ways to "combine openness at the global level with social integration at the domestic level," Soroka et al. 2007, p. 279. There is a burgeoning literature on ethnic diversity and public good provision; see Habyarimana, Humphryes, Posner, and Weinstein 2007, pp. 709–25, which notes that "the empirical connection between ethnic heterogeneity and the underprovision of public goods is widely accepted," though there is no consensus on "the specific mechanisms through which this relationship operates," p. 709.

[48] On the importance of remittances as an effective vehicle of poverty relief in the developing world, see, for example, Deaton 2015, pp. 323–4.

complainants: from those at the bottom in the USA and from poor potential migrants abroad. Which group's (if either's) complaints takes priority?

One feature of this conflict is worth highlighting: in the case of immigration policy in the USA, as in many cases in which our foreign and domestic obligations appear to conflict, the barriers to our fulfilling these unmet responsibilities are put in place by our own fellow citizens and public officials, rather than by sheer resource constraints or other forms of scarcity. As we have noted, immigration to the USA generates a collective economic surplus, and it should be possible to use that surplus to improve the situation of the least well-off Americans, including those made worse off by immigration. If enough Americans were willing to do their part on both the domestic and the global fronts, there is reason to believe that the trade-offs would disappear or at least be greatly lessened. Indeed, it is partly others' failure to support just institutions and contribute to the urgent needs of the global poor—their "noncompliance," in Rawls's terms—that makes the problem at hand one of non-ideal theory.[49]

So, let us suppose that we ought to redistribute the gains of immigration, so that both poor immigrants and poor Americans are made better off. But, we also know that high immigration will tend to unjustifiably reduce Americans' willingness to support such redistribution. We do not see why the latter point lessens the force of the objection coming from poor Americans, at least assuming that the unfortunate attitudes and voting behaviour of better off Americans cannot be easily altered through persuasion or in other ways.

If what is at stake is the basic needs of potential migrants, on the one hand, set against the relative standing of poorer Americans whose basic needs are being and will be met, on the other, then the former, we think, should take priority. In the actual case, the issue is a bit trickier, for while many actual and potential poorer migrants to the USA come from very poor circumstances, it is not clear that their basic needs will be unmet if they are denied the opportunity to migrate for work. The poorest people in the world, including those whose basic needs are unmet, typically do not have the resources needed to migrate. As Massey and Denton explain, labour migration is part of the development process, and requires that the process is already under way. Nevertheless, immigration does seem to provide great gains to migrants and their home communities, while only marginally worsening the relative position of American poor, and it is at least not obvious that a membership-based account of justice would forbid the USA from giving precedence to the interests of non-members in such a case.

In hard cases such as these, where there exist a variety of reasonable policy responses to conditions of partial noncompliance, it seems clear to us that states should be left free to act on their own considered judgement about how best to balance their competing responsibilities to members and non-members. For even if there are compelling reasons to favour a given policy over another, states have independent interests in being able to decide these difficult questions for themselves, at least insofar as they are internally

---

[49] See, for example, Rawls 1999b, pp. 7–8 and Rawls 1999a, p. 5, as well as Simmons 2010.

"well ordered" and can therefore act as the collective agent or representative of their individual members. These interests in *collective self-determination* would be undermined if some external agent, including the "cosmopolitan democratic institutions" favoured by some theorists,[50] were to impose a specific policy response on a well-ordered political community when other reasonable alternatives are available. The point, we believe, generalizes: if, as Rawls has suggested, we should allow a space for policies that are less than reasonable by the lights of liberal democratic values, yet at the same time "not fully unreasonable," then these, too, should be shielded from external control in order to respect the self-determination interests of specific states.[51]

While there is no precise way of demarcating the domain of policies over which states should enjoy political discretion in this sense, we might begin to give shape to this category with reference to the idea, mentioned above, that human rights specify a particularly urgent class of injustices that are a matter of international concern, in that violations of these rights give outside agents compelling reasons to undertake remedial and preventive action of various sorts. In cases in which the human rights of non-members are at stake, and the only way of preventing their violation is through some policy that will weaken the relative socioeconomic standing of current members (without dropping them below the threshold of human rights), we would suggest that a state's refusal to implement such a policy would be fully unreasonable and thus subject, in principle, to external sanction or interference. But where non-members currently enjoy basic human rights protection and stand only to increase their material position above this basic threshold of need, it would not be unreasonable for states to give precedence to considerations of domestic distributive equality, even if their members are better off in absolute terms than the outsiders seeking assistance.[52]

In the context of immigration policy, this proposal would require states to admit political refugees and other victims of human rights abuse if doing so is the only available means of securing those rights.[53] But it would give states the discretion to deny entry to low-skill migrants whose human rights are secure in their country of residence and whose admittance would foreseeably threaten the position of the domestically least advantaged. To be clear, we do not say that denying admittance in such a case would be the right policy to adopt, or even that it would be among the reasonable options available to policymakers in the developed world. Indeed, one of us has argued elsewhere that, in spite of immigration's likely negative effects on

---

[50] Abizadeh 2008, p. 48; see also Goodin 2007. As we make clear in Section 3, we think there is an important, though largely secondary and remedial, role for institutions of this sort to play in guiding the policy choices of particular states.

[51] Rawls 1999a, p. 74. For a fuller account of the value of self-determination, see Levitov 2015, sect. 2.

[52] Risse similarly proposes that states ought to secure the basic liberties of their members before turning to assist outsiders, but must prioritize non-members' human rights over the goal of mitigating domestic socioeconomic inequality; see Risse 2012, pp. 330–2.

[53] Compare Miller 2005b, p. 198 and Wellman 2008, at pp. 129–30. Because we view human rights as going beyond a mere right to be free from persecution, our approach would recommend a more expansive definition of refugees than that employed by the United Nations High Commission on Refugees; for a recent discussion and defense of the UNHCR definition, see Lister 2013.

distributive justice, the costs of excluding poor migrants to the USA appear to be too high.[54] Our point is only that a policy of this sort would not be so clearly *unreasonable* as to overcome the presumption in favour of states' collective self-determination. Within certain limits, states should enjoy the freedom to pursue policies that are nevertheless subject to valid moral criticism, and our suggestion is that the idea of human rights can help give content to these limits.

3. Conclusion: Human Rights and Self-Determination in International Practice

In a range of familiar if non-ideal conditions, states in the developed world must ultimately choose between policies that advance the interests of non-members in need and those that further the cause of socioeconomic justice at home. We have argued that, in confronting these hard choices, different societies may reasonably disagree about whose competing claims should take precedence, and that each has an independent interest in being able to decide such matters of moral weight and controversy for themselves, free from the interference of other states or multilateral bodies. So while the right of self-determination is by no means absolute, and must be constrained by the need to secure the human rights for all, states nevertheless ought to enjoy a moderate range of discretion over decisions, such as the choice of a national immigration policy, that affect the core interests of members and non-members alike.

At the same time, we recognize that well-ordered states, marked as they are by electorally accountable or at least popularly consultative institutions, may wind up systematically favouring the interests of members over non-members in practice. Worse, some states may use the rhetoric of compatriot priority to justify ignoring their responsibilities abroad without actually going on to address outstanding domestic injustices. A system of unbridled state-level discretion would thus seem to license widespread moral neglect and complacency, and would for this reason fail to do justice to the full range of commitments that underlie the cosmopolitan statism we favour.

Appropriately structured multilateral organizations, by contrast, could enable needy parties, or international organizations acting on their behalf, to bring public grievances against neglectful states, impelling powerful actors to justify their actions to those most acutely impacted by them and imposing reputational and perhaps material costs on egregiously irresponsible agents. While according states primary authority over their own political affairs, such a mechanism would nevertheless ensure that the interests of outside parties are adequately represented, and that the coercively backed decisions of states—including restrictions on movement across borders—are in due course "actually justified" (and not merely abstractly "justifiable") to all persons over whom that

---

[54] See Macedo 2011.

power is exercised.[55] By the same token, properly constrained multilateral institutions, far from undermining the collective self-determination of particular states, could in fact serve to heighten the level of transparency and improve the processes of deliberation and public justification already under way in well-ordered states.[56]

Needless to say, the details of this institutional proposal remain to be worked out. Without trying to settle these matters here, we will conclude by recapitulating three more general features of the cosmopolitan statist approach developed above. First, on our view, the statist account of social justice is fully consistent with, and most compelling when complemented by, a range of significant obligations to those beyond the borders of a given political society. Indeed, the very duties of justice that oblige us to support our local political institutions also enjoin us to advance the cause of justice abroad and assist those burdened by unfavourable natural and social conditions. Second, the defining commitment of statism—that our obligations to co-members are *more extensive than* those to non-members—does not imply that these obligations must *take precedence over* duties to outsiders in cases of conflict. We are instead permitted, and may at times be required, to prioritize the urgent interests of non-members over the demands of domestic justice when the two sets of responsibilities are for whatever reason mutually unrealizable. Third, and finally, even though cosmopolitan statism is committed to preserving the self-determination of particular states by according them a degree of discretion over matters of domestic policy, this discretion is limited by the global responsibility to secure basic human rights. So while states ought to enjoy primary authority over immigration policy and other questions calling for collective moral judgement, they must be able to demonstrate—before representative multilateral institutions, as necessary—that these decisions are ultimately consistent with treating the most urgent interests of all persons as matters of international concern. To this limited but not insignificant extent, our view shares the commitment to cosmopolitan democracy voiced by the most ardent critics of the traditional statist approach.

References

Abizadeh, Arash (2008) "Democratic Theory and Border Coercion," *Political Theory* 36, no. 1, pp. 37–65.

Beitz, Charles R. (2009) *The Idea of Human Rights* (Oxford: Oxford University Press).

Beitz, Charles R. (2011) "Global Political Justice and the 'Democratic Deficit,'" in *Reasons and Recognition: Essays on the Philosophy of T. M. Scanlon*, ed. R. Jay Wallace, Rahul Kumar, and Samuel Freeman (Oxford: Oxford University Press).

---

[55] Abizadeh 2008, p. 41. Our proposal diverges from Abizadeh's in that it does not require the "actual participation" of all coerced parties in the initial process of collective decision-making, although unlike Abizadeh, Goodin, and other cosmopolitan democrats, we doubt that democratic values are always or only served by procedural mechanisms that give equal decision-making authority to all affected individuals. For illuminating discussion, see Beitz 2011.

[56] See Keohane, Macedo, and Moravcsik 2009, esp. at pp. 18–22.

Blake, Michael (2001) "Distributive Justice, State Coercion, and Autonomy," *Philosophy and Public Affairs* 30, no. 3, pp. 257–96.

Borjas, George J. (1990) "The U.S. Takes the Wrong Immigrants," *The Wall Street Journal* (5 April).

Borjas, George J. (1999) *Heaven's Door: Immigration Policy and the American Economy* (Princeton: Princeton University Press).

Caney, Simon (2002) "Cosmopolitanism and the Law of Peoples," *Journal of Political Philosophy* 10, no. 1, pp. 95–123.

Carens, Joseph (1987) "Aliens and Citizens: The Case for Open Borders," *Review of Politics* 49, no. 1, pp. 251–73.

Carens, Joseph (2013) *The Ethics of Immigration* (Oxford: Oxford University Press).

Cohen, Joshua (2006) "Is There a Human Right to Democracy?," in *The Egalitarian Conscience: Essays in Honour of G. A. Cohen*, ed. Christine Sypnowich (Oxford: Oxford University Press).

Cohen, Joshua & Sabel, Charles (2006) "Extra Rempublicam Nulla Justitia," *Philosophy and Public Affairs* 34, no. 2, pp. 147–75.

Collier, Paul (2013) *Exodus: How Migration is Changing our World* (Oxford: Oxford University Press).

Deaton, Angus (2015) *The Great Escape: Health Wealth, and the Origins of Inequality* (Princeton: Princeton University Press).

Easterly, William (2006) *The White Man's Burden: Why the West's Efforts to Aid the Rest Have Done So Much Ill and So Little Good* (New York: Penguin Books).

Freeman, Samuel (2003) "Introduction" to *The Cambridge Companion to Rawls*, ed. Samuel Freeman (Cambridge: Cambridge University Press).

Freeman, Samuel (2007) "Distributive Justice and the Law of Peoples," in *Justice and the Social Contract: Essays on Rawlsian Political Philosophy* (Oxford: Oxford University Press).

Goodin, Robert E. (2007) "Enfranchising All Affected Interests, and Its Alternatives," *Philosophy and Public Affairs* 35, no. 1, pp. 40–68.

Habyarimana, James, Humphryes, Macartan, Posner, Daniel N., and Weinstein, Jeremy M. (2007) "Why Does Ethnic Diversity Undermine Public Goods Provision?" *American Political Science Review*, 101, no. 4, pp. 709–25.

Hart, H. M. & Sacks, A. M. (1994) *The Legal Process: Basic Problems in the Making and Application of Law*, ed. W. N. Eskridge and P. P. Frickey (Westbury, NY: Foundation Press).

Johannssons, Hannes and Shulman, Steven (2003) "Immigration and the Employment of African American Workers," *The Review of Black Political Economy*, 31, no. 1–2, pp. 95–110.

Julius, A. J. (2006) "Nagel's Atlas," *Philosophy and Public Affairs* 34, no. 2, pp. 176–92.

Kapur, Devesh and McHale, John (2006) "What Is Wrong with Plan B? International Migration as an Alternative to Development Assistance," *Brookings Trade Forum, Global Labor Markets?*, pp. 137–86.

Keohane, Robert O., Macedo, Stephen, and Moravcsik, Andrew (2009) "Democracy-Enhancing Multilateralism," *International Organization* 63, pp. 1–31.

Levitov, Alex (2013) "Legitimacy as Self-Determination" (doctoral dissertation, Princeton University).

Levitov, Alex (2015) "Human Rights, Self-Determination, and External Legitimacy," *Philosophy, Politics, and Economics* 14, no. 3, pp. 291–315.

Lister, Matthew (2013) "Who Are Refugees?," *Law and Philosophy* 32, no. 5, pp. 645–71.

McCarty, Nolan, Poole, Keith T., and Rosenthal, Howard (2006) *Polarized America: The Dance of Ideology and Unequal Riches* (Cambridge, Mass.: MIT Press).

Macedo, Stephen J. (2004) "What Self-Governing Peoples Owe to One Another: Universalism, Diversity, and *The Law of Peoples*," *Fordham Law Review* 72, no. 1, pp. 1721–38.

Macedo, Stephen J. (2007) "The Moral Dilemma of U.S. Immigration Policy: Open Borders vs. Social Justice?," in *Debating Immigration*, ed. Carol Swain (Cambridge: Cambridge University Press).

Macedo, Stephen J. (2011) "When and Why Should Liberal Democracies Restrict Immigration?," in Rogers M. Smith (ed.), *Citizenship, Borders, and Human Needs* (Philadelphia: University of Pennsylvania Press).

Malanga, Steven (2006) "The Right Immigration Policy: Not Amnesty or Guest Workers, but Newcomers who would Strengthen us," *CITY JOURNAL*, Autumn.

Miller, David (1995) *On Nationality* (Oxford: Oxford University Press).

Miller, David (2005a) "Reasonable Partiality towards Compatriots," *Ethical Theory and Moral Practice* 8, no. 1/2, pp. 63–81.

Miller, David (2005b) "Immigration: The Case for Limits," in Andrew I. Cohen and Christopher Heath Wellman (eds), *Contemporary Debates in Applied Ethics* (Malden, Mass.: Blackwell).

Miller, David (2007) *National Responsibility and Global Justice* (Oxford: Oxford University Press).

Miller, Richard W. (2010) *Globalizing Justice: The Ethics of Poverty and Power* (Oxford: Oxford University Press).

Nagel, Thomas (2005) "The Problem of Global Justice," *Philosophy and Public Affairs* 33, no. 2, pp. 113–47.

Pogge, Thomas (1992) "Cosmopolitanism and Sovereignty," *Ethics* 103, no. 1, pp. 48–75.

Pritchett, Lant (2006) *Let their People Come: Breaking the Gridlock on Global Labor Mobility* (Washington: Center for Global Development).

Putnam, Robert D. (2007) "E Pluribus Unum: Diversity and Community in the Twenty-First Century: The 2006 Johan Skytte Prize Lecture," *Scandinavian Political Studies* 30, no. 2, pp. 137–74.

Rawls, John (1999a) *The Law of Peoples* (Cambridge, Mass.: Harvard University Press).

Rawls, John (1999b) *A Theory of Justice*, rev. edn (Cambridge, Mass.: The Belknap Press of Harvard University).

Risse, Mathias (2008) "On the Morality of Immigration," *Ethics and International Affairs* 22 no. 1, pp. 25–33.

Risse, Matthias (2012) *On Global Justice* (Princeton: Princeton University Press).

Sangiovanni, Andrea (2007) "Global Justice, Reciprocity, and the State," *Philosophy and Public Affairs* 35, no. 1, pp. 3–39.

Scanlon, Thomas (1998) *What We Owe to Each Other* (Cambridge, Mass.: The Belknap Press of Harvard University).

Scanlon, Thomas (2003) "Human Rights as a Neutral Concern," in *The Difficulty of Tolerance: Essays in Political Philosophy* (Cambridge: Cambridge University Press).

Scheffler, Samuel (2010) "Cosmopolitanism, Justice, and Institutions," in *Equality and Tradition: Questions of Value in Moral and Political Theory* (Oxford: Oxford University Press), pp. 169–72.

Shue, Henry (1996) *Basic Rights: Subsistence, Affluence, and U.S. Foreign Policy*, 2nd edn (Princeton: Princeton University Press).

Simmons, A. John (2010) "Ideal and Nonideal Theory," *Philosophy and Public Affairs* 38, no. 1, pp. 5–36.

Soroka, Stuart, Banting, Keith, and Johnston, Richard (2007) "Immigration and Redistribution in a Global Era," in Pranab Bardhan, Samuel Bowles, and Michael Wallerstein (eds), *Globalization and Egalitarian Redistribution* (Princeton: Princeton University Press).

Stilz, Anna (2009) *Liberal Loyalty: Freedom, Obligation, and the State* (Princeton: Princeton University Press).

Tan, Kok-Chor (2004) *Justice without Borders: Cosmopolitanism, Nationalism, and Patriotism* (Cambridge: Cambridge University Press).

Waldron, Jeremy (2003) "Authority for Officials," in Lukas H. Meyer, Stanley L. Paulson, and Thomas W. Pogge (eds), *Rights, Culture and the Law: Themes from the Legal and Political Philosophy of Joseph Raz* (Oxford: Oxford University Press, 2003).

Walzer, Michael (1983) *Spheres of Justice: A Defense of Pluralism and Equality* (New York: Basic Books).

Wellman, Christopher Heath (2008) "Immigration and Freedom of Association," *Ethics* 119, no. 1, pp. 109–41.

Wenar, Leif (2002) "The Legitimacy of Peoples," in Pablo De Greiff and Ciaran Cronin (eds), *Global Justice and Transnational Politics: Essays on the Moral and Political Challenges of Globalization* (Cambridge, Mass.: The MIT Press), pp. 53–76.

Yong, Caleb (2012) "Rawls's Duty of Assistance: Transitional not Humanitarian or Sufficientarian," Nuffield Working Papers in Politics, November.

Ypi, Lea (2012) *Global Justice and Avant-Garde Political Agency* (Oxford: Oxford University Press).

14.1

The Slippery Slope of Statist Cosmopolitanism
A Response to Levitov and Macedo

Seyla Benhabib

I

Until recently, the movement of peoples across borders—whether as asylum seekers, refugees, or labour migrants—was hardly considered a pertinent topic in normative political thought. Although economics, anthropology, sociology, legal theory, and history paid attention to this issue, it was assumed that it hardly mattered for ideal political theory; rather, it seemed best confined to the judgement of law-makers, immigration officials, and border patrols. Proceeding from the assumption that "we are not seen as joining society at the age of reason, as we might join an association, but as being born into a society where we will lead a complete life,"[1] many Rawlsian theorists continued to believe that the movements of peoples across borders presented no special challenges to theories of justice. All this has changed radically. Levitov and Macedo's contribution is a fine example of Rawlsian theorists wishing to reconcile statist with cosmopolitan commitments, resulting in a position which the authors describe as "cosmopolitan statist."

What distinguishes the "cosmopolitan statist" from the simple "statist" view is that the former "holds that our obligations to non-members extend, for a variety of reasons, beyond the humanitarian minimum" (p. 417). The authors agree with the statists (sometimes also referred to as those holding the "membership" perspective) that "legitimate forms of collective self-governance are of considerable moral significance" (p. 471), and therefore result in obligations to our fellow citizens that are thicker and more extensive in kind than to non-citizens. Nonetheless, cosmopolitan statists also accept that significant moral duties extend across and beyond borders.

[1] Rawls 1996, pp. 40–1.

Levitov and Macedo recognize general *humanitarian duties* of beneficence and assistance to relieve those in distress, and to intervene in the event of gross violations of human rights. They further acknowledge a *general duty of assistance* to enhance just arrangements—"when this can be done without too much cost to ourselves."[2] There is an additional family of duties which the authors call "duties of reciprocity," and which include those of non-exploitation, non-domination, as well as not being a "free rider" on others in addressing common problems such as global warming, disaster relief, and humanitarian assistance. Duties of reciprocity lead to specific obligations of rectification, redress, and reform, all of which depend on the concrete history of interactions among states. Levitov and Macedo believe that there is no "general story to be told," only contingent historical circumstances which shape these relations (p. 479). If current institutional arrangements permit the domination of weaker by stronger states, then there is a duty to improve those institutions or create new institutions but no continuing obligations to change the lot of weaker states.

The cosmopolitan statist view is quite attractive insofar as it wants to reconcile strong moral obligations to "our compatriots" with demanding moral duties owed to others whether in virtue of obligations of beneficence or of justice. Yet I will argue that different assessments of the extent and intensity of duties of reciprocity, which arise out of historical patterns of interaction among states and peoples, remain one of the bones of contention between cosmopolitans and cosmopolitan statists. This disagreement is not only about the facts of human history,[3] it concerns deeper assumptions about individuals and peoples. For Levitov and Macedo, and unlike for cosmopolitans, peoples and not individuals are the primary unit of reasoning in such matters.[4] Movements across borders appear as anomalies and disruptions of an ordered universe of distinctly delineated and clearly identifiable peoples. In other writings, I have argued against the sociological naivety of this view and criticized its reduction of the dynamic histories of peoplehood to holistic generalizations about the moral qualities of supposedly clearly distinguishable peoples.[5]

In this chapter, I will claim that to analyse what privileges duties to compatriots over those we owe to foreigners and strangers, we must first distinguish among the anthropological, ontological, and political premises that underlie Levitov's and Macedo's view and which they fail to clarify (II). I will then show that in privileging the primacy of obligations to compatriots, they vacillate between a *contractarian* and an *identitarian*

---

[2] Rawls 1999, p. 99.

[3] There are significant divergences among Rawlsian theorists and other neo-Kantian cosmopolitans about the causes of the wealth of nations as well as the structure of the global economy as it gives rise to the continuing poverty and exploitation of some by others. This implies that, contrary to what Levitov and Macedo assert, there is indeed a "general story to be told." See Beitz 1979; Pogge 2008; and my discussion in Benhabib 2004a, pp. 97–106.

[4] See Macedo's statement: "The moral significance of *states* or *peoples* is not really so mysterious, but let us remind ourselves what a people has done in assuming the powers of self-government. They form a union usually understood as perpetual, and assert permanent control over a given territory, perhaps as the result of a violent struggle for independence." Macedo 2004, p. 1721 (emphasis added).

[5] See my discussion of "peoplehood" in Benhabib 2004b.

account. Turning to Thomas Nagel's much-discussed essay on "The Problem of Global Justice," I will maintain that for the contractarian tradition the boundaries of the demos are indeterminate, and that it is only identitarian assumptions concerning the primacy of national communities that can resolve this indeterminacy. But the moral arbitrariness in fixing the boundaries of the demos remains (III). If this conclusion is correct, then it has far-reaching implications for a just policy of the movement of peoples across borders: it complicates the central argument made by Levitov and Macedo that while there may be legitimate moral concerns to permit the migration of low-skilled workers into resource-rich countries of the north and the west, "states should be left free to act on their own considered judgement about how best to balance their competing responsibilities to members and non-members" (p. 482) (IV).

II

What special duties do we owe our compatriots and fellow citizens over those we owe strangers and foreigners? I suggest that the answer of the cosmopolitan statist may be of three sorts: anthropological, ontological, and political or polity-based. The *anthropological answer* suggests that the division of humanity into distinct human groupings, united throughout history via ties of family, kin, clan, language, religion, ethnicity, etc. is a fact. It is also a feature of humankind that such identification always entails differentiations between us and them, we and the others. Such differentiations may take the form of cooperation and collaboration as well as conflict, war, and confrontation. We are hard-wired, the cosmopolitan statist would argue, to identify with those like us, to feel affinity to them, and to carry strong moral obligations toward those to whom we belong.

Indeed, all this suggests an anthropological generalization which, nonetheless, tells us *nothing* about the specific group(s) with which we identify: it merely says that group differentiation and identification are constant features of human life. I can identify with the Workers of the World as well as the Universal Church of Christ, with Green Peace as well as the United States Military. In this account, there is no prioritization of the state or of the nation-state over other forms of association.

Suppose, however, that the argument is *ontological* and maintains that human beings may identify with all sorts of associations but only some among these are clearly primary. Certainly, the family is ontogenetically prior for the individual who is born into some kind of kinship unit; likewise, one's primary language or languages are the medium through which one becomes an adult person capable of agency, expressing wishes and desires, forming attachments to others, etc. We become a person insofar as we become a speaker of a natural language or a set of languages shared by some human group. If we accept the primacy of familial and linguistic ties, we arrive at the ontological priority for the individual of a familial and linguistic community of shared ties and belonging.

Yet such communities are not co-terminous with the nation or with the nation-state: Just as there may exist more than one language community within the boundaries of a given nation-state, language affinities may extend across national boundaries. Recognizing such ties is quite compatible with a more transnational, cosmopolitan sensibility. Again, we fail to reach the centrality of obligations to our compatriots or fellow citizens, with whom we may indeed share ties of language, memory, and sympathy, but these are neither exclusively shared with them alone nor are they so central to our lives that they ought to displace other attachments we may feel to our kin in dispersed diasporic communities.

Will Kymlicka has made a strong ontological argument for the priority of the national or "societal culture" over others.[6] He argues that only in sufficiently complex and differentiated human communities which are organized around a shared culture—whether they be mono or multi-linguistic—can we lead a life in which varieties of human goals, aspirations, and different pursuits of the good can be accommodated. Societal cultures are more comprehensive and resourceful in enabling more options of freedom to individuals than other communities of kinship, language, ethnicity, and religion. I suspect that Levitov and Macedo also subscribe to such a view, although they do not clarify it.

The position which they most explicitly endorse is the *political (or polity-centered)* one which they trace back to the social contract tradition. "We can live together with others in peace and security, cooperating on fair terms and respecting one another's rights, only when we all submit our competing claims to legitimate political institutions" (p. 474), they write. "From cradle to grave (and beyond)," they continue, "our interests, identities, relationships and opportunities are pervasively shaped by the political system that we create and within which we live" (p. 475). Note that this polity-based view consists of an amalgamation of two sorts of claims: one is the *justice-based* imperative of the social contract tradition that to live together with others in security and cooperation we must submit ourselves to a common authority; the other is the *identitarian* view, which emphasizes the pervasiveness of the political system in shaping interests, identities, and relationships. It is important to distinguish among them because in the social contract tradition, the *boundaries of the community of those who must submit to common rules of justice is indeterminate.* Neither in Hobbes, nor in Locke, nor especially in Kant, would one find the view that our identities, relationships, and opportunities are pervasively "shaped by the political system." Only in Rousseau's political theory do we note the beginnings of a culturalist identity argument which is then expanded upon by Herder and Hegel.[7] This conflation of the justice argument with the identitarian one

[6] Kymlicka 1995, pp. 76ff.

[7] Rousseau's Social Contract model is still quite indeterminate as regards the boundaries of the demos, with the sole caveat that "no man should be poor enough to have to sell himself and no one wealthy enough to buy another." It is only when Rousseau starts to characterize the attributes that people who are to be capable of such a form of government must possess that a certain ethno-cultural dimension enters into his argument. Cf. Rousseau 1968; Rousseau 1985. Hegel criticizes the view that the state can be based on a

permits Levitov and Macedo to leave the bases of the privileged obligations we owe to our compatriots quite murky.

III

I would like to clarify this point by turning to Thomas Nagel's reflections on these issues in "The Problem of Global Justice."[8] Levitov and Macedo's cosmopolitan statism, like Nagel's "political view," is a reinterpretation of Rawlsian principles to make room for moral duties which extend beyond and across borders, all the while insisting on the principle that only within the boundaries of a sovereign state can relations of thick socio-economic justice be realized. Nagel is quite explicit about the fact that "fellow participants in a collective enterprise" end up there quite arbitrarily. He writes:

What is interesting and somewhat surprising about this condition is that such co-membership is itself arbitrary, so an arbitrary distinction is responsible for the scope of the presumption against arbitrariness. We do not deserve to have been born into a particular society any more than we deserve to have been born into a particular family. *Those who are not immigrants have done nothing to become members of their society*...It is only the internal character of the system in which we arbitrarily find ourselves that gives rise to the special presumption against further arbitrary distinctions within it.[9] (My emphasis)

For Nagel what mitigates this arbitrariness of the "circumstances of birth and place" is that each one of us plays a dual role as one in whose name authority is exercised and as one who is subject to the authority thus exercised: we are subjects and authors of the laws and the schemes of cooperation in our states. On Nagel's contractarian and political account, the boundaries of the demos are arbitrary and what transforms those who happen to be included within such boundaries into fellow citizens toward whom one has special obligations is the principle of democratic authorship. I will not comment here on what this implies for relations of justice among the citizens of non-democratic societies who obviously cannot see themselves as authors and subjects of the laws of their societies in the same fashion. Here, I just wish to note that for Nagel, unlike for Levitov and Macedo, our special obligations to our co-citizens derive from duties and activities of democratic engagement and not from the mere *fact* of cultural or national membership. From the standpoint of a social-contract and justice oriented theory, the boundaries of the demos are arbitrary, both because the fact of birth on one territory rather than upon another is due to chance and not to morally relevant factors; but also because who is and who is not a full member of the demos cannot be decided upon democratically.

---

social contract altogether and introduces instead the concept of *Sittlichkeit* (ethical life) to define the boundaries of the demos. Cf. Hegel 1973; Herder 2002; and Taylor 1992.

    [8] Nagel 2005.   [9] Ibid., p. 128.

If we keep in mind that any demos is not composed of full citizens alone, but permits gradations of membership and affiliation, the well-known paradox of democracy can be stated as follows: the rights and duties of non-full members are decided upon through legislation that excludes them from having a voice over issues which affect their deepest interests. If democracy at a minimum entails that all those whose vital interests are affected by some law, practice, or institution should have a say in their articulation, then clearly the boundaries of the demos can never be set democratically. With this in mind, we can represent the democratic paradox of membership as follows: at time t1, the demos composed of members and non-members—call it d1—decides that in t2, some will be designated as non-members (aliens, the undocumented, etc.) and will be excluded from the circle of those who enjoy the privileges of full membership thus constituting d2. Likewise, in t3, d2 will decide who belongs to d3 and what privileges accrue to whom, etc... Although this paradox can never be quite resolved democratically since full members will continue to decide upon the status of non-members by excluding them from the conversation, it can be mitigated by the following procedure: The demos, d1, in t1 can redefine itself in such a way as to reconstitute itself as d2 in time t2 by redefining its rules of membership such as to diminish, alter, or even eliminate some the differential rights and privileges between members and non-members. Likewise, d3 in time t3 which now includes a new d2, including many non-members, may further contest these lines of division and so on. This is the deep theoretical structure underlying *all* immigration policy. Immigration policy is a process through which the demos reconstitutes itself by admitting or limiting, empowering or silencing those already within or those outside its territory.[10] Levitov and Macedo neglect the arbitrariness and paradoxical nature of democratic membership and attribute a moral primacy and urgency to obligations to our fellow citizens that is not fully grounded morally.

If we accept a political rather than an anthropological or ontological grounding of our obligations to our compatriots, then we also need to adopt a more nuanced understanding of political membership than Nagel or Levitov and Macedo do. Citizenship and membership in a society are different. In the current system of the world-society of states, citizenship is the pinnacle of membership and bestows upon one certain rights and privileges that are withheld from non-citizen members of our societies. Such members can be the undocumented children with whom we went to school; the nurse we hired to take care of our elderly parents; the newspaper columnist whose wise words we consume every morning. In the globalized world of interdependence and post-Fordist economies, we live together and benefit from relations with as well as the activities of many others who are not full citizens. Such relations generate what Ayelet Schachar has aptly called a "jus nexi"—that is, a bond and duty of justice that emerges through affiliations in civil society.[11]

---

[10] For a masterful historical account, see Zolberg 2008.
[11] See Schachar 2009 and my review, Benhabib 2013.

IV

Processes of migration are not only about foreigners *entering* a polity with well-defined borders. Throughout human history, peoples have been in motion but borders as well have moved. State borders have emerged out of historical contingencies that involve bloody wars as well as creeping annexations; conquests by ruse or by trade as well as accession of one polity to another; and the formation of federations among different groups. From a justice-oriented point of view, and from the standpoint of democratic legitimacy, we ought to recognize that the borders of our state-system are morally arbitrary.[12] Whatever arguments may be given in their defence ought not exaggerate their stability by transforming historical accident into conceptual necessity. Immigrants often say, "We are here because you were there!" "We did not cross the border, the border crossed us!"

There is hardly a state in today's world upon whose territory "others" do not live: among these, for example, are members of formerly colonial peoples such as Indians, Pakistanis, Punjabis in the UK; Algerians and Tunisians in France; Moluccans and natives of the Antilles islands in The Netherlands; Ethiopians in Italy; Iraqis, Persians, Syrians, and Palestinians in Turkey (all territories once under the dominion of the Ottoman Empire); Poles, Turks, and Hungarians, as well as thousands of Israelis in Germany (all peoples with complicated historical ties to Germany); and of course, Mexicans, Salvadorans, Hondurans, and many others in the United States. Those who are already upon the territory of a polity for whatever historical reason are often not full members: they may be undocumented migrants; guest workers; permanent residents; asylum seekers; or simply those whose legal status is murky and undefined. When considering immigration we should move away from the paradigmatic case of the outsider who wants in; we should think of the non-compatriots among us to whom we deny the status of citizenship and full membership as well.

If we shift our perspective from that of the *outsider looking in* to that of the *insider looking out*, we will note the following: although the movement of peoples is ubiquitous in human history, not everyone wants to migrate everywhere else. Migrations follow structured patterns of "pull" and "push" factors. With the exception of natural disasters and civil wars which compel people to cross borders wherever they can, the most significant "pull" factors are the presence of some network of kin, linguistic, and religious communities who already live in the preferred countries of emigration. Levitov and Macedo neglect the salience of one of the recognized universal human rights of migrants, namely family unification.[13] If we owe moral obligations to our compatriots,

---

[12] This case has been most forcefully argued by Abizadeh 2008.

[13] See Declaration on the Human Rights of Individuals Who Are Not Nationals of the Country in which They Live, GA res. 40/144. Annex, 40 UN GAOR Supp. (No. 53) at 252. UN Doc. A/40/53 (1985) (providing such "aliens" with rights to leave, liberty of movement within a country, as well as to have their spouses and minor children of legal aliens to be admitted to join and stay with them, and to protect them from expulsion by requiring opportunities for hearings and for decision-making not predicated on discrimination based on "race, colour, religion, culture, descent or national or ethnic origin").

who may or may not be full citizens, we also owe them special consideration in enabling their family members and kin to be reunited with them. Neglect of this fundamental human right has led recent US administrations to deport the undocumented parents of American-born children as well as not permitting entry to non-American children of long-term undocumented migrants resident within the United States.[14] Levitov and Macedo ignore the complexity of human ties and attachments underlying migratory movements and focus on the model of the migrant as an individual seeking to better his[15] economic condition by crossing borders.

The case which they consider is the increased migration of low-skill workers to the USA since the 1960s. They claim that such influx has led to a substantial decline in the wages of less well-educated drop-outs. The ethnic makeup of migration has also changed with the percentage arriving from Europe and Canada falling sharply in comparison with those arriving from Latin America and Asia (p. 480). Furthermore, "Recent patterns of immigration to the USA may, thus, worsen the relative lot of the least well-off Americans while also making redistributive politics less politically popular" (p. 481). Levitov and Macedo then ask: if immigration generates a collective economic surplus for the whole, while making the least-well-off Americans even more vulnerable, whose needs should be prioritized? Should we give precedence to the basic needs of potential immigrants or the relative standing of poorer Americans? They argue that if basic needs and the human rights of non-members are involved, they should take priority even if these are needs and rights of individuals who are not our compatriots. But they conclude that *once* these conditions are met states can be left free to act "on their own considered judgement about how best to balance their competing responsibilities to members and non-members" (p. 482).

While I find much in this argument plausible, what is implausible to me is the claim that increased influx of migrants has worsened the lot of the poor Americans while making redistributive policies less popular. The authors have confused correlation with causation. It is not increased immigration that makes redistributive policies unpopular in the United States; it is because such policies are already unpopular that there is an uncontrolled market in labour migration. The US free-market ideology gives preferential treatment to unorganized and politically vulnerable migrants who basically accept low-wage and hazardous work conditions—be it in agriculture, the meat-packing industry, and transportation—over organized labour that can exercise voice not only in labour-related issues but in migration politics as well. In countries such as Germany, for example, where the migrant percentage of the population has reached nearly 9 per cent, *sub rosa* hiring and employment practices are strictly penalized and migrant workers can become members of strong trade unions after a short period of time. As the example of migrations into more social democratic countries illustrates,

---

[14] See Bhabha 2009.

[15] There is much evidence that the rise of a post-industrial, service economy which generates jobs in nursing, elder and child care, tourism, hospitality, and other similar industries is in fact encouraging more female than male migration. Cf. Ehrenreich and Hochschild 2002.

it is not low-wage migration per se that undermines distributive politics, but rather, other structural and ideological factors shaping a country's economy which influence both redistributive politics and patterns of migration.[16]

My conclusion is different from Levitov and Macedo's: instead of privileging states' "considered judgement" about how to balance these obligations, I would ask states to respect the human as well as socio-economic rights of migrants, by penalizing unsanitary and exploitative work conditions, and by expediting the integration of undocumented migrants into the social network of the country in question through state or city-issued identity cards, the issuance of social security numbers, etc. Admittedly, such measures may discourage further undocumented labour migrants from wanting to enter a country. I agree with Levitov and Macedo that when the basic needs and rights of such individuals are at stake—as is for example the case with many African migrants to the European Union—they should have priority and stronger controls of undocumented migrants and their labour conditions should *not* lead to states neglecting those who are most vulnerable. Raising the level of protection offered to the most vulnerable undocumented migrants, instead of leaving them at the mercy of gangs, swindlers, and cruel bosses, can also lead to the increase in the rights protection of the working population at large.

One additional factor to consider in limiting the range of discretion that states believe they are entitled to in setting migration policy is what Levitov and Macedo have called "duties of reciprocity," which prohibit exploitation, domination, and free-riding. Migration debates often neglect the "pull" and "push" factors caused by states' own policies. Thus, the introduction of certain more resilient strains of corn by North American agro-business into Central American countries, and especially Mexico, had led to the closing down of Mexican farms and to unemployment in agriculture which, in turn, has contributed to migration across the US border. Likewise, protectionist policies on the part of the European Union meant that North African farmers could not compete on the European market with their cheap agricultural products subsidized by EU funds. This, in turn, intensified labour migration into the EU. Becoming aware of such causal nexi should lead to more mutually beneficial economic policies and increased development aid such as to enable migrant-sender countries to create employment at home. Migratory patterns are clear indicators of the degree of interdependence in a global economy, in which the main players continue to behave as self-centred monads with no windows to the outside—alas!

---

[16] I do not want to minimize the extent of xenophobia in European countries around migration. It is important to note though that some of this xenophobia does not concern migrants from Africa, the Middle East, etc. alone but is directed toward citizens from countries such as Poland, Romania, Bulgaria, and Greece who are members of the European Union and who have the right to labour mobility as EU citizens. The rejection of free movement from EU member countries to the UK was one of the principal causes behind the Brexit decision in 2015. For a judicious exploration of migration, xenophobia, and social-democratic politics, see Edsall 2014.

V

The statist-cosmopolitan position defended by Levitov and Macedo has many attractive features from a justice point of view, but it does not go far enough. The privileging of obligations to our compatriots is based upon a set of anthropological, ontological, and political (or polity-oriented) assumptions which are not clarified. Although the authors characterize their position as a political and contractarian one, they vacillate between identitarian and contractarian premises. From the standpoint of the social contract tradition, the boundaries of the demos are indeterminate and indeed arbitrary. Migration policies are the sites at which the arbitrariness of the boundaries of the demos are negotiated.

Levitov and Macedo try to minimize this arbitrariness from a moral point of view and they conceptualize migrations through the paradigm of the outsider wanting in. This leads them to ignore the presence of others within our polities, who are our compatriots without being our co-citizens. Migration policies are not just about letting the outsider in but also about changing the status of certain migrants already within our communities.

With regard to the example of low-skilled migration to the United States and how this affects distributive politics, I have argued that it is the presence of unregulated and free-market oriented policies and ideologies that affect both the patterns of migration to the USA as well asthe paucity of distributive politics.

In conclusion, I have urged Levitov and Macedo to consider the consequences of duties of reciprocity which result from states' economic policies in shaping migratory patterns beyond their borders.

Statist-cosmopolitanism is an unstable position, which prioritizes the fundamental moral and human rights of migrants but which also attributes more salience to duties to our compatriots than is defensible. It also privileges states and their policy makers as the sole proper addressees of the conversation about migration rather than focusing on individuals, communities, and civil society organizations who are the ones closest to the lives of migrants, temporary and undocumented workers, asylum seekers, and refugees.

References

Abizadeh, Arash (2008) "Democratic Theory and Border Coercion," *Political Theory* 36, no. 1, pp. 37–65.

Beitz, Charles (1979) *Political Theory and International Relations*, rev. edn. (Princeton: Princeton University Press).

Benhabib, Seyla (2004a) *The Rights of Others: Aliens, Residents and Citizens* (Cambridge: Cambridge University Press).

Benhabib, Seyla (2004b) "*The Law of Peoples*, Distributive Justice and Migrations," *Fordham Law Review* 72, pp. 1762–71.

Benhabib, Seyla (2013) "Birthright Citizenship, Immigration, and Global Poverty," *University of Toronto Law Review* 63, pp. 496–510.

Bhabha, Jacqueline (2009) "The 'Mere Fortuity of Birth': Children, Mothers, Borders, and the Meaning of Citizenship," in *Migrations and Mobilities: Citizenship, Borders and Gender*, ed. Seyla Benhabib and Judith Resnik (New York: New York University Press), pp. 187–228.

Edsall, Thomas B. (2014) "The Rise of 'Welfare Chauvinism,'" *NYTimes* <http://www.nytimes.com/2014/12/17/opinion/the-rise-of-welfare-chauvinism.html>.

Ehrenreich, Barbara & Hochschild, Arlie Russell (2002) *Global Woman: Nannies, Maids, and Sex Workers in the New Economy* (New York: Henry Holt and Company).

Hegel, G. W. F. (1973) *Hegel's Philosophy of Right*, trans. T. M. Knox (Oxford: Oxford University Press).

Herder, Johann Gottfried von (2002) *Philosophical Writings*, Cambridge Texts in the History of Philosophy, ed. and trans. Michael N. Forster (Cambridge: Cambridge University Press).

Kymlicka, Will (1995) *Multicultural Citizenship: A Liberal Theory of Minority Rights* (Oxford: Oxford University Press).

Macedo, Stephen (2004) "What Self-Governing Peoples Owe to One Another: Universalism, Diversity, and *The Law of Peoples*," *Fordham Law Review* 72, pp. 1721–38.

Nagel, Thomas (2005) "The Problem of Global Justice," *Philosophy and Public Affairs* 33, no. 2, pp. 113–47.

Pogge, Thomas (2008) *World Poverty and Human Rights*, 2nd edn. (Cambridge and Malden, Mass.: Polity Press).

Rawls, John (1996) *Political Liberalism* (New York: Columbia University Press).

Rawls, John (1999) *A Theory of Justice*, rev. edn (Cambridge, Mass.: The Belknap Press).

Rousseau, J.-J. (1968) *The Social Contract*, trans. Maurice Cranston (London: Penguin Classics [1762]).

Rousseau, J.-J. (1985) *The Government of Poland*, trans. Willmoore Kendall (Indianapolis: Hackett Publishing Company).

Schachar, Ayelet (2009) *The Birthright Lottery: Citizenship and Global Inequality* (Cambridge, Mass.: Harvard University Press).

Taylor, Charles (1992) "The Importance of Herder," in E. Avishai Margalit (ed.), *Isaiah Berlin: A Celebration* (Chicago: University of Chicago Press).

Zolberg, Ari (2008) *A Nation by Design: Immigration Policy in the Fashioning of America* (Cambridge, Mass.: Harvard University Press).

Index

Abizadeh, Arash 31n, 470, 483n, 495
Aesop 416
Afghanistan 189, 420, 421, 423, 424, 425, 426,
430, 435
Africa 54, 150, 164, 189, 190, 322, 325, 383, 384,
415, 423, 428, 455, 461, 462, 480, 486, 497
African Charter of Human Rights 150
African National Congress (ANC) 322
Algeria 461, 462, 463, 495
Alston, Philip 2n, 30n, 92n, 103, 108n, 171n,
183n, 193n, 197
American Bill of Rights 42
American Chamber of Commerce 101
American Convention on Human Rights
150, 194
Amnesty International 190, 191, 192, 193, 194,
197, 202, 259, 392, 417
Anderson, Mary B. 415
Anglo-American philosophy 70, 72
Annan, Kofi 99
Apartheid 322, 461, 462, 464, 466
Appiah, Kwame Anthony 322
Aquinas, Thomas 76, 77, 414n
Arab Spring 55
Arendt, Hannah 403, 406n, 436
Aristotle 47, 75, 414n
Ashford, Elizabeth 24–5, 337–62, 363–71
Athens 97
AusAID 415
Austria 187, 273

Badiou, Alain 412n
Balibar, Etienne 436
Barnett, Michelle 431
Barry, Brian 281, 401n, 402n, 404
BBC 418
Beitz, Charles 1n, 5, 7, 8n, 12, 14, 15, 23n, 26n,
71, 72, 73n, 80, 82n, 89, 97n, 99n, 106,
107, 119, 123, 128, 134, 135, 145, 150,
154–7, 158, 161, 162, 165, 166, 167n,
168n, 169, 172, 174n, 175n, 182n, 183n,
187n, 197n, 212n, 224, 225, 226n, 231,
238n, 280, 286, 332, 339, 352, 353, 356,
357n, 361n, 365, 376n, 380n, 381n, 383n,
385n, 396n, 442, 452, 454n, 466, 475n,
477n, 490n
Benhabib, Seyla 19n, 31n, 34, 110n, 205, 238n,
256, 263, 489–500
Besson, Samantha 19n, 21, 74, 175n, 212n,
225n, 243n, 262–8

Black Lives Matter 194, 195, 196
Borjas, George 480
Brems, Eva 270n, 272, 273, 274, 284, 328n, 337,
338, 343, 344, 345n, 346, 347n
Brett, Annabel 9–10, 42n, 45n, 49n, 61–8,
103, 110
Brexit 497n
Brownlee, Kimberley 19n, 24, 313–26, 327–35
Buchanan, Allen 1n, 3, 4n, 18n, 19–20, 31n, 152n,
165, 174n, 206n, 211–29, 230–7, 240n,
262n, 263n, 265n, 338, 385n, 453n, 455n
Burlamaqui, Jean-Jacques 51
Burma 322, 324, 330

Cambodia 411, 418, 419, 430
Cambridge School 62
Canada 384n, 397n, 446, 462, 463, 480, 496
Caney, Simon 477n
Card, David 480
Carens, Joseph 31n, 422n, 470
Carter, Jimmy 91, 108, 433
Cassin, René 63
Catholicism 42, 46, 49, 255, 417
Chalmers, David 185
China 132, 259, 322
Christianity 44, 49, 50, 75, 76, 255, 258, 276,
333, 411, 416
Christiano, Tom 19n, 227n, 454n
climate change 98
Coady, C. A. J. 10, 26n, 29, 316, 317n, 320, 329,
409–28, 429–37
Cohen, Jean 92
Cohen, Joshua 5n, 19n, 27n, 396n, 454n, 470,
471, 475n
Cold War 43, 63, 69, 86, 384, 423, 436
Colombia 393
Columbia Law School 259
Committee on Economic, Social and Cultural
Rights (CESCR) 23n, 345n
consumer boycotts 369
Convention on the Elimination of All Forms
of Discrimination Against Women
(CEDAW) 182n, 391, 393
Convention on the Prevention and Punishment
of the Crime of Genocide 30
Convention on the Rights of the Child 391
Council of Europe 269, 279, 281, 286, 287,
290, 303
Court of Justice of the European Union (CJEU/
ECJ) 238, 241, 242, 264, 288

Cranston, Maurice 17n, 19n, 22, 23, 24, 337n,
    338, 339, 340, 341, 343, 350, 351,
    352, 363
Cro-Magnon 117, 137
Cruft, Rowan 1n, 6n, 24, 27n, 31n, 180n, 313n,
    328–36
Cyprus 271

Darfur Conflict 192n
de Mably, Abbé Gabriel Bonnot 52
de Nemours, Pierre Samuel Dupont 51
de Soto, Domingo 44, 45n
de Vitoria, Francisco 44
de Waal, Alex 414, 418
Deaton, Angus 473n, 481n
Declaration of Independence 63
Declaration on the Human Rights of Individuals
    Who Are Not Nationals of the Country
    in which They Live 495
Declaration on the Rights of Indigenous
    Peoples 467
Déclaration des droits de l'homme et du
    citoyen 42–3, 52, 63, 244, 389–90
democratic paradox of membership 494
Democratic Republic of the Congo 420
Derrida, Jacques 63n
Destexhe, Alain 419
Devlin, Patrick (Lord) 248n
Dickinson, Emily 313
Diderot, Denis 51
dominium 44, 45, 47, 48n, 49, 56, 65, 110, 461
Donini, Antonio 431
Donnelly, Jack 30n, 31n, 442n, 450n
duelling 322
Dunant, Henry 411, 432
Dworkin, Ronald 1n, 121n, 176n, 245n, 277,
    280, 296, 297, 304n, 305n, 306, 307n

East India Company 46
East Timor 466
Eliot, T. S. 410
Ely, John Hart 281, 305n
Estlund, David 5n, 83n, 405n
Etinson, Adam 1–38, 103n, 154n, 157n, 160–73,
    186n, 228n, 230n, 269n, 270, 276, 297n,
    299n, 313n, 320n, 329n, 332n, 335n,
    379n, 397n, 425n, 429n, 441n
European Charter of Fundamental Rights 247
European Commission 101
European Commission for Democracy 281
European Commission of Human Rights 271
European Convention on Human Rights
    (ECHR) 21, 150, 189, 193n, 202, 241,
    246, 269, 279, 295
European Court of Human Rights (ECtHR) 21,
    22, 31, 134, 190, 195n, 197, 241, 266n,
    269–95, 295–310, 451n

European Court of Justice (ECJ) 238, 241, 242,
    264, 288
European Union (EU) 212n, 238n, 241, 264, 497
Evans, Gareth 123n, 434n
Evans, Tony 378n, 384

Fassin, Didier 111, 435
Feinberg, Joel 24n, 30n, 155n
FIFA 241
Finnis, John 91
First Amendment 252, 255
Flynn, Jeffrey 11, 103–12
Follesdal, Andreas 21–2, 269–94, 295–309
foreign aid 29, 384, 407–27, 472, 473
foreign intervention 26, 27, 29, 71, 80, 81, 171,
    407–27
Forst, Rainer 16, 21, 188n, 200–8, 239, 263, 266
Foucault, Michel 67, 403n
France 46, 50, 51, 66, 259, 453, 461, 463, 495
Frazer, Elizabeth 28, 379n, 397n, 400–8
French Revolution 66

Geneva Convention 412
genocide 30, 99n, 122, 125, 172, 192n, 339, 426,
    433, 463
German Federal Constitutional Court (GFCC/
    FCC) 241, 248, 253n
Geuss, Raymond 27, 28, 56, 64n, 83n, 314n,
    315, 327, 328n, 329, 334, 335, 379n
Gibbon, Edward 69, 76n
Gilabert, Pablo 1n, 4n, 10, 12n, 19n, 23n, 24n,
    25n, 27–9, 157n, 167n, 313n, 314, 317n,
    319n, 375–99, 400–8
Glennie, Jonathan 415
Goodin, Robert 471, 483n, 485n
Goodman, Ryan 2n, 26–7, 30n, 183n
Gould, Carol C. 30n
Gramsci, Antonio 383
Griffin, James 1n, 7n, 8, 11n, 12, 14, 16n, 17n,
    18n, 19n, 20n, 31n, 70, 89, 97n, 130n,
    145, 149–52, 153n, 156, 157, 158, 160,
    161, 162, 164, 165, 166, 168n, 169, 170,
    174n, 175n, 176–80, 187n, 211n, 226,
    232, 240n, 262n, 265, 332n, 343, 348,
    360, 410n
Grotius, Hugo 42, 46, 47, 48, 49, 50, 51, 55, 65
Guiding Principles on Business and Human
    Rights 19, 98–101

Habermas, Jürgen 17n, 18, 99n, 109n, 245n
Hart, H. L. A. 2, 17n, 248n, 296
Hassemer, Winfried 249n
Hassoun, Nicole 19n
Hawaii 461, 462
Hegel, Georg Wilhelm Friedrich 492, 493n
Henkin, Lewis 132n, 213n
Herder, Johann Gottfried 492, 493n

Hezbollah 424
Hobbes, Thomas 42, 51, 66, 492
Hohfeld, Wesley 30n, 349
Holbrooke, Richard 421
Honore, Tony 91
House of Lords 189, 295n
human dignity 16–17, 89, 96, 145, 151, 170, 172,
  186, 202, 204, 251n, 305n, 385, 388n, 441
human rights
  absolute vs. non-absolute 20, 45, 51n, 54, 127,
    149, 183, 238, 244–51, 265–6, 272, 283,
    297, 299n, 318, 347–9
  abstract vs. specific 76, 78, 84, 101, 108, 148,
    149, 151, 152, 156, 157, 158, 162, 243n,
    244, 246, 251–3, 257, 259, 262, 266, 270,
    276, 284, 297, 298, 301–2, 306, 307, 308,
    370, 376, 391
    see also specification of human rights
  activism 26, 52, 110, 164, 203
  against genocide
    see genocide
  against imprisonment for debt 245
  against slavery 1, 2, 3, 122, 271, 272, 284,
    308n, 321, 354, 355, 359
    see also human rights and slavery
  against tax fraud 177
  against the death penalty 245, 252, 255, 275
  against theft 46, 177
  against torture 23, 25, 28, 99n, 101, 122, 124,
    126, 127, 128, 129, 177, 182, 183, 239,
    245, 271, 272, 284, 297, 299n, 318, 321,
    322, 324, 338, 339, 342, 343, 344, 347,
    353, 364, 367, 368, 369, 382, 387, 392,
    409, 410, 412, 463
  against unreasonable punishment 252
  and animal rights 16, 187n
  and autonomy 17–18, 118, 145, 149–52, 177,
    204, 207, 214, 270, 295, 389, 402
  and basic rights 132, 206, 207, 343n, 476n
  and capitalism 55, 385, 388–92
  and children's rights 17, 179, 187, 194, 307,
    410, 465, 495
  and colonialism 27, 49, 53, 54, 56, 65, 381n,
    383, 394, 417, 426, 431, 460–8, 495
  and constitutional rights 14, 71, 72–3, 117,
    121, 129, 130–1, 134–6, 142, 148, 195,
    221, 240, 259, 281
  and democracy 19, 21–2, 25, 28–9, 94, 95, 97,
    191, 205, 227, 243, 244, 251, 256, 264,
    270, 279, 280–2, 303, 304, 305, 308, 382,
    394–7, 454, 469–500
  and development 30, 53, 117, 163, 356, 415,
    420n, 469, 473, 479, 482, 497
  and group rights 29–34, 55, 441–500
  and hegemony 42, 63, 383–6
  and human dignity
    see human dignity

  and humanitarian intervention 71, 122,
    124–5, 125–7, 128, 132–3, 133–4, 140,
    217, 222, 387, 410, 411, 414–23, 429–37
  and humanitarianism 43, 105, 106n, 409–13,
    414, 417, 419, 423–7, 429–36
  and immigration 31, 33–4, 469–500
  and manifesto rights 24, 155, 416
  and minimum core duties 23, 266, 344–5
  and national self-determination 30–4, 187n,
    193, 213n, 240, 251, 257, 266, 276, 382,
    394, 426, 441–500
  and national sovereignty 1, 5, 7, 12, 13, 14, 15,
    16, 20, 22, 31–2, 44, 45, 46, 48, 50, 65, 73,
    77, 90, 99n, 107, 120, 122, 123, 127, 131,
    132–3, 139, 140, 142, 143, 153, 154, 168,
    171, 172, 175, 182, 185, 194, 195, 200,
    213, 216, 219, 222, 224, 225, 226n, 234,
    235, 236, 251, 267, 269, 278, 284, 288,
    290, 295, 302, 303, 423, 433, 466
  interpretation of 132–3, 143
  and natural rights 1, 2, 7, 8, 43, 49, 50–1, 56,
    61–6, 74, 75, 78, 91–2, 96n, 98, 99n, 104,
    106, 108, 145, 150, 157–8, 212n, 328,
    332, 333, 334, 388, 410
  and non-domination 205–6, 239, 262, 279,
    280, 451, 478, 490
  and political legitimacy 1, 13, 63, 89, 168,
    220, 223, 254–5, 263n, 267, 270, 424,
    470, 471, 472, 474, 475, 476, 477, 478,
    489, 491, 492
  and prisoners' rights 180, 181, 192, 258, 275,
    302, 304, 307, 335, 385, 410
  and progressive realization duties 23n, 344
  and religion 55, 411, 491, 492
    see also human right to religious freedom
  and slavery 43, 49, 50, 53–4, 66, 151, 340,
    354–5, 359–60
    see also human right against slavery
  and standard threats 157, 394, 395, 466
  and structural injustice 4, 55, 57, 67, 337–71,
    388–92, 393, 401–7, 415, 435, 436,
    449, 497
  and the duties of corporations 19, 98–101,
    142, 187, 221, 340, 342, 357, 359,
    384n, 387
  and the Enlightenment 8, 42, 50, 53, 54, 77,
    149, 165, 244
  and the mirroring view 20, 214, 215, 216,
    217n, 226–8, 230–7
  and the right to justification 20, 188n, 204–7,
    239, 266
  and the rights of indigenous peoples 460–8
  and the white man's burden 386–8, 417
  and the 1940s 63, 81n, 106
  and the 1970s 43, 53, 54, 63n, 70, 74–5, 78,
    86, 91, 93, 99n, 105, 106, 108, 110, 111,
    259, 433, 455

human rights (*cont.*)
and the 1990s 29, 43, 53, 54, 79, 80, 99,
    419, 423
and utopia 5, 6, 54, 63n, 70, 71, 82–6, 94, 98,
    166n, 258, 313n, 345
and women's rights 97, 134, 151, 182n, 203,
    206, 242, 258, 295, 382, 385, 389, 390,
    391, 393, 402, 404, 465, 496
apparent objectivity of 1–2, 16, 45, 75, 77–8,
    80, 96n
aspirational character of 6, 23–5, 91, 314, 315,
    316, 327, 337–71, 379n
balancing of 55, 247, 250, 271, 273–4, 277,
    282, 285, 289, 306, 348, 479
civil and political 53, 55, 105, 205, 316,
    384, 394
    see also ICCPR
communitarian critique of 29–30, 388–92
culture 2, 80, 81, 82, 84, 85, 86, 92, 93, 97, 163,
    176, 201
demandingness of 22–5, 320, 323, 334
discourse-theoretical conception of 204–7
duty-bearers of 18, 155, 187, 221, 349–50,
    351, 357, 358, 359, 360, 361, 366–70
ethnocentricity of 96, 152, 158, 381–3
feasibility of 22–5, 26, 98, 167n, 178–9, 233,
    313–36, 340, 350–5, 356–8, 359, 364,
    365, 366, 378n, 393–4, 395, 453
fidelity to the practice of 4–5, 7–9, 10–11,
    15–16, 80–1, 82, 83, 88, 90, 139–44,
    163–72, 176, 178, 179, 180, 181, 182, 184,
    188, 190, 193, 196, 197, 201, 225–6
functionalization of 74, 76, 77, 78, 79, 81, 84,
    90–2, 108
history of 7–11, 41–117
inalienability of 16, 44, 54, 63, 65
indeterminacy of 13, 155, 166, 297n, 302,
    349, 350
individualism of 13–14, 29, 30–1, 42n, 72, 85,
    127–9, 134, 136, 217–18, 388–92, 442–3
indivisibility of 53, 54, 266
law 2, 3, 4, 9, 16–22, 131, 193n, 243, 263,
    405, 409
    domestic 2, 3n, 9, 16, 21, 26, 94, 112, 166,
        212n, 214, 219, 221, 223, 224, 228, 230,
        238n, 266, 267, 276, 277, 281, 284, 287,
        289, 304, 308, 376, 380
    European 20, 21, 150, 166, 189, 193, 202,
        212n, 238–69, 269–313
    international (IHRL/ILHR) 3, 5, 9, 16, 17,
        19, 20, 26, 29, 30, 31, 32, 33, 43, 89, 94,
        99n, 149, 152, 154, 165, 166, 171, 176,
        183, 192, 211–38, 240n, 243, 251, 266,
        267, 280, 288, 300n, 302, 304, 308, 309,
        337, 339, 383, 392, 433, 451n, 460, 461,
        463, 464, 465, 466, 467, 469
    purposes of 213–15

regional 2, 9, 16, 22, 134, 165, 193, 212, 223,
    238, 251, 257, 259, 266, 270, 280, 297
legal positivization of 2–4, 16–19, 19–20, 130,
    131, 206–7, 409–10
    see also human rights and the mirroring view
limitation of 244–51, 347–9
    see also absolute vs. non-absolute
    human rights
many lives of 5
minimalism 20, 73n, 149, 156, 177–8, 240n,
    257, 267, 319, 324, 343–6, 358, 360, 361,
    365, 366, 395, 396, 397, 476
    see also human rights and minimum
    core duties; human rights
    ultra-minimalism
movement 2, 3, 4, 83, 84, 85, 103, 106, 110,
    111, 181, 376, 387n, 391, 392, 409,
    411, 417
multidisciplinary nature of 6, 82, 88, 94–5,
    98, 104, 105
naturalistic character of 1–2, 30
non-legalist approach to 99–101
philosophical foundations of 5, 6, 11, 66, 89,
    90, 94, 95, 96, 108, 156–7, 160, 179, 200,
    236, 395, 429
polyfunctionalism of 81n, 145–59, 161–2
practice of 2–5, 7, 8–9, 11–13, 14, 15–16,
    21, 28, 81n, 82, 83, 85, 89–90, 96, 122,
    123, 125, 129, 130, 135, 140, 141, 142,
    143, 144, 150, 154, 155–6, 157, 158,
    164–6, 168, 169, 170, 171, 175, 188, 189,
    193, 200, 201, 226, 230, 232, 233, 238,
    239, 240, 246, 251, 253, 257, 264, 265,
    266, 267, 315, 375, 378, 379, 380, 381,
    383, 386, 387, 388, 394, 395, 400, 401,
    402, 407
    vs. culture, discourse, or movement 164–6
    unity vs. disunity of 168–70, 175, 186, 188,
        189, 193, 195, 197, 203, 332
proliferation of 93, 96, 98, 211, 337, 343
Rawls's conception of 152–4
    see also John Rawls
realization of 2, 10, 22–5, 26–7, 33, 93–5,
    96–101, 190n, 197, 313–26, 344, 401
sacredness of 142, 244, 337, 338, 343, 347
self-evidence of 43, 162
social and economic 30, 34, 64, 160, 205,
    242, 315, 316n, 337, 338, 344, 345n, 353,
    470n, 497
    see also ICESCR
specification of 94, 148, 149, 151, 188, 189,
    191, 194, 197, 205, 240, 244, 251–6, 257,
    259, 260, 262, 263, 266, 282, 297, 350,
    354, 360, 391, 394, 395
statist aspect of 99–101, 170, 213, 469–500
suprapositivity of 1–2, 16, 17, 27–8, 65, 204
timelessness of 44, 67, 77–8, 97–8, 212, 318

to a fair say in important family decisions 3, 17, 18, 168
to a fair trial 180, 181, 189, 272
to a good sleep 241
to adequate housing 24, 141, 142, 226n, 227n, 242, 344, 382
to an adequate standard of living 33, 98, 391
to asylum 31, 252, 469, 489, 495, 498
to bodily security 23, 25
to border control 31, 441–500
to breathable air 321n
to due process 24, 122, 243, 318, 328, 433
to education 148, 151, 154, 171, 178, 180, 181, 185, 193, 194, 195, 203, 325, 335, 344, 351, 390, 402, 403, 404, 405, 407, 415, 433, 434, 474, 480n
to food 24, 242, 344, 419, 426
to freedom of association 30, 180, 272
to freedom of thought and expression 30, 206
to health 3, 4, 19, 20, 24, 25, 98, 148, 171, 178, 214, 242, 246, 273, 283, 319, 325, 344, 348, 360, 390, 415, 416, 417, 433
to leave one's country 469
to life 63, 122, 204, 243, 252, 271, 272, 321, 391n
to national self-determination 30–4, 187n, 193, 213n, 240, 251, 257, 266, 279, 382, 394, 426, 441–500
to nondiscrimination 30, 122, 148, 264, 272, 382, 470
to periodic holidays with pay 19, 23, 171
to political participation 24, 28, 97, 148, 180, 204, 206, 318, 384, 396
to privacy 17, 18, 31, 241, 246, 252, 253n, 282, 295, 296n, 298, 307
to private property 45, 50, 53, 85, 388
to promise-keeping 177, 179
to religious freedom 30, 55, 105, 246, 251, 252, 255, 272, 282, 296, 299n, 378, 433, 451, 456
to romantic love 331n
to security 31, 55, 204, 476n
to shout fire in a crowded cinema 246
to subsistence 24–5, 204, 337–75
to vote 180, 181, 243, 275, 304, 307, 368, 482
ultra-minimalism 90, 122
universality of 23, 30, 54, 78n, 97, 136n, 137, 155, 212, 227, 251, 266–7, 285–6, 299, 335n, 352, 381n, 388–92, 410, 413, 451, 456, 465, 467n
urgency of 23, 25, 337–71
Human Rights Act 130, 189
Human Rights Watch 189, 192n, 194n, 420
humanitarian law 409, 410, 412
Hunt, Lynn 43n, 105, 106, 111, 390n, 433
Hussain, Saddam 424, 426
Hutu 419

Ignatieff, Michael 257n, 258n, 432, 435
International Committee of the Red Cross (ICRC) 410, 411, 412, 415
International Covenant on Civil and Political Rights (ICCPR) 1n, 3n, 16, 29, 30, 31n, 33n, 130, 131n, 134, 176, 190n, 193, 211n, 212, 220n, 243, 245n, 300n, 302, 376, 384, 393, 441, 457, 469
International Covenant on Economic, Social and Cultural Rights (ICESCR) 3n, 16, 23n, 29, 30, 33n, 171, 178, 211n, 265, 352, 376, 384, 441, 457
International Monetary Fund (IMF) 416, 420
International Rescue Committee 419
internet 77
Iraq War 122, 126, 184, 384, 411, 420, 423, 424, 425, 426, 430, 435, 495
Israel 251n, 424, 495
Israeli Supreme Court 251n

Jinks, Derek 26
Jones, Peter 1n, 31–3, 441–68
Jordan, Michael 190, 194

Kagame, Paul 420
Kant, Immanuel 1, 54, 118, 244n, 370, 413, 474, 490n, 492
Kennan, George 413
Keohane, Robert 385n, 485n
Kennedy, David 42n, 55n, 378, 380n, 381n, 386n, 392n, 394
Khmer Rouge 418, 419
Kosovo 126, 192n, 423, 432, 434n
Kouchner, Bernard 192n, 418, 422
Kuhn, Thomas 75
Kumm, Mattias 20–1, 238–61, 262–8
Kymlicka, Will 32, 453n, 455n, 460–8, 492
Koskenniemi, Martti 9–10, 41–60, 61–8, 103, 105, 107, 108n, 109, 110, 111, 278, 385, 467n
Kyi, Aung San Suu 134, 322, 324, 330

Lauterpacht, Hersch 17n, 53
Lebanon 424
League of Nations 8, 43
Letsas, George 21n, 22, 193n, 241, 266n, 269n, 270n, 271, 275, 279n, 282n, 286, 288, 295–313
Levitov, Alex 33–4, 469–500
Liao, Matthew S. 1n, 6n, 12n, 16n, 22n, 157n, 160n
Locke, John 49–50, 51, 66, 332n, 333, 474n, 492

Macedo, Stephen 33–4, 397, 469–500
MacIntyre, Alasdair 77
Macklem, Patrick 283, 466, 467

Make Poverty History 415
Mandela, Nelson 322, 325
margin of appreciation (MA) 21-2, 249, 253, 254, 269-310
Marks, Susan 54, 56n, 243n, 257n
Marx, Karl 29, 55, 80, 258, 388-92
Mayr, Erasmus 20, 228n, 230-7
McBeth, Adam 357
McCrudden, Christopher 92n, 96n, 195n
Médecins Sans Frontières (MSF) 192n, 411, 415, 418, 419, 420, 430
Middle East 411, 497n
Merry, Sally Engle 42n
Mill, John Stuart 19
Miller, David 31n, 97n, 178n, 245n, 331, 346, 370, 393, 453n, 455n, 470, 471, 474n, 475n, 477n, 483n
moralism 29, 409-27, 429-36
Morgenthau, Hans 413, 430n
Moyn, Samuel 4n, 10-11, 42n, 43n, 63n, 69-87, 88-102, 103-16, 192n, 257n, 411n, 433, 434, 436n
Mutua, Makau 27n, 43n, 378, 386n, 387n, 392

Nagel, Thomas 470n, 471n, 475n, 491, 493, 494
natural law 42n, 45, 46, 50, 51, 69, 70, 171, 413
Neibuhr, Reinhold 413
Neier, Arieh 183n, 192n
Nesiah, Vasuki 29, 429-37
Neuman, Gerald 16n, 17n, 130
NGO 120n, 165n, 141, 165, 187, 194n, 384, 410, 414n, 419
Nickel, James W. 1n, 2n, 13n, 14-15, 17n, 19n, 29n, 30n, 31n, 81n, 83n, 91, 122, 145-59, 160-73, 228n, 240n, 251n, 262n, 314n, 315, 327, 329n, 330, 332, 339n, 344, 355, 381n
Nietzsche, Friedrich 110, 252, 258
Nonhuman Rights Project 187n
North Korea 335
Nussbaum, Martha 4n, 111n

O'Neill, Onora 24n, 91, 160n, 349n, 350n, 353
Obama, Barack 417
Orford, Anna 44n
Organization for Economic Co-operation and Development (OECD) 101
Organization of African Unity 455
orthodox conception of human rights
  challenges facing the 69-87, 88-101, 117-18, 176-82
  defence of 1-2, 88-101, 117-39
  defined 1, 89, 106, 150, 174, 200
  different terms for 1
  historical facet of 7-8, 14, 88-101
Orthodox-Political debate

at cross-purposes 11-13, 14-15, 145-58, 160-1, 185, 200, 224
  historical facet of 7-9, 145-58
  overview 1-5, 11-16, 88-91, 117-211
Oxfam 392n, 411, 415

Pakistan 182, 184, 421, 495
Parfit, Derek 379n
Peace of Augsburg 46
Peoplehood (selfhood) 32-3, 452, 454-6, 490-3
Pettit, Philip 205n, 378, 458n
philosophy of human rights
  critique of 1, 41, 54-7, 97
    excessive abstraction of 76-7, 80-5
    uselessness of 1-5, 41, 69-87
  desiderata of 11-12, 89-90, 145-58, 169n, 175-6, 201
  methodology of 14-15, 89-90, 139-44, 145-58, 201
  normative vs. descriptive 1-5, 157, 162-3, 166-72, 225-6
  purpose of 1-5, 7-13, 64, 70, 71-87, 145-58
Philpot, Daniel 442, 454n, 455n
Pickering, Andrew 75
Pinochet, Augustus 384
Plato 2, 69, 75, 76, 77, 81, 83, 85, 94
Pogge, Thomas 174n, 187n, 342, 346, 359, 364, 366, 370n, 393, 422, 472, 490n
Pol Pot 411
political conception of human rights
  and practice-dependence 11-12, 139-44
    see fidelity to the practice of human rights
  challenges facing the 123-36, 182-5
  defence of 1-5, 139-44, 224-8
  defined 1, 4-5, 89, 118-20, 140-4, 174, 182, 200
  different terms for 1, 118-20
  historical facet of 7
  political knowledge 28, 401, 407
Posner, Eric 26n, 481n
Powell, Colin 421
Protestantism 42, 44-8, 49, 56
Pufendorf, Samuel 49, 50

Quong, Jonathan 5n

Rancière, Jacques 434, 436n
Rawls, John 1n, 4, 5n, 7, 13, 14, 15, 27, 33, 71, 72, 73, 74, 75, 77, 78, 79, 80, 81, 82n, 86, 89, 90, 91, 95n, 99n, 104, 106, 117-37, 145, 150, 152, 153, 154, 156, 157, 158, 160, 161, 162, 166, 168n, 169, 172, 175n, 203, 212n, 224, 238n, 240n, 245n, 257n, 263, 280, 333, 370, 442, 452, 454n, 470, 471, 472, 474n, 475, 476, 477, 478n, 482, 483, 490n, 493

Raz, Joseph 1n, 4, 5n, 7, 8n, 9n, 12, 13, 14, 20n,
    73n, 80, 81, 82n, 90n, 99n, 117–37,
    138–44, 145, 162, 163, 165, 166, 168n,
    169, 170, 171, 172, 175, 177n, 182n,
    211n, 212n, 226, 227n, 230, 231n, 233,
    234, 236, 238, 240n, 333, 442, 445–6,
    447, 448, 450n, 451n, 452
realism (in international relations) 26–7, 167n,
    413–14, 430–1
realism (in political theory) 70, 71, 82–6
realism (moral) 77–8, 84
Renzo, Massimo 6n, 16n, 188n
Responsibility to Protect 77, 123, 125, 172, 411,
    417, 423, 434, 435
Rieff, David 417, 418, 422
right to justification
    see human rights and the right
    to justification
Rights of Man 63, 64, 105, 106, 244, 388,
    389, 434
Risse, Matthias 19n, 31n, 471, 483n
Roman law 42
Rousseau, Jean-Jacques 51, 52, 54, 395,
    474, 492
Ruggie, John 19, 98–101
Rwanda 122, 192n, 419, 423, 430, 434n
Rwandan Patriotic Front 419

Sangiovanni, Andrea 1n, 5n, 15–16, 161n,
    167n, 174–99, 200–8, 470n, 475n
Scanlon, Thomas 475n, 476n
Schmitt, Carl 269, 291, 379n
Second Italian War of Independence 411
Second World War 7, 63, 88, 140, 165, 186, 246,
    252, 376
Sen, Amartya 3n, 17n, 19n, 91, 97n, 100, 178n,
    280, 314, 327, 329n, 382n
Shue, Henry 25, 30n, 313n, 314n, 327, 329, 330,
    331, 342, 343, 344, 345, 346, 349n, 354,
    395, 476n
Simmons, Beth 26, 81n, 94n, 171, 380n,
    382n, 383n, 384n, 387n, 392n, 393n,
    472n, 482n
Simmons, John A. 66n, 91
Singer, Peter 4, 38n, 365, 366n, 367, 370
Sinnott-Armstrong, Walter 22n
Skinner, Quentin 45n, 62
Solferino 411, 412, 419, 432
South Africa 189, 322, 325, 461, 462
Soviet Union (USSR) 7, 85, 384, 433, 455
Sreenivasan, Gopal 1n, 3, 4n, 18n, 19–20,
    211–29, 230–7
Stilz, Anna 474n
Stone Age 97, 98, 142
Suárez, Francisco 45–7, 49, 67
Sudan 192n

Tadros, Victor 15n, 332, 333, 334
Tasioulas, John 1n, 3, 7n, 8, 11, 12, 17n, 19, 70,
    72–86, 88–102, 103n, 104–9, 145, 162,
    163, 164n, 165, 166, 168n, 169n, 170,
    171n, 174n, 175, 176n, 177, 179, 180,
    181, 212, 240n, 267n, 319n, 331, 332n,
    335n, 350n, 451n
Taliban 424, 426
Tan, Kok-Chor 342n, 423n, 477n
Taylor, Charles 30n, 103, 493n
Terry, Fiona 415
Tierney, Brian 42n, 91
Tuck, Richard 61

United Kingdom (UK) 130, 166, 189, 192n, 255,
    271, 284, 289, 302, 307, 495, 497n
United Nations (UN) 8, 53, 99n, 135, 153, 338,
    411, 415, 421, 423, 433, 441, 453
    Aid 420
    Charter 338, 339n, 441
    General Assembly 7, 53, 123n, 172n
    High Commission on Refugees
        (UNHCR) 483n
    Human Rights Council 101, 238n
    Secretary General 99
    Security Council 154, 432
United States of America (US/USA) 131n, 167,
    192, 194, 195, 252, 255, 321, 383, 384,
    426, 462, 471, 472, 479, 480, 481, 482,
    484, 491, 496, 498
Universal Declaration of Human Rights
    (UDHR) 1n, 7, 8, 22n, 23n, 29, 30, 31n,
    33n, 43, 53, 63, 71, 74n, 75, 81n, 89, 90,
    91, 106, 122, 135, 150, 176, 191, 194, 195,
    243, 244n, 280, 376, 382, 387, 388n, 390,
    391n, 393, 412, 441, 465, 469
US Constitution 240n, 255
US Department of State 135

Valentini, Laura 1n, 5n, 393n, 405n, 406n
Vienna Convention on the Law of Treaties 53
Viet Cong 424
Vietnam War 92, 411, 424, 426
Voltaire 51

Waldron, Jeremy 5n, 13–14, 15, 17n, 19n, 72,
    73, 74, 76, 79n, 82, 85, 91, 111, 112,
    117–37, 139–45, 182n, 217n, 218n, 240n,
    263n, 334n, 345, 347, 348, 351, 442, 447,
    454n, 474n, 476
Walzer, Michael 217n, 425, 475, 478
Weber, Max 54, 406n
Weimar Republic 255
Weinstock, Daniel 25, 363–71
Wenar, Leif 1n, 148n, 475n
Western Sahara 466

Williams, Bernard 1n, 74, 75, 76, 83n, 423n
Wittgenstein, Ludwig 62, 64
Wolf, Susan 335
Wolff, Jonathan 19n
Wolterstorff, Nicholas 91, 181
World Summit Outcome (2005) 123n, 125, 172n
World Trade Organization (WTO) 143, 393

Ypi, Lea 477n
Yong, Caleb 477n
Yugoslavia 455

Zaire 192n, 414n, 419
Žižek, Slajov 381n, 384n, 386n, 389n
Zolo, Daniel 27n, 29n